Energy Law in Malaysia

Energy Law in Malaysia

Second Edition

Abdul Haseeb Ansari

This book was originally published as a monograph in the International Encyclopaedia of Laws/Energy Law.

Founding Editor: Roger Blanpain
General Editor: Frank Hendrickx
Volume Editors: Kurt Deketelaere & Bram Delvaux

Wolters Kluwer

Published by:
Kluwer Law International B.V.
PO Box 316
2400 AH Alphen aan den Rijn
The Netherlands
E-mail: international-sales@wolterskluwer.com
Website: lrus.wolterskluwer.com

Sold and distributed in North, Central and South America by:
Wolters Kluwer Legal & Regulatory U.S.
7201 McKinney Circle
Frederick, MD 21704
United States of America
Email: customer.service@wolterskluwer.com

Sold and distributed in all other countries by:
Air Business Subscriptions
Rockwood House
Haywards Heath
West Sussex
RH16 3DH
United Kingdom
Email: international-customerservice@wolterskluwer.com

Printed on acid-free paper

ISBN 978-94-035-0510-7

e-Book: ISBN 978-94-035-0511-4
web-PDF: ISBN 978-94-035-0512-1

Printed in the United Kingdom.

The Author

Professor Abdul Haseeb Ansari obtained his BSc from Gorakhpur University, India, and LLM, PhD from Banaras Hindu University, India. He has special interest in revenue law, environmental law, international trade law and comparative jurisprudence. He has extensively contributed on different aspects of these areas. He has a long experience of teaching and guiding research in these areas. Prof. Ansari has widely contributed to the knowledge by publishing fourteen books and over hundred articles. He is the editor of the *Journal of Islamic Law Review,* published by the Serials Publications, New Delhi, and he is on the editorial boards of several world-class journals. Professor Ansari has membership of some of the international institutions of high repute. He has the experience of working as the Deputy Dean of the Research Management Centre of the International Islamic University Malaysia, Head of Research at Ahmad Ibrahim Faculty of Laws, International Islamic University Malaysia, the Deputy Dean (Postgraduate and Research) of Ahmad Ibrahim Faculty of Laws of the university and a member of the Council of Professors of the university. He is working as professor at the Ahmad Ibrahim Faculty of Laws, International Islamic University Malaysia. In 2005, he got the best researcher award (Faculty Level) of the International Islamic University Malaysia. In 2008, he was honoured with the outstanding researcher award by the university, and he bagged the same award in 2012 and 2013. In 2009, he had the honour to receive outstanding paper award of the Emerald Literati Award, UK. He again bagged the most commended article award from them in 2013. In 2013, he got the maximum citation award from the IIUM. His postal address is: Faculty of Laws, International Islamic University Malaysia, Jalan Gombak, 53100 Kuala Lumpur, Malaysia.

The Author

Table of Contents

List of Abbreviations

AC	Appeal Cases
ACE	ASEAN Centre for Energy
AELB	Atomic Energy Licensing Board
AIR	All India Reporter
All ER	All England Law Reports
APEC	Asia-Pacific Economic Cooperation
	Asean Plan of Action for Energy Cooperation
APERC	Asia-Pacific Energy Research Centre
ASCOPE	Asean Council of Petroleum
ASEAN	Agreement of Southeast Asian Nations
ASEANTOM	ASEAN Network of Regulatory Bodies on Atomic Energy
ASFOC	ASEAN Forum on Coal
CCGT	Combined-Cycle Gas Turbine
CDM	Clean Development Mechanism
CE	Conservation of Energy
CETREE	Centre for Education and Training of Renewable Energy and Energy Efficiency
CLC	Civil Liability Convention
CLJ	Current Law Journal
CO2	Carbon Dioxide
COP	Conference of Parties
CPO	Crude Palm Oil reserve
DG	Director General
DOE	Department of Environment
EC	Energy Commission
EE	Energy Efficiency
EEM	Electrical Energy Manager

List of Abbreviations

EEPLS	Energy Efficiency Project Lending Scheme
EIA	Environmental Impact Assessment
EMS	Environmental Management System
EPRE	Electric Power Research Institute
EPSO	Floating, Production, Storage and Offloading
EPU	Energy Planning Unit
ERU	Emission Reduction Unit
ETP	Economic Transformation Programme
EU	European Union
FC	Fund Convention
FiT	Feed-in Tariff
FRIM	Forest Research Institute Malaysia
GDP	Gross Domestic Product
GDV	Gas District Cooling
GEF	Global Environment Fund
GHGs	Greenhouse Gases
GTFS	Green Technology Financing Scheme
HAPUA	Heads of ASEAN Power Utilities Authorities
HDI	Human Development Project
IAEA	International Atomic Energy Agency
IEA	International Energy Agency
IGCC	Integrated Gasification Combined Cycles
IPCC	Intergovernmental Panel on Climate Change
IPP	Independent Power Production
IUCN	International Union for Conservation of Nature
JPOI	Johannesburg Plan of Implementation
LCA	Life Cycle Analysis
LNG	Liquid Natural Gas
MDA	Middle Distillate Synthesis
MDTCA	Ministry of Domestic Trade and Consumer Affairs
MEAs	Multilateral Environmental Agreements
MESA	Master Energy Services Agreement
MIEEIP	Malaysian Industrial Energy Efficiency Programme
MINT	Malaysian Institute of Nuclear Technology
MITI	Ministry of International Trade and industry
MLJ	Malayan Law Journal
MNPC	Malaysian Nuclear Power Corporation

MPOB	Malaysian Palm Oil Board
MW	Mega Watt
NEPIO	Nuclear Energy Programme Implementation Organization
NDP	National Depletion Policy
NGOs	Non-Governmental Organizations
NGV	Natural Gas for Vehicles
NOCs	Asian National Oil Companies
NPAC	National Petroleum Advisory Council
NSG	Nuclear Suppliers Group
NPP	National Petroleum Policy
OIIP	Oil Initially in Place
OPEC	Organization of Petroleum Producing Countries
PA	Paris Agreement
PFBC	Pressurized Fluidized Bed Combustion
PIL	Public Interest Litigation
PPA	Power Purchase Agreement
PSC	Production Sharing Contract
QB	Queen's Bench
RAPID	Refinery and Petrochemical Integrated Development
RBI	Risk-Based Inspection
RE	Renewable Energy
REEM	Registered Electrical Energy Manager
REP	Renewable Energy Programme
REPPA	Renewable Power Purchase Agreement
RCM	Reliability Centered Management
RWEDP	Regional Wood Energy Development Programme
SCORE	Sarawak Corridor of Renewable Energy
SEDA	Sustainable Energy Development Authority
SESCO	Sarawak Electricity Supply Corporation
SIA	Social Impact Assessment
SREP	Small and Renewable energy Programme
TAPG	Trans-ASEAN Gas Pipeline Project
TNB	Tenaga Nasional Berhad
TTM	Trans Thailand Malaysia Gas Pipeline

List of Abbreviations

UNDP	United States Development Policy
UNFCCC	United Nations Framework Convention on Climate Change
UNEP	United Nations Environment Programme
WHO	World Health Organization
WLR	Weekly Law Reports
YDPA	Yang Di-Pertuan Agong

General Introduction

Chapter 1. Introduction

1. Ever since man started gaining civilization, energy has been one of the essential necessities. With the growth of the human population the need for energy also grew. Traditional energy production depended largely on the burning of biomass. Industrialization increased the use of fossil fuel, gas, coal and oil, for energy generation. Biomass, thus, remained the main source of energy in the rural areas, whereas urban population and industries, including vehicles, chiefly depended on fossil fuel.

2. Energy empowers human beings in manifest ways. Some of them are: by reducing drudgery, increasing productivity, transforming food, providing illumination, transporting water, fuelling transportation, powering industrial and agricultural processes, cooling or heating houses and facilitating electronic communications and computer operations. But unfettered and non-environment-friendly way of using biomass and fossil fuels contributed to a variety of social, economic and environmental problems and brought social menace in the form of health hazards and global warming-related problems. Developing countries are the worst sufferers because they do not have enough clean technology and spend huge amount of money on import of fossil fuels, especially oil and gas, which they could have used in upgrading the living standards of their people.

3. Thus, in particular, pertaining to energy, the poor population of the world is facing the following challenges:

(1) More than one-third of the population of the world, living in villages of developing and least developed countries, is deprived of electricity and cooking gas. They mainly depend on burning wood for fulfilling their energy needs, especially for cooking food and heating. Since they have no access to technology for safe energy use, they invariably suffer from all kinds of health hazards. What is required is to bring them electricity and gas. If it is not possible, they should be provided with rural power generation technology and financial assistance to protect their health even when they burn wood for cooking food or for heating their small houses.

(2) Related to point one, it is also necessary to make meaningful efforts to make them competent to use renewable sources of energy, especially to use the available biomass (appropriately cow dung) for producing gas that can be used

for cooking and illuminating gas-based lights. This will involve little bit of money that can be advanced to villagers as loans on easy terms by banks operating in villages. The government, on subsidized rate, can provide equipment for such plants.

(3) To improve energy efficiency is another challenge. This requires minimizing energy consumption at the end-user point, and increasing efficiency at the generation, transmission and consumption levels. Imperatives for minimizing consumption of energy are: efficient and well-organized generation system, appropriate wiring, efficient energy-consuming equipment, use of devices that protect houses from becoming hot in tropical countries and subtropical countries and from being cool in other countries and use of renewable energy sources like use of solar panels on the roof-tops and wind and solar energy for agricultural use. These kinds of efforts have also to be made at the industries level. Rather, it is necessary to have optimal consumption of energy in all kinds of industries because they are the main consumers of all kinds of energies.

(4) For the aspects mentioned in the third point, cash and tax incentives have to be given. Towards this end, exemptions and deductions in taxes should be provided to clean energy generation and research activities pertaining to this. Likewise, researches and use of renewable energy should also be supported with appropriate financial support and tax incentives. This is because clean energy innovations are imperatively demanded. Consumption tax can also be considered. But presently, efforts should be made to reduce subsidy on consumption of oil and gas.

(5) To give electricity to villagers for free, with the intention to boost agriculture, is not a good choice. It is, therefore, rightly suggested that the charges on supply of electricity to villagers should be low and on flat rate, and the financial resources mobilized from this source should be utilized in improving the conditions of the infrastructure in rural areas.

(6) On the sale of oil and gas, all countries should consider some kind of carbon tax. It is notable that presently only developed countries have resorted to this kind of tax. It is difficult for the developing and least developed countries to opt for this because of economic reasons. But it is necessary in some developing countries, where the number of vehicles on the road is increasing fast, to consider taxing supply of oil and gas if their economy permits to do so. It is also advisable to have higher excise duty, customs and sales tax on non-commercial vehicles. This will act as a disincentive, but this is a right choice to control the increasing number of non-commercial vehicles on the road.

(7) Developing countries should resort to gradually withdrawing subsidy given on oil and gas. The money generated from the withdrawal should be used in encouraging and supporting power generation by alternative and renewable means, especially in rural population. It will be a great help in keeping the promises made by them to the United Nations for reducing carbon emission under the Paris Agreement 2016.

(8) The idea of feed-in-tariff also requires to be practised in developing and least developed countries.

(9) Policies aimed at expanding modern energy technologies, as stated above, especially to rural areas, should be flexible enough to support a range of options depending upon what is appropriate to the situation. For instance, states should not resort to a centralized supply where village or household systems may be more cost-effective. Policies and programmes should encourage user participation in the choice of technologies and women should be targeted as users, operators and entrepreneurs in rural energy systems. They should foster the development of local capacity, especially in the areas of operation, maintenance and financial management. Local manufacture and marketing of energy technology offers a possibility of income generation along with important skill development. For these activities, appropriate incentives can be accorded.

(10) Markets play a crucial role in the energy sector. This has emerged due to privatization of the energy sector around the world. Privatization has proved to be better from the point of view of giving better as private companies compete to give better services and at the same time to make profit. Energy in private sector has reduced theft of electricity at the supply level and has increased efficiency at generation level. But power generation in private sector and exploration and distribution of oil and gas in this sector have to be put under certain standards, prescribed through suitable regulations, that ensure clean environment, care about human health and do not create unemployment. Strict adherence to the standards to venture into pollution-free energy is the most important factor in the whole process. So as to achieve prescribed standards, some oil companies have made innovations. Likewise, coal-fired power generation plants have developed environment-friendly devices.

Privatization of energy, however, demands the following aspects to be dealt with properly: Price of energy must suit both manufacturers/distributors and consumers. Investment in the clean energy sector should be encouraged by suitable financial and fiscal measures. Power companies should be encouraged to increase production and to diversify their energy generation and distribution activities. There should be limited number of companies, but they should work efficiently. Companies should be encouraged for rural electrification. Externalities, like protection of environment, human health and employment generation efficiency, should be given priority. The working of the companies should be transparent, and their working should be audited to assess these two aspects. Investment in these companies should be encouraged by all means.

It has to be noted here that private power producers (PPPs) engaged in producing electricity by renewable means, including mini-hydro projects, must get enough support from the government. Generally, as in Malaysia, they get licence from the Energy Commission. As they cannot sell electricity by themselves, they sell it to utility companies. They are closing down because the ventures for them did not prove to be enough profitable. Actually, it should be other way round; more and more companies should engage with this. It can be possible only when the venture is profitable and there is least technical and procedural hitch. The purchase price should be lucrative to them. They only will flourish rather than closing.

(11) On the top of all above-mentioned challenges, all countries, developed and developing, have to make appropriate endeavours for sustainable energy for sustainable development, which means fulfilling the energy needs of the present generation without compromising with the interests of future generations. Enormous successful efforts around the world are being made to make the ongoing development processes to be sustainable. The task seems to be furthering well in the right direction, and if it continues with the same magnitude and pace, it will certainly yield the desired results. Nevertheless, so far rural electrification is concerned, in spite of the fact that a lot of schemes are being suggested and being acted upon for increasing the number of beneficiaries, the success still seems to be far, as nearly one-third of the global population, living in developing and least developed countries, is still deprived of electricity and squarely depend on traditional energy sources. The task to provide electricity to all is quite big, which might take years. In addition to this, the energy output has to be expanded to fulfil the energy requirements of the coming generations. The expansion at the same time has to be safe, affordable, easy, convenient, reliable, equitable, economically viable and environment-friendly. We know that the existing energy supply mainly depends on fossil fuels, and these resources are limited. This is a compelling factor to intensify various renewable energy sources, which seems to be arduous, as the increase in these energy sources is not so encouraging. The Bonn Conference on Renewable Energy and other such conferences have recognized this fact and have emphasized on setting time frames to make a sizable population of the world mainly dependent on the renewable sources of energy. These targets can be achieved only when researches for generating and making use of renewable energy are properly streamlined and intensified. This will also demand international cooperation in capacity building of less technologically advanced and less resourceful countries. In this regard, South–South cooperation will also prove to be useful. In developing and least developed countries, there are two imperatives: one, to maximize generation and consumption through small units of renewable energy sources at local level; and second, to make efforts to generate electricity at large scale and to supply it through national grids.

Thus, to achieve that target of sustainable energy for sustainable development to all is a big challenge. What is necessarily required for achieving this is to make collective efforts by developed and developing countries, because without technological help and financial support extended by developed countries to developing countries, electricity needs of the rural mass in developing countries cannot be fulfilled. For a total success, the problems of developing and least developed countries will have to be given proper attention. This is because these countries have to develop, and presently their per capita consumption of energy is six to eight times lower than developed countries. Their future energy needs have to be addressed properly so that they could develop at the required pace. It is needless to mention that so as to meet the economic and environmental challenges of the world they have to develop at an increasingly faster pace. Their development cannot fulfil the thresholds of sustainable development unless developed countries help them by all means and in manifest ways. For example, sustainable and environment-friendly energy, based on fossil fuels, has to send least particulate matters into the atmosphere. It means oil has to be fully burnt. If possible, diesel has to be changed to another state so that it has fewer emissions of unburned carbon particles, carbon monoxide, ozone, hydrocarbons and oxides of nitrogen and sulphur. Likewise, petrol has to have least quantity of lead and sulphur. The use of gas should be maximized. Similarly, before coal is used its pollutants have to be reduced. Developing and least developed countries cannot face these challenges alone. Some developing and least developed countries import energy because they are not self-sufficient. If this trend continues, a substantial amount of money will continuously be drained out and, thus, their economy cannot sustainably develop. These can be possible only with the close cooperation between developing countries and developed countries with enhanced transfer of technology and financial resources. It got impetus under the Kyoto Protocol, made under the UNFCCC, via clean development mechanism (CDM). But it did not prove to be very successful. What is required is enough political will and commitment to boost environmentally friendly energy sources and boosting renewable energy sources, especially by tapping solar and wind energy. For this, solar panels (PV panels) and windmills should be available to developing and least developed countries on easy terms, and if need be, the fund created under the Paris Agreement 2016 should be utilized for it.

For setting up PV panels, there should be no problem, as solid waste dump sited can easily be converted into PV parks. Countries like India and China are already doing it. In Chennai, India has the biggest PV park on a huge dumpsite catering the energy needs of 250,000 people. Other developing and least developed countries can easily emulate India and China, but of course with help of developed and technologically advanced countries.

Conservation of energy is a related aspect of sustainable development. This implies to have an efficient use of energy, to reduce the use of energy in non-productive or less productive consumptions, like domestic consumptions and vehicular use, and to minimize the loss of energy. We have noted above that in the domestic sectors, by adopting some mechanical devices and using renewable sources of energy, its consumption can be reduced, and by using good-quality wires properly insulated, wastage of electricity in transmission can be minimized. The scope to reduce energy consumption in agricultural sector, including agro-based industries, is also imperatively required.

Likewise, towards conserving the energy, energy-efficient equipment are being manufactured. Energy-efficient or energy-saving equipment and appliances are becoming popular. They benefit in two ways: by reducing the electricity bills and by saving energy, which can be diverted to other sectors, including industries and agriculture. The emphasis areas are: smart thermostats, LSD lights, smart energy management systems, efficient charging stations, smart power trips, increasing the use of hybrid technology and converter technology. Moreover, these are: latest switchgears, control systems, transformers, cables, relay and measuring instruments designed to maximize energy use. States are encouraging this mode of conservation by all means. Incentives by tax exemptions and otherwise are being provided to companies involved in manufacturing and distributing such equipment.[1] These challenges have to be dealt with severally and collectively. Towards this end, first and the foremost requirements are to have a national policy on sustainable generation and consumption of energy so that it has compatibility with sustainable development strategies. The policy also has to be equitable so that those who are presently deprived of modern forms of energy also suitably get electricity and other forms of energy and their dependency on biomass considerably alleviates. The policy should encompass the above-mentioned challenges. It should be transformed into practice. Second, efforts should be made by all means, including suitably designed law, for sustainable energy. Third, developed countries and rich countries should help less fortunate ones so that they also become able to fulfil their commitments towards sustainable development. Malaysia has a national energy policy. It gave heed to the ASEAN Plan of Action for Energy Co-operation 1999–2004, which had been made a part of the ASEAN Vision 2020. The country is fully supporting the ASEAN Plan of Action for Energy Cooperation (APAEC) 2016–2025, phase of which is (2016–2020) in actions, made and working under the auspices of the ASEAN Center for Energy. The emphasis areas are: establishment of ASEAN Power Grid, having Trans-ASEAN Gas Pipeline, enhancing coal and clean coal technology, boosting energy efficiency and conservation of energy, enlarging and increasing renewable energy, developing a viable regional energy policy and planning and good civilian nuclear energy. For Malaysia, it is hard to meet the above-mentioned challenges. It has commitment for sustainable development, and for this, all measures are being adopted. It has a federal form of government with energy as a federal subject. Thus, the Parliament of the country has legislated suitable laws pertaining to energy. In addition to these laws, specific legislations are also there on protection of the environment that contains high environmental thresholds. The energy sector is privatized, but the government through appropriate legislation and enforcement authorities of the Ministry keeps proper control on all sources of energy. Malaysia is an oil-producing country, but to cater the needs of the country, local oil production and consumption is supplemented with gas imports. It opened its market and invited foreign direct investment in the country in the early seventies. With the result of that, rapid industrialization in the country took place. This phenomenon considerably increased the energy demand of the country. Rapid urbanization added to it. Now, industrial growth is steady, and is growing at a normal pace. The country has now laid emphasis on agriculture. This will lead to diversification of the consumption levels of energy in the country. With the result of that, the energy demand might grow further. Malaysia is making efforts to bring electricity to even remote places of the country and striving hard to make use of the renewable energy sources. Incentives, financial and fiscal, are being provided to renewable energy sources and R&D in the area of clean and renewable energy. So far sustainable energy for sustainable development is concerned. Malaysia has not yet made significant changes in its legal framework. The significant success in the area of sustainable development and sustainable energy is yet to be achieved.

1. *New Straits Times*, 15 Jun. 2004. Also see at: https://www.forbes.com/sites/trulia/2014/04/11/5-energy-saving-gadgets-that-are-totally-worth-it/#62f2296b2e2f (accessed on 24 Feb. 2018).

4. On 10 June 2010, while presenting the Tenth Malaysia Plan and explaining its salient features at the Parliament, the Prime Minister of Malaysia gave the 'New Energy Policy', which has emphasized on maximizing renewable and alternative energy sources and accelerating the implementation of energy efficiency imperatives. He put the policy under the following five points: (1) rationalizing energy pricing gradually to match market price, taking into consideration current economic conditions and affordability to the people; (2). understanding a more strategic development of energy supply by diversifying energy resources, including renewable energy sources. Nuclear energy will also be considered as an alternative source of energy; (3) accelerating the implementation of energy efficiency initiatives in the industrial, commercial, residential and transport sector; (4) improving governance to support the transition to market pricing while providing assistance to mitigate impact on the low-income groups; and (5) ensuring that the New Energy Policy is implemented based on an integrated approach and according to schedule to achieve energy supply security.[2] These points can be put as: pricing will be rationalized to gradually match market price; diversification of energy will be done in industrial and transport sector; energy efficiency will be speeded up; and efforts will be made to consolidate governance to support the transition to market pricing while helping the low-income groups. At the same time, the country launched the National Renewable Energy Policy, and an Action Plan, 2010 in order to prolong the oil and gas reserves in the country. They were added values to: the National Petroleum Policy (NPP) 1975 which strived to efficient utilization of petroleum resources of the country and to ensure that the country plays a major role in management and operation of the petroleum industry; the National Energy Policy 1979 which aimed to boost fast achieving the objectives to ensure adequate and cost-effective energy generation and supply, to promote best utilization of energy and conserve energy and to alleviate the negative impact of energy generation on the environment; the National Depletion Policy (NDP) 1980 which endeavours to increase the life span of the oil and gas reserves in the country; the Four-Fuel Policy 1981 strived to ensure reliability and security of supply of energy through diversification of fuels, coal, oil, gas and hydro; and the Five-Fuel Policy 2001, which aimed to encourage in addition to the Four-Fuel Policy power generation through biomass, solar and mini-hydro.[3] These have further been emphasized in the Eleventh Malaysia Plan with greater emphasis on increasing reliance on renewable energy sources. This was accentuated by the Prime Minster at the Conference of Parties (COP 15) of the UNFCCC 17 December 2009 in these words: '... Malaysia is adopting an indicator of a voluntary reduction of up to 40 percent in terms of carbon emission intensity of GDP by the year 2020 compared to 2005 levels ... .' He said about the Malaysia commitment prior to cut greenhouse gas emission as 'Malaysia is aiming to cut

2. *New Straits Times*, 11 Jun. 2010.
3. See 'Malaysian Energy Policy: Focusing on Sustainable Energy Development and the Way Forward', at: http://bseep.gov.my/App_ClientFile/df08bc24-99fb-47a3-937f-dc25df9d3997/Assets/BSEEP%20NCA2017/PAPER%204%20-%20KETTHA_Malaysia%20Energy%20Policy_04052017.pdf (accessed on 6 Mar. 2017).

greenhouse gas emission for each unit of economic growth 35 percent from 2005 levels by 2030 and 45 percent with international support.'[4]

Thus, in view of these, the Eleventh Malaysia Plan, which ends in 2020, has a comprehensive plans to boost renewable energy power generation in the country. It is because the country has to keep its promise under the Paris Agreement 2016.

5. There is a quest around the world to adopt renewable and other energy sources in place of traditional sources of energy so that environmental quality either does not degrade or their effect on it is minimal. Towards this end, along with encouraging the use of renewable energy sources, sulphur, lead and other pollutants from oil are also being reduced. Western countries have adopted stringent standards, and to meet those standards, all efforts are being made. Many Asian countries, including Malaysia, are also striving hard to adopt high standards of clean power generation. Since Malaysia is one of the biggest exporters of electronic goods, it has to follow international standards of manufacturing these; otherwise, its products will not have market in developed countries, where people are environmentally conscious. According to Reuters, Asia's uneven sprint to match the West's stringent fuel standards has roiled market, tightened supplies and forced refineries to gear up or bow out. By the year 2007, countries that consume more than half of Asia's 24 million barrels per day of oil will move to lower sulphur emission standards. By 2010, nearly whole of Asia will have to follow tightened specifications. Looming changes in Indonesia and Vietnam, Asia's leading importers of petrol and diesel, threaten to further strain clean fuel supplies after new specifications in India and the Philippines triggered a wave of imports. Further down the line, refiners in China face the challenge of satisfying more stringent rules in 2010 at the same time as rapidly rising demand and increasing high sulphur crude imports. Unlike the West, Asia has no harmonized standard on limit of sulphur, a cause of acid rain and lung problem. Nations are left to move forward at their own pace, causing sometimes sudden and irregular shift to clean fuel demand that can spike prices. Multi-billion-dollar investments have also taxed budgets at time when analysts say that world's refineries should be expanding capacity to meet soaring demands for transport fuels. The tightening of standards plus tightening of refining capacity will certainly drive margins and shift trade. Still haunted by the anaemic margins and costly overcapacity of the 1990s refiners are understandably reluctant to plough up to USD 30 billion; analysts say it is needed to meet higher environmental standards over the next decade. China alone needs 3 billion worth of investment. Asia, which has the faster rate of vehicle growth in the world, has a proven track record in catching up with the West when it comes to consumer fuels. Europe and US took twenty years to remove lead from petrol; most of Asian countries, including Malaysia, did it in shorter span of time. Now, Asian governments are racing to institute European fuel quality standard at a breakneck pace. In the next year alone, four Asian countries that consume 8.2 million barrels per day will reduce their sulphur limits to 500 parts per million or 0.05% – the so-called Euro II standard that came into force in Europe in 1996. More than half of Asian countries, including Malaysia, have already reached this standard. By 2010, nations with more than 8 million barrels per day

---

4. *Ibid.*

consumption of oil plan to cap sulphur at 50 parts per million, a move Europe officially made this year. Refiners who spent early enough can expect bumper profits, while those who waited will be under pressure to catch up or face a dwindling market and lower returns.[5]

6. The phenomenon of global warming, which is the result of increase of the ratio of carbon dioxide (CO_2) in the atmosphere beyond the sustainable limit, and for which burning of fossil fuels is responsible, has prompted states, especially those who burn more fossil fuels for fulfilling their energy demands, to reduce the ratio of the thermal power generation and resort to renewable energy sources. Kyoto Protocol that has been made under the Climate Change Convention and that has come into force strives to reduce CO_2 and bring it within the prescribed threshold. This has put further pressure to cut CO_2 emissions and increase dependency on renewable energy sources. It is for this reason that at the recent conference on energy held in Germany it has been decided that by the end of this decade the ratio of power generation by renewable energy sources will be increased up to 30%. Although developing countries, including Malaysia, have not to adopt any cut on the CO_2 emissions, they are also trying hard to maximize the use of renewable energy sources because prices of oil and gas are becoming unbearable to them. Malaysia is also trying hard to boost clean energy sources by all means. Following the West, Malaysia is also withdrawing the subsidy that the country is giving on oil and gas. The country is now thinking to impose some kind of carbon tax. For details, see *infra*.

5. *New Straits Times*, 30 Apr. 2005. For the detail of the Malaysian position, see *infra*.

Chapter 2. Energy Overview

§1. General

7. The energy system today mainly depends on fossil fuels, which together accounts for around 80% of the total primary energy consumption of the world. In order to make the Paris Agreement a success, there have to be considerable rise in power generation from renewable sources. But with the increase in the power demand, this percentage may remain for few more decades. According to the Institute of Energy Research, even in the US it is said that even by 2040 fossil fuels will be accountable for 80% of the energy demand. There will be increase in gas consumption increase by 13.4%, and consumption of coal will increase by 5.6% between 2017 and 2040. Thus, fossil fuels will cater 80% of the energy needs of the country. On this, 66.9% of the fossil fuels will be used for electricity generation. The position in other developed countries, barring Germany, will remain almost the same. Developing countries and least developed countries will far lag behind. However, efforts to maximize cleaner energy will continue which will alter the ratio in times to come. It is expected that the ratio will come down to 78% by 2040. According to the World Energy Outlook 2017, renewables may even rise up to 40%.[6] See Figure 1.

Figure 1 Comparative Primary Energy Consumption Over the Past Fifteen Years

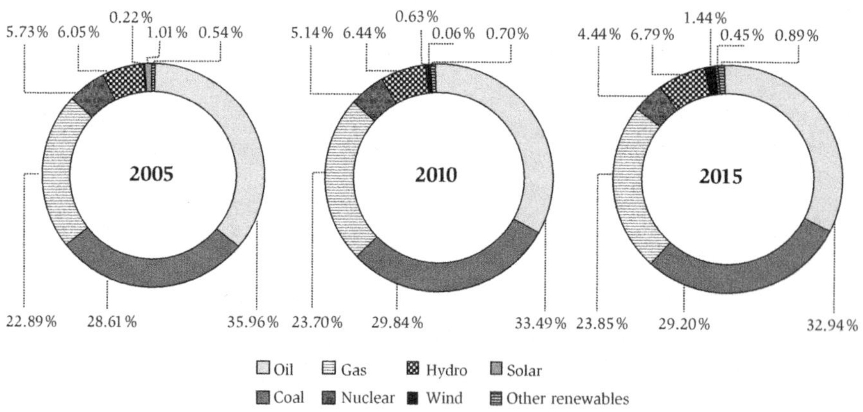

6. See https://instituteforenergyresearch.org/topics/encyclopedia/fossil-fuels/; http://www.globalization101.org/fossil-fuels/; https://www.iea.org/weo2017/ (accessed on 12 Dec. 2017).

8. The energy system now has the following characteristics:

(1) Total energy sales worldwide amount to over USD 150 trillion per year, which is around 3% of the Gross Domestic Product (GDP). This is expected to grow with the growth of states, especially in developing and least developed countries. Investment in electricity sector is going to grow steadily with the population growth and electricity demand. The rural electrification in developing countries, which is imperatively demanded by the equity, will invariably increase the sale.[7]

(2) Subsidies on the fossil fuel sales are about USD 1.27 tn (Trillion) per year. To date, Malaysia even after gradual withdrawal of subsidy on oil and gas is giving a substantial amount as subsidy on fossil fuels, especially on oil and gas, which could be utilized for boosting the GDP of the country. This should be noted here that as subsidies, in the interest of the sustainable and environment-friendly energy, have to be reduced, efforts to this effect, therefore, are being made all over the world, including Malaysia. But as the process has to be slow in developing economies, in these economies, subsidies are being reduced gradually. This is notable here that Malaysia has decided to use the money saved by reducing subsidies for enhancing infrastructure and improving transport facilities, so that people do not feel the pains of price rise, which might be the immediate consequence of withdrawal of subsidies. The least developed countries, which depend on imports of oil and gas, neither have enough money to buy oil and gas nor do they have sufficient facing real difficulties in the area of energy, because they do not have alternative energy for their people. A large number of their population depend on biomass, which sometimes is very dangerous and leaves deleterious effects on their forests and other vegetation. In these countries, there is no question of giving any subsidy on oil and gas.

(3) Sales of renewable energy equipment are around USD 30 billion. In view of the increasing emphasis on renewable sources of energy, which is evident from the Bonn Conference of May 2004 and which is necessary in view of the fact that oil might vanish by 2040 (this is according to one estimate; other estimates are slightly different. But it is for sure that this source of energy will sooner or later is going to vanish) gas will last for a longer period of time (but this source of energy will also vanish), and coal will last for the longest time, sales of such equipment will certainly multiply.

§2. Global Primary Energy Consumption by Sources

9. According to the World Energy Council, there have been dynamic changes in primary energy consumption between 2010 and 2015. Energy data show a shift from oil to other renewable energy such as solar and natural gas. Table 1 shows the distribution of primary energy sources and key facts, which identified significant

7. See, http://www.iea.org/publications/wei2017/ (accessed on 13 Jan. 2018).

transition in global energy sources. Table 2 shows the energy about each country group as stated in Tables 1 to 4. This should be noted at the outset that the data given in the figures are as of 1999, in such a long duration, no significant changes have taken place, except the slight increase towards gas and renewable sources of energy.

Table 1 Global Primary Energy Consumption by Source 2010 and 2015

Source	*2010 (%)*	*2015 (%)*
Oil	33.49	32.94
Coal	29.84	29.20
Gas	23.70	23.85
Nuclear	5.14	4.44
Hydro	6.44	6.79
Solar	0.06	0.45
Wind	0.63	1.44
Others renewables	0.70	0.89
Population: 5.9 billion		

Total Energy Use: 9,700 Mtoe (million tonnes of oil equivalent).

Per capita energy use: 1.6 toe per capita.

Source: World Energy Council, June 2016.

Primary Energy comprises only commercially traded fuels for primary energy, including modern renewables used to generate electricity. Traditional biomass is excluded.

Table 2 Primary Energy Consumption in Industrialized Countries by Source 1999 and 2016

Source	*1999(%)*	*2016 (%)*
Oil	41.3	36
Gas	21.1	26.9
Coal	20.3	17.1
Nuclear	11.0	9.8
Biomass	3.4	5.7
Hydro	2.2	2.3
Others	0.7	2.2

Population: 1.1 billion

Total energy use: 5.200 Mtoe (million tonnes of oil equivalent)

Per capita energy use: 4.7 toe per capita

Source: World Energy Council, June 2016.

Table 3 Primary Energy Consumption in non-Industrialized countries as of June 2016

Source	*Percentage*
Gas	43.1
Oil	23.8
Coal	26.0
Nuclear	4.9
Hydro	2.2

Population: 0.35 billion

Total energy use: 1,000 Mtoe (million tonnes of oil equivalent)

Per capita energy use: 2.9 toe per capita

Source: World Energy Council, June 2016.

Table 4 Primary Energy Consumption in Developing Countries as of June 2016

Source	*Percentage*
Oil	29.0
Coal	27.6
Biomass	26.0
Gas	13.5
Hydro	2.5
Nuclear	1
Others	0.3

Population: 4.4 billion

Total energy use: 3,500 Mtoe (million tonnes of oil equivalent)

Per capita energy use: 0.78 toe per capita

Source: World Energy Council, June 2016.

10. It may be noted here that the energy demand in developing countries will go on rising. In China and India, it will increase faster than other countries due to population growth, industrialization and urbanization. Between India and China, India will experience more demand as it has lesser number of nuclear power generation plants. The electricity demand in both the countries will rise. By 2040, the total energy demand will increase by 30% with the economic growth at the rate of 3.4% annually, rise of population from 7.4 billion to 9 billion and rise of process of urbanization. (See Figure 2) There will be rise of energy demand alone in India by 30%. China and South East Asian countries will also experience high demand. The ever-rising demand will prompt the generation levels.

11. This in turn will increase the primary energy consumption in these countries. As noted above, this demand will show a mark reduction only when renewable energy sources contribute to the total power generation substantially.

Figure 2 Change in Primary Energy Demand in Mtoe Between 2016 and 2040

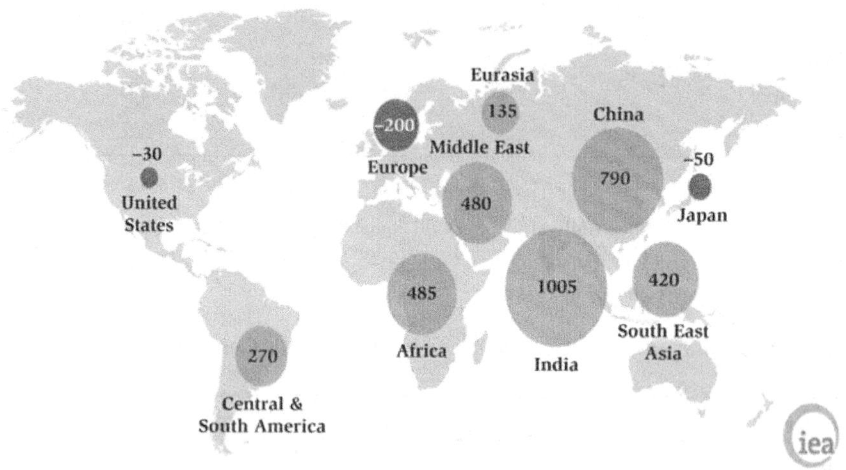

With the steady growth of energy demand, world energy production is also experiencing change. It is moving towards renewable and alternative energy sources. First emphasis is on the hydroelectric. Since it has its own limitations, the long-term but sustainable goal is to maximize renewable energy sources. All countries within the promises given by them to the United Nations under the UNFCCC are striving hard to maximize renewable energy sources to the best of their ability. Figure 3 shows the present energy mix in the world. According to the International Energy Outlook 2016, the strongest growth in electricity generation is among developing and non-OECD countries. In OECD countries increase in the use of electrical appliances and commercial services will prompt an increase by 2.5% from 2012 to 2040. In OECD countries, it will be 1.2% from 2012 to 2040.[8] In figure 3 we can notice the gradual rise in the renewable energy, whereas the use of coal for electricity generation remains almost the same with rise in the use of natural gas. The nuclear power, as it is understood, will have substantial share in the power mix, because developed countries will resort more to renewables but developing countries, especially India and China, will increase their power generation by this source.

8. https://www.e-education.psu.edu/egee102/node/1929 (accessed on 12 Feb. 2018).

Figure 3 Net Electricity Generation as the Primary Energy Source Between 2012 and 2040

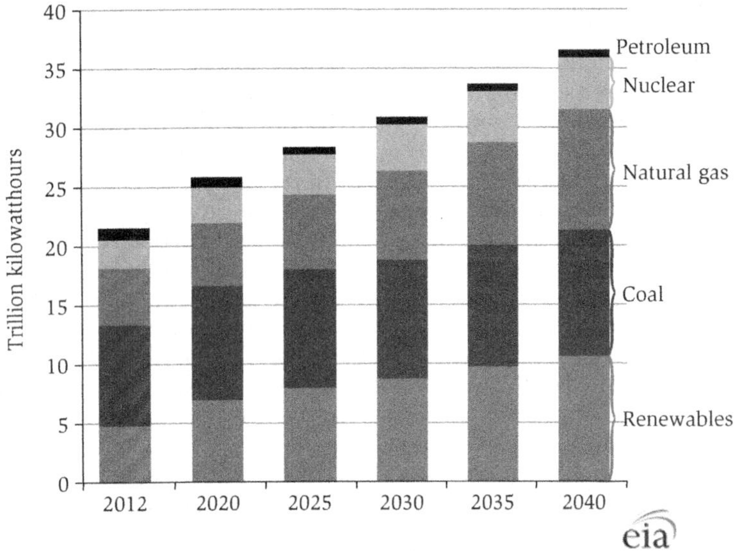

We can infer from the data above that in industrialized countries, main sources of energy are: oil, gas, coal and nuclear; renewable energy sources are picking up fast, especially in Germany and Japan. However, among them, oil is the main source. In the near future, their ratio is going to be more or less the same, but the ratio of the nuclear energy in the energy mix will remain substantial with increase in the power consumption; and thus there is increase of nuclear power generation plants. Contrary to this, in transition economies, gas is and will remain the main source of energy. Next to it will be hydroelectric plants. The ratio of coal and oil will not change significantly; there might be slight rise in the number of coal-fired thermal power generation plants in coal-rich countries and with the result of that the ratio of this source of energy might rise. There might be increase in nuclear power generation as India, China, Pakistan, Israel and some other developing countries that are generating a part of electricity from their nuclear power generation plants encourage other countries. This is notable that some developing countries are striving hard to have this source of energy also. However, presently, in many developing countries, oil is the main source of energy. Next to this are biomass and coal. In view of the protection of the environment, the ratio of coal and biomass will certainly reduce because emphasis on lesser consumption of biomass for energy is gradually reducing. The use of gas might increase. One thing is notable that per capita consumption of energy in developed countries is around eight times more than per capita consumption in developing countries. This ratio is also going to change, because the demand in developing and less developed countries is going to increase due to industrialization and urbanization. In Malaysia, gas is mainly used in power generation. Based on current projections, according to the IMF, Asia will have an annual growth of more than 5%, which is almost three times higher than that of industrialized nations of the world. Among them, the contribution of India, China and industrialized developing countries, like Pakistan, Malaysia, Thailand and Vietnam, will be significant. The expected growth in 2017 was about 5.5%, which is more than the world's average and the average of other developing regions of the world. In Asian countries, one of the big contributing factors is going to be agricultural sector. With the result of that, the oil demand in Asia will rise. It was estimated by the International Energy Agency (IEA) that world oil demand will grow by 1.65 million barrels per day (pbd) in 2005 and 2006. Two-thirds of which will come from Asia with China consuming half of it. This proved to be true. The IEA has also forecast that Asia will soak up 40% of the growth in world oil demand between now and 2025. The oil consumption then will be around 32 million barrels per day. This has to be noted here that projections from OPEC's World Energy Model see world oil demand from 77 million barrels per day (pbd) in 2002 to 115 million barrels per day in 2005 – an annual average growth rate of 1.7%, which proved to be true.[9] According to the IEA, the oil demand in South East Asian countries is going to grow relatively faster until 2040.[10] In Asia, China, Indonesia and Malaysia are the oil-producing countries. But their output is decreasing. So, they have to depend on the import of oil from major oil-producing countries of the world, mainly from Middle Eastern countries. In view of this, it is suggested that Asian countries should try hard to explore the possibility to find oil in deep sea off their coasts. Abdullah Ahmad Badawi, the then Prime Minister of Malaysia, while inaugurating the Ninth Asian Oil and Gas Conference, suggested that Asian National Oil Companies (NOCs) should work together to meet their energy needs.[11] These countries economically suffered due to fall in the crude oil prices. Their income from oil shrunk affecting their GDP. It prompted them to withdraw oil subsidy faster and look for market for their crude. The position has improved with the increase of oil price, discovery of other oil reserves and withdrawal of oil subsidy. This can also be suggested here that Asian countries should increase the number of sophisticated coal-fired power generation plants. This is because the region has huge coal deposits. Malaysia, China and India have already increased their coal-fired power generation plants, along with seriously working on increasing the contribution of renewable energy in the energy mix. Some experts are of the opinion that coal should not be used for power generation because it pollutes the environment the most. They suggest for having gas-based power generation as it pollutes the environment the least.[12] It can be argued here that gas also has its limitations and it will not last very long. What will happen after that? Their efforts, therefore, should be appreciated. Malaysia, China and India have already started working on it. Malaysia

9. See *New Straits Times*, 15 Jun. 2004.
10. https://www.reuters.com/article/us-asia-energy-iea/iea-sees-southeast-asia-oil-demand-growing-until-at-least-2040-idUSKBN1CT03R (accessed on 3 Jan. 2018).
11. *New Straits Times*, 15 Jun. 2004.
12. Robert Fisher, *New Straits Times*, June 2004.

has constructed its new coal-fired power generation plant at Janamanjung, Lumut. It is making few other such power plants, including one in Port Dickson.[13] The countries that have coal reserves will certainly resort to coal-fired power generation and they are doing it. But what is important is to make efforts to reduce polluting effects of these plants to the possible extent by using newer and environmentally friendly technology. For example, Malaysia upgraded its two coal-fired power generation plants in Melaka with the help of a German power company under the Clean Development Mechanism on the Kyoto Protocol of the UNFCCC. These countries are also striving hard to boost hydroelectric power generation. This is appreciable, but here also with proper Environmental Impact assessments (EIAs) and Social Impact Assessments (SIAs) followed by Audits, protection of environment and the society must be ensured. In the South East Asian countries, population is growing at the average rate of 4.4%. It will continue to grow more or less at this rate for at least thirty years to come. Oil in this region mainly comes from the Middle Eastern countries. Jakarta-based ASEAN Centre for Energy estimates that South East Asia's total energy demands will become more than double in twenty years' time. Despite efforts to promote the use of natural gas as an alternative to power generation plants and as a fuel to vehicles, the centre projects that oil will continue to be the region's largest source of energy even though the oil reserves of the region will decline in the near future. This may be noted here that Indonesia and Malaysia will experience decline in their oil reserves because they have limited amount of oil. South East Asia also buys oil from West African Nations like Nigeria and Angola, but distances involved make it more expensive. So, too, is the oil from Americas, which is shipped primarily from ports on the Atlantic in the United States. As a result, South East shares with Japan and South Korea a dependence on Middle Eastern oil imports. Middle Eastern suppliers take advantage of the situation by charging Asian buyers up to USD 1.50 more a barrel than the buyers in the United States and Europe. This is 'Business in business', said Kurtubi, who is the Director of the Centre for Petroleum and Energy Economics Studies in Jakarta. Thus, Asian buyers pay more. South East Asia is beholden to the Middle East for its oil may surprise students of history who remember that it was to secure South East Asia's oil, among other precious commodities, that motivated imperial Japan to this region of the world during the Second World War. But the region's rapid industrialization since has outstripped its ability to find and exploit new sources of oil. South East Asia has now lesser oil reserves than Europe. Only tiny Brunei produces more oil than they consume. Malaysia exported 100,313,029 barrels in 2016 and imported 322,280,617 barrels. The country wants to be a next oil exporter in times to come. But it depends on several factors, like discovery of oils and capacity to explore and potential to refine. Indonesia, which was the South East Asia's largest oil producer and a potent member of the Organization of the Petroleum Producing Countries (OPEC), in year 2016, is still a net oil importer. The country has left the OPEC as it did not agree with the production cut decided by it.

---

13. http://www.powerengineeringint.com/articles/2016/07/2-000-mw-coal-fired-power-plant-begins-construction-in-malaysia.html (accessed on 12 Dec. 2017).

12. South East Asia has a relative abundance of natural gas reserves, but more than half of these are tucked around more than 17,000 islands that make its excavation a risky and expensive venture. As a result, South East Asia is facing real difficulty to get its natural gas to the urban centres where it is needed. 'The problem with gas is that by its very nature it is a difficult commodity,' said Loh. He further said, 'Once you bring it out of the ground, you will either have to liquefy it or straight away put it in the pipe. And you are going to build a massive pipe without a contract that backs you up.' Indonesia is the world's largest exporter of liquefied natural gas, and because contracts are priced relative to oil, the country benefits from higher oil prices despite having to import more crude oil than to export. Most Indonesian liquefied natural gas, however, goes not to South East Asia but to Japan and South Korea. Building more plants to liquefy natural gas is prohibitively expensive, as are terminals to receive the liquid natural gas (LNG), and turn it back into gas. Both require first securing buyers willing to commit to contracts of up to thirty years. So do pipelines. ASEAN envisions someday having a network of gas pipelines crisscrossing South East Asia, enabling the region to have a spot market for natural gas like those already established in Europe and the United States. While pipelines have been built to get gas from Indonesia to Singapore and Malaysia, most pipeline constructions have been held up by the same concerns preventing exploration or construction of liquefied natural gas plants. Oil from the Middle East, therefore, remains South East Asia's most readily available source of energy.[14] In 2016, the natural gas accounted for 24% of the energy mix as the second largest source of energy after oil. This figure is almost not changed in comparison to the 2005 figure. The power generation by oil reduced during this period from 39% to 36%. However the power generation by coal has increased from 12% to 18%. In view of increased power demand in the region, for obvious reasons, the coal-fired power generation plants are going to increase. In view of the slow increase in the renewable energy sources, it can be said that in twenty years to come coal and gas will play a vital role in the energy sector. The table below may be referred.[15] It is notable here that Malaysia is the third largest exporter of liquefied natural gas in the world. Since West Malaysia imports coal for its coal-fired thermal power plants, it may shift power generation from coal to gas. The noticeable fact that in ASEAN, except for Thailand, the growth of renewable energy sources is not encouraging. In order to keep their promises under the UNFCCC, the Member States will have to put greater emphasis on the renewable sources.

---

14. See Wayne Arnold, 'At the Mercy of Oil', *New York Times*, 10 Jun. 2004; reprinted in *New Straits Times*, 11 Jun. 2004.
15. ASEAN Centre for Energy (2017): 5th ASEAN Energy Outlook, 2017.

Figure 4 ASEAN Energy Mix in 2005 and 2016

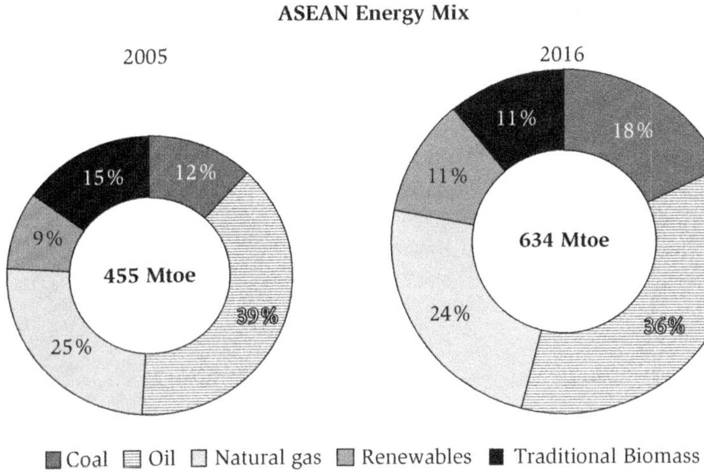

It is hoped that in the long run, South East Asian countries will properly exploit their own gas reserves and will also make use of the Indonesian gas through a proper networking of gas pipelines. States of the region are trying hard towards that end. In the recent meeting of the ASEAN Energy Ministers in the Philippines, the Ministers vowed for working seriously to have a viable gas networking.[16] Once pipelines are completed, all countries will benefit, and their dependency on Middle Eastern oil will considerably reduce. Thailand, for example, is fast shifting its electricity generation from oil to gas. So is the case in Malaysia. It is increasing its dependency on coal and gas. In addition to this, Malaysia is exporting 15% of world's total export of gas, placing it third among the top three exporters in the world. The goal of the Malaysian–Thailand Joint Authority Project, known as Trans Thailand–Malaysia Gas Pipeline (TTM), represented by the PETRONAS of Malaysia and the Petroleum Authority of Thailand is complete. It has been created and being developed to have two gas pipelines that are connected to each country, which will split the gas production between two processing plants of two countries. It is offshore as well as onshore. Another project initiated by PETRONAS, the Malaysian oil company, is the construction of two LNG liquefying Train 9 project which would boost the capacity of the plant. This project will be the largest liquefaction project in the world.[17]

13. Efforts are also underway to derive more power from renewable energy sources. Singapore is experimenting with both natural gas-powered vehicles and vehicles using hydrogen fuel cells. Malaysia is also providing all kinds of incentives to encourage renewable sources of energy; it will soon have vehicles run on

16. *New Straits Times*, 8 Jun. 2004.
17. https://www.hydrocarbons-technology.com/projects/petronas-bintulu-lng-complex-sarawak/ (accessed on 10 Feb. 2018).

hydrogen fuel technology. Liquefied natural gas is already being used for taxis. See *infra*. Thailand has signed a contract on 7 June 2004 with British Petroleum to develop a USD 20 million solar power project to supply electricity to rural areas. It also had a programme to promote the use of agricultural wastes, like rice husk, to produce biomass fuel. This kind of efforts is going to be doubled in the near future. With the result of that, dependency of the ASEAN countries will gradually reduce.

Chapter 3. Malaysian Position on Energy

§1. General

14. Malaysia has a peculiar character of energy sources. Few decades ago, its main energy source was oil. In 1980, it was decided to move away from the oil dependency and to adopt other strategy to diversify the power generation sector. With the result of that, coal, gas and hydropower were also resorted to in the power generation sector. Malaysia, thus, shifted the balance in the fuel mix from oil to natural gas, coal and hydroelectric. In that year, dependence on oil was 87.8%. It came down to 49.2% in 2000. It has further gone down. With the completion and commissioning of the Bakun dam, this dependency will experience further dip. Presently, hydropower generation accounts for around 11% of the total power generation. Although the country has abundance of biomass, it constitutes only 0.1% of the total energy supply. See Table 5 for comparative figure showing power mix as of 2017 and figures and tables between 2000 and 2014. Figure 6 shows that the main sources of energy in the Peninsular Malaysia are gas, oil and coal, whereas in Sabah, the main source is gas. In Sarawak, it is hydropower. It may be noted that the solar, biodiesel, biomass and biogas together constituted less than 1%. It is expected that the renewable sources of energy in the country will experience a mark rise.

Figure 5 Malaysia Energy Mix in 1994 and 2014

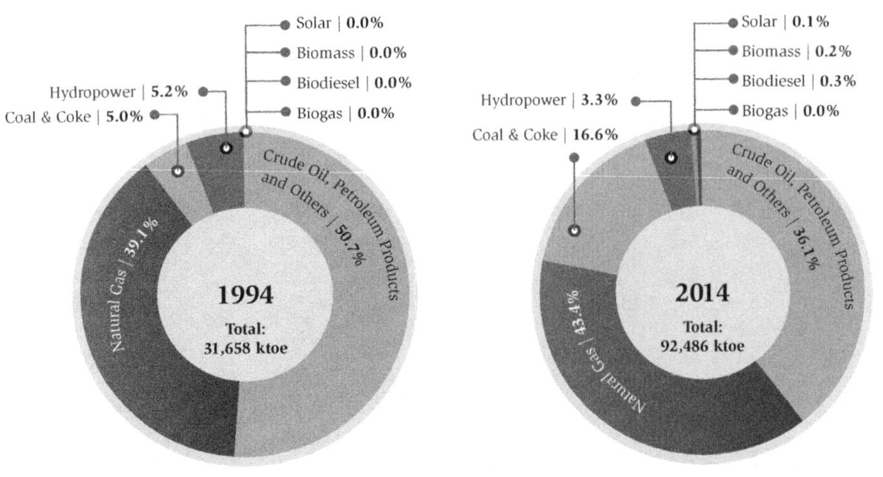

Source: Malaysian Statistics handbook 2016. Malaysia Energy Statistics Handbook 2016.

According to the Malaysia Energy Statistics handbook 2017, total generation will become 156003 GWh with: gas 43.5%; coal 42.5%; Hydro 13%; Biodiesel 0.4%; Oil 0.3%; and others 0.3%.

Figure 6 Energy Mix in 2017 in Peninsular Malaysia, Sabah and Sarawak

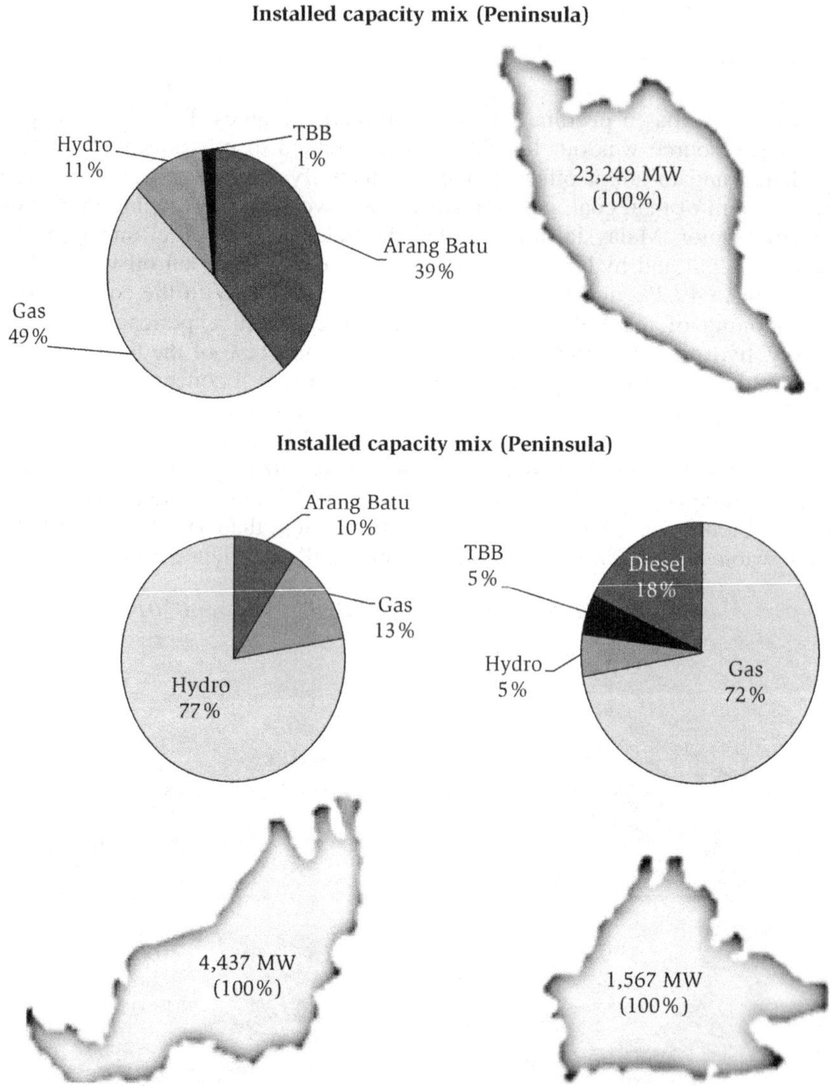

Installed capacity mix (Sarawak) Installed capacity mix (Sabah)
Source: KeTTHA Electricity Info February 2017.

The tabular presentations below demonstrate the energy mix positions the past and up to 2014.

Table 5 Primary Energy Sources in Malaysia 2000 and 2014

Source	*2000 (%)*	*2014 (%)*
Oil	71.4	30.1
Hydroelectric	11.6	3.1
Gas	8.8	64.2
Coal	7.6	1.7
Biomass	0.5	0.2
Others (biodiesel, biomass, solar and biogas)	0.1	0.9

Source: Energy Commission of Malaysia, Energy Statistics Handbook, 2016 report and.

15. According to the Ninth Malaysia Plan, total supply of energy increased from 2,003 PJ in 2000 to 2,526 PJ in 2005. The main sources of energy during this period were oil and natural gas. The ratio of coke and coal increased, but it relatively remained low. See Table 6 for comparative ratio.

Table 6 Energy Supply by Source 2000–2010

Source	*Petajoules*			*% of Total*			*Growth Rate %*	
Year/Plan	2000	2005	2010	2000	2005	2010	8MP	9MP
Oil	988.1	1181.2	1400.0	49.3	46.8	44.7	3.6	3.5
N. Gas	845.6	1043.9	1300.0	42.2	41.3	41.6	4.3	4.5
Coal	104.1	230.0	350.0	5.2	9.1	11.2	17.2	8.8
Hydro	65.3	71.0	77.7	3.3	2.8	2.5	1.7	1.8
Total	2003.1	2526.1	3127.7	100.0	100.0	100.0	4.7	4.4

Source: Ministry of Energy, Water and Communications and Economic Planning Unit.

16. It is evident from the above figures contained in Tables 5, 6 and 7 that since Malaysia has limited quantity of oil, it has now laid more emphasis on coal and gas as a source of energy. Accordingly the ratio, oil has reduced from 71.4% to 50.8%. But according to the Eighth Malaysia Plan, it has reduced from 54.3 (in 1995) to 53.1 in 2000; and it has been estimated that it had further reduced to 50.8% by 2005. The total picture can be seen in Table 7. But according to Table 6, which is contained in the Ninth Malaysia Plan, it went down to 46.8%.

Table 7 Primary Energy Sources in Malaysia in 1995, 2000, 2005 and 2014

Source	*1995*	*2000*	*2005*	*2014*
Oil	54.3	53.1	50.8	30.1
Gas	35.5	37.1	39.9	64.2
Hydro	5.0	4.4	3.4	3.1
Coal and Coke	5.2	5.4	5.9	1.7

Source: Eleventh Malaysia Plan

It refers to the supply of commercial energy that has not undergone a transformation process to produce energy.

It excludes flared gas, reinjected gas and exports of liquefied natural gas.

17. This may be noted that the total energy supply during the Eight Malaysia Plan period increased by an average of 5.3% per annum. This may also be noted from emphasis laid on the agricultural sector that the energy consumption will increase. Malaysia currently has energy reserves of around 3.39 billion barrels of oil, 89 trillion standard cubic feet of gas, 1,483 million tonnes of coal and 29,000 MW as hydroelectric reserve (123,000 GWh/year), which has increased with the operation of the Bakun dam. Presently, exploration of oil and gas is from more than forty-nine oil fields and thirteen gas fields. These fields are located within thirty-two offshore blocks awarded to and are currently operated by Petronas, the leading Malaysian oil and gas company, production sharing contracts (PSCs). It is notable that with the new discoveries of oil reserves, this projection might change. Because Malaysia has a large quantity of coal and gas deposits and its oil reserves are declining, it may be said that a time will come when Malaysia will have to fully depend on imported oil. In view of this, the country will increase its energy production based on coal-fired and gas-based power generation plants. This is shown by the estimated data prepared by the Gas Malaysia Bhd. The future projection can be seen in the below table which shows that reliability on coal and hydroelectric sources will increase with alleviation of consumption of oil and gas in the country. It is notable here that the 10 Malaysia Plan achieved: 1.33% reduction in greenhouse gases emission intensity of GDP compared to 2005 levels as of 2013; (2) EURO 4M for fuel are already implemented in 2013; (3) The Renewable Energy Act 2011 is already enforced with Feed-in-Tariff mechanism in place to support renewable energy. Greater and successful emphasis was made on upgrading the existing coal-fired power generation plants and maximizing the output of the Bakun Dam in Sarawak. In order to fulfil the cleaner energy demand in the country and to fulfil the promise to reduce the carbon emission under the UNFCCC, Malaysia in its 11th Malaysia Plan, 2016–2020, has undertaken to follow EURO 4 and EURO 5 standards for cleaner fuel and B15 (15% biodiesel blending) roll-out by 2020. There will be new generation capacity installed in Peninsular Malaysia by 2020, and additional refinery capacity by 2019. There will be additional import capacity through RTG-2 in Peninsular Malaysia; (4) 2080 MW electricity is aimed to be generated by renewable energy sources. In 2014, it was only 243 MW. Some important points in the 11th Malaysia Plan are the following:[18]

(1) The community involvement in rural electrification will be promoted with the help of relevant communities and NGOs in order to have sustainable electrification systems. By 2020 the rural electrification will become 99.9% with supply to 36,800 additional houses.
(2) The Strategy E4 will be geared up for managing supply diversity for security of electricity to support rural electrification. For that, rural infrastructure planning will be augmented.
(3) The areas that are too far from the grid, supply of electricity will be ensured through off-grid generation with the support of solar hybrid, and mini- and micro-hydro methods of power generation.
(4) Some 7626 MW new generation capacities will be installed in the West Malaysia.
(5) To ensure that electricity is affordable, the generation fuel mix will be made balanced to optimize the cost of supply. The Special Industrial Tariff will be abolished by 2020.
(6) In view of the Green Growth, energy efficiency will be one of the priorities. It is aimed that by 2020, 20% of government procurements will be green (for that, please see the Chapter dealing with energy efficiency, infra).
(7) Under the Strategy E4 and the Renewable Energy Action Plan, efforts will be made to substantially increase the share of renewable energy in the energy generation mix (please see the writing on Renewable energy).
(8) The sustainable energy use to support the growth of low-carbon power generation will be encouraged. The emphasis will be laid on both production and consumption. In order to facilitate it, appropriate regulations will be made. It is aimed that there will be 40% carbon reduction at 2005 level by the year 2020. These will be based on the Pollution Control Action Plan and the Decarbonization Strategy (for a detailed account, refer to the writing on protection of environment).
(9) The Enhanced Time of Use tariff scheme will gradually abolish the Special Industrial Tariff for energy-intensive industries (Strategy E5), focussing on sustainability, efficiency and reliability of the electricity sub-sector with sustainable tariff framework.
(10) The economic instruments such as green tax, carbon tax and REDD+ (reduction emission from deforestation and forest degradation) will be utilized wherever appropriate to develop green financing system.
(11) The use of CNG will be promoted.
(12) Under Strategy E2, secure security of supply and gas with increase in renewables will be an emphasis.
(13) There may be slight increase in the use of coal in the power generation.

18. See 'Eleventh Malaysia Plan, 2016-2020: Anchoring Growth on People' at: https://policy.asiapacificenergy.org/node/2508 (accessed on 15 Jan. 2018).

(14) Gas supply security will be ensured through the construction of pipelines from the Malaysia–Thailand Joint Development Area to Kertah, Terengganu; construction of RTG-2 in Pengerang, Johor and commissioning of two floating LNG units.
(15) The Refinery and Petrochemical Integrated Development (RADID) within the Pengerang Integrated Petroleum Complex (PIPC) will be encouraged.
(16) Under Strategy 3, independent power producers will be encouraged.
(17) Under the waste to wealth scheme, conversion of wastes into energy will be encouraged.
(18) Strategies will be developed to have more RE experts in the country.
(19) Efforts will be made to improve the security and reliability of the energy sector by addressing both supply-side and demand-side measures under the Strategy E1. Towards that, coordination and collaboration among the stakeholders will be enhanced.
(20) An independent Atomic Energy Regulatory Commission will be established based on a new comprehensive nuclear law for electricity generation.
(21) Initiatives will be taken to boost the clean energy technology research and develop skill in it with emphasis on renewable energy.

In view of the important features stated above in the Eleven Malaysia Plan and the strategies made for both the demand-side and the supply-side production projection until 2030 will be that the coal and gas will be the major sources of power generation. The renewable energy sources will still remain very low. It will be a moderate figure if we add hydropower generation source with it. The author is of the opinion that the renewable sources' energy generation should be given more attention, as they are clean and sustainable. Research and development in this area should be one of the priorities in the energy sector in the country. It should go hand-in-hand with energy efficiency, conservation and energy security strategies. For this purpose, it may be noted here that the Efficient Management of Electrical Energy Regulations 2008 requires that all installations on commercial and industrial premises that consume not less than 3 million kWh for a period up to six months need to appoint an Electrical Energy Manager (EEM) registered with the Energy Commission.

Table 8 Future Projections of Energy Sources in Malaysia on Percentage Basis: 2010–2030

Source	*2010*	*2020*	*2030*
Coal	36	45	50
Oil	1	1	0
Gas	56	48	45
Hydro	7	6	4
Others	1	1	1

However, it may be noted that Malaysia is planning under the 'Green Technology Policy', which has been one of the priorities of the Tenth Malaysia Plan and which is so in the Eleventh Malaysia Plan, to boost alternative and renewable energy sources. It might plan to construct few new dams also. It is also planning to have a nuclear power generation plant beyond the year 2030. Efforts are also being made to increase production of energy by using biomass and hydrogen cell (there is already motorcycle at the laboratory scale level under the leadership of Prof Dr Rashila Ramli of the University Kebangsaan Malaysia). There is possibility that in times to come, these clean sources of energy will significantly contribute to the energy mix of the country. In view of these, we can say that the figures given above might change.

Oil and Gas

18. Around half of the natural gas productions are in Sarawak. It is liquefied and exported as liquefied natural gas. In the Peninsula, natural gas comes from offshore Terengganu and is used domestically by industries, power, commercial and residential sectors. Petronas imports natural gas from Natuna, Indonesia, to support the demand in the Peninsula. Country's energy consumption initially was mainly on transportation and industrial sectors at 41.8% and 37.7% respectively, followed by commercial and residential sectors combined at 13.4% and the agricultural sector, which consumed only 0.39%. As stated above, in the near future, consumption on the agricultural sector will increase. In remote villages only biomass, such as wood or charcoal, is used, but the consumption of these is decreasing fast.[19]

19. Malaysia's crude oil reserves in 1995 were: off Sarawak – 26%; off Sabah – 14%; and off Peninsular Malaysia – 60%. The total oil reserve was 4.1 billion barrels. In 2000, it was: off Sarawak – 24%; off Sabah – 15%; and off Peninsular Malaysia – 61%. The total oil reserve fell to 3.4 barrels. It is said that the oil reserves are further declining and if new reserves are not discovered, by 2015, there will be no Malaysian oil. With discovery of new oil fields, this had proven to be wrong. The country is constantly working to find new oilfields within the country and to enter into agreements with foreign countries for exploration and exploitation

19. See 'Malaysia: Energy Profile and Future Estimations', <www.bu.edu/cees/classes/binna/304/energy_profiles/Malaysia.htm>; 'Extract from the Survey of Energy Resources 2001', <www.worldenergy.org/wecgeis/edc/countries/Malaysia.asp>; Institute of Energy Economics, Japan, 'Malaysia-Energy Overview', <www.ieej.or.jp/aperc/o/Malaysia.pdf>; International Energy Agency and Organisation for Economic Co-operation and Development, 'Energy Balances of Non-OECD Countries', Paris, France: OECD/IEA 2000. 1999–2000; Mohd Zamzam Jaafar, 'Malaysia's Energy Plan: The Way Forward', Malaysian Energy Centre, <www.ptm.org.my>; Komathi Mariyappan, 'Status of Renewable Energy and Energy Efficiency in Malaysia', <www.isep.or.jp/spena/2000/countryreports/malaysia.htm>; 'The Trends in Malaysia's Energy Consumption Up to the Year 2020', <www.ptm.org.my/ptmnews/Issue5-ED20.htm>; 'Eighth Malaysia Plan' (2001–2005), Economic Planning Unit, Prime Ministers Department, <www.epu.jpm.my/RM8/c11_cont.pdf>, 6 Apr. 2003; 'Malaysia', Energy Information Administration (2002), <www.eia.doe.gov/emeu/cabs/malaysia.html>, 6 Apr. 2003; Mohd Zamzam Jafaar, 'Greener Energy Solutions for a Sustainable Future: Issues and Challenges for Malaysia', *Energy Policy* 31 (): 1061–1072, <www.sciencedirect.com>, 6 Apr. 2003.

purposed. The county has recently entered into such agreements with Sudan and Nigeria. The country is also keen to improve and expand its refineries. It entered into an agreement to this effect with Saudi Arabia on 28 February 2017. It is known as RAPID. The project with USD 7 billion will be funded by the Saudi Aramco of the total project of USD 27 billion. Saudi Arabia will provide total of crude requirements. Malaysia will provide gas to be consumed by the project. The project is expected to be completed by early 2019. It will create 4000 jobs and will help boost the oil production in the country.[20]

20. Country's natural gas reserves in 1995 were: off Sarawak – 48%; off Sabah – 9%; and off Peninsular Malaysia – 43%. The total gas reserve was 84.7 tcf. This fell to 84.2 tcf in 2000: with 48% off Sarawak; 9% off Sabah; and 43% off Peninsular Malaysia. However, as at 1 January 2008, the gas reserve in the country was estimated at 88.0 tcf or 14.67 billion barrels. Of which 38% is there off the east coast, 48% off the Sarawak and 14% off the Sabah. Total gas produced in Malaysia was as under:

Table 9 Total Gas Produced in 1995–2015

Natural Gas Production, By Source 1995–2015 (mmscfd) Exploration Area	*1995*	*2000*	*2005*	*2015*
Off Peninsula	1440	2100	2800	1,949.69
Off Sabah	230	220	354	376.02
Off Sarawak	1881	2631	3888	4,147.00
Total	**3551**	**4951**	**7042**	**6,472.71**

Note: Total gas produced at wellhead.
Source: Eleventh Malaysia Plan.

21. Presently, the ratio of gas in production and consumption energy, according to the 2008 Report of the Energy Commission, is as follows:

- Production: Gas 60.7%; Coal 9.7%; Hydro 29.3%; and others 0.3%.
- Consumption: Gas 63.9%; Coal 6.9%; Hydro 29.1%; and others 0.1%.

It is notable that the percentage in power generation was different. We can see the estimated figures about production, consumption and present reserves of oil and gas in 2007–2008 in Table 10 below:

20. 'Mutually Beneficial Partnership for RAPID', *Energy Malaysia*, Vol. 11, p. 5.

Table 10 Malaysian Energy Situation (2007/2008) Estimates

Energy	*Production*	*Consumption*	*Reserves*
Electricity	102.9 billion kWh	95.58 billion kWh	-
Oil	753,300 bbl/day	501,100 bbl/day	4 billion bbl
Natural Gas	64.5 billion cu m	32.9 billion cu m	2.36 trillion cu m

Source: New Sunday Times, 28 June 2009.

22. According to the Energy Commission Report named 'Statistics of Distribution of Energy 2008', of the total gas production, 58.32% was utilized for power generation, 22.94% was used for non-power use, 12.27% was utilized for reticulation and the rest 6.48% is exported. This is well depicted by Table 11 below:

Table 11 Export and Utilization of Gas in Malaysia

Export	6.48%
Non-Power Sector	22.94%
Power Sector	58.32%
Reticulation	12.27%
Total	100%

23. On the basis of the Report of 2008 on the gas supply, the composition of gases was as shown in Table 12 as follows:

Table 12 Gas Composition in Peninsular Malaysia

Average Composition of Natural Gas supplied by Gas Malaysia Sdn Bhd from MT-JDA, Thailand and Kerteh, Malaysia

Source of Gas	*MT-JDA*	*Kerteh*
Gas	*Mol (%)*	*Mol (%)*
CH_4	85.86	95.17
C_2H_6	4.99	2.47
C_3H_8	1.54	0.43
IC_4H_{10}	0.12	0.02
nC_4H_{10}	0.09	0.02
$iC_5H_{12}+$	0.08	0.01
$nC_6H_{12}+$	0.04	0.01
$C_6H_{14}+$	0.02	0.01

Source of Gas	*MT-JDA*	*Kerteh*
CO_2	5.38	1.23
N_2	1.88	0.63

Source: Energy Commission: Statistics of Piped Gas Distribution Industry 2008.

Average composition of Liquified Petroleum Gas in Peninsular Malaysia

Gas	*Mol (%)*
C_3H_8	40.0
iC_4H_{10}	30.0
nC_4H_{10}	30.0

Source: Energy Commission: Statistics of Piped Gas Distribution Industry 2008.

Average Composition of Natural Gas supplied by Sabah Energy Corporation Sdn Bhd in Sabah

Gas	*Mol (%)*
CH_4	92.69
C_2H_6	3.54
C_3H_8	1.42
iC_4H_{10}	0.30
nC_4H_{10}	0.32
iC_6H_{12}	0.13
nC_5H_{12}	0.05
$C_6H_{14}+$	0.16
CO_2	1.28
N_2	0.14

Source: Energy Commission: Statistics of Piped Gas Distribution Industry 2008.

Average Composition of Natural Gas supplied by Sabah Energy Corporation Sdn Bhd in Labuan

Gas	*Mol (%)*
CH_4	91.22
C_2H_6	3.93
C_3H_8	1.99

Gas	*Mol (%)*
iC_4H_{10}	0.43
nC_4H_{10}	0.57
iC_5H_{12}	0.21
nC_5H_{12}	0.15
$C_6H_{14}+$	0.53
CO_2	1.36
N_2	0.13

Source: Energy Commission: Statistics of Piped Gas Distribution Industry 2008.

Average Composition of Natural Gas supply in Sarawak

Gas	*Mol (%)*
CH_4	85.09
C_2H_6	5.66
C_3H_8	3.97
iC_4H_{10}	0.86
nC_4H_{10}	1.10
iC_5H_{12}	0.37
nC_5H_{12}	0.27
$C_6H_{14}+$	0.48
CO_2	1.78
N_2	0.42

Source: Energy Commission: Statistics of Piped Gas Distribution Industry 2008.

24. Due to urbanization and use of gas in taxis, consumptions of natural gas and LPG are also increasing fast. From 2003, it had increased fivefold. This is clear from the statistics in the Table 13 below given by the above Report.

25. This may be noted that the total gas produced in the country is gradually increasing. This is because reliance for energy is increasing. The consumption of gas in power generation, running cars and household use are also increasing. It is notable here that Ranhill Power Bhd., which is a gas-fired power plant, is expecting up to 60 million RM that increases in the revenue by supplying more electricity from its Teluk Sulut plant to the Sabah state government. The company, thus, is increasing capacity at the plant to 190 MW from 120 MW and covering it from an open-cycle to a combined-cycle plant.[21] However, this source of energy will last for comparatively a longer time, and unless other gas reserves are found, the source of energy will totally deplete.

26. Malaysia had been trying hard to find new sources of oil and gas reserves. It was hoped that new oil reserves could be found in deepwater off Sabah. In view of this, Malaysian oil company Petronas developed a model deepwater PSC in 1996 and invited participants. This hope was brightened with the discovery of deepwater oil reserves in Kekeh, offshore Sabah in August 2002 by Murphy Oil Corporation. The area was estimated to have oil reserves between 400 million and 700 million barrels. In June 2004, the company registered another discovery in deepwater Kekap, located near the Kekeh area. Apart from MurphyOil Corporation, Shell announced that along with Petronas Cari Gali Sdn Bhd and Conoco Phillips it had discovered oil in deepwater Gumusut-1 well offshore Sabah in early 2004. Other deepwater oil players in Malaysia included Amerada Hess, French Total, Trenergy Bhd and Diamond Gas of the Netherlands.[22] ExxonMobil Corporation, one of the biggest American players in deepwater oil and gas exploration, but currently not engaged in such activities in Malaysia in deepwater exploration, had shown interest in exploring the possibility of finding oil and gas reserves in the deepwater off Sabah in future. The company had been operating in Malaysia for 110 years. It was thus the largest crude oil producer in the country and the largest supplier of natural gas in Peninsular Malaysia. The company had a working interest of 60% of crude oil in Malaysia and 70% working interest in gas offshore Peninsular Malaysia. ExxonMobil operates thirty-six platforms with a daily crude oil production of 280,000 barrels and a daily gas production of 1.3 billion cu ft. Esso Malaysia Bhd, its subsidiary company listed under Bursa Malaysia Bhd, operates a refinery in port Dickson capable of producing over 88,000 barrels a day. The then Chairman of its subsidiaries in Malaysia Robert Fisher said the company had no choice but to start thinking of exploring and producing more natural gas. They are already engaged in exploration of oil in the country, but emphasizing on exploration of gas because of the decline in the oil reserves. Hopefully, the company will grab the opportunity being offered by the Malaysian oil company Petronas.[23] Petronas planned and launched several new deepwater and ultra-deep water blocks (deepwater exploration involves the drilling of between 200 m and 1,000 m in water depth, while ultra-deep water exploration involves drilling beyond 1,000 m water depth.) offshore Sabah and Sarawak, which was prospected to be sold to multinational oil companies until July and November 2004. It was at that time and still notable that Malaysia has an exploration area of more than 600,000 sq km, which contains roughly over sixty blocks in shallow, deep and ultra-deep waters.[24] The former vice-president for exploration and production of Petronas, Datuk Shamsul Azhar Abbas, while presenting a paper entitled 'Up-Stream Prospects Challenges' at the Ninth Asia Oil and Gas Conference, Kuala Lumpur, June 2004, said that the company had

---

21. *New Straits Times*, 15 Jun. 2004.
22. *Ibid.*
23. *New Straits Times*, 14 Jun. 2004.
24. *New Straits Times*, 21 Jun. 2004.

just completed the demarcation of the blocks and they are ready for the take-up by exploration contractors. This may be noted here that one day ago at the same conference the President and Chief Executive Officer of Petronas Tan Sri Mohamad Hassan said that the company was focusing on developing ultra-deep water exploration as all the deepwater blocks had been taken up. Shamsul replied to this that he was referring to six other blocks, situated in open areas. He pointed out these areas fit for exploration of new reserves of oil and gas. He stated the estimated oil and gas reserves. He further said that Petronas has had an important discovery of oil in the area designated for exploration of gas.[25] Soon after this announcement some players including Trenergy Bhd indicated their willingness to explore the potential in deepwater exploration, particularly in the floating, production, storage and off-loading (FPSO) operations.[26]

27. Optimistically speaking, it could be said that if the search of deepwater and ultra-deepwater search of oil and gas prove to be successful and work well, the Malaysian oil will last for a fairly longer period, and it will be a good boost to the growing economy of the country. So will be the case of indigenous gas production and its contribution to the economy of the country.

28. According to the Eighth Malaysia Plan, Malaysian crude oil was largely exported due to its premium quality. The export decreased from 399,000 bpd in 1995 to 345,000 bpd in 2000. However, with the increase in the world oil prices, the export value of crude oil increased by an average annual rate of 16.3% from MYR 6.7 billion in 1995 to MYR 14.2 billion in 2000. Thus, in the near future, any increase in the oil price will not adversely affect Malaysia. With commissioning of the refinery in Malacca in 1997, Malaysia had six refineries with a total capacity of 520,000 bpd for domestic consumption and export. These refineries supplied more than 80% of the total domestic demand for petroleum products, thus reducing the import of petroleum products such as diesel, fuel oil and bitumen and increasing the export of certain products such as kerosene, liquefied petroleum gas and aviation fuel. Power generation plants and transport sector mainly utilize oil. The power sector has so far been the main consumer of gas accounting for 80.7% of total gas utilization in 2000. The non-power sector in this year consumed 19.3%, of which 45% was utilized by the petrochemical industry. With the implementation of the natural gas for vehicles (NGV) programme, the number of vehicles using LNG is increasing fast. The use of gas was further diversified with the introduction of gas district cooling (GDC) system, which produces chilled water for air conditioning and waste heat for power generation. It also helps to lower the peak load demand and reduces investment for peaking capacity. Gas is being exported to Japan, Taiwan and South Korea. The export was proposed to be increased.

29. All the same, it was stated in the Ninth Malaysia Plan that crude oil and condensate reserves increased from 4.4 billion barrels in 2000 to 5.3 billion barrels in

25. *New Straits Times*, 16 Jun. 2004.
26. *New Straits Times*, 21 Jun. 2004. A fully integrated FPSO is defined as having a spectrum of oil and gas-related activities from drilling to storage on a floating vessel.

2005. The average production of domestic crude oil and condensate increased from 681,000 barrels per day in 2000 to 727,000 barrels per day in 2005. Based on this production level, which is in line with the NDP, the reserves are projected to last for only nineteen years. Although the total refining capacity declined from 591,000 barrels per day to 546,500 barrels per day, it was sufficient to meet the demand for petroleum products. The export of crude oil and condensate increased to 369,000 barrels per day with a value of MYR 28.5 billion in 2005. The major export destinations were Australia, Thailand, India and the Republic of Korea.

30. At the advent of the 15th Asian Oil and Gas Conference, June 2010, Kuala Lumpur, experts noted that Malaysian exploration and supply of oil would increase in times to come. Alun Jones said that by the year 2014, Malaysia only would remain the net exporter of oil. According to Business Monitor International Report on Malaysian oil and gas outlook, Malaysia will account for 1.8% of Asia-Pacific's oil demand by 2014, while providing 8.36% of the total supply. Alun Jones said that the regional oil imports were growing rapidly because demand growth was outstripping the pace of supply expansion. He further said that the 2008 BP statistical energy survey revealed that Malaysia had proven oil reserves of 5.357 billion barrels as at the end of 2007. He stated that Malaysia was currently driving the region's subsea industry and had been at the forefront of the development through Petroliam National Berhad (Petronas), which was committed to augment offshore oil exploration at many places of the world. The country might become a regional hub if this trend continues, he said.[27] Bernard Di Tullio said that in terms of subsea industry, Malaysia was already a hub. Malaysia's deepwater industry was largely developed and it would soon become one of the four deepwater hubs. He appreciated Malaysia's efforts by saying that in past three years, Malaysia had shown fast development in this area. He further said:

> There have already been quite a number of fabrication works for Malaysia's deepwater oilfields, namely Kikeh and Gumusut. These include the manufacturing of flexible and ambilical pipes, spar and semi-submersible, installations of vessels as well as manufacturing of subsea wells.

It was notable that apart from these, there are other players like Malaysian Marine Heavy Engineering, Sapura and Aker Kvaerner. It will be possible by pouring in of foreign investments and internal efforts. It could be noted, for example, that Technip, which had investment of 800 million, planned to invest more. Likewise, ConocoPhillips will be investing USD 3 billon in the near future.[28] Exxon Mobil has already invested USD 15 billion in Malaysia. In late 2009, the company signed a twenty-five-year PSC with Petronas Cari Gali Sdn Bhd. to develop seven oil fields, namely Tapis, Seligi, Guntong, Semangkok, Irong Barat, Tabu and Palas. Under the terms of the PSC, the three parties spent around USD 2.1 billion to undertake major enhanced oil recovery projects, rejuvenation of facilities as well as development and

27. See Kamarul Yunus, 'Malaysia Region's Sole Oil Exporter by 2014', *New Straits Times* (*Business Times*), 8 Jun. 2010.
28. See *New Straits Times*, 9 Jun. 2010.

drilling activities in the fields.[29] Petronas mulled to expand all its capacities by finding new exploration sites around the world independently and in collaboration with other oil exploration industries, and by increasing the capacity of the Malacca refinery by 20,000 barrels per day. Petra Energy Berhad, an integrated oil and gas brownfield service provider, bided for contracts worth more than MYR 1 billion in the country for hook up and commissioning work. It is also bidding for brownfield maintenance contracts for all of Petroleum National Bhd's oilfields. This was revealed by its CEO K.B. Akbari at the 15th Asia Oil and Gas Conference, Kuala Lumpur, 14 June 2010. He further said:

> A new area we are moving into is subsea. We are evaluating the market potential for this. It is a natural migration for us as the water gets deeper. We understand the margins are good. We want to do something additional to what we have in our portfolio now.[30]

The Petronas Malacca Refinery complex houses two refining trains. The first train, known as PSR-1, is owned and operated by Petronas Penapinsan (Melaka) Sdn. Bhd., a wholly owned subsidiary of Petronas, while the second train, known as PSR-2, is owned by Malaysian Refining Co. Sdn Bhd, a joint venture between Petronas and ConocoPhillips. Each train has the capacity to process 100,000 bpd of sweet crude and condensates. Md Arif Mahmood vice-president for corporate strategic planning of Petronas said that the company would seriously consider potential opportunities for collaborations, alliances and partnerships, particularly in new growth areas that include unconventional oil and gas plays in other regions with high potential. He said that:

> The bottom line is to optimize value from several investments either in Malaysia or in other parts of the world to pursue growth and sustainability. Petronas is not just looking at foreign partnership with international oil companies and national oil companies, but beyond. Some of our production-sharing contractors are smaller and independent companies. Abroad, we are also collaborating with several players. The activities of the company will go beyond and work for manufacturing and selling unconventional oil and gas.[31]

Petronas negotiated with Iraq for concessions pertaining to exploration work in Iraq. There was probability that it would succeed in its efforts. Petronas has been shortlisted by the Iraqi government, and it did.[32]

Presently, Malaysia in South East Asia is the second largest oil producer after Indonesia. In 2016, it was estimated that it produced 744,000 barrels per day, which was 15% more than 2013 figures but slightly down from the 2003 figures, because of down oil price, production reduction around the world and maturing fields; more than a quarter of this originated from the Tapis oilfields. In 2014, exploration

29. See *New Straits Times*, 8 Jun. 2010; 10 Jun. 2010.
30. *New Straits Times*, 15 Jun. 2010.
31. See *New Straits Times*, 9 Jun. 2010.
32. *Ibid.*

started Lundin Petroleum's new Bertam oilfields of the Penyu Basin and the Gumusut–Kakap deepwater oilfields. This increased the total oil exploration and oil recovery in mature fields.

The consumption side has shown marked increase, which adversely affected the oil export in the country. The national oil company PETRONAS is trying hard to revert the situation by resorting to various measures and by inventing new oil reserves, mainly by risk service contracts, in which the company remains the owner and investors share the revenue for oil produced throughout the life of the agreed project. Contracts for exploring new deepwater offshore oil reserves of Sarawak and Sabah are being entered into, as they require advanced techniques and large financial investments. Since 2013, PETRONAS has also increased spending to support the exploration activities. The idea is to increase the export of oil. In addition to this, the national oil company with the help of some foreign companies, in 2014, started about ten enhanced oil recovery projects (EOR) ailed to increase the production lives of old and less productive oil fields. In this respect the partnership with ExxonMobil is notable. They are working together in several oilfields. It is expected that because of these projects the lives of oil fields will increase by about thirty years. Some foreign companies are also selling their exploration facilities to Malaysian companies. One such example is that in 2016 Shell sold its stake in the North Sabah EOR PSC to Malaysia's Hibiscus Petroleum.

As noted above, in addition to EOR projects, for maximizing oil production in the country, Malaysia also gave away several risk service contracts for about 100 small oil fields 580 million barrels of oil reserves.[33]

So far oil trade is concerned, at present import of oil is slightly more than the export of crude although Malaysia is the fourth oil producer in the Asia-Pacific after China, India and Vietnam. The country could be called as net oil exporter in 2016. In this year, it exported 333,000 b/d of crude oil, and imported some 200,000 b/d of crude oil. This difference is perhaps because of weaker economic growth in 2015 and 2016. In 1994, import of oil was only 7.4% (shown as lighter shade in Figure 7) and export was 92.6%. This figure changed to 45.1% and 54.9% (See Figure 7).

According to the Oil & Gas Journal, Malaysia might have around 3.6 billion barrels as of January 2017 in three basins, Malay Basin, Offshore Peninsular Malaysia and the Sabah and Sarawak Basins. As stated above, there are a large number of foreign and local companies in the Oil and Gas sector, but PETRONAS is the biggest player among them. It has equity in all upstream production share contracts (PSC). Foreign big players are: ExxonMobil, Shell and Murphy. Repsol, Lundin Petroleum, Roc Oil Company and Petrofac also come into the arena. It is notable here that the Indonesia's National Oil Company (NOC) has acquired 30% stake of the Murphy Oil in Malaysia in 2015. It is also to be noted that in view of the 2014 oil price slump, PETRONAS aimed to reduce its investment to the tune of 11.2 billion dollars between 2016 and 2020. But it is hoped that with the normalization of oil prices, the company may revise its investment policy.[34]

---

33. U.S. Energy Information Administration, Country Analysis Brief: Malaysia, 26 Apr. 2017.
34. *Ibid.*

Figure 7 Import and Export of Crude Oil in 1994 and 2014

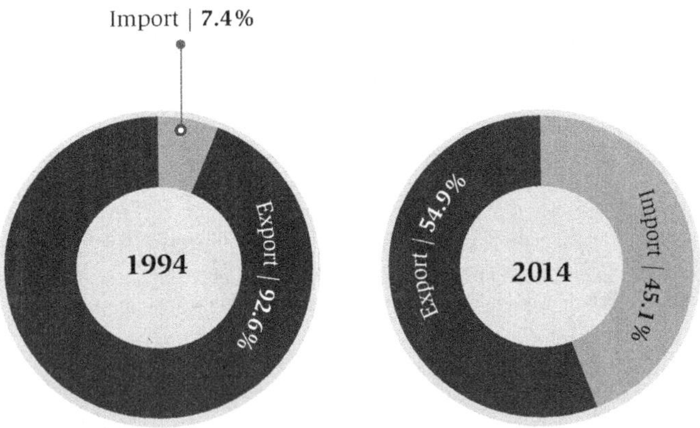

Sources: Energy Commission: Malaysia Energy Statistics Handbook 2016.

During this period, import petroleum products rose slightly from 56.5% to 60.6%. Export of petroleum products slightly fell from 40.5% to 39.4%. According to the Malaysia Energy Statistics Handbook 2017, in 2015, these figures changed to 65.8% and 34.2%. This is a good improvement. With the improvement in the oil prices, the figure change in favour of the country. (See Figure 8).

Figure 8 Import and Export of Petroleum Products in 1994 and 2014

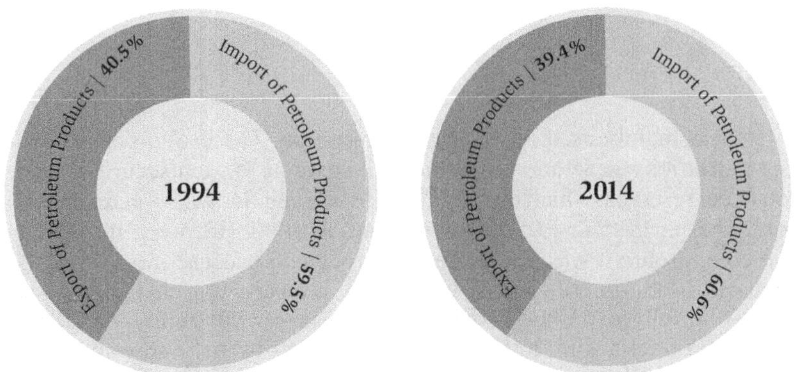

Source: Energy Commission: Malaysia Energy Statistics Handbook 2016.

According to the Malaysian Statistics Handbook 2017, in 2015, import of petroleum products rose to 41.8% and import fell to 58.2%. This is also good economic indicator.

We have noted above that in 2004, 91.5% of LNG and 4.5% of piped natural gas were exported, and 4% piped natural gas was imported. In 2014, this figure changed. Export of LNG fell to 74.3% and export of piped natural gas fell to 3%. Import of piped natural gas during this period rose to 17.3%. Still, Malaysia is the third highest LNG exporter in the world. It is expected that this position is going to remain for few more years to come. (See Figure 9).

Figure 9 Export of Piped Natural Gas and LNG in 2004 and 2014

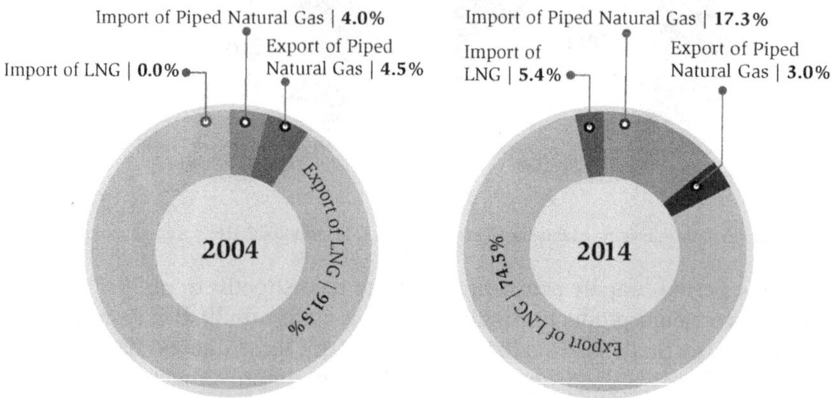

According to the Malaysia Energy Statistics Handbook 2017, the figures are: export of LNG 75.3%; report of piped LNG 3.0%; import of piped LNG 16.5%; and import of LNG 5.2%

§2. Coal

31. Coal is mainly used in electricity generation. The use of coal as an energy source in electricity generation was aimed at ensuring system security and reliability. Total coal reserves, which are mainly in Sabah and Sarawak, increased from 974 million tonnes in 1995 to 1,050 million tonnes in 2000. However, the development of local coal resources was not aggressively pursued because most of the deposits were located in the interior areas, which lack infrastructure and therefore uneconomical to be fully exploited. Coal production increased from 114,000 tonnes in 1995 to 310,000 tonnes in 2000, which was utilized by the Sarawak-based power generation plants. We have noted above that Malaysia has a plan to have some more coal-fired power generation plants. One has been started recently (Eighth Malaysia Plan, 315). One more will be started in the near future. (See Table 13)

32. According to the US Energy Information Administration, an average value during 1986 and 2014 was 919.55 thousand short tonnes with minimum of 24 thousand short tonnes in 1986 and a minimum of 3252 thousand short tonnes in 2012, which is slowly increasing.[35] In 2013, it was 3256 short tonnes. Coal consumption in Malaysia during this period has gradually increased because of gradual increase in the electricity demand. In 2014, it was 15.4 million tonnes oil equivalent. This increased to 16.9 in 2015 and 19.9 million tonnes oil equivalent in 2016.[36] This increase, as noted above, is due to construction of new coal-fired power generation plants in the Peninsular Malaysia.

Table 13 Existing and Planned Coal-Fired Power Plants 2000–2010

Plant	*Capacity*	*Completion*	*Coal Utilization*
TNB Kapar Ph. 2	600 MW	1988	1.5 mtpa
TNB Kapar Ph 3	1000 MW	2000	2.5 mtpa
TNB Janamanjung	2100 MW	2002/03	6.0 mtpa
SKS – IPP	2100 MW	2004/05	6.0 mtpa
Jimah – IPP	1400 MW	2005/06	3.0 mtpa

Source: John Thaddeus, 'Energy Scenario in Malaysia', at <http://eneken.ieej.or.jp/japac>./document/2 610319170913_2pdf>.

Since 2010 with the increase in demand in Malaysia, the power generation also experienced a considerable boost, especially in the Peninsular Malaysia. This demand was mainly fulfilled in this part of the country by upgrading and constructing new coal-fired power generation plants. In 2015, 42% of power generation was coal-fired and 51.8% was gas-fired. The country does not seem keen to have nuclear power in the near future. In view of that and in order to meet the growing energy demand by 2.3% annually atleast until 2030, it may be said that thermal power will be the main sources, and of this coal-fired power generation will be substantial. It is expected that the coal will dominate although coal in this part of the country has to be imported.

35. See, the Global Economy.com, Malaysia Coal production at: https://www.theglobaleconomy.com/Malaysia/coal_production/ (accessed on 20 Feb. 2018).
36. Statista, at: https://www.statista.com/statistics/612105/coal-consumption-in-malaysia/ (accessed on 12 Feb. 2018).

Table 14 Coal-fired Power Plants in 2015

Plant	*State*	*Coordinates*	*MW*	*Type*	*Owner/operator*	
Jimah Power Station	Negri Sembilanat Lukut	2°35'11″N101°43'21″E	1,400	Thermal (2 ST)	Jimah Energy Ventures Sdn Bhd	[15]
Manjung Power Station	Perak at Manjung	4°9'44″N100°38'48″E	2,295	Thermal (3 ST)	TNB Janamanjung Sdn Bhd	[15]
Mukah Power Station	Sarawak	2°55'56″N112°11'32″E	270	Thermal (2 ST)	Mukah Power Generation Sdn Bhd, a subsidiary of Sarawak Energy Berhad	[15][16]
PPLS Power Generation Plant	Sarawak in Kuching		110	Thermal (2 units)	PPLS Power Generation, a subsidiary of Sarawak Energy Berhad	
Sejingkat Power Corporation Plant	Sarawak at Kuching		200	Thermal	Sejingkat Power Corporation Sdn Bhd, a subsidiary of Sarawak Energy Berhad	[11]

Plant	*State*	*Coordinates*	*MW*	*Type*	*Owner/operator*
Sultan Salahuddin Abdul Aziz Shah Power Station	Selangor at Kapar	3°7'1″N101°19'1″E	2,420	Thermal (6 ST), open cycle (2 GT), natural gas and coal with oil backup	Kapar Energy Ventures Sdn Bhd
Tanjung Bin Power Station	Johor at Pontian	1°20'3″N103°32'55″E	2,100	Thermal (3 ST)	Tanjong Bin Power Sdn Bhd, a subsidiary of Malakoff

33. It is notable as of March 2018 that the coal capacity in peninsular Malaysia is 51%. In view of the cleaner energy and pledge of certain countries to do away with coal power generation, especially its phasing out by 2020, Malaysia is making its best efforts to diversify the energy mix of the country. However, the process of such a phasing out in ASEAN is not in the near future. ASEAN countries for this look at Japan, as it intends to develop more coal-fired thermal power generation in the near future, because the public opinion in Japan is against having nuclear power generation after the Fukushima accident. The world more so Japan is committed to producing clean coal as shown in the COP 21 at the time of Paris Agreement of December 2015. High Efficient and Low Emission (HELE) technologies such as Super Critical, Ultra-Super Critical and Advanced Ultra-Super Critical coal-fired power generation plants are being developed to operate at higher steam temperature and pressure to improve generation efficiency. It will produce more electricity with less coal. In line with the front runners, China and Japan, Malaysia commissioned its USC coal-fired plant in April 2015 and the second one in 2016. HELE due to its high cost may be in operation after some time. High cost is prompting Malaysia to look for renewable energy with Feed-in-Tariff facilities.[37]

34. It is estimated that by 2020, it will become 53%; gas-fired power generation will shrink to 30%.[38] This target is achievable with the emphasis laid to this power generation sector. Malaysian Company Malakoff Corporation commissioned an ultra-super critical coal-fired power generation plant of 1 GB capacity in March 2016. The construction of another 2,000 MW similar power generation plant with 2.6 billion Malaysian Ringgit has begun in Port Dickson. The main national power generation company TNB has 70% stake in it. It is expected to be completed by December 2019. Upon completion, Malaysia's generation capacity jumped to 26,940 MW from 22,748 MW by 2020. JEP project has further increased the power generation. They are: 1,000 MW Manjung 4 and 1,000 MW Manjung 5.[39] It may be noted here that Manjung 5 plant in Lumut, Perak, of RM 6 billion has started working from 1 October 2017. The other two similar plants of 1,000 MW capacity known as Jimah East Plants will be commissioned in 2019.[40]

35. In view of this, coal utilization mainly as fuel for power plants in the country, it was estimated that there will be increase from about 4.2 million tonnes oil equivalent in the year 2000 to about 13 million tones oil equivalent in 2005; and if some more coal-fired power generation plants are commissioned, the utilization will increase. Presently, in the energy generation mix of Tenaga Nasional Berhad (TNB), approximately 30% is coal.[41] This increase will be because of commissioning of new coal-fired power generation plants and government's licensing for independent

37. *See infra.*
38. Detail about these may be seen at: http://www.powermag.com/tanjung-bin-energy-power-plant-johor-malaysia-2/(accessed on 15 Feb. 2018).
39. *The Star Online,* 27 Mar. 2017.
40. *The Star Online,* 28 Sep. 2017.
41. *New Straits Times,* 23 Aug. 2005.

power production (IPP). Consumption by the cement industries is also expected to increase from about 1.8 million tonnes in the year 2000 to about 2 million tonnes in year 2005.

36. According to the Ninth Malaysia Plan, the consumption of coal for power generation and industrial use was expected to reach 19.0 million tonnes and 2.2 million tonnes, respectively, in 2010, mainly by the commissioning of two coal-fired power generation plants in Peninsular Malaysia. Efforts will be continued to enhance the security of supply by exploring the potential of developing local sources, particularly in Sarawak as well as securing long-term supplies from abroad.

The figures show the increase in the annual consumption of coal in power generation. It may be noted that, according to the Malaysian Statistics Handbook 2016, coal consumption rose from 5% in 1994 to 16.6% in 2014. (See figure 10).

Figure 10 Primary Energy Supply by Fuel Type, 1994 and 2014

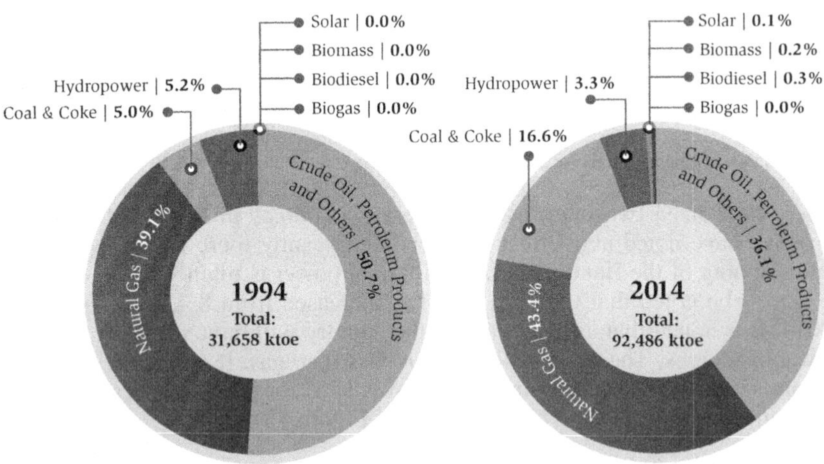

Source: Malaysian Energy Statistics Handbook 2016.

According to Malaysian Energy Statistics Handbook 2017, the figures in 2015 were: total energy supply rose to 100,721 ktoe, of which natural gas was 61.7%; crude oil was 32.2%; hydropower was 3.6%; coal and coke were 1.6%; biodiesel was 0.7%; biomass was 0.2%; solar was 0.1%; and biogas was 0.0%. We can notice that the gas source experienced tremendous rise.

Whereas, during this period according to the same source, input to power stations during this period rose from 9.3% to 9.6%. (See Figure 11).

Figure 11 Input to Power Stations by Fuel Type 1994 and 2014

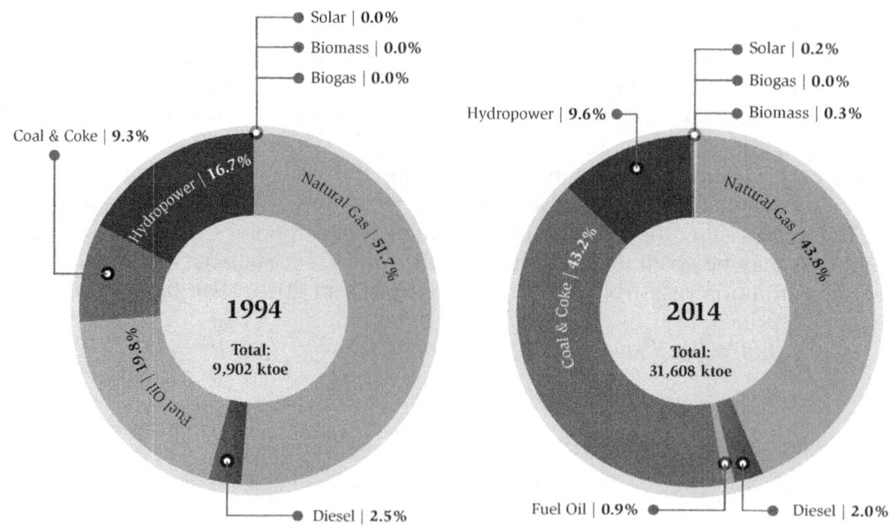

Sources: Malaysia Energy Statistics Handbook 2016.

There have been two main power generation sources in Malaysia, thermal and hydro. We have noted above that hydro is significantly there in Sarawak after the commissioning of the Bakun Dam. The thermal power is mainly based on coal and gas. It may be noted that the ratio of it has increased from 83.3% in 1994 to 87.7 in 2014. It is hoped that as stated above the country will have to revert seriously to renewable sources. The ratio of the coal is less than gas. (See Figure 12).

It may be further noted that in 1995 oil was used for power generation. In 2015, it is no more in use. It has yielded gas. (See Figure 13).

Figures 12 and 13 Energy Generation Plant Type in 1994 and 2014 and Power Generation Mix in 1995 and 2015

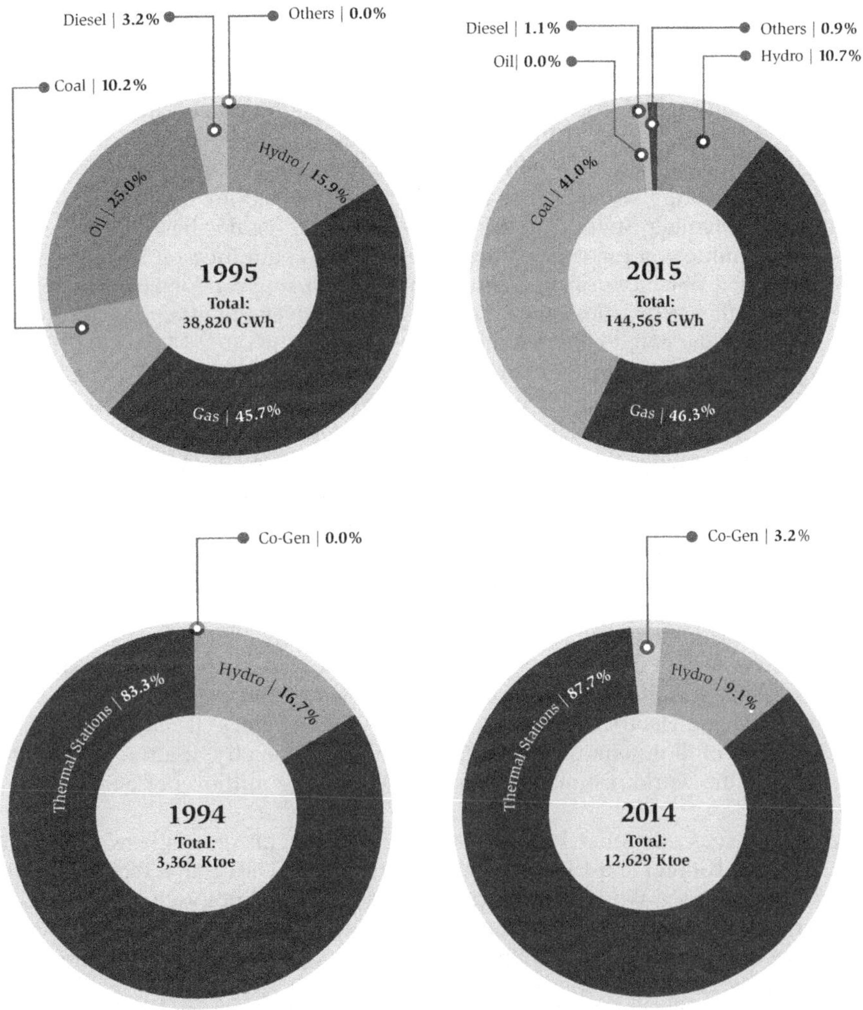

Sources: Malaysia Energy Statistics Handbook 2016.

§3. Wood Energy (Biomass Energy)

37. In 2008, wood energy accounted for 9% of total energy consumption in Malaysia. Statistics showed that most biomass energy was consumed by industries, but data on wood-fuel use by households were not available. In the domestic sector, biomass energy is mainly used for cooking. Malaysia proved to be exceptional among Regional Wood Energy Development Programme in Asia (RWEDP, 1985–2001) member countries for several reasons. One of them is that it has a rage quantity of wood and biomass resources. This is notwithstanding the fact that rubber wood is now much less available as most of it now being used in furniture industry. Likewise, the industrial wood wastes of palm oil industries and timber industries, which could have been used for burning, are being used for making furniture, especially tabletops, false ceilings and generating electricity. Prime Ministers Energy Planning Unit (EPU) quickly took up the challenge of wood/biomass energy planning, which was initially an ignored area in the country. EPU had already incorporating wood energy into the energy plans, thus taking a lead among the RWEPD Member States. The EPU took data on a regular basis. There exists a national committee on renewable energy, with a sub-committee on biomass energy. The underlined objective of the sub-committee is to suggest for utilizing biomass waste more efficiently as an energy source without adversely affecting the environment. This may be noted here that the Forest Research Institute Malaysia (FRIM) is working hard towards this and it has already developed devices that can produce heat with fewer emissions into the atmosphere. With regard to a wider range of fuels from biomass, research results from the Palm Oil Research Institute Malaysia (PORIM) on carotene from palm oil have been significant. Likewise, palm oil engine fuel is also of high value. They are technologically and commercially viable. They are already in use in some of the public buses.[42] The New Energy Policy 2010 and Add Energy Planning with various sustainable energy initiatives – Four-Fuel Diversification Policy 1981, Fifth Fuel Policy 2000, National Green Technology 2009, National Renewable Energy Policy and Action Plan 2010 – have increased the value and volume of biomass use in energy generation. The Malaysian Biomass Industry Action Plan 2020 has provided further boost to it. It aims to position the nation's biomass industry towards high value creation and boost sustainable practices in producing electricity from the biomass of the country. It may be noted here that 80 to 100 million tonnes of biomass is produced annually. It attracted investors from around the world, estimated at around MYR 82.9 million per annum.

38. A Japanese scientist Professor Yoshimitsu Umera, presently working with the Centre for Biofuel and Biochemical Research of the University Technology Petronas, claimed at the World Engineering, Science and Technology Congress, Kuala Lumpur, 27–28 June 2010, that the country had the potential to produce 30% of its energy needs by this source. Looking at the biomass generated in the country, what he said seems to be close to reality.[43]

39. The Minister of Energy, Communication and Multimedia of Malaysia, while speaking at the signing ceremony of Master Energy Services Agreement (MESA)

42. See <www.rwepd.org/c_cmal.html> (*Regional Study on Wood Energy Today and Tomorrow in Asia*, RWEDP Field Document 50, 1997; *Review of Wood Energy Data in RWEDP Member Countries*, Ch. 8, RWEPD Field Document 47, 1997; *Biomass Energy in Asean Member Countries*, RWEPD, Field Document 47, 1997.

43. See Yoshimitu Umera, 'Utilization of Biomass as Energy Source in Malaysia', paper presented at the World Engineering, Science and Technology Congress, Kuala Lumpur, 17–18 Jun. 2010.

between HeveaBoard Sdn. Bhd. and Mensilin Holdings Sdn. Bhd., 7 April 2003, said that the wood sector in Malaysia is one of the most energy-intensive sectors. There are more than 5,000 wood processing mills in the country, and at 3% intensity and an energy consumption growth rate of 19%, the wood sector is on the high-priority list of energy reduction programmes. This is notable that the agreement between the two companies replaced the oil-fired drying system or the combustion boiler, with a wood-fired drying system. This will lead to reduction of consumption of oil and gas and putting the use of wood waste, which is a byproduct of HeveaBoard, into useful energy sources. This way the company could save up to 90% of fossil fuel, which could be used for other activities.[44] These kinds of activities are growing fast in the country providing a productive use of wood-based industries.

40. Biomass is now used for heating, electric power generation and combined heat and power generation. Biomass in the country is mainly obtained from palm oil and timber industries. It is converted to electric power mainly by direct combustion. The other options are: gasification, pyrolysis and anaerobic digestion. Different processes require different types of biomass. In Malaysia, woody biomass is generally combusted for generation of electricity.[45] According to SEDA, with result of that in 2015, 18,090.00 MWh electricity was generated by biomass solid waste, but it reduced to 6,963.50 MWh in 2016. It is due to less availability of such wastes.[46] In Malaysia, in 2014 biomass electricity generation was 23% of the total renewable energy by all means. It is projected that by 2020, it will become 38%.[47] It is notable here that biomass energy is not growing fast because the purchase price offered to IPPs from this source is not lucrative. However, this energy source is growing. In Sabah, in spite of this, a group of Japanese investors, who had invested in Thailand in the same industry, advanced money under the Clean Development Mechanism of the Kyoto Protocol until 2012. Currently, the Malaysian company operates 2 biomass power plants together producing 23 MW which is sold to Sabah Electricity under the FiT Renewable Energy Power Purchase Agreement, allowing 1.5 MW to be used by the plant itself. Initially, these plants could not perform well, but in the long run, they performed well. They are performing well even now. Currently, there are seven such plants in Malaysia. It is said that in order to keep them running and encouraging new biomass energy plants to open, the tariff rate should be attractive.[48]

---

44. See <www.ptm.org.my/mieeip/speech.html>.
45. See, 'Biomass for Electricity Generation', 15 Sep. 2016, at: http:www.wbdg.org/resources/biomass-electricity-generation (accessed on 20 Feb. 2018).
46. 'East and Southeast Asia Renewable Energy Statistics Training Workshop', 12–14 Dec. 2016, Bangkok, Thailand, at: http://www.irena.org/events/2016/Dec/East-and-Southeast-Asia-Renewable-Energy-Statistics-Workshop (accessed on 3 Apr. 2018).
47. Ministry of Energy, Green Technology and Water, 'Malaysia Energy Policy: Focusing on Sustainable Energy Development and the Way Forward', at: http://bseep.gov.my/App_ClientFile/df08bc24-99fb-47a3-937f-dc25df9d3997/Assets/BSEEP%20NCA2017/PAPER%204%20-%20KETTHA_Malaysia%20Energy%20Policy_04052017.pdf (accessed on 12 Jan. 2018).
48. See, 'Powering Through Maximising Innovation to Spur Biomass', *Energy Malaysia*, Vol. 10, 2016, pp. 34–37.

§4. ELECTRICITY

41. According to John Thaddeus of TNB Fuel Services Sdn Bhd., the total installed generation capacity in Peninsular Malaysia as of 2001 was approximately 13,000 MW. The electricity generation industry in the country operates in private sector. Of the total installed capacity, 4,474 MW, which was around 34.4%, was owned and operated by five Independent Power Producers (IPPs). The entry of IPPs has taken a substantial slice of the generation market share from TNB, which prior to 1992 had a complete monopoly of the electricity supply industry. TNB also moved away from direct investment in power generation when all of its power stations were leased out to its wholly owned subsidiary, TNB Generation Sdn. Bhd. Most of the IPPs operating in Malaysia were developed on non-recurrence financing arrangement basis, where cost and performance management becomes a prime concern to the developers after debt payment.

42. The electricity supply industry experienced major changes during the plan period, particularly the restructuring of the three major utilities, namely TNB, SESB and Sarawak Electricity Supply Corporation (SESCO), which took place consequentially to the privatization programme. These included further streamlining of TNB's operations, divestment of its thermal plants as well as the privatization of LLS, which was subsequently known as Sabah Electricity Sdn. Bhd. With the operation of IPPs, the major utilities were relieved of the need to provide capital investments for new power plants to meet the nation's increasing electricity demands. Presently, estimated new generation capacity is projected at 12,649 MW. Relevant data pertaining to generation, generation mix, transmission and distribution are as follows:

Table 15 Installed Capacity, Peak Demand and Reserve Margin, by Source, 1995–2005

Year	*Generation by System (MW)*	*Accumulated Installed Capacity (MW)*	*Peak Demand (MW)*	*Reserve Margin (%)*
1995	Total	10,835	7,212	50.2
2000	Total	14,110	10,673	35.1
2005	Total	22,745	16,834	35.1

Source: Eighth Malaysia Plan.

System refers to utilities and the respective IPPs.

Peak demand is the maximum power demand registered by the system in a stated period of time.

43. Reserve margin equals accumulated capacity minus peak demand divided by peak demand multiplied by hundred.

44. The Ninth Malaysia Plan stated that in line with the strategy to ensure security and reliability of electricity supply as well as reduce the high dependence on gas, the source of fuel for power generation was further diversified with the increased use of coal. In this regard, two coal-based plants were commissioned by TNB while the Sejingkat plant was expanded by SESCO. During the plan period, a total of 6,240 MW of new generation capacity was installed.

45. In consonance with the growth of the economy, peak demand increased from 10,657 MW to 13,779 MW in 2005. With the expansion in the installation capacity, the reserve margin increased, which was more than adequate to meet demand. To enable sharing of costs for maintaining the reserve margin, the concept of demand risk sharing was introduced in power purchase agreements (PPAs). Installed Capacity, peak demand and reserve margin as projected by the Ninth Malaysia Plan were:

Table 16 Installed Capacity, Peak Demand and Reserve Margins, 2000–2010

Year	*Generation By System*	*Accumulated Installed Capacity (MW)*	*Peak Demand (MW)*	*Reserve Margin (%)*
2000	TNB	12,645	9,712	30.2
	SESB	785	391	100.8
	SESCO	861	552	55.4
	Total	14,291	10,657	34.1
2005	TNB	17,622	12,493	41.1
	SESB	639	543	17.7
	SESCO	956	743	28.7
	Total	19,217	13,779	39.5
2010	TNB	22,802	18,187	25.4
	SESB	1,100	802	37.2
	SESCO	13,56	1,098	23.5
	Total	25,258	20,087	25.7

Source: Tenaga Nasional Berhad Sdn, Bhd (TNB), and Syarikat SESCO Berhad (SESCO). Taken from Ninth Malaysia Plan.
System refers to utilities and IPPs.

Peak demand is the maximum power demand registered by the system in a stated time.

Reserve margin equals accumulated capacity minus peak demand, all of which divided by peak demand and multiplied by 100.

46. In view of the budget deficit in 2008 and 2009, the expected commissioning of the Bakun Dam Project was expected to be operative by the end of 2011. With respect to the generation in 2009 and consumption of electricity in the country, it was decided not to build new power generation plants. There was a proposal, accepted in principle, to build two more thermal power generation plants in the country. But these proposals were abandoned.[49] However, since the power demand in the country was increasing at that time by 5% per year, in June 2010, in order to meet this demand and save the country from any electricity crisis, government decided to go ahead with two coal-fired power generation plants. One of them worth 7 billion is proposed to be built in Manjung and to get it ready for generation by early 2011. For building this plant, TNB and MMC were bidding.[50] It was expected that the proposed two coal-fired power generation plants would have sophisticated technology so that they could emit minimum of CO_2. We have already noted that Malaysia is already modernizing its old coal-fired power generation plants in Malacca, Johor and Sarawak. We have also noted that the alternative and renewable sources of energy in the country are not so insignificant. Nevertheless, the potential of these sources of energy, especially solar energy is quite high. The government is a member of the Kyoto Protocol. By virtue of that the Prime Minister of Malaysia had already declared at the Copenhagen Conference in December 2009 for 40% cut on the carbon emission in the next ten years. Experts said that this was achievable with adequate technology transfer and transfer of financial resources under the Clean Development Mechanism (CDM) of the Kyoto Protocol. Gurmeet Singh, the director of the Centre for Environment, Technology and Development Malaysia, said that Malaysia needs USD 200 billion per year to keep its promise.[51] The author agreed with Gurmeet Singh because for upgrading the existing power generation plants, setting up new plants and embarking on renewable and alternative energy sources and energy-efficient equipment, the country needs technology and financial support (see *infra*).

47. It is notable that in view of the Malaysian promise on carbon emission reduction made to the UN under the UNFCCC before the Paris Agreement on 2015, which replaced the Kyoto protocol, the country is keen to report to clean power generation. The two old coal-fired power generation plants were upgraded under the CDM mechanism of the Kyoto Protocol. The other coal-fired power generation plants have already been commissioned. The Bakun Dam is already operative and claiming a substantial share in the energy mix of Sarawak state. (See supra). The installed capacity as of December 2016 was 29,253 MW. The installed capacity in Peninsular Malaysia was 23,249 MW, in Sabah it was 1,567 MW and in Sarawak it was 4,437 MW respectively. This has increased the electricity penetration to 99.83% in Peninsular Malaysia, 95% in Sabah and 93.7% in Sarawak, respectively, which are quite high. In the near future, these are going to be 100%. (See Table 17 below)

49. See *New Straits Times*, 23 Dec. 2009.
50. See *Business Times*, 19 Jun. 2010.
51. See *New Straits Times*, 25 Dec. 2009.

Table 17 Installed Capacity and Peak Demand in December 2016

As of Dec 2016	*Installed Capacity (MW)*	*Peak Demand (MW)*	*Reserve Margin (%)*
Pen. Malaysia	23,249	17,788	28.7%
Sabah	1,567	944.9	28.7%
Sarawak	4,437	3,315	34%

Sources: Ministry of Energy, Green Technology and Water.[52]

§5. Power Generation Fuel Mix

48. According to one estimate, which seems to be true in view of the price rise of oil and gas, the ratio of coal in the power generation fuel mix will increase. The estimated picture until 2010 is given in Table 18 below.

Table 18 Peninsular Malaysia Power Generation Mix 2000–2010 Percentage Basis

Year	*2000*	*2001*	*2002*	*2003*	*2004*	*2005*	*2006*	*2007*	*2008*	*2009*	*2010*
Gas	81.8	77.8	75.8	74.9	70.9	65.6	58.1	59.1	58.8	59.1	56.2
Coal	6.7	11.9	14.5	16.2	23.2	28.9	36.1	34.9	35.3	35.1	38.6
Hydro	7.9	6.9	6.4	6.0	5.4	5.0	5.5	5.8	5.5	5.0	4.5
Oil	3.6	3.4	3.3	2.8	0.6	0.5	0.3	0.4	0.4	0.9	0.7

Source: John Thaddeus, 'Energy Scenario in Malaysia', at <http://eneken.ieej.or.jp/japac>.

49. However, according to the Eighth Malaysia Plan, in the power generation fuel mix, in the year 2000 gas constituted about 78.7%. The ratio of gas increased because the consumption of oil in power generation as matter of state policy was reduced. However, in the year 2005, the ratio of gas reduced to 61.1% because of price rise and shift of emphasis to coal-fired power generation plants. This may be noted that with commissioning of the Bakun dam, the ratio of the hydroelectric power generation has considerably increased.

52. 'Malaysia Energy Policy: Focusing on Sustainable Energy Development and the Way Forward', at: http://bseep.gov.my/App_ClientFile/df08bc24-99fb-47a3-937f-dc25df9d3997/Assets/BSEEP%20NCA2017/PAPER%204%20-%20KETTHA_Malaysia%20Energy%20Policy_04052017.pdf (accessed on 12 Jan. 2018).

Table 19 Fuel Mix in Electricity Generation, By Source, 1995–2005

Year	*Oil*	*Coal*	*Gas*	*Hydro*	*Others*	*Total (gigawatthour)*
1995	11.1	9.7	67.8	11.3	0.2	41,813
2000	5.3	7.9	78.7	61.0	0.1	69,371
2005	3.0	30.3	61.1	5.4	0.3	102,341

Source: Eighth Malaysia Plan.

50. According to the 'interim report of the Energy Commission on the Performance of the Electricity Supply in Malaysia for the First Half Year 2009', as prepared by the Energy Commission, the maximum demand and installed generation capacity in Peninsular Malaysia, Sabah and Sarawak were expected to rise.

51. According to the Interim Report of 2009 of the Energy Commission, yearly sales of electricity of TNB, SEB and NUR are as follows.

52. This is notable here that TNB new power plant at Port Dickson, which is known as PD1, is 55.9% efficient compared to 30.1% efficiency of the older power generation plant it replaced and has the generation capacity of 735 MW. It is far less polluting than the old plant. The company had the plan to commission PD2 by 2010 and has done it. As of 2009, the company's energy generation mix was 35% coal, 34.7% natural gas and 18.2% hydro with the remaining 12.1% from oil and diesel for a combined installed capacity of 10,481 MW.[53]

53. The Ninth Malaysia Plan states that efforts were undertaken to reduce the high dependence on natural gas in the generation mix by increasing the use of coal. As a result, the ratio of coal to the total generation mix increased.

Table 20 Fuel Mix in Electricity Generation, 2000–2010

	Year	*Oil %*	*Coal %*	*Gas %*	*Hydro %*	*Others %*	*Total (GWh)*
Malaysia	2000	4.2	8.8	77.0	10.0	0.0	69,280
	2005	2.2	21.8	70.2	5.5	0.3	94,299
	2010	0.2	36.5	55.9	5.6	1.8	137,909
TNB	2000	2.3	8.7	79.6	9.4	0.0	63,634
	2005	0.5	22.5	71.9	4.9	0.2	86,242
	2010	0.1	38.1	56.8	3.4	1.6	126,718
SESB	2000	47.3	–	31.4	21.3	–	2,299

53. *New Straits Times*, 23 Aug. 2005.

	Year	Oil %	Coal %	Gas %	Hydro %	Others %	Total (GWh)
	2005	42.6	–	43.0	13.6	0.8	3,447
	2010	0.5	18.5	47.2	26.5	7.3	4,808
SESCO	2000	11.2	15.1	59.4	14.3	–	3,347
	2005	4.7	25.0	58.9	11.4	–	4,610
	2010	3.0	21.2	44.1	31.7	–	6,383

Source: TNB, SESCO. Taken from Ninth Malaysia Plan.

54. According to the Malaysia Energy Statistics Handbook, in 2014, the energy production mix was: natural gas 64.2%; crude oil 30.1%; hydropower 3.1%; coal and coke 1.7%; biodiesel 0.6%; biomass 0.2%; solar 0.1%; and biogas 0.0%. (See Figure 14).

Figure 14 Electricity Production by Fuel Type in 2014

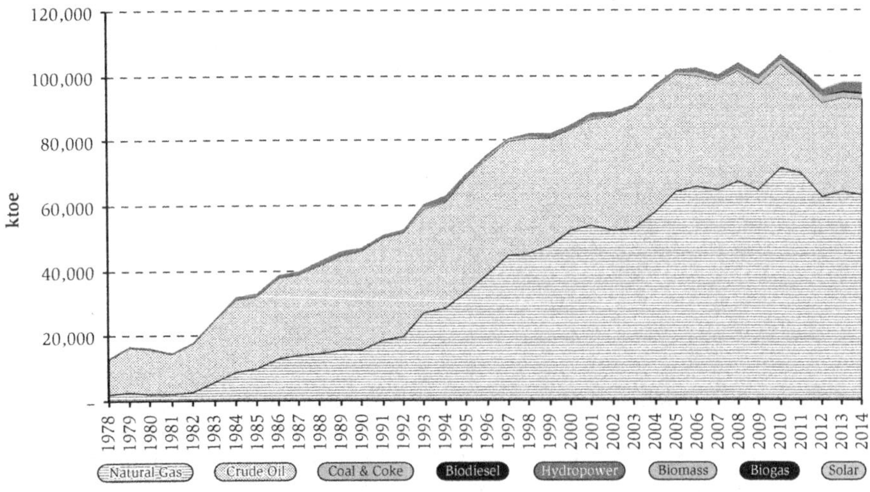

Source: National Energy Balance 2014.

55. In December 2016, the installed capacity mix in Peninsular Malaysia, according to KeTTHA Electricity Info. February 2017, showed: gas 49%; hydro 11%; coal 39%; and renewables 1%. In Sarawak the figures are: Hydro 77%; gas 13%; and coal 10%, whereas in Sabah, the statistics show: gas 72%; diesel 18%; hydro 5%; and renewables 5%.

§6. Transmission Network Capacity and Distribution Network Capacity

56. Along with the rise in the total power generation and rise in the power consumption in 2009, the transmission network capacity of the distribution network capacity of the utility companies had considerably enhanced. This had to be further strengthened as the electricity demand in the country was going to rise moderately. The rise was estimated to be more than other ASEAN countries of the South East Asia. The Eighth Malaysia Plan thus projected these as given in Table 21 below:

Table 21 Transmission Network Capacity, By Source, 1995–2005 (TNB, LLS, SESCO) (Circuit Kilometres)

Year	*500 kV*	*275 kV*	*132 kV*	*66 kV*
1995	–	4,891	8,588	868
2000	885	6,682	9,253	482
2005	1.300	10,679	10,495	116

Source: Eighth Malaysia Plan.

Table 22 Distribution Network Capacity, by Source, 1995–2005 (TNB, LLS, SESCO) (Circuit Kilometres)

Year	*33 kV*	*22 kV*	*11 kV*	*Total*
1995	6,117	4,044	52,727	62,888
2000	8,857	4,018	183,605	196,480
2005	16,820	100	357,733	374,653

Source: Eighth Malaysia Plan.

57. Presently, Malaysia does not have any nuclear power generation plant because it has enough gas reserves. The Malaysian Institute for Nuclear Technology Research (MINT) was set up in 1972 with a predominant intention to build nuclear power generation plant(s), but with the discovery of a large quantity of gas, the idea was kept in abeyance. MINT still exists but as a body focusing mainly on non-power use of nuclear technology. The country may have a nuclear reactor beyond 2030.

58. The Ninth Malaysia Plan states that the electricity transmission system was further expanded with the completion of the new transmission projects to link new generation plants to the main grids as well as provide connections to new industrial and commercial areas. These included the Manjung-Air Tawar line in Peninsular

Malaysia as well as the East Coast Grid and the Northern Grid in Sabah. The distribution network was also expanded to provide greater access and enhance electricity supply to consumers.

59. There was an overall improvement in the productivity and efficiency of the electricity supply services. TNB and SESCO recorded improved performance in terms of units sold per employee and reduction in the number of interruption incidences. This can be seen in Table 23.

Table 23 Performance Indicators of Electricity Supply System, 2000–2005

	2000	*2000*	*2000*	*2005*	*2005*	*2005*
Indicator	TNB	SESB	SESCO	TNB	SESB	SESCO
System Losses (%)	10.3	16.8	12.6	10.5	19.5	14.4
Units Sold per Employee (GWh)	2.43	0.94	1.40	3.05	1.29	1.93
Interruption Incidences (number)	46,896	14,543	8,145	23,213	20,385	4,489
SAIDI (minute/customer/ year	351	2,791	860	147	4,109	310

Source: TNB and SESCO. Taken from Ninth Malaysia Plan.

Notes:

1. This comprises utilities only.
2. SAIDI – System Average Interruption Index.
3. System Loss – Losses in generation, transmission and distribution.
4. Unit Sold per Employee – Total unit of electricity sold divided by the total number of employees.

At the advent of the Eleven Malaysia Plan, the position of electricity supply of electricity in December 2016 in Peninsular Malaysia was 99.83%; in Sarawak 95%, and in Sabah 95%. The suppliers are: TNB, Sarawak Energy and SESB. The transmission is now smooth and with least loss of electricity. It may be noted that in the near future there will be 100% supply of electricity in the country. In Peninsular Malaysia, TNB with internalizing the System Average Interruption Duration Index (SAIDI) and Enhanced Technical Operation and Maintenance System (TOMS).[54] According to the Energy Commission, Improvement of overall system reliability and efficiency continued when a total of 2,825.5 MW new power generation projects entered the grid system in 2016. The KPI of the Malaysian electricity supply companies seems to be at par with world class KPI.[55]

---

54. See statistics provided by the Malaysia Energy Information Hub, at: http://meih.st.gov.my/statistics (accessed on 1 Feb. 2018).
55. See TNB Handbook, Slide Presentation at the ASEAN Conference, Taiei, 22–23 Mar. 2016, at: https://www.tnb.com.my/assets/accolades/TNB_Handbook.pdf (accessed on 12 Jan. 2018).

§7. NUCLEAR POWER

60. It is known that most of the nuclear energy is produced and consumed by developed countries. Even fast-growing economies, like India and China, do not have enough nuclear energy. They are in the process of making more nuclear reactors for power generation so that they could reduce the burden of power generation by thermal power generation plants, and could fulfil the ever-growing power needs. Even upon their completion, their energy generation will mainly depend on thermal and hydroelectric power generations. In spite of the fact that many developing economies need nuclear power generation plants because oil will last some 50 years, natural gas will last 60 years and coal will last 133 years. They want nuclear energy because the known uranium reserves will last 241 years. It is also notable that 1 kg of uranium is equivalent to 9,000 barrels of oil and 3,000 tonnes of coal.[56] As of February 2018, nuclear energy now provides 11% of the total energy demand through 450 power reactors. In 2016, nuclear reactors supplied 2,476 TWh of electricity, up from 2,441 in 2015. Although developed countries warn about the adverse impacts of nuclear reactors, the power generation from this source is increasing. It is environmentally friendly power generation source as it is a low-carbon energy source. In addition to this, there are 225 research reactors in about 50 countries.

Figure 15 Nuclear Electricity Production from 1970 to 2016

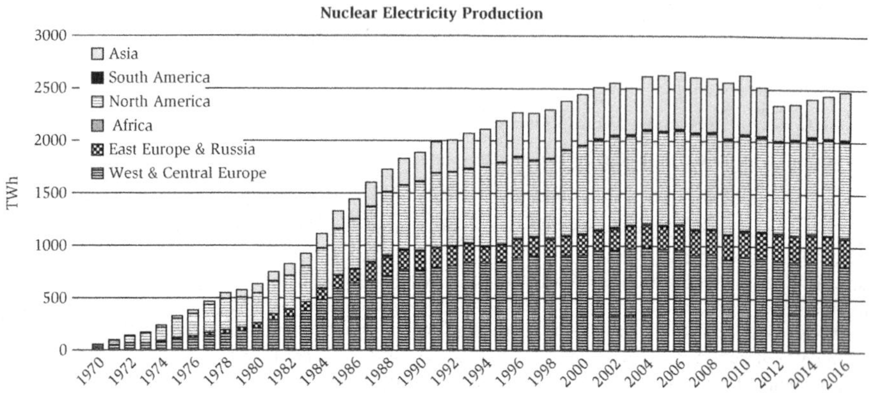

Source: World Nuclear Association, IAEA Power Reactor Information Service (PRIS).

Figure 15 shows the continuous rise in the power generation by nuclear source. In 2012, due to Fukushima accident, the sentiments went against it, but started to go up steadily. It is still below the 2010 level because some countries like Germany and Japan have decided to reduce the number of their reactors. We have noted above

56. *New Sunday Times*, 28 Jun. 2009.

that Japan is increasing its reliance on coal-fired power generation, whereas Germany is focussing on renewable sources. Figure 16 shows country-wise figures. This shows the big and small nuclear power countries.

Figure 16 Nuclear Power Generation in the world in 2016

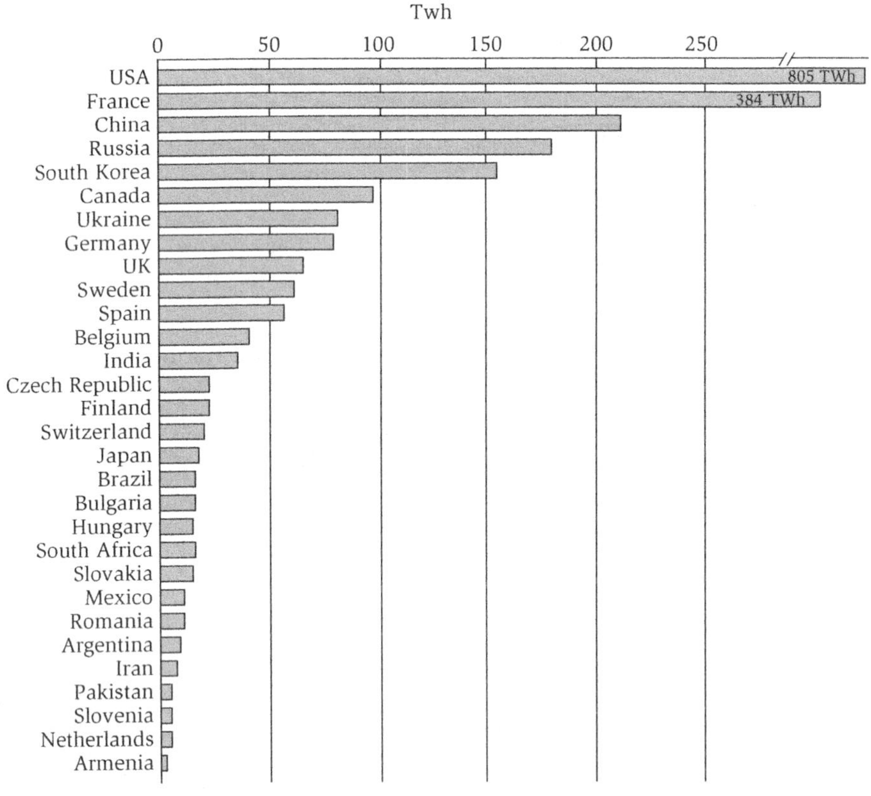

Source: IAEA PARIS Database.

Figure 16 reveals that USA, France, China, Russia, South Korea, Canada, Ukraine, Germany, UK and Sweden are the top ten nuclear power generators. It may be noted here that India is coming up fast although it is facing problem in getting nuclear technological assistance for establishing new reactors, and uranium for its existing reactors, as India is not there among the Nuclear Suppliers Group (NSG). China has been blocking it. But with the agreement with Canada and Australia on supply of uranium for its reactors will lease the problem. The problem will further ease if India becomes a member of the NSG. In the midst of the arguments in favour of and against nuclear power plants, the nuclear power generation, as noted above, is steadily increasing the percentage of nuclear power, as it is clean source of power generation.

It may be noted that in the world power mix scenario, coal, oil, gas and hydro had dominated. In the last decade oil yielded to gas. But the nuclear power has not increased much. However, it is expected that due to ever-growing high demand in populous countries like India and China, the ratio of nuclear power may increase, because this seems that presently this is the only way for them to fulfil the energy demand in these countries; otherwise, they will economically lag behind. (See Figure 17).

Figure 17 World Power Mix 2017

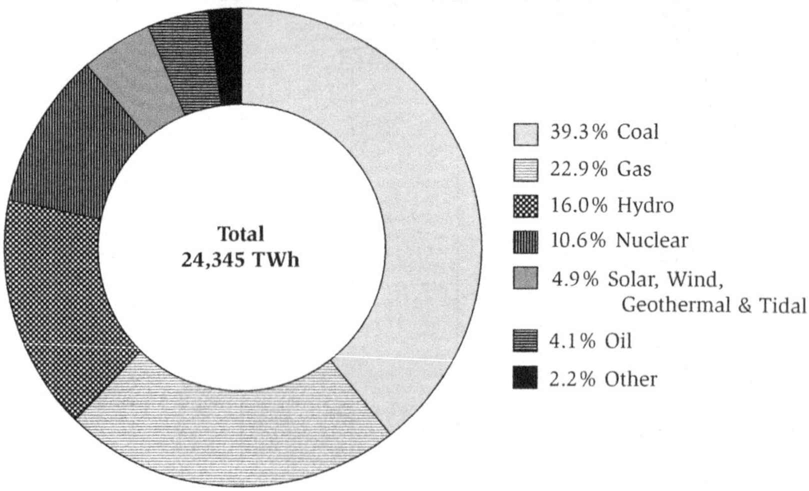

Source: IEA Electricity Information 2017.

We have noted above that among the top ten big nuclear power players, US, France, Russia and China are at the top. India is also coming up fast. (See Table 24).

Table 24 Top 10 Nuclear Energy Producers by Percentage in 2015

Countries	*TWh*	*% of World Total*
United States	830	32.3
France	437	17.0
Russia	195	7.6
China	171	6.7
Korea	165	6.4
Canada	101	3.9
Germany	92	3.6

Countries	*TWh*	*% of World Total*
Ukraine	88	3.4
United kingdom	70	2.7
Spain	57	2.2
World Total		

Source: International Energy Agency (2015).

Malaysia Position

61. Among the Association of Southeast Asian Nations (ASEAN), the Philippines took the initiative to have a nuclear power plant; and in 1984, it built the Batan Nuclear Power Plant costing about USD 2.4 billion, which, due to alleged corruption and poor design, is not competent enough to meet the international safety requirements and which has been converted into a tourism site.[57] This and the Fukushima incident did not act as deterrence to ASEAN countries; the Vietnamese nuclear energy project is on, and the construction work is expected to be completed by the end of 2020. Indonesia and Malaysia also have ambitions to diversify their energy mix by adding nuclear power to it beyond 2020. It is for this reason that Indonesia is keen first to have a small experimental nuclear reactor before embarking to prototype rectors of around 500 MW capacity, whereas Malaysia is working on feasibility study. It has to be noted here that these countries have capabilities to observe the international norms on nuclear safety, security and safeguards, which have been accentuated by the ASEAN normative framework enshrined in the Treaty on the Southeast Asian Nuclear Weapon-Free Zone, Bangkok 1995. The Treaty mainly focuses on nuclear non-proliferation. But it has some provisions pertaining to safety, security and safeguards. The members undertake: (1) To use nuclear materials and facilities exclusively for peaceful purposes. (2) To strictly follow the safety guidelines and standards designed by the IAEA. (3) To inform member about any conducted safety basements, if requested. (4) To strictly adhere to the IAEA Treaty on non-proliferation. (5) To dispose of nuclear wastes and other radioactive materials in accordance with the norms developed by the IAEA. Keeping these in view, the 2012 Phonm Penh Decoration agreed to give effect to these by improving nuclear safety and security in the development of nuclear energy for peaceful use, based on enhanced cooperation with IAEA and other relevant partners, and enhancing the ASEAN Network of Regulatory Bodies on Atomic Energy (ASEANTOM) network among the nuclear bodies of the Member States for exchanging relevant information of common interests. So far Vietnam, Indonesia and Vietnam and for that matter Thailand, Myanmar and the Philippines are concerned, they have capability to deal with safety, security and safeguard aspects of nuclear activities. But they might have to work on having a viable rector design with the help of a competent nuclear state an independent authority on the pattern of the Nuclear Regulatory Commission of the United States – created and supported with nuclear law

57. NorimitsuOnishi, 'A Nuclear Plant, and a Dream, Fizzles', *New York Times*, 13 Feb. 2012.

and policy of the country – to have management skill and expertise to strategies and supervise construction, operation of nuclear reactors, safe handling of nuclear materials, keep information secure, handle wastes generated from the plants with world-class waste management skill, meet the challenges posed by all types of emergencies and pay compensation to those who suffer damage from radiation.[58]

62. Like other fast-growing economies, increasing energy needs, due to fast-growing population, urbanization and industrialization, is pressing Malaysia to venture into alternative and renewable energy sources, including nuclear energy beyond 2020. The country has given its commitment under the United Nations Framework Convention on Climate Change 1991 (UNFCCC) to the United Nations, which became a pledge under the Paris Accord 2015, which states that it reduces CO_2 emissions by 40% at 2005 level. Of which, 25% will be attained without any foreign help, and the rest 15% will be achieved only with technological and financial help of developed countries. In view of the emphasis of the Paris Agreement and in order to accomplish their targets, countries will have to resort to renewable energy sources. Developing countries, including Malaysia, because of availability of fossil fuels, deficient in sophisticated technology in renewable energy sources, especially in geothermal and offshore wind mills and underwater turbines, and lack of financial resources, they squarely depend on fossil fuels, traditionally coal and now gas and coal. They know that renewable energy sources are the leanest and risk-free energy sources, but due to these reasons, they have to depend on fossil fuels, unless their developed counterpart show generosity and extend their helping hands. In fact, by doing so, developed countries will be observing polluter pays principle and will be serving the humanity. It is notable here that in the energy supply of 2015 of the country, natural gas was 44.3%, crude oil was 30.8%, coal and coke constituted 21.0% and hydro was 3.9%. Although Malaysia has great potential to substantially generate energy from renewable sources, like solar, wind, hydropower and biomass, the power generations from these sources are not so encouraging. It is only .6% of the energy mix.[59] Solar PV has the potential of 4.5kwh/m^2/day but it is generating 451.5 kWp; the potential of wind power is not estimated but it is generating only 15 MW; hydropower has the potential of 29,000 MW, but it is generating only 2,066 MW; biomass has huge potential of 29,000 MW but it is generating only 211 MW. These figures are pessimistic. They are going to be improved because, the government in order to keep its promise given under the UNFCCC, Malaysia will have to give full effect to the Renewable Energy Act 2011 by providing all necessary resources to the Sustainable Energy Development Authority (SEDA). Since renewable energy sources have their own limitations, as they may not be 100% replacement and they may give uninterrupted supply, Malaysia has to explore and venture for nuclear energy. In view of that, the country has a plan to have at least two nuclear reactors beyond 2020. To this effect, in 2010, the Economic Transformation Programme (ETP) was launched with a component to venture into nuclear power generation. Likewise, in the same year, in view of the New National Energy Policy, the 10th Malaysia Plan incorporated nuclear energy as a long-term option. Towards

58. See The practices of the US Nuclear Regulatory Commission at its website: www.nrc.gov.
59. Energy Commission, Malaysia Energy Statistics Hand Book, 2015, p. 56.

that, the Malaysian Nuclear Power Corporation (MNPC) – which was incorporated on 7 January 2011 and placed under the Prime Minister's Department, and which has superseded the 2009 Nuclear Power Development Steering Committee – acts as the Nuclear Energy Programme Implementation Organization (NEPIO) of the IAEA. As outlined by Dhana Raj Markandu of the MNPC,[60] it was, thus, aimed that the underlined national nuclear policy will have vision as: peaceful, safe and secure utilization of nuclear energy and technology for sustainable development of the country. It will have its mission as: to enhance the national capability and competency for peaceful, safe and secure utilization of nuclear energy and technology for sustainable development through technological innovation and appropriate legal and regulatory framework towards eventual technological self-sufficiency. The objectives to be achieved are: (1) to make nuclear energy as one of the fuel options post-2020 and (2) to enhance all the beneficial aspects by use of nuclear energy. These objectives are sought to be achieved via augmenting research and development in the area, by having a comprehensive legal regime which would establish an independent body governing all aspects of nuclear power generation with the emphasis on making nuclear energy generation safe, secure and sustainable, and a legal framework for civil liability, enriching human capital development, disseminating relevant information to the public and seeking public participation, and following international standards pertaining to nuclear power generation. The whole idea is to make Malaysia as a high-income country by fulfilling energy needs with the help of a substantial part of nuclear energy in the energy mix. The 11th Malaysia Plan provided impetus to the process by proposing to have an Atomic Energy Regulatory Commission (AERC) to be created under the proposed Atomic Energy Regulatory Act, to seek public acceptance of the nuclear power plant, and to put into operation of Nuclear Power Infrastructure Development Plan (NPIDP) developed under the 10th Malaysia Plan, which was thoroughly deliberated and discussed in the Nuclear Power Development Steering Committee, headed by the Minister of Energy, Green Technology and Water. The Committee also undertook to conduct study on feasibility and site selection. For this purpose, the Committee made three working groups namely, Nuclear Power Programme Development Working Committee, headed by the Malaysian Nuclear Agency, Nuclear Power Project Development Working Committee, headed by the TNB (the utility company in west Malaysia), and the Nuclear Power Legislative Development Coordination Working Committee, headed by the Atomic Energy Licensing Board (AELB) & the Energy Commission. The Committee worked as an interim NEPIO.

63. As a fully dedicated NEPIO, the MNPC is aiming to take Malaysia to a high-income economy significantly by providing a viable foundation supplementing the existing energy mix with safe, secure and sustainable nuclear power generation within the given time frame and to take necessary actions to establish first nuclear power plant with two prototype reactors post-2020. It should be noted here that initially the target is to have two reactors by 2021 and 2022. In wake of the Fukushima incident, the programme has been differed to 2024 and 2025 because the

---

60. See at: https://www.iaea.org/NuclearPower/Downloadable/Meetings/2013/2013-02-11-02-14-TM-INIG/3.markandu.pdf (accessed on 12 Jun. 2016).

government wants to be sure about safety, secure and sustainable.[61] The task of MNPC is arduous as it has to focus on the eighteen key areas recommended by the IAEA: (1) national position, (2) nuclear safety, (3) management, (4) procurement, (5) legislative framework, (6) regulatory framework, (7) radiation protection, (8) electricity grid, (9) nuclear fuel cycle, (10) stakeholder involvement, (11) funding and financing, (12) environmental protection, (13) emergency planning, (14) radioactive waste management, (15) site and supporting facilities, (16) security and physical protection, (17) industrial involvement and (18) human resource development.[62] In order to prepare a viable nuclear power infrastructure development plan (NPIDP), the MNPC had to conduct: risk assessment, human resource capability assessment, technological capability assessment, industrial capability assessment, public participation, self-assessment under the IAEA's (19) infrastructure development requirements, economic performance assessment, safety, security and safeguard assessment, financing assessment, emergency assessment, supply of nuclear material for reactors assessment, compensation mechanism assessment and decommissioning assessment. The MNPC has completed the legal and regulatory study and the Nuclear Energy Bill will be introduced shortly; it has completed 4-in-1 (FS, NPID, SE and BD) Nuclear Power Projection Development; it has also completed a ten-year Comprehensive Communications Plan and Strategies.[63] The tasks which are yet to be taken in order to ensure nuclear plant to be safe, secure and safeguard the following preventive measures have to be taken: (1) To conduct SIA under the Town and Country Planning Act 1976. (2) To carry out EIA under the Environmental Quality Act 1974. (3) If necessary, to conduct a transboundary EIA under the international law on it. (4) Radiological impact assessment (RIA) under the existing Atomic Energy Licensing Act 1984 (or under the proposed new law). It is to be noted here that these assessments should be repeated after lapse of a reasonable time or change in the geological conditions.

64. For the success of nuclear plants, participation of all stakeholders is necessary. Input of opinions of the public, NGOs, industries and researchers is required from time to time for successful operation of nuclear plants. It is necessary to tell stakeholders the pros and cons of the plan. For that, holding joint meeting is found

---

61. Some experts are of the opinion that Malaysia's plan is too ambitious and cannot be achieved within the given timeframe. See, Nuclear Forum.com, 'Malaysia's Nuclear Dream is overly ambitious', 4 Jan. 2016, at: http://nuclearforum.asia/policy-infrastructure/malaysias-nuke-dream-overly-ambitious-analyst (accessed on 13 Jun. 2016).
62. Footnote 38.
63. See MNPC, 'Malaysia: Engaging Stakeholders in the Process of Developing a National Position', presented at the IAEA Technical Meeting on Establishing a National Position for New Nuclear Power Programmes and Pre-Feasibility Studies, 27–30 Oct. 2015, IAEA, Vienna, Austria, at: https://www.iaea.org/NuclearPower/Downloadable/Meetings/2015/2015-10-27-10-30-NIDS2/16_Malaysia.pdf (accessed on 11 Jun. 2016). Also see, Jamal Khaer Ibrahim, 'Strategic Partnership Prior to the Nuclear Power Project Design-Making: Case Study of Malaysia', presented at the IAEA Technical Meeting on Establishing A Strategic Partnership & Contract Model for Expansion/Introduction of A Nuclear Power Programme Warsaw, Poland 10–12 Feb. 2016 at: https://www.iaea.org/NuclearPower/Downloadable/Meetings/2016/2016-02-10-02-12-NPES/12_Malaysia_Ibrahim.pdf (accessed on 12 Jul. 2016).

useful. It is necessary to mention here that stakeholders should have access to relevant document pertaining to the plan. The best way of their participation is to hold meetings, jointly or severally with them. Post-operation meetings have also been found useful. Such meetings will serve dual purposes: first, support from the people living within the permitted vicinity and second, peaceful operation of the plant. India has faced a lot of resistance from its people when it recently decided to set up few new plants. The people's resistance turned into support only after several sittings between the stakeholders. Malaysia might not face such problems because the country is not earthquake prone. It is also free from serious cyclones and tornados. However, certain corners of the country have echoed voices against the plan to resort to nuclear energy post-2020. Consumer Association Penang S.M. Mohamed Idris said that Malaysia was 'hell-bent', for nuclear energy. His concern actually was about the decision of the government and public opinion. According to him, the people of the country have not been consulted before about such decision.[64] He does not seem to be against the idea. The Malaysian Coalition Against Nuclear (MyCAN) urged the people and lawmakers to reject the Atomic Energy Regulatory Bill on the ground that nuclear energy power generation is unsafe, threatens public health and safety, and defeats any economic and environmental advantages. According to them, future energy needs can be fulfilled through demand management, energy conservation and efficiency measures. Comments offered by MyCAN do not seem to be reasonable because future energy needs can be fulfilled mainly by renewable and nuclear power generation. This has been proven in the world and widely practised by populous and technologically advanced countries, China and India. Ten ASEAN members have also expressed interest to develop nuclear technology. This is true that participation of all stockholders in the process is important. Undoubtedly, like other countries, Malaysian people will also support the idea, provided they are given proper information. Sometimes, views become irrational if government fails to properly put its viewpoint and they get motivated by adamant class of people. The abandoned Broga Incineration Project is the best example for this. The question of public opinion became very crucial and people went sceptical to nuclear energy because of the Fukushima incident. But the impact of Fukushima phobia did not last long. It faded when people around the world could know the reasons for the Fukushima incident. Moreover, it has been said time and again by nuclear experts that present-day nuclear reactors are quite safe, and nuclear radiation from them is extremely exceptional. In the meantime, the MNPC made excellent efforts on taking feedback from all the stakeholders by holding separate meetings with them.[65]

---

64. The *Nuclear News*, 'Consumer Groups in Malaysia Condemn Government That Is "Hell-Bent" on Nuclear Power', 1 Feb. 2015.
65. MNPC, 'Malaysia: Engaging Stakeholders in the Process of Developing a National Position', paper presented at the IAEA Technical Meeting on Establishing a National Position for Nuclear Power Programmes and Pre-Feasibility Studies, 27–30 Oct. 2015, IAEA, Vienna, Austria, at: https://www.iaea.org/NuclearPower/Downloadable/Meetings/2015/2015-10-27-10-30-NIDS2/16_Malaysia.pdf (accessed on 20 Jun. 2016). Also see, MNPC, 'Strategic Partnerships Prior to Nuclear Power Project Decision-Making: Case Study of Malaysia', paper presented at the IAEA Meeting on Establishing a Strategic Partnership and Contract Model for Expansion/Introduction of a Nuclear Power Programme, Warsaw, Poland, 10–12 Feb. 2016 (accessed on 12 Jul. 2016).

65. The Atomic Energy Licensing Act 1984 (AELA), with regulations made under it, constitutes the legal framework in the country. The Act provides for: the regulation and control of atomic energy; the establishment of standards on liability for nuclear damage; and other related matters. To carry out administrative duties, including duties pertaining to security, safety and safeguards, under section 3 of the Act, the AELB was created. The Board exercises its duties under the Ministry of Science, Technology and Innovation (MOSTI). For this, it has a Board of Directors, an executive secretary and two committees, namely Standing Safety Committee and Sub-Standing Safety Committee. In the Ministry, there is an AELB Director General with five divisions working under him: Nuclear Installation Division; and Technical Support Davidson; Administrative Services Division; Policy, Code and Standard Division; Licensing Division; and Enforcement Division. The main regulatory body in the administrative set-up is the Board. It has the mission to encourage innovation culture to ensure the safety and peaceful use of radiation and nuclear technology and the vision to remain as the relevant regulatory authority with credibility in radiation and nuclear safety, security and safeguard pertaining to peaceful use of nuclear power for sustainable development of the country. In order to achieve the vision and mission, it has five functions: (1) to control and supervise application and use of atomic energy and matters related to them; (2) to advice the Minister on matters arising out of the Act; (3) to establish, maintain and develop scientific and technical cooperation within the country and internationally; (4) to perform obligations arising out of agreements, treaties and conventions; (5) to perform such other acts arising from time to time or incidental to any provisions of the Act or agreements or treaties or conventions.

66. The AELB under the AELA issues licenses. Section 12(1) of the AELA provides that without a license issued under section 16(5) of the Act by the appropriate authority, no person shall site, construct or operate a nuclear installation, or deal in, possess or dispose of any radioactive material, nuclear material, prescribed substance or irradiating apparatus. It is notable here that the licence holder will have to fulfil the conditions, if any, imposed by the authority. Conditions appended to the licence may be enhanced, reduced or expunged. In order to particularize the functions of the Board in detail, initially there were four regulations made under the Act, which jointly constituted the subsidiary legislation under the Act and are enforced. They are:

(1) The Radiation Protection (Licensing) Regulations 1986.[66] These Regulations prescribe procedure norms for the licensing mechanism. Certain corrections were incorporated to it by P.U. (A) 355/86.
(2) The Radiation Protection (Basic Safety Standard) Regulation 1988.[67] These regulations prescribe safety standards for various activities. There are three orders under it: Atomic Energy Licensing (Exemption) Order 1988; Atomic Energy Licensing (Exemption) Order 1989; and Atomic Energy Licensing (Exemption) (Smoke Detectors) Order 1989.

---

66. P.U. (A) 149/86.
67. P.U. (A) 61/88.

(3) The Radiation Protection (Transport) Regulations 1889.[68] This also has two exemptions: Atomic Energy Licensing (Exemption) (Lightening Arrestor) Order 1990 and Atomic Energy Licensing (Exemption) (Leasing and Hire Purchase) Order 1990.
(4) Atomic Energy Licensing (Appeal) Regulations 1990.[69] This has one amendment, one corrigendum and four exemptions as follows: Radiation Protection (Transport) (Amendment) Regulations 1991; Corrigendum to Radiation Protection (Transport) Regulations 1989; Atomic Energy Licensing (Small Factory) (Exemption) Order; Atomic Energy Licensing (Exemption) (Scanning Electron Microscope) Order 1998; Atomic Energy Licensing (Exemption) (Irrigating Apparatus Below 5 Kilo Electron Volt) Order 2002; and Atomic Energy Licensing (Exemption) (Low Activity Radioactive Material) Order 2002.

67. Among all the regulations, the Radiation Protection (licensing) Regulations 1986 are the important ones. They cover two aspects: license for nuclear material and license for nuclear installations. The first one covers the activities, namely, for manufacturing, trade in, producing processing, purchasing, owning, possessing, using, transferring, handling, selling or storing nuclear material. The license may be given to a registered company, OBTL, ROP, radiation workers and approved registered medical practitioner. Technical requirements are: nuclear material, storage facility, radiation detector, personal monitoring or PPE.

68. So far latest development is concerned the Atomic Energy Licensing Act 1986 is proposed to undergo a large-scale amendment in order to make law comprehensive to cover fairly all the aspects of the nuclear power generation, to create an independent administrative body, as required by the IAEA to deal with all the aspects of establishing, securely and safely running and decommissioning of future nuclear plant, and to prescribe reasonable preventive and punitive measures. The bill to this effect was presented before the Parliament but due to some unfavourable remarks on it, it was held for further improvement. In the meantime, the Licensing Regulations 2009, the Basic Safety Standards Regulations 1988 and Transport Regulations 1989 were suitably amended. The following new regulations were made: the Waste Management Regulations 2009, the Nuclear Installation Licensing Regulations 2009, the Safeguards Regulations 2010, the Atomic Energy Licensing (BSRP) Regulations 2010, the Nuclear Security Regulations 2010 and the Atomic Energy Licensing (Radioactive Waste Management) Regulations 2011. Alongside, government kept on adopting IAEA standards. Towards this, about forty-nine documents with respect to research reactor and nuclear power plants of the IAEA have been internalized. For augmenting bilateral cooperation, the country has entered into MoUs with several countries' nuclear agencies and educational institutions for developing the Malaysian legal and institutional framework in line with international standards and practices, for example, with the Nuclear Energy Regulatory Agency, Indonesia; the National Commissions for Nuclear Activities Control,

68. P.U. (A) 456/89.
69. P.U. (A) 206/90.

Romania; Atomic Energy Agency, Hungary; Korean Institute of Nuclear Safety, Korea; USA; and the National University Malaysia.[70]

69. Other relevant laws pertaining to nuclear energy generation and supply are: the Electricity Supply Act 1990, the Occupational Safety Act 1994, the Machinery Act 1967, the Petroleum Act 1984, the Environmental Quality Act 1974, the Town and Country Planning Act 1976 and the Fire services Act 1988. In order to have an integrated approach, the AELB works with the Royal Malaysian Police (security aspects), the Energy Commission (nuclear energy policy aspects), the National Security Council (Nuclear disaster aspects), the Department of Occupational Safety and Health (occupational safety and health aspects), the Department of Environment (environmental protection aspects) and Ministry of Housing and Local Government (local authority and public participation aspects).

70. In order to consolidate their positions towards to garner support from foreign countries, especially nuclear power countries, states are becoming members of relevant treaties and conventions. For example, India ratified the Comprehensive Safeguards Agreement (CSA) before applying to be a member of the NSG. But it could not succeed because it was not a member of the Nuclear Non-Proliferation Treaty (NPT). Malaysia is a member of NPT, CSA. It is a signatory of the Additional Protocol, and a non-member of the Convention on Nuclear Test Ban (CTBT), the Convention on Physical Protection of Nuclear Material (CPPNM) and its 2005 Amendment, and the Small Quantities Protocol. With respect to other treaties and conventions, the Malaysian Position is:

No.	*Name*	*Status*	*Malaysia Position*
1	Agreement on the Privileges and Immunities of the IAEA	–	Non-party
2	Vienna Convention on Civil Liability for Nuclear Damage	–	Non-party
3	Optional Protocol Concerning the Compulsory Settlement of Disputes	–	Non-party
4	Convention on the Physical Protection of Nuclear Material	–	Non-party
5	Amendment to the Convention on the Physical Protection of Nuclear Material		Non-party
6	Convention on Early Notification of a Nuclear Accident	2 October 1987	Signature: 1 September 1987

70. See Department of Atomic Energy Licensing Board, Ministry of Science, Technology and Innovation, Malaysia, at: http://www.aelb.gov.my (accessed on 13 Jun. 2016).

No.	*Name*	*Status*	*Malaysia Position*
7	Convention on Assistance in the Case of a Nuclear Accident or Radiological Emergency	2 October 1987	Signature: 1 September 1987
8	Joint Protocol Relating to the Application of the Vienna Convention and the Paris Convention		Non-party
9	Convention on Nuclear Safety		Non-party
10	Joint Convention on the Safety of Spent Fuel Management and on the Safety of Radioactive Waste Management		Non-party
11	Protocol to Amend the Vienna Convention on Civil Liability for Nuclear Damage		Non-party
12	Convention on Supplementary Compensation for Nuclear Damage		Non-party
13	Revised Supplementary Agreement Concerning the Provision of Technical Assistance by the IAEA (RSA)	13 February 1981	Signature: 13 February 1981
14	Third Agreement to Extend the 1987 Regional Cooperative Agreement for Research, Development and Training Related to Nuclear Science and Technology (RCA)	26 March 2002	Acceptance: 26 March 2002
15	Application of Safeguard in Connection with the Treaty on Non-Proliferation of Nuclear Weapons (with Protocol)	29 February 1972	Signature: 29 February 1972

71. In view of the Malaysian position with the treaties and conventions, the author feels that in order to be one of the nuclear power generation countries and ultimately a member of the NSG, the country will have to think, keeping in view the Malaysian interest, about becoming party to the some of these treaties and conventions. This is because it should look beyond 2020. If Malaysia does so, the path to become a member of the NSG will become clear and it would ensure construction of nuclear reactors, supply of necessary equipment and continued supply of nuclear materials for the reactors. It is good that the country is maintaining transparency with respect to all nuclear activities in the country. It is working in close cooperation with the IAEA – IAEA as a party to agreements, as a forum of discussions and a depository, and as a body prescribing standards to be followed by all countries willing to engage with nuclear power generation, or already engaged with nuclear power generation and other nuclear activities, or willing to expand the scope of their nuclear activities, or decommissioning of nuclear installations, or keen to engage with terrorism prevention and control activities.

72. The main concern of the IAEA is to keep nuclear activities, including nuclear power generation to be safe, to be secure and to have enough safeguards in order to prevent harmful incidents and going nuclear materials in terrorists' hands. There is inhibition that if nuclear material (enriched) goes in terrorists' hands, they may produce dirty bomb, and that might yield disastrous results, which may even be beyond imagination. Likewise, they can cause sabotage to any nuclear installations resulting in large-scale and long-term damage to people and property. In order to meet such challenges there are: the Convention on Physical Protection of Nuclear Materials 1980 (in force; with 2005 amendment); the International Convention on Suppression of Terrorist Bombing 1997 (in force); the International Convention for the Suppression of Unlawful Acts Against the Safety of Maritime Navigation 1992; the Protocol for the Suppression of Unlawful Acts Against the Safety of Fixed Platforms Located on the Continental Shelf 2005 (in force); the International Convention on Suppression of Nuclear Terrorism 2005 (in force). The author is of the opinion that countries, including Malaysia, capable to resort to nuclear power generation are competent enough to keep nuclear materials and nuclear installations safe from the reach of terrorists. They should become members of these treaties. But in order to keep their commitments, they should have a competent legal framework supported with enough and competent enforcement personnel, if not must seriously work for it. It is to be noted here that Malaysia is competent to meet such challenges, because it has a good number of Acts and Statutes for it.[71] It has a competent regulatory author supported with relevant other Ministries and departments, including Police Diraja Malaysia and Malaysian Customs Department. It is also conducting, from time to time, radiation safety training and training for radiation protection and radioactive waste management. The country is also engaged with emergency planning nuclear disaster management through the Emergency Planning and Cooperation with National Disaster Management Centre with technical support from the Nuclear Malaysia Training Centre.

73. The proposed Atomic Energy Regulatory Bill is an updated version of the provisions of the Atomic Energy Licensing Act 1984. In specific, it might properly deal with all the aspects, through its substantive provisions and regulations covering health and medical, industrial as well as environmental issues. The further improved version will ensure safety, security and safeguard in a better way.

---

71. See Aisha Bidin, Faculty of Law, Malaysia, 'Nuclear Law and Malaysian Legal Framework on Nuclear Security', at: http://esi.nus.edu.sg/docs/default-source/event/presentation-3_aishah-bidin_nuclear-law.pdf?sfvrsn=2 (accessed on 12 Jun. 2016); A presentation of MOSTI and AELB, 'Latest Development on Decommissioning Plans regulatory Review Process: Malaysian Perspective', at the Workshop on Research Reactor Decommissioning Activities: project planning, management, regulatory review and safety assessment, 15–19 Sep. 2008, Manila, Philippines, at: http://www-ns.iaea.org/downloads/rw/projects/r2d2/workshop5/presentations/malaysia-reg-review-process.pdf (accessed on 10 Jul. 2016); MOSTI and AELB, 'Nuclear Regulatory Infrastructure in Malaysia', at: http://www.aelb.gov.my (accessed on 15 May 2016); Raja Abdul Aziz Raja Adnan and Noor Fitriah, 'Nuclear Security in Malaysia: Status and Strategy', paper presented at IAEA Workshop on 'Topical Issues on Infrastructure Development: Managing the Development of a National Infrastructure for Nuclear Power', at: http://www.iaea (accessed on 20 Jul. 2016).

§8. RURAL ELECTRIFICATION

74. Initially, a total of MYR 463.6 million was spent in the implementation of the rural electrification programme, which benefited an additional 101,530 rural households during the plan period of Eighth Malaysia Plan. Of this, 30,040 and 53,630 rural households were in Sabah and Sarawak, respectively. In addition, the Electricity Supply Industry Trust Account, funded by the industry, was established in 1997. Through its rural electrification programme, a total of 8,200 households in peninsular Malaysia were also provided with electricity. The trust fund still exists; and power generation and supply companies provide funding to it. The trust money is utilized for: rural electrification programme; R&D programme and new renewable sources; human resource development; energy efficiency projects; development and promotion of the electricity supply industry; and advance for projects approved by trustees of the Trust Fund. The Electricity Supply Industries Trust Account Committee manages it.[72] The Renewable Energy Fund created under the Renewable Energy Act 2010 and managed by the Sustainable Development Authority (SEDA) supplements this fund. This fund is funded by the 1% surcharge levied on consumers using more than 300 kwh electricity per month. This money comes around 300 million per month. This money is utilized for supporting renewable power generation in the country. In effect, the money is utilized in rural electrification because some of the independent power producers utilize the electricity for rural electrification. It may be noted that in the Peninsular Malaysia, 100% villages have got electricity, whereas in Sabah and Sarawak, they are short of 17%.[73]

75. By the end of the plan period, rural electricity coverage in Malaysia was 93%, as shown in the Table 25 below.

Table 25 Rural Electrification Coverage by Region, By Source, 1995–2005 (%)

Region	*1995*	*2000*	*2005*
Peninsular Malaysia	99	100	100
Sabah	72	79	85
Sarawak	67	80	90
Malaysia	92	93	95

Source: Eighth Malaysia Plan.

76. This may be noted that the rural electrification in the State of Sabah and Sarawak is below 100%. But the country is trying its best to provide electricity to

72. See at: http://mesita.kettha.gov.my/(accessed on 10 Jan. 2018).
73. http://www.malaysia.ahk.de/fileadmin/ahk_malaysia/Perspectives/MGC053-Sep-Oct16_iPAD.pdf (accessed on 12 Feb. 2018).

all villages and to each and every village household. Hopefully in the next Five-Year Plan, total rural electrification target will be achieved. The present achievement is commendable because transmission through forests and mountains in the country is an arduous task.

77. The rural electrification during previous plans and the projection for the Ninth Plan can be seen in Table 26.

Table 26 Rural Electrification Coverage by Region, 2000–2010 (in %)

Region	*2000*	*2005*	*2010*
P. Malaysia	97.5	98.6	98.8
Sabah	67.1	72.8	80.6
Sarawak	66.9	80.8	89.6
Malaysia	89.5	92.9	95.1

Source: TNB and SESCO. Taken from Ninth Malaysia Plan.
Notes: Coverage refers to rural housing units served as a percentage of total rural housing units. 2000 refers to Census 2000 data excluding housing units served with private individual generators.

78. The Tenth Malaysia Plan stated that the coverage of electricity supply in rural areas will be extended where about 6,000 more houses will be supplied with electricity in the Peninsula, 59,000 in Sabah and 76,000 in Sarawak. The author is of the opinion that these figures are not so encouraging.

79. As noted above, the Eleventh Malaysia Plan aims at community involvement in providing rural electrification. For that, under the Rural Electricity Supply Programme, it seeks to take help from NGOs to help power generation and supply in rural areas via renewable energy, mainly from mini and pico hydro, sources in the areas, which are too far from the grid. The plan has energy access to all as one of the priorities. It will be supported with IBR, which has been devised to incentivize to reduce cost and improve services of utility companies. The plan focuses on 99.9% electrification in Sabah and Sarawak by providing electricity to 36,800 additional households. The state government targets that by 2025, and there will be full electricity in Sarawak. The task of rural electrification in the state has been given to the Committee on Rural Transformation.[74] By then, Sabah will also have full electrification.[75] Right now, the state has about 95% electrification.[76]

74. *Borneo Post Online*, 19 May 2017.
75. Farhad M. Hossain, M. Hasanuzzaman, N.A. Rahim & H.W. Ping, 'Impact of Renewable Energy on Rural Electrification in Malaysia: A Review', *Clean Technology and Environmental Policy*, Vol. 17, Issue 4, pp. 859–871; H. Borhanazad, S. Mekhaiel, R. Saidur, & G. Boroumandjazi, 'Potential Application of Renewable Energy for Rural Electrification in Malaysia', *Renewable Energy*, Vol. 59, November 2013, pp. 210, 219.
76. See, Chen Shiun, 'Rural Electrification in Sarawak, Malaysia: Potential and Challenges for Mini-Hydro and Solar Hybrid Solutions', Paper presented at German Renewable Energy Symposium, 13

80. To conclude the trends of energy supply and use in Malaysia is similar to that of fast-growing economies of the world. Initially, energy supply in the country was between 5 and 10 Mtoe, but rapid industrialization process increased the demand, which was met by incorporation of gas in the fuel mix. Thus, in 1985, the supply went up to 30 Mtoe. This trend continued, and in nineties the supply went up further. Since Malaysia is growing at consistently a high growth rate, the energy demand has also to increase accordingly. It is estimated that by the year 2020 the energy demand will rise up to 100 Mtoe. Because the country has a large quantity of natural gas, power generation will not be a problem. But what are worrying environmentalists is the increasing trend of having coal-fired power generation plants and lack of enough renewable energy. Malaysia produces high-quality oil, which is exported. The country's oil needs are met by importation of oil from the Middle East. This brings profit to the country. After the Rio Conference 1992, all efforts are being made to have developments within the limits of sustainability. In the energy sector also efforts are being made around the world to generate and supply energy in such a way that provides impetus to sustainable development. Also, strategies are being made to craft the power generation process environment-friendly. Towards this end, conservation of energy, use of clean technology and encouragement of renewable energy have become necessary parts of the policy determination of all countries, especially developed countries and industrialized developing countries.

81. The following are notable prospects as stated in the Ninth Malaysia Plan:

– The overall energy demand is expected to increase at an average rate of 6.3% per annum.

Table 27 Final Commercial Energy Demand by Source, 2000–2010

	Petajoules			*% of Total*			*Average Annual Growth Rate (%)*	
Source	2000	2005	2010	2000	2005	2010	8MP	9MP
Petroleum Products	820.0	1023.1	13,72.9	65.9	62.7	61.9	4.5	6.1
Natural Gas	161.8	246.6	350.0	13.0	15.1	15.8	8.8	7.3
Electricity	220.4	310.0	420.0	17.7	19.0	18.9	7.1	6.3
Coal	41.5	52.0	75.0	3.4	3.2	3.4	4.6	7.6

Sep. 2016. at: https://www.google.com/search?q=Rural+Electrification+in+Sarawak%2C+Malaysia&oq=Rural+Electrification+in+Sarawak%2C+Malaysia&aqs=chrome..69i57.14821j0j8&sourceid=chrome&ie=UTF-8 (accessed on 10 Mar. 2018).

	Petajoules			*% of Total*			*Average Annual Growth Rate (%)*	
Total	1243.7	1631.9	2217.9	100.0	100.0	100.0	4.6	7.6
Per capita Consumption (gigajoules)	52.9	62.2	76.5			3.3	4.2	

Source: Ministry of Energy, Water and Communication and Economic Planning Unit.

Notes: Energy demand refers to the quantity of commercial energy delivered to final consumers but excludes gas, coal and fuel oil used in electricity generation. Joule is the unit of energy. Natural gas includes natural gas used as fuel and feedstock consumed by the non-electricity sector.

- The transport sector of the country was the largest consumer of energy, accounting for 40.5% of the total final commercial energy demand in 2005. This was followed by the industrial sector at 38.6% and the residential and commercial at 13.1%.

Table 28 Final Commercial Energy Demand by Sector, 2000–2010

	Petajoules			*% of Total*			*Average Annual Growth Rate (%)*	
Source	2000	2005	2010	2000	2005	2010	8MP	9MP
Industrial	477.6	630.7	859.9	38.4	38.6	38.8	5.7	6.4
Transport	505.5	661.3	911.7	40.6	450.5	41.1	5.5	6.4
Residential and Commercial	162.0	213.1	284.9	13.0	13.1	12.8	5.6	6.0
Non-energy	94.2	118.7	144.7	7.4	7.3	6.5	4.7	4.0
Agricultural and Forestry	4.4	8.0	16.7	0.4	0.5	0.8	12.9	15.9
Total	1243.7	1631.7	2217.9	100.0	100.0	100.0	5.6	6.3

Source: Ministry of energy, Water and Communication and Economic Planning Unit.

Notes: Industrial demand includes manufacturing, construction and mining. Non-energy includes natural gas, bitumen, lubricants, industrial feedstock and grease.

The energy consumption by fuel type has seen mark increase in natural gas and coal and coke for power generation.

Table 29 Final Energy Consumption by Fuel Type (ktoe), 2011–2014

Year	*Natural Gas*	*Pet. Products*	*Coal & Coak*	*Biodiesel*	*Electricity*	*Total*
2011	8,515	23,923	1,759	24	9,235	43,456
2012	10,206	27,215	1,744	115	10,011	49,291
2013	10,076	29,190	1,539	188	10,590	51,583
2014	9,641	29,517	1,709	300	11,042	52,209

Source: Malaysia Energy Statistics Handbook, 2016.

So far energy consumption is concerned, transport is at the top and next to it is industry. Consumption by residents comes at number 3.

Table 30 Final Energy Consumption by Sector (ktoe), 2011–2014

Year	*Industry*	*Transport*	*Residential*	*Non-Energy Use*	*Agriculture*	*Total*
2011	12,100	17,070	6,993	6,377	916	43,456
2012	13,919	19,757	7,065	7,497	1,053	49,291
2013	13,496	22,357	7,403	7,277	10,590	51,583
2014	13,162	24,327	7,458	6,217	11,042	52,209

Source: Malaysia Energy Statistics Handbook, 2016.

- The security, reliability, quality and cost-effective supply of energy will be enhanced through an optimum energy mix predominantly from domestic sources.
- Efforts will continue to be undertaken to reduce dependence on petroleum products while utilizing them efficiently. However, efforts will be made to increase their supply by finding new sources of oil and gas.
- The ratio of alternative fuel sources will be increased.
- The consumption of coal is expected to reach 19.0 million tonnes by the year 2010. This is because of commissioning of two new coal-fired power generation plants. Efforts will be made to enhance the security of supply by exploring the potential of developing local sources.
- The demand of electricity is expected to grow at an average rate of 7.8% per annum until 2010. All possible efforts will be made to meet this increasing demand. It is notable here that the new coal-fired power generation plants are possibly least polluting. Efforts are also being made to convert the old ones with new technology.
- Efforts will be made to increase the ratio of the renewable energy sources. It is expected that by the year 2010 about 300 MW will be generated and distributed through the TNB grid. 200 MW is expected to be generated and distributed

through the grid in Sabah. Other renewable energy sources to be privately generated and used will be encouraged. Towards this end, cost-effective technologies will be made available. Biofuel using palm oil of the country will be the matter of priority. Designated pump stations, mainly in the Klang Valley, will be chosen for distributing biodiesel. For this, appropriate law is being developed.

- The implementation of energy efficiency programmes will focus on energy-saving features in the industrial and commercial sectors. All possible efforts that are being made by developed world will be brought into practice. Towards this end, efforts will be undertaken to introduce the efficient management of Electrical Energy regulations, and the Uniform Building By-laws, label electrical appliances and use of high-efficiency motors.
- Efforts will be made for bringing awareness about renewable energy and energy efficiency at all energy consumption levels. To promote these, government buildings will be presented as models. It is noted in 2016 that government buildings, including buildings under twenty-five ministries, showed 10.9% increase in energy savings, which comes up to 28,900 million kwh. It is considered to be a robust achievement. In 2013, the target was set as 5% reduction. It is notable here that the 24-degree temperature set for air conditioners has helped in surpassing the target.[77] They will be subjected to good energy audit scheme. This kind of audit will be extended to other energy-intensive installations.
- Renewable energy sources, especially solar power and biomass energy, which have great potential in the county, will be a matter of priority.
- Green technology for energy efficiency will be boosted.
- Regional cooperation with ASEAN members will be enhanced. Proper heed will be given to ASEAN Plan of Action for Energy Cooperation (APAEC), the gas pipeline project, coal, EE and EC, etc.
- The APAEC, 2016–2025, which is the fourth series of implementation of such cooperation among the ASEAN countries, will serve as a blueprint for better cooperation towards enhancing energy security and sustainability under the framework of the ASEAN Economic Community for a designated period, says Dr Sanjayan Valautham, The Executive Director of the ASEAN Centre for Energy. The Fourth Phase focuses on: ASEAN Power Grid; Trans-ASEAN Gas Pipeline; Reduction of Energy intensity by 20 by 2020 based on 2005 level; increasing renewable energy component to 23% by 2025 in the ASEAN Energy Mix; and focussing on nuclear energy beyond 2030.[78]

77. 'Leading by Example', *Energy Malaysia,* Vol. 10, 2016, pp. 28–30.
78. See, 'Forging Regional Connections, ASEAN Plan of Action for Energy Cooperation', *Energy Malaysia,* Vol. 9, 2016, pp. 19–21.

Chapter 4. Policy Delineation in Malaysia

82. Energy is one of the Federal jurisdictions. Ministry of Energy, Communications and Multimedia at the Federal Cabinet is responsible in formulating a policy to be followed in the country. Initially, there was no formal policy determination on energy. However, on the basis of the practice in the area, the policy being followed can well be understood. The Ministry on its website outlined the objectives as: (1) to facilitate the establishment of an integrated, efficient and high-quality infrastructure for the energy; (2) to ensure a conducive climate to the development of energy; (3) to ensure continuous technological advancement for the energy through encouragement of research and development; (4) to ensure an efficient and effective universal delivery of energy services at affordable prices and to increase the productivity of business and quality of life; (5) to ensure a secured and reliable supply or provision of energy; (6) to establish a dynamic and progressive regulatory system for promoting market development and to manage the impact of energy on society and the environment. On the energy planning the Ministry said: The energy Division of the Ministry would work on formulation of energy policies, strategies and objectives in the energy industry (Electricity) aimed at ensuring sufficient and reliable supply of electricity at reasonable prices in the country. It would make efforts towards enhancing generation of electricity supply through independent power producers (IPPs) and dedicated power producers. The Division will work for diversification of sources of fuel used in the electricity supply industry through an optimum energy mix policy. It would also develop an efficient legal framework and an infrastructure. The Division will make short-term and long-term planning, and to cater the need of the country would make necessary changes in them. It coordinated in all activities especially in the areas of implementation of law, power generation and supply of various forms of energy.

§1. Oil and Gas Subsidy

83. As noted above, as a matter of policy, for economic reasons, Malaysia, like many other developing countries, used to give huge subsidy on oil and gas. In view of the soaring price of these around the world, developing countries decided to withdraw subsidy gradually. This is notable here that some developing countries, including Malaysia, India and Pakistan, had been gradually withdrawing the subsidy, but in 1995, Malaysia withdrew the subsidy three times; and in February 2006 the withdrawal was 30 Malaysian cents per litre, which is the highest of one-time withdrawal. The years 2008 and 2009 have been crucial from the point of view of gradual withdrawal of subsidy, and revising and re-revising oil and gas prices in the country. Prices in 2010 are stabilized. According to the author, revision of subsidies and consequential price rise of oil and gas have to be done only after appropriate economic and social studies. For example, if price of diesel is to be increased, its economic impacts and its burden on daily commuters, farmers and fishermen have to be studied. Malaysia did this kind of study before withdrawing subsidies on oil and gas and consequential price rise. Based on this study, diesel was made available to fishermen at relatively cheaper rate. It also adopted certain preventive measures to control export of diesel from Malaysia to its neighbouring countries.[79] The Prime Minister of Malaysia Datuk Seri Najib Razak said oil prices should reflect market realities and an increased oversight of financial systems was needed to prevent price manipulations. In today's environment, unjustifiably high oil prices would risk jeopardizing the fragile recovery and undermine the stability of the global economy. Since last year, we have seen oil prices strengthening. This strengthening had come about despite the fact that demand growth had been modest, particularly in the OECD countries, while global supplies remained ample, as reflected in an OPEC spare capacity above recent historic averages. Undoubtedly, Prime Minister Najib said this apparent mismatch between prices and supply and demand fundamentals raised questions over whether market had become 'overheated'. He further said:

> Some will view current and prospective demand increases as being sufficient to justify new, higher threshold price. Yet other will say that with oil increasing merely to be a source of energy, higher prices reflect the fact that commodity oil is today much sought-after financial asset. Whatever views may be on what is an appropriate price level, it can be assured that prices, even at these levels will come under renewed pressure as the recovery gains momentum. Over the longer term, population growth trends, utilization and industrialization in the emerging world, will continue to underpin historically robust growth in energy demand. Under these circumstances, an adequate supply-side response is critical if market stability is to be restored.[80] The then Prime Minister's statement is relevant in the context of giving and withdrawing oil and gas subsidies. For determining a stable and long-term policy about these, stability of their prices at the international market is a prerequisite. The Tenth Malaysia Plan stated that energy subsidies would be cut in stages on the basis of comprehensive studies conducted by economists. It further stated that supply of oil and gas would be strengthened through a more competitive market.[81] Some other countries, including China, Taiwan and Indonesia are studying plans to cut subsidies and to raise oil prices. In these countries, the broadly accepted notion that subsidies should be withdrawn keeping in view the economic conditions of the country; otherwise, it is going to leave undesirable impacts on the economy. The immediate impact that can be anticipated is inflation. This may have a long-lasting adverse impact on the growing economy. South Korea, Japan, Singapore and Hong Kong have been exception to the subsidy policy. This is because they had strong economies and they could have robust growth rate without giving any subsidy. Along with withdrawal of oil prices, these countries are emphasizing on increasing energy efficiency, conservation of energy and controlling the inflation by reducing road tax on heavy vehicles and not increasing toll rates.

---

79. See Abdul Haseeb Ansari, 'Socio-Economic and Legal Perspective of Withdrawal of Subsidy on Diesel and Petrol and Possibility of an Energy Tax: A Study with Special Reference to Malaysia', *The Law Review* (2009): 45.
80. *New Straits Times*, 8 Jun. 2010.
81. See *New Straits Times*, 11 Jun. 2010.

Malaysia is the best example of these. Thailand is also going to impose mandatory energy conservation in the country. Keith Bradsher writes that several big changes are making Asian governments more willing to review subsidies in 2005 than in the past. One change is the spreading perception that this year's price increases may prove more enduring than previous ones. But another change is the groping influence of traded companies that are much willing than state-owned enterprise to accept losses on their refining businesses. Huge government-owned businesses like Sinopec of China have been partly privatized and have issued stock, making them more sensitive to investor's needs and less concerned about helping governments hold down inflation by limiting increases in gasoline prices. At the same time, publicly traded companies like Reliance in India and Formosa petrochemicals in Taiwan have jumped into market previously monopolized by the government-run business.[82] Most economists are critical to oil subsidies, describing them an inefficient use of taxes, as the money can be utilized on other developmental activities. They favour direct payment as income supplements to impoverished households. Yet subsidies still have their defenders. Politicians across the political spectrum in Taiwan, including the opposition National Party, have supported the government's decision not to raise the wholesale prices Charged by Chinese Petroleum.

84. It may be noted that in 2013, the total fuel subsidies were around MYR 28 billion, which was about 2.8% of the GDP. At that time the fiscal deficit was 4% of the GDP. Government aimed to reduce the deficit to 3% by 2015 under the ETP.[83] In view of this, it became necessary to withdraw the fuel subsidies gradually. There was a time that Malaysia used to export gas. Now, in view of the increasing local demands, it has to import also. As a matter of fact it is not advisable to give subsidy on imported gas. Under the Subsidy Rationalization Programme (SRP), the subsidies are being gradually withdrawn so that the fiscal deficit could be reduced and the tax money could be diverted to other developmental activities. The price increase on gas may be seen in Table 31 below. Now the subsidies are withdrawn and the prices are revised with the increase and decrease of oil and gas prices. The recent oil price drop supported this move. But now the international oil price has gone up. In view of this, it is demanded that the some subsidy should be considered by the government in order to support power generation and other industries. But on the other hand, government claims that millions of dollars are still given as subsidies on oil and gas. The author is of the opinion that subsidies may or may not be given provided the economy of the county demands that as a measure to increase the GDP of the country.

From November 2016, Malaysia has removed subsidies given on cooking oil also. 1 Kg polybag and 5 Kilo bottles were excepted until December 2016. As of today, there are no subsidies on cooking oil. This stem may help boost biodiesel production in the country.

82. See Keith Bradsher, 'Why Asia Is Thinking Anew on Oil Subsidy', *New York Times*, 8 Sep. 2005; Re-printed in *New Straits Times*, 9 Sep. 2005.

83. Enerdata, 'Natural Gas Subsidies in Malaysia: Current Situation and Outlook', 12 Mar. 2015, at: https://www.enerdata.net/publications/executive-briefing/natural-gas-subsidies-malaysia.html.

Table 31 The Price Increase on Gas under SRP, 2010–2014

Natural Gas End-Use Sectors	*Planned Increase per MMBtu (2010–2014)*	*Actual Increase per MMBtu (2010–2014)*
Power	+MYR 4.65 in 2H2010; +MYR3 every six months from 2011 to 2014	+MYR3.0 in June 2011; +MYR 1.5 in January 2014
Industry	+MYR 2.52 in 2H2010; +MYR 3 every six months from 2011 to 2014	+MYR 2.65 in June 2011; +MYR 3.25 in May 2014, +MYR 0.45 in November 2014

Source: PEMANDU, Malaysia Energy Information Hub, Gas Malaysia Berhad.

§2. Energy Efficiency and Renewable Energy

85. In order to have sustainable energy for sustainable development, renewable energy (RE), energy efficiency (EE) and conservation of energy (CE) are important tools. They are also warranted for carbon emission reduction. Malaysia is committed to follow these to the possible extent. With respect to energy efficiency and renewable energy, during the Eighth and Ninth Malaysia Plans, the government aimed to a more sustainable national energy system through concerted efforts aimed at the efficient and productive utilization of energy resources as well as increasing renewable energy sources of energy in the country's total fuel mix and to encourage them by providing suitable financial and fiscal incentives. It also aimed at building national capacity and capability in renewable energy technologies through promoting R&D in renewable energy. It strived to promote new technologies and techniques in the generation, transmission, distribution and retail of energy aimed at increasing energy efficiency, promoting efficient utilization of fuel resources for the generation of electricity, and conducting information dissemination and awareness raining initiatives on energy efficiency and renewable energy. Towards promoting energy efficiency and renewable energy, the Eighth Malaysia Plan states that concerted efforts will be undertaken to ensure the sustainable development of energy resources, both depletable and renewable, in meeting the energy demand of the country. The energy sector will be further strengthened to support the development of Malaysia into a knowledge-based economy, thereby enhancing its resilience and competitiveness. Efforts will be intensified to ensure adequacy, quality and security of energy supply, encourage greater utilization of gas and renewable energy as well as provide adequate electricity generation capacity. In addition, the development of industries, the production of energy-related products and services will be supported for both the domestic and export markets.

86. Thus, Malaysia's energy policy evolved over the years since the early 1970s after the 1973 world oil crisis. The NPP was formulated in 1975. The policy aims at consistent supply of oil, gas and coal for meeting the energy needs of the fast-growing economy. The policy goals, according to the Asia Pacific Energy Research Centre (APERC), include: (1) making available adequate supplies at reasonable prices to support national economic development objectives, thus placing the application of oil and gas resources to serve the national needs as a first priority; (2) promoting greater Malaysian representation and providing a favourable investment climate, including creating opportunities for downstream industries; (3) affecting an optimal social and economic pace of exploration of the economy's endowments of exhaustible oil and gas resources, taking into account the need for conservation of these depletable assets and the protection of the environment. With the creation of PETRONAS, the national oil and gas company, through the PDA, the oil and gas sector was streamlined to ensure greater Malaysian participation in the ownership, management and control of oil and gas resources and activities. This was made possible through the introduction of a system of PSCs, replacing the system of concessions.

87. Under the NPP 1979, Petronas, as a state-owned enterprise, got exclusive rights of ownership, exploration and production. It comes under the direct control of the Prime Minister, office and is responsible for its own planning, investment and regulation of all upstream activities. The Minister of International Trade and Industry (MITI) and the Ministry of Domestic Trade and Consumer Affairs (MDTCA) through the Petroleum Regulations of 1974 (amended in 1975 and 1981) are vested with powers to regulate all downstream activities. MITI is responsible for the issue of licenses for the processing and refining of petroleum and the manufacture of petrochemical products, while MDTCA issues licenses for the marketing and distribution of petroleum products.

88. The national energy policy objectives, as stated by the APERC and as mentioned above, are: (1) The Supply Objective – to ensure the provision of adequate, secured and cost-effective energy supply through developing indigenous energy resources, both non-renewable and renewable energy sources using least-cost options, and diversification of supply sources both from within and outside the economy. (2) The Utilization Objective – to promote the efficient utilization of energy and elimination of wasteful and non-productive patterns of energy consumption. (3) The Environment Objective – to minimize the negative impact of energy production, transportation, conservation, utilization and consumption on the environment.

89. The details of these objectives are as under: in pursuit of the supply objectives, policy initiatives, particularly with respect to crude oil and gas, have aimed at both extending the life of domestic depletable energy resources, as well as diversification away from oil dependence to include other forms of energy sources, specifically coal and renewable energy strategies. The NDP of 1980 was aimed at safeguarding the depleting oil reserves and to explore the prospects of finding out other oil resources in the deepwater and ultra-deepwater. Towards safeguarding, the policy aimed at major oil fields of over 400 million barrels of oil initially in place (OIIP) and restricted their production to 1.75% of OIIP. However, in 1985, the ceiling was revised to 3%. As a result, the total production of crude oil increased. It is notable here that in view of the possibility of new discoveries of oil reserves in deepwater and ultra-deepwater, Petronas during the Asian Annual Oil and Gas Conference 2004, held in Kuala Lumpur in June 2004, declared plans to increase its oil and gas production by 3% a year within the next five years. Before the National Energy Policy, there was NPP 1975. It still works side-by-side the National Energy Policy. It aims at efficient utilization of petroleum resources and ensure that the country exercises majority control in the management and operation of the petroleum industry.

90. Initially, the NDP was limited to oil. It was later extended to gas and a limit on per-day extraction of gas was fixed. The objective of this policy was to prolong the life span of the nation's oil and gas reserves and to strive to find more reserves.

91. In 1981, Four-Fuel Policy supplemented the existing policies in order to ensure reliability and security of supply. The strategy under it maintains a workable diversification and balance between the four sources of energy, oil, gas, hydropower and coal. This strategy became successful in reducing dependence on oil. We have noted above that the ratio of gas and coal has increased. In the beginning, for the process of diversification of power generation, use of gas was chosen. Its ratio, thus, tremendously increased. But present situation is that relatively cleaner coal-fired power generation is also being boosted. This has reduced the burden on gas. But it is believed that in view of the environmental objectives, coal-fired power generation units will remain proportionately less, and efforts will be made to keep them possibly environmentally friendly, by reducing the pollution quotient to the achievable extent. In 2001, Five-Fuel Policy was launched with added emphasis on encouraging the utilization of renewable resources such as biomass, solar and mini-hydropower generation systems, and efficient utilization of energy. Thus, renewable energy was included as the fifth fuel in the energy mix of the country.

92. It is known that renewable energy sources cannot replace the conventional sources of energy, fossil fuel, but if it is properly fostered, it will reduce the burden on then. Malaysia as a matter of policy is encouraging all kinds of renewable energy strategies. Towards this end, all possible efforts are being made. After the Bonn Conference on Renewable Energy of June 2004, Malaysia has doubled its efforts for making appropriate use of renewable sources of energy. But a lot has yet to be done. It requires allocation of a substantial amount of financial resources and other incentives at production and consumption level. It seems that the country is determined to bear this kind of burden that is why exploitation of renewable source of energy is a part of the underlined energy policy.

93. According to APERC, there have been limited initiatives to pursue the utilization objective, relying heavily on the energy industry and consumers to exercise efficiency in energy production, transportation, conversion, utilization and consumption. Demand-side management initiatives by the utilities, particularly through tariff incentives, have had some impacts on efficient utilization and consumption. Government initiatives to encourage cogeneration are also aimed at promoting an efficient method for generating heat energy and electricity from a single energy source. This also contributes to a reduction in the cost of conversion. To enhance the utilization efficiency, legal measures are also being taken. Industries are being chosen to properly planning for reducing unnecessary and wasteful utilization of energy (see *infra*). All these have been there under the New Energy Policy enshrined in the Tenth Malaysia Plan.[84]

94. So far environmental objectives are concerned, APERC notes that there are limited policy initiatives. Major energy development projects have to undergo EIAs prepared on the basis of the guidelines developed by the Department of Environment (DOE), and subsequently approved by the DOE. The pressure on clean energy is increasing. For bringing the emissions and discharge levels of effluents, gas and other kinds of pollution within the acceptable limits, standards have been prescribed in specific legislations. These legislations have provision for penalizing the cases of non-compliance of the standards. Special attention is being given to monitor the air quality, for which vehicles and power generation plants are mainly responsible (see *infra* for a detailed account).[85]

95. According to M. Zamzam Jaafar, the Malaysian National Energy Policy, in line with the APERC discussed above, has three main objectives: supply – to ensure adequacy, security, cost-effectiveness of energy supply; utilization – to promote efficient utilization of energy and to discourage wasteful patterns of energy consumption; environment – to minimize the negative environmental impacts in the energy generation and supply chain. To fulfil these commitments, the country, according to him, faces the following challenges: (1) greater utilization of natural gas in power and non-power sectors, (2) development of renewable energy as the fifth fuel, particularly in power generation, (3) efficient utilization of energy through an effective regal regime and (4) adequacy of electricity generation capacity to ensure reliable, affordable and quality energy supply. Main challenge, as to developing and also to some extent developed countries, is to have clean energy for sustainable development. Towards this end, all countries, including Malaysia, are making possible efforts. The emphasis on renewable energy sources is being enhanced. It has been decided at the Bonn Conference on Renewable Energy on June 2004 that in twenty

84. See the Introductory Chapter above.

85. See T. Husniarti, 'Malaysian Energy Policy: An Overview', paper presented at the Malaysia–Japan Workshop on Energy Supply and Demand Forecasting, March 1998, Kuala Lumpur; Ministry of Energy, Communications and Multimedia, Malaysia, 'Notable Energy Developments', paper presented at EWG 18, Nov. 1999, Wellington; Ministry of Energy Communications and Multimedia, Malaysia, 'Proceedings of World Renewable Energy Congress (WREC)', December 1999, Kuala Lumpur; Eighth Malaysia Plan; Asia Pacific Energy Research Centre (APERC), Electricity Sector Deregulation in the APEC Region, 2000, Tokyo. 'Malaysia – Energy Overview', <www.ieej.or.jp/aperc/01Malaysia.PDF>; Dr Mohd Zamzam Jaafar, 'Malaysia's Energy Plan: The Way Forward', paper presented at 4th APEC Coal Trade and Investment Liberalization and Facilitation (TILF) Workshop, 6–8 Mar. 2002, Kuala Lumpur, <www.apec-egcfe.fossil.energy.gov/TILF_2002_KL/7.3_jaafar.pdf>.

years' time one-third of the world population should be able to exploit the renewable sources of energy. Malaysia also will have to augment the effort of exploiting renewable energy. For this, Malaysia will have to make efforts to upgrade its technology and to make fruitful efforts to acquire technology from developed countries.

96. In 2010, The Ministry of Energy, Green Technology and Water launched the National Renewable Energy Policy and Action Plan to overcome the main barriers to renewable energy development in the country. The strategy aims to address: market failure, inconsistency in the policies, mixed signals to investors and lack of robust and long-term sustainable growth. It thus aimed to enhance the use of indigenous renewable energy sources. Ensuring electricity supply in the out grid areas. One of its objectives is to maximize the RE in the country by providing incentives, technological support and increasing the purchase price. For these, an action plan based on FiT has been designed. The RE Action Plan sets a target of 24% of energy from these sources by 2050. It is to be noted again that in 2011 its share was 1%. It will go up to 9% by 2020.[86] If the set target is achieved, 30 million tonnes of CO_2 emissions will be reduced. This will help keep the promise made by the country under the Paris Agreement of 2015.

Alongside, the National Green Technology Policy was also launched by the Malaysian Prime Minister on 24 July 2009. The four objectives of the Policy are: to seek to attain energy independence and to promote efficient utilization of energy; to conserve and minimize the impact of energy generation and utilization on the environment; to enhance the national economic development through the use of green technology; and to improve the quality of life of the Malaysian people. In short, green technology will promote sustainable development with sustainable energy. It is submitted that the ultimate aim is to cut the greenhouse gas emissions by 35% at 2005 levels by 2030 and with international support 45%.

Towards this end, the Eleventh Malaysia Plan, as stated above, support them by: strengthening stakeholders coordination and collaboration in the energy sector; ensuring the security of supply and reliability for the oil and gas sector within a market-based approach; enabling the growth in the oil and gas sector; managing supply diversity for security of electricity subsector; and improving the sustainability, efficiency and reliability of the electricity subsector.[87]

It is expected that by 2020, which seems to be achievable, there will be 2,080 MW electricity generated by renewable sources. The various expected share of various sources are given in Figure 18.

86. International Energy Agency, 'Renewable Energy Policy and Action Plan', at: https://www.iea.org/policiesandmeasures/pams/malaysia/name-24985-en.php (accessed on 2 Jan. 2018).

87. 'Malaysia Energy Policy: Focusing on Sustainable Energy Development and the Way Forward', *Supra*.

Figure 18 Projection of Renewable Energy by 2020

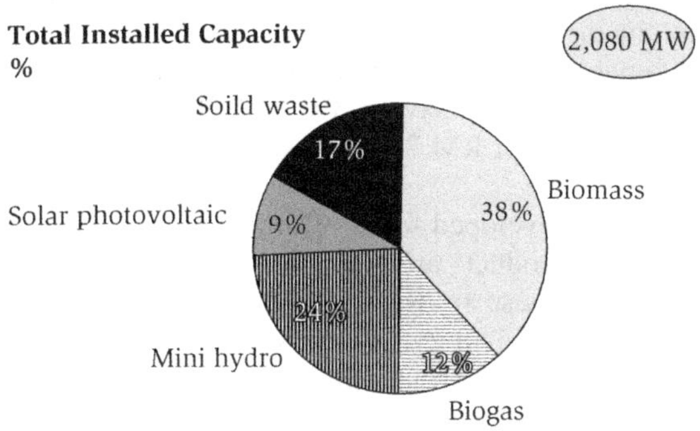

Source: Ministry of Energy, Green Technology and Water, 2016.

97. Energy Commission is entrusted to enrage the production energy by large-scale solar (LSS). It is being done under the Guidelines named 'Guidelines On Large Scale Solar Photovoltaic Plant for Connection to Electricity Networks' made under the Electricity Supply Act 1990 (Act 447). The Energy Commission for the time being has set the quota of 1,000 MW for 2017–2020 (250 MW/year), of which 800 MW is allocated to Peninsular Malaysia and 200 MW for Sabah. It may be noted that FiT fort this source of energy will cease to support duet to paucity of funds. However, the Prime Minister during the Budget 2016 announced that they will continue in the country and appropriate support will be provided to it. SEDA as the implementing agency has fixed quota to net energy metering (NEM) at 450 MW for Peninsular Malaysia and 50 MW for Sabah. In order to achieve the target, the state government is working at all levels. Notable among them is training the stakeholders on large-scale solar (LSS) photovoltaic plants and net energy metering scheme (NEM). Experts teach them about various international standards, processes and procedures that are relevant in the marketplace, and connecting generations to grids.[88] Now, NEM has an annual capacity of 100 MW, of which 90 MW is for Peninsular Malaysia, while the remainder is for Sabah, Sarawak and Labuan. Tjis has been set for five years, from 2016 to 2020.

98. In order to support the Green energy management in the country various strategies are there in place in the supply side also.

(1) There are: promotion of green energy offices and low-energy offices. For this, there is Green Building Index (GBI).
(2) Enhance the use of the Efficient Management of Electrical Energy Regulations (EMEER), 2008. The key provisions of the regulations are: it applies to

88. 'Coming Clean: Coaching Staff to Become Competent on Energy Matters', *Energy Malaysia*, Volume 10, 2016.

big energy users (3 mil kwh/6 months), and it requires appointment of EEM. There will be Electrical Energy Management Policy. There will be Energy Audit. There will be proper monitoring by appropriate authority and records will be maintained. There will be periodical reporting to the officer.

(3) There is Sustainability Achieved via Energy Efficiency (SAVE) Programme, 2011–2013. This resulted in saving 306.9 GWh from the domestic consumption resulting in saving of RM 78.4 million and reduction of 208,705 tonne of CO_2.

(4) A scheme has been developed for certifying standards and labelling the products. Least efficient products are given two stars, and the most efficient products have five stars. These are issued by the Energy Commission based on the certification issued to his effect by SIRIM. SIRIM also issues certification of fitness to electrical and electronic products.

(5) The Minimum Energy Performance Standard (MEPS), gazetted in 2013, is also there in place. It requires the product to show: energy rating from one star to five stars, appliance energy rating in numeral, model information, energy consumption (in kwh/year), energy saving compared to an average three-star model (in percentage). It is applicable now to: refrigerators, air conditioners, televisions, fans and lightings (fluorescent, CFL, LED and incandescent). The labelling scheme was initially successfully run between 2009 and 2012. Now, they have to be tested under the Malaysian Energy Efficient Standards. All applicants are required to follow the standards and have to follow the standards prescribed by the Department of Standards Malaysia (DSM) for them. SIRIM QAS International is the designated testing body for the certification to be granted by the Energy Commission. These standards are revised every five years in light of internationally practiced standards and the capacity of local manufacturers. This may be noted that with respect to certain items, MEPS is mandatory. This ruling came on 3 May 2013 as a part of the Electricity (Amendment) Regulations 2013. For appliances manufactured in a foreign county, that country's report is acceptable. As noted above, two star is acceptable, three star is good and five star is excellent as it saves 25% of electricity. The system is working successfully, as in 2015, 1215 appliances were certified; and in 2016 it went up to 2083 appliances. It is hoped that in future many more appliances will be brought under the MEPS scheme.[89]

(6) There is Energy Performance Contracting (EPC) for saving electricity from buildings. It came into force in 2013. It provides an effective mechanism for energy-saving measures for government buildings. The cost of its implementation is borne by ESCOs while the owners of government buildings are allowed to pay the cost of investment by the ESCOs from the savings. The author is of the opinion that some similar incentive-based scheme should be there for private buildings too.

(7) The National Energy Efficiency Action Plan (NEEAP) 2016–2025 has strategies to support energy efficiency activities. They are: to have a strong institutional framework; to encourage capacity development and training; to have

89. 'Certifying Energy Efficient Appliances', *Energy Malaysia*, Vol. 11, 2017, p. 26.

a fund to support EE; to promote investment in EE projects; to promote 5-star-rated appliances; to follow minimum energy performance standards (MEPS); and to conduct energy audit.

(8) The Home Energy Report (HER) programme, which is and educative programme on energy efficiency and energy-saving matters to household, has shown a remarkable results by saving 11 billion kwh electricity worth USD 1.5 billion in electricity bills, and reducing carbon emission by 13 billion in 2016. In Malaysia, TNB has started this programme. In 2017, Malaysia was number one in South East Asia and third in Asia, after Hong Kong and Japan. It is in line with the sustainable initiatives of the 11th Malaysia Plan. The programme is basically to educate electricity consumers. In 2015, 250,000 consumers were selected from the Klang Valley, Negri Sembilan and Melaka. They saved 13,979 MW hours. Under the scheme, customers are briefed about various methods and means of energy savings and the reports from them on energy savings are collected.[90]

(9) Energy audit of industrial and commercial buildings (2016–2018), and some financial support from the government to improve based on audit reports.

99. From the result of all the efforts indicated above, renewable energy in Malaysia is 392 MW, most of which are fuelled by solar PV, biomass, mini-hydro and biogas. In 2016, there was an increase by 7.1% from the 2015 figures. Of the 392 MW in 2016, 235 MW was from solar PV, 34 from biogas, 34 from mini-hydro and 89 from biomass. In order to keep its promise of 45% by 2030 (35% its own and another 10% upon receiving financial support and technological help from developed countries), Malaysia will have to re-strategize this sector of power generation.[91]

100. This is notable here that Malaysia is seriously thinking to embark on manufacturing, using and exporting biodiesel, mixing 5% palm oil with diesel and use it for running vehicles and generating power. This is because Malaysia is one of the biggest manufacturers of palm oil in the world. On 10 August 2005, the Malaysian Prime Minister has unveiled the biofuel strategy providing incentives for medium-term implementation in line with the awaited National Biofuel Policy, which is still being drafted. It is said that in the policy the medium-term initiatives will also include formulation of a national biodiesel industry Act, which will generally regulate manufacturing, storage, use and export of biodiesel. The policy, as stated, is aimed at encouraging the use of biodiesel as an alternative to diesel. The Government has decided to set up demonstration mills for the production of biodiesel for the cold climate, to appoint a plantation company to ensure consistent supply of palm oil for the production of palm oil-based biodiesel and to provide for warranty to automotive companies for biofuel engines that they will produce. There is a three-pronged plan: (1) biofuel production/use for transport/industries; (2) biofuel production for export to Europe; (3) commercializing biofuel as home-grown technology. The underlined proposals and incentives are: (1) biofuel demonstration

90. 'Nurturing an Energy Efficient Society', *Energy Malaysia*, Vol. 11, 2017, pp. 18–20.
91. See, 'Ming Sustainable Security', *Energy Malaysia*, Vol. 14, 2018, pp. 41–43.

mill for the cold climate, so that it could be exported to Europe, Canada and the United States. These countries use biodiesel for running trains; (2) appointment of a plantation company for consistent palm oil supply for production of biodiesel; (3) providing warrantee to biofuel engine carmakers; (4) 5% of palm oil in biofuel blends; (5) having biofuel pioneer stations; (6) fixing biofuel standards; (7) having a commercial biofuel mill in Labu, Negrisembilan.[92]

101. In 2004, the world demand for biofuel was 2.5 million tonnes. This is expected to rise at the rate of 25% per year because of two reasons: first, it has comparatively less pollutants, and second, it will be relatively cheaper. Malaysia has the potential and capability to fulfil the demand.

102. It is notable here that due to a flood of applications for constructing biodiesel plants in the country, government has imposed a temporary ban on opening new plants. On 29 June 2006, the cabinet Committee on the Competitiveness of the Palm oil Industry announced that the government would stop issuing new biodiesel manufacturing licenses. This has been done to protect the crude palm oil reserves (CPO) for that are mainly meant for food. The total numbers of biodiesel licensing are indicated in Table 32 below.

Table 32 Biodiesel Licensing in Malaysia

	Applications Made	*Applications Approved*	*Capacity (Tonnes)*
June 2006	87	32	3,000,000
Dec 2004	3	3	18,000
Dec 2002	2	2	6,000
Dec 2000	1	1	3,000

Source: Malaysian Palm Oil Council.

103. The biodiesel industry got impetus when Malaysian Biodiesel Industry Act (Act 666 of 207) was implemented. Applications for license for producing biodiesel can be made according to the Malaysian Biofuel Industry (Licensing) Regulations 2008 based on the guidelines prescribed by the Licensing Authority. Under this Act and the Regulations, fifty applications so far have been approved. Of them only twenty are operative. The author feels that this is not a good number. The government should make efforts to increase this number. The production of biodiesel in 2017 between 800,000 and 900,000, as noted below, is not an encouraging figure when compared to Indonesia.

104. It is further notable that this has been done to maintain the realistic level of biodiesel manufacturing in the country. The sudden and keen investment from the

92. See *New Straits Times*, 11 Aug. 2005.

private sector is being fuelled by the government's plan to create an assured local market and guaranteed export prospects. The government has left the option of the use of methyl ester to be used in manufacturing EnvoDiesel.[93]

105. Until February 2008, ninety-one permits were issued. Four major companies produced 300,000 tonnes of EnvoDiesel (Biodiesel). Seven other companies with 621,000 tonnes capacity were supposed to be operative soon. As the Biofuel Policy of 2006 of the country aims at boosting palm oil production, and a large part of it to be used in producing biodiesel so that the country gets cleaner energy indigenously produced which benefits a larger number of people, in future, the production of biodiesel will increase. It is notable that the country is also exporting biodiesel, and since overseas demand is increasing, this factor will also press the palm oil sector and companies oils, engaged with producing biodiesel to produce more.[94]

106. It is notable that the biodiesel industry in the country will flourish only when it gets support in the form of incentives from the government. Much depends on oil prices. Withdrawal of subsidy from oil may help boost the biodiesel industry. European countries' interest in it may provide further impetus to it. But EU Renewable Energy Directive II is quite discouraging to them. (See infra) Right now, investment in biodiesel industry is not encouraging. It is further to be noted that production of B5 (a blend of 5% vegetable oil and 95% natural diesel) biodiesel is postponed for the time being.[95] There is also on the card to have B10 biodiesel in the near future.

It was expected that the in 2017 production of biodiesel in the country would experience a notable boost. In 2016 the production was 500,000 tonnes, which was 173,000 tonnes lower than its production in 2015. It became between 800,000 and 900,000 tonnes.[96]

107. Professor Ottinger of the Pace University has rightly pointed out after a comprehensive socio-environmental study of biofuels that while promoting production of biodiesel, especially from edible oil, we have to conduct proper socio-environmental study. Otherwise, we might make edible oil unaffordable by the poor section of the world, and we can adversely affect the environment, because for facilitating growth of palm oil, we have to clear virgin forests, especially in tropical region, which play a positive role in maintaining the balance of CO_2, water cycle and retaining underground water.[97]

---

93. *New Straits Times*, 3 Jul. 2006.
94. See M. Nagarajan, 'Biofuel Development in Malaysia', paper presented at the 'International Symposium on Agricultural and Biofuel Policy', 25 Feb. 2008, Bangkok, Thailand.
95. www.mybiodiesel.org.my (accessed on 14 Mar. 2018).
96. *The Star Online*, 7 Mar. 2017, at: https://www.thestar.com.my/business/business-news/2017/03/07/malaysias-biodiesel-production-to-rebound-this-year/ (accessed on 25 Mar. 2018).
97. Richard L. Ottinger, 'Biofuels: Potentials, Problems and Solutions', *Environmental Law Review* (2009): 56.

108. European Union made guidelines, to be enforced from 5 December 2010, for imposing a levy on import of biodiesel and palm oil. It also requires for 'green certification'. These will adversely affect the export of biodiesel and palm oil to European Union countries. These, in fact, are a kind of protectionism in favour of locally manufactured oil to be used for making biodiesel and other biofuels, which will affect imports from Malaysia and Indonesia. Right now, these countries are exporting 40% of biodiesel and palm oil to the United States and EU countries.[98] It is for this reason that Malaysian and Indonesian governments have protested against the move. They are persuading the EU to withdraw this regulation. If persuasion efforts fail, they might go to the International Court of Justice. Some say it will not affect the sale of palm oil and biodiesel. But this does not seem to be true. There is going to be free trade agreement between the European Union and Malaysia. Malaysia might bring this issue in the discussions and might insist for lifting the requirement of 'green certification' and the levy. It has been reported in many issues of the local newspapers, especially in the *New Straits Times*. For a comprehensive account, we may refer to *Bernama*, 23 May 2010.

109. The Ninth Malaysia Plan states that efforts to promote the development of biofuel using palm oil as a renewable source of energy will be undertaken during the plan period in line with the initiative to make the country a world leader and hub for palm oil. Designated pump stations, mainly in the Klang Valley, to supply diesel blended with palm oil are expected to commence operation in 2006. For the initial phase, the blended diesel will be utilized by vehicles of selected government agencies. Along with local consumption, efforts will be made to export it.

110. Presently, EU is the world's biggest producer of biodiesel. Initially its production was 25 million tonnes. It rose to 400 million tonnes in 2005. All EU countries, except Finland Hungary, Ireland, Luxembourg and Netherlands, produce biodiesel. The break of the world production of biodiesel can be seen in Table 33:

Table 33 World Biodiesel in Million Tonnes

Country	*Million Tonnes*
EU	3.2
US	.25
Indonesia	3.5
Others	.11

Source: UN Food and Agricultural Organization; The European Commission; US Renewable Fuels association; and US Green Car Congress.

98. See Yusuf Basin of the TRUTH Foundation, 'Pushing the Case for Biodiesel, Palm Oil', *New Straits Times*, 27 May 2010.

111. As noted above, the Malaysian energy policy is in line with the collective energy policy of (ASEAN, also ASEAN) member countries. According to the ASEAN Centre for Energy, the economic developments in the ASEAN region received a boost with energy cooperation among the Member States. This cooperation received an impetus from the 1995 Bangkok Summit. The declaration at the conclusion of the summit stated, 'Asean will ensure greater security and sustainability to energy supply through diversification, development and conservation of resources, the efficient use of energy, and the wider application of environmentally sound technologies.' This was reinforced in the ASEAN Vision 2020, arising from the ASEAN second informal summit in December 1997 in Kuala Lumpur, and calling for cooperation on activities 'to establish interconnecting arrangements for electricity and gas within ASEAN through the ASEAN power grid and a trans-ASEAN gas pipeline, and to promote cooperation in energy efficiency and conservation, as well as the development of new and renewable energy sources'. This vision was fully stipulated in the Hanoi Action Plan of 1998, which provided direction towards this vision during the period 1999–2004. This ASEAN Action Plan for Energy Co-operation 1999–2004 provided basic principles on various aspects of energy generation and supply. The Action Plan merged the two programme areas, energy and environment. It considered energy security as a separate programme area. It urged the specialized bodies like ASCOPE, HAPUA, AEEMTRC, AFOC and the ASEAN sub-sector networks under SOME to further study the plan of action and submits to ACE the revised formulation. ACE was to finalize the document in time for consideration and adoption in the SOME/17th AMEM in July 1999, which it did. As provided for in the Hanoi Action Plan 1998, the energy sector shall have the following objectives for the stipulated period: (1) to ensure security and sustainability of energy supply, efficient utilization of natural energy sources in the region and to work for a rational management of energy demand, with due consideration of the environment; (2) to institute the policy framework and implementation modalities by 2004 for the early realization of the trans-Asean energy networks covering the ASEAN power grid and the trans-ASEAN gas pipeline projects (TAPGs) as a more focused continuation of the medium-term programme of action. The action plan is divided into six plan areas. There are designated bodies to work for implementation of the programmes:

Activities	*Designated Institution*
ASEAN Power Grid	Heads of ASEAN Power Utilities Authorities (HAPUA)
Trans-ASEAN Gas Pipeline	ASEAN Council of Petroleum (ASCOPE)
Coal	ASEAN Forum on Coal (AFOC)
Energy Efficiency & Conservation	The Energy Efficiency and Conservation Network in coordination with ACE

Activities	*Designated Institution*
New & Renewable Energy	New and Renewable Sources of Energy Sub-Sector Network
Regional Energy Outlook, Energy Policy and Environmental Analysis	ASEAN Centre for Energy (ACE)

Source: ASEAN Centre for Energy.

112. Cooperation and dialogue among the Member States of ASEAN (hereinafter Asean) are continued process. For policy determinations, for taking the stock of the progress already taken place, and for the future strategies and cooperation on the problems pertaining to energy faced by Asean countries, meetings of relevant authorities are regularly arranged. The powerful body to discuss these is Ministerial Meetings of the Member States. In the whole process, Malaysia is playing a significant role.[99]

113. Asean countries are now working together to implement the policy proclamation enshrined in the Five-year Action Plan for Energy covering 2004–2009, which lays greater emphasis on greater degree of reliance on indigenous energy sources, connecting the Asean region with a workable grid and natural gas pipelines, increasing the use of renewable energy, conservation of energy and enhancement of search for more oil and gas reserves. While speaking at the Meeting for Economic Integration and Energy Cooperation in Asean, H. E. Ong Keng Yong, the Secretary General of Asean, highlighted the importance of Asean cooperation in the energy sector. He suggested three things to be undertaken: (1) the Asean must invest more on energy production and infrastructural development so that the rising demand of energy is properly met. This is also necessary to provide adequate affordable energy and to improve human welfare and increase living standards; (2) energy sector should be modern and environmentally friendly. In the developing countries lack of modern technology and clean energy is the cause of degradation of the environment and impediment to sustainable development; (3) Asean must reduce its dependence on imported energy, particularly oil; (4) Asean must make more common and concerted efforts because it would offer significant benefits both in terms of security, flexibility and quality of energy supply and greater competition. For this, a power grid and interconnecting pipelines, which are already there, should be enhanced. The plans that are already in the building stage should be completed quickly.

114. He suggested that the Asean Secretariat would soon carry out a study on regional electricity trading, aimed at to promote greater understanding on the

99. See the website of the Asean Centre for Energy.

concept of electricity trading in Asean, its challenges, opportunities and options, as well as guide the formulation of common policy for regional power interconnection and trade.[100]

115. The Ninth Malaysia Plan States that at the regional level, Malaysia will continue to support the ASEAN Plan of Action for Energy Cooperation (APAEC). The APAEC covers four areas of cooperation, namely the TAPG Project; TAPG; Sustainable Utilization of Coal, Energy Efficiency and Conservation Programme; and Regional Energy and Regional Energy Policy and Planning Programme. In this regard, the interconnected network of electricity grids and gas pipelines will offer significant benefits in terms of energy security and sustainability. In addition, issues of energy security will also be given emphasis under the cooperation of ASEAN Plus Three as well as the Asia-Pacific Economic Cooperation (APEC).

116. Among all proposed plans, the gas pipeline programme is working well. Gas pipelines between Malaysia and Indonesia and between Malaysia and Thailand are notable breakthroughs. The author is of the opinion that since gas will last more than oil, gas pipelines among Asean countries will be promoted at least until 2020.

The Executive Summary of the SEAN Energy Cooperation Report 2017 shows encouraging progress in the cooperative concerted efforts in the cooperation among the Member States in the organization. The Executive Summary is:

> The 34 ASEAN Ministers on Energy Meeting (AMEM) held in Nay Pyi Taw, Myanmar in September 2016 expressed satisfaction on the strong start of the first year of implementation of the ASEAN Plan of Action for Energy Cooperation (APAEC) 2016-2025 Phase I: 2016-2020. The Ministers called upon Dialogue Partners (DPs), International Organisations (IOs) and the energy business community to strengthen collaboration to achieve energy security, accessibility, affordability and sustainability for ASEAN energy consumers. The Ministers agreed to publish the ASEAN Energy Cooperation Report (AECR) to help improve the profile of ASEAN internationally starting in 2017. This will promote the interactive flow of information on the key achievements of ASEAN energy cooperation activities in 2016/2017 and to highlight the strategic directions going forward with all the ASEAN energy stakeholders. The 5th ASEAN Energy Outlook (AEO5) of the ASEAN Centre for Energy (ACE) present the region's energy landscape for the period 2015-2040. The AEO5 shows that ASEAN is meeting the challenges of energy development both in terms of the business-as-usual (BAU) scenario and the AMS Targets Scenario (ATS) and underlines what needs to be done to strengthen the forward strategy of the ASEAN approach, especially within the parameters of cooperation to achieve progress at the level of APAEC. In particular, this means reinforcing the options and aspirations for renewable energy (RE) and energy efficiency (EE), which are increasingly seen as cornerstones for future energy policy

100. www.aseansec.org/16129.htm.(accessed on 12 Jan. 2018).

development. The AEO5 highlights that ASEAN is on track to reach the APAEC energy intensity (EI) target while the ASEAN's aspirational target to increase the share of RE to 23% by 2025 in the energy mix will require even greater effort than currently foreseen by AMS. The AEO5 will be launched at the 35th AMEM in September 2017 in Manila, the Philippines. ASEAN's cohesive cooperation in the energy sector is guided by the ASEAN Plan of Action for Energy Cooperation 2016-2025. Its theme is 'Enhancing Energy Connectivity and Market Integration in ASEAN to Achieve Energy Security, Accessibility, Affordability and Sustainability for All'. It serves as the single reference document comprising of seven (7) programme areas with specific outcome-based strategies and annual priorities and key action lines. The key achievements of the APAEC in 2016-2017 are as follows:

ASEAN has completed physical interconnections with capacity of about 1,723 MW, thus bringing the total capacity of the APG to 5,212 MW. Eight out of the sixteen planned APG projects have been completed. During the 34th AMEM in Myanmar, the governments signed the MOU to engage and implement the first phase of the 'Lao PDR-Thailand-Malaysia-Singapore (LTMS) Power Integration Project (PIP)' by January 2018, which will optimise the use of resources and promote economic cooperation on multilateral power interconnections and trading in the region.

Progress has been made in achieving 3,673 kilometre of existing pipelines connecting six (6) ASEAN Member States (AMS) and six (6) liquefied natural gas (LNG) regasification terminals with total capacity of 22.5 million tonnes per annum (MTPA).

The public image of coal in ASEAN has been advanced through conduct of capacity building and promotional activities on clean coal technologies (CCT). ASEAN has also established the focal point system and coordination mechanism in the AMS to submit data and information to the ASEAN Coal Database and Information System (ACDIS). Additionally, AMS participation has been on a voluntary basis.

As a result of collective AMS efforts, energy intensity reduction was about 19% in 2015 as compared to 2005 level. The 34th AMEM endorsed the Regional Policy Roadmap on Promotion of Higher Efficiency Air Conditioners and seven (7) AMS have now completed their National Policy Roadmaps. The draft ASEAN Regional Efficient Lighting Market Assessment Study is now completed and the development of Draft Policy Roadmap is underway.

The share of RE sources accounted for 13.6% in the ASEAN's total primary energy supply mix. In the power sector, RE contributes around 21.2% of total power generation producing 201 TWh of electricity in 2015 with a total installed power capacity of 50 GW. The 3-year ASEAN-Germany Energy Programme (AGEP) commenced the implementation of activities in 2016.

The AMS have aligned the key performance indicators and annual milestones of APAEC programme areas with the emerging trends and requirements of an integrated economy as identified by the AEC Blueprint 2025. Publications included the ASEAN Energy Cooperation Report 2017, 5th ASEAN Energy Outlook, ASEAN Energy Policy Review and Analysis Series Additionally the ASEAN Energy Database System was launched.

> The implementation of the ASEAN-Canada Work Programme commenced to enhance AMS capabilities on nuclear energy policy and regulatory systems. Other collaborations with partners have widely focused on improvement of public understanding and promotion of public education on nuclear power generation. The direction of future activities of the APAEC have been formulated collectively by the ASEAN Member States (AMS) including the Specialised Energy Bodies (SEB), Sub-sector Networks (SSN), ASEAN Secretariat and ACE. In 2018, the AMS will conduct the APAEC mid-term review to assess and update the annual priorities up to 2020. The preparation of APAEC Phase II: 2021-2025 will commence in 2019 for endorsement by AMEM in 2020. ASEAN welcomes collaborative partnerships with DPs and IOs to achieve the aspirations of the ASEAN Community Vision 2025. Engagement with DPs and IOs will play a key role in meeting ASEAN's energy objectives and targets under the APAEC 2016-2025. The APAEC strategies are broad and flexible enough to meet the ever-changing global and regional energy environments and to support the goals of the ASEAN Economic Community Blueprint 2025.

In view of the Paris Accord 2015, ASEAN has set a target of securing 23% of energy from renewable sources by 2025. As a part of it, Malaysia will make its best effort to meet the target; it has potential to do so. Malaysia has a target of 2,080 MW of renewable energy installed capacity by 2020 (excluding large hydro).[101]

101. *The ASEAN Post* at: https://theaseanpost.com/article/importance-renewable-energy-cooperation-asean-0 (accessed on 20 Jan. 2018).

Chapter 5. Energy Commission

§1. General

117. It is responsible to regulate the energy supply activities, enforce the energy supply laws and promote further development of the energy industry. Apart from its advisory role on policies and matters related to the energy supply activities, the Energy Commission is also responsible in ensuring adequate, secured and reliable supply of electricity and the supply of gas through pipelines at reasonable prices as well as promote efficiency and protect consumers. The Commission, in fact, had first to bring into practice the objectives stated in the National Energy Policy Objectives as stated in the Eighth Malaysia Plan: (1) To ensure the provision of adequate, secure and cost-effective energy supplies through developing indigenous energy resources using the least-cost options and diversification of supply sources both from within and outside the country. (2) To promote the efficient utilization of energy and to discourage wasteful and non-productive patterns of energy consumption. (3) To minimize the negative impacts of energy production, transportation, conversion, utilization and consumption on the environment. It also has to work in line with the NDP that strives: to safeguard the depleting oil reserves aiming at major oil fields of over 400 million barrels of OIIP, and restricting their production to 1.75% of OIIP, which was revised to 3% in 1985. With the result of that, the total production of crude oil tremendously increased. This has to be noted here that the NDP was later extended to include gas reserves also with an upper limit of 2,000 million standard cubic feet per day. This may also be noted here that with the inventions of new oil and gas reserves in the country, the expectancy has increased. For achieving these policy objectives, the following aims have been emphasized: (1) Diversification of fuel type and sources, technology, maximized use of indigenous energy resources, adequate reserve capacity to cater for contingencies. (2) Forecast demand, right energy pricing and formulate plans to meet demand. (3) Promote competition in the electricity supply industry. (4) Promote competition and provide indicative supply plan to meet demand based on least-cost approach using power computer software. (5) Promote the development of renewable and cogeneration as much as possible. (6) Match quality with customer demand with variable tariffs. (7) Benchmarking, auditing, financial and fiscal incentives, technology development, labelling, rating and correct pricing. (8) Monitor the impacts, improve efficiency of utilization and conversion and promote renewable sources of energy. The Commission's task has been to bring into practice the energy-related initiatives specified in the Five-Year Plans of the country, and to make proactive efforts towards achieving the targets set in them. The Commission is now working on achieving the green initiatives imperatives and to maximize the renewable energy and increase energy efficiency and conservation of energy so that the promise 40% carbon reduction target set by the Malaysian Prime Minister could be achieved.

118. Thus, the Commission is meant to create and enforce a regulatory framework for the achievement of a reliable, efficient and safe energy supply industry consistent with the needs for economic growth and sustainable development. It also works for protecting consumer's interests. Towards achieving these, the following objectives have been set by the Commission: (1) To provide timely and relevant advice on policies and strategies for the energy industry. (2) To provide an effective regulatory framework towards self-regulation in the energy sector. (3) To ensure efficient and safe supply and utilization of energy. (4) To ensure transparent and competitive energy market. (5) To protect consumers' interest. (6) To promote the use of renewable energy and the conservation of energy in general by developing viable strategies. (7) To promote research and development and maximize the use of new technology in the energy sector. It operates under: the Electricity Supply Act 1990 (Act 447) as amended in 2015; the Gas Supply Act 1993 (Act 501), as amended in 2016; the Electricity Regulations 1994 as amended in 2014; Licensee Supply Regulations 1990; the Electricity Supply (Compounding of Offences) Regulations 2001; the Efficient Management of Electrical Energy Regulations 2008; the Gas Supply Regulations 1997; and the Gas Supply (Compoundable Offences) Order 2006.

§2. Organization of the Commission

119. The Commission works under a Chairman and six members, two from the government and the other four members from outside. Chairman holds the post as a full-time officer.

120. Minister is the appointing authority. In case the Chairman is absent and travelling overseas or he/she cannot work for any reason, the Minister can appoint someone to act as the Chairperson. The tenure of the member of the commission is for a term not exceeding three years.

121. A member of the Commission will be eligible for reappointment but no member can hold office for more than two consecutive terms.

122. Minister has the power to revoke the appointment of any member of the Commission. Likewise, members are free to resign any time.

123. Remuneration is paid as the Minister finds to be suitable to be paid.

124. The office of any member will fall vacant if he/she dies or found guilty of any offence specified in section 10 of the Act.

125. Before a person is appointed as a member, he/she will have to make a declaration that he/she does not have any stake or interest in any undertaking engaged in energy sector.

We have noted that the Energy Commission has jurisdiction of the Peninsular Malaysia and Sabah. The Organization Chart of the Commission is:

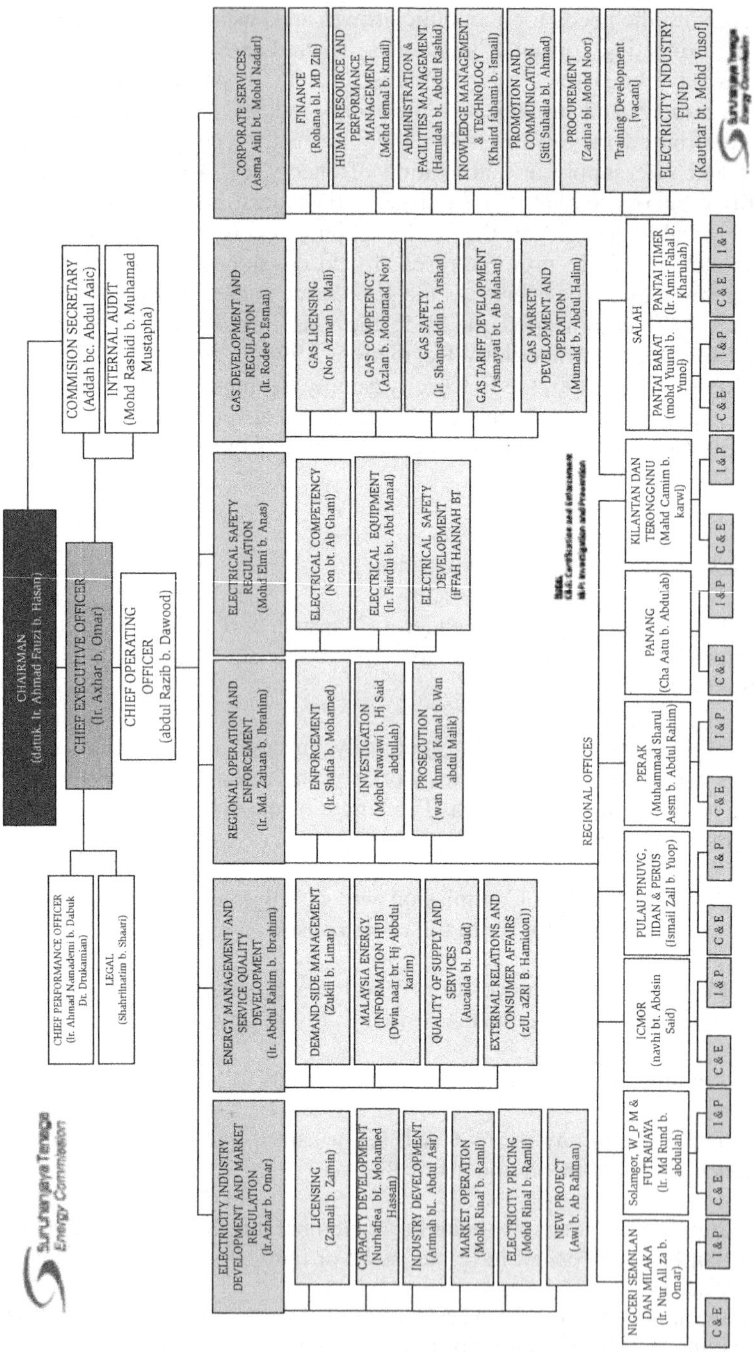
CHAIRMAN (datuk. Ir. Ahmad Fauzi b. Hasan)
CHIEF EXECUTIVE OFFICER (Ir. Axhar b. Omar)
CHIEF OPERATING OFFICER (abdul Razib b. Dawood)
COMMISION SECRETARY (Addah bc. Abdul Aaic)
INTERNAL AUDIT (Mohd Rashidi b. Muhamad Mustapha)
CHIEF PERFORMANCE OFFICER (Ir. Ahmad Namademi b. Dabuk Dr. Drukamian)
LEGAL (Shahrilnatim b. Shaari)
ELECTRICITY INDUSTRY DEVELOPMENT AND MARKET REGULATION (Ir.Azhar b. Omar)
LICENSING (Zamali b. Zamin)
CAPACITY DEVELOPMENT (Nurhafiea bl. Mohamed Hassan)
INDUSTRY DEVELOPMENT (Arimah bL. Abdul Asir)
MARKET OPERATION (Mohd Rinal b. Ramli)
ELECTRICITY PRICING (Mohd Rinal b. Ramli)
NEW PROJECT (Awi b. Ab Rahman)
ENERGY MANAGEMENT AND SERVICE QUALITY DEVELOPMENT (Ir. Abdul Rahim b. Ibrahim)
DEMAND-SIDE MANAGEMENT (Zukili b. Limar)
MALAYSIA ENERGY (INFORMATION HUB (Dwin naar br. Hj Abbdul karim)
QUALITY OF SUPPLY AND SERVICES (Aucaida bl. Daud)
EXTERNAL RELATIONS AND CONSUMER AFFAIRS (zUL aZRI B. Hamidon))
REGIONAL OPERATION AND ENFORCEMENT (Ir. Md. Zaluan b. Ibrahim)
ENFORCEMENT (Ir. Shafia b. Mohamed)
INVESTIGATION (Mohd Nawawi b. Hj Said abdullah)
PROSECUTION (wan Ahmad Kamal b.Wan abdul Malik)
ELECTRICAL SAFETY REGULATION (Mohd Elmi b. Anas)
ELECTRICAL COMPETENCY (Non bt. Ab Ghani)
ELECTRICAL EQUIPMENT (Ir. Fairdui bt. Abd Manal)
ELECTRICAL SAFETY DEVELOPMENT (IFFAH HANNAH BT
GAS DEVELOPMENT AND REGULATION (Ir. Rodee b.Esman)
GAS LICENSING (Nor Azman b. Mali)
GAS COMPETENCY (Azlan b. Mohamad Nor)
GAS SAFETY (Ir. Shamsuddin b. Arshad)
GAS TARIFF DEVELOPMENT (Asmayati bt. Ab Mahan)
GAS MARKET DEVELOPMENT AND OPERATION (Mumaid b. Abdul Halim)
CORPORATE SERVICES (Asma Ainl bt. Mohd Nadarl)
FINANCE (Rohana bl. MD Zin)
HUMAN RESOURCE AND PERFORMANCE MANAGEMENT (Mchd lemal b. kmail)
ADMINISTRATION & FACILITIES MANAGEMENT (Hamidah bt. Abdul Rashid)
KNOWLEDGE MANAGEMENT & TECHNOLOGY (Khaird fahami b. Ismail)
PROMOTION AND COMMUNICATION (Siti Suhaila bl. Ahmad)
PROCUREMENT (Zarina bl. Mohd Noor)
Training Development [vacant]
ELECTRICITY INDUSTRY FUND [Kauthar bt. Mchd Yusof]
REGIONAL OFFICES
NIGCERI SEMNLAN DAN MILAKA (Ir. Nur All za b. Omar)
Solamgor, W_P M & FUTRAUAYA (Ir. Md Rund b. abdulah)
ICMOR (navhi bt. Abdsin Said)
PULAU PINUVG, IIDAN & PERUS (Ismail Zall b. Yuop)
PERAK (Muhammad Sharul Assm b. Abdul Rahim)
PANANG (Cha Aatu b. Abdu'ab)
KILANTAN DAN TERONGGNU (Mahd Camim b. karwl)
SALAH
PANTAI BARAT (mohd Yuurul b. Yunol)
PANTAI TIMER (Ir. Amir Fahal b. Kharuhah)
C & E
I & P
Suruhanjaya Tenaga Energy Commission

It may be noted here that according to the Energy Commission Amendment Act 2010, the temporary CEO will be appointed by the Minister when the post of CEO is vacant, or When he is absent from duty; or for any other reason he unable to perform his duties.

§3. Power and Function

126. According to part III of the Energy Commission Act 2001, and as stated by the Energy Commission, under sections 14–17 of the Act the Commission has the following functions and powers.

127. The Commission shall have all the functions imposed on it under the energy supply laws and shall also have the following functions:

- to advice the Minister on all matters concerning the national policy objectives for energy supply activities;
- to advice the Minister on all matters relating to the generation, production, transmission, distribution, supply and use of electricity as provided under the electricity supply laws;
- to advice the Minister on all matters relating to the supply of gas through pipelines and the use of gas as provided under the gas supply laws;
- to implement and enforce the energy supply laws;
- to regulate all matters relating to the electricity supply industry and to protect any person from danger arising from the generation, production, transmission, distribution, supply and use of electricity as provided under the electricity supply laws;
- to regulate all matters relating to the supply of gas through pipelines and to protect any person from danger arising from the supply of gas through pipelines and the use of gas as provided under the gas supply laws;
- to promote efficiency, economy and safety in the generation, production, transmission, distribution, supply and the use of electricity and in the supply of gas through pipelines and the use of gas supplied through pipelines;
- to promote and safeguard competition and fair and efficient market conduct or, in the absence of a competitive market, to prevent the misuse of monopoly or market power in respect of the generation, production, transmission, distribution and supply of electricity and the supply of gas through pipelines;
- to promote the use of renewable energy and the conservation of non-renewable energy;
- to promote research into, and the development and the use of, new techniques relating to – the generation, production, transmission, distribution, supply and use of electricity, and the supply of gas through pipelines and the use of gas supplied through pipelines;
- to encourage and promote the development of the electricity and the supply of gas through pipelines including in the area of training;
- to encourage and promote the self-regulation in the electricity supply of gas through pipelines;

- to carry out any function conferred by or under the energy supply laws;
- to review the energy supply laws and to make the necessary recommendations to the Minister; and
- to carry out all such activities as may appear to the Commission requisite, advantageous or convenient for the purpose of carrying out in connection with the performance of its functions under the energy supply laws.

It may be noted here that according to the Energy Commission Amendment Act 2010, the Commission will not enter into any agreement without approval of the Minister and concurrence of the minister of Finance where the Commission has to pay or receive any amount exceeding RM 10 million.

The Amendment Act of 2010 further provides that the Commission will maintain accounts of the funds and will prepare proper reports. It will submit the audited accounts to the Minister.

§4. Consultative Panel

128. The Energy Commission takes its policy decision through its Consultative Panel. The Panel is operative under the Chair of the Commission with the members comprising representatives from relevant government agencies, energy utility companies and from various private sectors, consumer associations and professional bodies. The present members are: Ministry of Energy, Water and Communication, Economic Planning Unit, Ministry of Finance, Ministry of International Trade and Industry (MITI), MDTCA, TNB, Petronas, Gas Malaysia Sdn Bhd, Federation of Malaysian Consumer Association, Federation of Malaysian Manufacturers, Consumer Association of Sabah, Malaysian International Chamber of Commerce and Industry, Business Council on Sustainable Development Malaysia, Malaysian Association of Hotels, The Electrical and Electronics Association of Malaysia, Association of Independent Power Producers, Malaysian Economic Association and Institute of Engineers Malaysia.

129. The objective of the Consultative Panel is to create an interactive forum between the government, industry and consumers, besides functioning in the area of research and development (R&D) of the power sector of the country.

§5. Licensing Mechanism

130. Since the Energy Commission has all the powers that are there in the Electricity Supply Act 1990 and Gas Supply Act 1993, under section 11(1) of these Acts, the Commission is authorized to issue licenses for supply of gas through pipelines and installing any system of distribution of electricity. No person can operate in the distribution of these energy sources without the license. The Commission also has the power to suspend or revoke the license upon breach of any condition(s) appended to the license. This may be noted here that all companies operative in supply of gas and electricity have licenses issued by the energy Commission. On violation of any of the conditions, the license may be cancelled and other legal actions as provided in the Gas supply Act and the Electricity Supply Act may be taken. Recently, under this authority, the Commission cautioned on 28 March 2005 Syarikat Elektrik Pulau Ketam of its responsibility to ensure conditions and uninterrupted supply of electricity following news that the company has the plan to have power cut of six hours every day. It is in fact violation of the condition of the license issued to the company. Moreover, no such steps any license holder can take without taking permission from the Commission. The Commission warned the company that it will not hesitate to take any legal action against the company, and for that matter against any company, suspending or revoking the license under section 18 of the Electricity Supply Act, and taking criminal action under section 37 of the Act, which is punishable upon conviction with fine not exceeding MYR 10,000 and to a further fine not exceeding MYR 10,000 for every day or part of the day during which the offence continued.

131. Under the Gas Supply Act, for protecting the interests of customers as well facilitating the licensees' operations, a licensee is given certain obligations and also limited powers related to the construction and operation of pipelines and related installations. Among others, the licensee is obligated under section 14 of the Act to supply gas on request by owner or occupier of any premises situated within the area of supply. In return, he/she is allowed to levy approved tariff, recover expenses and require security for giving a supply of gas. Licensees may cause supply under prescribed circumstances including unsafe conditions such as failure of pipeline or fire, explosion or any other accident. Licensee may also enter any land other than state land after giving appropriate notice and compensation to occupier or officer in charge of the land to survey, install, maintain, repair or upgrade any pipeline or installation. They must also be notified before any third-party work is out in the vicinity of the pipeline route, as well as whenever there is any damage to the pipeline.

132. In order to have control over the safety of gas distribution or reticulation systems meant for own use, especially those installed in commercial or domestic premises, licensees are further classified into two categories, namely Gas Utility Licensee (those who supply gas to consumers) and Private Gas Licensee (those who supply gas for their own use).

133. Similar provisions are there in the Electricity Supply Act. Rather, the provisions enshrined in this Act are stricter. For details, see the next Chapter.

§6. Electrical Energy Managers

134. The jobs of energy managers are: to advice, monitor, supervise and audit generation and supply of electrical energy. On 29 October 2009, the Energy

Commission prescribed 'Guidelines for Prospective and Registered Electrical Energy Manager'. The salient features of the guidelines, as given by the Commission are as follows:

REGULATORY REQUIREMENTS
Registered electrical energy manager of installation

1. No person shall engage in, be employed or hold himself/herself out as a registered electrical energy manager for the purposes of these Regulations unless the person has been registered by the Commission.
2. Any person who fails to comply with subregulation (1) commits an offence under these Regulations.

QUALIFICATION REQUIREMENTS
Malaysian citizen aged 23 years and above; and is a Professional Engineer and possesses at least six months working experience in the efficient management of electrical energy, or holds a degree in Science, Engineering, Architecture or its equivalent and possesses at least one year working experience in the efficient management of electrical energy; or holds a certificate of competency as an Electrical Services Engineer or as a Competent Electrical Engineer as in the Electricity Regulations 1994 and possesses at least nine months working experience in the efficient management of electrical energy; and Demonstrates knowledge of the requirements of the Act and these Regulations; and the Commission may require the person to attend an interview.
SCOPE OF KNOWLEDGE AND EXPERIENCE
Knowledge about the related acts and regulations in electricity supply and installations and consumption
General obligations of the owner of installations; functions and duties of energy managers; and safety requirements in working with electrical installations.
Knowledge and hands-on/operational experiences in efficient management of electrical energy
Energy audit and its main components in performing energy audit in the installations (buildings, factories, and so on); basic equipment and its usage to perform energy audit; Involvement in energy efficient projects/programs at any installation (level of involvement, scope of works, operational/management and so on); familiar with the operation of electrical system/equipment at the installation; and common/specific energy saving measures that can be applied/implemented and its potential saving calculations.
APPLICATION PROCEDURE
Submit application form (FORM ST(DSM/PTE/2009)) and processing fee (First Schedule); and please attach information and supporting documents to substantiate track records as an electrical energy manager, or evidence to show that despite the lack of a track record, he/she has the necessary knowledge, skill and expertise to efficiently manage electrical energy.

FEES
No.
Types of fees
Fees(RM)

3. Application for registration as an electrical energy manager MYR 20.00 per application
4. Issuance/renewal of certificate of registration MYR 100.00 per year
5. Application for replacement of certificate of registration MYR 50.00 per copy
6. Application for certified true copy of certificate of registration MYR 10.00 per copy

FUNCTIONS AND DUTIES OF ELECTRICAL ENERGY MANAGER

To audit and analyse the total electrical energy consumption or generation; to advise in developing and implementing measures to ensure efficient management of electrical energy at the installation; to monitor effective implementation of the measures; to supervise the keeping of records on efficient management of electrical energy at the installation and verify its accuracy; and to ensure the timely submission of information and reports under the regulations.

INFORMATION REQUIRED FROM ENERGY AUDIT

Management of electrical energy at the Installation

Policy and targets; accounts and related documents; and compliance towards the regulations.

Electricity supply information

Total electricity supplied; sources of electricity supply from utility companies (TNB, SESB, public licensees) or own generation (private licensees) or both; and type of supply (voltage level, tariff).

Electricity Consumption Information

Electricity load profile of the installation (daily/weekly/monthly); estimated annual electricity consumption in kWh and the percentage (%) of load distribution according to electrical system/equipment such as HVAC, production machinery, lighting, and so on; and operating hours of the installation and major energy using system/equipment.

Energy Saving Opportunities

List of energy saving potentials identified; list of energy savings measures identified according to: no cost/low cost: housekeeping, minor repairs, and with high cost/major investment required: major repair/replacement of major system/equipment, introduction of new energy efficient technologies; estimated potential of energy savings in energy unit (kWh); energy saving measurements and calculations based on the potentials identified; estimated returns from the costs to implement energy saving measures (Simple Payback Period/ IRR); and proposed action plan and estimated time required to implement each energy saving measure.

CERTIFICATE OF REGISTRATION

Energy Commission will notify the applicant whether his/her application to be registered as an electrical energy manager has been approved or refused; Energy Commission shall register the applicant as an electrical energy manager, and upon payment of the fee as prescribed in the First Schedule; where the application is refused, Energy Commission may, upon the request of the applicant, provide reasons in writing to the applicant for such refusal; and the certificate of registration shall be in Form C of the Second Schedule, and Energy Commission may stipulate in the certificate any conditions or restrictions in respect of the registration.

MEDICAL EVIDENCE

The Commission may require medical evidence of the physical and mental fitness of the applicant, certified by a registered medical practitioner, to be produced by the applicant before a certificate of registration as an electrical energy manager is issued to him/her.

VALIDITY PERIOD OF REGISTRATION AND RENEWAL

The certificate of registration shall be valid for a period of not less than one year and not more than five years from the date of issue of the certificate; where the person who is registered shall, at least one month before the date of expiry of his/her registration, renew his/her registration; the Commission shall renew the registration of an electrical energy manager if the Commission is satisfied that – he/she has complied with the conditions or restrictions as stipulated in the certificate of registration; and he/she has paid the fee as prescribed in the First Schedule.

CANCELLATION OF REGISTRATION

The Commission may cancel the certificate of registration issued to a registered electrical energy manager under subregulation 14(2) if – contravened or failed to comply with any provision of the Act or these Regulations; certificate obtained by making or causing to be made any false or fraudulent declaration, certification or representation, either in writing or otherwise; used the certificate of registration for a purpose that differs from that for which it was issued or in a manner that is intended to mislead or deceive the public; or failed to carry out the functions and duties as specified in regulation 16. If Energy Commission intends to cancel the certificate of registration, the registered electrical energy manager will be notified in writing; the registered electrical energy manager shall within fourteen days from the date of issue of the written notice provide a written submission to the Commission stating the reasons why his/her certificate of registration should not be cancelled; Energy Commission shall give due consideration to the written submission made by the registered electrical energy manager before making any decision; after giving due consideration to the written submission, Energy Commission shall issue a notice of cancellation together with the reasons for the cancellation. The cancellation shall take effect on the expiry of twenty-one days from the date of the notice of cancellation; and where the Energy Commission is of the opinion that urgent action is required to protect the interest of the public and that action relates to the functions and duties of the registered electrical energy manager, it may immediately cancel the certificate of registration by serving upon him/her a notice of cancellation.

On 24 April 2010, the Energy Commission notified 'Continuous Development Program (CDP) for Registered Electrical Energy Manger'. The salient features of the CDP are as follows:

Engagement with Energy Efficiency Programs

Electrical energy managers registered with Energy Commission are required to participate or involve for at least eight (8) hours in programmes endorsed by Energy Commission related to efficient management of energy.

Types of Continuous Development Program

Courses or training sessions, conferences or seminars, workshop, participation in technical committees or working groups, and presentation of papers on technologies, management and research findings.

Types of Participation

As a participant, as a presenter or speaker, and as a member of committee or working group.

Topics and Contents of The Program

Topics or contents related to efficient management of electrical energy, and topics or contents can be proposed and will be considered to evaluate its suitability and later to be decided by Energy Commission.

Confirmation of Attendance for Registered Electrical Energy Managers

A registered energy manager shall submit the confirmation of his/her participation in the endorsed programme in the form of certificate of attendance or any written confirmation by the organizer, and a registered electrical energy manager shall submit a written confirmation by the programme organizer on his/her involvement as a speaker or presenter and other preparatory works related to the presentation or talk.

GUIDELINES:

The energy Commission has issued guidelines pertaining to electricity, and energy efficiency. These guidelines are related to licences, agreements, and generation, transmission and supply of electricity. There are guidelines for licenses for generation, import and supply of gas. Guidelines for also there for energy efficiency with respect to washing machines, refrigerators and air conditioners. Guidelines are also there for energy audit of energy efficient buildings and for registration of energy services company. As on 9 April 2018, these guidelines are:

(a) Electricity
- Guidelines on Business Plan Submission by Licensee
- Guidelines on The Connection of Solar Photovoltaic Installation for Self-Consumption
- Guidelines on Connection Charges for Sabah Electricity Sdn. Bhd. (SESB)
- Guidelines for Implementation of Gas Framework Agreement (GFA) in the Power Sector
- Guidelines for Implementation of Gas Framework Agreement (GFA) In the Power Sector (Amendment 1/2017)
- Guidelines for Ring-Fencing of The System Operator (Peninsular Malaysia) 2016

- Performance Standard of Electricity Supply Services of TNB
- Guidelines on Tariff Determination under Incentive Based Regulation for Tenaga Nasional Berhad
- Guidelines on Tariff Determination under Incentive Based Regulation for Sabah Electricity Sdn. Bhd
- Distribution Code for Peninsular Malaysia, Sabah & F.T. Labuan (Amendments) 2017
- Grid Code for Peninsular Malaysia
- Grid Code for Sabah And Labuan (Amendments) 2017
- Guidelines for Solar Photovoltaic Installation on Net Energy Metering Scheme
- Guide to NEDA's Trial Run
- Guidelines for Electricity Meters: Approval, Testing and Initial Verification Requirements
- The Installation of Electric Fence in Accordance to Procedures by Energy Commission
- Wayleave for Electricity Supply Lines
- Information Booklet on Approval of Electrical Equipment (Electricity Regulation 1994)
- *Garis Panduan Prosedur Tuntutan Kerugian Hasil Oleh Pemegang Lesen Bagi Kes-Kes Penggunaan Elektrik Dengan Curang*
- Guidelines for New Enhanced Dispatch Arrangement
- Single Buyer Rules
- Guidelines on Licensing under Section 9 of the Act [Electricity Supply Act 1990 (Act 447)]
- Guidelines on Large-Scale Solar Photovoltaic Plant for Connection to Electricity Networks
- *Garis Panduan Persempadanan Pengurusan dan Penyenggaraan Sistem Pepasangan Elektrik dan Gas Berpaip di Bangunan*

(b) Energy Efficiency

- Guide on Minimum Energy Performance Standard (MEPS) Requirement for Washing Machine
- Guide on Minimum Energy Performance Standard Requirements for Air Conditioner with Cooling Capacity $\leq$ 7.1kw
- Guide on Minimum Energy Performance Standard (MEPS) Requirements for Refrigerator
- Electrical Energy Audit Guidelines for Building
- Guideline for the Registration of Energy Service Company (ESCO)
- Guidelines on No-Cost and Low-Cost Measures for Efficient Use of Electricity in Buildings

(c) Gas

- Guide On New Applications And Renewal For Certificate Of Approval; Assemblers, Manufacturers Or Importers of Gas Fittings, Gas Appliances and Equipment & Gas Fittings, Gas Appliances and Equipment
- *Kaedah Penentuan Lesen Peruncitan Berdasarkan Akta Bekalan Gas 1993*

- Guidelines on Competition for the Malaysian Gas Market in relation to Market Definition, Anti-Competitive Agreements and Abuse of Dominant Position
- Guidelines on Licence Application
- Third Party Access Code for Malaysian Regasification Terminals
- Third Party Access Code for Malaysian Transmission Pipelines
- Third Party Access Code for Malaysian Distribution Pipelines
- Gas Responsible Person
- Guidelines for Copper Gas Piping
- Gas Supply Act and Regulations Guidelines
- Guidelines on Domestic Gas Piping System
- Garis Panduan Pelaksanaan Pemeriksaan Berkala Dan Ujian Kebocoran Sistem Gas Berpaip
- Gas Piping System Safety Handbook for Domestic Consumer
- Gas Safety Guidelines for School Laboratory.

§7. Circulars Issued by the Commission

135. The Energy Commission has issued the following a number of Circulars to streamline the manufacture, import, display, sell or advertise electrical equipment, generation and transmission of electricity and electricity safety. Circulars are also there pertaining to gas. The circulars pertaining to electrical equipment are:

I. Circular No. 1 Year 2003 (No. 1/2003)

136. This was issued on 31 March 2003. Procedures and Conditions for Obtaining the Certificate of approval to Manufacture, Import, Display, Sell or Advertise the Electric Equipment.

137. The list of electrical equipment-controlled item issued by the Energy Commission and the standards have been prescribed in the Attachment A.

138. The proponent will fill the form ST (PE) 3 and submit it with a processing fee of MYR 20.00 and the test report containing the list of components, instruction manual, technical specification and catalogue and the need to submit a sample of the product, if necessary.

139. Test report has to be taken from the approved institutions.

140. There will be a charge of annual fee of MYR 200.00 or MYR 300.00 depending on single phase or triple phase of the equipment.

Electrical equipment that have been approved for manufacturing shall enter the SIRIM's Product Certification Scheme and shall affix the label issued by SIRIM.

141. Electrical equipment that have been approved for import will apply the consignment test by SIRIM for every batch within the validity of the Certificate of Approval and will affix the label issued by SIRIM.

II. Energy Commission Circular No. 1 of 2004 (No. 2/2004)

142. The objective of the circular is to inform on the procedures and requirements for submitting the renewal application for Certificate of Approval to manufacture, import, display, sell or advertise the electrical equipment not less than fourteen days before the date of expiry of certificate that would come into force on the stipulated date. This circular is in conjunction with the Electricity (Amendment) Regulations 2003. This circular is further addition to the 2003 circular discussed above.

143. The circular requires the following to be appended with the renewal application: (1) A copy of the Certificate of Approval; (2) the latest type test report issued by laboratories recognized by the energy commission; (3) the certificate of approval for importation, receipt of SIRIM's label in the prescribed form; (4) renewal fee.

144. The application for renewal must be made before fourteen days from the expiry of the certificate. If not done so, the certificate will be deemed cancelled, and a new application will have to be made. It is submitted that entertaining the application with an appropriate late fee will be a correct approach in line with the general practice.

The other circulars are:

(a) Electricity

There are two circulars pertaining to electricity:

- ST(IP/PPTKP/KBP/16/19/1: Amendment to the Power Quality Standards under the Energy Commission's Circular No. 1/2017.
- JKPPE BIL.01/2012: Implementation of Performance Standard of Electricity Supply Services of TNB - Guaranteed Service Level and Minimum Service Level.

(b) Gas Supply and Safety

There are the following thirteen circulars pertaining to gas supply and safety imperatives pertaining to production and Gas Supply & Safety:

- 2017 - *Pemberitahuan berkenaan kelengkapan gas yang digunakan sebagai alat timbang dan sukat bagi tujuan perdagangan.*
- 2016 - Non Destructive Test (NDT) Requirement for welding works on gas pipe sized 4 inches and above.
- 2015 - Prohibition to install Liquefied Petroleum Gas (LPG) storage farms in areas that can hinder the ingress–egress structure of a building.
- 2015 - Direction to Display Approval to Operate (ATO) at Liquefied Petroleum Gas (LPG) Storage.
- 2015 - Direction to Display Private Gas License (PGL) at Liquefied Petroleum Gas (LPG) Storage.

- 2015 - Approval to Install (ATI) and Approval to Operate (ATO) application form updates for natural gas pipeline & additional piping installations.
- 2012 - *Pelaksanaan Langkah-Langkah Kawalan Keselamatan Sistem Talian Paip Gas Di Kompleks Membeli Belah Oleh Pemunya/Penduduk.*
- 2009 - *Keperluan Kedapan (sealed off) di mana-mana bukaan dihujung paip pada Sistem Pepasangan Paip Gas.*
- 2008 - *Keperluan Kedapan (sealed off) di mana-mana bukaan dihujung paip pada Sistem Pepasangan Paip Gas.*
- 2006 - *Had Pengendalian Sistem Paip Gas yang dibenarkan.*
- 2005 - *Kontraktor/ Sub Kontraktor Perlu Berdaftar Bagi Kerja Berkaitan Pepasangan Gas.*
- 2000 - *Mutu Kimpalan ke atas Pepasangan atau Talian Paip Gas.*
- 1998 - *Pemasangan Silinder Manifold Gas Petroleum Cecair (GPC).*

(c) Electrical Safety

Following are the thirty-six circulars pertaining to electrical safety:

- ST(IP/JKE)KE/16/12(04): *Notis Penangguhan Tarikh Kuatkuasa Perlaksanaan Arahan Mengemukakan No. Siri Kelengkapan Elektrik Bagi Setiap Batch Konsainmen Semasa Ujian Konsainmen SIRIM.*
- ST/IP/PPTKP/DSM/13/25/1 JLD2(25): *Notis Makluman Tarikh Pelaksanaan Minimum Energy Performance Standard (MEPS) Bagi Kelengkapan Elektrik – Peti Sejuk, Penghawa Dingin dan Mesin Basuh.*
- ST(IP/JKE) KE/16/12(03): Notice on Product Recall for Unlabelled Electrical Equipment As a Requirement for Reapplication of New CoA.
- ST(IP/JKE)KE/19/01/01: *Notis Pemakluman Pembatalan Perakuan Pendaftaran (Certificate of Registration) Syarikat yang Gagal Mengambil Tindakan Melupus/Menghantar Balik Kelengkapan Elektrik yang Gagal Ujian Konsainmen.*
- ST(IP/JKE)KE/01/01/02: Prohibition of Import, Manufacture, Exhibition, Advertisement and Sale of Electric Heated Pillow in Malaysia.
- ST(IP/JKE) KE/19/05 Jld 4 (28): Order of the Energy Commission for Manufacturers, Importers and Retailers of Electrical Equipment on the Condition of Compliance to MS1597-2-21:2015 (Installation of Isolation Barrier for Storage-Type Water Heaters).
- ST(IP/JKE)KE/19/01/01(01): Energy Commission's Directive to Electrical Equipment Manufacturers, Importers and Retailers on the Installation of Isolation Barrier for Storage Water Heater.
- ST(IP/JKE)KE/19/05 JLD4(25): Guidelines on the Adoption of the Validity Period for Test Reports for New Applications and Renewal of Certificate of Approval (CoA) Based on Risk Category of Electrical Equipment.
- ST(IP/JKE)KE/01/01/02(06): *Notis Pemakluman Tempoh Sah Laku Laporan Ujian Kelengkapan Elektrik.*
- ST(IP/JKE)KE/19/01(7): *Pendaftaran pengilang dan pengimport di Sistem e-Dik.*
- ST(IP/JKE)KE/19/01(16): Acceptance of new IEC Standards for double-capped LED lamp and audio and video for the application of Certificate Of Approval (COA).

- ST(IP/JKE)KE/19/01(17): Enforcement of Malaysian Standard (MS) to comply with the Minimum Energy Performance Standards (MEPS) requirements for five electrical equipments (refrigerator, air conditioner, television, domestic fan and lamp).
- No. 02/2014: Circular on Examination and Issuance of Certificate of Competency for Chargeman (Restricted) to meet current Industry needs.
- No. 01/2014: Upgrading of Certificate for Chargeman Categories A4-2, A4-1 to A4 or BO-2, BO-1 to BO and Termination of Examination and Issuing of Certificate for Chargeman Categories A4-2, A4-1, BO-2 and BO-1.
- ST (IP/JKE) KE/06/09: Announcement: Determination of one (1) Certificate of Approval (COA) for one (1) model of electrical equipment.
- ST(IP/JKE)KE/16/11(01) Announcement: Registration as a Manufacturer or Importer with The Energy Commission.
- JKKE Bil 01/2013: Training Conditions for Replacing Work Experience of Chargeman.
- JKPPE BIL.01/2012: Implementation of Performance Standard of Electricity Supply Services of TNB - Guaranteed Service Level and Minimum Service Level.
- JKKE Bil. 03/2012: The Usage of 1.5mm^2 Copper Power Cable in Fixed Wiring for Lighting Circuit.
- No. 04/2011: Requirement of installation of residual current device (RCD) on all final sub-circuits of electrical wiring systems.
- No. 03/2011: Buildings' Lightning Protection System.
- No. 02/2011: Approval to Manufacture and Import Fluorescent Ballast.
- No. 01/2011: Implementation of the Competency Examination System by the Accredited Institutions.
- No. 02/2010: Standardisation of Form for Testing and Calibration of Protective Relay and Device.
- No. 01/2010: Revised Criteria for Competency Examinations Conducted by Accredited Institutions.
- No. 3/2008: Procedure of Electrical Fence Installation.
- No. 2/2008: The use of Electrical Wiring Guidelines in Residential Buildings.
- No. 1/2008: Standards used in Electrical Installation.
- No. 4-2007: Requirement on Electrical Installation Inspection by Competent Person.
- No. 3/2007: The Termination of issuing Certificate of Competency for Chargeman.
- No. 5/2004: The use of Controlled Electrical Equipment for Electrical Works.
- No. 1/2004: Procedures & Requirements of Submission of the Renewal Application for Certificate of Approval.
- No. 1/2003: Procedures & Requirements of obtaining the Certificate of Approval to manufacture, import, display, sell & advertise the electrical equipment.
- JBE No. 10/1999: Frequency of visit and inspection by the competent person.

– Prohibition Notice for the Use of Residual Current Device (RCD) Voltage Stabilizer.
– Notification on Nominal Voltage.

Some of these circulars may be revised after coming into force the *Electricity Supply (Amendment) Act 2015*, gazetted 1 January 2016, because the provisions of this Act have to be implemented by the Energy Commission.

§8. Biofuel and the Commission

145. We have already noted above that in view of the limited oil and gas reserves and the soaring prices of these, countries around the world are embarking on biodiesel along with exploiting renewable sources of energy. They have very long way to go. There are two main sources of biodiesel, ethanol based and vegetable oil-based. In 2004, the world produced about 30 billion litres of fuel-ready ethanol from fermenting and distilling mainly sugar and corn. It was equivalent to 500,000 barrels of oil per day, around 2% of the total gasoline consumption of the world. The figure is relatively small. But it has potential in the longer term and become by 2025, 10% of the total gasoline consumption. This source of energy is being used mainly in Europe, United States and Brazil, but in the near future this has to become common because it is based on home-grown crop, provides cut on oil import bills and reduces GHGs emissions. Although presently the production cost is high, but in totality it will be beneficial to consuming countries. It will become a source of regular income to some of the big producers. So as to popularize the use of this biodiesel, incentives are being provided. United States and European Union countries are the examples.[102] In Malaysia also, efforts are being made to foster production of ethanol by utilizing fruit juice industries wastes. Scientists of the country are also engaged in research on ethanol, but it does not have a bright future because currently it is not producing enough corn or sugar cane. Malaysia is importing these two from various countries. However, Malaysia has a high potential to produce biodiesel because the country is the largest producer and exporter of palm oil. Palm oil can be used in manufacturing biodiesel. This is getting support from the MPOB and the Government. Malaysian Government is developing a policy to provide proper support to this industry. This is notable that presently the palm oil industry is exporting oil worth 31 billion annually. The Board has a small plant to produce 3,000 tonnes of biodiesel. It is exported to some European railway companies. There is a plan to set up a MYR 40 million palm in Labu, Negri Sembilan and to further widen the scope of such industries in the country. In the long run, biodiesel produced in the country will supplement the energy consumption within the country. It will also become a good source of earning foreign exchange.[103] This source of energy is to be taken care of by the MPOB. In 2006, the country invited applications for production of biodiesel in the country. It had a

102. *New Straits Times*, 10 Jun. 2005.
103. *New Straits times*, 13 Jun. 2005.

great response. A large number of companies, including some multinationals, showed interest through moving applications. But the government selected only some of the applications. It is notable here that there is a necessity to strike a balance between the amount of palm oil produced, consumptions of oil as edibles and allocation for producing biodiesel. Perhaps, the government is keeping this in mind. In future, when palm oil production increases, some more licenses may be issued. Restrictive attitude is also advisable to view the production of biodiesel and its economic efficiency in the country. The country wants to introduce biodiesel soon in the country. Towards this end, necessary modifications in engines of vehicles have already been aspired to be undertaken.

146. On the other hand, the Energy Commission of Malaysia is striving hard to encourage and properly develop the renewable energy sources in the country. The Commission will address the challenges faced by producers of renewable energy, as pointed out above, from biomass under the Ninth Malaysia Plan. Commission's Chairman Datuk Dr Mohd Anas Mohd Nor said:

> While we are encouraging renewable energy, it is still not going to be the answer to the country's energy needs … So in the Plan, while we are we are promoting renewable energy, we do not expect it to be more than 2 to 3 per cent of the electricity need in the grid … Malaysia still has to depend on the traditional energy sources, such as gas, oil, coal and hydropower … Renewable energy has been used in the palm oil industry. Most of the time, the palm oil industry depends on its own energy both for heat and electricity … Close to 1,000 MW of oil palm energy generation are available now but they are not connected to the electricity grid (which means they are not commercialized). … introducing renewable energy, what the government is trying to do is to get them connected to the grid … The idea started in the 8th Malaysia Plan … Towards this end, the government has launched the Small Renewable Energy Programme (SREP) and under the Programme, small power generation plants (10 MW and low) which utilize renewable energy can sell the electricity to the Tenaga Nasional Bhd and Sabah Electricity Board through the distribution grid.

147. He noted that the production of electricity by using biomass is a costly affair. Thus, the government is providing incentives to this. We have noted above that the pricing to the renewable energy sources is also a problem. He realized this and said that the purchase price of these sources of energy should range between 14 cents and 17 cents.[104]

148. If the incentive aspects and the pricing are properly taken care of, this renewable energy source will certainly flourish and it will attract investors; then only the commercial potential of this energy source will conspicuously be noticeable. The main problem is to prepare the utility companies to agree to the suggest

104. *New Straits Times*, 14 Jun. 2005.

price, but the problem can be solved if the interest of these companies is also protected. The Energy Commission can play a vital role in developing all kinds of renewable energy sources.

For further details of biofuel, see above. In short, Malaysia has a plan to phase out B7 with B10 biodiesel. But the plan has been delayed. The strategy is being looked into as how it can be made cost-effective and without hampering the oil as domestic consumption. It is undoubted that it has high potential in the county, as the country is one of the largest palm oil producers. Ethanol, in limited quantity, is also produced in the country derived from the Palm Oil Mill Effluents (POME). This also has to be made cost-effective. The National Biofuel Policy of 21 March 2006 aims to encourage this source of energy, as it emits relatively less carbon dioxide. The policy aims to produce biofuel to be used in transport industry locally and to export. In 2007 the Biofuel Industry Act was passed to successfully implement the idea of biofuel production in the country. And to implement the production and supply a licensing mechanism is there in the Malaysian Biofuel Industry (Licensing) Regulations 2008. However, production of biofuel could take place only from June 2011. Presently its production is there all over the country but limited to B7. The production of B7 in 2015 was estimated as 258 million litres, which will successfully reduce 1.05 million tonnes of carbon. The 11th Malaysia Plan to have B15 by 2020 for the on-road sector. It may be noted here that recently the European Parliament approved a resolution to introduce a single certification scheme for palm oil entering into EU by 2020. It means non-certified palm oil or biodiesel cannot enter. This is a matter of concern to Malaysia because EU is the largest importer of biodiesel from Malaysia.[105]

105. For a detailed account see at: https://gain.fas.usda.gov/Recent%20GAIN%20Publications/Biofuels%20Annual_Kuala%20Lumpur_Malaysia_10-24-2017.pdf(accessed on 9 Apr. 2018).

Part I. Regulatory Framework Concerning Electricity

Chapter 1. Electricity Supply Act 1990 (Act 447) (Amended by the Amendment Act 2001, and Electricity Supply (Successor Company) Act 1990): An Appraisal

§1. Electricity Supply Act 1990

149. The Electricity Supply Act 1990, which replaced the Electricity Act 1949, has been enacted to provide for the regulation of the electricity supply industry, the supply of electricity at reasonable prices, the licensing of any electrical installation, the control of any electrical installation, plant and equipment with respect to matters relating to the safety of persons and the efficient use of electricity. In short, the Act has provisions governing licensing, and control of electrical installations, plants and equipment, supply of electricity at reasonable prices as well as ensuring safety of consumers and operators, in general, efficient use of electricity in the country. Going by the provisions of the Act, 'electricity' means electrical energy or electrical power when generated, produced, transmitted, distributed, supplied or utilized for any purpose except for the transmission of any communication or signal. It may be noted that the definition is all-encompassing to include all kinds of generation and production of electricity.

150. It should also be noted here that the Electricity Supply Amendment Act 2001 has not made any major changes to the original Act though there are still few notable changes. Among the notable changes are: (1) The highest authority now is Commission in place of Director General. So, the Commission will be the authority in place of Director General, Deputy Director General, Assistant Directors of Electricity Supply and such other officers. (2) Deleting the word 'Director'. (3) Authorized Officer will be appointed by the Minister. (4) Repealing Part II of the Act. (5) Addition of Part VA for efficient use of electricity. (6) Authorizing the licensee to levy surcharge on the supply of electricity. (7) Substitution of subsections 4 and 5 of section 33 of the Act with new provisions with a view to making them more efficient and meaningful in case of accident or fire involving any electrical installation. (8) Adding subsection 1A to section 38 to authorize the police department to stop electricity supply under section 21A of the Gambling Act 1953. (9) No prosecution without the consent of the Public Prosecutor.

§2. Salient Features, as Originally were There

151. For a proper understanding of the various legal norms contained in the Electricity Supply Act 1990, the following points are notable.

I. Functions, Duties and Powers of the Commission

152. The Commission has the following powers under the Act: (i) To issue license under section 9 of the Act. (ii) To issue regulations. (iii) To promote the interest of consumers with respect to pricing, continuity of supply and quality of service. (iv) To satisfy the reasonable demand of electricity. (v) To ensure that licensees are able to finance the carrying on of the activities, which they are authorized by their licenses to carry on. (vi) To promote and encourage energy development. (vii) To regulate the manner in which any electrical installation or equipment will have to be inspected. (Viii) To prescribe the nature of test to be employed and to prescribe minimum qualifications and practical experience of the personnel involved. (ix) To investigate any accident or fire involving any electrical installation. (x) To provide for the registration of any installation, electrical contractor, manufacturer and importer, and any competent person. (xi) To prescribe the minimum standards and specifications and apprise and approve any electrical installation or equipment. (xii) To promote the efficient use of electricity.

153. It is notable here that under section 4A, which has been brought in by the Amendment Act, the Minister in order to exercise the powers of enforcement under the Act may authorize any Public Officer or any Officer of the Commission to exercise, including the power of examination and seizure, which is contained in section 5 of the Act. According to this section, the officer, bearing the official identity card, may enter into any land, house or building to inspect and examine any part of an installation or equipment on the basis of a search warrant issued by an appropriate magistrate under subsection 2 or on his/her own without such warrant, where he/she suspects that the delay in obtaining the warrant might be the reason for committing an offence under the Act. He/she is authorized to seize or seal any article, thing, book, document and installation. This power has been given to the police officer also.

154. A list of the seized items has to be given to the owner, and the seized things have to be produced before the magistrate. In the process of inspection, they are authorized to break open any door, forcibly enter any part of the premises, remove by application of force any obstruction and detain any person.

155. The person creating obstruction will be guilty of an offence and on conviction will be liable to fine not exceeding MYR 5,000 or to imprisonment for a term not exceeding two years or both.

156. Under section 6 of the Act, power to investigate and take statement pertaining to any offence committed under the Act has been given to the Commission. The Commission can ask the person to appear before the court.

II. Licenses and Registration of Installations

157. Part four of the Act comprising sections 9–22 deals with licensing and registration of installations. The Commission is authorized to issue licenses upon approval by the Minister for the specified duration for (a) use, work or operate or permitted to be used, worked or operated on any installations; or (b) supply to or for the use of any other person energy from any installation. They are issued on payment of fees specified by the Minister. On late payment of the fee, surcharge at the rate of 1% will be payable. A license for public installation sets out the following: (1) the area of supply; (2) the declared voltage and the variations permitted therefrom; (3) the maximum charges payable by the consumers; and (4) such other matters as the Commission may consider necessary.

158. Once the license is issued, the licensee has the following rights and duties: (1) Power to enter any land other than state land after giving twenty-four hours of notice and examine the suitability of the land from the point of view of installing the facilities. (2) He/she is not authorized to enter any building or cut down or clear away any vegetation or any fence or other erection. If the land is the reserved land, permission from the appropriate person will have to be taken. (3) The licensee is authorized to lay, place or carry on, under or over any land such as posts and other equipment as may be necessary or proper for the purpose of facilitating the licensed installations or for taking any other related activities for making the installations safe and efficient. (4) He/she will be liable to pay compensation according to section 16 of the Act with respect to any disturbance, damage or disability that may be caused. It would include the annual payment for land used for the purpose of posts or other equipment. (5) Acts undertaken by the licensee is subject to the supervision of the District Land Administration. The appropriate officer of the administration may allow any activity to go on or to issue an order to stop the work. If the licensee is dissatisfied with the order issued by the officer, he/she may appeal to the designate state authority. The decision on the matter by the State Authority will be final. The State Authority may issue an order for acquiring the land. In case of acquisition, necessary changes in the ownership register have to be made. (6) The State Authority if it deems fit may authorize the work to be carried on under or over the state land pertaining to supply lines, put posts and other equipment if necessary in the opinion of the Commission. (7) All equipment placed in or upon State land, which are not removed therefrom within six months, or such longer period as the State Government may permit, after the expiration or early determination of the license under the authority whereof the same was so placed, will vest in and become the property of the State. (8) The licensee has the right to enter upon any land, under or over which supply lines have been laid, placed or carried, or upon which posts or other equipment have been erected for the purposes of maintenance, repair and upgrading of such installations. (9) Since the convenience of the owner of the land is also given importance, the owner of the land for the sake of making best use of his/her land may ask the license holder to move the installations to another part of the land or to the land at higher or lower level or be altered in form suited to him/her without affecting the installation. In case the licensee does not listen to the owner of the land, he/she may apply to the State Authority. The State Authority after proper investigation, by himself/herself or through the District Land Administration, may reject the application or accept it with or without conditions. The authority also decides over the cost of removal or alteration by the licensee or by the person making the application. (10) The licensee instead of making desired alteration may apply to the State Authority to make an order for acquiring the land if necessary for the purposes of the line. Whenever such order of acquisition is made, the work is considered to be of public utility and any written law relating to land acquisition in force in the state where the land is situated will be enforced accordingly. (11) The situation pertaining to removal of installations is the same where the installations were on the state land and state has alienated the land to another person, provided that the cost of executing the removal or alteration will be defrayed by the person making the requisition. (12) The licensee has the right to enter into an agreement, commonly known as wayleave agreement, with the owner or occupier of any land for the purposes of carrying a supply line across the land, or amend any such agreement already existing between them. This agreement is appended in the ownership register. (13) The amount of compensation payable under section 11 or 13 has to be decided by the District Land Administrator. (14) In case the energy generated is not sufficient, the license holder may reduce the supply of electricity to any consumer. If he/she does so, he/she will not be liable to any loss suffered by the consumer; and in appropriate cases, abatement in the charges for the supply of energy will be made in proportion to the reduction made. (15) Any licensee will not be liable for any damage to any person or property or for any cessation of the supply of energy for the reasons given in section 17 of the Act. (16) Under section 18 of the Act, before the issuance of any license, the Commission may require necessary security system to be observed. (17) Upon breach of any condition or on default of payment or when the licensee ceases to work or operate the installation in respect of which the license was granted, the license may be suspended or revoked by the Commission. This order is appealable to the Minister. The decision of the Minister shall be final. The licensee will not be entitled to any compensation with respect to loss suffered by him/her during the suspension or revocation of his/her license. (18) Upon termination of his/her license, the licensee will remove all his/her paraphernalia within three months, failing which he/she will be liable to compensate the owner of the land. (19) According to section 19 of the Act, the license holder if restricted to using or supplying energy for specified purposes only, will not use or supply energy for any purpose other than that. (20) Section 20 of the Act provides for protection of the licensee by stating that in case any electrical equipment belonging to a licensee has been placed in or upon premises not owned or occupied by the licensee, it will not be subject to distress nor be liable to be taken in execution under any process of a court or in any bankruptcy or insolvency proceedings against any person. (21) Before the completion of the work, the work has to be registered with the Commission. On registration, a Certificate of Registration is issued. Before this, so as to facilitate the work a provisional certificate can be issued, which can be revoked or cancelled any time by the Commission. No person shall possess or operate an installation without possessing the Certificate of registration. The Certificate of Registration is not transferable. The Certificate has to be surrendered if the installation is no longer required to be used. In case the installation is restarted, it will be treated as a new installation and the formalities of licensing and Certificate of Registration will have to be done. (22) The cancellation of Certificate of Registration is done according to the Regulations made for this purpose (See *infra*). (23) Section 22 of the Act provides for periodical inspections of installations. It states that any person who intends to construct, extend or alter any installation will have to give notice of the purposes of construction, extension or alteration to the Commission. Such person will submit plans and obtain prior approval based on periodical inspections. Such periodical inspections have to be made even after the completion of the project provided it remains in the running condition. It is obligatory on the licensee to provide full facilities for inspection during working hours.

159. Under section 51 of the Act, the Yand di-Pertuan Agong (YDPA) may on the occurrence of any industrial unrest, strike, lockout or any other event which gives rise to an emergency or in the interest of public safety authorize the Commission to: (1) suspend the license, take temporary possession of any installation and operate it in such a manner as the Commission deems fit and (2) withdraw either partially or totally the use of any installation or facility from any person or class of persons or from the public at large.

160. Under the Electricity Supply (Exemption) Notification 1994, the Minister has issued an exemption order exempting certain persons from the license to be taken under sections 9(1)(a), 21(1), 21(2) and 23(1) of the Act. For details, the notification may be referred.

III. Control

161. According to section 23 of the Act, no installation or electrical plant equipment other than those owned or managed by a supply authority shall be worked or operated except by or under control of persons possessing such qualifications and holding such certificates as may be prescribed, and no person not possessing the qualifications or holding a certificate as aforesaid shall be in charge of any installation or shall control the operation of any electrical plant or equipment. Any person who contravenes this requirement will be liable to a fine not exceeding MYR 10,000 and, if the contravention continues, to a fine not exceeding MYR 1,000 for every day or part of a day during which the contravention continues after contravention.

IV. Supply of Electricity

162. According to section 24 of the Act, a licensee is authorized subject to regulations, if any, to give supply of electricity to those premises, and to provide supply lines or any electrical plant or equipment to the extent of necessity.

163. Where any person requires a supply, he/she will give to the licensee a notice specifying: the premises in respect of which the supply is required; the day on which the supply is required to commence; the maximum power which may be required at any time; and the maximum period for which the supply is required to be given. On receiving this, the licensee will give appropriate reply.

164. There will be no duty to supply electricity on the part of the licensee: (1) if the supply of electricity is already being given to the premises by another licensee and if such supply is given whether wholly or partly through the licensee's supply lines and electrical equipment or plant; (2) he/she is prevented from doing so by circumstances beyond his/her control; if circumstances exist by reason of which his/her doing so will or may involve his/her breach of any regulation under the Electricity Supply Act; or (3) if it is not reasonable in all the circumstances for him/her to be required to do so.

165. Under section 26 of the Act, a licensee is authorized for the prescribed levy having regard to any condition in the license, which relates to the supply of electricity in different areas and circumstances. The tariff fixed by the licensee has to be reasonable and it should properly be notified before it is actually taken. If the tariff rate has to be revised, it has to be subject to the permission by the Commission. The tariff may include the standing charge in addition to the charge for actual electricity supplied; a charge in respect of the availability of a supply of electricity and such charge may vary according to the extent of supply. The levy should not be discriminatory in nature.

166. The licensee is authorized to realize the expenses reasonably incurred in providing any supply line or electrical plant or equipment. It will include the capitalized value of any expenses likely to be so incurred on maintaining it, if such expenses cannot be recovered by the licensee as part of the tariffs levied by him/her for the supply.

167. Under section 28 of the Act, a licensee is authorized to require any person who requires a supply of electricity to furnish him/her a reasonable security for all monies which may become due to him/her with respect to the electricity supply or where any supply line or electrical plant or equipment has to be provided in respect of the provision of such facility, and if the person fails to give such security, the licensee may refuse to give supply or to provide the supply line or electrical plant or equipment until the security is paid.

168. If the person has not given the security or the security was insufficient, on the basis of seven days of notice the licensee may require him/her to pay full security. On failure to do so, the licensee may discontinue the supply of electricity until security is given.

V. Accident or Fire

169. Section 33 of the Act provides that in case of accident or fire in connection of any installation or electrical plant or equipment and it has resulted in death or injury to any person(s) or serious damage to property, the owner, licensee or supply authority and the management will be duty bound to report about the incident to the Commission within the quickest means of communication available and will submit the report in writing about the facts of the matter so far as they are known to them respectively.

170. Upon receipt of the first report, the Commission will direct an officer to visit the place of accident or fire; to make a preliminary enquiry; to record his/her findings in writing; and forward his/her report with all supporting documents and evidences. In case of any death or serious injury, he/she has to send his/her report to the Magistrate of appropriate jurisdiction.

171. In case of loss of life or serious injury, no alteration or addition will be made to the installation, electrical plant or equipment without the permission of the Commission. No alteration, if necessarily required, can be made without permission and completion of the report of the authorized officer, except where it is imperatively demanded for the general safety of life or property. Rescue work can also be done without any specific permission.

172. The Commission forwards the report to the Public Prosecutor for criminal action if it appears from the investigation that there was reason to believe that the accident or fire was due to any failure to comply the law or it could be prevented if proper precautions could have been taken and observed in the working of any installation or electrical plant or equipment as the case may be. This is to be noted here that violation of the provisions of this section is also an offence punishable with a fine not exceeding MYR 5,000.

VI. Procedure with Respect to Enquiry and Arbitration

173. Section 34 of the Act provides that in case of any dispute between a licensee and an authorized officer or between the management and owner pertaining to any installation or equipment or any matter affecting the construction, erection, maintenance or operation of any installation or equipment the matter will be decided by the Commission. The aggrieved party may move an appeal, within twenty-one days from the date of the decision of the Commission or within such period as allowed by the Minister, to the Minister for reconsideration of the matter in dispute.

174. On appeal application, the Minister appoints a person to act as his/her representative to hold inquiry into the matter along with two assessors who are experts not in the service of the Commission. On conclusion of the enquiry, the report along with summary of evidence and findings of the committee is submitted to the Minister. The Minister takes decision on them.

Where a matter is required to be resolved on the basis of arbitration, a board of three arbitrators is constituted. If there is no agreement on arbitrators between the parties, the Chief Judge appoints them. Although parties have right to appoint their assessors, the award is made by the board of arbitrators by majority. The arbitration has to be conducted under the legal provisions contained in the Arbitration Act 1952 (it is now Arbitration Act 2005).

VII. Punitive Measures: Penalties and Damages

A. *Offences and Penalties*

175. Section 37 of the Act declares sixteen offences and prescribes penalty for them. The important ones from them are as follows:

(a) Tampering with or adjusting any installation or part thereof or manufacturing or importing or selling any equipment so as to cause or likely to cause damage to human life or damage to any equipment or other property. This offence carries a fine not exceeding MYR 100,000 or to imprisonment for a term not exceeding five years or to both. In case the offence is not so serious, the liability will be to a fine not exceeding MYR 50,000 or imprisonment for a term not exceeding three years or to both.
(b) Dishonestly abstracting energy, consuming energy, using energy altering the index of any meter or other such instruments, or preventing any such meter or instrument from duly recording the production or consumption of energy. This offence carries a fine not exceeding MYR 100,000 or an imprisonment not exceeding three years or both. This is a *mens rea* crime.
(c) Working or operating any installation without any license obtained under section 9 of the Act. This offence carries the penalty of a fine not exceeding MYR 50,000 and to a further fine not exceeding MYR 1,000 for every day or part of a day during which offence continues after conviction.
(d) Supplying energy from an installation without obtaining a license under section 9 of the Act. This offence carries a liability of a fine not exceeding MYR 50,000, and to a further fine not exceeding MYR 1,000 for every day or part of a day during which the offence continues after conviction.
(e) Supply of energy or laying down any supply line or construction of any electrical work by the license holder outside the area of supply specified in his/her license without the express authority by the Commission. This offence carries a fine not exceeding MYR 500,000. The offender will have to remove the installation. In case the installation is removed by the Commission, the offender will be liable to pay the cost of the removal.

(f) Violating any condition specified in the license without any lawful excuse. This offence has been subjected to a fine not exceeding MYR 10,000, and to a further fine not exceeding one thousand for every day or part of a day during which the offence continues after conviction. This is notable here that if for the act there is a lawful excuse, there will be no offence.
(g) Failure or neglecting to register any installation under section 21 of the Act. This has the liability of a fine not exceeding MYR 25,000, and a further fine not exceeding MYR 1,000 for every day or part of a day during which the offence continues after conviction.
(h) Extinguishing or damaging any lamp or damaging or defacing any post, bracket or any other means of support of a public lamp. This offence carries a fine not exceeding MYR 5,000 or an imprisonment not exceeding one year or both.
(i) Affixing or causing to be affixed any advertisement, bill or notice or any paper against or upon, or otherwise defacing any building, post or bracket or any other equipment. This offence carries a fine not exceeding MYR 1,000.
(j) Wilfully or negligently causing energy to be diverted from its proper course, or braking, throwing down, causing to fall or damage any supply line, post, pole, or other equipment, installation or any part thereof connected with the supply of energy. This offence carries a fine not exceeding MYR 50,000, or to an imprisonment not exceeding three years or both. This offence is a *mens rea* crime.
(k) Undertaking any work or engaging in any activity in the vicinity of any electrical installation or part thereof in a manner likely to cause interference in the operation of the installation. This offence carries a fine not exceeding MYR 5,000 or an imprisonment not exceeding one year or both.
(l) With respect to any unlawful act to which no penalty has expressly been prescribed, there will be liability of a fine not exceeding MYR 5,000:

Wherever any agent or servant in the course of his/her employment does or omits to do any act the doing or omission of which by his/her principal or employer would be an offence, and such agent or servant as the case may be shall be guilty of the offence, and the principal or employer as the case will be liable unless it is proved that the principal or the employer has taken reasonable precautions to prevent the act or omission.

This has to be noted here that some of these offences are compoundable. The compoundable offences are those which have been committed under sections 8, 37(9), 37(10), 37(12), 37(13), 37(14), 37(15), 45 and 59 of the Act. Section 45 rules that the execution of all work in connection of generation or supply of electricity will have to be carried out in the prescribed manner without prejudice to any public or private safety. Any person who fails or contravenes to comply with this will be guilty of an offence under the Act. Section 49 prescribes certain procedural norms to be followed in case of dangerous defects in installation or part thereof either noticed by the Commission or communicated to the licensee, or the licensee has himself/herself detected the defect. Contravention of these amounts to an offence under the Act.

B. Disconnection of Supply of Energy

176. With respect to three offences specified in section 38 of the Act, supply of electricity can be disconnected. Reconnection can be made only on the order of the reconnection given by the licensee. On reconnection, the offender will pay the expenses incurred by the licensee to him/her.

C. Compensation for Damage

177. Any person who removes, destroys or damages whether wilfully or otherwise, any installation or any part thereof, or any public lamp or any post, bracket or any other means of support of a public lamp, or any instrument used in connection with any installation for recording the output or consumption of energy shall, in addition to any penalty to which he/she may be liable in the Act, be liable to pay full compensation for the damage he/she has done and the compensation shall be recoverable by civil action. Subsection (2) of section 41 says that without prejudice to this, any court before which a person has been with an offence under this Act may assess the amount of compensation payable and can make an order to for its payment. Any such order may be enforced as if it was a judgment in a civil action or suit.

D. Prosecution/Compounding of Offences

178. According to section 42 of the Act, prosecution can take place only with the written consent of the Public Prosecutor. Under section 43, Chairman of the Commission with permission of the Public Prosecutor can compound offences under various sections on the basis of payment of the 50% of the amount of the maximum fine for that offence. The money received on compounding offences will be sent to the consolidated fund of the state. By virtue of section 44, a part of the fine as determined by the prosecuting officer may be paid to the informer. This is a kind of award and it should not be more than half of the fine imposed.

E. Other Relevant Provisions

179. The following are the other relevant provisions:

(a) Execution of all works in connection with the generation or supply of energy which may affect infrastructure or facilities like supply of water, drainage, telegraph, telephone, radiocommunications etc., will be carried out in the prescribed manner and without prejudice to public or private safety, violation of which will be considered as an offence (section 45).
(b) If any work or operation of any installation causes electrical interference radiocommunication or telecommunication, the Commission may ask for abatement of such interference. Even after such order, disturbance continues fourteen days

or more, the matter will be referred to the Minister and the Minister may order for revocation of the license. In genuine cases, the licensee can claim damages from the Government for the damage if any caused by such revocation order (section 46).

(c) Any Governmental department or any other consumer taking or using energy from any installation if demanded will provide such means for obviating any risk of damage to such installation by atmospheric electricity as may be directed by the Commission or as may be prescribed by regulations made under this Act (section 47).
(d) Any generation, transmission, supply or use of electricity can be connected to the earth according to the provided mode (section 48).
(e) Government, on the request made by the Commission, may declare any lake, river or waterway or any part thereof with suitable conditions to be a source of water for any licensee (section 52).
(f) Minister has the power to make suitable regulations to facilitate and bring into action various provisions of the Act (section 53).
(g) Minister has the power to grant exemption from any provision(s) of the Act or any regulation(s) made under it to any installation of any supply authority or any other particular class of installation, plant or equipment. It has to be notified. He/she also has the power to cancel any exemption so notified (section 54).
(h) Any license granted under any law promulgated prior to this Act will be deemed to have been granted under this Act and will remain valid until it is revoked. For them, conditions contained in this Act will be applicable. The licensee cannot do the following without prior permission of the Commission: acquiring any land or building; commencing any new scheme for the supply of energy; extending any existing installation or area of supply; and installing any new or replacing any existing plant or equipment for the purposes of such installation. On violation of any of these, the lines may be revoked (section 55).

§3. The Electricity Supply (Amendment) Act 2015 (Act A1510)

180. The Electricity Supply (Amendment) Act (hereinafter 'Amendment Act') has rationalized the provisions of the Act and has made them more realistic and meaningful to meet the cotemporary challenges in supply of electricity for domestic use and commercial and public installations, and to enhance the safety features pertaining to it. The Amendment Act has brought about the following notable changes – related to safety, governance, enforcement and protection – in the 1990 Act:

(1) Under section 33A of the Amendment Act, two new Codes have been developed, namely The Non-Domestic Electrical Installation Safety Code and the Electrical Installation Safety Code. Under these Codes, the licensee for electricity supply is required to create an infrastructure safety management plan in light of the Electrical Infrastructure Safety Code. These Codes contain general

regulations that already exist added with some innovative provisions for making it more comprehensive. It may be noted here that the Energy Commissions already had Distribution Code and Grid Code under the 1990 original Act but since they were purely administrative in nature, these new Codes became necessary so that they could also cover technical the aspects of safety. In Contravention of these Codes, they will be liable for a fine of RM 100,000 or a jail term not exceeding two years, or both. Non-Domestic installation operators are also required to prepare such programme, failing which, they will also be liable for the punitive measures. In order to make all to be aware of these Codes, the Energy Commission is organizing meeting in the Peninsular Malaysia and Sabah. In line of these Codes, there is 'Electrical Safety Management System Audit Checklist'. Audits have to be conducted according to the checklist.[106]

(2) The safety section of the Amendment Act provides for compliance inspection to be conducted by the Energy Commission and take necessary action if the safety management programme applicable to it is flawed. Offenders that tamper electricity installations, public or private, risking human lives or causing or threat to cause damage to property will be liable for a fine up to RM 1 million and/or a jail term not exceeding ten years. Tampering with electricity meters is subject to fine RM 100,000 or a jail term up to five years or both. It is for domestic consumers. For non-Domestic consumers, it is RM 5 million or ten years jail term or both. According to Vo. 7 of *the Energy Malaysia*, the Official Magazine of the Energy Commission, the offences and penalties altered by the Amendment Act, are:

Offence	*Penalties (Electricity Supply Act 1990)*
Tampering/adjusting any electrical installation, or manufacturing/ importing/selling equipment that may endanger other people or property	RM 100,000 fine/five years of imprisonment/both penalties
Causing damage to any person or property, through either rash action or negligence	RM 50,000 fine/three years of imprisonment/both penalties
Illegal consumption of electricity/ tampering or preventing normal operation of electricity metres	RM 100,000 fine/three years of imprisonment/both penalties

106. See, 'Sringent Measures, Achieving Better Safety Management Practices', *Energy Malaysia*, Vol. 9, 2016, pp. 15–18.

Under the Amendment Act, these penalties are changed to:

Offence	*Penalties (Electricity Supply (Amendment) Act 2015)*
Tampering/adjusting any electrical installation, or manufacturing/importing/ selling equipment that may endanger other people or property	RM 100,000 fine/ten years of imprisonment/both penalties
Causing damage to any person or property, through either rash action or negligence	RM 100,000 fine/five years of imprisonment/both penalties
Illegal consumption of electricity/ tampering or preventing normal operation of electricity metres	**Domestic Consumers:** First offence: RM 1,000–50,000 fine/1 year of imprisonment/both penalties Second and subsequent offences: RM 5,000–100,000 fine/three years of imprisonment/both penalties **Non-domestic Consumers:** First offence: RM 20,000–1,000,000 fine/five years of imprisonment/both penalties Second and subsequent offences: RM 100,000–5,000,000 fine/ten years of imprisonment/both penalties

(3) The Amendment Act requires the Energy Commission to be more actively involved in PPAs so that interests of utility company and of independent power producers (IPPs) could amicably be protected. The same goes with the consumer supply agreements (ASAs) so that the genuine rights of consumers are protected according to the law. The electricity tariff has to be fixed by the Energy Commission with approval of the Ministry.

(4) The Amendment Act separated the functions of single buyer be separated from the utility in order to ensure independence and transparency in electricity supply, because this way the Energy Commission can keep better eyes on both of them.

(5) In order to have better deterrence, penalties for various offences have been enhanced. It is for this reason that there are stringent penalties for repeat offences. The quanta of penalties are higher for factories because that can inflict greater harm to the economic interests of the country and may pose bigger safety risk to people. It will also deter them from being negligent. It also extends to a third party's negligence. For example, there is drainage work and

because of that electricity supply is interrupted, the person at work will be libale for the loss to consumers and will also be penalized for being negligent. Likewise, if there is electric surge because of the negligence on the part of the supplier (licensee) and because of that consumers' equipment got damaged, the supplier of electricity has to compensate.

(6) The Amendment Act has provisions to protect transport of communications. Thus, a broadband service provider if registered with the Communication and Multimedia Commission has right to use power lines for its network. Section 44A of the Amendment Act governs the use of supply lines and electrical installations and infrastructure means of communications registered under the Communication and Multimedia Act 1998. To this effect, the Energy Commission may issue guidelines/code in future. Thus, the Energy Commission under the Amendment Act has power to regulate use of smart meters in order to ensure accurate metering.

In an interview conducted by *Energy Malaysia,* a Senior Director of the Electricity Supply & Market Regulation Department of the Energy Commission Ir Azhar Omar, as he then was, outlined the imperatives of the Amendment Act 2015 that customers are supposed to know Are:

(1) The role of electricity supply industry with respect to competition, compliance, safety and consumers' interest, he said: 'The amendments would enhance transparency, planning, compliance monitoring and enforcement, to create a level playing field for the all players in the industry, and to improve safety management and protection of consumers' interests.' He further said with respect to the role of the Energy Commission with respect to these: 'The Energy Commission's role in planning will ensure the coordinated and orderly development of the MESI in meeting the needs of reliable and cost-efficient electricity supply. To instil confidence in investors in the industry, a transparent and level playing field has to be established, particularly as TNB, being a major player in the industry, has control over most activities.' He further said, 'In protecting consumers' interests, the amended Act will enhance the role of the Energy Commission in regulating supply applications and requirements; tariff-setting processes; meter testing and verification; and safety of equipment and installations. The terms and conditions of supply, charges imposed by licensees and meters to be installed have to be approved by the Energy Commission. The performance of licensees will be gauged through an approved standard of perform and safety will be enhanced through the establishment of safety management plan/programmes and the stipulation of standards for equipment and installation. In ensuring cost-effective electricity supply, a tariff-setting process through the implementation of Incentive-Based Regulations (IBR) has been established. The procurement of electricity supply through Power Purchase Agreements (PPAs) will be scrutinised by the Energy Commission.'

(2) 'New power plants, according to him, will have to be in line with the approved plan and subject to approval of the Energy Commission. Transmission and distribution projects will be subject to the Energy Commission's security under

the IBR Mechanism. Implementation of the smart grid and smart meters will have to demonstrate the cost benefit of such programmes before being approved by the Energy Commission to be included under the IBR investment.'

(3) About the establishment of the Electricity Industry Fund (EIF), he said, 'Recognizing the need to soften the financial effects the Amendment Act has established an industrial fund for tariff stabilization and other such purposes. Contribution to the fund will be through various means such as input by licensees, savings from operational efficiency, and savings and penalties under PPAs. A trust deed for the fund will be created to determine allocation and distribution of the fund for various purposes … The Energy Commission will be the custodian of the Fund, and will be responsible for managing the collection, allocation and investment of the funding line with the established procedure.'

In *Energy Malaysia,* Vol. 7, 2016, Ir Othman Omar, The Director of the Regional Operation and Enforcement, as he then was, emphasized on enhanced penalty in the Amendment Act 2015. It is hoped that with the severe penalties in certain serious matters, the compliance of law will be there and people will deter from committing such crimes. Additionally, he recorded that amendments will clarify and widen the scope of authority given to officers of the Energy Commission, allowing them to conduct audit of non-domestic electrical installations. Under the amended Act, according to him, the Energy Commission is authorized to issue directives to the industry to ensure players' strict compliance to the Act. He stated that the Energy Commission has already started conducting safety audits of several players in the country. According to him, best practices will get the way in the system. He added that the amendments would enable the Energy Commission to determine the standards applicable to licensees and non-domestic owners or operators, and any installation or equipment they oversee.

§4. Electricity Supply (Successor Companies) Act 1990

181. The Electricity Supply (Successor Company) Act 1990 has only nine sections. It provides for the vesting of property, rights and liabilities of the National Electricity Board of the states of Malaysia in a company, to make financial arrangements for that company, to provide for matters relating to staff and for other matters connected therewith. That company is known as Successor Company. This can be done by the Minister by making an order to this effect. As a consequence of this, the successor company will issue such securities of the company as the Minister of Finance may from time to time direct (a) to the corporation or (b) to any person entitled to require the issue of the securities following their initial allotment to the corporation. This order is not issued if the successor company has ceased to be wholly owned by the Government of Malaysia.

182. If immediately before the transfer date any person holds any share in the Board, all such shares will as from the transfer date be held by such person in the successor company and the successor company will issue shares to such person of a value not less than the value of the shares held by such person in the Board immediately before the transfer date.

183. The Minister has the following powers pertaining to Government investments in securities of the successor company: (a) He/she can acquire securities or rights to subscribe for any such securities. (b) He/she can dispose of any such securities or rights. (c) Expenditures in this process will be treated as investments. (d) Any dividend on them or profit on their disposal will be sent to the Consolidated Fund.

184. For the purposes of initial government holdings in successor company, the Minister of Finance may appoint any person(s) to act as his/her representative(s). Thus securities of the successor company may be assigned to such nominee of the Minister.

185. If the Minister of Finance so desires at any time before the successor company ceases to be wholly owned by the Government such sum, not exceeding the accumulated realized profit of the Board, as may be specified in the Direction will be transferred by the successor company to a reserve, which will be referred as 'the statutory reserve', which can be applied by the successor company in paying up unissued shares of the company to be allotted to members of the company as fully paid bonus shares. The vesting so affected will be taken to have been a vesting of all property, rights and liabilities to which the Board was entitled. The value of any asset in question will be the amount assigned to that asset or liability for the purposes of the corresponding statement of accounts prepared by the Board. For the purposes of any statutory accounts of the successor company, the amount to be included in respect to any item will be determined as if anything done by the Board.

Chapter 2. Electricity Regulations 1994

186. To enforce the substantive provisions of the Electricity Supply Act 1990, the Minister made an order known as the Modification of Electrical Inspectorate Regulations Order 1990, which came into force on 1 September 1990, wherein it modified by substituting for the words 'Electrical Inspectorate Regulations 1984' the words 'Electrical Supply Regulations 1990'. But regulations were reframed as Electricity Regulations 1994, which came into force on 30 January 1994; and by Regulation 123 of the Electricity Regulations 1994, the Electricity Supply Regulations 1990 were revoked. The 1994 Regulations contain a number of provisions to deal with various aspects pertaining to the supply of electricity in the country. This has been amended from time to time. Amendments have been made to amend various fees and charges and to substitute 'Electricity Commission' in place of 'Director General' and 'Authorized Officer' in place of 'Director'. The salient features of the regulations are the following.

§1. Registration of Installation

187. Regulations 3 to 7 are to facilitate the registration process. According to them, the proponent will be moved for fresh registration or renewal of registration, which has to be made two months before the expiry of the registration, with the payment of the fee prescribed for them. Application is given in Form A.

188. With respect to new installation, inspection has to be made; for which written information is given to the applicant in Form D. With respect to any follow-up inspection information is given in Form F. The applicant has to do necessary preparations for the inspection, and to pay the fee prescribed. Certificate of registration and renewal are given in Forms B and C respectively.

189. Registration can be cancelled if: the installation is no longer is required to be used; or installation is found unsafe for use; or the person to whom the certificate was issued uses it for a purpose other than that for which it was issued; or the person has contravened or failed to comply with any of the provisions of the act or Regulations. On the cancellation of the registration, within fourteen days the certificate has to be surrendered.

§2. License for Installation

190. A license for a public installation is to be given in the form, which the Commission deems fit and appropriate. However, for private installation, license is given in Form F. For fresh license and for renewal of the license, fee as prescribed for the purpose will have to be paid.

§3. Supervision and Test of Installation

191. Regulations 11 to 14 deal about this. According to these, only an electrical contractor or a Private Wiring Unit obtain permission by the licensee or the supply authority as the case can make wiring or re-wiring or extension of the wiring. This has to be noted here that with respect to the domestic wiring if the maximum current demand is not changed, which has been prescribed in the Third Schedule, permission is not required. The job of the wiring has to be done under the supervision of a Wireman, who has to be employed on full-time basis by the Electrical Contractor or a Private Wiring Unit, and upon completion of the wiring in the installation the Wireman issues the Completion Certificate and test certificate in Forms G and H respectively.

192. Upon completion of an installation or extension to an existing installation on higher than low voltage, the installation shall be tested by an Electrical Services Engineer, employed on a full-time basis by the Electrical Services contractor and who shall issue a test certificate for the installation.

§4. Material, Equipment and Installations

193. Regulations 15 to 43 deal about these. A brief account of these is as follows:

(a) Any apparatus, conductor, or accessory will be of sufficient size, power and number and will properly be constructed, installed, arranged and protected (Regulation 15).
(b) Any switch, switchfuse, fuse switch, circuit, breaker or isolating link should be installed according to the requirements contained in Regulation 16.
(c) Any part of the generator, motor, transformer or other equipments operating and at high or extra high voltage which is within the reach of a person will be properly protected so that it does not cause any danger. For this purpose, the switch, switchgear, auto-transformer and underground substation must have proper preventive measures (Regulation 17).
(d) Proper means of isolation will be provided for making dead every part of the system and every branch and subcircuit of the system (Regulation 18).
(e) The general arrangement of switchboard will be: all parts that are to be adjusted should be easily approachable; the course of conductor should be properly drawn and should be traceable; a conductor not to be used for the system should be apart; and a bare conductor should be properly protracted. The ground of the switchboard should have a rubber mat. A competent person only should handle the switches or conductor. An apparatus necessary to a switchboard and requiring handling should be properly placed or arranged. Before any work is commenced on the switchboard, the board will be made dead and the conductor earthed. Switchboard operating at high or extra high voltage will properly be protected and earthed (Regulations 19 to 21).

(f) Underground supply line will be all through insulated and protected to the satisfaction of the authority appointed for this purpose. It should also be easily detectable. The underground work will have to be carried out by the licensee or through the person authorized by him/her according to the requirement of the authority. Except emergency, repair works will have to have permission (Regulation 22).

(g) Any electrical joint, connection or termination will be constructed and made to serve its purpose with regard to its conductivity, insulation, mechanical strength and mechanical protection. Joining will have to be carried out by a proper cable jointer (Regulation 22).

(h) Where a flexible cable has to be joined with a portable apparatus, the joint has to be permanent or with appropriate plug and socket. The portable apparatus has to be controlled by effective means and the exposed metallic part has to be earthed and insulated.

(i) A portable apparatus on a dredge structure has to have 50 Volts between conductors and it should be connected to the main. A portable apparatus having 100 Volts should be attached with a transformer and should properly be earthed (Regulation 25).

(j) No circuit for an electric sign will use voltage exceeding 7,500 volts to earth, measured on an open circuit and will be an effective means of disconnection or isolation. It should have double pole switch and should be installed in an easily accessible position. Any exposed part of it will be earthed.

(k) For any exterior electric sign and interior electric sign, there will be a firemen's switch. It has the following requirements: there should be proper arrangement; it will be painted red; it will be fixed in a conspicuous position so that it is easily approached; Swathes will be right below the sign; Internal switch will be on the main entrance with proper signage; Switch will be provided with a lock or catch designed to prevent the switch from being accidentally 'ON'; If there are more than one switches, each one of them will a sign; and there will be a danger notice (Regulation 27).

(l) The owner or management of an installation will maintain the electric sign to ensure adequate safety to avoid danger from arising, and will take adequate precautions to prevent any unauthorized person from coming into contact with any part of the electric sign (Regulation 28).

(m) Following points are to be taken into consideration with respect to other installations: Installations not in use will be isolated from the source of energy and will not be allowed to remain alive. When an installation is found to cause undue interference in the supply of electricity, the owner or the occupier will be asked to make necessary adjustments or alterations. Electric smelting and X-ray installations will be operated according to the instructions given by the Commission. Meter or main switch at the place of public entertainment will be installed in an enclosure made up of fire resistant material and necessary precautions as prescribed for this will have to be taken (Regulations 29 to 33).

(n) All installations mentioned in Regulation 24 will have appropriate earthing system with acceptable materials. At the place of public entertainment special care will have to be taken for protection against earth leakage (Regulation 34).

(o) As general requirement of installations: there should be adequate lighting; there should be no obstruction; there should be enough space for safe operation or maintenance; there should be a conspicuous notice indicating 'DILARAG MASUK'; a standard conspicuous notice of 'BHAYA' should also be there near the switchboard; there should be instruction to provide first-aid to a person having received an electric shock; person employed to handle installations should be competent; and there should be fire extinguishers (Regulation 37).

(p) General conditions to be followed with respect to aerial lines are: the line conductor will be hard drawn copper, cadmium, aluminium, steel-cored aluminium or any other suitable material approved by the Commission; it should be effectively insulated. There should be proper height of the conductor; there should be proper earthing; if necessary, there should be proper earthing; any multiple earth neutral cannot be installed without permission of the Commission; precautions will be taken to protect it from corrosion of metals and deterioration of wooden poles; a service line will be connected to a line conductor at a point of support only and shall be fixed to an insulator; and adequate provision shall be made for any line conductor forming part of a system at different voltages, erected on the same pole or support to guard against danger to any person who works on the system and to guard against the lower voltage caused by leakage from, or when it comes into contact with the higher voltage system. There are other conditions contained in Regulation 41. They will have to be followed (Regulation 41).

(q) With respect to aerial lines operating at low voltage there are less stringent condition to be followed. These are: The aerial line will be protected from any leakage; it may cross over or under any overhead telecommunication line provided it is properly protected; the clearance between a line conductor and a building will be maintained; and no person, without the lawful authority, will undertake any work (Regulation 42).

(r) The following conditions are applicable with respect to an aerial line operating at high or extra high voltage: every metalwork will properly be earthed; if it crosses over a road, a suitable cradle guard will be erected; no line will run along the road without prior approval of the Commission; When lines are crossing any telecommunication line, should properly be protected; it should be marked with numbers; adequate provision should be made for climbing the tower; a danger notice should be put; a person engaged in any work must have the authority for it; and it should not run parallel to any telecommunication line (Regulation 43).

§5. Operation of Installations

I. Examination of Competent Person

194. Regulations 44 to 65 deal about this. The salient features of these sections are as follows:

(a) For examining competent persons a Board of Examiners has been made (Regulation 44).
(b) Any Electric Service Engineer, Engineer, Electrical Supervisor, Chargeman, Wireman or any other such a technical person must possess a Certificate of Competency issued by the Commission. They can apply competency test, which is conducted by the Board of Examiners (Regulation 45).
(c) A person seeking certificate of competency in Electrical Services Engineer must be a Malaysian citizen, an electrical engineer with enough working experience and proficiency of local language. The applicant will have to face an interview board and will have to appear in the examination. After the interview if the Board so desires, the candidate may be exempted from appearing in the exam. It happens when the person proves that he/she has enough expertise in the area of electrical engineering (Regulation 45).
(d) A person in order to be considered as an Electrical Engineer will have to satisfy the Board that he/she complies with the following conditions: A degree of electrical engineering, registered with the Board of Engineers, five years of working experience, proficiency in the national language. Before he/she gets the Certificate, he/she will have to face an interview, and if necessary will have to pass an examination. In this case also, the Board has the power to exempt (Regulation 46).
(e) In order to get a Certificate of Competency as an Electrical Supervisor a person must have the following qualifications: a Malaysian citizen, a diploma or equivalent, five years of working experience, proficiency in the national language. He/she will have to face an interview and if need be will have to appear in the examination (Regulation 47).
(f) A person in order to be considered for Certificate of Competency as a Chargeman must have the following qualifications: a Malaysian citizen, 20 years of age, suitable educational qualification, three years working experience, proficiency in the national language. He/she will attend interview and if necessary, will appear in the examination (Regulation 48).
(g) Likewise, a person to be considered for a Certificate of Competency as Wireman will have to satisfy the Board that he/she has the following qualifications: a Malaysian citizen, 18 years of age, suitable educational qualification, suitable working experience, proficiency in the national language. He/she will also have to attend an interview, and if need be, will have to appear in the practical examination (Regulation 49).
(h) Similar provisions are there for Certification of Competency for a Cable Jointer (Regulation 51).
(i) A temporary Certificate of Competency is issued to a competent foreign national if he/she satisfies that he/she possesses the necessary qualifications, experience, and he/she has necessary work permit. This has to be noted here that before a person is registered as an Electrical Services Engineer or a Competent Electrical Engineer, he/she has to get himself/herself registered as Professional Engineer with the Board of Engineers. The person is issued Certificate of Competency by the Commission not exceeding twelve months, which can be renewed (Regulation 52).

(j) Pertaining to all, the Commission may require a certificate of fitness (Regulation 53).
(k) The Commission has the power to restrict the use of Certificate of Competency to any type, class, duration or location. It can endorse the Certificate of Competency for a wireman (Regulations 54 and 55).
(l) There are different forms for each category of certificate of competency. The Certificate holder will surrender certificate if any has already possesses under any other law. In case the certificate is lost, stolen, destroyed, mutilated or defaced, a replacement certificate is issued. The certificate can be confiscated if a person is involved in criminal activities. If the certificate was taken by way of fraud or misrepresentation, it can be suspended or revoked. A Certificate can be endorsed, suspended or revoked by the Commission on the ground of serious misconduct. Instances of 'serious misconducts' have been specified. In case of misconduct, a committee will be set up and actions will be taken based on the report (Regulation 56).

§6. Competent Person

195. The competent person to work, operate or be in control of any work or operation of installation, when it does not exceed 600 volts, can be recommended by the following persons: (a) Electrical Services Engineer; (b) Competent Electrical Engineer; (c) Electrical Supervisor; or (d) Resident Competent Electrical Engineer. When this limit is more than 600 volts but below 132,000 volts, recommendation can be made by: (a) Electrical Services Engineer; (b) Competent Electrical Engineer; or (c) Resident Competent Electrical Engineer. Above this limit, the recommending authority is only resident Competent Electrical Engineer. The owner, management or licensee of the installation or equipment is bound to comply with such recommendations, unless it is disapproved by the Commission (Regulation 60). This is notable here that the competent person required by a licensee of a public installation shall work, operate or be in control of the operation, and shall be responsible for the work or operation in the installation of any person under this control (Regulation 61).

196. If the work is to be carried on in more than one shift, the competent person for each shift has to be specified. Any person who holds a Certificate of Competency will have to register himself/herself with the Commission, which will be valid for not less than one year and not more than five years. This can be renewed on the request of the holder of the certificate (Regulation 63).

§7. Inspections by the Competent Person

197. Installations can be visited and inspected by the competent person: if the operation is operating at low voltage, it can be inspected by Electrical services Engineer, Competent Electrical Engineer or Electrical Supervisor. If the operation is at high voltage, it can be inspected by the designate Electrical Services Engineer or Competent Electrical Engineer. Depending on installations, minimum visits can be one to four in a month (Regulation 67).

198. On each inspection, the inspecting officer will have to report to the Commission and the owner, management or licensee of the installation with his/her recommendations within two weeks of the inspection. There has to be book of records pertaining to installations and that book will have to be open for inspection by the Commission at all times (Regulation 68).

199. If any defect is discovered on inspection, it has to be informed immediately to the owner, manager or licensee, and a report will be submitted to the Commission.

§8. Registration of Electrical Services Contractor

200. Any person who wants to perform any work of maintenance, repair, overhaul, service, calibration, test and commission of any installation or equipment and location of cable faults must possess Certificate of Competency of the Electrical Services Contactor. This is issued by the Commission and certificate is valid for one year. The application to this effect can be made by him/her if he/she is registered under the Business Act 1956 (if it is a company, it has to be registered under the Companies Act 1965), he/she employs Electrical Services Engineers or himself/herself act in that capacity and he/she has insurance coverage for his/her employees under the Employees' Social Security Act 1965 (Regulations 71 to 72).

201. He/she is also required by the Commission to furnish the details of partnership if there is any, names of Directors, managers and shareholders in case of a company.

§9. Registration of Electrical Contractor

202. There are different categories of Electrical Contactors (Class A to Class D). They also have to be registered with the Commission. All provisions pertaining to registration are the same except that they appoint wiremen (Regulations 75 to 78).

§10. Registration of Private Wire Unit

203. Registration of Private Wire Unit also has the same kind of provisions applicable to them. They are competent to employ on full-time basis wiremen with three-phase restriction. He/she should employ at least one wireman (Regulations 80 to 83).

§11. Registration of Electric Sign Contractor

204. Electric Sign Contractors are registered with the Commission. In this case also, the provisions are same like registration of Private Wire Unit (Regulations 84 to 87).

§12. Registration of Electric Repair Contractor

205. Their job is to perform or carry out any checking, servicing or repair of any electrical appliance. Like above they have to be registered with the Commission (Regulations 88 to 91).

§13. Registration of Switchboard Manufacturer

206. They have to be registered and the provisions applicable to them are similar to registration of above experts (Regulations 92 to 96).

§14. Approval of Equipment

207. The following statutory law has to be taken into account for approval of equipment to be used in installations and wirings: (1) Only equipment that are approved by the Commission can be sold. (2) All approved equipment must bear the mark of approval. (3) Samples of equipment, if to be done so, have to be delivered to the Commission. (4) Approval is given only after proper testing. (5) Dangerous equipment will be seized (Regulations 97 to 101).

I. The Electricity (Amendment) Regulations 2013 [(P.U. (A) 151]

208. The Electricity (Amendment) Act 2013 has brought about several useful amendments in the Electricity Regulations 1994 to make the existing regulations more meaningful and facing the contemporary challenges faced by the electricity supply in the country. The following changes are worth mentioning:

(1) Regulations 97A, 97B, 97D, 97E and 97F have been added in order to grant recognition to foreign conformity assessment bodies. According to regulation 97A it provides that for certifying any equipment under regulation 97, a foreign conformity assessment body can be recognized and authorized by the Energy Commission provided that body is duly registered for this purpose in its own country. The authorization will remain until it remains like that there. Under regulation 97B, a local conformity assessment bodies can be registered with the Energy Commission provided the body is accredited by the accreditation authority. Regulation 97C provides that a person who manufactures or imports any equipment under regulation 97 will apply to be registered with the

Commission. It can be granted a certificate by the Energy Commission a Certificate of Registration to manufacture or import specified equipment. Under regulation 97D the person can submit test reports duly issued by a certified laboratory, about equipment that they comply with the safety standards prescribed by the Energy Commission. It can also submit to the Commission a certificate of conformity issued by a local conformity assessment body. They have to be submitted within the validity period of not less than one year before the expiry date, because it has to be done on annual basis. Under regulation 97E, any importer issued with a certificate of registration under regulation 97C is entitled to submit to the Commission a test report pertaining to equipment(s) in conformity to safety standards and issued by a recognized laboratory, and a certificate of conformity issued by an authorized for it. It also has to be done on annual basis. It means, the importer has to ensure that such test report or certificate of conformity has a validity period of not less than one year before the expiry date. Regulation 97F provides that a manufacturer or importer issued with a certificate of registration under registration under regulation 97C will have to keep all technical files of any equipment issued together with a test report or certificate of conformity, as the case may be, for not less than ten years after the last equipment has left the production line. The testing laboratory and the local conformity assessment body have to keep all records for not less than six years.

The terms 'accreditation authority', 'certificate of conformity', 'conformity assessment body', 'foreign conformity assessment body' and 'local conformity assessment body' are defined in the Amendment Regulations 2013.

(2) In Part III of the Principal Regulations, new regulations 101A, 101B and 101C have been added. They pertain to approval of equipment. For ensuring efficient use of electricity equipment are required under regulation 101A to meet the energy performance testing standards, the minimum energy performance standards and the efficiency ratings as set out in the Fourth Schedule. For this purpose, a manufacturer of importer is required to submit the energy performance testing report pertaining to the equipment in accordance with regulation 101B. Based on that, the Energy Commission will issue the rating label. The testing reports are prepared by the manufacturer of importer based on the tests conducted by authorized laboratories. They have to be done on annual basis. Regulation 101C authorises the Energy Commission to ask manufacturers, importers, who sells or offers for sale or lease such equipment to deliver within such period as may be specified in the notice, samples of the equipment for an examination and a test. If the Commission determines that the equipment does not fulfil the requirements of efficient use of electricity, the Commission may prohibit the manufacturing or import of such equipment and to recall all equipments sent out for leasing or for sale. In such a situation the Commission will not be liable for any financial losses suffered by the manufacturer of importer.

(3) A new regulation 109A provides that the Commission is authorized to carry out market surveillance to determine if any such equipment is safe and is affixed a required label or an efficient rating label or both as the case may be. Anyone who removes such labels or otherwise creates hindrance to officials of

the Commission for exercising of its powers in this regard, or harbours, keeps, conceals or is in the possession of any unlabelled equipment, commits an offence punishable under the Electricity Supply Act 1990.

II. Electricity (Amendment) Regulations 2014 [P.U. (A) 73]

209. The 2014 amendment regulations have not made any significant changes in the principal regulations. In the substantive provisions the notable changes are that initially provisions of regulation 10 were applicable to biomass only, now they are applicable to biogas also. Otherwise, the amendment regulations are to revise the fees for issuance of certificate of registration, fees for inspection and test of installation, fees for public installation other than generation referred to in subregulation 10(2), fees for the issuance of a licence for a private installation, fees for public installation for generating electricity using biomass, biogas, hydropower, solar power, geothermal power, wind power, waves and tides sources with aggregate power not exceeding 5 MW (previously it was 10 MW), fees for issuance of temporary certificate of competency, fees for processing examination application, examination, endorsement, replacement and reissuance of certificate of competency, fees for registration of competent person, fees for certificate of registration as an electrical services contractor, fees for certificate of registration as a private wiring unit, fees for certificate of registration as an electrical design contractor, fees for certificate of registration as an electric repair contractor, fees for certificate of registration as a switchboard manufacturer and fees for certificate of approval to manufacture, import, display, sell or advertise equipment.

It is notable in the Amendment Regulation 2014 that the fees chargeable for various activities of the Schedule Second have suitably been increased so that they could become meaningful in view of the annual inflations.

Chapter 3. Efficient Management of Electrical Energy Regulations 2008

210. In order to further give effect to the substantive provisions of the Electricity Supply Act 1990 (Act 447) and in exercise of his powers conferred by sections 23A and 53 of the same Act, the Minister made regulations known as 'Efficient Management of Electrical Energy Regulations 2008' which came into force on 15 December 2008. This legislative framework on the efficient use of electricity energy covers all installations or users with total electricity consumption of 3 million kWh or more over six consecutive months.

§1. Application

211. The scope of application of these regulations is limited to such installation or user which receives energy from licensee or supply authority with total electricity consumption of 3 million kWh or more over a period not exceeding six consecutive months. If such installation receives supply authority before or on the effective date, the electricity consumption mentioned will be calculated from the effective date. However, if such installation receives electricity supply after the effective date, the 3 million kWh will be calculated over any period not exceeding six consecutive months from the date the electricity energy was connected. The same rules apply to any installation used, worked or operated by a private installation licensee (Regulation 3).

212. The prescribed fees under these regulations which shall be paid to the Commission are set out in the First Schedule (Regulation 4). The types of fees include application for registration as an EEM (MYR 20 per application), issuance/renewal of certificate of registration (MYR 100 per year), application for replacement of certificate of registration (MYR 50 per copy) and application for certified true copy of certificate of registration (MYR 10 per copy).

§2. Electrical Energy Management

213. The regulations place an obligation on the licensee or supply authority to submit necessary information or documents to the Commission. Regulation 5(1) to (4) covers the licensee or supply authority who supplies electrical energy under paragraphs 3(2)(a), 3(2)(b) and a private installation licensee under paragraphs 3(2)(c) and 3(2)(d). The submission must be made not later than one month after six consecutive months from the effective date. However, despite the foregoing provisions, the Energy Commission can, at anytime, direct any licensee, supply authority or private installation licensee through a written notice to provide any information or document within a specified period stipulated in the notice (subregulation (5)). Such statutory information or document required by the Commission must be true, accurate and complete. The licensee, supply authority or private installation licensee must ensure this by including a representation to that effect as required by subregulation (6).

214. It becomes an offence under the regulation if a licensee, supply authority or private installation licensee fails to comply with the regulation, or fails to disclose any relevant information or document or provides misleading or false information or documents (Regulation 5(7)).

215. Any private installation licensee or consumer with a total net electrical energy generation or total electrical energy consumption up to or more than 3,000,000 kWh may be required by the Commission through a written notice to appoint or designate a registered electrical energy manager (REEM) to carry out the functions and duties under Regulation 16. Such licensee or consumer may also be required to submit a written confirmation of such appointment or designation containing the names and particulars of the REEM. In addition, the licensee may also be required to submit information regarding the statement of policy, objectives and accounts and documents for the efficient electrical energy management of the installation. The report is to be submitted in accordance with Form A of the Second Schedule; and it must be duly signed. The Commissioner can also require the licensee to submit any other information as it deems fit (Regulation 6(1)).

216. The report required under Regulation 6(1) must be submitted by the private installation licensee or consumer alongside with a declaration by the REEM for the installation in Form B of the Second Schedule. More importantly, the licensee or consumer must ensure that the information is true, accurate and complete and a representation must be provided to that effect (Regulation 6(3)). It becomes an offence under the Regulations if such licensee or consumer fails to comply with subregulations (1) or (2) or fails to disclose or omits any relevant information or document or provides misleading information (Regulation 6(4)).

217. The private installation licensee or consumer is under an obligation to submit the information required by the Commission not later than three months from the date of the written notice from the Commission. In addition, it must also submit the information and report regarding the statement of policy, objectives and accounts and documents for the efficient electrical energy management of the installation, and any other document required by the Commission with the necessary declaration not later than thirty days after the expiry of six consecutive months from the end of the three-month period specified in Regulation 7(1) *(a)*. These reports as specified in paragraph (1) *(a)* and (1) *(b)* must subsequently be submitted to the Commission according to the specified periods; failure to comply to that is an offence under the Regulations. The Commission may also request for additional information or documents, which must be provided. Failure to furnish the Commission with additional information is an offence (Regulation 8).

218. After the submission of the information and report, the Commission may review the obligations of the private installation licensee or consumer considering the total net electrical energy generated or consumed for the reported period, full compliance of the private installation licensee or consumer with the regulations, and any other reason which the Commission deems fit to show efficient management of electrical energy at the installation for the reported period. After the review, the Commission shall, by written notice, notify the private installation licensee or consumer not to submit further information and report. Once the private installation licensee or consumer receives the notice, he/she shall cease to submit the information and report with effect from the date in the notice from the Commission (Regulation 9).

219. The Commission may withdraw a written notice issued under Regulation 9(2) at any time if the total electrical energy consumption or total net electrical energy generation over any period of six consecutive months equals to or exceeds 3,000,000 kWh or for any other reason as the Commission deems fit especially if it is satisfied that efficient management of electricity energy has not been practiced after the issuance of the notice. Once the notice is withdrawn, the private installation licensee or consumer shall become subject to the Regulations with effect from the date of withdrawal of the notice. There is a fundamental requirement that any withdrawal of the written notice must be made in writing and duly served.

§3. Registered Electrical Energy Manager

220. A fundamental rule laid down in the Regulations is that every electric energy manager must be registered by the Commission. It is an offence for someone to engage in, be employed or hold himself/herself out as a registered electric energy manager without being registered by the Commission (Regulation 11). For the Commission to register a person as an EEM, he/she must apply to the Commission and satisfy the following requirements: Malaysian citizenship aged 23 years and above with a certificate of registration as a Professional Engineer and six months working experience in the efficient management of electrical energy, or hold a degree in Science, Engineering, Architecture or its equivalent with a one-year working experience in the efficient management of electrical energy, or holds a Certificate of Competency issued by the Commission as an Electric Services Engineer or a Competent Electrical Engineer with at least nine months working experience in the efficient management of electrical energy. Such applicant must also demonstrate knowledge of the requirements of the Electricity Supply Act and the Regulations. These requirements will be ascertained at an interview, which may be conducted by the Commission at a date and location as determined by it (Regulation 12).

221. Eligible candidates as electric energy manager who satisfy the requirements may apply in writing to the Commission for registration. The following documents must accompany such application: application fee and supporting documents. However, additional information or document may be requested by the Commission upon the receipt of an application. If such additional information or document is not submitted within the specified period, the application will be deemed withdrawn but this will not affect any fresh application.

222. Within forty-five days of the receipt of an application or any additional information or document requested for, the Commission shall inform the applicant in writing whether such application is approved or not. If such application is approved, the applicant shall be registered as an EEM and will be issued the certificate of registration upon the payment of the prescribed fee. On the other hand, if the Commission refused such application, it may provide reasons in writing to the applicant for such refusal upon the request of the applicant (Regulation 14). For an applicant whose application has been approved, before a certificate of registration is issued to him/her, he/she may be required by the Commission to produce a medical evidence of physical and mental fitness certified by a registered medical practitioner (Regulation 15).

223. The functions and duties of a REEM are: to audit and analyse the total electrical energy consumption or total net electrical energy generation including the significant end use of electricity, advise the private installation licensee or consumer in developing measures to ensure efficient management of electrical energy, monitor effective implementation of the measures referred, supervise the keeping of records on efficient management of electrical energy and verify its accuracy and ensure that the private installation licensee or consumer submits the information and report required by the Commission from time to time within the specified periods (Regulation 16).

224. The validity period of certificate of registration shall be a period not less than one year and not more than five years. The certificate can be renewed at least one month prior to the date of expiry. However, the Commission will only renew such registration of an EEM if it is satisfied that he/she has complied with the conditions or restrictions as stipulated in the certificate and he/she has duly paid the required fee (Regulation 17).

225. The certificate registration of a REEM may be cancelled by the Commission under any of the four circumstances where he/she has contravened or failed to comply with any provision of the Act or the Regulations; obtained the certificate of registration by making or causing to be made any false or fraudulent declaration, certification or representation, either in writing or otherwise; used the certificate of registration for a purpose that differs from that for which it was issued or in a manner that is intended to mislead or deceive the public; or failed to carry out the functions and duties of a REEM. Nevertheless, the Commission must notify the REEM in writing of its intention to cancel the certificate of registration. Such notice of intention to cancel the certificate of registration must be duly answered through a written submission by the REEM within fourteen days from the date of issuance of the notice stating the reasons why his/her certificate should not be cancelled. This written submission will be duly considered by the Commission before any decision is made. If the Commission decides to cancel the certificate of registration, it shall issue a notice of cancellation to the REEM containing the reasons for such cancellation. This cancellation shall take effect on the expiry of twenty-one days from the date of the notice of cancellation. In some extreme situations, the Commission may, in line with public interest, immediately cancel the certificate of registration by serving upon the REEM a notice of cancellation notwithstanding the provisions of Regulation 18(1)*(a)*–*(d)*.

§4. REGISTER

226. A register of every REEM to whom a certificate has been issued shall be maintained by the Commission. This register will include the name and particulars of the REEMs. Whenever the Commission cancels the certificate of registration of any REEM, it shall consequently delete his/her name and particulars from the register (Regulation 19).

227. In the case of defacement or loss of a certificate of registration, the REEM may apply in writing to the Commission for a replacement. Such application must be accompanied with a police report or statutory declaration in the case of loss of the certificate or a defaced certificate of registration in the case of defacement of the certificate of registration. In addition, the application must be accompanied with the prescribed fee and any other information required by the Commission. If the Commission is satisfied that the loss or defacement of the original certificate of registration was not tainted with fraud or negligence, it will issue a replacement certificate of registration, which will be endorsed with the word 'DUPLICATE' (Regulation 20). The Commission may also issue a certified true copy of the certificate of registration on the application of the REEM and upon the payment of the prescribed fee (Regulation 21).

228. There are provisions relating to offences under the Regulations. Anybody who commits any of the offences mentioned above shall be liable to a maximum fine of MYR 5,000 or maximum imprisonment for a term of one year or both upon conviction (Regulation 22).

229. A general proviso to so many provisions in the Regulations is given here. It is observed that so many applications, notices or conditions to be fulfilled are replete in the Regulations. So, in order to ease the processes and procedures, a person affected in any notice issued by the Commission or a condition required to be fulfilled may request for an extension of time in writing. The Commission will grant such application for extension of time as it deems fit (Regulation 23). This proviso is very important considering the seriousness of the previous provision on the offences under the Regulations.

230. The notices mentioned in the Regulations may be served personally or through registered post. Service is deemed to have been effected in the case of a registered post on the day succeeding the day on which the notice would have been received in the ordinary course of post if it is addressed to that registered office in the case of a company, partnership or body of persons having a registered office in Malaysia. If the registered office is not in Malaysia, then if it is addressed to any registered office of the company, partnership or body of persons wherever that office may be; or to the principal place of business or other activity of the company, partnership or body of persons wherever that place may be situated; or to any individual authorized to accept service of the notice. If such addressee is an individual, it will be deemed to have been delivered if such is addressed to his/her last known address as contained in the register (Regulation 24).

Chapter 4. Case Law on the Electricity Supply Act 1990

§1. General

231. Under the Electricity Supply Act 1990 there are important cases under sections 11, 13, 16, 37, 38 and 56. Under the Electricity Supply Regulations, cases are generally there in Regulations 22 and 23. In this chapter, some important cases will be discussed. There are some cases under the old law, the Electricity Regulations of 1951 and the Electricity Act of 1949. Important ones among them will also be discussed. Some cases are there on torts of negligence and trespass. A brief account of those cases will also be given.

§2. Cases

I. *Ong See Teong & Anor v. Tenaga Nasional Bhd* [2008] 5 MLJ 717

232. In this case, the applicant sought judicial review of the respondent's decision dated 21 June 2007, pursuant to notice issued under section 13 of the Electricity Supply Act 1990, whereby the respondent sought to, *inter alia*, enter into the lands belonging to or occupied by the applicants: (i) to carry out works to upgrade the distribution supply lines and to lay and place supply lines within the areas where posts had been erected and to construct and to reserve a five-foot pathway for the inspection of the said lines; (ii) to use the existing access road and lanes for the construction and completion of all of the above works; and (iii) to carry out maintenance, repairs and upgrading of the electrical installation from time to time. In or about 2005, the respondent began upgrading its transmission line in the central area of the peninsular Malaysia, as part of its long-term plan to enhance the electricity supply system under the Central Area Reinforcement Project ('the CAR project'). It was meant to prevent the recurrence of the massive electricity supply disruption of 13 January 2005, which had caused huge damages and losses to the country. The applicants' ground was that: (i) the impugned decision was illegal for both procedure ultra vires and substantive ultra vires since section 13 of the Electricity Supply Act was not applicable for work involved for the CAR project and as such the respondent did not have the power to proceed with the work over the applicants' lands; (ii) the respondent had failed to take into consideration relevant matters and/or had taken into consideration irrelevant matters in making the impugned decision; (iii) the respondent in deciding to proceed work on the applicants' lands had acted in a manner a reasonable body charged with the same functions and responsibility would not have done; (iv) the respondent failed to take into consideration the proportionality and effect of its decision to the extent that monetary means could not compensate the applicants adequately in them not proceeding with the proposed alternative route. The facts disputed, among others, were: the proper location or a boundary of the existing posts; the existence of the wayleave granted by the state authority; and the viability of the alternative route proposed by the applicants. The applicants averred that section 56 of the Electricity Supply Act 1949 ('1949 Act') required wayleave agreement to be endorsed on the issue document of title. In the absence of such endorsement, it was said, there was no wayleave agreement. The applicants argued that the respondent had not issued the required section 11 notice of the Electricity Supply Act and therefore could not proceed under section 13 of the Electricity Supply Act.

233. Wan Afrah J. dismissing the application held that the grounds advocated by the applicants were too general in nature lacking the necessary precision. It was insufficient for the applicants to state merely that the exercise by the respondent was illegal, unreasonable or other commonly acceptable grounds without linking to the specific or particular facts alleged. The court was not duty bound to fill in the gaps left open by the applicants. Therefore, based on the facts, while there remained doubts as to the proper boundary and location of the existing pots, it was however patently clear that at all material time the lands were under the status of state land from 1950s until the alienation of the lands to the applicants in the 1980s. The applicants did not dispute the fact that the existing posts had been erected as early as around 1974–1975. On this premise, this was consistent with the respondent's averment that LLN (the respondent's predecessor in title) was allowed by the state government to enter into the said state land for the purpose of installing and carrying its transmission lines. It was self-evident from the unequivocal wording of section 52 of the 1949 Act that there was no requirement for the land authority to endorse any wayleave granted pursuant to this section. In fact, this court was ready to find that there was no mention of any wayleave in this provision at all. All that was required from the respondent was to secure the approval from the land authority for the installation of posts upon the state land. Thus, there was no support in the applicant's contention that the section 13 notice was bad as there was no wayleave agreement endorsed on the applicant's issue document of titles when the lands were alienated to them in 1980s.

234. The judge further held that the applicants took no steps since 1985 to object or to resort to section 55(5) of the 1949 Act to have the existing posts removed from the current locations. As such, the applicants could not now dispute the very existence of the posts upon their lands. The wording of section 13 is clear; the exercise of the respondent was only conditioned for the purpose of maintaining, repairing or upgrading any license installation or any part thereof. In the absence of any conclusive evidence tendered by the applicants showing otherwise, the court was left with no room but to accept that the current posts were installed validly. In this premise, the natural conclusion would be that the issuance of section 13 notice was perfectly within the procedure envisaged for its current purpose of upgrading the transmission line from 33kV to 275kV. The report prepared by the chief engineer of the respondent clearly showed that the feasibility of the alternative route had been considered in detail and it had been rejected based on well-reasoned rationales. It was suffice to mention the major technical hindrance associated with the alternative route, as highlighted in the report, which included dismantling the existing transmission lines for considerably long period that might result in power outage, and delay occasioned in event to proceed on with the alternative route. In asserting whether public interest outweighed the applicant's private interest the court was mindful of the main objective of the CAR project which was to prevent the disruption of electricity supply. The scale of justice weighted in favour of the public interest in the construction of the electricity transmission and distribution system in the instance case. The applicants were not without any remedy as claimed. The remedy was in the form of monetary compensation. The court therefore dismissed the application for judicial review on the foregoing grounds.

II. *Tenaga Nasional Bhd v. Teobros Development Sdn Bhd* [2008] 6 MLJ 391

235. The appellant in this case is a public listed company licensed to supply electricity under the Electricity Supply Act 1990 ('the Act'). In order to carry out the business of supplying electricity the appellant has the right to enter private land to erect pylons for its electricity transmission lines provided it complies strictly with the requirements of the Act. Alternatively the appellant has the right to choose to acquire the land, whereon it wants to erect the pylons, permanently by resorting to the Land Acquisitions Act 1960 ('the LAA'). The respondent purchased six lots of land at a public auction held at the Malacca High Court. According to the respondent the register documents of titles of the six lots of land showed no endorsements at all of any right of entry of the appellant. Furthermore, a director of the respondent company gave affidavit evidence that the land title searches carried out prior to the auction revealed that there were endorsements of land acquisition in respect of three of the six lots of the land but upon enquiries being made it was learnt that they were minor acquisitions for the purpose of road widening. When the respondent later drew plans to convert the six lots of land into a housing estate they made enquiries at the appellant's office about the future supply of electricity for the new housing estate. The appellant then disclosed their plans to construct electricity pylons across three of the six lots of land (the lands) purchased by the respondent. It was only then that the respondent learnt that the appellant had issued a notice under section 11(2) of the Act to the previous owner of the lands and therefore possessed a wayleave right over the lands and was by virtue of this right a licensee of the lands.

236. Upon this discovery the respondent applied to the High Court for, *inter alia*, declarations which would have the effect of annulling whatever rights the appellant had to enter the lands. At the same time the respondent applied for an interlocutory injunction to preserve the status quo pending the disposal of the respondent's substantive claim and/or some directions or orders to be issued to the appellant by the State Authority of Malacca. The respondent's substantive claim against the appellant centred on the appellant's failure to comply with section 11(10) of the Act. The respondent cited that under section 11(4) of the Act if the owner or occupier of the land chooses to object to the section 11(2) notice then the objection may be made to the District Land Administrator either verbally or in writing. Since an objection could have been lodged by the owner verbally, it became necessary for the appellant licensee to comply with section 11(10) of the Act that is to obtain a written statement from the district land administrator stating that no objection had been lodged by the owner or occupier. The appellant's stand at the High Court was that they had an absolute right to enter the respondent's land and that the search results were in their view immaterial. The High Court judge after reading and examining the whole of section 11 of the Act, and in particular section 11(10) of the Act, granted the interlocutory injunction. In this appeal against that decision, the appellant submitted that the High Court judge erred in dealing with section 11(10) of the Act at length and that, in any case, the appellant's duty to comply with section 11(10) of the Act was directory and not mandatory. The appellant also faulted the High Court judge for failing to consider section 11(5) of the Act which had allegedly created a perpetual right of entry for the appellant. In addition the appellant submitted both orally and in its written submission that as a 'public authority' it ought to be regarded favourably by the court.

237. The Court of Appeal, dismissing the appeal with costs, held that the identity of the parties in any case is not a factor that will influence the court in its decision-making process. Judgments will be rendered according to the facts and the law and not influenced by whether the appellant is the government or a government-linked company. In short it is the law and justice of the case that matters. The court added that if the High Court judge was not supposed to consider and construe section 11(10) of the Act, how could he/she consider and construe section 11(5) of the Act in isolation. Section 11(5) of the Act had to be viewed in its correct perspective because on its own it did not create any right of entry for the appellant. Section 11 and its ten subsections were legislatively enacted to provide a mechanism for a licensee under the Act to obtain a right to enter land to construct electricity pylons and/or lay electricity cables, to protect the rights of the owners and occupiers of the land who are affected by such a right of entry and to ensure that the endorsement of the register document of title of the affected land by giving notice to those who conduct a title search in the future. Although the process starts with the licensee issuing a notice under section 11(2) of the Act to the owner or occupier, for the notice under section 11(2) of the Act to create any right of entry under section 11(5) of the Act, the licensee must first obtain a statement from the District Land Administrator stating that there was no objection lodged by the owner or occupier. If there is any objection lodged by the owner or occupier of the land then section 11(5) of the Act does not create any right of entry at all. This is because the effect of a notice under section 11(2) of the Act is completely nullified even if there was a verbal objection lodged by an occupier. Therefore the High Court judge had exercised his discretion judiciously in finding that the respondent had a bona fide serious issue to be tried as to whether a licensee could be said to acquire rights under section 11(5) of the Act without complying with section 11(10).

238. The court added that it is now trite law that the failure to endorse on the register document of title was fatal. Therefore this again showed that there were serious bona fide issues for the High Court to consider and it followed the decision in *Pow Hing & Anor v. Registrar of Titles, Malacca* [1981] 1 MLJ 155. Furthermore, the issue of whether there was negligence on the part of the appellant for not entering the respondent's land for the last ten years and nine months after issuing the notice under section 11(2) of the Act and whether the doctrine of estoppel could be correctly invoked against the appellant in these circumstances were substantive observations for the High Court to consider and not be considered in an interlocutory application. However, the court observed that the totality of the facts disclosed yet another bona fide serious issue to be tried. Although the provision of electricity by the appellant is definitely a public purpose activity, this public purpose is not intended to grant blanket immunity to all licensees under the Act. The public purpose factor is intended to literally put the interest of the public above other considerations. At this point, the court considered if 'public purpose' could be used as a shield by the appellant to avoid the consequences of failing to comply with an important provision of the Act that is section 11(10) of the Act. At the same time it is necessary to bear in mind that non-compliance with section 11(10) of the Act defeats the conclusiveness of the register document of title. The fact remains that the National Land Code is based on the Torrens system of conclusiveness of the register document of title. Therefore the respondent who had purchased the land from an auction held in the Malacca High Court and not from the previous registered proprietor and who was on the balance of probabilities a bona fide purchaser for value of the lands was entitled to presume that there was no error in the register document of title. In addition, the appellant's failure to comply with section 11(10) of the Act had nothing to do with the public purpose of providing electricity. Thus, based on the facts, the court observed that it was only fair and reasonable to conclude that a licensee under the Act, such as the appellant, was entitled to invoke public purpose only when it concerned their public purpose function of supplying electricity. Otherwise it would be tantamount to granting the appellant absolute immunity to ignore the provisions of the Act, which had been carefully drafted to protect the interests of the public.

239. On the issue of adequacy of damages, the court held that the justice of the case took precedence and where there was any doubt as to the adequacy of the remedy of damages, it was incumbent upon the court to regard damages as an inadequate remedy and move on to consider the question of the balance of convenience and thereafter take whichever course that appears to carry the lower risk of injustice. The respondent in the present case being an innocent purchaser who relied on a search of the register document of title to purchase the lands from a public auction could not have known of the notice under section 11(2) of the Act issued by the appellant some ten years and nine months earlier. In addition there was further evidence that it was not impossible for the appellant to realign the proposed transmission line but for the costs. Although no ruling regarding any realignment of the transmission line could be made in this application, this factor was relevant in considering where the justice of the case lies and whether the status quo should be preserved while awaiting the substantive judgment to be made by the High Court. For such reasons, it was decided that the exercise of the discretion by the High Court judge ought not to be disturbed and the interlocutory injunction should therefore be maintained following the decision in *Alor Janggus Soon Seng Trading Sdn Bhd & Ors v. Sey Hoe Sdn Bhd & Ors* [1995] 1 MLJ 241.

III. *Claybricks & Tiles Sdn Bhd v. Tenaga Nasional Bhd* [2007] 1 MLJ 217

240. On 7 December 2004, the respondent issued a letter to the appellant claiming that the installation of the electric meter at the business premises of the appellant was tempered and called the appellant to its (respondent's) office for explanation. During the discussion at the respondent's office, the appellant was informed that a check was carried out by the respondent and it was found that the electric meter which had been installed was not functioning well and the appellant was required to pay MYR 1,723,304.17, that is 30% loss calculated from the month of January 2001. The appellant questioned the basis of the respondent's claim. On 12 May 2005, the respondent issued a notice of discontinuance of the supply of electricity and the appellant was given a duration until 23 May 2005 to settle the said sum, failing which the supply of electricity would be cut off on 24 May 2005. The appellant sent its letter in reply dated 17 May 2005 and they also attended discussion held at the respondent's office on 18 May 2005. Later, the appellant was informed that the supply of electricity to the said premises would be cut off. The appellant then filed a claim in the High Court against respondent. The appellant also vide its summons in chamber prayed for an ex parte injunction order to be granted to prevent the respondent or its agent from cutting off the supply of electricity to the appellant's premises. The High Court allowed the appellant's application and ordered an ex parte injunction issued. The High Court then fixed a date for the application to be heard inter parte. After hearing the submission of both parties, the High Court dismissed the appellant's application and set aside the ex parte injunction order. The High Court was of the view that there was no issue to be tried as section 38(1) Electricity Supply Act 1990 ('the Act') gives full interim rights to the respondent to cut off the electricity supply and the appellant has other remedies available to it against the respondent if the disconnection was mala fide. This is an application by the appellant for an Erinford injunction to prevent the respondent or its agent from cutting off the electricity supply to the appellant's premises pending the hearing of the appeal made by the appellant against the decision of the High Court.

241. Dismissing the application, the court held that section 38(1) of the Act does not require the offence to be proven before the Court prior to an action is taken to cut off the electricity supply by TNB; *Tan Yeong Kim v. Tenaga Nasional Berhad* [2000] 8 CLJ 629; [2000] MLJU 447 followed and *Dai-Ichi Electronics (M) Sdn Bhd v. Tenaga Nasional Bhd* [1996] 4 MLJ 506 not followed. If the proving of guilt process by the court is required, it will take a long time before the power under section 38(1) of the Act could be exercised. Section 38(1) of the Act is specifically provided to safeguard the interest of the respondent and to enable the respondent to act expediently to prevent abuse such as stealing the electricity supplied by the respondent. If the legislative body intended that the offence is to be proven before the court is required before the power under section 38(1) of the Act could be exercised, it has to make a clear provision. However, there was no such provision made. The interpretation submitted by the appellant could not be accepted because if the court did so by inserting its own words to be used in the Act, it would be against all the principles of statutory interpretation. The court emphasized that with regards to the claim of the appellant that the respondent was acting mala fide in its process of cutting off the electricity supply and the written statement produced by the respondent for the loss of revenue amounting to MYR 1,723,304.17 which was claimed by the appellant as inaccurate and is disputed, the court was of the view that these issues even if they have merits must be raised by the appellant in the different forum or cause of action. The appellant could not question the power granted to the respondent with regards to the discontinuance of the electricity supply and further, the power of the respondent to claim payments imposed on the appellant when the respondent made the re-calculation on the actual total usage of electricity. The appellant was bound by the conditions as contained in the supply contract executed between the appellant and the respondent whereby the appellant must comply with the terms contained therein, the Act and the regulations made thereunder.

IV. *Tenaga Nasional Bhd v. Teck See Plastic Sdn Bhd* [2007] 5 MLJ 430

242. On 15 August 1990, the plaintiff installed a meter at the defendant's factory to record the electricity consumed by the factory. On 11 July 1996, the plaintiff discovered that the meter installed was faulty which caused the meter to record lesser units of electricity consumed at the defendant's factory. The plaintiff had all this while billed the defendant monthly and the defendant had duly paid the bills. The plaintiff had made an estimate loss calculation of MYR 2,270,209.70 for the said irregularities of the meter for the period from September 1990 to August 1996 and demanded the same from the defendant. The defendant contended that the plaintiff was formerly known as Lembaga Letrik Negara Tanah Melayu, a statutory body incorporated under section 3 of the Electricity Act 1949. The Electricity Act 1949 was repealed and replaced by the Electricity Supply Act 1990. The plaintiff thereon was no longer a statutory body. The defendants said the plaintiff ought to have known that the defendant would price the manufactured products for sale to its customers by taking into account the cost of electricity consumed in the manufacture of the products. It would not be equitable to burden the defendant with the alleged loss suffered by the plaintiff. The defendant admits there were irregularities in the metering system but that these irregularities were caused by the negligence of the servants or agents of the plaintiff who had changed the metering system by installing a meter system which was defective. The plaintiff was also time-barred under section 6 Limitation Act 1953. The main issues for determination were: (i) whether it was right at law that the defendant should burden the loss of MYR 2,270,209.70 as a result of using electricity which have already been sold and delivered; (ii) whether the plaintiff was entitled to claim from the defendant for an alleged 'under billed' electricity consumption due to the wrongful installation of the meter by the plaintiff's servants/agents at the defendant's premises; and (iii) whether the plaintiff's claim was time-barred.

243. The court held, allowing the plaintiff's claim, that LLN was entitled to claim from the consumer any amount undercharged for electricity energy supplied notwithstanding that the undercharging was due to error or mistake by LLN and/or its agent/servant (see *Public Textiles Berhad v. Lembaga Letrik Negara* [1976] 2

MLJ 58). The Electricity Supply Act 1990 (Act 447) and the Electricity Supply (Successor Company) Act 1990 both came into force on 1 September 1990. All rights and liabilities to which LLN is entitled to or subject to immediately before 1 September 1990 arising from the contract were transferred to the plaintiff. Thus the right enjoyed by LLN under the laws of Malaysia immediately prior to 1 September 1990 was vested in the plaintiff by virtue of section 3 of the Electric Supply (Successor Company) Act 1990. Therefore it was right at law that the defendant should burden the loss of MYR 2,270,209.70 as a result of using electricity, which had already been sold and delivered. Furthermore, the Licensee Supply Regulations 1990 (the Regulations) permits the plaintiff to raise a claim against the defendant for the amount undercharged for the supply of electrical energy as stated in a similar unreported High Court case of *Hock Seng Company Sdn Bhd v. Tenaga Nasional Berhad* [2000] MLJU 571. It must however be noted that the amended Regulation 11(2) of the Regulations only allowed undercharging of not more than three months from the date the consumer had been informed about being undercharged which came into force only on 15 December 2002 after this suit was filed and hence after the present cause of action arose. The amendment should be construed as a prospective and not retrospective provision. It was therefore clear that, at the time of breaches complained by the plaintiff, the earlier rule would still be applicable. The date which the plaintiff's cause of action accrued was on the date when the defendant denied liability (see *Tan Boon Yen dan Lain-Lain lwn Maybank General Assurance Bhd* [2003] 5 MLJ 315). According to the defendant the breach accrued in September 1990 from which date the plaintiff claimed for the alleged under billed amount. Nevertheless, this was not the date when the breach occurred but rather when the damage occurred. The court opined that the breach occurred on 12 June 1998 when the defendant's solicitors informed the plaintiff's solicitors that the defendant was denying liability to pay the undercharged sum. Since the action was filed by the plaintiff on 5 September 1998, the action was not time-barred.

V. *Karupasamy a/l Silliah and Others v. Tenaga Nasional Bhd* [2006] 3 MLJ 347

244. In this case, the plaintiff applied for an order for an interim injunction to be granted specifically to the defendant himself, his workers or representatives to reconnect the electricity supply to the plaintiff's premises as well as to prohibit the defendant himself, his workers or his representatives from disconnecting the electricity supply to the plaintiff's premises. In addition to that, there were five other relieves sought by the plaintiff against the defendant. The plaintiff's application was heard by the earlier judge and an ex parte application was made pursuant to O 29 r 2A of the Rules of the High Court 1980. This case is an inter parte hearing for an injunction order application.

245. The court having examined the position of this case as a whole, examined the contents of the affidavits which were filed whether by the plaintiff or by the defendant, had decided that in this claim there were no serious contentious issues which required a determination to be made in trial. In this matter, there was only one question of importance which needed to be determined here, which was the interpretation of section 38(1) of the Electricity Supply Act 1990 (Act 447). The provision of this section does not require the proof of an offence as a precondition before a disconnection is made by TNB as the license holder. The section is not required until an offence is firstly proved by the court before the exercise of the power to determine the disconnection is carried out. This power is given by parliament only to protect TNB as the electricity supplier, from not bearing any prolonged and continuous losses from all activities, which are not allowed. The power to charge for the offence is clearly contained in the said Act and there is no particular fixed period depending on TNB. However, it is not a condition that the offence in the court must be proved first before TNB is able to carry out the disconnecting power. The wording in section 38(1) of the said Act is clear and therefore should be given a normal and literal interpretation. The plaintiff cannot use the excuse in relation to the business' goodwill and the effect on the business in the event the electricity supply is disconnected as the issue that needs to be considered. Questions, which are private in nature, should not be made the basis of recourse in law. From the point of balance of convenience as well, it is found that the balance of convenience is in favour of the defendant for the order of interlocutory default not to be issued.

VI. *Tenaga Nasional Bhd v. Calsonic Compressor (M) Sdn Bhd* [2009] 8 MLJ 793

246. On 27 November 2001, the plaintiff and the defendant entered into an electricity supply agreement. On 26 October 2004, the defendant applied for an increase in the supply of electricity to its premises. When the plaintiff's representative visited the defendant's premises on 2 November 2004, pursuant to the defendant's request for an increase in its electricity supply, it was discovered that the original meter installed by the plaintiff had not been recording the actual unit of usage of electricity. On the same day, the original defective meter was replaced with a new meter and the defendant was billed for the correct sum of charges from that date that is from 2 November 2004. These bills were duly settled by the defendant. On 28 March 2005, the plaintiff served on the defendant a notice informing the latter of the defect in the original meter installed by it and claimed MYR 2,110,792.53, which was the undercharged sum for the electricity supplied to the defendant. By way of a letter dated 14 April 2005, the defendant refuted the plaintiff's claim. The plaintiff vide a letter dated 8 June 2005 amended the sum claimed to MYR 316,144.22, based on a purported calculation of the bills for the months of August, September and October 2004. The defendant again refuted its liability to make such payments. The dispute was referred to the Energy Commission, which under section 30 of the Electricity Supply Act 1990 was conferred with the power to hear disputes between the plaintiff as the licensee and its customers. After hearing both the plaintiff and the defendant, the Commission found that the plaintiff was not entitled to claim the sum of MYR 316,411.22 from the defendant. The Commission's decision was based on the provisions of law that provided that the plaintiff could only claim for an undercharged sum for the period of three months from the date the defendant was notified of the said undercharged sum. Since the defendant had settled all its electricity bills after the installation of the new meter on 2 November 2004 until the date the defendant received the plaintiff's notice of claim, dated 28 March 2005 on 12 April 2005, there was no undercharged sum for the period of three months that is for the period of 12 January 2005 to 12 April 2005. The decision of the commission was conveyed to the plaintiff and defendant by way of a letter dated 8 November 2005.

247. However, vide a letter dated 24 January 2007, the plaintiff once again claimed for the sum of MYR 316,411.22 from the defendant and thereafter on 24 January 2007 demanded the sum of MYR 2,110,792.53. On 28 July 2007, the plaintiff filed a writ of summons and statement of claim for the sum of MYR 2,110,792.53 against the defendant. The defendant filed its defence. This was an application under O 18 r 19(1) of the Rules of the High Court 1980 by the defendant to strike out the plaintiff's writ and statement of claim. At the hearing of this application, the plaintiff submitted that it was not appropriate for the court to consider the application to strike out the claim because there were serious and bona fide issues, which merited a trial in this case. One of the issues for determination raised by the plaintiff was whether the plaintiff was entitled to claim from the defendant for alleged undercharging for electricity consumption due to the wrongful installation of the meter by the plaintiff's servants and/or agents in the defendant's premises. The plaintiff further submitted that the dispute relating to the undercharging of electricity did not fall under the jurisdiction of the Commission and that the latter did not have the authority to decide on the dispute brought before it by the defendant. In addition, the plaintiff submitted that the Commission's decision was not binding upon the parties because the Commission had acted in excess of its function and powers.

248. The court, allowing the defendant's application with costs, held that there is a plethora of weighty authorities to say that 'where the issue raised is one of the laws and it is clear-cut and can be decided upon, the judge hearing it should decide on it rather than let it go to trial'. In this case, having carefully scrutinized the facts of the case, it was clear that the sole dispute involved a question of statutory interpretation. The question of law to be resolved was whether the plaintiff's claim should rightfully come under subregulation 11(2) of the Licensee Supply Regulations 1990 ('the Regulations'). As the interpretation of a statute and its application to undisputed facts are questions of law, it should be decided without the rigmarole of a full trial. Applying subregulation 11(2) of the Regulations to the instant case, the reading of the consumer's meter shall be prima facie evidence of the amount of electricity consumed. As the plaintiff had referred to its conduct in wrongfully programming the original meter installed at the defendant's premises as a mistake, that is an incorrect meter reading for the purposes of subregulation 11(2), it could be concluded that under the Regulations, the plaintiff had a right to claim against the defendant for the amount undercharged for the supply of electricity. However, the amended subregulation 11(2) only allows undercharging of not more than three months from the date the defendant had been informed about being undercharged. As the defendant in this case was only informed of the undercharging on 12 April

2005, the plaintiff was only entitled to claim for the undercharged sum from the period 12 January 2005 to 12 April 2005. However, since the meter had been replaced since 2 November 2004 and the correct sum of charges had been billed to the defendant and duly settled by the defendant since that date, the plaintiff's claim for MYR 2,110,792.53 against the defendant was misconceived in law and unsustainable.

249. As the commission was established by the statute, that is the Energy Commission Act 2001, it is settled law that the commission's powers, duties and authority are only those conferred expressly or impliedly by statute. Under section 14(1)(d) and (e) of the Energy Commission Act 2001, the commission is empowered to regulate all matters relating to the electricity supply industry. The dispute in the present case is regarding 'meter inaccuracy' or 'incorrect meter reading' and related to the supply of electricity. Hence the Energy Commission was conferred with the jurisdiction to hear the dispute and any party to the dispute may refer the dispute to the commission. Therefore, the contention by the plaintiff that disputes relating to the undercharging of electricity under subregulation 11(2) of the Regulations did not fall within the Act was misplaced given the clear provision of the Act. Further, the commission clearly stated its determination of the dispute was in accordance to section 30 of the Act and its interpretation should be accorded great weight deference. This is called the 'doctrine of operative construction'. The decision of the Commission was correctly decided and not ultra vires as contended by the plaintiff. The plaintiff's attempt in contending that the Commission's decision was ultra vires would appear to be an afterthought. The plaintiff should be estopped from asserting that the Commission's decision was not binding on the plaintiff. In the instant case, estoppel by silence arose because the plaintiff had the opportunity to make a challenge to the jurisdiction of the Commission but refrained from doing so, thereby leading the defendant to believe in an erroneous state of facts. Further, the plaintiff did not make any contemporaneous challenge as to the jurisdiction and authority of the Commission by way of judicial review. There was no doubt that the decision complained of fell within the public law sphere and therefore judicial review laid against the Commission. However, the plaintiff having realized that it was out of time to file a judicial review on the decision of the Commission was now seeking to invalidate that decision in these proceedings which was not permissible. Only in a judicial review can it be determined whether the decision of the Commission was ultra vires of the Act but as the plaintiff had failed to do so, it was now precluded from raising that issue.

VII. *Everhome Furniture Manufacturing (M) Sdn Bhd v. Tenaga Nasional Bhd* [2009] MLJ 715

250. In this case, the defendant's investigation team inspected the installation of the electricity at the plaintiff's premises and found that there had been tampering which had caused the calculation of the use of electricity by the plaintiff to be lesser than the actual use. Thus, the defendant had sent to the plaintiff a back billing for the amount of MYR 114,096.66 and MYR 253,138.54 that is being cost of use of electricity that had not been recorded in the meter reading due to the tampering by the plaintiff on the installation. The plaintiff thereafter commenced this proceedings against the defendant and sought the orders: (i) that the defendant deduct the sum of MYR 114,094.66 and MYR 253,138.54 from the plaintiff's bill; (ii) that the electricity supply at the plaintiff's premises not disconnected by the defendant; and (iii) for the damages suffered by the plaintiff due to the defendant's actions. The defendant had counterclaimed for the back-billing sums as well as the operational cost and the cost of repairing the meter reading.

251. The court held, dismissing the plaintiff's claim with costs and allowing the defendant's counterclaim with costs, that there was no direct proof given as to why the plaintiff should not pay the defendant's claim with regards to the back billing. Whereas, the evidence showed that there were tampering to the meter reading, which had caused error. The meter reading recorded lesser usage of electricity than the actual use of electricity by the plaintiff. The back billing that had been prepared was done according to the procedure stipulated by TNB.

VIII. *Ong See Teong & Anor v. Tenaga Nasional Bhd* [2009] 5 MLJ 85

252. The appellants and other residents of Kampung Sungai Terentang were occupying a piece of land as licensees. Subsequently, most of the residents were issued with titles to their land. The respondent undertook upgrading exercise as part of long-term plan to enhance the electricity supply system under a project known as CAR. The appellants objected to the alleged upgrading work and argued that a notice under section 13 of the Electricity Supply Act 1990 was inapplicable for the anticipated work. The respondent had intended to construct within the appellants' land a main supply line, five-foot pathway reserved for inspection of the supply line, the use of existing roads and lane to carry out upgrading work and to carry out maintenance and related works when necessary. The appellants applied for a judicial review in respect to the respondent's decision, which came in the form of notice issued by the respondent under section 13 of the Act. The appellants alleged that the notice did not merely permit the respondent to carry out and complete the proposed upgrading work as the respondent ought to take into consideration the rule of proportionality and effect of the upgrading work towards the appellants. The appellants also argued that the respondent had also failed to take into consideration an alternative route. The learned High Court judge in dismissing the appellants' application concluded, *inter alia*, (i) that entry to the piece of the appellants' land for carrying out the installation works depended on the existence of posts that had been lawfully erected earlier; (ii) that public interest to prevent nationwide electricity disruption outweighed the private interest of the appellants; and (iii) that new grounds were raised which were not pleaded by the appellants in their statement. Further, the learned High Court judge opined that the intended work by the respondent was for the purpose of maintaining, repairing or upgrading any installation on the piece of land, hence the notice fell correctly within the procedure and purpose of section 13 of the Act. Prior to the appeal the respondent had consented that the appellants could use fresh evidence for the appeal and file a supplementary record of appeal.

253. The court held, allowing the appeal with costs here and court below, that the government had in the interest of the appellants and twenty-three other residents of Kampung Sungai Terentang (the affected residents) suggested either to undertake acquisition of the said piece of land or to consider alternative routes. However, the respondent irrationally and unreasonably persisted to enforce the notice issued under section 13 of the Act. The factual evidence conspicuously revealed the irrationality of not acquiring the lands involved. Evidence adduced also confirmed the negative medical effect on people, especially children who are more susceptible to leukaemia and like diseases, when bombarded by the flow of electricity passing over the affected residents' houses. Despite these hazardous life-threatening factors, the respondent argued that adequate monetary compensation would be given to the affected residents for their discomfort. The subtle and unconscionable way of driving and depriving the affected residents of their properties were in effect an acquisition of their land by the respondent (a power exercisable only by the state authority), which would contravene their constitutional rights (Article 13 of the Federal Constitution). With a mega project in the offing, the affected residents would witness a major emplacement of the transmission lines together with the structures holding them and affecting the area involved directly. The respondent's upgrading works could not be construed as an exercise to repair and maintain the existing part in the ordinary sense when the new superstructures would radically and fundamentally alter the landscape and become permanent features. The respondent's argument that public interest must override the grievances of the appellants and the affected residents would be trampling over a minority's rights, though in certain circumstances may be acceptable, sounds hollow when there were other alternative ways to solve the problem. Although the appellants' pleadings did not state anything about the notice pursuant to section 13 of the Act suffering errors of law, it is trite that courts are more concerned with the justice of a matter rather than being overly concerned with format or procedure. The court concluded that the respondent was not at any juncture caught flatfooted or prevented from replying the issues that were not pleaded; thus, the respondent's submission of being caught unaware and unprepared was without merit.

IX. *Tenaga Nasional Bhd v. Trans Resources Corp Sdn Bhd & Anor* [2009] 5 MLJ 673

254. The plaintiff alleged that an electrical installation belonging to it, viz. a 33-kV electricity cable, was damaged due to construction piling work carried out by the defendants. The plaintiff sued the defendants in the High Court to recover compensation for consequential losses. On the day of the trial, counsel for the defendants informed the judicial commissioner ('JC') that he had instructions to cease representing the defendants and had that very morning filed an application to discharge himself as counsel. He sought a stay and/or adjournment for the defendants to engage a new counsel. The learned JC, having considered all relevant circumstances, refused to stay and/or adjourn the hearing. Counsel then informed the JC that he could not participate in the trial and that the trial would proceed in the absence of the defendants and/or their agents. However, counsel remained in court to listen to the proceedings but refused to cross-examine witnesses for the plaintiff when invited by the JC to do so. The issue for the High Court was whether the plaintiff had proved its case; that is, whether the defendants were in fact responsible for the damage caused to the plaintiff's cable.

255. The court held, allowing the plaintiff's claim with costs, that the witnesses for the plaintiff testified that the defendants were the only contractors working at the site where the cable was damaged at the material time. This was evidenced by heavy machinery and lorries belonging to the defendants at that site. Further, the defendants had by letter informed several parties, including the plaintiff, that it would be carrying out piling works at the site. The plaintiff had even responded by letter to the defendants' consultant suggesting measures to protect the plaintiff's 33-kV cable. Section 41(1) of the Electricity Supply Act 1990 imposes strict liability on anyone who causes damage to any installation belonging to the plaintiff. This is made clear by the words 'whether wilfully or otherwise'. Thus, once the plaintiff was able to prove that it was the defendants who caused the damage to its installation, the defendants would become liable to compensate the plaintiff for the damage sustained. The defendants were aware of the plaintiff's cable. The act of the defendants in damaging the cable due to their piling works constituted prima facie evidence of negligence. The burden was thus on the defendants to introduce evidence to explain or show that the damage occurred without any negligence on their part. However, there was no such evidence and they even failed to attend the trial. Thus, the court concluded that negligence had been proven on the part of the defendants. They were therefore liable for damages to the plaintiff.

X. *Tenaga Nasional Bhd v. Dolomite Industrial Park Sdn Bhd*, [2000] 1 CLJ 695

256. In this case, respondent brought an action against the appellant for trespass claiming that the appellant had, without lawful authority, constructed a pylon on the respondent's land. The High Court decided in favour of the respondent and granted *inter alia* a declaration that the appellant was not entitled to build the pylon found on the respondent's land and an injunction restraining the appellant from building any pylon on the respondent's land. In the Court of Appeal, the appellant claimed that it had a wayleave agreement and relied on the Electricity Act 1949 and the Electricity Supply Act 1990 to contend that as a result of such an agreement, it was justified in having the pylon on the respondent's land. However, no wayleave agreement was produced by the appellant. There also was no evidence to indicate that the appellant had given notice of its intention to use the area of land in dispute.

257. On this fact, Justice Gopal Sri Ram of the Court of Appeal upholding the High Court's decision ruled:

> Before the Appellant can take advantage of s. 56 of the Electricity Act 1949, it must satisfy s. 53 of the said act, in particular the procedure prescribed by subsections 2, 3 and 4. Unfortunately the Appellant was not able to produce the

> document prescribed by section 53 of the said act. Under these circumstances. ... there was no leave agreement as pleaded by the Appellant.

However, in view of the fact that the pylon was the part of the National Grid for the conveyance of electricity, he ruled that mandatory injunction could not be maintained as it would affect the electricity supply in the peninsular Malaysia, and disruption of electricity supply would not be in the public interest. He held that the public interest in this matter outweighs the respondent's interest.

258. The plea of trespass was accepted. He ordered for award of damages to be assessed by the Senior Assistant Registrar of the High Court.

XI. *Tekali Prospecting Sdn Bhd v. Tenaga Nasional Berhad and 1 Or*, [2002] 1 MLJ 113

259. In this case, on 23 December 2000 the first respondent, a statutory corporation, issued a notice to enter private land belonging to the applicant. This notice was served on 12 January 2001 on the applicant. The notice was said to be issued pursuant to *section 11 of the Electricity Supply Act 1990* which permits for the purpose of installing system of distribution of energy entry into private land by the first respondent as a licensee appointed under the Act in order to lay, place or carry on posts or other equipment as may be necessary or proper for the purposes of the licensed installation, as the case may be, and may take such other action as may be necessary to render the installation safe. The notice required the applicant to remove all buildings and keep clear 7,064 acres of land and stated that the first respondent proposed to construct posts (tiang) or towers (menara). The applicant seeks an order to remove the notice to this Court for the notice to be quashed or alternatively a declaration that the notice is invalid, null and void. The applicant is also seeking a stay of all proceedings pursuant to the said notice. The respondents contend that the 1st respondent has correctly proceeded under *section 11 of the Electricity Supply Act 1990.* They also contend that there is provision in the Electricity Supply Act 1990 to deal with objections and to provide compensation. The applicant contends that section 11 was not intended for a situation such as the present one.

260. It is notable that the notice is said to be issued pursuant to *section 11 of the Electricity Supply Act 1990.* Under *section 11 of the Electricity Supply Act 1990* if an objection is not lodged by the applicant with the land administrator within fourteen days of service of the said section 11 notice, the first respondent can enter the applicant's land for the purpose stated and do all of the acts stated in the notice. *Section 11 of the Electricity Supply Act 1990* provides for payment to the applicant landowner of full compensation for any 'disturbance, damage or disability that may be caused' by the acts done and also provides that such compensation shall include 'an annual payment for land sued for the purpose of the posts (tiang) or other equipment'. *Section 11 of the Electricity Supply Act 1990* permits such a notice to be given for the 'purpose of installing any system of distribution of energy under this Act', and 'a licensee may lay, place or carry on, under or over any land, other than

State land, such posts (tiang) and other equipment as may be necessary or proper for the purposes of the licensed installation, as the case may be, and may take such other action as may be necessary to render the installation safe and efficient'. Before entering the land the licensee is required to give a notice stating as 'fully and accurately as possible the nature and extent of the acts intended to be done'. The first respondent is the 'licensee' under the Electricity Supply Act 1990. The *section 11* notice does not state what is the 'licensed installation' that the acts intended to be done are in aid of, but it appears that the installation is the 'national grid' system. The first respondent sets up a system of distributing and selling electricity to consumers all over Malaysia. Although there was currently no buildings on the land the applicant had applied for planning permission with a view to developing their land into a low-cost and medium-cost housing estate.

261. The High Court held that when there was the Land Acquisition Act 1960, which was the appropriate law, there was no reason to ask the court to extend the provisions of the Electricity Supply Act to accommodate the section 11 notice to carry out the work which is not covered by the section.

262. The Court supports by saying that section 11 is limited to installations of posts and the word 'post' should be limited to normal lampposts. The word 'other equipment' cannot be construed to mean large steel structures called 'menara' or 'tower'. It is notable here that the word 'instrument' has been defined in the definition clause of the Act, which in no way can cover towers. Putting many towers on someone's land will amount to taking possession of the land. Section 11 of the Act is not meant and does not appear to be intended for assuming such power. A land can be acquired under section 19 of the Land Acquisition Act 1990, which provides for entry into the land in urgent cases for land to be used for public purpose. Proper interpretation of Article 13(2) of the Federal Constitution reveals that sections 11 and 16 of the Act were not intended to cover compulsory acquisition or use of land. Thus, the provisions are only intended for the purpose of entry into private land to erect post and provisions for payment of compensation for such specific incursion. It is not intended for construction of towers or large-scale constructions.

XII. *Tenaga Nasional Bhd v. Tekali Prospecting Sdn Bhd,* [2002] 2 MLJ 707

263. Against the decision of the above case, the Tenaga Nasional Bhd. (TNB) went into appeal to the Court of Appeal. Justice Gopal Sri Ram, Abdul Kadir Sulaiman and Alauddine JJ of the Court of Appeal reversed the decision of the High Court for the following reasons: (a) The relevant words in section 11(1) of the Electricity Supply Act 1990 that 'such posts and other equipment as may be necessary or proper for the purposes of the licensed installation' did not confine the appellant as licensee under the Act to merely constructing posts. The expression 'such purposes as transmission' in the definition of the word 'equipment' in section 2 of the Act must *a fortiori* include pylons designed to carry electricity from one point to another point in the country. It can therefore be concluded that the notice given by the TNB was not illegal. (b) When Parliament uses technical words, they must be given their technical meaning (see *DP Vijandran v. Majlis Peguam*, [1995] 3 MLJ 576). (c) The issues such as the inappropriateness of the compensation and the inapplicability of the Act to the case where land had to be set aside were more appropriate for the hearing before the land administration under section 11(6) of the Act. (d) The respondent's fear that the payment of compensation under the Electricity Supply Act will be lower than the payment under the Land Acquisition Act is illusory. Section 11 of the act has made it abundantly clear that 'full compensation in accordance with section 16' will have to be paid to 'all persons interested for any disturbance, damage or disability suffered by them'. (e) This is the purposive approach of interpretation as stated by Lord Griffith in *Pepper v. Hart*, [1993] AC 593. (f) There can be judicial review if the compensation is considered by the party to be inappropriate. The court thus concluded that deprivation of land can be well compensated under the Act itself.

264. The author is of the opinion that the reasons given by the Court of Appeal are realistic. If section 16 of the Act is read with sections 2 and 11, we can draw a conclusion that under section 16 of the Act the landowner can be awarded full compensation. In case he/she thinks that the compensation is not adequate, he/she can apply for judicial review.

265. Upon an alleged discovery that the blue power supply wire and the circuit board seal in the plaintiff's factory had been tampered with, the defendant ('TNB') issued and forwarded to the plaintiff a special bill dated 15 March 1995 for the sum of MYR 247,943.27 and a 'bil rampai' (supplementary bill) dated 16 March 1995 for the sum of MYR 2,000 ('the two bills'). TNB also threatened to cut off the supply of electricity to the plaintiff's factory. This compelled the plaintiff to make 10% payment on the two bills and to arrange for a bank guarantee for MYR 223,148.94 to cover the balance amount in the two bills. The plaintiff thereafter instituted a suit against TNB. Pending the trial of the suit, the plaintiff obtained two interim injunctions ex parte. The present matter before the court was an inter partes application by the plaintiff which prayed for interlocutory injunctions: (a) that TNB be restrained from disconnecting the electrical supply to the plaintiff's factory and (b) that TNB be restrained from demanding the instalment payments on the two bills or to enforce the bank guarantee which was issued by the plaintiff to the defendant on 20 March 1995. Counsel for the plaintiff submitted that there was a serious dispute of fact in this case. However, TNB contended that they were entitled to issue the two bills and to disconnect the supply of electricity to the plaintiff's factory under section 38(1) of the Electricity Supply Act 1990 ('the Act').

266. The High Court granted the injunction order and gave the following reasons for its judgment:

> (1) Though s 38(1) of the Act *ex facie* appears to allow TNB to disconnect power upon giving 24 hours' notice, it is doubted whether the legislature intended to endow 'any person employed by' TNB such drastic and decisive power. Section 38(1) should be read in conjunction with s 38(3) and the phrase 'which in his opinion' cannot be interpreted in isolation from other words in s

38 and other provisions of the Act. The words 'proves that an offence has been committed under s 37(1), (3) and (14)' following the words 'in his opinion' in s 38(1), when read in the light of s 38(3), would indicate that disconnection followed by reconnection of electrical supply are the approved steps that can be carried out by TNB only after the consumer is proved by evidence in the court of law to have committed an offence under s 37(1), (3) or (14). The word 'proves' appearing in s 38(1) envisages proof before a court of law and not before an employee of TNB.

267. Therefore the power envisaged in section 38(1) should be dependent, as its sole basis, on the outcome of court proceedings under sections 37 and 38(5) of the Act. (2) It should be remembered that the legislature had already placed sufficient protection for TNB in the form of civil and criminal remedies under sections 37 and 38(5) of the Act. (3) The fact that TNB finally conceded to the granting of the interlocutory injunction to restrain itself from disconnecting the electricity supply to the plaintiff's factory clearly showed that there were serious questions to be tried and that the balance of convenience lay in favour of the plaintiff. (4) When granting an interlocutory injunction, neither the court nor the parties can impose any extraneous condition other than the condition as to damages, unless of course both parties agree to such extraneous conditions. However, in cases where a plaintiff is resident out of the jurisdiction of the court and it is shown that the plaintiff has no assets within the jurisdiction then the court may order fortification of the undertaking. In the present case, as it had not been contended that the plaintiff had no assets within the court's jurisdiction, the bank guarantee of MYR 223,148.94 should not remain. (The authorities relied are: *Ashtiani v. Kashi,* [1968] 3 WLR 647; *Allen v. Jumbo Holdings Ltd*, [1980] 1 WLR 1252*; Z Ltd v. A*, [1982] 1 All ER 556; and *Third Chandris Corp. v. Unimarine* 1979] 1 QB 645). (5) Defendant thus restrained from disconnecting the supply of electricity to the plaintiff's factory and from demanding instalment payments on the two bills.

268. In this judgment some notable points are: (a) In construing the statutory provisions the courts ought to presume the intention of the parliament for enacting that law. (b) We ought to be mindful that the parliament has already put in place in favour of the utility company, sufficient protection in form of civil and criminal remedies under sections 37 and 38 of the Act.

XIII. *Abdul Ghani Hamid v. Abdul Nasir Abdul Jabbar & Anor.*, [1995] 4 CLJ 317

269. The plaintiff had suffered severe third-degree burns as a result of an explosion that occurred at an electric substation owned and managed by the second defendant, the electric undertaker of the country. The plaintiff sued the defendants and claimed damages for breach of statutory duty contained in Regulations 22 and 23 of the Electricity Supply Regulations 1990 (as it then was) and negligence at common law. At the material time the plaintiff and one Ridzuan were doing service and repair work at the said substation and, while so engaged, were being supervised by the first defendant Nasir, the engineer in charge of the substation. The facts showed that just prior to the explosion, Nasir had directed the plaintiff and Ridzuan to repair some cables in the switch panel of the switch gear room of the station, assuring both of them that it was safe for such works to be carried out. However, unknown to the plaintiff and Ridzuan, electricity was flowing through the cables as the switch cable had not been switched off. The result was that an electrical explosion occurred when the spanner held by Ridzuan came into contact with the live cable. The facts also showed that the defendants had not affixed any warning notices at the entrance of the switch gear room or anywhere near the explosion site.

270. On these facts Justice Dato Hj, Abdul Malik Bin Hj and Ishak decided the case in favour of the plaintiff allowing his petition for breach of statutory duty and ordered for payment of adequate damages for pain and suffering and special damages for loss of earning to him. The following points from the judgment, as noted by the CLJ, are as follows:

(a) The substation is the property of the second defendant and they are responsible to ensure that both the plaintiff and Ridzuan be adequately protected from danger. It is their responsibility as the 'management' to afford such protection as envisaged by Regulation 32(5) of the Electricity Supply Regulations 1990.
(b) The defendants had failed to display the standard warning notices such as the 'danger' signs at the relevant portions of the substation. This was in clear breach of Regulation 22(12)(a) & (b) and Regulation 22(16)(a) & (b) of the Regulations. There was also a blatant disregard of Regulation 32(5) & (7) when the switch cable had not been switched off prior to the repair works. On the evidence the defendants had clearly breached their statutory duty and were negligent in not ensuring that the substation was safe.
(c) In relation to the Electricity Supply Regulations, the defendants' statutory duty can be said to be absolute. In the event, once it has been proved, as the plaintiff herein had, that the duty has not been performed, it becomes actionable without having to prove any lack of care or diligence on the part of the defendants. In the circumstances, the plaintiff's claim must succeed.
(d) The defendants were also liable for negligence at common law. The second defendant, as the undertaker of the electricity and the owner of the substation, owed a duty of care to take reasonable care to avoid acts or omissions, which the second defendant could reasonably foresee, would injure the plaintiff. In the instant case the duty of care arose when Nasir assured both the plaintiff and Ridzuan that the substation was safe, and that duty was breached when the defendants failed to earth the panel and switch off the supply of electricity to the substation. The defendants were negligent in not ensuring that the substation was safe.
(e) There is no merit in the contention that the plaintiff and Ridzuan had undertaken the risk of performing their task with full appreciation of the danger. The plaintiff and Ridzuan could not be said to have voluntarily taken any inherent risk in undertaking the repair work, as they did not know that there was electricity in the substation. On the facts there was just no evidence to show a lack

of reasonable care by the plaintiff for his own safety. As the plaintiff was not part author of his misfortune the defendants must be wholly liable.

(f) The plaintiff had sustained extensive burns on his face, both arms and hands and it went down to the lower limbs. The plaintiff had been unconscious for some eighteen days and there is no doubt that he had suffered tremendously from the severe burns. In the circumstances MYR 120,000 would be a fair award for pain and suffering. As for special damages, a sum of MYR 171,820 encompassing compensation for loss of earnings, future medical expenses and nursing care seems appropriate and reasonable.

(g) Although it is logical that some part of the plaintiff's earnings must have been devoted to his own maintenance, it can only be deducted if the amount is either admitted by the plaintiff or proved by the defendant. Here there is neither admission nor proof, and therefore no deduction would be made from the plaintiff's income.

271. It is noticed that the court followed the widely accepted principle that once it is proved that a particular statutory duty has not been performed, it becomes actionable without having to prove any lack of care or diligence on the part of the person on whom the duty is imposed. In short, what matters is simply to show the non-performance of the act that the statute requires a person to perform, and that non-performance is itself negligence on the part of that person.

XIV. *Lembaga Letrik Negara Tanah Melayu v. Syarikat Klang Electric*, [1974] 1 MLJ 209

272. On 12 September 1968 the Syarikat Klang Electric (respondent) submitted to the Lembaga Letrik Negara, Klang, an application for a license for the installation wiring at premises No. 63 Jalan Kapar, Klang. Later in carrying out this installation work the respondent had to drive in an earth pipe 7 feet long into the ground, 6 inches away from the road-side drain. Subsequently on 31 January 1969 the Lembaga Letrik Negara, Klang, was notified that the work was completed. However, electricity was supplied to the premises only on 14 March 1969.

273. The day before this supply was given, that is on 13 March 1969, Hud bin Daud (PW1), the Assistant Engineer attached to the Lembaga Letrik Negara, Klang, received a phone call of a likely breakdown in the distribution feeder. So he carried out an inspection of the substation at Jalan Kapar and traced the faulty section to be at one of the distribution feeders. After having isolated the faulty section he contacted the Meter Protection Department, Petaling Jaya, for assistance.

274. On the recommendation of the Meter Protection Department, an excavation work was carried out in the presence of PW1 at this site fronting premises No. 63. After the excavation had been done, PW1 noticed that a two-inch galvanized iron pipe connected to a small installation wiring for earthing had penetrated through the brick cover and scraped against the cable sheathing, thus exposing a section of the lead sheet through which water had seeped in and caused the breakdown. As a result 26 yards of the damaged cable had to be replaced.

275. However, it was not until about six months later that the respondent informed the appellant of the damage to the cable by a letter dated 18 September 1969 – P1. In the same letter the appellant informed the respondent that the cost of replacement of the damaged section of the cable was USD 3,390 and demanded payment of this amount. The respondent replied on 22 September 1969 (P2) denying liability. Finally on 5 June 1970, the appellant filed an action for damages against the respondent in the Sessions Court, Klang vide Civil Action No. 48 of 1970. At the trial the appellant alleged that the respondent was vicariously liable in damages because the damage to the cable was caused by and due to the negligence of its servants. Alternatively, the appellant contended that in any case the respondent would be liable under section 88(1) of the Electricity Ordinance No. 30 of 1949 to pay the amount claimed by the appellant.

276. The learned President of the Sessions Court found that the appellant had failed to prove that the respondent knew or ought to have known that the cable had already been laid under the ground when the respondent drove in the pipe and in the circumstances the respondent could not have foreseen the danger. The President of the Sessions Court, therefore, rejected the appellant's allegation of negligence on the part of the respondent. Further, on the alternative claim under section 88(1) of the Electricity Ordinance the President of the Sessions Court found that the respondent had complied with the requirements of the Lembaga Letrik Negara and had exercised the care of a skilled man in doing the operation because the Lembaga Letrik Negara approved the work and connected the supply on 14 March 1969. Similarly, the alternative claim of the appellant was also dismissed by the President of the Sessions Court.

277. The High Court dismissed the appeal for the following reasons:

> For the Appellant to succeed on common law negligence it would be necessary for him to prove that the Respondent owed a duty of care to the Appellant and as a result of the Respondent's failure to exercise that duty of care the Appellant has suffered damage. It is the contention of the Appellant that the failure of the Respondent to consult all the Government Departments before carrying out the works amounted to negligence. However, in the present case the respondent had obtained at least the permission of the Lembaga Letrik Negara, Klang, before carrying out the works and there is no evidence to show that the Respondent had committed any breach of any of the conditions of the licence granting the approval to carry out the works. The damage caused to the cable was not something, which the Respondent could reasonably have foreseen because there was no marker anywhere near the site. Moreover, the Respondent drove the earth pipe 7 feet deep into the ground only after having taken the precaution of digging a hole 3 feet wide and 3 feet deep and finding nothing at that site. In my view the Appellant has failed to prove negligence on the part of the Respondent and the appeal on this ground will therefore fail.

278. In the circumstances, the court held that section 88(1) of the Electricity Ordinance would had to be read within the context of section 75. Since the respondent had obtained the prior permission of the Lembaga Letrik Negara and had taken sufficient precautions before driving in the pipe it is also my view upon reading the two said provisions together that the respondent cannot be liable under section 88(1) to pay compensation for the damage to the cable and therefore the appellant also fails on this ground. The appeal is, therefore, dismissed with costs.

XV. *Jaswant Singh v. Central Electricity Board and Anor*, [1967] 1 MLJ 272

279. The plaintiff sued the defendants for damages arising out of the death of five buffaloes and one dog belonging to him as a result of their being electrocuted by coming into contact with a telephone wire belonging to the second defendants (the Government of Malaysia). The wire had been snapped on the 30 November 1962 and was lying on the ground and resting on top of the aerial electricity lines belonging to the first defendants. It remained so resting till the day of the death of the buffaloes, 3 December 1962. The claim was based on the negligence of the servants of both defendants or alternately the negligence of the servants of one or other of the defendants. In the claim against the first defendants, the plaintiff also alleged breach of statutory duty under Regulation 16, section B(2) and/or section C(4) of the Electricity Regulations, 1951.

280. The defendants contended that they owed no duty of care to the plaintiff because the buffaloes were trespassers on the highway, that they were not being led by nose strings as required by section 2 of the Buffaloes Enactment (F.M.S. Cap. 194) and that they were not negligent.

281. The Court held that the defendants owed a duty of care towards the plaintiff, as he was a neighbour irrespective of the fact that buffaloes were or were not trespassers on the highway. This is notable that the buffaloes were being nicely taken along the road.

282. The judge writes that:

> in applying to the facts of the present case the principles of the law of negligence which I have discussed, the first question which I have to consider is whether in view of what happened the defendants can be said to have created a situation of peril, however blamelessly, which generated a consequential duty to adopt precautions before it culminated in injury. In other words, were the circumstances in which damage was caused to the Plaintiff capable of giving rise to a notional duty of care? It is clear from the evidence that the telephone wire by itself was not a dangerous thing. What made it dangerous was the fact that it was resting on top of an electric wire by reason of which it was capable of becoming live with electricity, thereby causing damage to anyone who came in contact with it. It was the omission on the part of the defendants to remove the telephone wire from the top of the electric wire, which created the situation

> of danger and consequently gave rise to a notional duty of care. The Defendants have not sought to deny the existence of such notional duty. In any event, I do not think it can be seriously argued that no reasonable person could foresee some damage arising to someone in all the circumstances of the case.

On the facts of the case I have made a finding that the telephone wire in fact snapped on the 30 November 1962. The accident took place three days later. When electricity is carried overhead by wires or cables great care must be taken, in addition to any precautions required by statute, to see that it is not likely to become a source of danger. In my opinion, the defendants were negligent in allowing the telephone wire to remain resting on electricity wires for such a long time. It was as much the duty of the first defendants as it was of the second defendants to see that the telephone wire was taken off the electricity wires. In all the circumstances of the case, both defendants failed to observe the standard of care required of them and were thus in breach of a duty to take care.

Before concluding the matter I must deal briefly with the allegations against the first defendants of breaches of statutory duty as laid down in the Electricity Regulations, 1951. It is clear from the evidence that they complied with Regulation 16, section B, subsection 2(a)(iv) and that the whole of section C under Regulation 16 did not apply in this case because the electricity wire on which the telephone wire had fallen was a low voltage service wire. There was, therefore, no breach of statutory duty, so that if the plaintiff was relying on breach of statutory duty alone as the basis of his claim against the first defendants, he would not succeed.

283. It is notable that in spite of the fact that court did not find statutory duty, the damage was not too remote, it was reasonably foreseeable; and thus court found negligence and awarded damages.

XVI. *Yusoff v. Central Electricity Board*, [1964] 1 MLJ 374

284. The plaintiff sued the defendant on behalf of the estate of his son who died from electrocution as a result of coming into contract with a defect in the installation erected by the defendants for the supply of electricity to the plaintiff's house. The plaintiff claimed damages under sections 7 and 8 of the Civil Law Ordinance, 1956, and rested his claim on two alternative courses of action, that is (a) breach of statutory duty as provided in section 67 of the Electricity Ordinance and/or (b) negligence at common law. The defendants denied that they were in breach of statutory duty or guilty of negligence. They contended that the deceased caused and/or contributed to his death by his own negligence and failure to take care of his own safety. In the alternative, they alleged that the deceased knew or ought to have known that tampering with the electrical installation involved a risk of injury and that the deceased in acting as he did consented to running the said risk.

285. The court thoroughly discussed the law of negligence and its applicability on different negligent situations. The court decided that in this case, there was no proof of breach of section 67(1) of the Ordinance; there was not an evidence of negligence on the part of the defendants; and the cause of accident was solely due to the deceased's own act in tampering with the defendants installations.

XVII. T*enaga Nasional Bhd. v. Ong See Teong & Another*, [2010] 2 CLJ 1

286. A licensee under the Electricity Supply Act 1990 wanted to carry 270-kV transmission line which ran across the new village, built on a land alienated by the Selangor Government. The owners on the new village objected to it. This was actually to be carried out at the existing rout of 33-kV existing cable line. The residents filed a suit in the High Court to quash the appellant's such decision. They pleaded that it is a new transmission under disguise of upgrading. The High Court rejected the request. But Court of Appeal reversed the decision of the High Court. Before the federal Court the main legal question was the meaning of the word 'upgrading' in section 13 of the Act. The Federal Court said that it would mean 'improvement by replacement of components and raising in rank of electricity cables'. The Federal Court by 2:1 majority allowed the appeal with cost. The Court gave two reasons to support its decision: (1) The words repair, maintain and upgrade do not have same meaning. (2) The word is improvement by replacement ... therefore fell within the meaning of 'upgrading'.

XVIII. *Tenaga Nasional Berhad v. Pearl Island Development Sdn Bhd,* Civil Appeal No. P-02 (NCVC) (W)-897-04/2013. Decided on 13 January 2015

287. This case was an appeal from the Penang High Court to the Court of Appeal. The Penang High Court had dismissed the monetary claim of the TNB against the Pearl Island Resort Development Sdn Bhd arising out of supply of electricity. Under the electricity supply agreement, the resort was supposed to pay Connected Load Charges in certain situations. The resort claimed that the amount due was time-barred. This was accepted by the High Court. And it is not claimable under section 26 of the Electricity Supply Act 1990 which was accepted by the High Court. The Court of Appeal upheld the decision of the Penang High Court.

XIX. *Kamalanathan Ponnumbalan v. Tenaga Nasional Berhad*, Civil Suit No: MT(3)22-585-1998. Decided on 7 March 2006

288. The High Court of Malaya, Johor Bahru heard this appeal against the District Court, which had the claim of damaged for breach of contract and defamation. The defendant had sent a bill foe payment of electricity dues to him. The plaintiff rejected the bill land subsequent bills. The defendant disconnected and reconnected the electricity supply several times. The defendant denied any liability under section 30(1) of the Electricity Supply Act 1990. The High Court held that the defendant's claim was not justified under the Act. The claim should be based on the actual meter reading, which was not. If they felt that they were justified, they should have gone to the court. So the defendant's action was breach of the electricity supply contact between them. Disconnecting electricity supply again and again was arbitrary and coercive.

XX. *Sabah Electricity Sdn. Bhd. V. Kkip Power Sdn Bhd.* Civil Appeal No. S-02(w)-1123-06/2016 (CA)

289. This case is an appeal from the High Court at Kota Kinabalu. The High Court dismissed the claim of the appellant. The Court of Appeal also dismissed the appeal. The appellant company, having power to supply electricity in the state under section 9 of the Electric Supply Act 1990, had taken over the property, rights and liabilities of the Lembaga Lectric Sabah. The dispute started with the announcement of the Ministry to the effect that restructured tariff rates would apply from 15 July 2011 to the general public under section 26 of the Act. The appellant wrote to the respondent notifying that the new rates will also apply to the bulk purchases of the respondent with effect from 15 July 2011. The respondent disagreed with the revised rate. The matter went to the Energy Commission under section 30(2) of the Act, but not as a formal reference by the parties to decide the matter. The Energy Commission decided that the new rates would be applicable from 1 December 2012. Despite the decision of the Energy Commission, for the period between 15 July 2011 until 30 November 2012 the respondent did not pay the electricity charges based on the new tariff rates but instead paid the charges based on the old rates. They argued that there was no decision by the Energy Commission. The respondent, thus, paid new rates from 1 December 2012. The appellant then claimed arrears. This argument was accepted by the High Court. The Court of Appeal agreed with the High Court that the case was not formally referred to the Energy Commission. Thus, there was no legal decision by the Commission on the dispute.

XXI. *Nikmat Maju Development Sdn Bhd v. Tenaga Nasional Berhad*, Civil Appeal No: W-02(NCVC)(W)-949-04/2013 (CA)

290. Upon inspection, the TNB found that the meter in the hotel of the appellant was tampered. The meter then was corrected. According to the utility company, the tampering resulted in an under-recording or an error rate of -32.44% and thus claimed additional charges. The appellant refused to settle the charges. So the company went to the court. The appellant was not charged under the Electricity Supply Act 1990, which was, according the appellant, a condition precedent. The High Court accepted that there was tampering of the meter and asked the appellant to pay the claim of the utility company. The Court of Appeal approved the company's claim, and ruled that for enforcing 38, a prosecution case under section 37 is not a condition precedent.

Part II. Regulatory Framework Concerning Gas

Chapter 1. Gas Supply Act 1993 (Act 501)

§1. General

291. The Gas Supply Act 1993 provides for the licensing of the supply of gas to consumers through pipelines at a reasonable price, and the control of the pipelines, installations, appliances and related matters. The Act was amended through the Gas supply Act (Amendment) 2001 (Act A1126) to further enhance the industry and the new amendment was effective from 2 January 2002. It has further been amended by the Gas Supply Amendment Act 2016, which along with other amendments has introduced provisions for 'Third Party Access'. The Amendment Act 2016 has replaced the long title with an extended title: 'An act to provide for the licensing of the import into regasification terminal, regasification, shipping, transportation, distribution, retail or use of gas in the supply of gas through pipelines and related matters, the supply of gas at reasonable prices, the control of gas supply pipelines, installations and appliances with respect to matters relating to safety to persons in the distribution retail or use of gas and for purposes connected therewith.' The Amendment Act provides for extending it to Sarawak also. The Act is applicable throughout Malaysia, but subject to order of suspension by the Minister (Minister for the time being charged with the responsibility relating to petroleum). It governs and regulates supply of gas to consumers through pipelines downstream of the last flange of the city gate station, and pipelines from the filling connection of a storage tank or cylinder specifically used for reticulation or delivery of gas to any apparatus in any premises. 'City Gate Station' means a station with gas measurement and pressure-regulating facilities where gas is received directly from the gas transmission pipelines (from the outlet of the gas processing plant or receiving terminal to the inlet of the city gate station) and subsequently delivered through the pipeline distribution system for the supply of gas to consumer. The amendment Act has widened its scope to by allowing third party access, which broke the monopoly of Gas Malaysia Berhad and Pertonas Gas Berhad and made it more competitive.

292. Originally, according to section 2, 'gas' means methane, ethane, propane, butane or hydrocarbons, which may consist of one or more of the aforesaid gasses either in the form of gas or liquid. The new definition is: ' … natural gas, liquefied natural gas, or liquefied petroleum gas'. Here, 'natural gas' means hydrocarbon gas mixture consisting primarily of methane, and 'liquified petroleum gas' means a mixture of hydrocarbon gases primarily propane and butane at various proportions and stored in liquid form. 'Supply of Gas' is defined as the delivery, transportation, distribution or reticulation of gas through pipelines, while 'consumer' simply means a person who is supplied with gas or whose premise are for the time being connected for the purpose of supply of gas by a license.

293. Section 4 provides for functions and duties of the Energy Commission (established under the Energy Commission Act 2001) (hereinafter referred to as the Commission). Among some notable functions are: to secure license authorized under this Act satisfies all reasonable demand for gas; to protect the interests of the consumers in respect to prices, continuity of supply and the service quality; to regulate the composition, pressure, purity and volume of gas supply; to protect the public from dangers arising from gas supply services; and to investigate any accident or fire involving any gas pipeline. These functions may be carried out by any of the Commission's officer, duly appointed in writing by the Commission for such purposes.

I. Functions and Duties of the Energy Commission

294. According to the new section 4, the Commission will have the following functions and duties:

(1) To secure that licensee … is capable to fulfil all reasonable demand of gas.
(2) To ensure that a regasification, transportation or distribution licensee satisfies all reasonable demands for access to the facility.
(3) To ensure that the lisensee has enough financial capability to carry out his tasks.
(4) To protect the interests of consumers.
(5) To develop and issue codes, directions and guidelines.
(6) To regulate the quality of gas.
(7) To promote efficiency and economy on the part of licensee or other person to import, utilize and transport and distribute gas.
(8) To protect the public from dangers in the whole process.
(9) To maintain a competitive atmosphere.
(10) To investigate any accident or fire.
(11) To inspect pipeline or piping system.
(12) To carry out audit.
(13) To carry out all such other activities as may appear to the Commission … necessary for carrying out the provisions of the Act.

These functions can be carried out by an officer authorized by the Minister. He may be any public officer or an officer of the Commission. According to the amended section 6, the authorized officer can carry put investigation if he has reason to suspect that any prohibited act is done or being done. While doing so, he will have power of a police officer. Upon completion of his investigation of any offence, he will submit the matter to a police officer who may arrest the alleged offender. In case of violation of any prohibitory order, he will submit the papers to the Commission for further action under 28L and 28O of the Act.

§2. Powers of Entry, Investigation and Prosecution

295. The powers of enforcement under the Gas Supply Act may be exercised by the authorized officer, that is, any public officer or officer of the Commission authorized in writing by the Minister. He/she may enter a house or building at any reasonable time upon any land to investigate and examine any pipelines or for such other purposes. He/she may also take samples of gas from the premises and test or cause it to be tested at any convenient place. Later, if he/she has reasonable cause to believe that it is likely to cause danger, he/she may require rectification of the defect by notice in writing, or discontinue the supply; or remove or seal the defective part.

296. In case where there is information given under oath to any Magistrate that an offence under this Act is carried out upon any premises, the Magistrate shall issue a warrant to the authorized officer (named in the warrant), and he/she may enter the land and premises at any reasonable time by day or night, and seize or seal any incriminating materials. He/she may also enter such premises without warrant provided that he/she has the reason to believe that by reason of delay in obtaining search warrant, such materials is likely to be removed or destroyed. In doing so, he/she may break open any outer or inner door and also to detain every person found in the place until search is completed (section 5).

297. The authorized officer shall have the power to investigate the commission of any offence under this Act and the regulations thereunder. In doing so, he/she may exercise the special powers in relation to police investigation except power to arrest without warrant under the Criminal Procedure Code. Upon completion of the investigation, he/she shall immediately give all the information to a police officer in charge of a police station who may later effect an arrest by warrant (section 6).

298. During investigation, the authorized officer may, by order in writing, require attendance before himself/herself of any person acquainted with the case for the purpose of obtaining information, and such person shall attend as required. If he/she fails to attend as required, the authorized officer may report it to a Magistrate who shall issue a summon to secure attendance of such person (section 7). The authorized officer may examine such person, and the latter shall be legally bound to answer all questions put to him/her truthfully, except any question the answer to which would expose him/her to a criminal charge, penalty or forfeiture. Statements made by such person shall be reduced into writing whenever possible, signed or affixed with his/her thumb print, after it has been read to him/her and he/she has given opportunity to make any corrections (section 8).

299. Prosecution under this Act shall only be instituted with the Public Prosecutor's consent in writing (section 9). Interestingly, in case of a conviction involving a fine, part of the payment of the fine (maximum half) may be directed to the person who gives the substantial information leading to conviction (section 10). The Commission or the authorized officer is expressly protected against any action or prosecution for his/her act or omission done in good faith in exercising his/her power under this Act (section 37).

§3. Licence

300. New section 11 makes licence as a mandatory condition for: import into regasification terminal, regasification of gas, shipping of gas, transportation of gas, distribution of gas, retail of gas and use of gas. Thus, appropriate licence issued under this Act is a condition precedent for supply of gas through pipelines (section 11), unless otherwise exempted by the Minister under section 42 of the Act. Previously, licences required approval by the Minister. Now, it is exceptional. There are two situations where license is granted, on application by the Commission with the approval of the Minister if it is for the regasification or distribution of gas or if it is for the transportation or distribution of gas. It will be subject to the terms and conditions of the licence, on payment of fees as prescribed under this Act. Under new section 11A, 11B and 11C, a person applying for a licence shall submit to the Commission the necessary details for the supply, such as area of supply, site location plan of the proposed location, piping layout, technical specifications and certification of the pipelines or installation, and any other information as may be required by the Commission. In case of a licence for import into regasification terminal, regasification, shipping or transportation of gas, any details as required by the Commissioner. Section 11B states that '… a license will not be granted to any person: if it, in the opinion of the Commissions give rise to conflict of interest, or who is not incorporated in MALAYSIA or does not have a place of business in Malaysia, except for a licence for the import into regasification terminal'. The Commission may grant more than one licence to one person. Subject to approval of the State Authority, the licensee may carry out any necessary work involving ground. The license is non-transferable, neither it can be assigned nor sub-licensed except with written consent of the Minister. The licence will only be valid for a term as specified by the Commission in the license. By virtue of the licence, the licensee is authorized to lay, place and carry on, under and over the State land, subject to approval of the State Authority, the pipelines and installation, and other necessary equipment. New section 11C states that the Commission may at any time impose additional terms or conditions, or can amend the terms and condition previously imposed.

301. Before issuing any licence, the Commission may require a security to be furnished based on the licensee's construction costs or operational costs or both, and such amount may be reviewed from time to time. The Commission may suspend or revoke a licence at any time upon breach of any conditions or in default of any payment. The licensee later may appeal to the Minister against the suspension and revocation whose decision shall be final (section 12(2)). The licensee shall not be entitled to any compensation for any loss arising thereof. Upon the suspension of a licence, the Commission may require the licensee to rectify any breach of conditions or to pay any monies due; and/or for the sake of public, authorize another person to continue operating the pipeline or the part thereof has been in operation for the period of suspension. If the Commission is satisfied with the above-said rectification, the suspension may be lifted; if not, the licence may be revoked. Upon revocation of a licence, the Commission may require the licensee to remove his/her pipeline and installation at his/her own costs, within a reasonable period of time; or acquire the pipeline and installation on payment of adequate compensation, and appoint another licensee to complete the work. If a license is revoked under this section, the security shall be forfeited as the Commission thinks fit (section 12(7)).

The Guidelines on Licence Application Amendment 4/2018 under section 11A of the Act. It is to facilitate the TPA mechanism introduced in by the amendments in 2016 and the consequential necessary amendment in the same year in the Gas Supply Regulations. It says that other departments may also have jurisdictions with respect to certain matters, for example Occupational Safety and Health under the Petroleum (Safety Measures) Act 1984 and the Factories and Machineries Act 1967. It further clarifies that the Commission may grant licences with appropriate fees chargeable for: import into regasification terminal licence; shipping licence; regasification licence; transportation licence; retail licence; and private gas licence. The guidelines are to establish a framework for the issuance of the TPA system and the appropriate conditions, which may be imposed together with the issuance of such licence.[107]

I. New Section 13A, 13B, 13C and 13D

302. The amendment Act 2016 has introduced new section 13A, 13B, 13C and 13D governing obligation to submit business plan some other matters:

(a) **OBLIGATION TO SUBMIT BUSINESS PLAN:** Section 13A requires the licensee submit a five-year or such other period as determined by the Commission, a rolling business plan pertaining to the licence. Contravention tot his will be considered as an offence.

(b) **STANDARDS OF PERFORMANCE OF GAS AND SERVICES OF LISENSEE:** Section 13B authorises the Commission to issue guidelines with respect to supply of gas and provision of services to consumers by retail linsensee, and services in relation to the activities of regasification, transportation or distribution lisensee. This will include: reasonably meeting consumer requirement; the handling of consumer complaints and disputes; procedures for

107. See at: file:///Users/ahaseeb/Downloads/Guidelines%20on%20Licence%20Application%20-V2.pdf (accessed on 20 Mar. 2018).

the compensation of consumers in case of a breach of the standards of performance, consumer service standards or for a breach of any of its obligations under the Act that affects consumers; and the protection of consumer information. The lisensee will have to publish their own consumer service standards in accordance with guidelines. Any action taken under this section will not affect other remedies, such as remedy under the Consumer Protection Act 1999. Additionally, contravention to section 13B will be an offence subjected to RM 300,000 (maximum) fine and a further fine of RM 10,000 for every day or part of a day during which the offence continues. There will be liability to compensate the loss incurred.

(c) **SEPARATE ACCOUNT FOR ACTIVITIES UNDER THE LICENCE:**Under section 13C, the licensee is required to maintain separate and distinct account having all details for the business under each licence. It has to be submitted to the Commission as and when requested. Contravention to this requirement will be subject to a fine not exceeding RM 500,000 and a further fine of RM 1,000 for every day the offence is continued after conviction.

(d) Upon contravention of any law contained in the Principal Act or subsidiary legislations made under it, or the terms and conditions appended to the licence, the Commission may write to the licensee for rectification.

§4. Provisions Relating to License, Supply of Gas, Entry into Land, Etc.

303. Section 13 empowers the licensee to fix tariffs, which may include a standing charge (i.e., a fixed charge approved by the Commission for supply of gas and includes the cost to maintain the system), a charge in respect of availability of a supply of gas and rent of any gas meter or installation. The proposal tariffs may be approved by Minister in writing, and then shall be framed by the licensee as to indicate the methods the tariffs being made and the prices to be charged, and shall be published in such manner to secure adequate publicity for it. In fixing tariffs, there should be no undue preference or discrimination.

Amended section 16 has thoroughly amended section 16 which provided for duty of retail licensee to supply gas to consumers upon request or duty of the regasification, transportation or distribution lisensee to allow utilization of their faculties by third parties. This section now provides for smooth and effective mechanism of gas supply to consumers. Sections 16 and 17 have suitably been amended. Section 18 has been deleted. Section 19 has been made more rational with respect to measuring the supply of gas by metering.

304. The licensee has the duty to supply gas on request of the owner or occupier of the premises and this includes providing all things reasonably necessary for that purpose. The owner or occupier of such premises shall first give a notice to the licensee specifying the premises, the day on which the supply is required to commence, the quantity and the pressure required and the minimum period of the gas supply. As soon as practicable, the licensee shall then reply with a notice stating the extent of the proposal acceptable to the licensee, prices and terms to be charged, whether by a tariff or by special agreement, specifying any payment to be made and also the security required. There are, however, circumstances where the licensee is exempted from the duty to supply gas. For instance, if it is contrary to any law, or he/she is so exempted under any agreement, or he/she is prevented from doing so by malfunction or failure of any pipeline or installation beyond his/her control, or if the Commission thinks that it is not reasonable for him/her to do so, or in case there is already a supply of gas given to the person (section 15).

305. In providing the gas supply to the consumer under section 14, by virtue of section 16, the licensee has power to recover expenses reasonably incurred from the consumer, provided with the Commission's approval. It is, however, notable that the expenses in providing pipeline and installation from the outlet of the meter to the internal piping within the premises shall definitely be borne by the consumer (section 16(3)). Apart from that, the licensee may also require security to be furnished for all monies due to him/her in respect of the work necessary to gas supply and the supply of gas itself. If the person fails to give such security, he/she may refuse to provide pipeline until security is given (section 17). The return of such security shall be with interest, at a prescribed rate (section 17A).

306. A person who requires a supply of gas may enter into a special agreement with the licensee for the supply on the terms as specified in the agreement, and hence sections 13–17 shall not apply. Any term relating to tariff shall be submitted to the Commission (section 18). The charge for supply of gas shall be ascertained by an appropriate meter, of the approved type by the Commission. The meter is to be provided by the licensee whether by way of sale, hire or loan to the consumer, and installed on the consumer's premises. If the consumer refuses any payment for that purpose, the licensee may refuse or discontinue giving the supply (section 19).

307. The licensee may cease the supply of gas or reduce the quantity supplied under circumstances laid down in section 15. If it happens, there shall be no liability on part of the licensee as to any loss or damage caused, except if it is shown to have resulted from the negligence of the licensee, his/her employees, servants or agents, or from his/her faulty construction of pipeline and installation. In such cases, the licensee is bound to rectify such damages or defects (section 20).

308. The licensee has the right to disconnect supply of gas in premises which is suspected in commission of any offences under section 30(5), (6), (7) and (9) by giving twenty-four hours of notice, and then shall immediately inform the Commission about it. The Commission shall immediately direct an authorized officer to inspect such premises and later forms an opinion whether an offence has been committed or not. If no offence is committed, the supply shall immediately be reconnected. If offence has been committed, then investigation shall be carried out and if later it discloses no commission of any offence, the Commission may pay for adequate compensation. If it discloses otherwise, then the licensee may require the consumer to pay him/her for the loss of revenue as well as the expenses for reconnection of gas. These provisions and other provisions of this Act do not however affect the licensee's liability either civil or criminal arising under this Act (section 22).

309. Apart from that, the licensee also has the power to enter on and examine land whenever it thinks necessary for exercising the rights under this license, for constructing pipeline, etc. This must be done by first giving twenty-four hours of notice to the occupier of the land or in case of reserved land, to the District Land Administrator. This power however does not authorize the licensee to cause damage, disturbance upon the land or to clear away trees, fence or building (section 23). This power is extended by section 24, whereby the licensee may lay, place or carry on pipelines, etc. on the land for the purpose of installation, and he/she have to pay full compensation (in accordance with section 28) to all interested persons for any disturbance or damage caused. This section further provided for the procedure of such entry of land for the purpose of construction.

310. First the licensee shall give a notice (as set out in the First Schedule), stating the nature and extent of the proposed activity upon the land, and served to the owner or occupier of the land who shall have the right to object such activity verbally or in writing to the District Land Administrator, within fourteen days of the receipt of the notice. If there is an objection lodged, the District Land Administrator shall hold an inquiry giving all parties right to be heard. Upon the conclusion of the inquiry, the District Land Administrator may make an order authorizing or prohibiting the intended activity which may be subject to terms and conditions. Any party dissatisfied with the order may appeal to the State Authority within twenty-one days from the order is made, whose decision shall be final. If the State Authority thinks fit, he/she may alternatively direct the acquisition of the land. The licensee then is required to produce the notice (if no objection) or the original order (made after inquiry) to the Registrar (as defined in the National Land Code) who shall make a note of the existence of such rights on the register document of title. The licensee may also enter upon any land for maintenance, repair and upgrading of pipeline or installation (section 25).

311. Later, if the owner or occupier of the land desires to use his/her land, which requires removal or alteration of the pipelines and installation, he/she may require the licensee to do so under section 26. If the licensee omits to comply with the requisition, that person may apply in writing to the State Authority which may decide after inquiry, whether to reject the application or to make an order for removal or alteration of the pipelines, specifying the person who shall borne such cost. If such order has been made, the licensee may apply to the State Authority to direct acquisition of the land (section 26(4)). If acquisition is authorized, the pipeline and installation shall be deemed to be a work for public utility.

312. By virtue of section 27, the licensee shall always have the right to enter into wayleave agreement with the owner or occupier of any land for purpose of constructing a pipeline or installation. The original and the certified copy of the agreement shall be produced before the Registrar who shall make note of it on the register document of title.

313. Section 28 specifically deals with the amount of compensation, payable under sections 23, 24 and 25. It shall be assessed by the District Land Administrator after an inquiry. The assessment shall be in the form set out in the Third Schedule. No compensation to be payable in respect of any tree within 50 feet of the centre line of any public road. Any person aggrieved by the assessment may appeal within twenty-one days after the assessment to the State Authority whose decision shall be final.

§5. Inquiry

314. Procedure for inquiry is provided by section 29. Any dispute arising between the licensee and the consumers under sections 13–21 may be referred to the Commission, who shall determine the dispute and make order accordingly, or sometimes with the approval of the Minister form a committee for inquiry. The committee shall consist of three members led by a person appointed by the Minister. The committee may summon person for attendance, to produce any documents and examine him/her as a witness. Failure to comply with such summon, or offer any disrespect to the committee, and refusal to give evidence when required to do so, or giving false evidence are offences under subsection 5, and liable to a fine not exceeding MYR 3,000 or to imprisonment for a term not exceeding one year or to both. Pending the determination of the dispute, the licensee shall continue to supply gas (subsection 7) unless otherwise directed by the Commission. Any person feels aggrieved by the Commission's decision may appeal to the Minister, by application in writing within twenty-one days of the decision. The decision of the Minister shall be final (section 29(10)).

§6. Offences and Penalties

315. In addition to what we have noted above, section 30 lists down the offences and penalties under the Act. They are:

(1) Contravene section 11, supply gas through pipelines without any license. Penalty: Fine not exceeding MYR 100,000 or imprisonment for five years, and a further fine of maximum MYR 1,000 per day for continuing offence; and any pipelines and installation be forfeited (section 30(1)).
(2) Carrying out business in contravention of section 11 carries a fine not exceeding MYR 5,000,000 as fine or imprisonment not exceeding five years or both. And a further fine not exceeding MYR 1,000 for every day with respect to continued offence.

(3) Failure to have to meet the published standards is subject to under 13B in case of retail licensee a fine not exceeding RM 300,000, and RM 1,000 per day for repeated offence. In case of regasification, transportation or distribution licensee, it is MYR 1 million, and MYR 10,000 per day for repeat offences.
(4) Refuse access to any authorized officer, assault, obstruct or delay entry of such officer, refuse to give information, or give false information to an authorized officer. Penalty: Fine not exceeding MYR 5,000 or two years imprisonment (max.) or to both (section 30(3)).
(5) Failure to comply with any terms and conditions in the license without lawful excuse. Penalty: Fine not exceeding MYR 10,000, and a further fine of maximum MYR 1,000 per day for continuing offence (section 30(4)).
(6) Extend, adjust, remove or destroy any pipeline or installation wilfully, dishonestly or negligently, by act or omission. Penalty: Fine not exceeding MYR 50,000 (section 30(5)).
(7) Tamper with or damage pipeline or installation (wilfully, dishonestly or negligently, by act or omission) so as to cause or likely to cause injury to human life or property. Penalty: Fine not exceeding MYR 500,000 or imprisonment not exceeding five years or both (section 30(6)).
(8) Cause any pipeline to divert from its proper cause, alter the index of any meter, prevent it and damage any meter or dishonestly abstract or consume gas. Penalty: Fine not exceeding MYR 100,000 or imprisonment not exceeding three years or both (section 30(7)).
(9) Undertake any pipeline work without lawful authority of the licensee, in a manner likely to cause danger to person or property unless the licensee has taken all reasonable steps to give proper notice for the protection of pipelines and installations (section 30(8)). Penalty: Fine not exceeding MYR 50,000 or imprisonment not exceeding two years or both. (section 30(6)).
(10) Section 30B is on threat and reprisal committed. It provides for a fine not exceeding MYR 1 million. For a second and subsequent offence, it provides for a fine not exceeding MYR 5 million. If such person is not a body corporate, there will be a fine not exceeding MYR 500,000, and for second and subsequent offences, a fine not exceeding MYR 1 million.
(11) Section 30C provides for penalty for disclosure of confidential matters. It provides penalty for it not exceeding MYR 1 million, and for a second and subsequent offence, a fine not exceeding MYR 5 million. If such person is not a body corporate, there will be fine not exceeding five hundred thousand or a jail term of five years or both. For a second or subsequent offences, there will be a fine not exceeding MYR 1 million or to imprisonment not exceeding five years or both.
(12) Any act or omission contravenes any provision under this Act or regulation. Penalty: Fine not exceeding MYR 100,000, and a further fine of not exceeding MYR 2,000 per day for continuing offence.(section 31).

316. For offences committed by body corporate, it shall only be liable to fine as provided in the Act. In charging the corporate body, a director or officer of it (at the time of the commission of the offence) may be jointly charged, and he/she shall be deemed guilty unless it is proved that the offence was committed without his/her knowledge, or that he/she took all reasonable precaution to prevent its commission. If the offence is committed by an agent, the principal (person) shall also be liable to the same penalty unless he/she proves that he/she took all reasonable precaution to prevent its commission (section 32). A new section 32A provides penalty for attempt and abetment. It provides that abettors and where a person attempts to make or to make on behalf of another person an incorrect return, account or statement will be punishable with the punishment provided for such offence under the Act provided that any term of imprisonment imposed will not exceed one-half of the longest term provided for the offence. For the offences under this Act, the existence of artificial, which could be used for altering any pipeline, installation or meter, in committing such offence shall be prima facie evidence that dishonest alteration has been carried out (section 33).

317. In addition to the aforesaid offences, there are also offences, which may be compounded, that are prescribed by the Minister, by order in the Gazette. The Chairman (of the Energy Commission) with written consent of the Public Prosecutor may compound such offences by collecting a sum of money not exceeding 50% of the maximum fine for that offence, from the offender. All monies collected shall be part of the Consolidated Fund (section 34).

318. Section 35 generally requires that all pipeline works must be carried out under the supervision of and certified by a competent person, unless otherwise exempted (by the Minister, under section 42, by notification in the Gazette). Whenever any serious accidents happen, that is involving damage to person or property, the consumer or the licensee shall have the duty to report it to the Commission by the quickest means possible, and also submit report in writing with the least possible delay. Failure to do this is an offence under section 36. In emergency case (on occurrence of any industrial unrest, lock out, etc.), or in the interest of public safety, the Yang di-Pertuan Agong (YDPA) may authorize the Commission to suspend any licence, or to take possession any pipeline or to withdraw the use of any pipeline (section 38).

319. Section 39 expressly empowers the Minister to make regulations under this Act for purposes laid down therein. Among them are to provide for procedures for exercising the Commission's functions, to limit the variation of composition, pressure and purity of gas, management, storage and distribution of gas through pipeline, the fees payable, the standard and method for pipeline works and equipment, and any other matter generally to give effect to provisions of this Act.

§7. Extent of Applications, Savings and Transition

320. Certain sections of this Act shall not apply to supply of gas through pipelines within factories as defined under the Factories and Machinery Act 1967. Those sections are sections 5, 35, 36, 39(c), (d), (f), (i), (j), (m) and (n) (section 40).

321. In case where there is any conflicting provisions in the Petroleum Development Act (PDA) 1974, Petroleum (Safety Measures) Act 1984 or the Factories and Machinery Act 1967, provisions of this Act shall prevail to the extent of its inconsistency (section 41). Whoever was supplying gas through pipelines before the commencement of this Act may continue doing so for the period of six months after its commencement, in which he/she shall make an application for a licence or an exemption from licence, pending the outcome of his/her application. Whereas, any existing pipeline or installation used may continue to be used until determination by the Commission or an authorized officer.

§8. First Schedule: Notice of Intention to Enter And Do Work on Land under Section 24

322. This notice is issued by the licensee to the owner or occupier of the specified land and stating that he/she has the right to lodge any objection within fourteen days of the date of receipt, the appointed date of hearing and also stating that he/she will be paid proper compensation.

§9. Second Schedule: Order of the District Land A422. Administrator in Respect of Objection on the Entry on Land

323. This order is made by the District Land Administrator after holding the inquiry. It may allow entry to the licensee with or without conditions or may not allow such entry.

§10. Third Schedule: Assessment

324. This is an assessment of compensation by the District Land Administrator after inquiry, stating the amount of compensation payable to the owner or occupier by the licensee.

I. Some Notable Amendments Brought About by the Gas Supply (Amendment) Act 2016

325.

(1) The Gas Supply (Amendment) Act 2016, which was gazetted on 9 September 2016 and came into force on 16 January 2017 and by adding Part VIA entitled 'General Competition Practice', comprising section 28A to section 28AD, it introduced 'Third Party Access' (TPA) – A third party (other than the two players in the country) accessing and utilizing the capacity of gas facility, which are regasification terminals, transmission pipelines and distribution pipelines, for the purposes of delivering gas to consumers – breaking the

monopoly of two nation players in the gas industry. This has made the industry more competitive because a health competition is always warranted in any kind of business venture, as it has benefits to consumers, keeps price competitive, improves the quality of products and services, and enhances the sustainability of supply. Under the TPA, the licensed activities are: regasification, transportation, distribution, import into regasification terminals, shipping, use of gas and retail supply. The players can be local and foreigners. Section 28 provides for anticompetitive agreement/Conduct as illegal. They may be: fixing purchase–selling prices; limiting or controlling production, market outlet/ access, technical developments or investments in the gas industry; sharing of market or sources of gas supply; and bid-rigging. Section 28G prohibits abuse of dominant position. They are: imposing unfair purchase/selling price or trading condition; limiting/controlling production, market access, technical developments or investments in the gas industry; applying different conditions to investment transactions; and making conclusion of agreements conditional upon acceptance of unrelated obligations. On contravention, the offender will be liable 10% of the worldwide turnover or MYR 500,000. Individuals and block may be exempted on the ground of: significant identifiable technical, efficiency or social benefits; benefits could not reasonably have been provided without the agreement having the effect of preventing, restricting or distorting competition; detrimental effect on competition is proportionate to the benefits provided; and the agreement does not allow complete elimination of competition in respect of substantial part of licensed activities.[108] It may be noted that the provisions are in line with the Competition Act 2010. The status of industry previously was unclear given that only activities under the Petroleum Development Act 1974 were expressly excluded from the provisions of the Competition Act 2010. The Head of the Gas Market Development and Operation Mr Rumaizi Abdul Halim rightly says that with the introduction of the TPA system, it creates an existing market structure. The players will be swayed by the supply and demand and it could set the tone of the market price. It is because the TPA system enables third parties to access gas facilities on the same terms and conditions as applicable to other parties for similar utilization. We have noted that it covers liquified natural gas regulation terminals, gas transmission pipelines and gas distribution pipelines. It may also be noted that the Act prohibits the all kinds of anticompetitive behaviours. In order to run the TPA system smoothly the Commission has issued TPA Codes. It is about to issue guidelines also. The Guidelines for Licence Application is already in place. The best thing is that the two existing players, Gas Malaysia Berhad and

108. Energy Commission, 'Gas Supply (Amendment) Act 2016 and the TPA System', at: file:///Users/ahaseeb/Downloads/1-Gas%20Supply%20Amendment%20Act%202016%20and%20the%20TPA%20System%20(4).pdf (accessed on 13 Mar. 2018); Energy Commission, 'Frequently Asked Questions on Third Party Access System (TPA)', at: https://www.google.com/search?ei=iLEDW9vtM8rLvgSS_p34DQ&q=Frequently+Asked+Questions+for+Third+Party+Access+System&oq=Frequently+Asked+Questions+for+Third+Party+Access+System&gs_l=psy-ab.3..33i160k1.27593.36103.0.38023.20.20.0.0.0.0.767.2010.0j2j0j1j0j1j1.5.0....0...1c.1.64.psy-ab..15.3.1475...33i21k1.0.NPzgJUjv7kA (accessed on 12 Mar. 2018).

Pertonas Gas Berhad, are supportive of the TPA system as it will create more flexibility in the gas market which will provide better bargaining power to gas users.[109] The CEO of Gas Malaysia Berhad Mr Ahmad Hashimi Abdul Manap comments on the TPA system as: 'In general, market forces will balance the dynamics of demand and supply in segments of the industry where competition is feasible. Competition in turn will increase the economic efficiency through precise pricing signals and better utilisation of the gas infrastructure. It would also remove disparities between competitive sources, eventually ensuring competitive pricing.'[110]

(2) The TPA provisions provide for procedural remedy also. It establishes Gas Competition Appeal Tribunal. They provided structure and procedural mechanism of the Tribunal. Any person aggrieved under section 28C and 28G may appeal to the Tribunal. Likewise, any person aggrieved from the decision of the Commission under section 28J and 28N can appeal to the Tribunal.

109. 'Gas What', *Energy Malaysia,* Vol. 14, 2018, pp. 29–31.
110. *Ibid.* pp. 33–34.

Chapter 2. Gas Supply Regulations 1997

§1. General

326. These regulations are made pursuant to power conferred by section 39 of Gas Supply Act 1993. It was made by the Deputy Prime Minister, having been directed under section 51 of the Interpretation Acts 1948 and 1967 to exercise the powers of the Prime Minister. These Regulations come into force on 17 July 1997, except some regulations listed in Regulation 1(2), which came into force a year later that is on 17 July 1998. The Regulations apply to gas pipeline or gas installation, gas fitting and gas appliances (Regulation 3). Installation here includes conversion of a pipe, fitting, meter, equipment, etc. for supply of gas through pipelines. 'Gas fitting' means an item in a piping or tubing system that is used as a connector but does not include a functioning item (functioning items is referred to as gas equipment), whereas 'gas appliance' is appliance designed for use by the consumer of gas for heating, burning, motive power, etc. including gas appliance regulator (Regulation 2). The following points are notable. Regulations have been amended twice, in 2014 and 2017.

§2. Licence

327. There are two categories of license for gas supply through pipeline under section 11 of the Act. They are gas import into regasification terminal licence and gasification licence, and shipping licence, transportation licence, distribution licence, retail licence and private gas licence. [Regulation 4 as amended by the Gas (Amendment) Regulations 2017]. Application for all licenses shall be made to the Commission together with the details mentioned in section 11(3), and the fee shall be at a rate determined by the Commission, and for renewal fee shall be as prescribed in Part I of the Third Schedule. For private gas licence, the application must be attached with the approval to install under Regulation 15, and the approval to operate under Regulation 16. Regulation 12, as amended by the 12017 Amendment Regulations, requires that all distribution, retail and private gas licensees to maintain records.

328. Application for renewal of licence shall be made at the time specified in the licence for gas utility licence, and in not less than two months before the expiry of the private gas licence. Such application may be approved by the Commission, after an inspection or without making an inspection (Regulation 10). Any licence issued may be suspended or revoked by the Commission if the gas installation is no longer required; it is found to be unsafe for use; or the licensee has failed to comply with these Regulations. If a licence is revoked or suspended, the licensee is required to surrender the licence within fourteen days from the date of notification in writing (Regulation 11). It may be noted that by the 2014 Gas Supply (Amendment) Regulations, all act of the Commission will be performed by the Energy Commission.

329. The Gas Utility Licensee shall have the duty to keep and maintain proper record of gas installation containing the location of installation, name and address of the owner and occupier of the premises, Certificate of Completion, Test Certificate or other necessary information for inspection and approval of the Commission. In addition to that, the licensee shall keep the record of the quantity of gas sold per month, number of breakdown of pipeline, lists of all consumers and other necessary information, which shall be produced to the Commission whenever required.

§3. Gas Installation

330. All gas installations shall be classified as in Table 1 of the Second Schedule (Regulation 13) and must be carried out in accordance with these Regulations and conditions as determined by the Commission. Any work of installation, additional gas installation or extension of gas installation must be done after getting an approval from the Commission by an application made under Regulation 15, with the attached drawings of the system which is endorsed by a Gas Engineer, Gas Engineering Supervisor, Class I Gas Fitter or Class II Gas Fitter as the case may be. Upon completion of a new gas installation work, the applicant shall apply for an approval to operate it from the Commission by a written application together with the Certificate of Completion and Test Certificate (as in Form B and Form C of the First Schedule) which shall be issued and signed by a competent person as specified in Table 2 of the Second Schedule (Regulation 17). Test Certificate simply certifies that the gas installation is safe and free from leakage (Regulation 18). It may be noted that a subregulation added to section 16 by the 2014 Amendment Regulations states that 'The Commission may approve the application if it is satisfied that the applicant has fulfilled the requirements of these regulations and subsequently issue an approval to operate, containing such terms and conditions as it deems fit'.

331. As to work on any existing gas installation, it shall be carried out only after notification in Form D is made to the Commission or the Gas Utility Licensee as the case may be. If no such notification, the Commission may order the work to be suspended or stopped. Every installation work shall be supervised by a competent person employed by the particular Gas Contractor (Regulation 21). Regulation 22 provides that the Commission or the Gas Utility Licensee shall determine point of termination of the gas main pipe, gas service pipe and riser in the premises supplied by gas.

It may be noted that the 2014 Amendment Regulations have substituted the word extension with the words 'additional gas installation or extension of gas installation'. (Section 15).

§4. Information, Excavation and Safety of Gas Installation

332. The location of a gas installation shall be indicated either by measurement from a surface datum point, surface staking or surface marking. Marking by concrete marker, warning sign post and pipeline marker for traffic area shall be done as prescribed in Figures 1, 2 or 3 of the Fourth Schedule (Regulation 25).

333. No installation in vicinity of underground structure shall be carried out except with written permission of the Commission. Similarly, no installation of underground structure that will interfere with a gas installation is required, until an agreement has been entered with the licensee to remove the installation (Regulation 27).

334. For construction of underground structure within 1 m of a gas installation, or excavation in vicinity of a gas installation, a written notice in not less than three days before the excavation should be given to the licensee or his/her agent. Before any excavation work may commence, the excavator, licensee or his/her agent shall first determine the exact location of a gas installation. Any person who intends to excavate shall request in writing for information on location of the gas installation from the licensee or his/her agent in not less than four days before the proposed excavation (Regulation 29), and the information shall be provided twenty-four hours prior to the proposed excavation (Regulation 30). No excavation shall commence before such information is received (Regulation 31). If no excavation commences within ten days after the information is given, the excavator shall have to verify it before excavation (Regulation 41).

335. The indicated location of a gas installation shall be confirmed by excavator by means of hand digging before using any mechanized excavation equipment (Regulation 34), and probing with pointed tools is strictly prohibited (Regulation 35). The excavator shall have the duty to maintain and keep visible the markings placed by the licensee identifying location of gas installation (Regulation 38). Excavation work shall be carried out under supervision of competent person (Regulation 33), and it shall not be in a manner which is damaging or dangerous to a gas installation (Regulation 39). The same procedure applies to blasting, a written notice as to the proposed blasting shall be given to the licensee not less than three working days before the blasting. If it is in the process of construction, such notice shall be submitted to the Commission at least one working day before carrying out the blasting (Regulation 40).

336. All the procedures above shall not apply to emergency excavation, provided that verbal notice is given (Regulation 42). Notwithstanding all the procedures complied with, an authorized officer may order excavation to be stopped if he/she considers that it may damage gas installation or cause leakage, and may require licensee to cut out or repair faulty pipeline (Regulation 43).

337. Any person who causes damage to a gas installation shall immediately notify the Commission or the licensee of the damage. If it results in gas leakage, he/she shall immediately take reasonable steps to notify and warn all persons in the building, and the nearby traffic, as well as the nearest police station, and extinguish all flames and source of ignition (Regulation 45). While carrying out excavation, any person who exposes a gas installation for more than 3 m, or exposes a bell-and-spigot joint, etc. shall immediately notify the Commission or the licensee. This also applies to damages done to cathodic protection device (Regulation 48), and protective wrapping (Regulation 49). Regulation 50 provides for backfilling activity of an excavation.

338. No gas pipeline or installation shall be used for earth connection or as an electrical earth continuity conductor (Regulation 59). For safety purpose, a service gas pipeline shall be installed above the ground level when entering a building or structure (Regulation 51), and work on gas installation shall only be done if the gas is turned off (Regulation 52). Turning off and turning on the gas supply must first notify all the affected consumers (Regulation 53). Installation of gas pipeline shall be in accordance of these Regulations, and the requirements of Regulation 61 must be complied with. Furthermore, only gas pipeline, gas fitting or gas equipment made from materials resistant to being corroded or suitably protected from being corroded shall be used in a place exposed to a corrosion substance (Regulation 56). Moreover, those things must be supported and protected from damage (Regulation 57). New gas installation must be ensured that it has been tested for gas tightness (Regulation 60).

339. Where there is an escape of gas, the responsible person or his/her representative shall immediately take all reasonable steps to shut off the supply of gas and inform the Commission (Regulation 63). Due to that reason, sometimes an odorant shall be added to odourless gas as a warning agent for detection of leakage (Regulation 55). As to gas installation, it shall be marked for identification in a manner prescribed in Figure 4 of the Fourth Schedule (Regulation 62).

340. The owner of rented premises has duty to ensure the gas appliance is maintained in safe condition, and to display a notice on safe operation of gas appliance (Regulation 54). Any alteration made on such premises must be in accordance with these Regulations and in a manner as determined by the Commission (Regulation 58).

§5. Connection for the Supply of Gas to Consumer

341. Before connection of gas supply from the gas main pipe, Regulation 65 requires that an agreement must have been entered into, all expenses payable under this Act have been paid and the gas installation has been tested and found safe. The Gas Utility Licensee may also require security from the consumer, which sum shall be sufficient to cover the estimated charge for two-month supply of gas and rental of pipeline and installation (Regulation 66). This security shall be refunded within two months after disconnection and vacation of the premises. Apart from that, the licensee is also entitled to recover any charges for gas supply and maintenance of the pipeline (Regulation 68). A bill demanding gas supply fee shall be charged monthly of which default payment may cause the supply to be disconnected. For reconnection, licensee may impose reconnection fee which shall be paid in advance (Regulation 69). Then only the licensee shall restore the gas supply.

342. Before vacating any premise, the consumer shall send a notice of his/her intention to the licensee, otherwise he/she shall be liable to pay for all the charges for the supply of gas accruing up to the day from which a subsequent occupier requires gas supply. If a consumer vacates his/her premise without paying the amount payable to the licensee, the latter may refuse to supply gas to him/her at any other premise until it is settled (Regulation 71). Gas Utility Licensee may disconnect any gas supply, if it is made in contravention of these Regulations (Regulation 73). The authorized officer also may disconnect gas supply immediately upon knowing that a gas installation is unsafe for use, and in such cases may refuse reconnection (Regulation 72).

§6. Inspection and Test

343. The Commission may inspect and test gas installation after giving notice as in Form E, which shall be valid for twenty-one days from date of issue, and the responsible person of the particular premise shall make all the necessary preparation for inspection (Regulation 23), and a fee as prescribed in Part I of the Third Schedule shall be charged (Regulation 24).

344. A person authorized by a Gas Utility Licensee may enter into premises to inspect a gas pipeline or gas installation, to ascertain the register of a meter, remove or inspect it, in case of emergency (Regulation 74), for reconnection of gas supply (Regulation 75) and for replacing or repairing gas pipeline or installation (Regulation 76). Such person may be accompanied by some appropriate persons and shall ensure that the premises are left secured after the entry. Any damage caused during such entry shall be made good or compensated by the Gas Utility Licensee (Regulation 77).

345. For every supply of gas, the Gas Utility Licensee shall provide and fix a meter to measure the amount of gas supplied. The consumer shall pay for an additional meter, and also indemnify for any damage done to the meter (Regulation 78). The reading of the meter shall be prima facie evidence of the amount of gas consumed; however, if there is a fault in the meter, the licensee may impose a provisional charge. In case where licensee is unable to provide meter, he/she may fix a monthly charge, provided with approval of the Commission (Regulation 79). The consumer shall have the right to ask the licensee to test the meter, by making request in writing together with the payment of fee. If the meter's reading is found to be defective, then the fee shall be refunded and the consumer's account will be adjusted (Regulation 80).

§7. CERTIFICATE OF COMPETENCY

346. Only a competent person may carry out or personally supervise work on gas pipeline (Regulation 81). Competent person here refers to any person who holds and possesses a valid Certificate of Competency issued under these Regulations, who can either be a Gas Engineer, Gas Engineering Supervisor, Gas Fitter of Class I, Class II and Class III. The Certificate shall be as prescribed in Forms F and G of the First Schedule, and signed by the Commission. The scope of work of the competent person is prescribed in Table 2 of the Second Schedule (Regulation 83). These competent persons must be medically healthy and fit, physically and mentally as evidenced by a certificate certified by a registered medical practitioner, before Certificate of Competency may be issued (Regulation 84).

347. The Certificate however may be modified, suspended or cancelled by the Commission, if there is false or fraudulent declaration (Regulation 85) or if there is serious misconduct or an offence under this Act and Regulations has been committed (Regulation 86). Regulation 86 further lists down the activities, which will amount to 'serious misconduct' and also the procedure before suspension or cancellation is to be made. If the Certificate is lost, stolen, destroyed, etc., the holder may apply for a replacement Certificate, upon production of statutory declaration (of it being lost whatsoever) and payment of fee as prescribed in Part II of the Third Schedule (Regulation 88).

348. Regulation 89 requires competent person to register himself/herself with the Commission, which shall only be valid for twelve months. It shall be renewed annually subject to payment of fee in Part II of Third Schedule. Generally, no competent person of more than 65 years of age is allowed to do any work on gas pipeline but this restriction may be waived on a year-to-year basis by the Commission.

§8. EXAMINATION OF COMPETENT PERSON

349. Before a person may be issued with a Certificate of Competency, he/she must pass the examination before the Panel of Examiners appointed under Regulations 90 and 91. The Panel of Examiner consists of the Commission as a Chairman (appointed by the Minister), who later appoints an authorized officer as a Deputy Chairman and two other officers as members of the Panel. Only eligible candidate may apply to sit for the examination (Regulation 95) and must pay the examination fee as in Part II of Third Schedule (Regulation 94). Regulation 97 provides the eligibility to become a Gas Engineer, Regulation 98 for Gas Engineering Supervisor and Regulation 99 for Gas Fitter.

350. Only the successful candidate will be awarded with a Certificate of Competency, and if a candidate fails, the Panel may bar him/her from the subsequent examination within the next six months (Regulation 96). Upon issuance of the Certificate, the Panel may impose restrictions or endorsements on the Certificate (Regulation 100). The Panel also may exempt any candidate who is a Malaysian resident from examination if he/she holds a Certificate of Competency equivalent to that is issued under these Regulations, and upon payment of fee, be issued with Certificate of Competency under these Regulations (Regulation 102). Furthermore, the Panel may also issue a temporary Certificate of Competency for a term of maximum twelve months, to a foreign person (i.e., non-citizen or permanent resident of Malaysia), if he/she fulfils all the requirements under Regulation 101(2). He/she may apply for renewal of the Certificate upon its expiry.

§9. Registration of Gas Contractor

351. Certificate of Registration as a Gas Contractor issued under these Regulations is required before one can carry out work of installing, constructing, testing, commissioning, maintaining and repairing gas pipeline (Regulation 103). The Certificate shall be in Form H of the First Schedule, and valid for twelve months from the date of issuance or renewal. There are four classes of Gas Contractor, Classes A, B, C and D (as described in Regulations 105, 106, 107 and 108 respectively) and the scope of work is prescribed in Table 3 of the Second Schedule.

352. Before the Certificate is issued, the Gas Contractor must fulfil all the requirements in Regulation 109, and the Commission shall require the person to submit information as to name and addresses of the all the partners, directors, shareholders, etc., the premises for business rented or owned, and other necessary information (Regulation 110). The person must also pay the fee for issuance of Certificate and also for its renewal, which shall be made not less than two months before expiry. The Certificate is not transferable except with written permission from the Director General. Similarly, his/her approval is required for any change in name or address of the Gas Contractor.

353. The name of Gas Contractor shall be removed from the Register if the Certificate has expired and no renewal is made, or if it is cancelled by the Commission if the Gas Contractor ceases to carry on business, bankrupts, goes into liquidation, or contravenes any provision of this Act and Regulations. When the Certificate is cancelled, it shall be returned within fourteen days from notification of cancellation (Regulation 114). Regulation 115 provides that upon removal from the Register, the Gas Contractor may appeal for reinstatement within thirty days to the Commission. A further appeal for reconsideration of the matter may be made to the Minister whose decision shall be final.

Under new regulation 114A added by the 2014 Amendment Regulations, if a certificate of registration of gas contractor issued by the Commission is lost, stolen, destroyed, mutilated or defaced, a replacement of the certificate may be issued by the Commission on the production of a statutory declaration by the holder of the original certificate has been lost, stolen or destroyed or upon surrender of the mutilated or defaced original certificate. For that, the prescribed fees will have to be paid. Similar provisions have been inserted in regulation 118 also.

§10. Gas Fitting, Gas Appliances and Gas Equipment

354. Assembler, manufacturer or importer of gas fitting, gas appliances and gas equipment must first get Certificate of Approval of the Commission as in Forms I and J. Similarly, all gas fitting, gas appliances and gas equipment cannot be used or sold, unless it has been tested and get Certificate of Approval as in Form K. Both Certificates shall be valid for twelve months and may be renewed two months before its expiry. The fee for issuance and renewal is prescribed in Part II of the Third Schedule. All the approved fitting, appliances or equipment shall be marked in a manner determined by the Commission.

355. Application for the Certificate shall be made to the Commission, and the applicant shall deliver samples for the gas fitting, gas appliances and gas equipment, attached or affixed with labels describing the applicant and the samples. The Commission shall not be liable for any damage or loss of the samples. The samples shall then be examined and tested to ensure that they are safe for use. Dangerous gas fitting, appliances and equipment shall not be installed, and if so, shall be removed and seized.

356. Installation of gas appliances must be easily accessible for operation, inspection and maintenance. Immediately after installation, it shall be tested to verify that the connection is tight, installed in compliance with these Regulations, and all gas safety controls are working in proper order. Unsafe gas appliances are strictly prohibited from use, and irreparable gas appliance shall be discontinued from use and immediately notification to an authorized officer shall be made.

§11. Maintenance

357. A gas installation shall be maintained in good and efficient working order to ensure safety is observed at all time. A domestic gas installation shall be checked, tested and certified by the appropriate competent person every three years, and other gas installation, in every two years. The Commission shall have power to inspect or order inspection on gas installation. Only competent person may undertake maintenance work, which scope is prescribed in Table 2 of the Second Schedule, and only persons authorized by the licensee, owner or occupier may do certain work; open or make connection of pipe, disconnect the inlet of a meter or move a meter. A specific valid certificate of qualification is required for welding on a metallic gas piping, installation and interconnect of non-metallic piping. After disconnection of the outlets of a meter from the house piping is done, the competent person is required to do testing on the meter to ensure no other outlets are open, and then to turn it on again. A meter shall be replaced every ten years and upon malfunction. If the competent person realizes that there is a need to repair any part of supply system, he/she shall immediately notify the responsible person, and in emergency cases, may himself/herself make the necessary repair. A person engaged in maintenance work shall be adequately protected from danger, and he/she shall take all precautions for his/her safety, as well as the gas installation and pipeline. The responsible person shall keep a maintenance book record for all maintenance works (Regulation 131).

§12. Miscellaneous

358. Official identification card of an authorized officer shall be in Form L of the First Schedule (Regulation 138). All fees payable under these Regulations shall be paid in advance (Regulation 139). Serious accident shall be reported and investigated, and if the Commission is of the opinion that an offence under this Act or these Regulations has been committed, a copy of the report shall immediately be forwarded to the police. Any person involved in the investigation is entitled to receive the summary evidence and decisions upon payment of MYR 50 of fee (Regulation 140). Regulation 141 lists down all the records to be kept by the Commission, which have to be numbered according to chronological order. Among them are all inquiries conducted, licences, Certificates of Competency, technical and administrative instruction issued by him/her, all accidents and fires occurred, all registered competent persons, Gas Contractors, assemblers, manufacturers, and importers, all registered gas appliances, fitting and equipment and other necessary records. Failure to comply or contravention of these Regulations is an offence by virtue of Regulation 142.

§13. First Schedule

359. The First Schedule has the following forms:

FORM A	– Private Gas Licence
FORM B	– Certificate of Completion (of Installation), signed and stamped by the competent person and witnessed by the owner or representative of the premise.
FORM C	– Test Certificate
FORM D	– Notice of Work on a Gas Installation
FORM E	– Notice of Inspection and Test of Leakage of Gas
FORM F	– Certificate of Competency as Gas Engineer / Gas Engineering Supervisor
FORM G	– Certificate of Competency of Gas Fitter
FORM H	– Certificate of Registration of Gas Contractor
FORM I	– Certificate of Approval to Manufacture/ Assemble Gas Fitting/ appliance/ Equipment
FORM J	– Certificate of Approval to Import Gas Fitting/ Appliance/ Equipment

FORM K	– Certificate of Approval Gas Fitting/ Appliance/ Equipment
FORM L	– Identification Card of Authorised Officer

§14. Second Schedule

360. The Second Schedule has the following tables:

Table 1	– Classification of Gas Installation
Table 2	– Scope of Work of Various Classes of Competent Person
Table 3	– Scope of Work of Various Classes of Gas Contractors
Table 4	– Competent Person Required for Certain Classes of Gas Contractors

§15. Third Schedule

361. The Third Schedule prescribes Fees. FEE. (See the Schedule). The fees have suitably been revised by the 2014 and 2017 Amendment Regulations.

§16. Fourth Schedule

362. The Fourth Schedule contains the following figures:

Figure 1	– Concrete Marker
Figure 2	– Warning Sign Post
Figure 3	– Pipeline Marker for Traffic Area
Figure 4	– Marking on Gas Pipeline

Part III. Regulatory Framework Concerning Petrol

Chapter 1. Petroleum Development Act 1974 (Act 144)

363. (Act came into force: 1 October 1974, P.U. (B) 501/74).

§1. General

364. As stated in the preamble, the purpose of the Petroleum Development Act 1974 is to provide for exploration and exploitation of petroleum in Malaysia, including matters connected with and incidental to it. It also provides for the establishment of a Corporation in which will be vested the entire ownership in and exclusive rights and powers with respect to exploration and exploitation of petroleum, control the downstream activities and development relating to petroleum and its product. The word 'petroleum' is defined in section 10 as any mineral oil or relative hydrocarbon and natural gas existing in its natural condition and casing head petroleum spirit including bituminous sales and other stratified deposits from which oil can be extracted. [SLIGHTLY DIFFERS FROM PMA 1966]. By virtue of section 3, the word 'Corporation' specifically refers to Petroleum Nasional Berhad or in short form PETRONAS, a company incorporated under the Companies Act 1965. According to section 2, the Corporation will be vested with the entire ownership in, and exclusive rights, powers, liberties and privileges of exploring, exploiting, winning and obtaining petroleum, whether onshore and offshore, which shall take effect on the execution of an instrument of grant contained in the Schedule of the Act. The grant (as stated in the instrument) will be for perpetuity, irrevocable and shall ensure for the benefit of the corporation and its successors (section 3(3)). In return for the ownership of the said exclusive entire ownership, the Corporation is bound to make cash payment to the Government of Federation and the Government of any relevant State as may be agreed between the parties concerned (section 4). The following points are notable.

§2. Power to Takeover and Acquire

365. In additional to the Corporation's powers in its Memorandum and Articles of Association, and under this Act or any written law, the Corporation shall have the power to take over or acquire the whole or any part of any commercial undertaking, business or enterprise of whatever form of any person or body of persons (corporate or unincorporated) and carry out or enter into any activity (which was carried out prior to such taking over), whether mentioned in this Act or not. This however does not apply to any person who is licensed under the Gas Supply Act 1993, to supply gas to consumers through pipelines (section 3A).

§3. Cash Payment to Governments

366. Section 4 requires from Petronas to pay to the Federal Government and State Governments the agreed sum, agreed between the parties concerned. By virtue of this section the company is regularly paying the agreed amount to the respective Governments.

§4. Prime Minister's Control

367. The Corporation shall be subject to control and direction of the Prime Minister, and the direction so issued shall be binding on the Corporation, notwithstanding other written law to the contrary (section 2(2), (3)). The Prime Minister will receive advice from the National Petroleum Advisory Council (NPAC) on national policy, interests and matters pertaining to petroleum, petroleum industries, energy resources and their utilization. The establishment of NPAC is provided by section 5, consisting of persons appointed by the Prime Minister from the relevant States.

368. The Prime Minister's permission is required for downstream operations by any person other than PETRONAS (section 6). Downstream operation refers to business of processing or refining of petroleum or manufacturing of petrochemical products from petroleum. However, any person who is carrying on such business on the commencement of the Act may continue doing so but must apply in writing for the Prime Minister's permission, not later than six months from the date of the commencement. This also applies to any business of marketing or distributing of petroleum or petrochemical products. In granting permission, the Prime Minister, on his/her discretion, may impose terms and conditions, as he/she deems fit. Section 6 makes failure to obtain the Prime Minister's permission for downstream operations and failure to comply with any of its term and condition, offences under the Act. It may be noted here that the Prime Minister may delegate his power, except the power under section 3(2), section 5(1) and section 7, with certain conditions and restrictions, to any person. Under section 6, on conviction, the person shall be liable to:

(1) a fine not exceeding MYR 1 million, or to imprisonment for a term not exceeding five years or to both;
(2) for continuing offence, a further fine not exceeding MYR 100,000 for each day, or part of a day during which the offence continues after the first day of the conviction recorded; and

(3) all the machinery, tools, plant, buildings and other property or thing used or intended to be used in the commission of the offence and any petroleum or its products thereby obtained shall be liable to forfeiture.

369. However, Prime Minister may also exempt any of the said business or any company carrying on such business from the provisions of the section by notification in the Gazette (section 6(6)).

§5. License and Compensation Mechanism

370. As to any licenses, leases and agreements issued pursuant to the Petroleum Mining Act (PMA), 1966 or any written law in force relating to prospecting, exploration or mining for petroleum, such licences shall be valid for six months from the commencement of the PDA, and will cease to have effect afterwards, unless the period is extended by the Prime Minister (section 9). To remedy this situation, section 9 further provides for payment of compensation to be made by the Federal Government to the aggrieved party under such licences whose rights been so determined.

371. Section 7 of the Act empowers the PM to make regulations, for the purpose of carrying into effect the provision of the Act, particularly in respect of:

(1) the conduct of or the carrying on of any business or service relating to the exploration, exploitation, winning or obtaining of petroleum; any business involving the manufacture and supply of equipment used in the petroleum industry; and downstream activities and development relating to petroleum.
(2) the marketing and distribution of petroleum and its products;
(3) penalties in the form of a fine not exceeding MYR 100,000 or imprisonment not exceeding five years or both for breach of any of the regulations and for non-compliance with any term or condition of any license, permission or approval issued or granted under the regulations; and
(4) the forfeiture of anything used or intended to be used in the commission of any such breach or non-compliance.

§6. Corporate Criminal Liability

372. If any offence against this Act or against any regulation made under this Act has been committed by any company or body, by virtue of section 7B, the director, manager, partner, other similar officer or who was acting in such capacity at the time of the commission of the offence shall be deemed to be guilty of that offence. And, where the offence has been committed by any clerk, servant or agent in the course of his/her employment, the principal shall also be liable. The competent court to try offences under this Act is the Sessions Court, or in Sabah and Sarawak, the First Class Magistrate's Court (section 7C).

373. It should be noted here, that, section 7A expressly provides that the Prime Minister by notification in the gazette may delegate to any person described by name or office, his/her powers under this Act, other than power to issue directions (section 3(2)), power to appoint members of NPAC (section 5(1)) and power to make regulations under section 7.

§7. Saving

374. Section 14 of the PMA 1966 shall not apply to the Corporation, and any reference to the licensee (in the section) shall be construed as referring to the Corporation, and the reference to any rights contained in the license shall be construed as to the Corporations rights under this Act (section 2(1)).

§8. Sarawak Is Disputing Enforcement of the Act in the State

375. The state government of Sarawak has always disputed the enforcement of the authority of PETRONAS on the state. It argues that under the state laws, under section 12 of especially the Land Code, state has the exclusive rights on its lands, including the territorial waters and the continental shelf. It may be noted there that the state has territorial rights only up to 3 nautical miles. The state is planning to have its own Regulations governing petroleum development in the State. The State had made similar objections with respect to the enforcement of the Gas Supply Act 1993 in the State of Sarawak. It passed the Sarawak Gas Supply Services (Operating Company) Ordinance 1995. It may be noted here that such a demand is there even when PETRONAS is giving due favour in financial and employment matters to Sarawak. Perhaps the demand is because according to the Energy Commission at the end of 2015, Sarawak had 28.7% of known national oil reserves and 52.7% of known gas reserves.[111]

§9. Selected Cases

I. *Petroleum Nasional Bhd v. Kerajaan Negeri Terengganu* [2004] 1 MLJ 8

376. By a vesting instrument of 22 March 1975 ('the vesting instrument'), the State Government of Terengganu ('the plaintiff') vested Petroleum Nasional Bhd ('the first defendant') with the entire ownership in, and the exclusive rights, powers, liberties and privileges of exploring, exploiting, winning and obtaining petroleum whether onshore or offshore of Malaysia. Under an agreement of the same date ('the principal agreement'), the first defendant agreed to pay to the plaintiff a sum

111. 'Why Sarawak Is Questioning the Law That Created Petronas', *The Edge Markets*, 27 Jan. 2018, at: http://www.theedgemarkets.com/article/why-sarawak-questioning-law-created-petronas (accessed on 12 Mar. 2018); 'Regulatory Framework for Petronas', *Borneo Post Online*, 16 Jun. 2016.

equivalent to 5% of the value of petroleum won and saved in the State of Terengganu and sold by the first defendant. Payments were made by the first defendant from 1978 until March 2000, when the first defendant stopped the payment. The stoppage triggered the plaintiff to file this suit against the first defendant and the Government of Malaysia ('the second defendant'). The defendants, by separate applications, applied before the High Court, for certain proposed questions of law to be determined under O 14A and O 33 r 2 of the Rules of the High Court 1980 ('RHC'). The questions were, *inter alia*, whether: (a) the plaintiff had any right over petroleum in the continental shelf prior to the enactment of the PDA 1974 and the execution of the principal agreement ('the first question'); (b) the plaintiff vested any right to petroleum won and saved in the continental shelf of the coast of Terengganu in the first defendant pursuant to the vesting instrument and the principal agreement ('the second question'); and (c) the plaintiff was entitled to the payment as stipulated in the principal agreement ('the third question'). The learned High Court judge dismissed the applications. The defendants appealed.

377. The court held, allowing the defendant's appeal, that the primary issue in the suit was whether the plaintiff had, at any time, sovereign rights over petroleum in the continental shelf adjacent to the coast of Terengganu. This primary issue was contained in the first three questions posed in the defendants' applications. All the questions were purely questions of law. If the answer to the first question was in the plaintiff's favour, the answers to the second and third questions should also be in the plaintiff's favour. Hence, the answers would be decisive of the main or a substantive part of the suit. Therefore, what remained to be done was the determination of liability in damages and its assessment, if any, against the defendants since each of the defendants had made a concession not to contest the plaintiff's claim should the questions be answered in the plaintiff's favour. On the other hand, if the answer to the first question was against the plaintiff, the subsequent two questions would suffer the same fate and consequently, its action was doomed to fail because without the said right the plaintiff had nothing to vest in the first defendant and hence would not be entitled to the payments under the principal agreement. Therefore, the determination of the threshold issues as preliminary issues would be decisive of the whole litigation or essentially the main part of the suit. This would result in a substantial saving of time and cost as it would significantly cut down the costs and time involved in pretrial preparation or in connection with the trial proper. As the first defendant had paid the plaintiff continuously for twenty-two years, the plaintiff's counsel contended that the subsequent conduct can be used to interpret the principal agreement. The first defendant's subsequent conduct was inadmissible to interpret the vesting instrument and the principal agreement, although it was admissible to show whether there was a contract and what the terms of the contract were, either originally or by variation, or as the basis for an estoppels relying on the following cases: *James Miller & Partners Ltd v. Whitworth Street Estates (Manchester) Ltd* [1970] AC 583; *L Schuler AG v. Wickman Machine Tool Sales Ltd* [1974] AC 235; and *Sussex Caravan Parks Ltd v. Richardson (Valuation Officer)* [1961] 1 All ER 731 followed; *Watcham v. AG of East Africa Protectorate* [1919] AC 533 not followed.

378. Where either O 14A or O 33 r 2 of the RHC applied, the reluctant party had no choice but to accept the risk, and the party was no longer entitled to the benefit of the ordinary process of law and the right to a trial. Hence, there was no distinction as to whether the party making the application for determination under O 14A and/or O 33 r 2 was the plaintiff or the defendants. The High Court judge had merely considered the pleadings and the submissions of the parties and concluded that this case was far from being plain and simple because it raised a number of complex legal issues. The High Court judge did not identify and make proper appraisal of the material facts pleaded which were obviously undisputed or which should not have been disputed. Had he done so he would have been able to appreciate the facts and the magnitude of the case better and would have arrived at an appropriate conclusion and finding. His consideration on the matter was inadequate, incomplete and unsustainable. Hence, his exercise of discretion was incorrect. In any case, even if the case appeared to be or was complicated, it did not mean that the court must shy away from considering the applicability of O14A and O 33 r 2 of the RHC in relation to the questions of law which were clear and definite.

II. *Petroliam Nasional Bhd & Ors v. Khoo Nee Kiong* [2003] 4 MLJ 216

379. The first plaintiff was a well-known national petroleum corporation. The second plaintiff was one of the marketing arms of the first plaintiff and the third plaintiff was in the business of processing and transmitting natural gas and it conducted its gas business under the trade name 'Petronas Gas'. The defendant was an individual carrying out trading operations as a registered sole proprietor under the trade/business name 'Araneum Consulting Services' and was in no way associated with the plaintiffs. Sometime in 2001, the plaintiffs made a series of searches of domain names on the Internet using the search engine 'better-whois.com' and discovered that the defendant had registered the domain names 'petronasdagangan.com', 'petronasgas.com', 'mypetronasdagangan.com' and 'mypetronas.com' ('the said domain names') for purposes of sale. The defendant had also maintained a website under the name <www.petronasgas.com.> ('the Petronas website') which purported to provide information on, *inter alia*, the locality of the plaintiffs' service stations. A printout of the main webpage of the Petronas website showed that it was maintained by the defendant. The Petronas website was also accessible via URL <www.searchmalaysia.com> ('the searchmalaysia website'). On the searchmalaysia website, the domain name 'petronasgas.com' was described as a subsidiary of 'searchmalaysia.com'.

380. In response to a request from the first plaintiff to the defendant to transfer to the first plaintiff the registration of the said domain names on the ground that 'Petronas' was the first plaintiff's trade name worldwide and the intellectual property rights in the trade name belonged to the first plaintiff, the defendant had published certain statements via e-mail ('the impugned statements') which the plaintiffs averred clearly referred to the plaintiffs and were defamatory. In this application, the plaintiffs sought the following reliefs on the grounds of passing off of domain names and defamation: (a) an inter partes interim injunction to restrain the defendant from:

(i) passing off or attempting to pass off any website with a domain name comprising the word 'Petronas' which was not related to a website connected with the plaintiffs; (ii) making any representation to any registrar of domain names that the defendant was connected or associated with the plaintiffs and/or the name 'Petronas' and the goodwill subsisting therein; and (iii) registering or attempting to register on the internet any domain name containing the word 'Petronas'; and (b) an inter partes interim injunction to restrain the defendant from publishing or posting or disseminating the impugned statements.

381. The court held allowing the plaintiff's application that the plaintiffs had shown that the name in the e-mail address was that of the defendant and that the defendant was the sole proprietor of Araneum Consulting Services and that both the websites were operated by Araneum Consulting Services. The searches conducted by the plaintiffs on the said domain names showed that the registrants were the defendant, Araneum Consulting Services and 'Araneum@email.com for sales'. Further, the offensive e-mail also carried the hand phone number of the defendant. In the circumstances of this case, the court was more than satisfied that it was most probably the defendant who had sent the e-mail and who had set up the webpage and it followed, therefore, that the plaintiffs had sufficiently identified the defendant for the purposes of the injunctive relief sought by the plaintiffs in this application. It was not mandatory for the plaintiffs to exhibit a certificate pursuant to section 90A of the Evidence Act 1950 ('the Act') in respect of the computer printouts containing the impugned statements in the affidavit-in-support of their application for the interim injunctions. This was because at this stage of the proceedings, the plaintiffs only had to show a bona fide case or a serious question to be tried and there was no necessity for the plaintiffs to show a prima facie case. The deponent of the plaintiffs' affidavit-in-support had deposed that the contents of the affidavit were within his personal knowledge unless otherwise stated. The defendant had not challenged nor disputed the deponent's affidavit-in-reply. The plaintiffs would only have to tender the section 90A certificate if the plaintiffs did not wish to call the officer who had personal knowledge as to the production of the computer printouts by the computer to testify to that effect in the trial proper.

382. The impugned statements were manifestly defamatory. The plaintiffs had shown that the natural and ordinary meaning of the impugned statements was that: (a) the plaintiffs did not have any lawful claim to any domain name containing the word 'Petronas'; (b) the plaintiffs were in the habit of resorting to strong-arm tactics to oppress and intimidate other local companies and/or local business entities; (c) the plaintiffs were attempting or have in the past attempted to extort money from local companies or business entities by forcing them to transfer domain names to the plaintiffs for free; (d) the plaintiffs consistently behaved in an arrogant or high-handed fashion to oppress and intimidate other local companies and/or local entities; (e) the plaintiffs had acted like a 'robber' and their actions may be likened to a form of theft; and (f) the legal services department of the plaintiffs was generally incompetent and/or ignorant. Second, the plaintiffs had shown that the impugned statements were: (a) calculated to injure the reputation of the plaintiffs by exposing them to hatred, contempt or ridicule; (b) intended to lower the plaintiffs in the estimation of right-thinking members of society generally; (c) calculated to injure and disparage the plaintiffs' reputation in the plaintiffs' office, profession and trade; and (d) intended to bring the plaintiffs, by virtue of their standing, honour and integrity, into public scandal, odium and contempt. Third, the plaintiffs had sufficiently demonstrated that the impugned statements had been published to third parties. Fourth, the plaintiffs had shown that by reason of the publication of the impugned statements, the plaintiffs had suffered grave injury to their trading personality and irreparable loss and damage and would continue to suffer such irreparable loss and damage. Fifth, the court was satisfied that there had been no improper delay on the part of the plaintiffs in bringing this application because the existence of the Petronas website maintained by the defendant was only discovered by the plaintiffs on or about the end of November 2001 and the defendant's official response to the plaintiffs' solicitors was only received on 5 December 2001. Finally, the plaintiffs had given an undertaking as to damages and the court was satisfied that the plaintiffs were in a strong financial position to meet their undertaking should the defendant win at the trial. By registering the said domain names which contained the word 'Petronas', there was a serious issue to be tried in that the defendant was making a false representation to persons who may have consulted the register that the registrant, 'Araneum Consulting Services' was connected or associated with the name registered and thus the owner of the goodwill in the name 'Petronas'.

383. By registering the said domain names, the defendant had eroded the exclusive goodwill in the name 'Petronas' which had caused damage to the plaintiffs. The said domain names were instruments of fraud and any realistic use of them, as domain names would result in passing off. This would cause irreparable injury and damage to the plaintiffs and by virtue of this, the balance of convenience tilted in favour of the plaintiffs. The plaintiffs had sufficiently demonstrated that since the said domain names contained the word 'Petronas', the court can assume that the intention of the defendant in using the said domain names was to deceive the public by passing off himself as part of the Petronas group of companies or his business or products as those of the plaintiffs'. In the circumstances, the plaintiffs had shown that there was a threat of passing off and trademark infringement on the defendant's part which was likely to cause confusion in the minds of consumers of the plaintiffs' products, thereby resulting in irreparable injury and damage to the plaintiffs' trade, business and goodwill. Therefore, the court concluded that as the plaintiffs had provided an undertaking as to damages, the interim injunction sought for ought to be granted relying on the decision in *British Telecommunications plc and Another v. One In A Million Ltd and Others and Other Actions* [1998] 4 All ER 476.

III. *Petroliam Nasional Bhd (Petronas) & Anor v. Cheah Kam Hiew [1987] 1 MLJ 25*

384. In this case the respondent who was an account holder of Bank Bumiputra Malaysia Berhad had applied by Originating Summons for declarations that the acquisition of shares in the bank by Petronas was ultra vires the PDA, 1978, and so was the purchase or acquisition of the loans of the bank by Petronas. The appellants applied to strike out the Originating Summons on the ground that no reasonable cause of action was disclosed against either of them and that the action was misconceived, frivolous and vexatious as well as an abuse of the process of the court. Before the hearing of the summons of the appellants, the second appellant, the Government of Malaysia, tabled a Bill in Parliament which was later enacted as the Petroleum Development (Amendment) Act, 1985. This Act in effect gave the necessary powers to Petronas and gave them with retrospective effect. The result was that when the Summons in Chambers to strike out the Originating Summons was heard the respondent could no longer dispute that he had no cause of action. The learned trial judge struck out the Originating Summons but awarded costs to the respondent. The appellants appealed.

385. The general principle envisaged in the Rules of the High Court is simply that costs follow the event and that the successful party is entitled to be paid his/her costs except when it appears to the court that in the circumstances of the case some other order should be made. An appellate court does not interfere in the question of costs without reluctance. This is because the court below has an absolute discretion except that the discretion must be exercised judicially. An appellate court should not interfere unless it can be shown that there has been an error of law or the purported exercise of discretion was based on grounds wholly unconnected with the cause of action. The court concluded that in this case the appellate court could not say that the learned judge had exercised his discretion wrongly in the circumstances of the case.

Chapter 2. Petroleum Regulations 1974, PU(A) 432/1974

386. (These Regulations are made pursuant to section 7 of Petroleum Development Act 1974).

§1. Substantive Part

387. Under Regulation 2, all existing bodies or companies who are issued with exploration licence, or have entered into petroleum agreements under the Petroleum Mining Act 1966, are required to submit all data, information and records in respect of any survey, research, exploration and production carried out by them to PETRONAS, for no consideration.

388. Applications for commencement and continuation of licence shall be made to:

(1) The President of PETRONAS with respect to licence for exploration, exploitation, winning and obtaining of petroleum (upstream activities), and licence to supply of equipment, facilities and services for that activities (Regulation 3).
(2) The Secretary General, MITI relating to downstream activities of processing or refining of petroleum or manufacture of petrochemical products from petroleum (under section 6(1) of the Petroleum Development Act) (Regulation 3A(1)).
(3) The Secretary General, Ministry of International Trade and Consumer Affairs, with respect to marketing or distribution of petroleum or petrochemical products (under section 6(3)) (Regulation 3A(2)).

389. After the Chairman and Chief Executive of PETRONAS processed the application, it shall be forwarded to the Prime Minister. The same goes to other applications, which will be forwarded to the Prime Minister who shall reject or approve such applications (Regulation 5). Any permission and licences granted shall be subject to the payment of fees as specified in the Schedule, and may be subject to all or some conditions relating thereto with respect to items listed down in Regulation 5(2); among others are the payment of royalties, fees, method of working, inspection, etc. Every application shall contain details and information as may be required from time to time (Regulation 4). Furthermore, under Regulation 7, the Prime Minister may from time to time authorize any officer, by notice under his/her hand, to require the person granted permission or licence under this Regulation to give in writing all information required in the notice within stipulated time. Failure to comply with that notice without reasonable excuse is an offence, punishable with a fine not exceeding MYR 5,000 or to imprisonment for a term not exceeding two years or with both. Likewise, furnishing false information is also an offence, punishable with a fine not exceeding MYR 10,000 or imprisonment for a term not exceeding four years or both.

390. Another offences prescribed in the Regulation are commencing or continuing business mentioned in Regulation 3 without licence and failure to comply with any condition of such licence. On conviction, the offender will be liable to a fine not exceeding MYR 50,000 or imprisonment for a term not exceeding two years or to both, and in case of continuing offence, a further fine of MYR 1,000 for each day after the conviction is recorded.

391. Any licence or permission granted under the Petroleum Development Act 1974 and the Regulation shall continue to be in force so long as it is not superseded, revoked or terminated, and where such licence expressly validates only for definite period, it will be invalidated at the expiration of the period, unless it is renewed (Regulation 10).

§2. Schedule

392. The schedule (made under Regulation 5) lists down the amounts of fees chargeable for a licence or a permission to commence and continue any business or service specified in Regulations 3, 3A(a) and (b).

Chapter 3. Petroleum Mining Act 1966 (Act 95)

§1. General

393. The provisions of this Act mainly concern on mining of petroleum and matters connected with it.

394. The word 'petroleum' is defined in section 2 to include any mineral oil or relative hydrocarbon and natural gas existing in its natural condition in strata but does not include coal or bituminous sales and other stratified deposits from which oil can be extracted by destructive distillation. This definition is slightly wider than the definition of the word contained in section 10 of the PDA. The definition in this Act is:

> the expression 'petroleum' means any mineral oil or relative hydrocarbon and natural gas existing in its natural condition and casing head petroleum spirit including bituminous shales and other stratified deposits from which oil can be extracted.

395. By virtue of section 3 of the Act, no exploring, prospecting and mining for petroleum upon any land shall be carried out except in pursuant to an exploration licence or a petroleum agreement. The word 'land' in section 2 means onshore (defined as inclusive of foreshores and the submarine areas beneath the territorial water of the States) and offshore land in relation to West Malaysia and for Sabah and Sarawak means offshore land only. Offshore land means the area of the continental shelf as defined under section 2 of the Continental Shelf Act, 1966. Exploring etc. petroleum without such licence or agreement, or in breach of any of its condition, is an offence (section 3(2)), punishable with a fine not exceeding MYR 20,000 (the Act still uses the word 'dollar'), or imprisonment for a term not exceeding two years or both; and all machinery, tools, buildings and other property together with any minerals or products obtained from the land shall be liable to forfeiture (section 3(2)).

§2. Licences

396. For those who want to carry out such activities, application for exploration licence or a petroleum agreement in accordance with this Act in respect of any area of land may be made to the Petroleum Authority who shall consider and decide whether to approve or to refuse it (section 4). The Petroleum Authority refers to the Ruler or the Governor of the particular State, in which the area of onshore land is situated, and in respect to offshore land, shall be the YDPA (section 4(3)). Section 5 provides for the procedure of making the application, among others:

(1) it must be made in writing in the Form set out in the First Schedule of the Act, addressed to the Menteri Besar or the Chief Minister of the State or to the Minister for consideration by the Petroleum Authority;
(2) it must be accompanied with the prescribed fees (see Rule 4, Petroleum Mining Rules 1968), two copies of a survey office map showing delineated boundaries of the proposed area of land. Where two or more separated area involved, a separate application must be made in respect of each area;
(3) upon request, it must be furnished with such evidence as to the financial position and technical qualification, within three month from the request. Failure of this would render the application deemed to be withdrawn.

397. All information furnished under this Act is confidential (section 5(5)).

398. Once approved, the petroleum agreement must be executed within six months from the date of the approval, otherwise the approval shall be lapsed, unless the Petroleum Authority considers that the delay is not attributable to the fault of the applicant.

I. Exploration Licence and Petroleum Agreement

399. Section 2 of the Act simply defines exploration licence as licence issued under section 7, and petroleum agreement as agreement entered into under section 8 and section 9.

400. According to section 7, the Petroleum Authority may issue the exploration licence in respect to the whole or any part of the area specified in the application. There can be more than one licence issued in respect of the same area, but no exploration licence shall be issued, in area which has already been covered by a petroleum agreement entered into under section 8. Nevertheless, the licensee may at any time apply for a petroleum agreement in respect of the whole or part of the area licensed to him/her, and upon issuance of the petroleum agreement, he/she will not be entitled to any compensation from the Petroleum Authority. Every exploration licence shall be issued for initial period of two years, and thereafter may be extended from time to time upon application. An exploration licence shall be in the form set out in Second Schedule, but it is subject to modifications, exclusions and additions of ancillary matters by the Petroleum Authority.

401. With regards to petroleum agreement, section 8 provides that, the Petroleum Authority may enter into petroleum agreement with the applicant in respect of the specified area. The area of land covered shall not exceed 4,000 square miles, and shall be in the form of the model petroleum agreement (made by the YDPA pursuant to section 12 of the Act), but subject to modification and amendment by the Petroleum Authority. However, by virtue of section 9, there can also be a single petroleum agreement covering more than 4,000 square miles. But this only applies to contiguous areas, which means 'areas which are situated on the same geological structure or cover a group of geologically similar and related structure' (section 9(3)).

402. By virtue of section 10, there may be more than one exploration licence or petroleum agreement being issued to or entered into at the same time in favour of the same person. Section 11 then makes it mandatory for the Petroleum Authority to publish a notification in the *Gazette* stating the name of the person with whom the petroleum agreement is entered into, the name of any assignee and the situation of the area concerned.

403. If the licensee or the person who is a party to a petroleum agreement has been refused entry upon any alienated land by its owner, he/she may apply to the State Authority for permission to enter upon that land. The State Authority, after giving to the owner of the land the right of being heard, may grant the permission, on condition that the applicant undertakes to pay compensation for all the damage which may be caused by such entry. The permission so granted will be final and shall not be questioned in any court. The owner shall then be bound by the permission granted, of which, if he/she refuses entry, shall be guilty of an offence and liable to a fine not exceeding MYR 500 and a further fine not exceeding MYR 10 for each day when the refusal continues. And for the purpose of this section (section 14), the word 'owner' includes chargee, lessee, occupier or any person having interest in the land; and the word 'entry' includes the exercising of rights contained in the exploration licence or the petroleum agreement.

II. Power of the YDPA

404. Regulations under this Act may be made by the YDPA under section 12, with respect to:

(a) the appointment of officers to enforce this Act, fees to be paid, and the form and contents of the model petroleum agreement;
(b) the prevention of fires in areas where oil mining is carried out; and
(c) the establishment of safety areas, as well as the general safety, health and welfare of the workers.

405. Item (a) mentioned above shall only be effective in States if it is concurred to by the State Authority of the respective States. As to item (b) above, it may provide that the regulations shall be in addition to or in substitution for the written law relating to labour. This section also empowers the YDPA to amend the First Schedule of the Act (Application for Exploration Licence or Petroleum Agreement).

§3. Section 13. Repeal and Saving

406. By virtue of this Act, all references to oil prospecting licences and oil mining leases in the Mining Enactments of the States in West Malaysia shall be deemed to have been repealed, except for licences and leases for the duration of time shall remain valid until the expiration of that duration.

407. The Mining Ordinance of Sabah, the Oil Mining Ordinance of Sarawak and any other State law in force in Sabah and Sarawak with respect to exploration of petroleum onshore land shall remain in force, and the provisions relating to exploration of petroleum offshore land shall be deemed to be repealed. Nevertheless, any licence, lease or agreement relating to offshore land issued under the Ordinance, before 8 November 1969, shall remain in force. However, it will be construed subject to this Act, and all rights and liabilities borne by the Government of Sabah and Sarawak shall be borne by the Federal Government. By virtue of subsection 2(e), YDPA may before 31 December 1972 make further transitional or saving provision by order.

§4. First Schedule: Application for an Exploration Licence or for a Petroleum Agreement

408. The application may be made by either individuals or a company. The following must contain in the application:

(a) The full name and the details of the applicant: address, nationality and occupation for application by individuals.
(b) The details of the company/applicant must consist of all the followings: the law under which it is incorporated, its principal place of business, name and address of its authorized agent in Malaysia (for companies whose principal place of business is outside Malaysia), the nature of the business, name and nationality of each director and name of each principal shareholders together with the amount of shares held.
(c) Whether onshore or offshore activity, the situation and approximate area of the proposed land.
(d) Brief particulars of previous experience in petroleum prospecting work, and particulars of interest in and access to refining and marketing facilities outside Malaysia.
(e) Name and qualifications of technical experts or advisers, and amount of capital for operation of the exploration applied for, available at the time of presentation of the application, as well as amount and the source of capital which can be made available.

At the end of the application, the applicant declares the particulars stated are correct, followed by his/her signature at the bottom right of the application.

§5. Second Schedule: Exploration Licence

409. (Section 7(5) – Form of Exploration Licence)

I. General

410. At the centre top of the licence, there should be the name of the particular government which is issuing the licence. Exploration licence is issued in respect of the area of land specified in the Schedule, which can either be of offshore or onshore land. The licensee will be named under the interpretation of the word 'licensee' in Clause 1 of the licence, including his/her successor in title and also person deriving title under him/her. Petroleum Authority refers to either the Ruler or Government of the State, and in some cases also includes the Menteri Besar or the Chief Minister as the case may be. Any other terms and expressions undefined under the licence will have the meaning as assigned in the PMA, 1966.

411. The licence is given in consideration of payments of a sum stated under Clause 9 to the Petroleum Authority, whereby subject to the terms and conditions of the licence, the licensee will be granted licence and liberty to search for petroleum in the exploration area (Clause 2) for the term of two years unless sooner determined or extended (Clause 7). The right to search for petroleum conferred by the licence shall include prospecting geological, geophysical, topographic survey and chemical means and drilling for geological information but shall not include any right to drill well and to get petroleum (Clause 6).

412. This licence may exist in common with other licensees' rights. The licensee however, at any time during the licence term, has the right to determine this licence by giving to the Petroleum Authority not less than six months written notice to that effect. Likewise, the licensee may apply for extension to the Petroleum Authority not less than three months before the expiry of the licence, and extension for a further term of one year on the same terms and conditions set out in this licence will be given in consideration for a further consideration (Clause 8).

413. The Petroleum Authority reserves the right and liberty to enter in or upon the licensed land, liberty to search for, work and get petroleum and other minerals upon the exploration area, and liberty to authorize any person or to grant leases or licences for that purposes. The reservations however shall not be exercised in such a way as to hinder or interfere with the licensees' rights and power granted by this licence (Clause 3). Petroleum Authority shall also have the right at any time to exclude any part of the exploration area required for public purposes. Such part shall continue to be part of the exploration area, but no operation shall be carried out upon it, without permission in writing of the authorities. Thus, the licensee shall be relieved from all liabilities in respect of the excluded part (Clause 4). The Petroleum Authority has the right to determine any part of the exploration area by entering into petroleum agreement in respect of the whole or any part of the exploration area with the licensee or other persons (Clause 2), or by reducing the exploration area (Clause 9), without being liable to pay any compensation to the licensee.

II. Restrictions of the Licensees' Powers and His/Her Obligations

414. The licensee's powers are restricted in relation to:

- Parts held to be sacred as decided by the Menteri Besar or the Chief Minister.
- Parts appropriated for public purposes, parts situated or occupied by township, cemetery or occupied by the Federal or the State Government, parts which is the site of or 50 yards of any building, public road, etc., and parts actually under cultivation, unless written permission from the Petroleum Authority is obtained.
- Part consisting of alienated land, unless written permission from the owner of the land is obtained.

415. Moreover, the licensee must always comply with all written laws in force in Malaysia, and shall not hinder or prevent any person from having access to any road constructed under this licence.

416. Written consent of the Petroleum Authority is required before commencing or recommencing the drilling of any well (including boreholes – Clause 1), and it shall be not less than 125 m from any of the exploration area's boundaries (Clauses 10 and 11). The licensee shall maintain all the apparatus, appliances and wells in good repair and condition and shall execute all operations in a proper and workmanlike manner in accordance with method and practice of exploration customarily used in good oilfield practice. Furthermore, the licensee shall take all the precautionary steps practicable in preventing the escape or waste of petroleum discovered, conserving the exploration area and preventing damage to petroleum, and petroleum-bearing strata. If any such event occurs, the licensee shall notify the Petroleum Authority within three days of the occurrence of that event (Clause 12).

417. The licensee is prohibited from cutting or taking any timber or protected trees unless there is consent from the appropriate authority on payment of fees and royalties prescribed by law, together with payment of fair and adequate compensation (Clause 13). The licensee is also prohibited from exercising his/her rights under this licence in a manner which will unjustifiably interfere with navigation or fishing in the waters of the exploration area or with the conservation of the living resources of the sea (Clause 15).

418. The licensee shall comply with all instructions relating to safety, health and welfare of the employees. He/she also shall keep accurate records of the operations in a form approved by the Petroleum Authority, which shall contain the items listed in Clause 16 of the licence, including the geological and geophysical plans of the exploration area. He/she shall, every three months during the licence term, furnish a return containing the required particulars of the operations, and its progress to the

Petroleum Authority. Correspondingly, the licensee shall forthwith report of any discovery of petroleum and petroleum-bearing strata to the Petroleum Authority.

419. As far as reasonably practicable the licensee shall correctly label and preserve samples of the seabed and of the strata encountered, for reference for a period of twelve months. The Petroleum Authority shall be entitled to require and retain the samples, in order to inspect and analyse them. All records and information furnished shall be treated as confidential. Any person authorized by the Petroleum Authority may inspect and make abstracts or copies of any records which the licensee is required to keep, at all reasonable times.

420. Failure on part of the licensee to perform the obligations under Clauses 10, 12 and 15 shall entitle the Petroleum Authority after giving reasonable written notice of his/her intention, to execute any works and to provide equipment necessary to secure the performance of the said obligations and also to recover the cost and expenses for doing so from the licensee. The licensee shall not assign any of the rights granted under this licence in respect of the whole or any part of the exploration area or grant any sub-licence of any such rights.

421. The Petroleum Authority may revoke this licence if any of the following events occur:

- any payment of consideration in arrear or unpaid for two months from the date it ought to have been paid;
- any breach or non-observance of any of the terms and conditions of this licence;
- the bankruptcy of the licensee;
- any arrangement or composition made by the licensee with his/her creditors; or
- if the licensee is a company, the appointment of a receiver or any liquidation, voluntary or compulsory.

422. Any dispute or question arising from this licence shall be referred to arbitration in accordance with the Arbitration Act, 2005, by a single arbitrator who in default of agreement between the parties as to his/her appointment shall be appointed by the Lord President of the Supreme Court for the time being (Clause 27).

423. The last clause is then followed by the Schedule, specifying or describing the exploration area, date of issuance of the licence, and signature of the Minister or Menteri Besar, or the Chief Minister, as the case may be, on behalf of the particular government issuing the licence.

Chapter 4. Petroleum Mining Rules 1968

424. The Petroleum Mining Rules 1968 came into force on 1 December 1966 (Regulation 1). It has two annexes of model petroleum agreements: Annex I, relating to offshore land (Regulation 2); and Annex II, relating to onshore land (Regulation 3). The last rule, which is Rule 4, prescribes the fees payable under section 5(2) of the Petroleum Mining Act that are MYR 500 for exploration licence and MYR 1,000 for petroleum agreement. The following are the notable points.

§1. The Two Model Agreements in Respect of Offshore Land

425. The agreements start with the execution date of the agreement, followed by identification of the parties involved. The main difference between the two model agreements is due to the different reference made to the word 'Petroleum Authority' under section 4(3) of the Petroleum Mining Act. By implications, it shows that offshore land is a matter under the Federal Government power, whereas the onshore land is under the Government of the particular State, where the mining activities will take place. Thus, as regards to offshore land (annex I), the agreement is between the Government of the Federation and the named company, whereas in onshore land, the agreement is between the Government of the respective state and the named company (including also its successors and assigns).

426. The preambles of the two agreements are exactly the same. It says that the company (i) has applied to the Government for a petroleum agreement under the Petroleum Mining Act 1966, in respect of land specified in the First Schedule of the agreement and (ii) has entered into a bond in the form set out in the Second Schedule with the stated sum of ringgit conditioned for the due and faithful carrying out of the provisions contained in the Agreement, and that the Government has agreed to enter into a petroleum agreement under the terms and provisions specified in the Agreement.

427. Most of clauses of the two model agreements have been substantively worded exactly the same, except that the numbering is not the same. This is due to the fact that generally, model agreement for onshore land has some additional clauses that are absent in offshore agreement. Examples are clauses under the particular Part (of the agreement) relating to 'Rights Reserved by Government' and 'Restriction on the company's rights' as we will see later. However, offshore agreement also has one distinctive clause that is Clause 45 – Land required by the company for its operations, while on the other hand, onshore agreement has one clause – Land for shore installation (Clause 54). The rest are exactly in *pari materia.*

428. The first Part of the Agreement is definitions under Clause 1. The only difference between the two model agreements here is the word 'Minister'. The word 'Minister' under the offshore agreement refers to Minister charged with the responsibility for lands and mines, whereas in onshore agreement, it refers to the Menteri

Besar or the Chief Minister of a state. To note, the word 'petroleum' here has similar meaning with that of the definition in the PMA 1966, but it includes also the casing head petroleum spirit, which is defined as:

> Any mineral oil or relative hydrocarbon and natural gas existing in its natural condition and casing head petroleum spirit but does not include coal or bituminous shales or other stratified deposits from which oil can be extracted by destructive distillation.

429. 'Agreement Period' of the agreement means the period during which this Agreement subsists as determined under the provisions of Clause 59 or Clause 75 respectively. The Agreement shall subsist for a period of forty years from the date hereof, and shall be divided in two phases: (1) exploration phase and (2) development phase. 'Exploration phase' means the period for finding and searching for petroleum activities, and 'development phase' means the period which the companies' activities are directed towards the production of petroleum from the Scheduled Land.

430. Part II states that under Clause 2 Government grants to the company holding the Agreement the rights specified in Part III, to exercise and enjoy all the said rights subject to the provisions of this Agreement, particularly under Parts IV, VII to XII. This general grant is given in consideration of the expenditure commitments and payments to be made by the company specified in Parts V and VI.

I. Rights of the Company under the Model Agreements

431. In both Agreements, rights of the company are spelt out under Part III – 'Rights of the Company over Scheduled Lands', particularly in Clause 3 of this part. Under this clause, the rights are more or less the same but for onshore agreement, it has two additional rights, as we will see later. It is interesting to note here that the wording used for onshore agreement is stronger. It reads 'the Company shall have the sole and exclusive rights' whereas in offshore agreements it uses the word 'the Company shall hold the exclusive rights'. See the following chart:

Offshore Land	*Onshore Land*
– The Company shall have the right to enter upon the Scheduled Lands, explore and search for petroleum, including making geological, geophysical and topographic examination on the Scheduled Lands.	– same.

Offshore Land	*Onshore Land*
– to bore for and work out all or any petroleum lying within and throughout the Lands.	– same.
– to carry away and dispose of any petroleum, the produce of the Lands for the use and benefit of the Company.	– to use, collect, impound and bore for water upon the land for any purpose connected with the borings for petroleum or refining operation; provided that: – the Company must get prior approval from the Government (of the Federation). – it shall not deprive of a reasonable supply of water to any land, villages or accustomed watering place for cattle.
– to use and occupy a sufficient part of the Lands as necessary and convenient for the said borings and operations.	– same.
– to refine or treat the aforesaid petroleum in and upon any lands within the Federation, for the purpose of sale or otherwise, save as hereinafter provided.	– to refine or treat the aforesaid petroleum in and upon the Lands (Scheduled Lands), for the purpose of sale or otherwise, save as hereinafter provided.
– to store, take, lead, pipe and carry away, on, under or over the Lands the aforesaid petroleum and the product, and to dispose of the same at its own will and pleasure, save as hereinafter provided.	– same.
– to erect and operate in, upon and over the Land and the sea lying over: – such structures, machineries, pipelines, storage tanks, telephone and power lines; – radio transmitting and receiving apparatus, loading places (for ships, aircraft and helicopter);	– to erect and operate in, upon and over the Land, the infrastructures and facilities necessary for the exercise of the several rights and privileges hereby granted. (In addition to the things mentioned in Clause 3(g) of offshore agreement, here this also includes offices, houses, schools, hospitals, recreation ground, sport facilities, etc.)

Offshore Land	*Onshore Land*
necessary and convenient for effectually carrying out any operations hereunder, provided that the Company shall get prior permission or approval as may be required by any written law in force.	
– to search for, dig and obtain for free of charge: water, gravel, sand, clay and stone being within and throughout the Scheduled Land, for the purpose of the Company's operation. However, the Company has no right to sell these items.	– same; Provided that, at the expiration of the Agreement, any excavations shall be fenced or filled in or levelled and left the Land suitable for cultivation as far as reasonably practicable if so required by the Government.
– –	– to cut down trees (including timber, except the protected trees) on the Land for the purpose of ingress and egress to and from the Land, for the erection of machinery and plant (for the operations), for protection against damage by fire and for erecting dwelling houses; provided that the Company shall pay a reasonable price for all timber and the felled trees, such price is to be assessed in default of agreement as provided in arbitration clause (Clause 80). This however does not apply to 'reserved forest', where prior written consent of the Government is required.
– –	– to enclose the surface of any of the Scheduled Land with a fence, subject to provisions of this Agreement provided that the Company shall secure permission required by any written law in force, before doing so.

§2. Part IV: Surrender Provisions

432. There are two types of surrender: voluntary surrender (Clause 5) and compulsory surrender (Clause 4). Any area or areas of the Scheduled Land to be surrendered, shall so far as reasonable, be areas which are of sufficient size and convenient shape for enabling effective oil operations carried out thereon (Clause 6). The company is free to decide which area to be surrendered, and shall, not less than two calendar months before the due date of surrender, notify the Minister in writing of the areas to be surrendered (Clause 4(3)).

433. For voluntary surrender, the company shall be entitled to surrender at any time during the Agreement Period, its right in any area of the Scheduled Land by giving not less than two calendar months' notice to the Government, and shall be effective upon expiration of such notice. Agreement Period for the Agreement is forty years from the date of the Agreement (Clause 59 (offshore) or Clause 70 (onshore)).

434. So for compulsory surrender is concerned, by virtue of Clause 4, the company shall surrender any area or areas of the Scheduled Land:

(1) on the expiration of five Agreement Years (from the date of the Agreement), areas amount to 50% of the area originally contained in the Scheduled Land (including areas which have already been surrendered voluntarily); or
(2) on the expiration of ten Agreement Years, areas amount to 75% of the area originally contained in the Scheduled Land (including areas which have already been surrendered).

435. The only excuse on which the company may not surrender land under this clause is that by reason of such surrender the areas retained by the company would be too small for effective development. The company, however, will have to satisfy the Minister, by making written representation to him/her not less than three calendar months before the due date of such surrender, whereby the Minister may waive his/her rights to such and subsequent surrender (Proviso to Clause 4(1)).

436. After any such surrender, if the Scheduled Lands retained do not form a single entity, the company shall be granted wayleaves over any Scheduled Land surrendered provided the company so requires for the purpose of this Agreement. Such grant shall be subject to reasonable payment and other stipulations and provisions as may be agreed between the parties. The said wayleaves shall not be calculated as part of the Land retained (Clause 4(4)).

437. By virtue of subclause 5 of Clause 4, the Minister may in his/her discretion upon application made in writing to him/her by the company, at any time, re-include in this Agreement any part of the Land surrendered under this clause, provided that:

(1) if such resumption would make the aggregate of the Scheduled Land greater than the amount authorized by subclause 1, the company shall surrender other parts of the Land so as to make up with the authorized aggregate; and

(2) if no rights inconsistent with the rights under this Agreement (resumption) have been granted to any third party, and in the event where there are also mining rights other than petroleum has been granted to over the (resumed) Land, the company shall exercise its rights in the manner not to interfere or hinder with such existing rights (of others).

The Land once surrendered shall be deemed to be excluded from the Scheduled Land, and any reference to the Scheduled Land thereafter would mean only the Scheduled Land as reduced by such surrender (Clause 7). And in the event where any area has inadvertently been included under the Agreement (may be of two reasons: first, upon proof that the Government is not entitled to the rights over the area of land, and second, that the area has already been granted to other companies or individuals), this Agreement shall be deemed to have been amended by the exclusion of the said particular area of land, effective from the date of such proof or grant (Clause 8).

The company shall on its own expense, unless Minister otherwise determines, carry out survey on the boundary line of the Land, and erect and maintain substantial boundary marks of brick stone or concrete not less than 1 foot high. Such boundary marks shall be connected in such a manner that the boundaries of the Scheduled Land can be accurately traced. However, the company shall ensure that the area demarcated on the ground shall conform as closely as possible to the area delineated on the plan annexed to this Agreement (Clause 9).

§3. Part V: Expenditure Commitment and Fixed Yearly Payments

438. Clause 10 provides the following working obligation and expenditure commitment of the company during the exploration phase:

(1) To carry out scheme of prospecting including geological and geophysical surveys and examination, and may employ contractors for these purposes.
(2) To submit, during the first month of each Agreement Year to the Minister a programme of prospecting which the company intends to carry out during the year, together with the estimated cost.
(3) To submit, within three months of the end of each Agreement Year, to the Government detailed audited account, showing the sum of money expended by the company in carrying out prospecting during that year.
(4) To spend on exploration and operations, not less than the sum specified under subclause 4. For the first and second year, MYR 200,000 each; the third and fourth year, MYR 500,000 each and for the fifth year up to the tenth year, the amount of MYR 2 million each. If the exploration phase is extended, then the company shall spend MYR 3 million for the subsequent eleventh to the fifteenth year.
(5) The company shall pay the difference between its liability (sum required under subclause 4) and its actual expenditure (as shown by the audited accounts submitted under subclause 3), if the sum expended falls short of that required sum, resulting from the sooner determination of this Agreement:

- to the Accountant General in Kuala Lumpur within three months of the end of either of the said second five Agreement Years or such lesser period, during which the required sum fell short; and
- to the Government within three months of the end of the extended exploration phase during which the required sum fell short. If the abovementioned short fall is during any Five Agreement Years, in the opinion of the Government, not due to lack of diligence on the part of the company, then, such short fall may be carried forward and made good in the next succeeding five Agreement Years; and if the total actual expenditure during any five Agreement Years exceeds the total amount required, then such excess shall be carried forward to set off against any short fall which may occur in the next succeeding five Agreement Years, provided that the amount carried forward is not exceeding 25% of the total expenditure to be incurred in the next succeeding five Agreement Years.

(6) Where the Scheduled Land held by the company during the first five Agreement Years exceeds 4,000 square miles, or exceeds 2,000 square miles during the second five Agreement Years, or exceeds 1,000 square miles for the subsequent Agreement Year, the company shall, in addition to the sum required under subclause 4, spend for each and every square mile held in excess, a further sum of MYR 170 per annum during the first five Agreement Years, MYR 1,000 per annum during the second 5 Agreement Years and MYR 3,000 per annum during the third 5 Agreement Years.

439. Apart from that, the company shall make fixed yearly payments to the Government as specified under Clause 11. During the exploration phase, the company shall pay for every square mile of the Scheduled Land, MYR 20 in respect of each of the sixth, to tenth years of the Agreement, and MYR 40 for each of the extended years (11th to 15th). To note, the first five years of the Agreement is exempted from payment under this clause. Whereas, during the development phase, the company shall pay for every square mile of the Scheduled Land, MYR 50 in respect of each of the first to fifth year, MYR 1,000 for the sixth to tenth years of the Agreement and MYR 2,000 for each of the subsequent years (11th to 15th). The payment shall be made in two instalments, first, on the first day of January, and second, on the first day of July of each respective year.

440. By virtue of subclause 3, the said fixed yearly payments during the first five years of the development phase may be deducted from the amount of royalties payable in that year under Part VI, in respect of acreage within a petroleum field, and in respect of acreage outside such petroleum field, the said fixed yearly payment may be reduced by expenditures incurred in that year for exploration of petroleum. Any deduction of the said fixed payment from royalties shall be treated as part or full payment of such royalties, provided that such royalties, for income tax purpose, shall be treated as if it were fixed yearly payments. In this subclause, the expression 'acreage within a petroleum field' means the area occupied by petroleum at the time of its discovery plus 20%. The boundaries of petroleum field once established will continue throughout the Agreement Period but may be extended by application if additional petroleum-bearing areas are subsequently discovered.

441. However, in case when the company's rights over any area of the Scheduled Land are determined or surrendered, the Government shall refund to the company an apportioned part of any fixed yearly payment made by the company in advance in respect of such areas. This refund shall be in respect of the date of such determination or surrender for which payment has already been made.

442. In addition to the above financial commitment, in onshore agreement, the company shall pay to the Government additional yearly payment of an agreed sum per acre of the surface State lands actually occupied by the company for any purpose of this Agreement. Such payment shall be made in accordance with provisions of the National Land Code and Rules made thereunder.

§4. Part VI: Royalties and Taxes

443. The company shall pay to the Government, within two months from the first day of January and the first day of July in each year of the Agreement Period, in Malaysian currency unless otherwise agreed, the royalties set out in the succeeding three clauses (14, 15 and 16), in respect of the half-year period ending on the said dates. If there is dispute affecting the amount of royalties, then the payable amount shall be the minimum amount admitted by the company, and no further royalties shall be payable in respect of that half-year period until the amount is finally determined. Basically, royalty should be paid on crude oil, casing head petroleum spirit and natural gas won and saved by the company from the Scheduled Land in the preceding half-year period at a rate equal to 12% of the value. 'Crude oil' is mineral oil in its natural state before refinery or otherwise treatment, excluding water and foreign substances, 'casing head petroleum spirit' means any liquid hydrocarbons obtained from natural gas by separation or by any chemical or physical process, and 'natural gas' means obtained from boreholes and wells and consisting primarily of hydrocarbons (Clause 2).

444. For crude oil, the value shall be the value obtained by applying the rate of posted price effective at the end of the period of which the royalty is to be paid. To note, any crude oil or casing head petroleum spirit used for drilling and production operations shall be excluded in calculation of the quantity obtained, for the purpose of this clause. 'Posted price' means the f.o.b. price published by the company under the pricing clause (Clause 18–offshore, Clause 19–onshore). If no posted price published, in respect of crude oil not exported, the value shall be ascertained in a manner to be agreed between the company and the Minister.

445. However, where it is shown to the satisfaction of the Minister that any part of the crude oil is consumed within Malaysia, such value shall be the actual selling price obtained by the company from the sale of such crude oil.

The Government may, in lieu of the royalty, elect to take a portion of each type of crude oil not exceeding 12% of the total volume of each type, by giving not less than four calendar months' notice to the company, and when made shall continue for the period specified in the notice, or if not stated, until terminated by the Government by giving further notice not less than four calendar months.

446. For both casing head petroleum and natural gas, the value shall be the value in the field of production. Such value shall be the actual selling price obtained less an appropriate allowance for the cost of processing and transportation.

§5. Measurement of Petroleum for Royalty Purposes

447. The company shall measure or weight by a method or methods customarily used in good oilfield operations and from time to time approved by the Minister, and no alteration in the methods used shall be made without first informing the Minister. For crude oil and casing head petroleum spirit, the measurement is based on the quantity obtained and recovered, while for natural gas, it is based on the quantity obtained and sold (the volume is calculated at an absolute pressure of 1 atmosphere and at the temperature of 60°F). Any officer authorized by the Minister shall be entitled to be present in the measurement process.

§6. Taxation and Audit

448. The company shall be liable to pay to the Government the income tax payable by the application of the Petroleum (Income Tax) Act 1967 only, and not under any other Act. Apart from payments which would be made under this agreement, the company shall only be liable to pay for charges, fees for services rendered by the governmental authorities so long as it is reasonable and non-discriminatory, and the taxes and fees of general application such as import duties, stamp duties and registration fees, provided they are at rates no higher than those generally applicable in the Federation. The company will have to pay tax on: (1) Payments made in accordance of the agreement and the provision of the Petroleum (Income Tax) 1967 Act. (2) Charges and fees for services rendered by governmental authorities on request or to the public general provided that they are reasonable and non-discriminatory. (3) Taxes and fees of general application such as import duties, stamp duties and registration fees provided that they are at the rates no higher than those generally applicable in the Federation.

449. As to audit, the Government will have the right from time to time to appoint a qualified, independent auditor who shall have the right to audit revenues and not otherwise the books and account of the company. For that, the company will have to make available all such books, records, accounts and other documents and information as may be reasonably required, to such auditor all such documents reasonably necessary required by him/her.

§7. Part VII: Rights Reserved by Government

450. There is only one common right reserved by the Government under both the model agreements. It is basically the right of the Government to permit, license or authorize any other person of exploration rights over the Scheduled Land for any substance other than petroleum. Such person shall have the right to enter and occupy the land for exercising his/her rights under the licence as stipulated under clauses (a), (b) and (c), in a manner not to interfere or hinder the rights of the company under this Agreement. The company is also entitled to fair compensation for all loss or damage that may incur due to the exercise of such rights.

451. Onshore agreement has four additional clauses for rights reserved by the Government as restrictions on company's rights under Clauses 22, 23, 24, 25 and 26. They are: limitation of rights over sea areas and reclamation; installation in sea areas; pollution prevention; and not to use Lands other than the purposes of the agreement; and not to obstruct working of other minerals. Exercising of those rights shall be in a manner not to interfere or hinder the rights of the company under this Agreement, and if any loss or damage incur incidental thereto, the company shall be entitled to fair compensation.

452. Those rights are:

(1) Right of the Government and any other person authorized by the Government to enter into and upon the Scheduled Land to make or maintain such reservoir, roads, etc. for any purposes in the interest of the public, and also to obtained stone, etc. from the Land for that purposes. The Government shall also have right at all times to draw water from the Land and free access thereto.
(2) Right of the Government at any time to alienate all or any area of the Scheduled Land to any person subject to the company's rights under this Agreement.
(3) Right to alienate surface in certain cases so as to interfere with the company's rights. Before doing so, the Government will give notice to the company that application to acquire rights over the surface has been made to the Government, and if there is no objection by the company within ninety days of the notice, then only the alienation will take place. The company shall hold the priority over that area if it subsequently become available. Note however, the company shall always have the right to enter into agreement with the acquirer of the land and his/her successor in order to occupy such area.
(4) Right to exclude any area or areas of the Scheduled Lands for public purposes provided that the areas so excluded shall not exceed 10 square miles (in one

area), or in all shall not exceed 50 square miles. However, the areas so excluded shall continue to be part of the Scheduled Land, subject to this Agreement.

§8. Part VIII: Restrictions on Company's Rights

453. The onshore model agreement has some additional provisions with regards to restriction on the company's rights. They are:

(1) Restriction as to alienate lands. The rights of the company over any area or areas of the Scheduled Land which happen to be held by a third party shall be subject to the written law applicable thereto (e.g., The National Land Code). To exercise its right over such land, the company needs consent from the Minister by satisfying him/her that it would not tend to the religious prejudice of the community:
   - agreement has been made between the company and the owner of the land, providing for compensation to be paid; or
   - reasonable effort has been taken but they failed to enter into an agreement though no fault of the company; or
   - agreement cannot be entered into due to the fact that the owner cannot be found or out of the State or for any such reasons.

(2) Occupation of the scheduled lands for surface purposes. Before occupying the Land for surface operation, the company shall give the Minister not less than twenty-eight days' notice specifying by name, the details of the land proposed. Furthermore, the company must always pay compensation to the occupiers of that land before occupying the land, or at least offer reasonable compensation to them. The amount of compensation shall be determined by agreement between the Government and the company, and any dispute shall be referred to arbitration.

(3) The company cannot exercise its rights under this Agreement in a way, which may cause damage by water, or otherwise to land not occupied by the company.

(4) Timber cutting in reserved forest restricted. Where any area or areas of the Scheduled Land has been proclaimed to be a Reserved Forest, then the following restrictions shall apply:
   - A plan of the area that is proposed to develop or cleared shall be given to the State Forest Officer.
   - Clearings shall be strictly limited to the actual area necessary for the efficient conduct of the operation, and necessary for protection from fire and other hazard. Clearing for well sites shall not exceed 2 acres.
   - Due care shall be exercised in felling trees so as not to damage trees outside the area.

(5) Limitation of right over foreshore. The company shall exercise its right on the foreshore lying between high-water mark and low-water mark at usual spring

tides only when it is necessary to carry out the operation effectively, and it shall not cause any reasonably avoidable obstruction to the use of such foreshore for other purposes.

454. Common restrictions on the company's rights in the two model agreements are:

(1) Limitation of rights over sea area and reclamation. The company can only exercise its rights over sea area and reclamation which is necessary for effective operation, and nothing more, other than expressly mentioned in this Agreement.
(2) Any works or installation erected in or over any part of seabed shall be made, equipped and maintained in such a way to leave it in conditions safe and convenient channel for shipping. If required by the Government, the company must also maintain the audible and visible navigational aids.
(3) The company shall adopt all the practicable precautions including modern equipment, to prevent pollution to the sea water or shore line.
(4) The company shall not use the lands other than the purposes of this Agreement.
(5) The company shall not obstruct working of other minerals within the Scheduled Lands or the adjacent lands. It shall always give means of access and passage on and across the Scheduled Land for that purposes.
(6) Boreholes or wells shall not be drilled within a distance of 600 feet from the boundaries of the Scheduled Land, except with the Minister's consent.
(7) No drilling operations shall be carried out on the Scheduled Land at any place within 100 yards of any reservoir, railway, public road, etc., or within 100 yards from any other public works. Moreover, no storage tanks shall be erected within 300 yards of such places.
(8) The company shall without avoidable delay report the discovery of petroleum or petroleum-bearing strata to the Minister.
(9) The company shall notify the Minister as soon as the site of any borehole or well has been decided, and describe it by a certain number in the records, maps and plans. Before commencing or recommencing work on borehole or well (which operation has been discontinued for more than six months), the company shall give seven clear days' notice in writing to the Minister.
(10) Prior consent of the Minister is required for abandonment boreholes and it shall be plugged in order to prevent entry and exit of water in and from any portion of the strata bored through.
(11) The company shall proceed to carry out exploration and development work with all due diligence at a reasonable and economically justifiable rate. It shall also maintain all the apparatus in good repair and condition. All operation shall be carried out in a workmanlike manner and in accordance with generally accepted standards of good petroleum field operations and conservation practices.
(12) The company shall use generally accepted standards of good petroleum field operations for confining the petroleum obtained in tanks, gasholders, pipes, pipelines or other receptacles constructed for the purpose.

(13) The company shall drain all waste oil, salt water and refuse from tanks, boreholes and well into proper receptacles at a safe distance from those tanks, boreholes and well. Disposal of such waste must be in a manner approved by the Minister.
(14) The company shall comply with any instructions given by the Minister for maintaining health and safety of the company's employees.
(15) The company shall be prepared to supply some of its production of crude oil (if requested) as shall be necessary for the supply of refined products for local consumption in the Federation (Clause 35; Clause 67).
(16) Unit development – If there are more than one petroleum agreements in force, in respect of the common petroleum reservoir, there should be a unit development in cooperations by all the persons. The company will be given a notice requiring it to work with those persons (referred to as the other operators) to prepare a development scheme in respect of the common petroleum reservoir. If no development scheme is submitted within the prescribed period in the notice, then the Minister may prepare a development scheme which shall be fair and equitable to the company and the other Operators, and which the company shall obey. Any objection shall refer to arbitration within twenty-eight days from the notice given.
(17) Right of pre-emption in emergency. Whenever a Proclamation of Emergency has been issued under Article 150 of the Constitution of Malaysia, the following provisions shall apply:
   - The Government shall hold the first right to purchase all crude oil obtained by the company and its products.
   - The company shall endeavour to increase the supply of crude oil and/or products to the extent required by the Government and to deliver all crude oil or products so purchased. The price shall either be agreed separately by the parties, or in default of agreement, at a fair price set by arbitration.
   - The Government shall also hold the right to take control of the plant and premises of the company, and if happens, reasonable compensation shall be paid.

§9. Part IX: Records, Accounts, Etc.

455. This part lists down obligations of the company with respect to records, account, etc.:

- The company shall keep full and accurate record, in a form approved by the Minister containing the particulars required (the drilling, etc., the strata and subsoil, the casing inserted, any petroleum, water and minerals encountered), and shall also keep accurate geological and geophysical maps and plans. These shall be made available for inspection, and copies shall be delivered whenever required. Moreover, there are several provisions, which make it mandatory for the company to give summary of records or estimates (required) to the Minister, for each quarter-year period, each half-year period and also for each year (refer to Clause 38(2) of offshore agreement and Clause 48(2) of onshore agreement).

- The company shall also keep samples of the water encountered in any borehole or well, samples of any petroleum found in the Scheduled Land, and also samples of the strata found in any borehole and well. The Minister or his/her representative shall have access and may retain any of such specimens.
- The company shall keep accurate accounts of the gross quantity of crude oil, and natural gas obtained, the method and result test on them, the quantity sold together with name of purchaser, quantity and price, the quantity consumed for drilling and production operations, the quantity refined or treated, etc. Summary of the said particulars shall be delivered to the Minister within two months after the first day of January, and July for each half-year period.
- The company shall furnish copies of agreements relating to the Scheduled Land or any interest therein, to which the company is a party directly or indirectly, to the Minister within two months from the date of its execution.
- All information supplied by the company shall be at the expense of the company, and it shall be treated as confidential during the terms of the Agreement and five years thereafter. It, however, can be used by the Government for the purposes listed down in the particular clause (Clause 42 and Clause 52).
- The Minister or his/her duly authorized representatives shall hold the right at all reasonable times to enter into the Land for inspection and examination purposes of the plant, records, etc., and also for carrying out operations which the Government entitled to conduct under this Agreement.

§10. Part X: Miscellaneous Provisions

456. Clause 45(1) of the offshore agreement is a distinctive clause. It provides that the Government shall grant to the company rights over the continental shelves outside the Scheduled Land and over territorial water for its operations. The Government shall also make available (at the request and the expense of the company) such land onshore, on the mainland or island for its operation, provided that if such land is alienated land, the company must first offer to acquire or to lease the land at a reasonable price and terms.

457. On the other hand, onshore agreement distinct clause is Clause 45(2). It provides that the Government shall make State land outside the Scheduled Land but within the State, available to the company (if required), for shore installation, etc. as necessary for exercising its rights under the Agreement.

458. The rest of the provisions are commonly shared by the two agreements. Some notable ones among others are:

(1) The company shall pay reasonable compensation for all damages to person or property or rights of third person, which may be done by the company, its agents or servants in exercising rights under this Agreement.

(2) The company shall at all times indemnify the Government, the Minister and every public officer of the Federation against third-party claims in connection with anything done or purported to be done by the company under this Agreement.

(3) The company shall report to the Minister of any fresh issues of capital and any alteration made to its constitution.

(4) The company shall not transfer its interests or rights under this Agreement to any person except with prior consent in writing of the Government.

(5) If the company at any time fails to do its obligations required by this Agreement, the Government shall be entitled to do things necessary to ensure compliance with such obligation after giving reasonable notice, and also to recover the costs and expenses for that purpose from the company.

(6) The company shall endeavour to employ and train citizen of the Federation in and for the company's operation and management, subject to availability of suitable candidates.

(7) The Government shall have the first option to purchase of the surplus of the natural gas, at the price no higher than the normal price. If no acceptance by the Government within twenty-eight days from the offer (to sell), then it shall be deemed to have been refused.

(8) The company before commencing any operations on the Scheduled Land must furnish to the Minister, name and address of the manager resident in the locality of the Land.

(9) The company shall have the right to remit, retain abroad and to dispose freely of all funds and assets acquired, provided that the Malaysian Government shall have the option to demand payment of royalty and income tax in foreign currency, and that the Malaysian Exchange Control formalities are complied with. The company shall also have the right to convert freely any Malaysian currency, which the company considers as surplus, into foreign currency acceptable to the company.

(10) The company shall pay the agreed sum of money to the Government upon signing of this Agreement.

(11) If and whenever there are any royalties or the fixed yearly payments in arrear or unpaid (two months from the due date for the payments), the Government authorized officer may enter into the land occupied by the company, and may seize, and sell off the properties of the company found, including any stocks of petroleum and any products thereof. The proceeds of sale may be retained to pay all the arrears and also the costs and expenses for the distress.

(12) The company shall peaceably and quietly hold and enjoy the rights and privileges granted under the Agreement.

(13) This Agreement shall be determined if the company becomes controlled directly or indirectly by a national of a country that do not permit companies incorporated in that country to be controlled directly or indirectly by citizens of Malaysia.

§11. Part XI: Extension and Determination

459. This part mainly concerns the Agreement period, its extension and determination in one part, and the determination of assets in another part.

460. Agreement Period as stated earlier will be forty years from the date of this Agreement, including both the exploration and development phases. The exploration phase shall subsist for a period of ten years, from the commencement of the agreement, unless sooner terminated. If it appears that no petroleum is likely to be found before the expiry of the exploration phase, the company upon making application for extension not later than three months before the expiry shall be entitled to an extension of maximum five years. The extension however can only be granted in respect of areas not more than 25% of areas originally contained in the Scheduled Lands. If at the expiry of the exploration phase the company has not notified the Minister that it has discovered petroleum in commercial quantity, this Agreement shall be automatically determined. ('Petroleum in commercial quantity' means the discovery of reserves of petroleum in such quantity, which will permit their being economically developed, taking into consideration the location of the reserves, the depth and number of wells required to be drilled and the transport and terminal facilities needed to exploit the reserves, which has been discovered) (Clause 1)). Conversely, if such notification has been made, the Agreement shall continue to subsist, but the exploration phase shall automatically be terminated and the company shall enter into the development phase. The development phase shall commence thereon (from the date of such notification) and shall subsist for a period of thirty years. If such notification is given during the exploration phase, then the development phase shall be automatically extended for such further period as to balance of the exploration phase. This will not apply in case of extension of the exploration phase.

461. If the company complies with all obligations under this Agreement, then it shall have right to an extension of the Agreement, by giving notice to the Government, not less than one year but not more than two years, before the end of the Agreement Period. Such extension shall be for a further agreed period upon terms and conditions contained in any written law in force, and under this Agreement. If the extension given is only to any part of the Scheduled Land, then the company shall be released from all liability in relation to such (excluded) land.

I. Right to Determine the Agreement

462. The company, under Clause 61, shall hold the right to determine the Agreement at any time by giving twelve months' notice in writing to that effect to the Government. On the other hand, under Clause 62, the Government shall hold such right if any of the following takes place:

- The company has not paid any required payment under this Agreement for six months after its due date.

- The company fails to comply with any obligations required to be complied with under this Agreement.
- The company ceases to exist either voluntarily or compulsorily (except voluntary cessation of a solvent company for amalgamation or reconstruction purposes).
- The company fails to comply with any unit development scheme prepared under the respective clause.
- The company fails to produce petroleum five years after the commencement of development phase.

463. Provided, however, the Government must give notice to the company specifying the particular matter causing the said power to arise, and asking the company to remedy the matter (if possible), and to pay reasonable compensation within a reasonable time.

464. According to Clause 63, the effect of such determination will be on all rights and obligations of the parties under this Agreement shall cease altogether, subject and without prejudice to rights and obligation expressed to arise under this Agreement on the determination thereof, and the liability arising out of an earlier failure to comply.

II. Right of the Government on Assets

465. The company shall deliver to the Government if so requested, any buildings, machinery and other assets of permanent nature constructed or moveable assets used by the company on the Land, at the price not exceeding the written down value for tax purposes, at the end of the Agreement Period or any earlier determination of this Agreement. Within five years before the end of the Agreement, the company shall not remove or sell any assets of permanent nature, and assets in the nature of public utility, which might be deliverable to the Government under this clause. However, subject to this clause, the company may from time to time sell or otherwise dispose of any assets in the land that are no longer required. Furthermore, within two months after the end of the Agreement, the company shall deliver up all productive boreholes or well made by the company in good repair and condition for further working, and if required, to plug all abandoned boreholes and wells.

§12. Part XII: Ancillary Provisions

466. Following are the ancillary provisions:

(1) Force Majeure provision. No claim against the company may be made by the Government in respect of the company's failure to fulfil its obligations under this Agreement due to any exceptional or unforeseeable circumstances that are not within the control of the company.
(2) Arbitration clause.

Any reference to arbitration under this Agreement, and any question or disputes relating to this Agreement, shall be referred to arbitration in Geneva, Switzerland or other place as may be mutually agreed. The parties shall seek to agree upon appointment of a single arbitrator, failing which each party will have the right to appoint one arbitrator, and the two arbitrators shall jointly appoint a third arbitrator who shall be the chairman. If this also fails, then the matter (of appointment) shall be referred to the competence of the President of the Federal Tribunal of Switzerland upon the request of either party. Such arbitration shall be conducted in accordance with the laws and custom at the place of arbitration, and the award shall be final and binding upon both parties. Each party shall bear its costs and shall contribute 50% of the fees and expenses of the arbitration.

(3) Any dispute with regards to pricing shall be referred to an expert or the Price Committee of experts, members of which are similarly appointed and have power, procedure and decision as which the Controller may refer pricing question under the Petroleum (Income Tax) Act 1967.

(4) This Agreement shall be construed in accordance with the law of the Federation, and nothing in this Agreement shall entitle the company to contravene that law.

(5) All notices and communications under this Agreement must be in writing, and it may be sent to the company's registered office in the Federation (if any) or at its statutory address for service of notice. For the Government, it may be sent to the Minister at any address notified by him/her, or at his/her office. Any notice sent by registered post shall be deemed to have been received three days after the date of posting in the Federation.

(6) So far the alteration of terms of this Agreement is concerned, the company will on request consult with the Government whether any alteration of terms in this Agreement would be made and that are equitable to the parties.

467. Towards the end of this agreement, there shall be execution: signed by the Minister on behalf of the Government, supported with Common Seal affixed by the company and attested by witnesses.

468. It is later followed by the First Schedule of the Agreement containing and describing the Scheduled Lands, and the Second Schedule that is about the Bond for a sum of money issued by the company, in respect of the Petroleum Agreement.

Chapter 5. Petroleum (Safety Measures) Act 1984 (Act 302)

§1. General

469. The Petroleum (Safety Measures) Act 1984 is to consolidate laws relating to safety in the transportation, storage and utilization of petroleum and matters relating to it.

470. The Act was supposed to come into force on the appointed date (date appointed by the Minister by notification in Gazette). However, there may be some provisions which come into force on different prescribed date, for different area or locality, and as such, reference to the appointed date shall be construed as reference to the prescribed date. It is to be noted that all its provisions have now come into force.

471. In this Act, the word 'petroleum' is defined in section 2, the interpretation section as: any mineral oil or relative hydrocarbon and natural gas existing in its natural condition and casing head petroleum spirit including bituminous shales and other stratified deposits from which oil can be extracted (same like section 10 of Petroleum Development Act), including petroleum products.

472. For the purpose of this Act, petroleum has been classified into different classes (section 2). They are:

Class I – petroleum having flash points <37.8°C	Class II – flash point ≥37.8°C, <60°C	Class III – flash point ≥60°C
IA – flash point <22.8°C, and boiling point < 37.8°C IB – flash point <22.8°C and boiling point ≥37.8°C IC – flash point ≥22.8°C <37.8°C		IIIB – flash point ≥60°C, < 93.4°C. IIIB – flash point ≥ 93.4°C.

§2. Transportation of Petroleum

473. Basically, the Act provides four means of transportation of petroleum, by road and railway, by water, by air and by pipelines. The word 'transportation' as defined in section 2 means the action of taking petroleum from any place or vessel by any means or mode of transportation such as land, air, water and includes conveyance by pipelines both onshore or offshore, on land or underground, in water and underwater.

474. It is notable that the provisions of this Act are restrictive in nature in the sense that generally no petroleum shall be dealt with except in accordance with this Act and regulations made thereunder. It also provides that non-compliance is an offence, and prescribes the punishments/liabilities for the offences (mostly fine).

475. The Act strictly prohibits transportation of petroleum by air, unless there is prior authorization of the Minister for doing so (i.e., Minister charged with the responsibility for petroleum (section 2)). Petroleum used solely for the propulsion of the particular aircraft is not subject of this provision (section 15).

476. The Minister may make regulations for the safe transportation of petroleum by road or railway and for safeguarding persons and property from danger in connection with the transportation, and for regulating and authorizing of workshops for liquefied petroleum gas (LPG) fuel system. LPG fuel system means an assembly consisting of one or more containers with a means for conveying LPG from containers to dispensing or consuming devices and which incorporates components intended to achieve control of quantity, flow, pressure or state (section 2).

477. The owner (person having ownership, dominion or title of property as stated in section 2) or operator of a vehicle used for conveying petroleum by road shall take all necessary measures to ensure all his/her employees are informed and carry out the provisions of this Act. If any person contravenes any provisions of the Act, he/she shall be guilty of an offence, and liable to a fine of maximum MYR 10,000. If it involves petroleum of Class IA or IB, the maximum fine is MYR 15,000.

478. For transportation by water, loading or discharging petroleum can only be done at a port or other places appointed for that purpose by the Minister by notification in the Gazette (section 6(1)). In respect of those places, the Minister may appoint persons as he/she thinks fit to carry out the duties and functions as a port officer. By virtue of section 2, port may be either of the following: a port, or place declared to be a port under the Merchant Shipping Ordinance 1952, or under the Merchant Shipping Ordinance 1960 of Sabah, or under the Merchant Shipping Ordinance 1960 of Sarawak, or an area declared to be Bintulu Port under section 3 of the Declaration of an Area in the Bintulu District to be a port under the Federal Port Act 1979. Likewise, 'port officer' has same meaning as defined under those Ordinances.

479. The word 'vessels' under the Act includes every kind of vessel whether propelled by machinery or sails, junk, boat, sampan or any kind of craft (section 2).

480. The provisions of this Act provide for the obligations of the person in control of the vessels, and non-compliance of them is an offence subject to penalty. They are as follows:

(1) Vessel carrying petroleum on board as cargo shall not enter into any ports without first obtaining the permission of the port officer in writing (section 7). Upon giving permission, port officer may impose reasonable terms and conditions. Breach of this provision is an offence, and the master of the vessel shall be liable to a fine not exceeding MYR 15,000, and the petroleum being seized and forfeited.

(2) On arrival at the port, the master of the vessel shall notify the Inspector (Inspector of Petroleum appointed under section 38) of the arrival, and shall include in that notification other particulars necessary for inspection of the petroleum (section 8). If there is any contravention (of this provision), the master, owner and agent of such vessel shall be guilty of an offence, and be liable to a fine of maximum MYR 5,000. Unloading, discharging or storage of the petroleum if made thereafter shall be made with licence issued under section 19, as soon as possible after the granting of permission (section 10). Breach of this provision shall be liable to a fine of maximum MYR 10,000, and the petroleum being seized and forfeited.

Inspector of Petroleum is appointed by the Minister under section 38 of the Act for the purposes of carrying out the provisions of the Act into effect, and he/she shall be deemed to be a public servant within the meaning of the Penal Code. He/she shall have the power to make examination and inquiry as may be necessary to ensure the provisions of this Act are complied with and also empowered to do things listed down in section 38(2). Obstructing the Inspector's duty is an offence, liable to a fine of maximum MYR 5,000. Any Inspector or any person authorized under section 19 may take samples of any petroleum on payment of the value and may test or cause it to be tested at any convenient place, at any reasonable time as he/she may appoint. The Inspector or any police officer not below the rank of Sergeant is entitled (on demand) to a free and unobstructed ingress to all reasonable facilities for inspection. He/she may even break open any doors or windows of such premises, enter it forcibly, and to remove any obstruction by force (section 40).

(3) Section 9 is a general provision for unloading or discharging petroleum from any vessel, that it shall be with the permission of the port officer, and in accordance with the stipulated conditions, at the time and place so stated. Contravention of this section shall be liable to a fine of maximum MYR 10,000, and the petroleum being sized and forfeited.

(4) By virtue of section 10A, no petroleum shall be loaded or unloaded between the hours of sunset and sunrise except with permission of the port officer. This provision does not apply to petroleum in bulk from any vessel to or from any shore installation. Petroleum in bulk means a homogeneous cargo of petroleum stored loose in free-flowing tank and required to be handled by pumping or by gravity flow (section 2). Breach of this section shall be liable to a fine not exceeding MYR 10,000 and the petroleum being seized and forfeited.

(5) Vessels carrying petroleum shall follow the direction of the port officer, if ordered to proceed to the petroleum anchorage within or without the limit of the port (section 11). Petroleum anchorage means a place prescribed as anchorage by regulations made under this Act (section 2). Default of compliance with the order/direction, the master of the vessel shall be liable to a fine not exceeding MYR 20,000.

(6) Loading or carriage of petroleum shall only be made under the conditions and restriction imposed by the Act and regulations made thereunder (section 12). Any breach of conditions or restrictions, the owner, master and agent of the vessel shall be liable to a fine not exceeding MYR 10,000.

(7) Section 13 clearly states that no vessel carrying Class I or Class II petroleum shall remain in any port for a longer time than is reasonably necessary for loading or unloading petroleum, unless there is prior written permission of the port officer. Breach of this provision shall be liable to a fine not exceeding MYR 5,000. This section is not applicable to such vessel if the receptacles or containers for the storage of such classes of petroleum are approved by a Surveyor of Ships. 'Surveyor of Ships' means a surveyor of ship as appointed under section 10 of the Merchant shipping Ordinance 1952, section 130 of the Merchant Shipping Ordinance of Sabah, and of Sarawak, 1960, and shall include the Surveyor General of Ships (section 2).

(8) Likewise by virtue of section 14, no person shall place, or permit petroleum to remain on any quay, bank or other place, for a longer time than is reasonably necessary for the loading or unloading in connection to transportation, and in no case between sunset and sunrise. Any person who commits a breach of this section shall be liable to a fine not exceeding MYR 5,000.

§3. Transportation of Petroleum Through Pipelines

481. According to section 2 of the Act, pipelines means all parts of those physical facilities through which petroleum moves in transportation including pipes, pumps, compressor units, meters, regulators and fabricated assemblies, while 'pipeline works' means any works of the following kinds: placing, adjusting, changing or removing pipelines, and breaking up or opening land and tunnelling for that purpose.

482. Section 16 envisages that no pipeline works shall be done by any person except under authorization granted by the Minister, within the authorized limits/areas. If no substantial pipeline work has been done after twelve months from the date such authorization is granted, or at the expiration of any extension period allowed, the authorization shall be of no effect, except as regards to works previously executed. However, no authorization is needed for emergency pipeline works that is to prevent danger and interruption of the conveyance of petroleum (section 17), so long as the Minister is notified within twenty-four hours of the commencement of such works, and the map and details of the works are submitted to him/her as soon as practicable. The Minister shall also have the power to require rectification of the pipeline works, if it does not meet the safety measures and standard enforceable under this Act. Any person contravening sections 16 and 17 shall be guilty of offence, and liable to a fine of maximum MYR 20,000, and a further fine of MYR 5,000 per day for continuing offence. This part however shall not apply to the supply of gas to consumer through pipelines under the Gas Supply Act 1993, and the terms 'gas', 'consumer' and 'pipelines' here are defined in the said Act.

§4. Storage and Handling of Petroleum

483. According to section 2, storage includes the processing, dispensing or transfer of petroleum, the action of putting into store, or stacking at a place or in an aircraft, motor vehicle, motor trailer or vessel, while handling includes the action of touching, feeling, grasping, transferring or decanting with the hand or assisted by any means.

484. Only the holder of a valid petroleum storage licence or a valid petroleum handling licence granted under this Act shall store or handle any petroleum, in accordance with the licence (section 19(1)). This also includes person acting lawfully under the supervision or instruction of such licensee (section 19(1A)). This however does not apply to the exempted categories of petroleum under section 27, provided that the petroleum shall always be subject to any provisions of this Act and the regulations pertaining to the design and specification of such containers or receptacles.

485. The grant of licence under section 9 is authorized by the Minister and in respect of the area under a Local Authority, or in Sabah, after consultation with the respective State Authority, or Local Authority. 'State Authority' in reference to the Federal Territories of Kuala Lumpur and Labuan means the Minister charged with the responsibility for local government. In contravention of these provisions, the occupier of the premises shall be guilty of an offence and shall be liable to a fine not exceeding MYR 10,000, and a further fine of MYR 2,000 per day for continuing offence. Apart from that, any petroleum, tools and containers used may be seized and forfeited.

486. The occupier of the premises shall ensure a notice setting out the conditions attached with the licence, to be kept posted on the premises in a readable form. Failure to do this is an offence and shall cause him/her liable to a fine not exceeding MYR 5,000, and a further fine of MYR 1,000 per day for continuing offence. Whereas, any person pulls down or damages such notice, or any employee contravenes any conditions in such notice, shall on conviction be liable to a fine of maximum MYR 5,000.

487. Where any petroleum is kept, or sent/conveyed, or sold/exposed or offered for sale, there shall be a label showing the required information (section 20(1)), be attached to or displayed near the container of the petroleum. Failure to have such label is an offence, carried liability of fine not exceeding MYR 5,000, and the petroleum and vessel being forfeited or dealt with in any manner as the court thinks fit.

488. Section 21 empowers the Minister to make regulations, in special circumstances, if he/she is satisfied that the petroleum or any mixed substance is likely to affect safety or health. Contravention or attempt to contravene with the regulation shall be liable to a fine not exceeding MYR 5,000 and a further fine of MYR 1,000 per day for continuing offence, and the petroleum and vessel being forfeited or dealt with in any manner as the court thinks fit.

489. The occupier of the premises is obliged to notify the Minister, whenever any accident involving petroleum occurs, within twenty-four hours of such occurrences, failing which he/she shall be liable to a fine of maximum MYR 5,000. Upon receipt of such notice, the Minister may direct any person to hold inquiry into the cause of the accident. He/she may also appoint any person possessing legal or special knowledge to assist in the inquiry. These persons shall conduct the inquiry in most effective way in order to make the report. Such person will have the power to summon any person to appear before him/her. Failure to appear without reasonable cause will give him/her right to certify the failure to attend to the High Court, by instrument in writing. The High Court may then order the person to comply with the requirement at hearing before the person conducting the inquiry (section 23). Moreover, section 24 expressly prohibits any person from insulting, interrupting or contempt a hearing before the person conducting the inquiry. Doing such prohibited acts is an offence and shall be liable to imprisonment for a maximum term of three months or a fine not exceeding MYR 2,000 or both. Any persons involved in the inquiry, including the advocates, and witnesses have the same privilege and immunity as in proceedings in the High Court (section 25). Evidence taken under this Act shall not be admissible in any civil or criminal proceedings against the person who gave the evidence, except when he/she is charged with perjury.

§5. Utilization of Equipment, Building, etc., and Installation

490. Utilization means the action of utilizing or the fact of being utilized and includes facilitating or performing any such act where petroleum or petroleum products are involved (section 2). Any equipment, gadgets, materials, plants, appliances, buildings, structures and installations used or intended to be used for storage, handling, transportation and utilization of petroleum shall not be used, sold or offered to be sold, unless it is declared as of approved types by the Minister by publication in the Gazette. 'Approved type' means the equipment, etc., is of similar design and specifications as those specified in the list of equipment tested and found safe and suitable for such use. To ensure due compliance with this section, a duly authorized person or authority may conduct tests or any verification methods as necessary, and thereafter a certificate shall be issued on such equipment. It is important to note that the Minister shall always have the power to vary list of approved type equipment, etc., and any change suggested by the Minister must be complied with (section 29). Any equipment, etc., which is later rendered contrary to the list shall not be used until rectification is made. Breach of these provisions is an offence, and liable to a maximum fine of MYR 20,000, and a further fine of MYR 2,000 per day for continuing offence. The application of these provisions is confined to equipment for commercial and industrial purposes and also applicable to selling or offer to sale equipment as far as domestic purposes is concerned.

§6. Existing Equipment

491. As to the existing equipment, etc., it may continue to be used with the approval of the Minister, if he/she is satisfied that such usage does not constitute hazard to safety, life or property (section 32). The person wishing to continue using the existing equipment in the licensed premises (i.e., premises licensed under the Petroleum Ordinance 1949 and Petroleum Ordinance 1960 of Sabah, which are expressly repealed by this Act (section 48) shall apply in writing to the Minister for approval within ninety days from the date of the declaration published in the Gazette).

492. Any existing equipment other than stated in section 32 shall not be used unless rectified in accordance of this Act and its regulations. Rectification shall be effected within three years from the date of publication of the declaration in the Gazette. This period may be extended by the Minister for a further two years (maximum), provided that the application is made not later than six months before the expiry of the initial period. Contravention of these provisions is an offence, liable to a fine of maximum MYR 20,000, and to a further fine of MYR 200 per day for continuing offence. Note that the Minister shall always have a power to require rectification of any equipment that is detrimental to the safety of life or property.

§7. Liability

493. Where verification is required by Regulations in respect of any plan, drawing, description, calculation or construction of any buildings, it shall be in the Form prescribed by such Regulations; and by virtue of section 36 of this Act, it shall contain the undertaking to accept full responsibility by a person making such verification.

§8. Miscellaneous

494. Any person conferred with powers under this Act may delegate the power to any person and subject to conditions as he/she thinks fit. The delegated power shall be revocable at his/her will.

495. Where any person would be liable under provision of this Act, he/she shall be liable to the same punishment for every similar offence done by his/her agent or servant employed by him/her in the course of his/her business (section 41). Revocation of licence (section 42).

496. The authority granting any licence under this Act shall have the right to revoke such licence or suspend the licence (if it appears to be expedient and necessary in the circumstances of the case), if he/she is satisfied that:

- the apparatus or premises have become unfit for carrying out the licensed purpose; or
- the licensee has breach any of the conditions of the licence, or
- the continuance of the licence is against public safety.

497. The authority however must first call upon the licensee to show cause as to why the licence should not be revoked. This can either be in writing or in hearing. If the person fails to do so, his/her licence may be revoked.

498. Any aggrieved person by any decisions made under this Act may appeal to the Minister within twenty-one days of the receipt of the decision. On appeal, the Minister may on the evidence before him/her confirm, annul or vary such decision. For this purpose, he/she may appoint any officers of technical or appropriate skills to assist him/her. Such officer shall have power to inspect any relevant premises (section 43).

499. Besides all the powers given to the Minister, by virtue of section 44, he/she may, by order, whether conditionally or absolutely, exempt any person, vehicle, vessel or place from all or any provisions of this Act or Regulations. He/she may also exempt from all or any of such provisions any petroleum under the control of the Armed Forces, the Royal Malaysian Police and other lawful forces of the Federation, as well as petroleum under the control of the Government of the Federation and any Government of any states.

500. Furthermore, section 45 empowers the Minister to make regulations and rules for carrying out the purpose of this Act generally, and for the specific purposes listed down in that section (e.g., to determine classification of petroleum and to regulate safety of transportation of petroleum). Likewise, he/she may also be prescribed code of practice, which shall take effect upon publication in the Gazette (section 46). Code of practice is a document prescribing recommended practices for the design, manufacturing, setting up, maintenance or utilization of equipment, installations, structures or products (section 2).

501. Any fees (as authorized by the Minister) collected in respect of any licence issued shall be the revenue of the local authority issuing the licence (section 47).

§9. Schedule

502. Section 2(1) –Petroleum products means all materials derived from petroleum as are listed in the schedule. Thus, the schedule listed down eleven petroleum products such as methane, gasoline, kerosene and lubricating oil. To note, by virtue of section 2(2), the Minister may by order amend, vary, delete from or add to the

Schedule, which includes methane, ethane, propane, hydrocarbons, gasoline, neptha, reformate, kerosene, diesel, fuel oil, base oil, lubricating oil asphalt/ bitumen and grease and wax.

The Director general of the Department of Occupational Safety and Health of the Ministry of Human Resources, which is responsible for administering and enforcing legislation to ensure the safety, health and welfare of workers and others at the place of work, under section 30 of the Occupational Health and Safety Act 1994, requires from the employer of 40 or more employees to establish a safety and health committee at the place of work. The primary task of the committee is to review from time to time safety and health measures taken by the employer and to investigate, if need be, to investigate any safety or health incidents. In view of this, it is required from the employers to notify the Department of any accident, dangerous occurrence, occupational poisoning or disease which occurred or likely to occur at the place of work.[112]

It may also be noted here that the Ministry of Domestic Trade, Cooperation and Consumers, as it then was until April 2018, had the Petroleum Safety Unit under it. It was responsible in assuring and observing the safety of petroleum industry by operating and updating the principle, enactment and regulations especially pertaining to the 1984 Act and regulations made thereunder. In specific: observing the execution and coordination about the enforcement of the provisions of the Act and Regulations; to have a secretariat to Petroleum Safety Industry Venture Team; to compile the data and information on the petroleum safety matters; to bring about awareness and understanding safety aspects; helping and advising related organizations and others for ensuring safety.[113]

---

112. For further details about the Safety and Health Committee, see 'Occupational Safety and Health (Safety and Health Committee) Regulations 1996.

113. Ministry of Domestic Trade, Co-Operatives and Consumers, 'Petroleum Industry Safety', at: https://www.kpdnkk.gov.my/kpdnkk/petroleum-industry-safety/?lang=en (accessed on 2 Jan. 2018).

Chapter 6. Part I The Petroleum (Safety Measures) (Transportation of Petroleum by Pipelines) Regulations 1985

§1. General

503. Regulations under The Petroleum (Safety Measures) (transportation of Petroleum from Pipelines) Regulations have been made by the Minister pursuant to power conferred by section 45 of the Petroleum (Safety Measures) Act 1984, and come into force on the 1 March 1985. Words and expressions in these regulations shall have the same meaning as in the said Act, unless otherwise defined in the Regulations.

504. These Regulations shall apply to pipelines transporting liquid petroleum between the delivery and receiving points; pipelines transporting natural gas from outlet of separators or traps at gas wells until the outlet of the customer's meter set assembly; and distribution piping in a LPG system, from the first state regulator of the storage tank to the outlet of the customer's meter set assembly. The Regulations however do not apply to pipelines within petroleum refineries and gas processing plants; pipelines within industrial plants, bulk plants and service stations; and piping system from the delivery point to the connections with each gas utilization device (Regulation 3). Interpretation Regulation 2 defines 'bulk plant' as that portion of a property where petroleum is received by tank vessel, pipelines, tank car or tank vehicle and is stored or blended in bulk for the purpose of distributing such petroleum; and service stations as service station (automotive) and (marine). Service station (automotive) means that portion of a property where liquids used as motor fuels are stored and dispensed from fixed equipment into the fuel tanks of motor vehicles, while service station (marine) means that portion of property where liquids used as fuels are stored and dispensed from fixed equipment on shore, piers, wharves or floating docks into the fuel tanks of self-propelled craft and shall include all facilities used in connection therewith.

505. By virtue of Regulation 4, all the design, fabrication, installation, testing and the safety aspect of the operation, maintenance of petroleum and gas pipeline shall meet the requirements of the American National Standard Institute Code for Liquid Petroleum Transportation Piping System ANSI/ASMEB 31.4 or for the Pressure Piping Gas Transmission and Distribution Piping System ANSI/ASMEB 31.8. Note however, the Approving Authority (i.e., any person whom the Minister has delegated his/her power under section 37 of the Act to exercise his/her functions under sections 16 and 17 of the Act (Regulation 2)) may ban the use of certain material or fitting in a petroleum and gas pipeline system, even if it meet the Code's requirements. He/she may also permit the use of any material, fitting, component, etc., not prescribed by the Code provided that there is sufficient evidence to substantiate any claim made regarding to the safety of such alternative.

506. These Regulations require written permission from the Approving Authority to be obtained before commencement of any installation (Regulation 5), operations of any pipelines (Regulation 6) and any modification work on a pipeline which affect the basic design and specification (Regulation 14). However, such modification may be carried out without permission in case of emergency, that is necessary to prevent imminent danger, but it must be immediately informed to the Approving Authority (Regulation 14(2)). Regulations 5 and 6 also provide for procedure, things to be submitted in an application for permission.

507. In pipelines operation, the pressure shall not be greater than the maximum allowable pressure approved by the Approving Authority. Such operations including installation shall be subjected to inspection by the Approving Authority, who shall determine the types of inspection and the interval between inspections, after considering any representation made by the owner or operator (Regulation 9). If during the inspection the Inspector (i.e., Inspector of Petroleum appointed under section 38 of the Act and who is from the office of the Approving Authority (Regulation 2)) is of the opinion that any part of the pipelines is likely to cause damage, he/she shall give a written notice to the owner, operator or contractor as the case may be, requiring such defects to be made good within the 'grace period' specified therein. Such part of the pipelines shall not be resumed usage until and unless the Inspector is satisfied that the defect has been made good. The Inspector has the right to immediately prohibit any installation or operations of pipelines without prior notice in writing, if he/she thinks that the defect is likely to cause imminent danger to life and property (Regulation 9(2)).

508. After any inspection, the Inspector may issue a written notice specifying the conditions and limitations for such operation as he/she thinks fit, including to reduce the maximum working pressure (Regulation 10). Failure to comply with any notice or order given by the Inspector is an offence under the Regulations. The following points may be noted for a complete picture of Regulations.

§2. Obligations of the Owner, Operator or Contractor

509. So far obligations of the owner, occupier or contractor is concerned, the following points are notable:

(1) The operator shall maintain record of the items listed down in Regulation 8(1), and shall produce them for inspection whenever directed by the Approving Authority. The Approving Authority may also request other additional information or documents to be submitted (Regulation 8(2)).
(2) The owner, operator or contractor of a pipeline or his/her authorized representative shall afford every reasonable facility to enable the Approving Authority to discharge its duties effectively (Regulation 12).

(3) The owner, operator or contractor of a pipeline or his/her authorized representative shall immediately notify the Approving Authority of any dangerous occurrence; or any gas leak which may affect the safety of property and person (Regulation 13(1)).
(4) The owner or operator of a pipeline shall, as soon as he/she becomes aware of any defect in the pipeline, rectify the defect, or stop the operation of the defective pipeline and inform the Approving Authority (Regulation 13(2)).
(5) Owner or operator of any pipelines prior to the commencement of these Regulations shall inform the Approving Authority of the existing pipelines within sixty days after the Regulation come into force (Regulation 15). The Approving Authority may direct the owner or operator to submit any records or particulars as it deems fit. The existing pipelines are exempted from provisions in Regulations 4(1), 5(1) and 6(1).

510. Contravention of any provisions in the Regulations is an offence, and the person shall be liable to a fine not exceeding MYR 20,000, and a further fine of maximum MYR 5,000 per day for continuing offence. Any aggrieved person by an order made by the Inspector under Regulations 9(3) and 10(1) may appeal to the Inspector's Head of Department within twenty-one days of such order. The Head of Department may, by order in writing confirm, annul or vary such order. A further appeal may be made, within twenty-one days of the order to the Minister, who may confirm, annul or vary the order.

511. The Regulations (made on the 23 February 1985) expressly repeal Rule 53(1) and 53(3) of the Petroleum Rules 1960 (Regulation 17).

Chapter 7. Part II Petroleum (Safety Measures) (Transportation of Petroleum by Water) Regulations 1985

§1. General

512. These Regulations have been made by the Minister pursuant to power conferred by section 45 of the Petroleum (Safety Measures) Act 1984, and have come into force on the 1 March 1985. It is notable that these Regulations basically provide for procedure of entering into port and the matters incidental thereto. It generally provides for vessel carrying any class of petroleum, but gives more concern on vessel carrying Class IA, IB and IC petroleum.

513. Words and expressions in these Regulations shall have the same meaning as in the said Act, unless otherwise defined in the Regulations. The word 'vessel' in the Regulations shall be deemed to be a vessel constructed to carry petroleum of Class 1A, 1B or 1C in bulk, or in packages as the case may be, and such vessel possesses a certificate issued by a Classification Society and endorsed by the Surveyor General of Ships, or certified by the Surveyor General of Ships.

514. For the purpose of these Regulations, the areas in port shall be divided into dangerous petroleum anchorages, prohibited areas and non-dangerous areas of the port as specified in columns of the First Schedule. The Schedule however is always subject to amendment by the Minister, by notification in the Gazette Regulation 3(1). The Regulations also provide the rules within those areas: the prohibited area (Regulation 18), the dangerous area (Regulation 19) and the non-dangerous area (Regulation 20).

515. Within the prohibited area and the dangerous area, no petroleum shall be transported or loaded into any boat or similar craft unless with a licence obtained from the appropriate authority in Form C, and the amount of petroleum shall not exceed 23,000 litres, and there shall be a certificate in Form D, for petroleum to be carried under deck. Whereas, within the non-dangerous area, loading and transportation of petroleum are permitted in a vessel constructed to carry petroleum, or any boat or similar craft with licence or certificate issued by the Surveyor General of Ships.

§2. General Provisions Relating to Vessels Loaded with Petroleum (Class I, II or III)

516. The following provisions are notable.

I. Procedures for Inspection and Transportation

517. An application for permit to land or transship petroleum must first be made in writing as in Part I of Form A (Consignee's Notification), to the Port Officer (the nearest Port Officer through an Inspector). Then, permit will be issued as in Part III of Form A (Regulation 5).

518. Upon arrival of such a vessel, the master, owner, agent or consignee shall send to an Inspector a notice in Part I of Form A of the Second Schedule giving all the necessary particulars for inspection (Regulation 4), and upon receiving it, the Inspector may board the vessel and take samples of the petroleum to be tested. Immediately upon completion of the testing, the Inspector shall issue a certificate as in Part II of Form A, to the Port Officer together with the said notice. Where the Inspector dispenses with inspection, he/she shall forthwith send Part II of Form A to the Port Officer and notify him/her the existence of Class IA, IB or IC petroleum on board.

519. After that, the Port Officer may, for some special reason, refuse to give permission for discharging of petroleum into lighters or ashore (Regulation 6). Where samples have been taken, no petroleum shall be landed until the Port Officer has received the Inspector's reports. In case of petroleum in bulk, permission may be given to discharge it direct into the tanks of a bulk installation, and discharge of any petroleum, being a dutiable goods, shall only be with the authority of a senior officer of Customs (as defined in the Customs Act 1967).

520. The agent or master of any vessel about to leave a Malaysian port with petroleum on board is required to give a notice (export notice) in writing to the Port Officer of the intention to carrying petroleum as cargo and of the maximum quantity intended to be carried. Such notice must be given not less than six hours before applying for the port clearance (Regulation 7).

521. Regulation 9 provides lengthy provision to be observed by any vessel carrying petroleum within any port. Most of it centred on the dealings with Class IA, IB and IC petroleum.

522. Regulation 10 provides that every boat or similar craft carrying petroleum must have a licence as in Form C, which shall only be issued if it has been certified by a Surveyor of Ships to be fit to carry the particular class of petroleum in accordance with the requirements of the Third Schedule; or in case of petroleum loaded below deck, a certificate as in Form D shall only be granted after it has been examined by the Surveyor General of Ships and it shall be subject to any conditions as provided in the Fourth Schedule. Application of the said licence or certificate must be made in writing to the Surveyor General of Ships at least twenty-four hours before the boat or craft's departure. By virtue of subregulation 3, the licence or certificate shall be valid for one year, and is revocable at will by the Surveyor General of Ships.

523. In case where any class of petroleum I, II, III is carried as cargo under deck of a boat or similar craft not constructed for carrying petroleum in bulk, then the provisions from (a) to (f) have to be observed (Regulation 16), among others: the petroleum shall be stowed in watertight compartment, and shall not be contiguous to any other cargo in that hold; it shall be separated from the engine, boiler space, crew space, store, etc., and the gas freeing arrangements and hatchways shall be to the satisfaction of the Surveyor General of Ships.

524. In case where the petroleum is to be carried as deck cargo in any vessel or in the open hold of any undocked boat or similar craft, provisions (a) to (c) of Regulation 17 shall be observed:

(1) there shall be a distance of not less than 3 m between the petroleum and the cooking galley; and not less than 1.22 m between the petroleum and the engine room, boiling casing or exhaust;
(2) the petroleum shall be stored in a distance of not less than 3 m from any part of the deck occupied or accessible to the passengers; and
(3) conspicuous notice shall be put up drawing attention to the danger of smoking or using or exposing naked flame near such class of petroleum.

525. Class I, II or III petroleum not carried in bulk shall be carried either in appropriate receptacles constructed according to the International Maritime Dangerous Goods Code, as published by the International Maritime Organization, each containing not less than 35 litres petroleum but not more than 95% of liquid, marked with the correct technical name, and identified with distinctive labels on stencils in accordance with the above-said Code for inflammable gasses and liquids (Regulation 21(1)(a)), or in steel drums each containing not more than 200 litres petroleum but not more than 95% of liquid (Regulation 21(1)(b)). 'International Maritime Organization' means the organization formerly known as the Inter-Governmental Maritime Consultative Organization established by the convention in the Inter-Governmental Maritime Consultative Organization 1948 (Regulation 2).

526. Loading of petroleum into any vessel, boat or similar craft within the limit of any port shall only be made under direct supervision of a competent person, who shall remain in charge of that vessel during the whole time that any class IA, IB or IC is on board (Regulation 21(3)).

527. For safety purpose, petroleum when not carried under deck shall be under a specially constructed wooden covering or suitable tarpaulins during transportation (Regulation 21(4)). In addition to that, smoking, fire or any kind of artificial light other than what is necessary for navigation shall not be allowed within 9 m of petroleum carried as deck cargo on any vessel, boat or similar craft (Regulation 21(5)). Likewise, no flame shall be used or exposed in the hold of any vessel carrying petroleum as cargo under deck, and no artificial light shall be used other than approved self-contained battery lamps (Regulation 21(6)). In case where inflammable liquid having a flash point below 60°C is on board, smoking, lighting of fire or artificial light is strictly prohibited (Regulation 37). Wooden vessel carrying packed cargoes of petroleum to outposts shall leave on courses specified in the Port Rules for that port (if any) (Regulation 21(8)).

528. By virtue of Regulation 30, use of containers which is (from the opinion of the Port Officer) likely to cause escape of petroleum in form of liquid or vapours is strictly prohibited. Shipping petroleum in such containers or allowing or causing it to be shipped is an offence. It is also an offence for the master or owner of any vessel to receive such petroleum on board.

529. Every vessel carrying petroleum, when berthed alongside, shall have or provided by the terminal operator with wire hawsers and ropes of sufficient strength and length to tow the vessel (Regulation 24(1)). Then the master, owner, agent or consignee of the vessel shall be obliged to ensure that the provisions relating to wire hawsers and ropes have been complied with (Regulation 24(2)). It must always be noted that immobilization of vessel, boat or similar craft carrying petroleum as cargo shall only be made with the written permission of a Port Officer (Regulation 25).

530. Apart from the above, under Regulation 26, the master has to ensure that there shall be a no smoking symbol of a minimum size of 15.24 cm displayed at all entry and exit points of the vessel. He/she shall also take adequate steps to prevent any person from smoking, carrying matches or any appliances for producing ignition, at or near the place for loading and discharging petroleum (especially petroleum Class IA, IB and IC) or ballast water, or place where gas freeing or tank cleaning work is carried out. Moreover, he (the master) or the owner, agent or consignee of the vessel shall ensure that a watchman shall be stationed at each gangway leading on to any vessel, etc., to prevent smoking, unauthorized access and to warn every person that Class I, II or III petroleum is being loaded or unloaded.

531. Repair or other similar operations to any compartment or pipeline of a vessel which contains petroleum other than Class IA, IB or IC shall not be commenced within the limits of a port, unless an Inspector has certified as in Form B that he/she has examined such compartments or pipeline and such other parts, and that he/she is of the opinion that those parts are free from inflammable vapour (Regulation 34). This provision however does not apply to repairs carried out externally and do not involve the use of burning, welding or riveting.

II. Provisions Relating to Vessels Loaded with Petroleum Class I (A, B or C): More Restrictive in Nature

532. Vessels loaded with Class 1A, 1B and 1C petroleum shall only anchor or berth within the dangerous petroleum anchorage for the purpose of handling and discharging the petroleum, unless otherwise permitted by the Port Officer in writing

(Regulation 3(2)). Dealings with such class of petroleum within the limits of any port shall only be done under direct supervision of a competent person (Regulation 8).

533. No such petroleum may be loaded or transported within the prohibited area of a port, unless with written approval of the Port Officer (for quantities not exceeding 400 litres water capacity of such petroleum, in a vessel licensed under Form C, if it is not intended to be shipped as cargo), or unless the petroleum is required for consumption on board (Regulation 11). The transportation and loading of such petroleum within the dangerous area of a port are permitted provided that the total quantity does not exceed 45,000 litres, has been loaded at shore installation and carried by a vessel under licence in Form C. If the total quantity exceeds 45,000 litres, then loading of such petroleum may only be permitted if it is required for consumption on board (Regulation 12). Transportation or loading of such petroleum within the non-dangerous area of a port is permitted for vessels constructed to carry such class of petroleum, or a boat, or similar craft or vessel permitted under this regulation, or with licence or certificate in Form C or Form D as the case may be (Regulation 13).

534. When class IA, IB or IC of petroleum is to be carried on deck as cargo which plies beyond the limits of any port in Malaysia, a local-trade or home-trade ship, or a foreign-going ship, such petroleum shall be properly fenced off and stored on the main deck at a distance of not less than 9 m from any galley, funnel or exhaust, and not less than 3 m of any part of the ship occupied or accessible to the passenger. Furthermore, a conspicuous notice shall be put to draw attention to the danger arising from smoking or exposing naked flame near the deck cargo (Regulation 14). The word 'local-trade ship', 'home-trade ship' and 'foreign-going ship' here shall have the same meaning as defined in the Merchant Shipping Ordinance 1952, the Merchant Shipping Ordinance 1960 of Sabah and the Merchant Shipping Ordinance 1960 of Sarawak (Regulation 2). The quantity of such petroleum on deck shall not exceed 400 litres (within the prohibited area, or the dangerous area; or on ship which plies only within 50 km of any port), or 300 litres (for every 25,500 kg of gross weight of a local-trade ship, up to a maximum of 23,000 litres for a passenger ship and 36,600 litres for a cargo ship) or 3,600 litres (on a local-trade ship or a foreign-going ship).

535. As to transportation of such petroleum under deck, it is strictly prohibited in relation to any passenger ship by virtue of Regulation 16(2). It is again emphasized in Regulation 21(9) that no passenger shall be allowed on any boat or similar craft carrying such class of petroleum under licence in Form C, while the petroleum is on board.

536. If Class IA, IB or IC petroleum is not carried in bulk, it shall be carried in tins, provided that such tins shall be carried in a boat or similar craft which has licence in Form C, and complies with conditions of the Third Schedule. The tins shall not contain more than 95% of liquid, and need not to be packed in cases (Regulation 21(2)). The loading of more than 400 litres of such petroleum shall only be carried out at dangerous petroleum anchorages, or an installation situated at dangerous or non-dangerous areas and licensed for the storage of such petroleum, or such other places as may be specifically approved by the Port Officer (Regulation 21(7)).

537. By virtue of Regulation 22, vessels carrying class IA, IB or IC petroleum as cargo not exceeding 1,300 litres may berth at the wharf of any port, with written permission from the Port Officer, previously obtained, and subject to the regulations and by-laws relating to dangerous goods.

538. For safety purpose, Regulation 23 strictly prohibited smoking and use of fire or any artificial light in any vessel handling such class of petroleum, except in specifically designated areas on board. Also the use of iron and steel hammer or other instrument capable of causing spark for opening and closing hatches, tank lids or loading arms is expressly prohibited under Regulation 28. Similarly, chipping, scaling or hammering of iron or steel is also prohibited except with the written approval of the Port Officer (Regulation 29).

539. Furthermore, Regulation 31 expressly stated that no vessel having such class of petroleum on board whether the whole or part as cargo, certified by a recognized authority as free from inflammable vapour, shall enter the limits of any port, unless the master has certified in Form B that all empty cofferdams and all compartments which contained petroleum have been thoroughly cleansed by washing, or by an alternative standard methods approved by an Inspector, and that the vessel is free from inflammable vapour (to the best of his/her knowledge); and an Inspector has certified in Form B that he/she has examined every accessible part of the vessel, and it is, in his/her opinion, free from inflammable vapour. The said certificate shall be forwarded to the Port Officer as soon as possible after the inspection is completed (Regulation 32). The same goes before any repairs or similar operation to be carried out on vessels carrying such class of petroleum (i.e., Inspector's Certification in Form B).

III. Miscellaneous Provisions

540. The Surveyor General of Ships may delegate his/her power under these regulations to any person he/she thinks fit (Regulation 35). All fees under these Regulations shall be in accordance with the Fifth Schedule (Regulation 36). Breach of any provisions of these Regulations is an offence, and on conviction shall be liable to a fine not exceeding MYR 5,000.00 and a further fine of maximum MYR 5,000 per day for continuing offence (Regulation 38).

541. These Regulations except Regulations 37 and 38 do not apply to acetic ether (ethyl acetate), acetone or methylated spirit (Regulation 39). The Regulations expressly repeal Part I, II, III and IV of the Petroleum Regulation 1953 and Part II of the Petroleum Rules 1960. However, any certificate, license, etc. granted under any of the said Regulations or Rules shall still be valid until superseded, revoked or cancelled or otherwise terminated, or if it is expressly stated to be valid for a definite period of time, then it shall not remain in force after expiry of such period, unless it shall be renewed in accordance with the provisions of these Regulations (Regulation 40).

IV. First Schedule

542. It describes the dangerous petroleum anchorages, prohibited areas, dangerous and non-dangerous areas of ports throughout the Federation of Malaysia, including Sabah and Sarawak.

PENANG: Penang	TERENGGANU: Kuala Terengganu, Kerteh, Kemaman
KEDAN: Kuala Kedah, Pulau Langkawi – Kuah, Pulau Langkawi – Teluk Ewa, Tanjoing Dawai	PAHANG: Sungai Kuantan, Tanjong Gelang.
SELANGOR: Port Kelang	JOHORE: Johor Bharu
MALACCA: Malacca, Sungai Udang	SABAH: Kota Kinabalu, Kudat, Labuan, Lahad Datu, Sandakan, Semporna, Tawau
NEGERI SEMBILAN: Port Dickson	SARAWAK. Bintulu, Kuching, Sibu, Miri

V. Second Schedule

543. It provides the format of various Forms.

A. *Form A*

PART I – CONSIGNEE'S NOTIFICATION
This part shall serve as an application for landing. It is signed by the 'Importers' whose address appears at the top right of the Form, issued to the Inspector, giving the name of the vessel, the quantity and the description of the petroleum on board, the name of the owner, agent or consignee and any other relevant information (such as the date and time the vessel is about to arrive, the place of storage).

PART II – INSPECTOR'S REPORT – It may be either of these Forms:

(1) It is the chemical report of the samples of petroleum taken from the vessel, etc. It is issued by the Inspector of Petroleum of the particular department of chemistry (which appears at the top right of the report), to the Port Officer certifying that the sample petroleum result shows that such petroleum is from which class, the flash point and the brand of the petroleum.

(2) The Inspector certifies that he has dispensed with inspection of the particular vessel, the reason for that and that such vessel has on board Class IA/ IB/ IC petroleum. It is endorsed with the departmental stamp and date of issuance.

PART III – PERMIT

The permit is issued by the Port Officer of the department of marine (which appears at the top right of the permit), to the above named Importers, stating that the permission to land is granted, and endorsed with the departmental stamp and date of issuance. If this permit is not made use of the day it is issued, then it must be returned within 24 hours to the Port Officer. A copy of this permit will be given to the General Manager. At the bottom left, there appears the name of the particular Port Authority.

B. Form B

MASTER'S CERTIFICATE

This certificate must be completed before the Inspector's Certificate is issued. The certificate is issued by the master of the vessel certifying that the vessel has been thoroughly cleaned.

INSPECTOR'S CERTIFICATE

This certificate is issued by the Inspector of Petroleum of the particular department of chemistry (which appears at the top right of the report), to the master of the vessel certifying that he has examined the accessibility of the vessel, and in his opinion free from inflammable flame. It is followed by his observation, departmental stamp and date and time issued. Note: This certificate must be forwarded to the Port Officer as soon as possible after the vessel's inspection. The validity of the certificate minimizes any likelihood of the need for repeated inspection during the period of repairs.

C. Form C

PART I – LICENCE TO CARRY CLASS 1A AND CLASS 1B PETROLEUM

The numbered licence (as appears at the top left of the Form) is actually issued by the Surveyor General of Ships from the particular department of marine to the Port Officer, certifying that he has inspected the (named) vessel and find it fit the understated quantity of Class IA and IB and other classes of petroleum in accordance with the requirements in the Third Schedule, within the understated areas of the port. It is endorsed with the departmental stamp and dated.

PART II

It is actually a licence issued by the Port Officer of the respective Port to the master of the named vessel, to carry the above-mentioned quantities of Class IA and IB petroleum in accordance with the Act, provided that the quantity does not exceed the maximum quantity permitted under this licence. The lifespan of the licence is expressly stated, followed by departmental stamp.

D. Form D

A certificate (as numbered) issued by the Surveyor General of Ships from particular department of marine certifying that inspection has been made of the named vessel on the stated date, as to its fitness for carrying the particular class of petroleum (as specified), and that it complies with the requirements of the Fourth Schedule to the Petroleum Regulation 1985. The expiry date for the certificate is expressly stated, followed by the departmental stamp and date of issuance.

VI. Third Schedule

LICENSING REQUIREMENTS FOR ANY VESSEL USED TO CARRY CLASS 1A, 1B, 1C AND CLASS II PETROLEUM (CLOSED CUP TEST) WITHIN A PORT LIMIT OR WITHIN 50 KM LIMIT VOYAGES.

544. There are eighteen requirements listed down in this schedule. Among others: doors shall be resistant to fire, and where required, to be self-closing and reasonably gastight (item 7); all electrical wirings etc. shall be flameproof (item 9) and all engine exhaust piping shall be lagged with heat resistance material (item 10).

VII. Fourth Schedule

545. This Schedule Provides For:

CONDITIONS TO BE COMPLIED WITH BY VESSELS TO WHICH CERTIFICATES TO LOAD AND CARRY CLASS 1A, 1B, 1C AND CLASS II PETROLEUM BELOW DECK ARE ISSUED IN FORM D.

1. The cargo carried must be destined for out-ports and loaded at a dangerous petroleum anchorage.
2. The requirements of regulations 16 and 20 shall be complied with.3. One or more fire-extinguishers must be fitted as ordered by the Surveyor General of Ships.

CONDITIONS TO BE COMPLIED WITH BY VESSELS TO WHICH CERTIFICATES TO CARRY PETROLEUM BELOW DECK ARE ISSUED IN FORM D.

3. The cargo carried must be destined for out-ports.

4. The requirements of regulations 16 and 20 shall be complied with.3. One or more fire-extinguishers must be fitted as ordered by the Surveyor General of Ships.

VIII. Fifth Schedule

546. It provides for fees to be levied by the Department of Marine. It shall be MYR 20 for each, a permit in Part III of Form A, a licence in Form C and a certificate in Form D.

Chapter 8. Petroleum (Income Tax) Act 1967 (Act 543)

§1. Part I: Preliminary

547. The Petroleum (Income Tax) Act 1967 (Revised 1995) is a specific legislation enacted to govern the imposition of tax upon the income derived from petroleum operations in Malaysia and it will have effect to related incidental petroleum operations throughout Malaysia for the year of assessment 1968 and the subsequent years. Petroleum income tax is assessed on the income earned in the preceding year. Currently, exploration, development and production of crude oil and natural gas are actively being undertaken and managed through petroleum agreements or the model of production sharing contracts (PSCs) entered into between Petronas (Petroleum Nasional Berhad) and a number of international oil and gas companies as well as with its subsidiary Petronas Cari Gali Sdn Bhd.

§2. Part II: Imposition of the Tax

548. Petroleum income tax is charged for each year of assessment on the income of every chargeable person – a person carrying on petroleum operation under a petroleum agreement with PETRONAS or Malaysia Thailand Joint Authority (MTJA), and there may be different chargeable person for each petroleum agreement, for example when a person carries on operations under more than one petroleum agreement, he will be considered as a separate chargeable person for each of such agreements – being income derived by such chargeable person from petroleum operation. 'Petroleum operations' means searching for and obtaining of petroleum in Malaysia, and any sale or disposal of the obtained petroleum including the transportation within Malaysia to any point of sale or delivery or export, excluding any process of refining or liquefying of petroleum and any product thereof and services involving the supply and use of rigs, derricks, ocean tankers and barges (section 2). It is notable that for this purpose, where a person, other than Petroleum Nasional Berhad or the Malaysia–Thailand Joint Authority, carries on petroleum operations under more than one petroleum agreement, he/she shall be regarded as a separate chargeable person in respect of each of those agreements. Likewise, where a partnership is succeeded by another at any time and at least one of the original parties to the petroleum agreement who was a member of a succeeded partnership, both partnerships shall be treated for the purposes of imposition of tax.

549. Currently, exploration, development and production of crude oil and natural gas are being actively undertaken and managed through petroleum agreements or the model of PSCs entered into between PETRONAS and a number of international oil and gas companies as well as with its subsidiary Petronas Cari Gali Sdn Bhd. However, the chargeable income from the petroleum operations of any person other than PETRONAS or MTJA shall be ascertained by reference to each petroleum agreement separately (section 4(3)).

550. The method used to ascertain the tax upon the chargeable income of a petroleum company is discussed in length in the Chapter 1 to Chapter 5 of Part III of the Act. The tax assessment will include the ascertainment of variable revenues of the petroleum companies encompasses the gross income, adjusted income or adjusted loss, statutory income and assessable income as stipulated by the Act (section 4(1)).

§3. Part III: Ascertainment of Chargeable Income

551. Chargeable income of a chargeable person refers to the net income of the petroleum operations that is taxable after computing the deductions and relieves available under the Act.

§4. Chapter 1: Basis Period

552. The accounting period that is the basis period of the tax assessment is twelve months. It begins on the date of the first sale of chargeable petroleum by or on behalf of the chargeable person or it can commence and end at any chosen date by the chargeable person with the approval of the Director General of Inland Revenue (hereinafter Director General). The accounting period may also be a shorter period than the twelve-month time ending up on the date chosen by the chargeable person with the consent of the Director General or on the date the chargeable person ceases from the petroleum operations or ceases to get profit from the petroleum operations whichever is the later (section 5(2)).

§5. Chapter 2: Ascertainment of Gross Income

553. Gross income of a *chargeable person* from his/her *petroleum operations* for a basic period for the year of assessment includes: (a) the proceeds from the sale of crude oil, natural gas or casing head petroleum spirit ('casing head' means any liquid hydrocarbons obtained in Malaysia from natural gas by separation or by any chemical or physical process but before the same has been refined or otherwise treated (section 2)); (b) the market value of crude oil or chargeable petroleum that is delivered to refinery and; (c) miscellaneous income incidental to petroleum operations (section 8). Gross income does not include: (a) any transportation of petroleum outside Malaysia; (b) any process of refining or liquefying of petroleum and; (c) any dealings with products so refined or liquefied; (d) service involving the supply and use of rigs, derricks, ocean tankers and barges (section 8).

§6. Chapter 3: Adjusted Income (Gross Income – Deductions/Capital Allowances = Adjusted Income)

554. Adjusted income of a chargeable person for the basic period for a year of assessment refers to an amount that can be ascertained by deducting from the gross income of the chargeable person for all outgoings and expenses in the production of the gross income. Various deductions and relieves are available against the gross income assessed for petroleum income tax liability.

555. The deduction shall include any loan of money and the interest upon thereof, any investment in movable or immovable property, rent payable by the chargeable person in respect of land or building occupied by him/her, expenses incurred for the repair of premises, plant, machinery or for the renewal, repair or alteration of any equipment or utensils which have working lifespan less than two years under normal condition of use. The deduction however shall not include the cost of reconstructing or rebuilding any premises, buildings, plant and machinery. The deduction will also include the assessment rates payable for that period to local authorities in respect of any property used for the petroleum operations (section 15).

As of January 2016, The Notable allowances are in the form of initial allowance and annual allowance. The notable ones are:

Secondary Recovery	40% and 10% respectively.
Any other case	20% and 8% respectively.
Fixed, Offshore platform	only annual allowance at the rate of 10%.
Environmental protection equipment and other such facilities	40% and 20% respectively.
Computer software	20% and 40% respectively.
Building secondary recovery	20% and 3% respectively.
Any other case pertaining to building	10% and 3% respectively.

The qualifying exploration expenditure incurred in course of exploration and development period is accumulated and carried forward until the first sale of petroleum. It is allowed as a deduction gradually in the form of initial allowance and annual allowance: Initial allowance at the rate of 10%; and Annual allowance (a) at the rate of 15% of the residual expenditure, or (b) output from petroleum operations for the basis period x residual expenditure (output from petroleum operations for the basis period + total potential future output of the petroleum operations).

556. In addition, the deduction from the gross income will embrace irrecoverable debt owing to chargeable person, contribution to employee's remuneration scheme such as Employees Provident Fund (EPF), expenditure of any equipment necessary to assist any disabled employee (section 16(7A)), services, public amenities and contribution to charity or community project pertaining to education, health, housing infrastructure as well as information and communication technology approved by the Minister of Finance (hereinafter known as 'the Minister') (section 16(7B)), maintenance of a child care centre for the benefits of persons employed by him/her in his/her business (section 16(7C)), activities related to establishing and managing a musical or cultural group approved by the Minister of Finance (section 16(D)) or sponsoring any arts or sculptural approved by the Ministry of Culture Arts and Tourism provided that the amount deducted shall not exceed MYR 200,000 (section 16(E)).

557. Apart from that, the deduction of the relevant gross income of the chargeable person will also include scholarships provided by the chargeable persons to a student of any course of study leading to an award of diploma or degree including a degree at a Masters or Doctorate level undertaken at a higher educational institution established or registered under the laws regulating such establishment in Malaysia (section 16(7F)). It shall also include any expenditure for the purpose of obtaining certification for recognized quality systems and standards evidenced by a certificate issued by a certification body as determined by the Minister (section 16(7G)) along with any practical training in Malaysia in relation to his/her business to an individual who is the resident of Malaysia and not an employee to the chargeable person (section 16(7H)).

558. Section 17 of the Act provides that in ascertaining the adjusted income of the chargeable person, the value of stock in trade ('stock in trade' of a chargeable person means his/her chargeable petroleum which he/she holds in his/her stock and which he/she has not: (i) delivered to a plant for refining or liquefying; (ii) exported; or (iii) sold (section 2)) shall be taken into account. In ascertaining the adjusted income, section 18 of the Act further stipulates that it will not be subject to deductions, which comprise of:

- any disbursement or expenses not being money expended wholly and exclusively for the purpose of producing the gross income, any sum of money employed to be the capital;
- any amount in respect of any payment to any pension, provident savings, widow and orphans or other similar fund or society which is not an approved scheme;
- rent or cost of repairs to any premises or any part thereof not used for the purpose of the petroleum operations, expenditure incurred to the depreciation of any premises;
- buildings, structures, works of permanent nature, plant, machinery or fixtures;
- any expenditure qualifying the expenditure for the purpose of First Schedule or Second Schedule;
- interest, royalty, services, technical advice, assistance, rent or other payments made under the agreement or arrangement for the use of moveable property derived from Malaysia or contract payment to a non-resident contractor from which tax is deductible under the provisions of law enforced in Malaysia relating to income tax;
- any amount chargeable tax payable under PITA or CITA;

- any sum paid by way of rentals in respect of motor vehicle, other than a motor vehicle licensed by the appropriate authority for commercial transportation of goods or passengers in excess of MYR 50,000; and
- a sum of 50% of any expenses incurred in entertainment ('entertainment' includes the provision of food, drink, recreation or hospitality of any kind or accommodation or travel for the purpose of facilitating the entertainment of the chargeable person on his/her employee in connection with petroleum operations (section 2)).

559. It shall not however include any expenditure pertaining to a benefit or amenity to an employee consisting of a leave passage within or outside Malaysia.

I. Adjusted Loss (Deductions Exceeds Gross Income)

560. In ascertaining the adjusted income, when the amount of deductions exceeds the amount of gross income from the petroleum operations, the amount will be regarded as adjusted loss for that year of assessment (section 19).

It may be noted here that any unabsorbed allowances can be carried forward and set off against income of subsequent years as long as there is a succeeding partnership.

§7. Chapter 4: Statutory Income (Adjusted Income + Balancing Charges = Statutory Income)

561. The statutory income of a chargeable person for a year of assessment shall consist of the amount of adjusted income and the amount of any balancing charge (paragraph 18, Second Schedule – when the value of disposable asset exceeds the residual expenditure, the excess will be charged upon the chargeable person as a balancing charge) or the aggregate amount of the balancing charge to be made for that year of assessment under the Second Schedule after reducing the amount of any allowances to be made for that year under the Schedule (section 20). If there is adjusted loss which has not been deducted from the statutory income for the years of assessment preceding or before the relevant year, the deduction of the adjusted loss will be made in the relevant year of the assessment (section 21(2), (3)).

I. Assessable Income

562. The assessable income of a chargeable person shall consist of the amount of statutory income for the relevant year after reducing any deduction to be made in that year. The assessable income shall also include the deduction for: (a) donation to the Government, a State Government, a local authority or an approved institution or organization (approved by the Director General) provided that it shall not exceed 5% of the statutory income from his/her petroleum operations; (b) gift of artefact or manuscript or painting to the Government or State Government (the value which will be determined by the Department of Museums and Antiquities or the National

Archives); (c) public facilities for disabled persons; (d) gift of medical equipment to healthcare facility (approved by the Ministry of Health and that amount shall not exceed MYR 20,000); and (d) gift of painting given to the National Art Gallery or any state gallery the value of which will be determined by the respective galleries (section 21(1), (1A), (1B), (1C), (1D)).

§8. Chapter 5: Chargeable Income

563. Chargeable income of a chargeable person is the income derived from petroleum operations after computing the allowable deductions, non-allowable deductions, adjusted loss, balancing charges, capital allowances, donation, etc. in the petroleum operations.

Tax Computation Format

Gross Income – Allowable Deductions + Non-allowable Deductions = Adjusted Income
Adjusted Income + Balancing Charges – Capital Allowances = Statutory Income
Statutory Income – Adjusted loss before = Assessable Income
Assessable Income – Donation etc. = CHARGEABLE INCOME
TAX PAYABLE = CHARGEABLE INCOME @ 38%

§9. Part IV: Ascertainment of Chargeable Tax

I. Chargeable Tax

564. Section 23 of the Petroleum Income Tax Act 1967 stipulates that the rate of tax imposed on chargeable income of the chargeable person for the year of assessment to be an amount equal to 38%, while the chargeable tax for any year of assessment of a chargeable person on income derived from petroleum operations in the Joint Development Area shall be as follows:

Tax Rates for Joint Development Areas	
First eight years of production	0%
The next seven years	10%
Subsequent years of production	20%

565. The rates of tax have been:

- Assessment year 1976–1993: 45 percent;
- Assessment year 1994–1997: 40 percent; and
- Assessment year 1998 to date: 38 Percent.

Petroleum operations in marginal fields are subject to 25 percent tax.

By virtue of section 2 of the Malaysia–Thailand Joint Authority Act 1990, The joint development area is an overlapping economic zone located offshore between Malaysia and Thailand in the Gulf of Thailand known as the Malaysia–Thailand Joint Development Area. The joint development area was established to resolve the overlapping claims between Malaysia and Thailand over the hydrocarbon resources in the area. The area is divided into three blocks – Block A-18, Block B-17 and Block C-19 and is administered by the Malaysia–Thailand Joint Authority (MTJA) established under the Malaysia–Thailand Joint Authority Act 1990, of which Malaysia and Thailand each owned 50%. Through MTJA, both countries agree to adopt Malaysia's model of the production sharing contract. The income from the joint development area would be subject to both Malaysian as well as Thai taxes. As quoted from: <www.petronas.com.my/business/index.htm>.[114]

566. If the chargeable income relates to income from two different production periods, the tax liability will be calculated according to each period of the production period (section 23(2)).

II. Chargeable Persons

567. The Act has listed out the chargeable persons and the persons on his/her behalf who are subject to the tax. The chargeable persons can be either a company or a body of persons who are responsible for all acts and things required to be done according to the Act. In the case of company the responsibilities rely upon the manager or other principal officer in Malaysia, the directors, the secretary and any other persons who exercise the duties on their behalf. With regards to the body of persons, the manager, the treasurer, the secretary and the members of its controlling authority are duly assessable and chargeable for the tax in respect to the petroleum operations (section 27).

568. In case of a company who has been wound up, the liquidator shall not distribute any of the assets of the company to the shareholders unless the payment of the tax charged upon the company has been made. Upon any failure on the part of the liquidator, he/she shall be liable for the penalty equivalent to the accrued amount of the company's tax. In this matter the penalty shall be subjected to section 64(2) of the Act that the accrued tax shall be recovered as if it were part of tax payable by the person but not for the purpose of any provision of tax of the Act (section 27(5)).

---

114. Also refer to: Sykirah Bt. Md. Nor, 'Petroleum Fiscal Regime-Malaysia's Experience', at: http://www.imf.org/external/np/seminars/eng/2015/natrestax/pdf/syakirah.pdf (accessed on 12 May 2018).

III. Power to Appoint Agent

569. The power to appoint agent lies solely on the hand of the Director General when he/she thinks there is a need to appoint an agent that would serve on behalf of the chargeable person in any responsibilities including to be assessed and charged on tax. The Director General also has power to revoke the appointment at any time. The Act also mentioned that if the representative of the chargeable person is aggrieved with the appointment he/she can appeal under section 43 as if the notice to serve upon him/her were a notice of assessment (section 28).

IV. Vicarious Responsibility and Chargeability of the Agent

570. According to the Act, the agent will step in the shoe of the chargeable person also known as the principal to be assessable and charged to tax. The representative has right to require any person who receives or controls the income or being paid the income to supply full particulars of any income and any expenses of the company. The representative will also be treated in the same manner the principal is treated in the tax assessment and charge including the penalty for any default payment of the tax. He/she however will not be liable to any fine for the offence committed by the principal (section 29).

V. Returns

571. Section 30 of the Act mentions that it is the duty of the chargeable person to prepare accounts of his/her profits and losses arising from the petroleum operations for the basic period for each year of assessment. Within three months after the expiration date of assessment, he/she has to deliver a copy of his/her accounts to Director General, which shall contain the declaration that the same is true and complete.

572. The Finance Act 2010 replaced section 30 with a different mechanism of filing returns. According to the new section 30, a return has to be filed to the Director General on the prescribed form within seven months from the date following the end of the basis period for that year of assessment. New section 30A, a return to be filed with respect to expenditure, incurred during exploration period within seven months from the date following the end of period a return in the prescribed form. New section 30B provides that the chargeable person may make amendments in the return filed by him in respect to the amount of tax or additional tax payable by him on the chargeable income.

573. In ascertaining whether or not a chargeable person is subject to tax liability, the Director General has vast and absolute power through a notice to acquire specific information of the company's account from any person from the company, to require any person to attend personally before him/her and produce for examination all books, accounts, returns and other documents which the Director General deems necessary, to require any person to give orally or in writing all information concerning income, assets or liabilities of a chargeable person (section 34), shall have full and free access to all lands and buildings (section 33) and to require further returns/reports on any matter under the Act (section 35). The specific information must be completed and delivered to Director General less than thirty days from the date of service of the notice (section 31(a)). A return made by any person shall be presumed to be made by him/her or on his/her authority until the contrary is approved and it shall be deemed that any person signing such a return to be aware of its content (section 36). Any change of address by the chargeable person must be informed to the Director General in written notice (section 37).

New section, inserted by the Finance Act 2010, requires from the chargeable person carrying on petroleum operation to keep relevant records, electronically or otherwise, for a period of seven years to enable the Director General or an authorized officer to ascertain the expenditure or income and income or adjusted loss.

§10. Part VII: Assessment and Appeals

I. Assessments, Payment of Tax and Failure to Furnish Return

574. Upon furnishing of return under section 30, the Director General shall be deemed to have made assessment on the day on which the return is furnished. It may be noted here that the Finance Act 2014 requires that accounts submitted by the chargeable person must be audited by a professional accountant together with a report made by the accountant. If the return has not be filed under section 30 of the Act, the Director General will make assessment on the basis of his best judgement; it is popularly known as best judgement assessment, provided that the making of assessment does not affect any liability otherwise incurred by the reason of his failure to deliver the return. New section 39A, inserted by the Finance Act 2010, has the provision about deemed assessment on the amended return. It provides that upon furnishing of the amended return, the Director General will be deemed to have made assessment on it.

The Finance Act 2010 has replaced section 48, which provided the mechanism for payment of tax. It provides that the tax will be due and payable on the due date whether or not the chargeable person appeals against the assessment made. Under sections 38, 39, 40 or 45, it is from the date of service of the relevant notice. The position will be the same if additional assessment has been made under section 39A of the Act. The best thing is that the assessee may request the Director General for payment of tax on instalment basis. But in case of default in all situations there will be liability to pay 10% additional tax on unpaid amount of tax. It may be noted here that upon request the Director General has discretion to make an order to refund the additional payment of tax. The section 39A, inserted by the Finance Act 2010, provides conditions for estimating tax payable by the chargeable person. It also has provisions for determining tax to be paid in instalment by him. The provisions are liberal providing payments of tax easy to the chargeable person.

The Finance Act 2010 replaced section 51 with a new one. The new section has slightly stringent penalty with power to the Director General to impose penalty instead of prosecuting the offender. Thus, a defaulting person for not furnishing appropriate return under section 30 or 30A as the case may be will be guilty of an offence punishable with a fine not exceeding five years or to a jail term not exceeding one year or both. And he will not be exonerated from filing the return and paying the tax. However, the Director General may require the person to pay a penalty equal to treble the amount of tax payable in that year. If he pays that penalty, he will not be liable to be charged. The Director General may require a person to pay an additional amount of penalty in respect to any additional tax payable by that person for a year of assessment.

The Finance Act 2015 inserted a new subsection (6) in section 39 for making adjustments in the assessments. It says, where in a basis period for the year of assessment, any adjustment is made in respect to any input tax paid under the Goods and Services Tax Act 2014, the Director General may suitably make an assessment or a reduced assessment. It may be noted here that in May 2018, after the 14 General Election in Malaysia, the Prime Minister made announcement for abolishing goods and services tax. If it happens so this provision will become redundant. There are few other amendments brought about by the Finance Act 2015, for example amendments in First Schedule and Second Schedule of the parent Act, in order to make the law compatible with the Goods and Services Tax Act. The author is of the opinion that will also have to be recharged.

Section 82A, a new section inserted by the Finance Act 2010, authorises Director General to allow any chargeable person to use the electronic version of any form. He may authorise his agent to use such form(s). In this regard the Director General may prescribed any condition(s). The chargeable person will have to keep a hard copy of such form duly signed by him for seven years.

The Finance Act 2013 has introduced a new section 57A prescribing punishment for failure to keep records. If records under section 34A is not kept as required, the offender will be liable a fine not less than 300 and not more than MYR 10,000 or to imprisonment for a term not exceeding one year or both.

575. According to section 40, an assessment shall be made in the appropriate prescribed form. The assessment upon the chargeable person is considered to be final when there is no appeal made within thirty days after the service notice of assessment or any extension thereof. In case there is an appeal towards the assessment, any decision determined on the appeal shall be final and there is no right for future appeal.

II. Appeals

576. Any chargeable person (the principal) or his/her representative who is aggrieved by an assessment may appeal to the Special Commissioners against the assessment by giving the Director General a written notice of appeal in a prescribed form stating the grounds of appeal and other relevant particulars within thirty days after the service of the notice of assessment (or within an extended period thereof) (section 43(1)). The Act specifically states that there should be three or more of Special Commissioner of Petroleum Income Tax and a Clerk to the Special Commissioners who are appointed under the law relating to income tax to examine the appeal of the aggrieved persons (section 42(1), (2), (3)). If possible, an appeal by the principal and the agent or the representative against an assessment may be dealt with together (section 43(2)). The Third Schedule of the Act which exclusively deals with appeals stipulates that the agent may represent and act generally on behalf of the principal (section 43(3)).

577. On receipt of a notice of appeal, the Director General will review the assessment against which the appeal is made. In this matter, the Director General may require the appellant to equip the particulars the Director General thinks necessary with respect to the income of the appellant in the petroleum operations that may include the submission of all books or any other documents in the appellant's custody that are relevant to the assessment. He/she may also summon anybody to attend before him/her to provide evidence relating to the assessment and examine any person on oath or otherwise. If the investigation requires a longer period than twelve months, the Director General may seek permission from the Minister for an extension period not later than thirty days before the expiry of the twelve-month period (section 45(1)). The Minister may grant the extension when he/she thinks it fits under any reasonable circumstances not later than thirty days of the twelve-month period and his/her decision in this matter shall be final (section 45(1B), (1C)).

III. Extension of Appeal

578. As far as the extension of time for appeal is concerned, a chargeable person through a written application in prescribed form may seek for an extension from the Director General. If satisfied, the Director General for any practical reason may extend the period to a suitable time frame that suits the circumstances and he/she shall serve a notice of the extension to the applicant. If the Director General is not satisfied, he/she shall forward the application to the Clerk of the Special Commissioners with a statement of the reasons for his/her dissatisfactions. The Commissioner then will decide on whether or not to extend the period of appeal and his/her decision in this matter is final (section 44(4), (5)).

579. The result of the review by the Director General that may lead to a mutual agreement between them shall be enunciated in a written contract and shall be treated as having been confirmed, reduced, increased or discharged in accordance with the agreement (section 45(2)). If the result of the review is rejected by the appellant, the matter will be brought before the Special Commissioners and the decision by one of the Special Commissioner is final (section 45(5)).

580. The Director General may send the application of appeal from the chargeable person against the assessment of income and the payable tax to the Special Commissioners at anytime within the twelve-month period from the date of receipt of the notice of appeal or if extension under subsection 45(1B) has been granted and he/she shall give a written notice to the appellant that he/she has done so (section 46(1)). However if there is an agreement between the Director General and the appellant about the assessment, no appeal shall be forwarded to the Special Commissioners (section 46(3)). Where an appeal is brought upon the Special Commissioners, it will be regulated and determined according to the Third Schedule of the Act (section 46(4)). At any time before the hearing of the appeal, the Director General and the appellant may come to an agreement of any kind mentioned in subsection 45(2) and the appellant may at anytime withdraw the appeal (section 46(5)(a) and (b)).

581. Section 47(1) of the Act stipulates that if the Director General is not satisfied with the determination of the market value of chargeable petroleum, either the Director General or that chargeable person may refer the matter to the Price Review Committee. The committee shall determine the matter referred to it and its decision shall be final (section 47(9)).

§11. Part VIII: Collection and Recovery of Tax

582. The chargeable person has to pay the tax or additional tax by virtue of incurred assessment at the place specified in the notice whether or not the chargeable person appeals against the assessment or the increased assessment (section 48(1), (2)). The payment can be made on lump sum or on instalment basis the amount of which will be determined by the DG (section 48(3)). The payable tax must be settled within thirty days after the service or any extended period agreed by the Director General.

583. In the event of default in the tax imbursement, a sum of 10% will be charged to the unpaid or outstanding amount of tax and the increased shall be deemed as if it were tax payable under the Act. When the tax instalment is paid, the Director General may consider that it has been paid on its due date. Furthermore, Director General for any good reason also has the power to remit the increased sum chargeable upon the outstanding tax balance (section 48(5), (6)).

I. Recovery by Suit

584. Tax due and payable may be recovered by the Government by proceedings as a debt due to the government and the proceedings in this matter will be carried out by the Director General or officers authorized by the Minister (section 49). The Finance Act 2017 redefined the term 'secondary recovery'. The term would mean a project, which has its object the production of quantities of hydrocarbons by the application of external energy to the underground reservoir for the purpose of additional and accelerated recovery of those hydrocarbons which is carried out subsequent to the earlier recovery process.

II. Refund of Overpayments

585. If there is any excess of the amount of payable tax under the Act, the chargeable person shall be refundable by the Government after the endorsement by the Director General. The claim of the refund must be made within six years after the end of the year of assessment to which the claim relates (section 50).

§12. Part IX: Offences and Penalties (Section 51 – Section 64A)

586. The following points are notable:

(1) Failure to make or deliver accounts without any reasonable reason shall on conviction be liable a fine not exceeding MYR 5,000 or imprisonment for a term not exceeding one year or to both.
(2) Incorrect return by omitting or understating any income/give any incorrect information – penalty – a fine not exceeding MYR 50,000 and shall pay a special penalty of double the amount of tax which has been undercharged (section 52).
(3) Wilful evasion – any person who wilfully and with intent to assist a chargeable person to evade tax – penalty – MYR 100,000 or to imprisonment not exceeding five years and shall pay a special penalty of treble the amount of tax which has been undercharged (section 53).
(4) Obstruction of Officers – obstructs or refuses to permit the entry of the Director General or an authorized officer into land, building or any place, refuses to produce any book or other document in his/her custody, fails to provide reasonable facilities or assistance and refuses to answer any questions by the Director General or his/her unauthorized person – penalty – a fine not exceeding MYR 20,000 or imprisonment not exceeding three years or both (section 54).
(5) Breach of confidence – communicates classified material to another person or allows another person to have access to classified material – upon conviction – a fine not exceeding MYR 2,000 or imprisonment not exceeding one year or to both (section 55).
(6) Any person having an official function under the Act and acting beyond and against his/her official duties for example demands from any person an amount in excess of the tax or penalties due under the Act, withholds for his/her own use any portion of such tax or penalty collected or received by him/her, makes a false report or return (orally or in writing) of the amount of any such tax or penalty collected or received by him/her, defrauds any person, embezzles any money or uses his/her position to deal wrongfully with the Director General or any other person, shall be guilty of an offence and shall, on conviction, be liable to a fine not exceeding MYR 10,000 or to imprisonment for a term not exceeding three years or to both (section 56). Any unauthorized person who collects or attempts to collect tax or penalty is guilty – penalty – fine not exceeding MYR 10,000 or to imprisonment for a term not exceeding one year or to both (section 57).

(7) Any person without any reasonable excuse fails to comply with a notice by the Director General to furnish information for the purpose of assessment of income and tax – penalty – a fine not exceeding MYR 5,000. Any person who aids, abets or incites any person to commit an offence under section 52 (incorrect returns/reports), section 54 (obstruction of officers into land/building, refuse to produce books/documents/assistance), section 56 (not acting on good faith of his/her official functions) shall be deemed to have committed the same offence and shall be liable for the same penalty.

I. Compounding the Offences

587. The Director General at any time before the conviction has power to compound the offences and order that person to pay a sum of money not exceeding the maximum fine (section 62). He/she also has power to abate and remit penalties imposed under this Act before the conviction (section 63). The subordinate court shall have jurisdiction to try any offence under this Act (section 64A).

§13. Part X: Remission and Other Relief

588. The Act has provided remission to the chargeable persons on the tax paid or payable, which may be wholly or partially with the consent of the Minister on ground of justice and equity (section 65). The Minister also has power to make double taxation arrangements (section 65A) and to order any exemption from tax the income of chargeable person in overlapping areas for the joint exploitation or exploration of petroleum with the government of any territory outside Malaysia.

589. The chargeable person, who has paid tax, is entitled for a relief with respect to excessive payment of tax because of error or mistake in any year of assessment if he alleges that an assessment relating to that year is excessive. For this, he has to move an application to the Director General within six years of the assessment. The Director General will take an appropriate decision after an enquiry conducted by him. (section 66).

§14. Part XI: Supplemental

I. Administration

A. The Director General

590. The Director General of Inland Revenue appointed under the law relating to income tax shall have the care and management of the tax (section 67). The Director General is directly responsible to the Minister who has power to ascertain the general characters of a Director General in exercising his/her functions. It is the duty of a Director General to serve and give effect to the directions (section 68).

B. Identification of Officials

591. Any person who is purporting to be a public officer or an employee of the Inland Revenue Board in exercising his/her duty shall have an identification/warrant issued by the DG (section 70). Any person who is an official who deals with information classified as confidential must not disclose any information to others (section 71). The Director with reasonable reasons has right to disregard and make adjustments to any transactions which is believed to have direct and indirect effect of altering the incidence of tax which is payable or suffered by any chargeable person, relieving him/her from any duty or liability which has arisen to pay tax or to make a return or preventing the operation of this Act in respect (section 72(1)). In this section 'transaction' means any trust, grant, covenant, agreement, arrangement or other disposition or transaction made or entered into orally or in writing (whether before or after the commencement of this Act), and includes a transaction entered into by two or more companies with another company or companies (section 72(7)).

II. Miscellaneous

A. Evidential Provisions

592. The production of any certificate under section 49 (recovery of tax) signed by the Director General shall be sufficient evidence for the court to give judgment. While in criminal or civil proceedings under this Act the certificates signed by the Director General or other authorized officer can be authoritative evidence until the contrary is proved and provided that the punishment for the offence is not punishable by imprisonment (section 73).

B. Errors and Defects in Assessments, Notices and Other Documents

593. No assessment, notice or other document purporting to be made or issued for the purposes of this Act shall be quashed or deemed to be void or voidable for want of form, or be affected by any mistake, defect or omission therein, if it is in substance and effect in conformity with this Act or in accordance with the intent and meaning of this Act (section 74).

C. Power to Direct Where Returns, Etc. Are to Be Sent

594. By statutory order, the Director General may direct any information, returns or documents to be sent or supplied to any public officer or to such addressed in the order (section 75).

D. Service of Notice

595. Notices relating to tax may be served personally or by ordinary or registered post and shall be deemed to have been served on the person to whom it is addressed. Where a person to whom the letter is addressed, a registered letter containing notice under the Act, is informed that there is a registered letter awaiting him/her at the post office and he/she refuses or neglects to take delivery of the letter, then the notice shall be deemed to have been served on the date he/she was informed about it (section 76(3)).

E. Authentication of Notices and Other Documents

596. Every notice or other document issued, served or given for the purposes of this Act by the Director General or an authorized officer shall be sufficiently authenticated if the name and office of the Director General, the Director of Inland Revenue, Sabah, or the Director of Inland Revenue, Sarawak, are printed, stamped or otherwise written thereon. A notice or other documents issued by an authorized officer must be signed in manuscript by that officer. A notice or documents served and given by the Director General or an authorized officer shall be presumed to have been signed by him until the contrary is proved (section 77).

F. Free Postage

597. According to section 78, all returns and all remittances of tax made under this Act may if posted in Malaysia be sent free of postage to the Director General, to the Director of Inland Revenue, Sabah, to the Director of Inland Revenue, Sarawak, or to an officer or address specified in an order made under section 75 except in certain cases that the Director General by notice in writing require any person to send any return, document or correspondence by registered post.

G. Provision as to Approvals and Directions Given by Minister or Director General

598. It is notable that the Minister or the Director General has power to give an approval or direction of any kind (provided that is not a power exercisable by statutory order), and an approval or direction given shall not be regarded as subsidiary legislation. According to section 79, the authority given will include power to give any approval or direction with retrospective effect and power to vary or revoke any approval or direction retrospectively or otherwise. The approval and the direction shall take effect immediately or on the specified date.

H. Annulment of Rules and Orders Laid Before House of Representatives

599. The House of Representatives has statutory right to resolve any rule or order or any provision of it be annulled, and such rule and order shall cease to have effect without any prejudice to anything previously done thereunder (section 80).

I. Procedure for Making Refunds and Repayment

600. In making refunds and repayments, the Director General must certify the amount of the sum to be refunded or repaid and it shall be taken from the Consolidated Fund (section 81).

J. Forms

601. The Director General, by statutory order, may prescribe a form according to the Act or suitable substitute for that form in connection with the operation of the Act. In order to comply with any provision of this Act a person is required to use the prescribed form or its substitute (section 82).

K. Power to Make Rules

602. The power to make rules is laid upon the hand of the Minister. The Minister may make rules to prescribe anything that is required to be prescribed by the Act (section 83(1)) and to facilitate the Act generally. Any rules made under subsection 83(1) shall be laid before the House of Representatives (section 83).

L. Any Other Law Not Applicable

603. This Act shall govern matters relating to income tax for the year of assessment 1968 and subsequent years where the assessable income of the company derived from petroleum operations, and dividends being paid by any company out of its income derived from petroleum operations. Hence, the company shall not be chargeable to tax under any other law (section 84).

§15. First Schedule Deductions for Capital Expenditures on Exploration

604. The First Schedule provides for the allowable deductions upon the capital expenditure on the petroleum exploration. The qualifying exploration expenditure for the purpose of this schedule is expenditure which is incurred by a chargeable person in connection with his/her petroleum operations to include the acquisition of petroleum deposits, searching for, discovering and testing or winning access to petroleum deposits, the construction of any works or buildings or general administration or management before the date any sale or disposal of petroleum so won or obtained. The qualifying exploration expenditure is subject to two kinds of tax deductions namely the initial allowance which is imposed only once and the annual allowance which is imposed in every year of assessment. For the first year of assessment, the initial allowance for the 'secondary recovery' means a project which has as its object the production of quantities of hydrocarbons by the application of external energy to the underground reservoir for the purpose of additional and/or accelerated recovery of those hydrocarbons (section 2). In general, there are three stages of oil field development: primary recovery, secondary recovery and third recovery.[115]. For the primary or other recovery the deduction is 10% of the qualifying exploration expenditure. The annual allowance for a year of assessment and the subsequent years would be any permitted fraction or 15% whichever is greater. The deduction will be made from the gross income of the chargeable person for the basic period for the year of assessment.

605. If the chargeable person transfers an exploration asset (an asset on which the chargeable has incurred qualifying expenditure in connection with the preparation of the petroleum operations (paragraph 7)) for a consideration, the value of the consideration shall be deemed to be recovered expenditure in the petroleum operations and to be received by the chargeable person on the date of transfer.

§16. Second Schedule: Capital Allowances and Charges

606. Paragraphs 8, 9, 12, 13 and 14 of the Second Schedule of Petroleum (Income Tax) Act stipulate specific rates of initial and annual allowances for qualifying expenditure incurred on plant and machinery, fixed offshore platforms and industrial buildings. The expenditure for the plant will include the alteration of the existing building and land preparation activities (cutting, tunnelling or levelling the land) for the purpose of installing machinery or plant, construction of fixed offshore platforms for drilling or other petroleum operations. The qualifying building expenditure comprised of the construction or purchase of a building or industrial building.

607. The amount of initial allowances for qualifying plant expenditure is 40% in secondary recovery and 20% in any other case. While for the qualifying building expenditure the allowance is 20% in secondary discovery and 10% in any other case.

608. Annual allowance for plant expenditure incurred on alteration of an existing building for installation purposes, and on preparing a site for installation is equal to 10% in secondary recovery or 8% or other prescribed rate. If the chargeable person has incurred qualifying plant expenditure on the construction of fixed offshore

115. See at:www.britannica.com/eb/-81767> is 20% (accessed on 20 January 2017).

platforms for petroleum operations, the allowance is equal to 10% or other prescribed rate. In respect of building on construction or purchase of a building used as industrial building for the petroleum operations the allowance rate is 3% or any other rate may be prescribed of that expenditure.

I. Balancing Allowances and Balancing Charges

609. In case the chargeable person disposes his/her asset, which he/she has incurred qualifying expenditure and the residual expenditure at the date of the disposal of the asset exceed the disposal value of the asset, the allowance for him/her for that year of assessment shall be equal to the amount of the excess. If the disposal value of the asset exceeds the residual expenditure, he/she will be charged an amount equal to the excess. The amount referred above shall be known as balancing allowances and balancing charges respectively.

II. Disposal Subject to Control

610. When the chargeable person disposes an asset in relation of which the initial or annual allowance has been made or would have been made, after the transfer, the disposer still has the control over the asset along with the other chargeable person or the acquirer. The disposer controls over the asset shall cease, that is the disposal of the assets shall be deemed to take place on the first day of the disposer's final period for a sum equal to the disposer's residual expenditure on that day.

§17. Third Schedule: Appeals

611. When there is no mutual agreement between the Director General and the appellant regarding the assessment of payable tax over the income of the petroleum operations, either of the parties may extend an appeal to the Special Commissioners of petroleum Income Tax. Every appeal shall be heard by three Special Commissioners, at least one of whom shall be a person with experience as advocate, as a member of judicial and legal service of the Federation or as the holder of and office to which the Judges Remuneration 1963 apply. The hearing of the appeal will be held in any place where the Special Commissioners think appropriate. A notice will be sent by the Clerk to both the Director General and the appellant at least twenty-eight days before the date and placed are fixed. In an appeal, the onus of approving that an assessment is excessive or erroneous is on the appellant. In the trial, the appellant may be presented by an advocate or an accountant or both and if the appellant is a principal, he/she may be presented by a representative.

I. Power of Special Commissioners

612. The Special Commissioners shall have power to summon any person to attend at the hearing of any appeal or any person who might be able to give evidence respecting the appellant. They have rights to examine the person as a witness under oath or otherwise. By the statutory provision, the Special Commissioners have authority to require the person, who is summoned to produce any books and documents in his/her custody or control or any other evidence, which he/she considers necessary for the appeal. The power is also in the hands of the Special Commissioners to admit or reject any evidence whether oral or documentary in the hearing along with the power to postpone or adjourned the hearing of appeal including power to adjourn to consider their decision.

613. In addition, the Special Commissioners have powers of the subordinate Court with regards to the enforcement of attendance of witness, hearing evidence on oath and punishment for contempt. For the person who is summoned to attend the hearing, the expenses of his/her attendance shall be borne by the appellant or by the Government as ordered by the Special Commissioner. The Special Commissioners in the exercise of their functions shall enjoy the same judicial immunity as enjoyed by the person presiding in a subordinate court.

II. Further Appeals

614. Either party to proceedings before the Special Commissioners may appeal on a question of law against the deciding order by requiring the Special Commissioners to a case for the opinion of the High Court. The writing requisition must be delivered to the Clerk within twenty-one days after the order by the Special Commissioner or within any extended period allowed by the High Court. The decision of the High Court may be forwarded to the Court of Appeal by either party who is not satisfied with the judgment on a question of law.

III. Supplemental Provisions

615. Proceedings under this Schedule before the Special Commissioners or the Court may take place in camera provided that the Director General applies to the Special Commissioners or the court that the proceedings or any part thereof shall be made by way of hearing to public where he/she deems necessary. The Special Commissioners or the Court may allow such application notwithstanding any objections by any other party. Any authorized publication may be obtained from the Special Commissioners or the Court on certain fees that may be prescribed from time to time by the Minister.

§18. PETROLEUM (INCOME TAX) DEDUCTIONS RULES

616. Under the powers conferred by section 83(1) of the Act, the Minister makes the following deductions rules for the purpose of ascertaining the adjusted income of a chargeable person:

(1) Deductions of Research Expenditure Rules 1989:
- shall be deemed to take effect from the year of assessment 1976 onwards;
- any contractual payment of research cess made under a petroleum agreement, or in case of Petronas, payment made to Petroleum Research Fund shall be allowed as deduction under section 15 of the Act.

(2) Deductions for the Employment of Disabled Persons Rules 1989:
- shall take effect from the year of assessment 1989 onwards;
- The remuneration payable by the chargeable person to disabled employees, physically or mentally, shall be allowed as a kind of remuneration deduction under section 15 of the Act, provided that the chargeable person shall prove to the satisfaction of the Director General the employee is physically or mentally disabled and is not able to perform the work of a normal person.

(3) Deductions of Insurance Premiums for Importers Rules 1989:
- has taken effect from year 1989 onwards;
- Any premium payable in respect of insurance of cargo imported by the chargeable person, so long as the risks are insured with any insurance company incorporated in Malaysia, shall be allowed as deduction, in addition to allowable deduction under section 15 of the Act.

(4) Deductions of Abandonment Expenditure Rules 1997:
- is deemed to have effect for the assessment year of 1984 onwards;
- Any contractual payment of abandonment cess under a petroleum agreement, and in case of Petronas or the Malaysia–Thailand Joint Authority, such payment made to the Abandonment Cess Fund, shall be allowed as deduction under section 15 of the Act.

§19. PETROLEUM (INCOME TAX) (QUALIFYING PLANT ALLOWANCES) (COST OF PROVISION OF COMPUTER SOFTWARE) RULES 2003

617. These Rules were made on 3 April 2003 but are deemed to have effect from the year of assessment 1999. The application of the Rules covers the qualifying plant expenditure incurred on the cost of provision of computer software used for the purpose of petroleum operations. The initial allowance under subparagraph 8*(a)*of the Second Schedule to the Act on qualifying plant expenditure shall be calculated at the rate of 20%, while the annual allowance under subparagraph 12(1)*(a)* of the same Schedule shall be calculated at the rate of 40%.

§20. PETROLEUM (INCOME TAX) (QUALIFYING PLANT ALLOWANCES) (COMPUTERS AND INFORMATION TECHNOLOGY EQUIPMENT) RULES 2003

618. Though these Rules were made on 3 April 2003, they are deemed to have effect from the year of assessment 1996.

619. They apply to qualifying plant expenditure incurred on the cost of provision of computers and information technology equipment used for the purpose of petroleum operations. These equipment include equipment used in the gathering, processing and communication of information through computerization and telecommunication. The initial allowance under subparagraph 8*(a)* of the Second Schedule to the Act shall be calculated at the rate of 20% while the annual allowance under subparagraph 12(1)*(a)* of the same Schedule shall be calculated at the rate of 40%.

§21. PETROLEUM (INCOME TAX) (QUALIFYING PLANT ALLOWANCES) (SECONDARY GAS RECOVERY) RULES 2003

620. Though these Rules were made on 24 July 2003, they are deemed to have effect from the year of assessment 2000. The initial allowance under paragraph 8 of the Second Schedule to the Act on qualifying plant expenditure shall be calculated at the rate of 40%, while the annual allowance under paragraph 12(1) of the same schedule shall be calculated at the rate of 10%.

§22. PETROLEUM (INCOME TAX) (QUALIFYING PLANT ALLOWANCES) (ENVIRONMENTAL PROTECTION EQUIPMENT AND FACILITIES) RULES 2004

621. Though these Rules were made on 18 November 2004, they are deemed to have a retrospective effect from the year of assessment 1996 and subsequent years of assessment.

622. In order to encourage renewable energy with the use of environment-friendly equipment and facilities, these Rules were made to apply in respect of qualifying plant expenditure incurred on the provision of equipment and facilities used for the purpose of petroleum operation. They include storage, treatment and disposal facilities and environmental monitoring system. The first category includes effluent treatment plant facilities, air pollution control equipment and facilities, renewable energy and environment-friendly equipment and facilities, and safety and spill equipment and facilities. The second category includes water pollution monitoring, air pollution monitoring, underground water monitoring and analytical equipment.

623. The initial allowance under paragraph 8*(b)* of the Second Schedule to the Act shall be calculated at the rate of 40%, while the annual allowance under paragraph 12(1)*(b)* of the Second Schedule to the Act shall be calculated at the rate of 20%.

§23. Petroleum (Income Tax) (Deduction for Audit Expenditure) Rules 2006

624. The Petroleum (Income Tax) (Deduction for Audit Expenditure) Rules was made by the Minister in exercise of the powers conferred by paragraph 83(1)(*a*) of the Petroleum (Income Tax) Act 1967. These Rules provide for a deduction of an amount equivalent to the amount of statutory audit fees expenditure incurred in the basic period for the year of assessment. This is required for the purpose of ascertaining the adjusted income of a company from its business in the basic period for a year of assessment. The Rules were made on 17 May 2006.

§24. Latest Rules and Regulations (Providing Incentives)

625.

(1) On March 2013, three new incentives were given to help small oilfields. These are effective from 30 November 3010:

   (a) **Petroleum (Income Tax) (Accelerated Capital Allowances) (Marginal Field) Rules 2013, [P.U. (A) 119]:** These rules provide for an accelerated capital allowance at the rate of 15% for a term of five years with a bonus allowance of 25% in the year of acquisition of qualifying machinery for carrying out petroleum operation in marginal filed. It has to be written off in five years by adjusting against the income. This incentive will continue until 2024.

   (b) **Petroleum (Income Tax) (Investment Allowances) Regulations 2013 [P.U. (A) 120]:** For encouraging capital intensive projects, these regulations provide an annual investment allowance on qualifying capital expenditure incurred with respect to qualifying project at the rate of 60%. For this, qualifying projects are: enhanced oil recovery projects; projects engaged with high carbon dioxide gas; and any infrastructure asset determined by the Minister. This will be in addition to the normal 8% annual capital allowance and 20% of the bonus allowance.

   (c) **Petroleum (Income Tax) (Exemption) Order 2013 [PU (A) 122]**: This Order provides an incentive to petroleum operation in qualifying marginal field determined by the Minister. For this purpose qualifying statutory income will be determined on the basis of formula (A/B x C), A is the chargeable tax of a chargeable person in respect of his petroleum operations in a marginal field which is equal to 38% of his chargeable income reduced by the chargeable tax which is equal to 25% of his chargeable income, B is the chargeable tax of a chargeable person which is equal to 38% of his chargeable income and C is the amount of such chargeable income. This order does not apply to if petroleum operation is being carried (a) in a marginal field within an area in respect of a deepwater project which has been granted investment allowance under the Petroleum (Income Tax) (Investment allowance) Regulations 2013; (b) if the operation is in a joint development area; or (c) it is in an area under any agreement or arrangement made by the government with the government of any territory outside Malaysia for the joint exploration and exploitation of petroleum in overlapping area.

(2) On 29 March 2013, **Petroleum (Income Tax) (Marginal Field) Regulations 2013 [PU (A) 121]** were notified, which came into force on 30 November 2013. These Regulations define the term 'Marginal Field' and provide for determining 'gross Income', 'Adjusted Income', 'Adjusted Loss', 'Statutory Income', 'Assessable Income' and 'Chargeable Income'. These regulations apply to all chargeable persons carrying on petroleum operations in a marginal filed, which is, as determined by the Minister, a field in a petroleum agreement area which has potential crude oil reserves not exceeding 30 million stock tank barrels or natural gas reserves not exceeding five hundred billion cubic feet. Since this is a separate head of income, the chargeable person has to maintain separate accounts for income derived from this source (marginal field).

(3) **Petroleum (Income Tax) (Deduction for Participation in and Approved Career Fair) Rules 2013 [PU (A) 14:** These rules were made on 18 January 2013. It was made applicable from the assessment year 2012 and remained enforced until assessment 2016. The following expenses incurred on approved career fair will qualify for deduction: (a) travelling expenses; expenses on marketing and promotional materials; payments made to the organizer of the fair; and any other expenses directly incurred in connection of the fair.

Petroleum (Income Tax) (Deduction for Expenditure Incurred for the Provision of an Expenditure Incurred for the Provision of an Approved Internship Programme) Rules 2012 [PU (A) 334: These rules provide expenditure on approved internship programmes in higher educational institutions incurred on internship programmes with the maximum of RM 5,000 per student per year. It covers monthly allowances, food, travel, accommodation and money paid to the organizer.

Part IV. Regulatory Framework Concerning Sustainable and Renewable Energy

Chapter 1. Energy for Sustainable Development

626. Initially, development was not considered as a threat to the environment as the absorption capacity of the environment was immensely high. But when development became unbridled and was brought forward without any predominant sense of protection of the environment, the adverse effects of the unfettered development activities started becoming conspicuous. Then the right-minded people ruled that we must strike a balance between development and environment, so that development takes place without impairing the quality of the ambience around. This was reflected in the Stockholm Declaration (Declaration on the conclusion of the United Nations Conference on Human Environment). Consumption of biomass generally in villages and fossil fuels in urban and industrialized areas posed threat to the environment by degrading it lower than sustainable levels, and brought hardship and wretchedness to the people in general. The phenomenon of global warming was considered as the natural consequence of that, which has brought peril to all countries in the form of adverse weather conditions and natural calamities of deluge and drought. Imports of fossil fuels are empowering many less developed countries. In view of these, the idea of sustainable development and sustainable energy for sustainable development received strength. The Brundtland Report (the Report of the World Commission on Environment and Development, 1987) put the concept of sustainable development as: A form of economic transformation that ensures the development needs of the present generation without compromising the ability of future generations to meet their own needs. This has two aspects: one, to ensure the needs of the existing generation, and two, to provide equal opportunity to coming generations. This implies both intra-generational equity and sustainable development. For fulfilling this requirement, not only uninterrupted flow of energy is indispensable for all times to come but also it should conform to the social and economic imperatives of the supply of energy. In order to achieve these, efforts should be doubled: for searching new sources of fossil fuels; for gradual reduction of dependency on the traditional sources of energy; for making energy from fossil fuels clean and environment-friendly; for conservation of energy and increasing energy efficiency; and for inventing and enhancing the renewable sources of energy. Efforts are being made for all these but the result is not so encouraging. Fossil fuels are still one of the main sources of energy in developed countries and industrialized developing countries, because the generation and use of renewable source of energy is not so significant, and dependency on biomass burning in less developed countries is still high. In addition to these, law in many countries has failed to play a notable positive role in energy management strategies. The Brundtland Commission realized this situation. It states the situation as:

> A safe, environmentally sound and economically viable energy pathway that will sustain human progress into the distant future is clearly imperative. It is also possible. But it will require new dimensions of political will and institutional cooperation to achieve it.

For achieving a successful sustainable energy for sustainable development, along with a strong political will, social, economic and technological strategies have to be augmented in the light of relevant principles enshrined in the Agenda 21, a document negotiated at 1992 Conference on Environment and Development, popularly known as Rio Conference. The chapter will discuss relevant social, technological and legal aspects of sustainable energy for sustainable development. The chapter will also discuss about the 'Transforming the World: The 2030 Agenda for Sustainable Development', UN 2015, which is actually a plan of action for people and the planet. It focuses on eradication of poverty for achieving sustainable development.

§1. Sustainable Energy/Sustainable Development: Agenda 21

627. The Brundtland Report paved a safe and sustainable energy pathway to be crucial to achieving sustainable development. Use of fossil fuels and coal for generation and use of electricity for economic growth and social development have led to a plethora of environmental problems. Thus, for a sustainable growth, energy also has to be sustainable. The World Energy assessment describes sustainable energy as energy produced and used in ways that support human development over the long term, in its entire social, economic and environmental dimensions. The term is not meant to refer solely to a continuing supply of energy, but also to the production and use of energy resources in ways that promotes, or at least are compatible with long-term human well-being and ecological balance. The key elements of sustainable energy identified by the Brundtland Report are to be: sufficient and sustainable growth of energy supplies to meet the needs of humanity for all time to come (including an allowance for development in less developed countries); increase and improvement in energy efficiency and conservation measures; shifting the current energy mix more towards renewable resources; public health, recognizing the safety risks posed by energy use and production; and protection of the biosphere and elimination of local pollution problems. Fossil fuels are exhaustible natural resources, so is the case of uranium for atomic power generation. Thus, these energy sources are not sustainable. Renewable energy sources are sustainable energy sources in the true sense of the term, because they are never enduring and environment-friendly.[116]

---

116. See Michael I. Jeffery, 'Capacity Building for Sustainable Energy Regimes and Effective Compliance and Enforcement: Foundations in University Education', paper presented at IUCN Colloquium, Shanghai, November 2003; The Brundtland Report, 'Our Common Future', Ch. 7, at:

628. Energy for sustainable development was neither discussed at the Rio Conference, nor was it dealt with in a separate chapter in the Agenda 21. It is just a part of Chapter 9 entitled Atmosphere, Chapter 14 entitled Agriculture and Chapter 7 entitled Human Settlements. It has been succinctly stated under the head Energy Development, Efficiency and Consumption that much of the world's energy is produced and used in ways that could not be sustained if technology were to remain constant and if overall quantities were to increase sustainability. This is particularly true insofar as atmospheric emissions are concerned. The international community should continue to strive for economically efficient energy development paths that are increasingly safe and environmentally sound. This will require reliance on environmentally safe and sound energy system, increasingly based on efficiency at energy production, transmission distribution and consumption, as well as on the use of new and renewable source of energy. All energy sources will need to be used in ways that respect the atmosphere and the environment as a whole. The constraints in the pursuit of energy for sustainable development existing in developing countries were realized, and were suggested to be removed. Broadly identified objectives towards energy for sustainable development are: (1) As a long-term objective, one has to adopt methods and techniques which move towards less polluting and more efficient energy systems, as well as to increase use of economically viable energy, and new and renewable sources of energy, which causes least adverse effect on the environment and serves the needs of developing countries. (2) To promote efficient, safe and environmentally sound energy production, transmission, distribution and use. (3) To promote the use of safe, efficient and less polluting technologies in the production and consumption of energy from fossil fuels and other safe conventional and renewable sources. (4) To increase the environmentally safe and sound energy systems in the energy supply and consumption mix, in particular distribution and development of renewable sources of energy. (5) To promote and enhance adequate and equitable energy availability in economically viable and environmentally safe and sound ways to respond to the increasing energy needs for sustainable social and economic development, particularly in developing countries. (6) To cooperate in undertaking the necessary technical, research development and adaptation of measures to support a transition to environmentally safe and sound energy systems. Special consideration will need to be given to countries heavily dependent on the production, export and consumption of fossil fuels to ensure that the transition does not adversely affect their development and export revenues. Activities suggested for achieving these objectives are: (1) There should be a meaningful cooperation for achieving the specified objectives, especially in developing countries because the task in these countries due to limited resources and less advanced technologies is difficult. (2) Cooperation should be maximized in the development of appropriate methodologies for making integrated energy, environment and economic policy decisions in a sustainable and long-term framework, and furthermore they should be encouraged to adopt certain preventive measures like

---

<www.en.wikipedia.org/wiki/world_commission_on_environment_and_development>; UNDP/Un DESA/WEC, *World Energy Assessment: Energy and the Challenge of Sustainability: An Overview*, UNDP, 2001; A. Bradbrook, 'Energy and Sustainable Development', *Asia Pacific Journal of Environmental Law* 4, no. 4 (1999): 309–317.

EIA. (3) Development and use of improved energy-efficient and environmentally friendly technology and their transfer have to be encouraged. (4) Review should be done of the present energy supply mixes to determine how the contribution of environmentally safe and sound energy systems as whole, particularly new and renewable energy systems, could be increased in an economically efficient manner. (5) It is necessary to coordinate regional energy plans, and study feasibility of efficient distribution of safe energy from new and renewable energy sources. (6) It is necessary to consider, with a view to increasing research, development and the introduction of environmentally safe and sound energy systems. (7) Cooperation should be enhanced to increase the availability of capacity, capabilities and relevant technologies, including biotechnology for utilizing and producing environmentally safe and sound renewable resources, including wood-fuel resources, keeping in view the sustainable development imperatives and minimizing adverse effects on the environment. (8) A suitable policy at national level should be developed for energy for sustainable development that outlines and ensures clean energy supply to coming generations. This will also require developing standards about generation, transmission and consumption of energy by all sources. These standards should be mandatorily followed and should be enforced by appropriate legislations having punitive sanctions. People should be educated about conversation of energy.

629. The Agenda 21 also stipulates strategies to be adopted for transportation systems. It suggests for promoting cost-effective programmes and strategies to limit and reduce, as appropriate, emissions of pollutants into the atmosphere and other adverse environmental effects of the transport sector, taking into account development priorities, as well as the specific local and national circumstances and safety aspects. It suggests that for planning and developing of a safe, more efficient and less polluting transportation systems, especially mass transit, to support economic development efforts in an environmentally safe and sound way. Special attention has to be given to urban and metropolitan areas because these areas suffer the most due to air vehicular pollution. Agenda 21 suggests for improving the energy consumption patterns in rural areas of developing countries so that reliance of wood burning for energy is reduced and village inhabitants get clean and environmentally friendly energy. For this, it suggests that renewable energy sources should be maximized and traditional and other energy sources are streamlined. It also suggests for conservation of energy, taking into account the need for efficient use and environmentally sound technologies.

630. We have noted above that in spite of the fact that energy in Agenda 21 should have been discussed with due importance because energy is the key component for sustainable development. This was realized by the General Assembly as in its 19th Special Session while reviewing the progress on Agenda 21, and thus reached to a conclusion that the Commission on Sustainable Development – which was established to strengthen international cooperation and rationalize the intergovernmental decision-making capacity for the integration of the environment and development imperatives, and to know the progress on Agenda 21 at the national, regional and international levels – it was said that it should consider energy at its

9th session; it did so in several sessions and COPs. Thorough discussion on sustainable energy was also warranted in view of the Kyoto Protocol negotiated under the UNFCCC. We know that the Protocol demanded 5% reduction on 1990 levels between 2008 and 2012. Although the threshold was not so stringent, some countries, including the United States, are reluctant in accepting this. Some countries, however, supported the so-called Marrakesh Agreement, which is considered to have settled key details pertaining to the implementation of the Kyoto Protocol. Cut on the CO_2 emissions and emissions of other green hose gases are directly related to burning of fossil fuels. It would require the use of cleaner energy and rural electrification so that wood burning for energy is alleviated. We have noted above that the Kyoto Protocol could not do much. For some, it was a failure. Now, in view of the Paris Agreement, which replaced the Kyoto Protocol, and which strategizes to put a cap on the CO_2 and other greenhouse gas emissions by maximizing generation of energy by renewable sources in order not to let the average global temperature go beyond sustainable limits.

I. UN Agenda 2030

631. The 'UN 2030 Agenda For Sustainable Development' 2015 focuses primarily on eradication of poverty and ameliorating the overall conditions of the people of the world. It has seventeen goals and most of the goals cannot be achieved without sustained supply of energy from sustainable sources. Thus, sustainable energy is central to them. Goal 7 focuses on ensuring access to affordable, sustainable and modern energy for all by 2030. It requires to: ensure universal access to affordable, reliable and modern energy services; increase substantially the share of renewable energy in the global energy mix; double the global rate of improvement in energy efficiency; enhance international cooperation to facilitate access to clean energy research and technology, including renewable energy, energy efficiency and advanced and cleaner fossil fuel technology, and promote investment in energy infrastructure and clean energy technology; and expand infrastructure and upgrade technology for supplying modern and sustainable energy services for all in developing countries, small islands developing states and landlocked developing countries, in accordance with their respective programme of support.[117]

In short, Energy is inextricably interlinked with many of the Sustainable Development Goals (SDGs), including poverty eradication, food security, clean water and sanitation, health, education, prosperity, jobs creation and the empowerment of youth and women. Access to affordable, reliable, sustainable and modern energy for all is fundamental to human development. A shift toward sustainable energy solutions is also essential to the achievement of the Paris Agreement on Climate Change.

Recognizing the importance of energy for sustainable development, the 2030 Agenda established SDG 7, the first-ever universal goal on energy, with five targets on access, efficiency, renewables and means of implementation. SDG 7 represents a significant milestone, especially since the Millennium Development Goals did not

117. See at: https://sustainabledevelopment.un.org/content/documents/21252030%20Agenda%20for%20Sustainable%20Development%20web.pdf (accessed on 12 Apr. 2018).

include an energy goal. Energy is – for the first time – recognized as a core part of the global sustainable development agenda of the United Nations system.[118]

§2. CSD-9: Energy for Sustainable Development

632. Kui-Nang Mak & Friedrich Soltau write that energy was one of the three sectoral themes considered at CSD-9 and was dealt in considerable details. The other two themes were atmosphere and transport, with information for decision-making and participation and international cooperation for an energy environment falling under the heading of crosscutting issues. The Commission's decision on energy begins by affirming, 'Energy is central to achieving the goals of sustainable development.' The Commission explicitly casts the challenge in terms of some two billion people, who have no or inadequate energy services while at the same time recognizing that current patterns of energy production, distribution and utilization are unsustainable. The Commission also noted clearly that the foremost in developing country priority is the eradication of poverty and energy can play a meaningful role in that. It was recognized that energy for sustainable development will be achieved by providing cost-effective access to a mix of energy sources, and by improving energy efficiency and greater reliance of advanced energy technologies, including fossil fuel technologies. The decision on energy is notable. The basic approach advocated was to give a greater share of the energy mix to renewable energies, improving energy efficiency and greater reliance on advanced energy technologies, including fossil fuel technologies. Seven areas of challenge were identified as: accessibility, energy efficiency, renewable energy, advanced fossil fuel technologies, nuclear energy technologies, rural energy, and energy and transport.

633. The work of the Commission marked the first such detailed level consideration of energy issues at the intergovernmental level and established a baseline consensus. This remains true even in the absence of numerical targets and new means of implementation. The negotiations demonstrated that the nexus of energy, environment and development is a knotty one, and the process frustrated many, especially those lacking familiarity with the limit of the intergovernmental process. However, it is true to say that the importance of the conclusions reached at the CSD-9 was revealed at the WSSD, where they formed the starting point for the negotiations and served as a basis for the decisions on energy. In part, this reflected the fact that the CSD-9 negotiations had foreshadowed the same splits between the North and the South that were demonstrated at the WSSD. Looking at the future, the Commission decided at its 11th Session in 2003 that its multi-year programme of work would be organized on the basis of seven two-year cycles, with each cycle focusing on selected thematic clusters, as well as crosscutting issues. The two-year cycle will consist of a review session and a policy session, with the idea being to make the work of the Commission more focused and consistent towards achieving

118. UN, Dept. of Economic and Social Affairs: Energizing the 2030 Agenda-the Glogal SDG 7 Conference, 16 Feb. 2018, New York, at: https://www.un.org/development/desa/en/news/sustainable/global-sdg7-conference.html (accessed on 12 Feb. 2018).

sustainable energy for sustainable development. Energy for sustainable development, atmospheric pollution, industrial development and climate change comprises the thematic cluster of water, sanitation and human settlements. Although energy is thus not specifically on the Agenda of the Commission for the next one year, it is of relevance to the topic of human settlements. It is now the job of the United Nations to find the ways and modalities for implementing the decisions taken at the CSD-9 and the Johannesburg Plan of Implementation (JPOI), adopted at the WSSD, and to evaluate the progress made on them.[119]

§3. World Summit on Sustainable Development

634. At the World Summit on Sustainable Development (WSSD), the importance of energy for sustainable development got proper attention, and thus decisions therein were made in line with the CSD-9. Among other things, there was also agreement that the action should be taken to increase the use of renewable energy, ensure more efficient use of energy and promote greater reliance on advanced and cleaner fossil fuel technologies. Although the lack of agreement on target for renewables was viewed by many as setback, the summit agreed that the countries should 'with sense urgency sustainably increase the global share of renewable energy sources'. Renewable energy, energy efficiency and cleaner fossil fuel technologies were referred to several times in relation to their development, dissemination and diversification of the energy supply. It was also recommended that the policies of international financial institutions and other agencies support developing countries, as well as economies in transition, 'in their own to establish policy and regulatory frameworks which create a level playing field between the following: renewable energy, energy efficiency, advanced energy technologies, including advanced and cleaner fossil fuel technologies, and centralized, distributed and decentralized energy systems'. The plan of implementation also requires the energy policy to be streamlined to support and encourage supply of energy for sustainable development. Towards this end, bearing in mind the development needs of developing countries, withdrawal of subsidy, restructuring the tax system and enhancing the energy market have been suggested. The plan of implementation also suggested for stabilizing concentrations of greenhouse gases (GHGs) by following the treaty norms of the Kyoto Protocol.[120]

---

119. See Kui-Nang Mak & Friedrich Soltau, 'A United Nations Perspective on Law and Energy for Sustainable Development', paper presented at Colloquium on Energy for Sustainable Development, 4–6 Nov. 2003, Shanghai; Jayarao Gururaja, 'Financing Energy for Sustainable Development', paper presented at Colloquium on Energy Law for Sustainable Development, 4–6 Nov. 2003; Randall Spalding Fetcher, Harald Winkler, & Stanford Mwakasonda, 'Energy and the World Summit on Sustainable Development: What Next', *Energy Policy* (Winter 2003): 34–51; Jayarao Gururaja, 'Energy for Sustainable Development: Framework and Methodology', *Natural Resources Forum* 27 (2003): 58.
120. See Kui-Nang & Friedrich Soltau, *supra* n. 118, *World Energy Outlook*, International Energy Agency, 2002.

635. Thus, at the WSSD, the participants agreed in principle that sustainable development requires special attention on energy. It also agreed, towards this end, that access to energy to the maximum number of people around the globe and protecting environment from being degraded by various kinds of energy generation, especially by burning of fossil fuels, are central in the relationship of energy and sustainable development. In view of this, paragraph 8 of the JPOI is notable because by virtue of this states agreed to take joint actions to improve access to reliable and affordable energy so that poverty on the globe could be alleviated by the year 2015. This is because energy is central in providing other basic amenities to indigent people of the world. In the plan there are following six notable points:

(1) To improve access to reliable, affordable, economically viable, socially acceptable and environmentally sound energy services and resources. It would require priority to rural electrification and a decentralized energy system at places where centralized energy system is not so feasible. This will also require use of alternative source of energy, such as renewable energy, and energy based on biomass, including producing gas by using cattle dung.
(2) To improve access to modern biomass technologies – This will entail use of biomass for generating energy at small-scale level.
(3) Support the transition to the cleaner use of liquid and natural gas – This is because the use of liquefied natural gas is considered the best choice among fossil fuels for generating clean energy. It pollutes the air less than other fossil fuels. But it will release CO_2. This aspect of energy mix has not been addressed in the plan.
(4) To develop a national energy policy and a regulatory framework that will help to create the necessary economic, social and institutional conditions in the energy sector – This would require developing a legal mechanism that ensures environmentally friendly and economically viable energy to the maximum number of people in a country. This will include licensing, EIA, environment auditing, energy efficiency mechanism, incentives and disincentives to energy sectors, and affordable pricing. For all these, an appropriate substantial legislation supported with suitable rules, guidelines and regulations will be required.
(5) To enhance international and regional cooperation in order to meet the goals stated above with special attention to rural desolate areas – This will require an appropriate system that facilitates, coordinates implementation and suggests future strategy for enforcing the above-mentioned policy determinations. It is notable that this kind of international body is urgently required but unfortunately lacks in the recommendations.
(6) To assist and facilitate on an accelerated basis, the access of the poor to energy systems as stated in the recommendations – This is necessary because one of the priority matters among energy for sustainable development conform to the element of equity so that poor could also have access to energy sources. This is how poverty can be alleviated.[121]

---

121. See The Johannesburg Plan of Implementation, UN Doc. A/CONF.199/20, 4 Sep. 2002.

636. Professor Robinson is of the opinion that two elements will be required to realize these recommendations. First, basic principles, which have been pioneered in the context of environmental law, will need to be applied consistently to the realm of energy law, and with greater effectiveness. These include the principles set forth in the UN World Charter for Nature,[122] in the 1992 Declaration of the Rio Conference, and in the earlier Stockholm Declaration. These principles are implemented in many nations' laws, in the Directives of the European Union and several multilateral environmental agreements (MEAs). This is a basic question of ethics as the JPOI states. Nonetheless, those who developed utilitarian and short-term economic objectives of energy sector have largely ignored these principles. Ignoring these principles is against the widely accepted principles for energy for sustainable development. Energy law, according to him, must be grounded on reuse and recycling of energy. This is true because energy changes only its form; it never dies. He also emphasized that waste avoidance and robust use of procedures for environmental impact assessment and public participation are also imperatively demanded. Assurance of basic electricity and other fuel needs for the poor must be a priority. Second, guided by principles, financial and technological resources should be deployed to put on line, where geographic conditions permit, renewable energy systems and to refine and deploy hydrogen fuel cell technologies for motor vehicles design in transport systems and for supply of electricity on a decentralized rural basis.[123]

637. It will be better if the COPs of the Climate Change Convention develop basic principles for future law on energy for sustainable development. Detailed practicable rules for implementation of the treaty norms of the Kyoto Protocol have been incorporated in the Marrakesh Accords. The rules are in fact operational guidelines for creating a transparent market in credible emission reduction. It provides a workable mechanism for forests, monitoring, reporting, review, compliance and enforcement, and funding for developing countries. David R. Hodas on these writes that the key provisions of the Accords concern the establishment of concrete rules and guidelines to support a market-based approach to greenhouse gases (GHGs) emission reductions and sink enhancement. To do this, the Accords create a trading vehicle in the form of the 'emission reduction unit' (ERU), which is equal to one tonne of CO2 equivalent (calculated using IPCC global warming potential and can be used to meet emission reduction targets). A supervisory committee of the ten members of the parties to the Kyoto Protocol or independent entities accredited by the supervisory committee must verify all ERUs generated by the GHGs reduction projects. To participate in a project and be allowed to earn and trade ERUs, a nation must be a party to the Kyoto Protocol and have in place a national system of GHGs emission measurements that meet IPCC guidelines. Projects must first be approved, after undergoing review in a transparent process that includes establishing baselines for measurement. Once implemented, projects must be verified by a certified independent entity. The same process must be followed for credits under the CDM and

122. See UNGA Res. 37/7 (1982).
123. See Nicholas A. Robinson, 'Foreword', in *Energy law and Sustainable Development*, ed. Adrian J. Bradbrook & Richard L. Ottinger (IUCN, 2003); Nicholas A. Robinson, 'Befogged Vision: International Environmental Governance a Decade after Rio', *Law & Policy Review* (May 2002).

other flexible mechanism under the Kyoto Protocol. All credits will be issued and transferred by the supervisory committee, which will be compensated for its administrative expenses by receiving a share of the project credits. Strong compliance and enforcement provisions were also agreed and included in the Accords. It appears that the Accords create all the necessary elements for a global market in GHGs emission reduction credits and sink managements. Such a system if implemented could unleash an enormous demand for renewable energy technology and energy efficiency supply-side and demand-side technology. Taken together, the texts from the FCCC to the Marrakesh Accords comprise an emerging international legal structure to control GHGs emissions.[124]

638. Ultimately, each nation will be responsible for its own reductions and for that they will have to choose modalities best suited to them. So, the kind of strategy stated in the Marrakesh Accords might not prove very useful in the beginning because of varied interest of individual countries, but in the long run it will serve as a workable guide to those countries who will really be serious and will be really interested to develop a legal regime for energy for sustainable development. This is because a good energy law for sustainable development is a must and many states have started thinking on this line, and others will very soon have to think about it. Energy in its various forms is essential for achieving the sustained aspirations of comprehensive and sustainable development of the better future to all measured in terms of GDP, Human Development Index (HDI) and job creation potential. It is desired that a competent energy management will keep the entire three moderated and sustained.[125]

639. At the Copenhagen Conference of December 2009, there was consensus among the states, including Malaysia, that all states will maximize, along with the conventional sources of energy, renewable and alternative energy sources. The Copenhagen Declaration stressed on the Annex I countries of the Kyoto Protocol go ahead with various strategies, like emission trading, cooperating with developed and least developed countries in increasing the number of CDM industries, and transferring technology. It contains an important decision that developed countries will financially help these countries so that they could fight with the menace caused by the phenomenon of global warming. The author is of the opinion that developed

124. See David R. Hodas, 'Energy, Climate Change and Sustainable Development', in *Energy Law and Sustainable Development*, ed. Adrisn J. Bradbrook & Richard L. Ottinger (IUCN, 2003), 11, at 27–28. Also see, M. Vespa, 'Climate Change 2001: Kyoto, Bonn and Marrakesh', *Ecology Law Quarterly* 29 (2002): 395.

125. See O. Mielnik & J. Goldemberg, 'Covering to a Common Pattern of Energy Use in Developing and Industrialized Countries', *Energy Policy* 28 (2000): 503–508; J. Goldemberg, 'Development and Energy', in *Energy Law and Sustainable Development*, ed. Adrian J. Bradbrook & Richard L. Ottinger (IUCN, 2003), 1–9; I.G. Grassi, 'Potential Employment Impacts of Bioenergy Activity on Employment', *Proceedings of the 9th European Bioenergy Conference* 1 (1996): 419–423; A.K.N. Reddy, 'Energy Technologies and Policies for Rural Development', in *Energy for Sustainable Development*, ed. T.B. Johansson & J. Goldemberg (IIIEE and UNDP, 2002).

countries will have no problem if a part of that money is utilized for encouraging and developing alternative and renewable energy sources in developing and least developed countries.[126]

640. Malaysia is serious about encouraging by all means, cash grants, subsidies and tax incentives, renewable energy sources. The Sustainable Development Authority (SEDA) is proposed to be set up soon to spearhead the implementation of the proposed Feed-in Tariff (FiT) scheme for renewable energy some time in 2011. Energy, Green Technology and Water Minister said that SEDA would serve as a central body for all national-level RE and FiT matters. FiT is a mechanism that allows electricity produced from renewable energy sources like solar, biomass, biogas, mini-hydro, solid waste and wind to be sold to power utilities at fixed premium price for a specific duration. The tariff structure, according to him, will be finalized by the end of year 2010. He said at present, the government is looking at the tariff rate of between MYR 1.25 and 1.75 per kilowatt hour (kWh) for 21 years for solar photovoltaic (PV), and 23 cents to 24 cents per kWh for 21 years for mini-hydro sources. For biomass and biogas, it will be between 24 cents and 35 cents per kWh for 16 years; and for solid waste and swage, 30 cents to 46 cents for 21 years. For instance, if the capital investment for 3 kWp using solar PV is MYR 57,000 (excluding loan financing cost), the collective income after 21 years is said to be MYR 113,400. The business and home owners would be able to recover their investments between seven and ten years' time, the Minister said. Government is aiming to increase renewable energy contribution to 6% of the total power generation of the country. The ratio will increase to 11% between 2015 and 2010.[127] The Minister said that for all these, a Renewable Energy Act would be enacted. He will be presenting the bill for it soon. The proposed FiT scheme will certainly boost renewable energy because presently it is not popular because of the low purchase rates. The total picture of the FiT can be seen in the below table:

Renewable Energy Technologies/ Resources	*FiT Duration (Years)*	*Range of FiT Rates (MYR/ kWh)*		*Tariff Degradation (5)*
Min	Max			
Biomass (palm oil, agro-based)	16	0.24	0.35	0.5
Biogas (palm oil, agro-based, farming)	16	0.28	0.35	0.5

126. For negotiations and comments see, Richard. L. Ottinger, 'Notes From Copenhagen Blog', at: <http://web.pace.edu/page.cfm?doc_id=35345> (20 Jun. 2010).
127. *New Straits Times*, 5 May 2010.

Renewable Energy Technologies/ Resources	*FiT Duration (Years)*	*Range of FiT Rates (MYR/ kWh)*		*Tariff Degradation (5)*
Mini-Hydro	21	0.23	0.24	0
Solar PV	21	1.25	1.75	8
Solid Waste and Sewage	21	0.30	0.46	1.8
Wind	21	0.23	0.35	1.5
Ocean, Geothermal	21	0.28	0.46	1

Note: Range of FiT rates and Tariff are subject to final confirmation upon enactment of the Renewable Energy Law
Source: New Straits Times (Business Times), 5 May 2010.

641. We have noted that the FiT system in Malaysia has been enforced by the Renewable Energy Act 2011, which came into force on 1 April 2011, under which those installations which consume 300 kwh/month and above have to pay 1% additionally on their electricity bills. This money goes to the RE Fund, which is ultimately given to Feed in Approved RE installations by the Sustainable Development Authority (SEDA). They generate energy and sell it under agreement with utility companies of the country. Presently, FiTs are ranging over 21-year period for PV and mini-hydro and 16-year period for biomass and biogas. In May 2015, it was decided that geothermal projects up to 30 MW may also benefit[128] (See the detailed account in the Chapter on Renewable Energy Act, infra).

642. We have noted above that Malaysia and Indonesia are critical of the proposed EU's Renewable Energy Directive (EU-RED) (Directive 2009/28/EC of the European Parliament and of the Council of 23 April 2009 on the promotion of the use of energy from renewable sources and amending and subsequently repealing Directives 2001/77/EC and 2003/30/EC), which will come into force in December 2010, because they consider it as discrimination against palm oil and biodiesel manufactured blending natural diesel with palm oil, and this will adversely affect the export of palm oil and biodiesel to European countries. Malaysia will press this issue when it discusses free trade agreement with the European Union. Actually, the EU-RED aims to 20% reduction in energy use. In order to achieve this target, it lays emphasis on cleaner biofuels, especially ethanol and other biofuels. It requires that

128. International Energy Agency, 'Renewable Energy Act establishing feed-in-tariff (FiT) system', at: https://www.iea.org/policiesandmeasures/pams/malaysia/name-24984-en.php (accessed on 20 Jan. 2018).

biofuels must have GHG savings of at least 35%. It does not mean that the Directive rejects import of biodiesel produced using palm oil. Sustainable palm oil will have access to European countries. Right now, palm oil-based biodiesel has only 19% GHG savings. What is bothering to Malaysia and Indonesia is the certification provisions of the EU-RED; it lays down the requirement of certification schemes that had to be recognized by European Community (EC). In the presence of this certification provision, Malaysian and Indonesian palm oil cannot be exported to EU countries. In order to increase the export of biodiesel from Malaysia to EU countries, this figure has to be increased, which seems to be difficult at least for coming five years. It can be done by capturing methane during production of palm oil, which is not easy, as it requires sophisticated technology. Nevertheless, while defending the EU-RED, Vincent Picket, EU Ambassador said, 'it gives clear guidelines to Malaysian palm oil producers on what they need to do to meet the EU's sustainability criteria for biofuels, including palm oil-based biodiesel'. Defending the export of palm oil policy to EU countries he said:

> The sustainability criteria do not apply to exports of Malaysian palm oil for consumer products such as food and cosmetics, which currently represents about 95 percent of Malaysia's palm oil export to EU.[129]

The author is of the opinion that the EU-RED will adversely affect palm oil exports and palm oil-based products, especially biodiesel in EU countries. EU should have different criteria for palm oil-based biodiesel and Ethanol and other biodiesel. If it is not done it will amount to equal treatment of unequals. However, the author feels that in view of the sustainable forest management principles developed by the International Tropical Timber Organization (ITTO) should properly be adhered to. And towards achieving 100% compliance of these principles, timber-importing countries should help timber-exporting countries in a big way under the ITTO and the Kyoto Protocol via emission trading. If there are sufficient such helps, then only we can justify EU-RED type restrictive measures.

International Air Transport Association (IATA) aims to use 50% to 60% of biofuels for national and international flights. It is confident that by 2035, 40% of jet fuels will be in the form of biofuels. The ideal ratio is 100%. Paul Steele, its aviation environment director, at the IATA annual general meeting in Berlin, Germany, on 11 June 2010, said that various kinds of biofuels were no longer a technological challenge. The only questions that are agitating minds of policymakers, scientists, economists and other stakeholders are as to how productions of biofuels can be diversified, produced more, made cost-effective and environment-friendly. In 2009, US fuel certifying body ASTM approved a new specification enabling the use of synthetic (e.g., Fischer–Tropsch) fuel blends up to 50% in aviation (ASTM D7566). This certification is proposed to be extended to 100% in the last quarter of 2010 or beginning 2011. Hydro-treated renewable fuel is set to get certification, by the end

129. See *New Straits Times*, 14 Jun. 2010.

of the third quarter of 2011. Biojet fuels, new and second generation, are produced from sustainable, non-food biomass sources such as algae, babassu, camelina, halophytes, jatropha and switch grass. Steele said, 'We are not are looking for a one size that fits all approach. Environmentally we see different feedstocks being used in different parts of the world.' On the issue of Aviation European Union Emission Trading Scheme (EST), Steele said IATA was operative of calls to push back the implementation of the scheme by a year. He further said that we experienced the biggest distortion in air traffic that the industry had ever seen this year. Lufthansa's chief executive officer Wolf Gang called for postponement of the Aviation EU Emissions Trading Scheme at least for one year due to market distortions caused by the grounding of aircrafts during the volcanic ash cloud incident in April 2010. This emission trading scheme is scheduled to start in 2012.[130] The author is of the opinion that postponement of the emission trading scheme is not a good advice because it will not be in the interest of developing and least developed countries.

Several airlines are already conducting test flights using biofuels. The details are there in the below table:

Carrier	*Aircraft*	*Partners*	*Date*	*Alternative Fuel*	*Blend*
Virgin Atlantic	B747-400	Boeing GE Aviation	23 Feb. 2008	Coconut and Babassu	20% One Engine
Air New Zealand	B747-400	Boeing Rolls-Royce	30 Dec. 2008	Jatropha	50% One Engine
Continental Airlines	B737-800	Boeing GE Aviation, CFM, Honey Well UoP	7 Jan. 2009	Algae and Jatropha	50% One Engine
Japan Airlines	B747-300	Boeing Pratt and Witney	30 Jan. 2009	Camelina, Jatropha, Algae blend	50% One Engine
Qatar Airways	A340-600	Airbus Shell	12 Oct. 2009	Gas Liquid (Not Biofuel)	50% All Engine

130. See Presenna Nambiar, 'IATA Optimistic Biofuels Will Take Off in Big Way', *Business Times*, 14 Jun. 2010.

Carrier	*Aircraft*	*Partners*	*Date*	*Alternative Fuel*	*Blend*
KLM United Airlines	B747-400 A319	GE, Honeywell UoP Rentech	23 Nov. 2009 30 Apr. 2009	Camelina Gas Liquid (Not Biofuel)	50% One Engine 50% two Engines

Source: IATA; taken from Presenna Nambiar, Business Times, 14 June 2010.

643. In the whole scenario, it is crucial to develop efficient enforcement machinery; without this, law will remain as dead letters in the statute books. Efficient enforcement machinery has enough trained and competent workforce. International cooperation can play a constructive role in this area.

644. We have noted above that the Kyoto Protocol rules that CO_2 emission levels have to be brought down by 5.2% from 1990 levels by 2008–2012. Most of the countries, which are responsible for the phenomenon of global warming by burning fossil fuels for energy generation, have accepted this. The United States, who has the largest share of CO_2 emissions, has not yet ratified the Protocol. For total success, participation of the United States is crucial. President Bush's opposition to the Kyoto Protocol has been to protect the American industries and to continue to develop the GDP of the country. There has not been a constant reason for not ratifying the Protocol. At first, he doubted the phenomenon of global warming and asked the U.S. Academy of Science to evaluate the findings of the IPCC. When Academy supported the IPCC, Bush came with other arguments, like Protocol does not require the developing countries to reduce emissions, reducing the emission by 7% on the part of the United States will require the current emissions to be levered by about 30% and most of the industries are in private sector and they cannot be compelled to reduce burning fossil fuels. United States objection on developing countries is absurd. Since they are much below the threshold, they cannot be compelled to accept any cut on emissions of greenhouse gases (GHGs), especially CO_2 emissions. It is notable here that at the time of negotiation of the Climate Change Convention it was agreed in principle that developing countries will develop first and then to accept any cut on GHGs emissions, because they have to develop at a faster rate, and for that, they will have to continue increasing burning fossil fuels. The crux of the problem of the United States is that, it does not want to impede its development process that is why it is arguing to purchase the status of developing and less developed countries, which also seems to be foolish. David R. Hodas has rightly written that in rejecting Kyoto, Bonn and Marrakesh, the Bush Administration is obstructing the emergence of global market-based mechanisms that could be beneficial to all countries of the world, big and small. This will also motivate technologically competent countries to develop technology that is efficient enough to produce more energy with consumption of less fossil fuel. This will help mobilize investment in the energy sector, which has priority for environmentally friendly energy and energy efficiency. United States is competent to provide leadership in these strategic researches. This will also encourage carrying out research in the area of nuclear power generation plants that are really safe and competent enough to treat radioactive effluents.[131] It is expected that sooner or later the United States will have to become part of the Kyoto Protocol and the Marrakesh Accord.

645. Keeping the American issue apart, it is also important for each state to design a workable modality and to work on it so that the commitment pertaining to the Kyoto Protocol is kept. There cannot be a uniform modality. It will differ from state to state. But workable guideline towards this end can be provided. International bodies responsible for implementation of the Protocol should do a viable mental exercise for coming out with some kind of guidelines. This task is difficult, not impossible.[132]

646. Malaysia has given a serious thought to most of the recommendations stated above. But revamping the energy laws, from the point of view of transforming them in line with universally accepted principles of energy for sustainable development, is yet to be achieved. It is hoped that the process has already started and further changes will take place in the near future (see *infra*). Although Malaysia is much below the threshold, it has started working to uphold the treaty norm of the Kyoto Protocol. It has decided to maintain 50% of its territory covered with forests, which act as a sink for CO_2. It generates the major part of electricity by using liquefied gas. One new coal-fired power generation plant has been started, but efforts are being made to keep it environmentally clean to the possible extent. Rural electrification is more than 90%. This has reduced the burning of wood in the rural sector to a considerable extent. For vehicles, standards of emissions have been prescribed that are comparable with standards followed by many developed countries. Stringent law has been made to curb open burning. This law has proved to be successful. Malaysia is cooperating with Indonesia for meeting the challenges of forest fires, which occur in Kalimantan and Sumatra. For discouraging influx of vehicles, the duties are high. Malaysia is gradually withdrawing the subsidy given on oil.

647. Sustainable energy for sustainable development is soon going to be a reality. Efforts by all means are being made by states jointly and severally to maximize electricity generation by renewable sources. Ban Ki-moon in 2012, while inaugurating the Rio+20 Conference, said, 'It (clean energy) is the golden thread that connects economic growth, increased social equity and preserving the environment. We are here to build a new energy future that harnesses the power of technology and innovation in the service of people and the planet.' Sustainable energy for all calls

131. See David R. Hodas, *supra* n. 123.
132. See David R. Hodas, 'Energy, Climate Change and Sustainable Development', in *Energy Law and Sustainable Development*, ed. Adrian J. Bradbrook & Richard L. Ottinger (IUCN, 2003), 11–29; UNDP, *World Energy Assessment: Energy and the Challenge of Sustainability* (2000), 370; Richard L. Ottinger, *Environmental Cost of Energy* (Oceana Publications, 1989); M. Vespa, 'Climate Change 2001: Kyoto at Bonn and Marrakesh', *Ecology Law Quarterly* 29 (2002): 395; D. Writh, 'The Sixth Session (Part 2) and Seventh Session of the Conference of Parties to the Framework Convention on Climate Change', *American Journal of International Law* (July 2002): 45; IPCC Reports.

for private sector and national participation to meet three objectives by 2030: (1) Achieving universal access to modern energy services; (2) High profit and high growth; and doubling the share of renewable energy in the world's energy mix.[133] The Rio+20 stressed on maximizing electricity generation so that the target of sustainable energy for sustainable development for all could be achieved. A synthesis of energy-related issues were highlighted in National Reports of Rio+20, 2014. This report is important because it synthesises the energy issues discussed in the national reports, intended to help strengthen implementation of the Rio+20 directions and commitments. It identifies lessons and best practices across all regions, underscoring the nexus of energy-related concerns with other sustainable development factors. It addresses in particular the issues relating most directly to the three focal areas indicated in the Ban Ki-moon's address. This report has become a good guide to all countries in energy matters in keeping their promises made for achieving the targets set under the Paris Accord.

133. *The Guardian*, at: https://www.theguardian.com/sustainable-business/rio-sustainable-energy-for-all-accenture-ungc (accessed on 20 Feb. 2018).

Chapter 2. Strategies for Sustainable Energy

§1. Petroleum Sector and Sustainable Development

648. Much of the environmental issues pertaining to oil and gas have been discussed above. Energy in general and generation of electricity in specific has been linked to sustainable development. This aspect has been agitating the minds of industries in this sector. Ever since the development of this concept, oil and gas industries are making efforts by R&D for achieving sustainability in the excavation of energy sources and their consumption in different sectors that contribute to the economic development, especially transportation and power generation. This encompasses to have corporate economic growth, corporate environmental stewardship and corporate social progress. Since developing countries have high rate of GDPs, they need to have a continued and uninterrupted supply of oil and gas. But the supply has to be clean and environmentally friendly. Otherwise, there will be undesired results, like air pollution. If developing and least developed countries do not by all means venture in the field of generation and distribution of renewable energy, debt arising out of import oil and gas in them will increase. This will lead to poverty at the national level and economic inequality at the international level.

649. We have noted above that liquefied natural gas, which is Methane (CH_4), has less percentage of carbon. Thus, its use as energy source (fuel) in cars and other industrial facilities is cleaner than oil and gas because they emit far less CO_2. It does not have sulphur, toxic metals like mercury and lead. It does not emit gases like ozone and oxides of nitrogen. So, it is a preferable source of energy from the point of view of sustainable development. Because of this and other reasons like easy and affordable availability of gas, it is for this reason that the Malaysian Palm Oil Board (MPOB) has suggested Sabah to use methane to generate electricity instead of building coal-fired power generation plants in order to meet the power shortage in the state. It is also said that other than the natural sources of Methane, state's 117 palm oil mills instead of emitting methane can trap them for power plants.[134] The author is of the opinion that the process will work only if it is incentive-based. It is notable that the purchase price of renewable energy and alternative energy is going to be increased in the near future. This has prompted countries like India, China and Malaysia to use gas at large scale in their thermal power generation plants. Developed countries also prefer it. This has resulted in slowing down of CO_2 emissions to some extent and has also reduced air pollution hazards locally. So far power plants are concerned, if gas is used for gas turbine and steam turbine built jointly, it will double the power generation efficiency because the heat that is wasted in gas turbine can be trapped for running a steam turbine alongside. Natural gas-powered vehicles are efficient and less polluting. The New Delhi success story is worth referring here. When oil was used for vehicles used for public transport, Delhi was rated

134. See *New Straits Times*, 24 Dec. 2009.

as one of the most polluted cities of the world. Under a public interest litigation (PIL) the Supreme Court ruled that, instead of oil, liquefied gas should be used for running vehicles used for public transport, and ordered the State of Delhi to implement it. After three months Delhi was free from air pollution by 66%.

650. Liquefied natural gas is considered to be ultra-clean fuel because it has carbon content reduced to about 50%. Countries like Germany and Japan, where people are really environmental conscious, prefer to use the kind of fuel in their vehicles that leaves less polluting effects. Liquefied gas is the best fuel for them. We have noted above, as Malaysia is the third largest exporter of liquefied natural gas, it has plenty of gas to be used to cater the needs of its thermal power generation plants. It is the number 1 source of power generation in its energy generation mix. Although it is not environmentally friendly source of energy, as methane causes several times more greenhouse effect that carbon dioxide, natural gas is being preferred because it is cleaner source of energy in comparison with oil and coal, and it is less expensive. It has a bright future especially in developing and least developed countries until 2050. It will be a good choice if coal-fired power generation plants are replaced by gas.[135] Oil companies, in view of this, have Middle Distillate Synthesis (MDS) process that uses natural gas as feedstock to produce high-quality middle distillates, such as diesel and kerosene, which are non-toxic, easy to transport and biodegradable. MDS diesel burns much more cleanly than standard fuels making it a cost-effective way to reduce emissions of CO_2, hydrocarbons, oxides of sulphur and nitrogen, unburned carbon particles and carbon monoxide. MDS products can be delivered using the existing oil products manufactured to power standard diesel engines.[136]

It is said that availability and price of liquefied natural gas will determine its further use. Right now, it is popular because liquefied gas is easily available at affordable price; it will be preferred over oil and gas because their prices are soaring. But in future if these two factors turn unfavourable, countries might go back to oil and coal again or any other affordable energy sources. There are countries like China, India and Malaysia that have a large deposit of coal. This is an alluring factor for them to have coal-fired power generation plants also. We have noted above that Malaysia has recently opened one coal-fired power generation plant in the Peninsular Malaysia and has a plan to have one of 300 MW in the State of Sabah. For this state advantage is that coal is available in the state and the government wants to phase out the existing diesel-based plants. Countries like China, India and many other countries already have coal-fired power generation plants. They also might have some more in future if they face the circumstances mentioned above. For example, right now, about 60% of the total energy needs of India are fulfilled by the coal-fired power generation plants. It is planning to have more coal-fired power generation plants, hydroelectric plants and five nuclear power generation plants. India

135. Irina Slav, 'Cleaner and Cheaper: The Future of Natural Gas', *Oil Price.com,* 22 Feb. 2018, at: https://oilprice.com/Energy/Natural-Gas/Cleaner-And-Cheaper-The-Future-Of-Natural-Gas.html (accessed on 12 Apr. 2018).

136. See Nick Wood, 'The Business Case and Approach to Sustainable Energy', paper presented at I IUCN Academy on Environmental Law 2003 Colloquium on The Law of Energy for Sustainable Development, October 2003, 83–108.

has no choice but to have more coal-fired power generation plants as a large section of population of the country does not have power supply at all, and another sizable population face daily power cut. Coal-fired power generation plants will continue to fulfil the need until twenty-five more years to come. The country wants to add 78.7 gigawatts of power generation during the current Five Year Plan ending in March 2012, most of which will come from coal-fired power generation plants. Although the country is on the track of alternative and renewable source of energy, 55% energy will come from coal-fired power generation plants until 2030 as other sources of energy have their own limitations. Renewable and alternative energy sources will account only 8.8% of the energy mix by the year 2022.[137] This ratio can increase only with substantial help from developed countries in terms of transfer of technology and financial resources, more importantly help in building the proposed nuclear power generation plants. The scenario in China is slightly better, but China also will have to have more nuclear power generation plants in order to reduce energy reliance on coal-fired power generation plants.

§2. Renewable and Other Sources of Energy

651. We have noted above that as compared to gas, oil pollutes the atmosphere more. Liquefied gas if used as energy or for power generation, it emits only CO_2 and that too considerably less than use of coal or gas. It emits several other gases, including oxides of sulphur, oxides of nitrogen, ozone, oxides of harmful metals and hydrocarbons. Diesel has more oxides of sulphur than petrol. This is one factor that turned the attention towards the use of gas as energy and power generation. The other factor, which is more important and in fact acted as a driving force, is the soaring oil prices. Initially, the world squarely depended on the oil reserves of the Middle Eastern countries. But for many reasons, especially political reasons like threat of use of oil as weapon and burning of oil by Saddam Hussein during the Gulf War as a war strategy, the prices of oil escalated fast. This prompted nations, especially the countries of the West Europe and the United States, to adopt two strategies to reduce the dependency on the oil coming from this region: one, states attempted to find oil reserves elsewhere in the world and they got substantial success in it; and two, they concentrated towards exploiting renewable and other sources of energy and discover energy efficiency strategies. The process of discovering these is faster now because the oil politics is still on, oil installation in Saudi Arabia and Iraq are subject to terrorist attacks and states know that oil has a life. Thus, total dependency on oil will be suicidal. This has received an impetus after the Bonn Conference on Renewable Energy of June 2004. The success story of these strategies can be known from the energy profile of the United States. Now the United States has become 25% more energy efficient and 32% more oil efficient since 1974. The country is also striving hard to boost renewable energy sources. The energy profile of the Organisation of Economic Co-operation and Development countries (OECD countries) also gives more or less the same picture. Liquefied

137. See Krittivas Mukherjee, 'India Finds Prosperity Still Depends on Coal', *New Straits Times*, 8 Dec. 2009.

natural gas has provided a relief, but this also has a limited life. States now are compelled to think about having nuclear power generation plants, further enhancing energy efficiency, increasing use of renewable and other energy sources. Some states like Malaysia and China, in addition to boosting their renewable energy sources, are resorting to coal-fired power generation plants also. As discussed above, it is notable that seventeen out of twenty-eight nuclear power generation plants that are under construction are in Asia for a simple reason that their energy demand is going to increase at a faster rate. There is no harm in it, provided safety of such plants is ensured and radioactive effluents are properly treated. The Western countries right now do not look interested in increasing the number of nuclear power generation plants. But in future, the position might change. Al Baradai, the Secretary General of IAEA, has rightly stated that they would have to resort to this source of energy.

652. The potential of renewable energy is immense, but this source of energy is not properly exploited. The success story rests only in the United States, Brazil and some countries of the Western Europe. Developing countries exploit this source as less than 1% of their total energy consumption because of the availability of fossil fuels. They are cheap and easily available. When oil prices started shooting because of increased demand and the reasons mentioned above, liquefied natural gas came for the rescue and proved to be a cheaper and cleaner source of energy. But as envisaged at the Bonn Conference, by the year 2020 one-third of the total energy consumption must come from this source of energy; otherwise, the world cannot be saved from its dooming. In some countries biomass is also being used for energy, but their contribution in the total energy consumption of those countries is negligible. Malaysia can be quoted as an example for the use of biowaste of its palm oil industries for power generation. Presently, it is at a small scale but it has potential to become a noticeable source of energy in future. So is the case of Malaysian biodiesel. It also has tremendous scope to be used as a potential source of energy (for details, see *infra*). India also has potential in exploiting cow dung for making methane gas that can easily be used for cooking and generation of light for domestic uses.

§3. Conservation of Oil

653. Conservation of petroleum has been considered to be a potential measure to increase the energy supply for maintaining sustainable development. In the beginning, trillions of cubic feet of gas were vented or flared into the atmosphere, as there was no technology to catch them and use ultimately as fuel. Due to inefficient technology, a large quantity of oil and gas was left unexplored in the reservoir. Now, the United States has applied an efficient technology that leaved the least quantity of oil and gas in the reservoirs. Some developing countries have still high rate of flaring of gas while exploring oil, but in the near future, with the help of the developed counterpart, their capability is going to be boosted to trap gas to the maximum extent by increasing the maximum efficient rate of recovery (EMR). Jacqueline

Lang Weaver pertinently writes that for the first half of the nineteenth century, sustainable development of oil and gas meant adopting the laws and regulations necessary to prevent the underground waste of oil and gas through well spacing and permitting requirements, prorating controls, no-flare orders, and pooling and unitization statutes that prevented competitive drilling and production. In the United States, where oil and gas can be owned by private landowners, these regulations are largely the jurisdictions of conservation commissions in each of the producing states. In rest of the world, including Malaysia, where oil and gas are public property, the exploration and production work is done either by state-owned oil companies or by private companies on profit-sharing basis. In both the cases, the whole process is controlled by suitable legislations. In these countries conservation measures have also been adopted to some extent. The player companies are multinationals with sophisticated technologies, and trained personnel, wastage of oil and gas in the process of exploration and production are minimal. The exploration activities and the end use of oil and gas are generally measured in terms of their contribution in the GDP of the country. The wasteful exploration and production of oil and gas is non-sustainable. Initially, it will not be felt because the growth will not be affected, but in the long run, it will become conspicuous. This has been anticipated by all petroleum-rich countries. That is why these countries through multinational companies have adopted conservation measures. Wastage of oil and gas while used as energy is also significant in all countries. This has resulted in degrading the environment and costing the economy to a considerable extent. Some countries have measure to remedy it by creating a trust fund to be used in emergency. Jacqueline about modalities and beneficial use of such funds writes that some resource-dependent states and nations have adopted trust funds that place a certain percentage of the royalties and tax revenues from resource extraction into a fund reserved for future use. When the resource gets depleted, the fund will continue to generate interest payments that can provide services to those citizens who can no longer benefit from the resource-generated rent enjoyed by earlier citizens. These trust funds can be a useful device to assure intergenerational equity, but they reduce the investment funds currently available for social infrastructure and economic diversifications. In nations with pressing immediate needs to solve problems of social equity, poverty and health, such trust funds may seem a luxury. Nonetheless, all resource-extracting nations should engage in long-term planning for the day when their resources run out. At a minimum, sustainable development requires that such nations save and invest in social capital at a rate that replaces the natural resource capital being depleted. Her observations are not far from truth. But very few developing countries have resorted to this kind of device. Many countries provide incentives and subsidies rather than creating a fund and enriching it by allocating a part of the tax and royalties imposed on supply of oil and gas. On the contrary, they subsidize them, so that GDP of the country is not affected. It is, therefore, suggested that subsidy should gradually be withdrawn and supply of oil and gas should be subjected to some kind of tax. But for this, a workable balance will have to be created between intergenerational equity – that demands sustainable use and utilization of energy sources so that interests of coming generations may be protected – and immediate need of fast economic development of the country. This is very pertinent in developing and underdeveloped countries of the world, including Malaysia. This task is not so easy. It requires a feasible study.[138]

654. Environment-friendly devices have been developed that cause minimal harm on the surface of the earth in the course of exploration. With the use of sophisticated exploratory equipment, especially in case of exploratory drilling that requires making deep hole into the earth followed by explosion of the biodiversity and the geography of the earth and the ocean, as the case may be, is not seriously affected. Even drilling in the process of excavation of oil and gas does not have much adverse impact on the environment above the surface of the earth except accidents, which relatively causes much more harm to the surface of the earth and the atmosphere with the release of gases that are there on the top of the oil. In case of offshore drilling, the possibility of degradation of marine environment is not less, but in case, there are international treaty norms that have to be followed by all states. If in the drilling process technology of international standards is used, the requirements of the norms can easily be kept. It is notable here that almost all exploration and exploitation works are done by multinational oil companies and they follow the standard prescribed by treaty norms. However, accidental explosions might cause exceptional harm to the marine environment because it might release unexpected quantity of oil and gas into the marine water. This may also be noted that the excavation process of oil has some natural devices of injecting water and gas to push the oil from the reservoirs and failure of such devices might cause environmental harm. Gas reserves are different. It is relatively safe, but exceptional release of gas might cause inconvenience and harm to the biodiversity including the nearby human settlements.

655. The Prime Minster of Malaysia, while presenting the salient features of the Tenth Malaysia Plan in the Parliament, said that the Plan has laid emphasis on sustainability of the environment. He said it was, in fact, our responsibility. He further said:

> Emphasis will be placed on the use of renewable energy and increasing energy efficiency. The government will introduce the Feed-in Tariff and Renewable Energy Fund to encourage the implementation of renewable energy projects. Relevant guidelines standards and laws will also be introduced to ensure efficient use of energy, and to reduce greenhouse gas emission. We must also seize opportunities that arise from emerging trends, where green products services and technology are increasingly in demand. In this respect, I call upon industries to take this opportunity and use the incentives provided by the government through the Green Technology Financing Scheme (GTFS), worth RM 1.5 billion, to enhance the application of green technology in the production of

138. See Jacqueline Lang Weaver, 'Sustainable Development in the Petroleum Sector', in ed. Adrian J. Bradbrook & Richard L. Ottinger 99 (IUCN, 2003); R. Gavigan, 'Siberia's Environment: A Challenge to Traditional Thinking', *Georgetown International Environmental Law Review* 8 (1996): 333; S. McDonald, *Petroleum Conservation in the United States: An Economic Analysis* (John Hopkins University Press, 1971); B. Field & M. Field, *Environmental Economics: An Introduction* (McGraw Hill, 2002), Ch. 5.

> goods and provision of services. The government will also promote environmentally friendly housing by introducing guidelines and a green rating system. Houses that do not depend or least depend on electricity from outside will be known as smart houses. New government buildings will be designed to meet the green standards. Energy efficiency of these buildings will be enhanced.[139]

It is notable here that the GTFS was created by the government right on 26 January 2010. Response to the MYR 1.5 billion Green Technology Financing Scheme (GTFS) has been overwhelming, Energy, The then, Green Technology and Water Minister Datuk Seri Peter Chin Fah Kui said on 14 June 2010. The scheme was launched on 26 January 2010, by the government to attract the private sector to participate in green technology entrepreneurship. The fund is aimed at facilitating and fast tracking efforts by companies pursuing green technology and businesses. 'We fear that the fund will run dry before the year ends,' Chin said in his speech at the opening ceremony of the Green Energy, Technology and Innovation Summit 2010. 'However, I am optimistic that the government will provide more funds for this if the impact of green technology on the economy proves to be resounding,' he said. Chin said the government envisaged that the setting up of the fund will unleash the potential for growth in new areas of economy. Moving forward, the government has approved the Renewable Energy Policy and Action Plan, which will be implemented in 2011, once the institutional framework for the Renewable Energy Law and implementing agency are in place. 'One of the highlights of the Renewable Energy Policy and Action Plan is the FiT mechanism which is being widely used around the world to promote renewable energy development in a systematic and holistic approach,' he said. The Renewable Energy Law was now in the drafting stage, the minister said. 'The government has also approved the setting up of the renewable energy agency in the form of a statutory body that will oversee and facilitate renewable energy growth in Malaysia,' he said. According to Chin, it is projected that Malaysia will have 11% or 2,000 MW of power generation mix coming from renewable energy sources by 2020.[140]

656. Green Technology: According to the Ministry of Energy, Green Technology and Water, green technology means: It is the development and application of products, equipment and systems used to conserve the natural environment and resources, which minimize and reduces the negative impact of human activities.

Green technology refers to products, equipment or systems, which satisfy the following criteria:

- It minimizes the degradation of the environment.
- It conserves the use of energy and natural resources.
- It has zero or low greenhouse gas (GHG) emission. It is safe for use and promotes healthy and improved environment for all forms of life.
- It promotes the use of renewable resources.

139. See *New Straits Times*, 11 Jun. 1010.
140. *Bernama*, 15 Jun. 2010.

It has the following important pillars:

- Energy – Seek to attain energy independence and promote efficient utilization.
- Environment – Conserve and minimize the impact on the environment.
- Economy – Enhance the national economic development through the use of technology.
- Social – Improve the quality of life for all.

Its objectives are:

- To minimize growth of energy consumption while enhancing economic development.
- To facilitate the growth of the Green Technology industry and enhance its contribution to the national economy.
- To increase national capability and capacity for innovation in Green Technology development and enhance Malaysia's competitiveness in Green Technology in the global arena.
- To ensure sustainable development and conserve the environment for future generation.
- To enhance public education and awareness on Green Technology and encourage its widespread use.

It has several priority areas. Prominent among them pertaining to clean energy are the following:

- Energy Supply Sector: Application of Green Technology in power generation and in the energy supply-side management, including cogeneration by the industrial and commercial sectors.
- Energy Utilization Sector: Application of Green Technology in all energy utilization sectors and in demand-side management programmes.

Its national objectives pertaining to energy are the following:

- Secure supply: Diversification of fuel type and sources and technology maximize use of indigenous energy resources, adequate reserve capacity to cater for contingencies (adequate reserve margin for generation, upgrading transmission and distribution networks and distributed generation) (islanding).
- Sufficient supply: Forecast demand, right energy pricing and formulate plans to meet demand.
- Efficient supply: Promote competition in the electricity supply industry.
- Cost-effective supply: Promote competition and provide indicative supply plan to meet demand based on least-cost approach using power computer software such as WASP.
- Sustainable supply: Promote the development of renewable and cogeneration as much as possible.
- Quality supply (low harmonics, no surges and spikes, minimal variation in voltage): Match quality with customer demand with variable tariffs.

- Efficient utilization of energy: Benchmarking, auditing, financial and fiscal incentives, technology development, promotion of ESCOs, labelling, ratings, correct pricing, energy managers.
- Minimizing negative environmental impacts: Monitor the impacts, improve efficiency of utilization and conversion and promote renewable.
- In 2010, Malaysian Government introduced the GTSF under the Malaysian Green Technology Corporation (Green Tech Malaysia), a body working under the Ministry of Energy, Green Technology and Water. This is for catalysing green initiatives under the National Green Technology Policy 2009. The focus is on: to develop sustainable and widespread green technology markets; to strengthen the local green technology industry; to enhance human competency and capacity in green technology applications; to formulate support policies and financing frameworks to promote green technology growth; and to promote and create awareness of green technology. There are four flagship projects of Green Malaysia Plan, Green Procurement, Electric Mobility and Sustainable Living in energy, transport, building, waste management and water management. The financing scheme has been working well. It has been carried forward until 2022. USD 1.2 billion are supposed to be spent on these projects. Giving soft loans encourages these projects. It shows government's commitment to sustainable energy for sustainable development. As of October 2017, the GTFS has approved total of 315 projects with the cost of nearly USD 1.7 billion. The maximum approvals are for renewable energy sector. The approved renewable energy projects upon complete functioning will be able to reduce CO_2 emissions by 3.7 million tonnes and will create 5,200 jobs. The GTFS has been instrumental in encouraging the participation of private financial institutions to invest in green projects. It is hoped that the GTFS will further be expanded in order to further reduction of carbon emission.[141]
- There has been a general practice of all states that as a regulatory measure all operational activities of oil and gas are subjected to a licensing mechanism. This is because there cannot be zero adverse impact on the environment surrounding the exploration work and the governments want to keep the record of exploration activities. Be it land or sea, there are chances that the ambience around the site of operation will certainly be affected. But with the application of sophisticated technology, trained personnel and competent legal framework this adverse effect can be mitigated. It is universally accepted now that to keep the requirements of sustainable development lofty in exploration, exploitation and production of oil and gas projects, environmental impact assessment (EIA) is necessarily required to be done; many countries have made it mandatory. If people are also going to be affected or displaced for facilitating the proposed exploration work, SIA is also done; this supplemented with a suitable relocation if relocation is required. The scheme that is generally followed is that the proponent company gets an EIA prepared by the authorized person or group of persons (generally company or partnership firm) for the proposed project on the basis of guidelines, if any, prescribed by the government, and submits it to the appropriate authority prescribed by law,

141. Green Bank Network, 'Malaysian Green Technology Corporation', 22 Jan. 2018, at: https://greenbanknetwork.org/malaysia-green-technology-corporation/ (accessed on 20 Apr. 2018).

which is generally the Director General of the Department of Environment working under the Ministry of Environment. The authority at his/her level, with help of experts of the DOE, evaluates the suggested impacts and mitigating measures suggested by the proponent. If it is considered to be suitable, the project is allowed to go ahead with or without certain condition(s) to be adopted either in advance or in the process of the work. On the contrary, the proponent is either asked to submit another EIA with necessary modification as suggested by the DOE, or the EIA is outrightly rejected. The DOE also looks into the SIA and monitors relocation process if required. In some countries, the DOE prepares Environment Impact Statement (EIS) that contains all information about the condition of the environment around the proposed project, probable harm to it due to the project, probable adverse effects on the people living in the vicinity of the project and future preventive measures that are necessary to be taken. Before EIS is finalized, opinion of the people to be affected from the proposed project is taken into consideration. In the whole process, it is necessary to strike a balance between the expected harm to the environment and/or people and the benefit of the exploration and exploitation work has to be maintained. In case of grave economic necessity, up to the permissible limit, harm to the environment or the people can be compromised. But in case the balance goes much in favour of the economic aspect of the project, the whole preventive measures will have to be reconsidered. For this purpose environmental auditing is done. The company does the internal auditing and external auditing is done under the supervision of the DOE. In some countries, on the adverse auditing results, the project is stopped. The halted project can be restarted if enough preventive measures have been taken or when there is a grave economic necessity. In case of critical economic necessity or priority of the project, contravention licence can be issued. Thus, contravention licence is an exception, which can be revoked if the adverse effect on the environment becomes conspicuously harmful to the environment. The requirement of EIA and SIA is also there in transportation through pipelines and distribution of oil and gas.

657. In some federal systems, where environment is not only a central subject or where land is a state matter the situation of conflict of laws has arisen, and this has caused difficulties in enforcing the above-stated preventive measures. The problem has been resolved by making the environment as a central subject, or by suggesting the State DOE to have similar provisions as that of the Federal Government in respect to making, approving and enforcing EIAs and SIAs. But the second option has created a lot of difficulties and confusions. It is, therefore, suggested that environment should be a central subject.[142]

142. See G. Cronman, D. Felio & T. O'Connor, 'International Oil and Gas Ventures: A Business Perspective', *American Association of Petroleum Geologists* (2000); G. Marsh, 'The Environmental Realities of Petroleum Exploration', in *The Business of Petroleum Exploration*, ed. R. Steinmetz (American Association of Petroleum Geologists, 2000); J. Hickey, 'International Law', in Energy Law Group, *Energy Law and Policy in 21st Century*, ed. Energy Law Group (Rocky Mountain Mineral Foundation, 2000), 4–18.

658. Malaysia follows more or less the same preventive measure as discussed above. Oil and gas explorations and exploitations require compulsory EIAs, which are monitored in future by regular auditing, which is done under the supervision of the DOE. Environment in Malaysia is a central subject, but since jurisdictional problem arose in the Bakun Dam case, the term environment has to be interpreted in the context where it exists (see *infra*).

659. In Malaysia, national oil company 'Petronas' under the Petroleum Development Act 1974 has power to venture independently or with cooperation of other oil and gas companies and to grant licence as 'third party contract' to explore and exploit oil and gas. The contracts are PSCs, on the basis of sharing both cost and profit, not simply awarding concessions. To date there are more than 100 awarded contract areas by more than 26 operators. Through this process, the country has diversified the oil and gas exploitations around the world. In addition to that there are about 4,000 registered service providers comprising international oil companies, independents, services and manufacturing companies. The company is projecting to be one of the biggest in the region by 2020 and provide a hub for other players in oil and gas sector. Petronas is active in other parts of the world. The country has huge gas reserves. In short, the future of oil and gas in the country is bright. They will last in many more years to come.[143]

660. Dr Shahino Mah Abdullah writes: 'In Malaysia, the transition from fossil fuels to green energy resources has become an issue in the country's quest to become a developed nation. As the government aims to reduce carbon emissions by 45 per cent by 2030, various incentives have been given to encourage investment in green technology industries and the adoption of green technology by the private sector. One of the most compelling measures towards green technology development is the financial support offered by the government and financial institutions. Under the ETP, the government of Malaysia has created GreenTech Malaysia, a financing platform for new green projects that is supported by participating financial institutions (PFIs). GreenTech Malaysia introduced the scheme, the GTFS, aimed at promoting investment in types of green technology with the potential to minimise the degradation of the environment, reduce green house gas emission, promote a healthy environment for life, and promote the use of renewable energy and natural resources.

GTFS was originally proposed by Prime Minister Datuk Seri Najib Razak during the tabling of the 2010 Budget with an allocation of RM 1.5 billion. In 2013, the fund for GTFS was increased by RM 2 billion while the application period for companies to apply for GTFS was extended to Dec 31, 2015, and during Budget 2016 it was further extended to Dec 31 this year. As stated by Green Tech Malaysia, 272 projects benefited from this scheme between 2010 and 2016, involving RM 2.962 billion of financial support. According to a news release on March 2, the Green Technology and Climate Change Council meeting chaired by the prime minister has

143. *Star Online*, 28 Nov. 2018, at: https://www.thestar.com.my/business/business-news/2017/11/28/malaysias-oil-journey/ (accessed on 12 Dec. 2018).

agreed to extend the fund for five years with an additional allocation of RM 5 billion. The extension will definitely benefit companies that are producers and users of green technology. This national initiative has opened great business opportunities for the people, and also encouraged them to appreciate the environment and support sustainable development in Malaysia.'[144]

661. In order to carry out the Green Initiatives, the Energy, Green Technology and Water Ministry established Malaysian Green Technology Corporation (Green Tech Malaysia) for catalysing green technology development. It is working within the scope of the Malaysian Green Technology Policy 2009, which has the following objectives: developing sustainable and widespread green technology markers; strengthening the local green technology industry; enhancing the human competence in capacity building in green technology; formulating support policies and financing framework to promote green technology growth; and promoting and creating awareness of green technology. These initiatives are carried out so far energy is concerned via electric mobility and sustainable living. The scheme is extended until 2022. It has lots of incentives, including easy loan, for those who engage with green power generation. Since the inception of the GTFS in 2010, as of October 2017, the GTFS has successfully approved a total of 315 projects with a total cost of nearly USD 1.7 billion. The amount of loans that have been approved under the scheme is USD 829 million. The bulk of projects approved are in the renewable energy sector. The approved projects are anticipated to contribute to the avoidance of over 3.7 million tonnes of CO_2 equivalent every year and create more than 5,200 green jobs. The GTFS has been instrumental in encouraging the participation of private financial institutions to invest in green ventures, as it has brought together a total of twenty-eight banks and financial institutions to participate in the Scheme. With increasing numbers of entrepreneurs venturing into the green technology sector, GTFS will continue to be an important enabler bridging financing gaps and empowering emerging green businesses in the country.[145]

§4. SUSTAINABLE ELECTRICITY FOR SUSTAINABLE DEVELOPMENT

662. Electricity is an energy carrier, which is generated by a variety of ways. It is not a fuel; it is a physical phenomenon happening simultaneously and almost instantaneously throughout entire interconnected technological system of generation, transmission and consumption. For generating it, fossil fuels or nuclear fusion or fission is generally used. It can also be produced by solar energy, by using appropriate photovoltaic cells. It is different than fossil fuels, because unlike electricity, they can be produced, stored, transported and supplied in batches or as a continuous flow through pipe lines. Because of these reasons, the whole process of generation, transmission and consumption of electricity is different than other sources of energy. Law to deal with these also has to be different.

144. *New Straits Times*, 24 Mar. 2017.

145. Green Bank Network, Malaysian Green Bank Network, 22 Jan. 2018, at: https://greenbanknetwork.org/malaysia-green-technology-corporation/ (accessed on 12 Mar. 2018).

663. Sustainable energy will generally mean adequate supply of energy to all coming generations. Electricity for sustainable development means the sustainable development process should not suffer from shortage of electricity. It is evident from the painful facts that electricity has not been sustainable. One-third of the population of the world, mainly in developing countries, is deprived of this divine gift. In these countries, electricity generation is increasing. This is evident from the fact that these states are trying hard to increase power generation by all means, including renewable energy, nuclear power generation, so that energy needs of these countries could be met. But in these countries, population will keep on growing in at least three decades to come at about 4% per year. This phenomenon will shatter their energy planning if renewable energy is not exploited at its maximum. These countries are hard-pressed by the rural electrification imperative. It does not mean that rural electrification in developing countries is a myth. There are countries, like Malaysia, that have achieved the success of providing electricity to more than 90% of their villages. It is suggested that by resorting to sophisticated technology for electricity generation and competent and honest workforce, the object to provide access to electricity to all can be a reality. But for this, developed states will have to provide all kinds of support for capacity building and for supporting the process of generation, transmission and supply of electricity. Only then electricity supply can be reliable, affordable and uninterruptedly available. Some are of the opinion that in view of the rising energy demand, these countries if can afford must resort to nuclear power generation. This is notable here that this is of no use to least developed countries and many developing countries, for they cannot afford to have nuclear power generation plant as it is expensive, unsafe and requires treatment of wastes generated by it. So, the first choice for them will be a viable choice. For sustainable electricity population, control is also necessary; otherwise, no planning and no policy will turn the page of success. It is rightly said that a policy to foster sustainable development must include policy to make electricity services available to all on a sustainable basis.

664. Walt Patterson, Anton Eberhad and Carlos E. Suarez have rightly written that the circumstances pertaining to electricity generation has been propitious. Technical and institutional evolution in the beginning was not so encouraging, but in due course of time, conditions changed and a lot of innovative researches were done that have brightened the hope of millions of people who are deprived of electricity. These researches have received modest support from favourable electricity policies. Initially, the focus was on retaining the best of traditional forms of power generation, coal-fired and diesel-based, where new technologies cannot be used, and renovate it for increasing its efficiency. This has failed to meet the requirements of sustainable electricity and electricity for sustainable development. The attention then was shifted to use of gas for power generation. The use of modern technology proved it to be environment-friendly and a sustainable source of sustainable development.

665. Traditional electricity systems, replicated all over the world, shared a common technical model and key institutional mechanisms. The power generation was in public sector. So, the government was responsible for power generation, transmission and ultimate supply to consumers. There were big power generation plants connected with grids and a large number of workforces to manage the whole process of generation, transmission and distribution. This required investment of huge amount of money and involvement of a large number of technical and support staff. They were impressively successful for a very long time. Despite a variety of problems, their services were ubiquitous and fulfilled the needs of urban societies, especially industrial energy needs during the industrial revolution after the Second World War. Bigger power generation plants require huge investment, take five to six years to be operative and have long redressal period. In due course of time, when population increased and electricity needs of the countries around the world accordingly increased, the centralized system in developed countries was replaced by decentralized power generation and supply. This system proved to be more feasible, because it requires less investment, investments can easily and comparatively return in shorter time, it is easy to manage, it does not have monopoly and it divides the risk of failure. There are added advantages that in case of failure of one unit or power brake down for any technical or natural reasons, other units can support, there will be no unnecessary risk of high-tension lines. Later on, these power generation units were given, fully or partially to private sectors. This brought power generation and distribution closer to consumers and avoided the hassle that existed with bigger and centralized power generation plants and long transmission lines. It also made the electricity market competitive, which in turn benefited the consumers and increased efficiency. It then became easier for the DOE to properly enforce the environment protection legislations. This system solved the financial difficulties also, especially in developing countries. Now, the countries have not to bother for investments in the electricity sector; private corporations will ably do it. The use of gas in place of oil in power generation has provided a boost to such units. It is comparatively easier to install a gas turbine, and it pollutes considerably less than oil and coal. Government easily earns revenue in the form of tax on consumption of electricity and corporation tax on the income of the company. This system has not fully been adopted by all countries. Some have partially resorted to and some others have not yet adopted it at all. The main contra factor is that the privatized system will generate unemployment. This is because private sectors generally encourage automation and stick to the exact requirement of workforce.

666. Walt Patterson[146] and his two co-authors have rightly stipulated that the policy implications of such a transition are daunting. It imposes intensifying stress on electricity systems originally built and operated as integrated monopolies. Moreover, some traditional interests inevitably oppose such changes. Governments and regulators must consider reconciling consequent conflicts to create a stable framework for the transition, to minimize disruption and to maximize the potential to

146. See Walt Patterson, Anton Aberhard & Carols E. Suarez, 'Towards Sustainable Electricity Policy', in *Energy for Sustainable Development: A Policy Agenda*, ed. Thomas B. Johnson & Jose Goldemberg (UNDP, 2002), 77–113.

move towards sustainable electricity services. It is needless to say that the decentralized system of electricity fulfils the imperatives of sustainable electricity for sustainable development. In the parts of the world where traditional system is already operative, the challenge is to devise electricity policy that can keep the light reliably, affordably and sustainably. In China, India and other developing countries the challenge for policymakers is to cope with growing demand and wider access to electricity services at breathtaking rate, without intolerable environment impacts.

667. Developing countries are lagging in terms of privatization and opening up their borders for foreign electricity players. Many developing countries, including Malaysia, are cautious in inviting foreign companies to compete with local companies engaged in power generation, transmission and supply. The job is done by few companies active at the national level. But the whole process is subjected to a competent legal regime that regulates the operation and distribution of electricity. Tenaga National Berhad (TNB) of Malaysia is the best example. This company is operative in the Peninsular Malaysia. Sabah Electricity Sdn Bhd (SESB) is in the State of Sabah and SESCO is operative in the State of Sarawak. The major shareholder of TNB is the Government of Malaysia; the major shareholder of SESCO is the State Government of Sarawak while SESB is a subsidiary of TNB. All the three utilities are basically vertically integrated except that the generation facilities of TNB have been leased to its wholly owned subsidiary, TNB Generation Sdn Bhd, for operation and selling back of electricity energy generated to TNB. Besides the three state-owned utilities, there are currently six IPPs operating in Peninsular Malaysia, five in Sabah and two in Sarawak. As of December 2002, the six IPPs operating in Peninsular Malaysia contribute approximately 4,449 MW (34%) of the total grid-connected capacity of 12,975 MW in the Peninsular Malaysia and the five IPPs in Sabah contribute 305 MW (39%) out of total 777 MW installed capacity in Sabah, while the two IPPs in Sarawak contribute 318 MW (36%) of the installed capacity of 872 MW in the state. The balance of the grid-connected capacity is provided by TNB, SESB and SESCO respectively.[147]

668. We can notice that in Malaysia the power sector is gradually becoming competitive. The government has been considering restructuring the electricity generation and supply industry aiming at bringing it in line with the system used by the Western countries and making it more competitive. For these, various models, which are already being practiced in some parts of the world, are under consideration. However, Malaysia has a cautious approach to transform the system; it is thus doing it gradually. Total privatization, thus, does not seem to be near. The Energy Commission of Malaysia is working on it.

669. At institutional levels also, big units of public sector power generation and distribution system situated in developing countries have unique problems. Some of them are: (1) Mismanagement – The power generation system is mainly in public

147. See Keong Kwok Yan, 'Developing Coal-Fired Generation: A Legal Perspective', paper presented at 4th APEC Coal Trade and Investment Liberalization and Facilitation Workshop, 6–8 Mar. 2002, KL, <apec-egcfe.fossil.energy.gov/TILF_2002_KL/17.1_lky.pdf>.

sector, and generation, transmission and distribution are done by some huge establishments having a large number of workforces. To manage such a huge establishment is an arduous job, the high-level officials cannot keep eyes on the day-to-day functioning. With the result of that, actual and effective control of those officials lack; and officials at the lower levels thus get laxity to execute works according to their own choice, which sometimes goes against the policy of the Electricity Department. It also sometimes overlooks legal requirements pertaining to generation, transmission and distribution. For example, in an area there cannot be further load and the officer at the ground grants permission for a new connection without bringing it in the knowledge of the higher officials. In addition to this, there is no commercial and competitive environment. This kind of environment does not develop unless management and employees working under it really work for a private sector company and make potent attempts to create competitive environment of the company. So long a company has monopoly or its employees do not involve in corruption, this kind of environment cannot be expected. (2) Financial Loss – Many of government establishments because of mismanagement instead of yielding profit run in loss, which in turn put burden on the revenue of the state. In some countries financial loss is quite big. (3) Corruption – This is a big problem in some developing countries, like India, Pakistan and Bangladesh. There are various forms of corruptions. The most common are: advancing bribe for taking power connections even if the situation is that the area is already overloaded. This results in regular load shedding in evenings when domestic power consumptions and power requirements of bazaar increase. Jamming the meter or readjusting it is another type of corruption. This puts the electricity department at a big financial loss. (4) Theft of electricity – This is quite common. People have devised various kinds of theft. Among them, having defective meters and taking electricity without meter are common. (5) Electricity to Rural Areas – To stop this kind of practice in the rural areas, payment on average consumption basis was devised, but this also did not work. In some states, villagers get electricity free. This seems to be unacceptable as it is discriminatory and the money, which could have been used for development of the state, especially improving the conditions of the infrastructure, is unnecessarily going to the rural sector. This practice thus overburdens the state. (6) Poor Quality of Transmission wires – Poor quality of transmission wires and outdated transmission equipment waste a lot of electricity. In spite of best efforts made by many states, quality of transmission wires could not be improved. (7) Poor Quality of Power Generation Equipment – In many countries, due to lack of enough financial resources, power generation equipment are not so sophisticated. With the result of that power plants are less efficient and suffer from breakdowns. Very few countries are using two turbines together, one gas turbine and the other one steam turbine, in gas-based power generation plants. (8) Overemployment – In many developing countries, where power generation is in public sector, there are overemployment. This contributes to the loss to the electricity departments. (9) Strikes – In democratic countries evil use of human rights is trade unionism and strikes. Every now and then workers come forward, most of the time for no genuine reasons, and on non-fulfilment of demands they go on strike. This also adds to the loss of the electricity department. The position is significantly lower when generation, transmission and distribution are with private companies. These are the compelling factors for giving away power generation plants to private sectors. Private sectors will actually run power generation plants for profit. Therefore, they will not allow these things to be practiced. These factors are, in fact, a driving force for expediting to reform the whole mechanism of power generation, transmission and distribution. Walt Patterson and his allies have also pointed out a number of factors driving changes in the electricity systems of most countries in the world. According to them, following are the lashing forces: (1) Need to Improve Operating Efficiency – Government-owned infrastructure industries historically have played an important role in underpinning economic development. However, weak performance in finances, investment, operation and poor management accountability has caused governments to embark on fundamental reform and restructuring the electricity systems in a desire to improve investment allocation and operation. (2) Broadening Customer Choice – Government-owned electricity systems had few incentives to improve efficiencies. Now, however, many governments are aiming to lower cost and prices by commercializing and exposing the industry to greater competition and private ownership. In this new environment, even previously well-regarded companies often show market gains in efficiency. A commercial and competitive environment exposes the performance of investment planners and managers to market security. It sharpens incentives to reduce operating costs and drive wholesale prices to their lowest economic levels – although the economic quantification may still not adequately account for subsidies, other market failures and similar issues. It exposes investment decisions to their associated risk and stimulates innovations. It also provides an avenue to access private capital at a time when government budgets are hard-pressed to fund investments. (3) New Technologies – Traditional ways to reduce costs, for example scaling in power plant construction by large integrated electricity systems, have largely been exhausted. Innovative technologies, including combined-cycle gas turbines and distributed generation options such as fuel cells have different scale attributes from those of traditional electricity generation. Smaller-scale technologies with different risk profiles allow new smaller entrants to come and compete into the market. Moreover, new information and communication technologies now enable the system control more sophisticated than was previously possible, by potentially facilitating short-term electricity trading and including a wide range of participants. (4) Financing and Market – Further pressure to reform electricity systems comes from changes in capital markets, sector finance and various fiscal concerns. Public finance from governments and multilateral funding agencies are inadequate for large infrastructure projects. Governments face growing pressures to reduce their fiscal borrowing requirements and to sell off public assets. At the same time, globalization of international capital markets has created new financing opportunities, often linked through purchase and sale of equity shares. The consequent financial difficulties have slowed investments in many countries in the large coal-fired and nuclear plants favoured by the large traditional electricity systems. (5) Environmental Imperatives – Concern about global warming because of traditional fossil fuel burning for generating electricity intensified with the confirmed scientific opinion that the phenomenon of global warming and climate change are true and they are responsible for unusual weather condition. So, the traditional fuels – coal and oil – were replaced by liquefied natural gas. But this concern is renewed with some countries' decisions to resort to coal-fired power generation plants. Now, environmentalists want it to be clean as much as possible. They also emphasize on maximizing the use of the renewable sources of energy so that the burden on traditional electricity generation is reduced. (6) Need to Address Specific Issues in Individual Countries – Individual countries also have specific reasons to reform electricity systems. In Chile and the United Kingdom, for example, the governments in power are ideologically strongly committed to privatization. The UK government also wanted to undermine the power of coal mining trade unions; it expected that private generations would purchase imported coal. The rapid emergence of gas-fired power generation was only one of many expected consequences of liberalization. In some countries, the reform process may be initiated by a crisis, or perceived crisis, such as the droughts in New Zealand and in Colombia in the early 1990s, which affected hydrogenation and caused both governments to consider whether their power sectors could be organized differently. In South Africa, where widening economic ownership and promoting black economic empowerment are key policy objectives, reforming the electricity system and privatizing electricity assets could make a major contribution to achieving these objectives. In some countries, so as to discourage the use of coal for power generation, mining subsidies are being withdrawn and transportation charges are being inflated.

670. As noted above, in Malaysia, with the discovery of liquefied natural gas deposits, emphasis was shifted from coal and oil-based power generation plants to gas-fired power generation system preferably with two turbines, gas turbine and steam turbine. Since Malaysia has a large quantity of coal in its Sarawak state and since technology to keep the power generation system from coal as clean to a considerable extent has been developed, country is attempting to have some coal-fired power generation plants also. In addition to this, the country is making successful efforts to maximize power generation through hydroelectric sources. Towards this end, the country has already started power generation from a huge dam in its state of Sarawak, which is now covering the major supply mix of the state.

671. In general, the role of liberalization towards delivering electricity services to the two billion people around the world urgently requires a profound and careful appraisal of the positive measures to make the electricity available to the maximum number of people, especially in rural areas. In this perspective, along with increasing present system of clean power generation, the following aspects need to be emphasized: to increase power efficiency along with adoption of proper conservation measures and measures to eradicate corruption, and to accept maximizing the use of renewable and other sources of energy as a *sine qua non.* Along with these, electricity should be affordable. In order to make electricity affordable, it is necessary that this necessary supply should be governed strictly under the rules made by the governments that are suited to their circumstances and conditions of their people. This has to be there even in those countries where power generation is under corporatized private sector. It will be appropriate in these countries that private companies are under control of an appropriate Public Body. In Malaysia, for example, corporatization has been done but the government has control on the distribution process through appropriately designed legal regime enforcement by the Energy Commission. It is notable that in Malaysia electricity charges are controlled by the government and government is vigilant through Energy Commission about ensuring about following of standards prescribed by law at all levels, including uninterrupted supply of electricity. On one occasion, there was black out in some parts of the Peninsular Malaysia and because of that people in general suffered inconvenience and business and trading sectors suffered loss. In many developing countries these kinds of phenomena are regular features and governments are helpless. But Malaysia took it seriously and ordered the corporation to give 10% discount on the next month's bill.

672. We have noted above that in many countries, efforts are being made by all means to make the power sector competitive. This is because monopoly is regressive and competition has its own advantages. It is natural that in a competitive market, services improve and prices go down. This will prompt the competitors to have new and sophisticated technology so that with less input more could be generated, and to concentrate on increasing of conservation and enhancing electricity efficiency strategies. A competitive market might result in relatively small power generation units closer to the place of consumption. It will, thus, diffuse the pollution hazards and save from the hassle of transporting the electricity via high-tension wirings. This type of power generation system is suited to all countries, developing and developed. It is already in practice in many countries, including OECD countries. But even in this type of power generation system, proper legal control is necessary. It is also necessary that all units are connected *inter se* so that in case of breakdown in one of such units others could support.

673. But this is notable that in the South East Asia and some other developing countries, including Malaysia, governments have generally introduced the system of independent power producers (IPPs). They have sales of power through power production agreements (PPAs) entered into with the utility company. Like in the Peninsular Malaysia, TNB is the only utility company to sell electricity. This is known as single buyer model. This denies competitive atmosphere. This may lead to monopoly, which might in turn prove to be regressive and harmful to ultimate consumers. But if governments have proper vigilance on generation of power and its supply, as it is there in Malaysia, the scourge of monopoly cannot harm the people, and thus economy of the country may grow steadily. But this system should be changed to a competitive kind of thing as stated above. It might take some time, but ultimately these countries will also have to move to that system because this system along with other benefits noted above protects the interests of all consumers, big and small, alike, provided the electricity is kept as a controlled service and price of electricity is not allowed to shoot up. If considered to be feasible and useful, a distinction between commercial use and domestic use can be made. Likewise, a distinction between rural consumers and urban consumers can also be made. But in all cases giving electricity for free to certain class of people, especially to the rural mass, is not advisable at all. Some countries are giving electricity to rural sector for free. It is not a healthy tradition. This has neither yielded the desired result of boosting the agricultural produce, nor have they been able to benefit the rural poor. From this kind of thing, rich farmers have been benefited, which is not at all the object. Instead of giving total exemption, a subsidized flat rate can be a better choice. The rest of the money can suitably be utilized in proper transmission of electricity and improving the infrastructure of the rural areas.

674. Privatization and corporatization of the power generation sector in many countries including Malaysia, as stated above, have provided a boost to research and development. The breaking of big power generation units into small ones also prompted augmenting research in developing small gas turbines that could be run along with steam turbines. Scientists now have made it true and it is in practice in many countries, including Malaysia. This system has increased the efficiency by 40% to 50%. Use of liquefied gas reduced around 50% of CO_2 emissions. Thus, total gain, so far environmental protection is concerned, with the modern technology, has been around 100%. Another breakthrough invention is atomic power generation plants. We have noted above that if safety measure is ensured and the waste generation is properly taken care of, it will be sustained for fairly a longer period and will be a clean source of energy. But the problem with this source of power generation is that we cannot afford to have so many of them in a country and that the plant has to be in a desolate place. Scientists have developed competent technologies that can keep such plants safe, but this technology can only be handled by expert technocrats, who have had proper training. Because of this reason, it is advised that this area of power generation should be collaborative. Developed countries or other countries that have enough technological expertise in this area and have been managing such plant(s) can collaborate with beginners. The problems that have to be properly addressed are: a secured reactor because this requires an advanced and competent technology, and an efficient treatment of nuclear wastes generated by nuclear power generation plants because it requires a sophisticated technology and involves large amount of money. We still remember the incident when USSR wanted to dump nuclear wastes somewhere near an island under the Japanese sovereignty, and this was strongly opposed by Japan and other developed countries because it would have caused disastrous effects on the marine environment that would have specifically be detrimental to Japan and would have set an unhealthy tradition. USSR was insisting to dump the nuclear waste in spite of the fact that there is total moratorium on dumping of nuclear wastes in the ocean. USSR agreed to abstain only when Japan promised to pay for the treatment expenses of the wastes. The problem of nuclear wastes is still a big and intricate problem associated with nuclear power generation. However, a collaborative venture will not pose that kind of situation. One thing is important in this context that the treatment of nuclear wastes should be done closest possible to the power generation plants, because safe movement of such hazardous wastes cannot be guaranteed. We have not yet forgotten when nuclear wastes were carried from one country to another country through the Straits of Malacca and Singapore, which is one of the busiest waterways in the world. This was done in spite of loud protests staged by NGOs and the three littoral states of the Straits of Malacca. In wake of these, it is advisable that further research should be directed towards making treatment of nuclear wastes at the place of power generation, as a possibility. Research has also successfully been done in the area of reducing pollutants from diesel and making it more efficient for oil-based power generation. Sulphur is being reduced form diesel used for running vehicles, trains and ships or for generating electricity. This is being done by states around the world because it is not very difficult to reduce sulphur content from diesel and because states are duty bound to do so under the Sofia Protocol made under the Long-Range Transboundary Air Pollution Convention. Further breakthrough is converting diesel into gas before it is used as fuel. This is not yet common in the area of power generation (see *infra*).[148]

675. Along with the change in the system of power generation from big centralized power generation plants to small power generation units, a marked shift in the law governing power generation sector became imperative. In the beginning, when power generation, transmission and distribution were in public sector, to govern these there were a set of legal regulations. With privatization and corporatization, law had to be changed. The law is further being changed in all countries, including Malaysia, for encouraging renewable energy sources for increasing the energy efficiency and for making energy sustainable so that coming generations are not deprived of it. The change has generally been done in the area of providing financial and fiscal incentives to these, in making these part of the policy determination of the state, and linking renewable energy with the national grid.

§5. Usage of Coal in Sustainable Power Generation

676. Initially, around the world, power generation was done by coal-fired power generation plants. But this system of power generation was not environment-friendly. Because of this, the use of other less polluting options of power generation, especially the gas-fired power generation, became the preferable choice, and the coal-fired power generation became the last choice. In spite of the fact that much of the pollution effects, with the application of pollution prevention measures, of the coal-fired power generation are reduced, it still remains the last choice. We have noted above that presently gas-fired power generation plants are preferred. Coal-fired power generation plants are being discouraged and efforts are being made by all means to have clean energy sources to the possible extent. In this process, incentives provided to coal mining operations are being withdrawn by Western countries. But since some countries have a large deposit of coal, like China and South Africa and Indonesia, gas is in limited quantity, and if they use coal for power generation, they can sell out the gas deposits that they have to those countries that do not have gas deposits. Malaysia is one of them. But the problem in Malaysia is that it is difficult to excavate coal from coalmines. Thus, for its coal-fired power generation plants, coal is mainly imported from China, Australia, South Africa and Indonesia. May be in future, with the increase in coal demand exploration of locally available

148. See, Man-Sung Yim and K. Liang Murty, 'Material Issues in Nuclear Waste Management', *JOM*, 52 (9) (2000), pp. 26–29, at: http://www.tms.org/pubs/journals/JOM/0009/Yim-0009.html (accessed on 12 Mar. 2018).

coal is increased. It seems that ultimately this will have to be done because the country cannot rely on imported coal for a very long period. The first coal-fired power generation was started in Malaysia in 1988. With discovery of gas deposits and availability of gas in the market, gas-fired power generation received impetus and became the preferred option for power generation. At times, it constituted around 75% of total power generation in the country. But recently, some new coal-fired power generation units have been commissioned and there is a plan to phase out the oil-based power generation plant of the State of Sarawak with a coal-fired plant. This plan may be carried forward in future. The existing and planned coal-fired power plants until 2010 were as follows:

Plant	*Capacity*	*Completion*	*Coal Utilization*
TNB Kapar Ph.2	600 MW	1988	1.5 mtpa
TNB Kapar Ph.3	1,000 MW	2001	2.5 mtpa
TNB Janamanjung	2,100 MW	2002/2003	6 mtpa
SKS-IPP	2,100 MW	2005/2006	5.7 mtpa
Jimah-IPP	1,400 MW	2005/2006	3.5 mtpa

Source: M. Zainal bin Azirun, 'Coal Usage in Malaysian Power Sector – Opportunities and Challenges', Keynote address delivered at 4th APEC Coal Trade and Investment Liberalization Facilitation Workshop, 6–8 March, 2002, Kuala Lumpur. <apec-egcfe.fossil.energy.gov/TILF_2002_KL/1.1_mohd.pdf>

677. We have noted above that Malaysia is now on the track of sustainable energy for sustainable development. Towards this end, the country is upgrading its oil coal-fired power generation plants, opening new coal-fired power generation plants with environment-friendly technology, giving more importance to gas-based power generation plants, maximizing hydropower and renewable energy sources, and working on producing energy-efficient electrical appliances, widening the application of 1-5 stars system of energy efficiency certification system, and conservation and energy education in both urban and rural areas.

678. The Malaysian programme to increase reliance on coal-fired power generation plants is bothering the environmentalists of the country. Some of them resoundingly hold the opinion that the increasing reliance of coal-fired power generation will increase air pollution, especially the greenhouse effect (GHE). This may be noted here that as stated above, a better plant efficiency strategy, which makes use of newer technologically, will certainly reduce the pollution effect to a considerable extent because it will reduce coal consumption. This is also notable that Malaysia has adopted a clean technology, which polluted 50% less, and has started shifting its old coal-fired power generation plants into new ones in its Malacca State. The company that owns and operates these plants has a plan to convert all coal-fired plants with the new technology. Some of such technologies are: advanced clean coal technology such as pressurized fluidized bed combustion (PFBC) and integrated gasification combined cycle (IGCC). But the problem with these technologies is that they are yet to be proven technologically efficient and economically viable. These technologies are not easily available and most of them require further experimentations and trial operations before they can be recommended for common use. Towards suitable use of technologies at particular place, environmental impact assessments (EIAs) followed by periodical auditing are being carried out. The central in the process of doing EIAs is to have input of the local people. In addition to this, power generation plants can comply with the Environment Management System (EMS) pertaining to coal-fired power generation plants contained in the ISO 14000. Malaysia is following these. It has done EIAs to its power generation plants and its establishments have ISO 14000 certification. Some notable measures taken by TNB are: use of clean coals that has less sulphur and less ash content; installation of electrostatic precipitators; having chimney heights as internationally recommended; having sophisticated ash handling ponds; having enclosed coal handling systems and provision for water spray facilities at the coal stockpiles to mitigate dust problems; having fly ash handling system completely enclosed and that ensures prompt disposal; diversified use of ash (presently in Malaysia, ash is used by cement industries, but there are other commercial applications also); setting up air quality monitoring stations located in the various populated areas around the power generation plants; continuous monitoring of the boiler fuel gas emissions quality; having preparation to meet any eventuality; and to give heed to the public complaints. This may be noted that these measures can successfully mitigate the polluting effects, but use of new and clean technologies is the real solution. Thus, that they have to be resorted to ultimately.

679. Most of the old coal-fired power generation plants are being made with the use of sophisticated equipment to bring them up to the international standards so that they pollute the environment the least. It is proven from the upgrading of two coal-fired power generation plants situated in Malacca and TNB write up of April 2008. The best example of this is upgrading of two coal-fired power generation plants in Malacca under the Clean Development Mechanism of the Kyoto Protocol. According to the write up, 'The coal-fired Sultan Azlan Shah (SJSAS) power plant at Manjung, Perak, already demonstrates TNB's efforts in complying not only with national environmental standards but also with the World Bank environmental standards.' The plant runs on clean coal technologies, including employing an Electrostatic Precipitator (ESP) to trap fly ash and using Flue-Gas Desulphurization (FGD) to reduce emission of sulphur dioxide (SO_2) to the atmosphere. The plant, fondly known to TNB as Janamanjung, demonstrates the following World Bank standards on emissions:

Comparison of Emission Standards

Emission	*DoE M'sia*	*TNB Manjung Plant*	*World Bank*	*Typical Bank*	*Typical Asian*	*Typical North American*	*Typical European*
Particulates	400	50	50	400	100	40	100
SOx	3,500	750	750	850–1,700	1,430	980–1,480	400
200							
NOx	1,700	650	650	640	720	615–1,640	500–560
2000							

More recently, discussions have been made with Danish engineering consultant firm sanctioned by the Royal Danish Embassy to examine the feasibility of implementing Biomass Co-Firing in the power station. The Embassy just recently conducted a site visit to the SJSAS station to assess the site condition. The discussions have reached a stage where pre-feasibility has been established. The public can be assured that TNB can achieve its own internal targets on the energy efficiency of its plants and hence always working to improve our plants' efficiency. Currently, the target for efficiency improvement is to have from 0.5% to 1% reduction in heat rate (better efficiency) for its power plants. The latest TNB's 750 MW Combined-Cycle Gas Turbine (CCGT) plant at Port Dickson is the most efficient thermal plant in the nation (56% efficiency). Construction of the second phase is currently ongoing for a second CCGT block. We would like to point out that coal constitutes 32% of generation mix in Peninsular Malaysia. The other fuel mix is gas and hydro. Gas is known as less polluting than coal whereas hydro is considered renewable energy and has a very small carbon footprint. Our decision to embark on utilizing coal is to create a more balanced generation mix in Peninsular Malaysia, therefore enhancing the security and reliability of energy supplies. Efforts to improve existing power plant availability and efficiency include the implementation of Reliability Centered Maintenance (RCM) and Risk-Based Inspection (RBI) on all TNB generating plants. This has resulted in an improved thermal efficiency achieved in the Financial Year (FY) 2007 (37.58%) as compared to that achieved in FY 2006 (36.22%). We are pleased to note that all our TNB power plants are certified MS ISO 14001 (Environment). Annual Environmental Management Audits (EMS) based on MS ISO 14001 are conducted at all power stations by both TNB's internal auditors and SIRIM QAS International (external auditors). 'Co-firing of biomass with coal gives partial relief. It has been experienced that in addition to the use of coal, it has played a positive role in the reduction of GHG emissions. It is thus the good avenue to use biomass, which is generally disposed off, for generating electricity. The review of a number of Life Cycle Analysis (LCA) reveals that using 5% biomass for co-firing could reduce GHG emissions by 5%. If this biomass is replaced by regrowth, GHG emissions could be reduced by up to 10%. Co-firing has been found to provide positive benefits for sulphur and nitrogen emissions also. This is a breakthrough in reducing the pollution effects of coal-fired power generation units. But it does not seem to be very useful. If reduction of CO_2 emissions goes down to 10% or more, this technology can really prove to be helpful.[149] However, if we look at the practicability aspect of the research, we can appreciate it because it, in addition to reducing CO_2 emissions, helps in beneficial use of biomass wastes that have to be dumped somewhere as landfill. This is already practiced in a country like Malaysia as it has a lot of biomass waste from its palm oil industries. This waste is already being used at some scale for power generation in the country (see *infra*).

680. Some type of coal mixed with minute particles scatters coal dust at the time of handling such as loading, unloading, conveyance and storage and pollutes the surroundings which cause health hazards to those who are engaged in such activities and those who live in the near vicinity of such places where these are carried out. We have noted above that dust management at coal-fired thermal power stations is one of the strategies that has been recommended for being entitled to get ISO 14000 certification. In some countries, this problem is becoming acute and efforts are being made to alleviate it to a possible extent. High-degree anti-dust measures are specially applied at locations close to human settlements or national parks. Domed or silo-type sealed coal storage is the most ideal anti-dust solution, but it is a costly device. Because of this reason, all places cannot be equipped with this device. But for open-air storage of coal, it is essential to take anti-scattering measures. The best method applied is erecting windbreak fences, growing trees and sprinkling water. For unloading coal, the conventional club-bucket method has suitably been replaced by the continuous unloader system in recent years, and a conveyor in airtight housing is also being followed. It is also demanded that safety control should address generation of heat and ignition. If coal remains in contact of air, it slowly oxidizes, invariably generates heat and in exceptional situations catches fire. To control generation of heat, stockpile should be kept in compact so that it gets minimum contact to the air. Precautions have to be taken in taking out of coal from the stockpile so that air does not enter into the storage. The incidents of combustion and fire may occur generally when coal remains stored at one place for a longer period. It is therefore suggested that coal is repiled. Longer period storage also results in release of CO, O_3, methane and other harmful gases. In exceptional cases explosion has also been experienced, which throws a large quantity of coal dust into the atmosphere and that in turn causes widespread health hazards. To prevent such adverse effects of storage of coal, proper vigil has to be kept.[150]

---

149. See Peter Coombes, 'Renewables and Coal: Co-firing for Greater Efficiency', paper presented at 4th APEC Coal Trade and Investment Liberalization and Facilitation Workshop, 6–8 Mar. 2002, K.L. <apec-egcfe.fossil.energy.gov/TILF_2002_KL/3.4coombes.pdf>; Allen Robinson et al., 'Fireside Issues Associated with Coal-Biomass Co-firing', *BioEnergy* (1998): 34–43.

150. See Masahiro Ikezawa, 'Pollution and Safety Controls in Coal Handling at the Thermal Power Station', paper presented at 4th APEC Coal Trade and Investment Liberalization and Facilitation Workshop, 6–8 Mar. 2002, K. L. <apec.egcfe.fossil.energy.gov/TILF_2002_KL/3.3_ikezawa.pdf>.

681. Coal gasification is also one of the methods, which is being adopted in some countries as a measure for reducing the adverse environmental impacts. In this process, gas is produced from coal. A country like China has tremendous potential in this area because it has one-third of the total coal deposits of the world. In this country nearly two-third of its population uses coal for cooking, heating and other domestic activities. In India also, this source of energy, along with wood burning, among the urban population is quite popular.

682. Coal gasification is a partial combustion of carbonaceous materials, such as coal and petroleum coke, which uses only 20% to 30% of the amount of oxygen that would normally be required to achieve complete combustion. It is generally a dry process that uses nitrogen gas to transport powered coal to burners. The primary product is syngas, which is a mixture of carbon monoxide and hydrogen. The syngas contains about 80% of the original energy in the coal. Another 15% of the energy is recovered in the form of steam. Energy losses during gasification are only around 5%.

683. Syngas can be used to manufacture pure hydrogen and to synthesis ammonia, methanol, oxochemicals and their derivatives, such as urea fertilizer and synthetic hydrocarbon fuels. It can also be used directly as a fuel to generate heat, steam and electricity in power plants and can be supplied to town gas grids. In this process, none of the constituents of the coal are wasted. The added advantage of this process is that pure sulphur is extracted and sold to the chemical industries. In this process ash is recovered as clean slag, which can easily be used to make ceramic tiles and bricks. The process consumes only little water and the wastewater can easily be cleaned by any of the popular methods and reused. Another advantage is the flexibility of the process to be able to operate on wide range of coal qualities, including low-quality sub-bituminous coal and lignite. Shell Oil Company has a very long practical working experience in this technology and is successfully supplying it in China in the fertilizer industry providing clean and affordable source of energy recovered from coal, which is considered to be the dirtiest kind of energy source. It has a 50:50 joint venture with Cinopec in Yueyang, Hunan, to build a 2,000 tonnes a day coal gasification plant, which will be complete soon, to supply synthetic gas as feedstock to the Cinopec Baling Fertilizer Plant.[151] This type of activity is in practice at many other places. But use of this technology is too limited. If this is widely used, it would really revolutionize the source of energy from coal. What is solicited is that this technology should be diversified and gas produced should be made available to common people who are presently using coal for energy and with the result pollute the environment and damage health. Efforts are being made around the world to use oil and electricity for running rails, but total success in this sector is also yet to be achieved. It will be better if this technology benefits the rural sector also. Towards this end, states should make positive endeavours by encouraging the

151. Nick Wood, *supra* n. 135.

application of this technology by all means, by enhancing research and development and by providing suitable incentives. Countries that have abundance of coal reserves should give priority to the technology development and should maximize its use.

§6. Hydroelectric Power Generation (DAMS)

684. Hydroelectric power generation has always been an option for power generation, especially in those countries that have opportunities due to favourable geographical conditions to build dams. Although its share in the total power generation of the world is not encouragingly big, it is one of the sources of power generation. In countries like China and India, it is one of the preferred modes of power generation. In some other countries like Malaysia, it is going to play a substantial role in the power generation sector. However, hydroelectric power generation has always been a debatable issue. It is not considered to be environment-friendly for many reasons. Some of recurrently asserted reasons are: (1) Dams require clearing a big area, which is generally covered with forests. Clearing of such a large area adversely affects the climatic conditions of the area. It can also affect the water cycle of the area. (2) A dam requires a large water catchments area. The water catchment areas have to be undisturbed and covered with forests, preferably virgin forests. The dam that does not have enough catchment areas may adversely affect the environmental conditions. Also, in that case the dam might not have enough waters for fulfilling the power and irrigation needs. Generally, for building a dam, people living in the dam area and the catchment areas have to be relocated. Relocation is not an easy exercise. It has several socio-economic problems that are needed to be solved before the project of building dam is allowed to go ahead. Some problems like providing suitable place to the people to be relocated, providing them relocation amount that includes the payment for the building a house, managing for a source of income and monetary support for the time consumed for relocation. It has been experienced that the process of the location has been slow, people are not given suitable place to live and the money given to them is not enough to meet the expenses of proper location. Apart from these, the inhabitants of forests want same kind of locality. Thus, for an acceptable relocation, all these factors should be given due consideration. It has rightly been said that in every relocation scheme an amicable balance between the interests of the state and of the people relocated should be created. It has to be faster also. In India, for constructing a dam, a large number of people had to be relocated, and there was delay due to inefficient administrative mechanism. In PIL, the Supreme Court then decided to set up a special tribunal to decide over relocation issues and dispose of all cases within one month on the basis of summary proceedings. The problems could then be settled accordingly and people had no grudge thereafter. In Malaysia, pertaining to the Bakun Dam project, which is still going on, around 10,000 people had to be displaced. Initially, people to be displaced were not happy with the package of displacement given by the government. But when the government revised the relocation package, people were satisfied and there was no complaint. It is advised, therefore, that if any proposed dam project involved relocation of people, proper SIA with special emphasis on relocation should be done, and in the process of finalizing the SIA, participation of the people relocated must be given due importance. This is because for the convenience and benefit of certain class of people, we should not put the other class of people in a miserable condition. Now, the practice of SIA is becoming common where any proposed project is considered to affect, now or in future, certain class of people. (3) We have noted above that normally construction of a dam involves clearing of a large area covered with trees. In addition to this, construction of a dam changes the configuration of the topography of the soil. Also, when a dam is constructed, we put a large quantity of water at a place, which either did not have water at all or there were small quantity of it. Putting huge quantity of water at one place is creating imbalance on the earth. It has been experienced that the places of the close proximity of the Sardar Sarover dam suffer from mild tremors every day. In fact, they are living in fear. Also, if a dam unfortunately breaks or suffers from big breaches, it can wash away all kinds of vegetation and settlements coming in the way of the gushing water. World has many times experienced this kind of disaster. To avoid this kind of situations or to mitigate them by adopting preventive measures, a comprehensive EIA is done. It is normally done by a conglomerate of experts pertaining to the activity. In many countries, including Malaysia, this is a mandatory requirement. In Malaysia, for the Bakun Dam project a comprehensive EIA was done by an expert team comprising locally and also by a team of foreign experts. In some countries, including India, a replica of the dam is made and testing is done on it for about a month. During the testing all kinds of eventualities to which the dam can come across are taken into consideration. The pressure of the water flow, normally and in case of probable emergency, is taken into consideration. In spite of these, breaches and collapse of dams have proved to be very dangerous and have left behind long-lasting adverse effects on the environment and sufferance to the people. It is therefore suggested that EIA should sincerely be done and no compromises on the interest of the environment and people should be made. Rather, EIA should be a mandatory requirement for construction of dams, and to the possible extent, the best available experts in the world should be consulted. (4) The EIA should not be considered valid to infinity. It should be repeated as and when felt necessary. (5) In addition to EIAs, environmental auditing should also be done by a group of competent people. On the basis of the audit report, preventive measures should be advised. In case audit report concludes that the dam should be abandoned, it should be discarded. Otherwise, for a smaller and short-term benefit, we might come across a bigger loss. (6) In many countries, including India and Malaysia, the height of dams has also been debatable issue. It is known to all experts that the height of the dam should be within the bearable limits. If the height is high, we store more water, and more water means more regular tremors and more damage in case of eventual disaster. Sardar Sarover dam of India is the best example of this. In Malaysia, the height and capacity of the dam are already decided. (7) Although it is well understood that for environmental and social reasons dams should not be constructed on hills, in some countries dams are being constructed at hills. One example in India is of Tehri dam. Sundar Lal Bahuguna launched a movement against this dam. His arguments are plausible, but the government did not abandon the project. There is no doubt in it that dams on hills might in certain circumstances be able to cause more loss than benefit. So, it is better not to have a dam on the hill. (8) It is advised that instead of one big dam we should have more than one small dam, because small dams have less effect on the environment and in case of accidents, they prove to be less disastrous. This idea is also considered to be understandable from the point of view of power generation and supply. This kind of decentralized system is already in practice in Indian Kashmir and China. But this is not possible in all countries; it is possible only in those countries that have plentiful sites and opportunities of building smaller dams. (9) To maintain dams is also an arduous task that requires a good number of competent personnel on their toes. During rainy seasons, where countries have rainy seasons, their job becomes more arduous and responsible. (10) Dams have a life. After that, they have to be discarded and dismantled. To keep them operative after the expiry of their lives is very dangerous. In China, for example, some dams are operative although they have technically become old enough to de discarded. The country is keeping them for fulfilling the power needs of those areas or to cater the irrigation needs of the farmers. Countries keep them operative for economic and geographical reasons also.

685. The above-discussed imperatives are more relevant in respect to big dams, as small dams might pose environmental, social and economic problems of lesser degree. There are 45,000 big dams around the world and every now and then one or the other poses environmental and social problems. To meet challenges posed by big dams, the World Commission on Dams through its report 'Dams and Development: A New Framework for Decision-Making' submitted in November 2000 has issued clearest and most comprehensive call to action for the legal fraternity and law-making constituencies and has offered suggestions to make big dams efficient and safe that are considered to be of immense value in successful management of dams around the world towards optimizing social, environmental and economic performances. The Commission proposed five core values and a 'rights-and-risks' approach, with supporting strategic priorities and guidelines to better integrate these perspectives in decision-making on water and energy development.

686. The five values, which are to be given priority, are: (1) To assess the water and electricity needs of the area. (2) To identify the preferred development plan, among the available alternatives, that is best suited in the social, economic and environmental conditions. (3) To prepare the project via verifying that agreements among stakeholders are in place before tendering construction contracts. (4) To confirm before commissioning that the conditions that were considered necessary for a viable dam have been complied with. (5) After the dam has been operational for a considerable period and thereafter condition(s) have changed, these have to be met properly.

687. The rights-and-risks approach has best been discussed by Achim Steiner and Lawrence J. M. Hass ('The Report of the World Commission on Dams: Some Implications for Energy Law'. In *Energy Law and Sustainable Development*, edited by Adrian J. Bradbrook & Richard L. Ottinger. IUCN, 2003, 143–144) in these words: Few disagree that large dams fundamentally alter rivers and transform resources, frequently allocating benefits and entitlements from local riparian users to new groups of beneficiaries at the regional or national level. In the Commission's view, issues of equity, governance, justice and power to decide entitlements were at the heart of the dams' debate, and negotiated approaches serve best to reconcile the competing needs and entitlements. The commission felt that the rights-and-risks approach provided an effective framework to determine who has a legitimate place in consultation on overall water and energy policy, what issues need to be on the agenda and what legitimate groups need to be at the negotiation table on specific project. The rights-and-risks approach empowers decision-making processes based on the pursuit of negotiated outcomes, conducted in an open and transparent manner and inclusive of all legitimate actors involved in the issue. While this will present greater demands at early stages, it leads to greater clarity and legitimacy for subsequent steps in project-level decision-making and implementation and reduces the risks faced by all stakeholders. It shifts the basic perspective on management of resources to place more emphasis on human development dimensions.

688. The Commission did not have to look far to identify principles on rights. They are the same principles that merge from the global debates on human rights, development and sustainability. But in practice these have to be translated to the context. For upstream and downstream inhabited communities affected by dams, there is a spade of rights that potentially may come into play. These range from customary and traditional rights of ownership, tenancy, resources access and livelihood benefit. Rights may also belong to the individual, household or family, a traditional user, or neighbourhood groups, or to a company or public body, or other defined social entity such as indigenous people. At the other end of the spectrum are the rights of those who may be recipients, or the main beneficiaries from a resource transformation occurring elsewhere, and include their right of access to water and energy services essential to their right to develop, welfare and livelihood.

689. The second element in the rights-and-risks, the risk assessment, adds an important dimension to understanding to what extent an intervention may impact the people's rights in a significant and systematic way. Traditional practices have been to restrict the definition of risk to that of national economy in terms of avoided cost, or nationally defined water or energy security, or to the corporate investor or developer, in terms of loan repayment and expected return on equity. In contrast, the Commission's global review showed that risk faced by far larger group of stakeholders in dam projects was not addressed. Often these groups had risks imposed on them involuntarily and managed by others, including risk that directly affects their livelihoods, quality of life and culture. Typically, these involuntary risk bearers have little or no say in overall water and energy policy, in choice of specific projects to meet their needs or in subsequent project design and implementation, thus denying them to participate in the decision-making process commensurate with their exposure to risk. In the Commission's view voluntary risk takers have the capacity to define the level and type of risk they wish to take and explicitly to define its boundaries. Involuntary risk bearers must engage with risk takers in a transparent process to negotiate equitable outcomes, in ways appropriate to the governance context. What the Commission proposed was that governments have responsibility to establish the enabling framework for good faith negotiations to take place. To be effective, this framework would include procedures for more effective mediation, and adjudication either through political or judiciary means, in the case of intractable disputes. Governments nonetheless retained ultimate responsibility for all processes, decisions and their sovereignty.

690. According to Achin Steiner and Lawrence J. M. Hans (*supra*), The Commission's Report is certainly not the last word on large dams, or on how the issues raised on the dams' debate should be tackled. It derives its significance from the rapidly changing context into which the Commission's recommendations are offered, at a time when suitable water resources management concerns are rapidly moving to the top of the global development agenda, as is most evident from the United Nations Millennium Declaration and Plan of implementation. They are right to say that Commission's own legitimacy in offering a way forward was that it engaged the entire spectrum of participants in the dams debate, and at all levels, in an open process. It offered itself as a model for what can be achieved at the national level. Certainly after two years of intense study, dialogues and reflection, the Commission felt its rationale and framework offered scope for progress on this issue that no single perspective on its own may offer. In their 'call to action' the Commission declared that its Report itself was not a blueprint. They encouraged all parties to use it as 'a starting point for discussions, debates, internal reviews and reassessments of existing procedures'. As the Commission hoped, stakeholders have moved on with the dams debate, largely informed by, and in large measures with constant reference to the Commission's work. The necessary task now is to move from policy to practice. And in this respect, the legal fraternity in countries and working at international level will have significant role to play.

691. Commission's approach on rights-and-risks framework appended to big dams is commendable. All states should have to undergo the processes suggested by it. In fact, state is responsible for all probable consequential effects of a dam, and it is the bounded duty of the state to strike a meaningful balance between the water and energy needs of the area for sustainable development and the rights of the people. Even if people living in the close vicinity of the proposed site of construction of a dam voluntarily concede to certain proposals, the state should take decision, which is broadly in the interest of all. People's participation is very important. It will be a healthy tradition to involve NGOs in the negotiation process. All parties should think with free minds and should make endeavours to protect interests of all stakeholders. The five pointers suggested for strategic planning by the Commission are also imperatively demanded to be given due consideration. If these pointers are given proper consideration, economic, social and environmental interests can aptly be protected.

692. Dams on the rivers passing through more than one country have been a matter of dispute between the beneficiary countries. This is because when a country builds a dam on the river that passes to another country, it regulates the movement of water to another country. The internationally accepted rule in this connection is to have equitable distribution of water between the beneficiary countries, what is equitable is not so easy to determine. These kinds of problems have been resolved on the basis of bilateral of multilateral agreements, as the case may be. The example of India and Bangladesh is the best. It will, therefore, be better to have necessary agreements between the beneficiary countries in advance about sharing of water and if possible about sharing of power to be generated from the proposed dam so that the interests of all countries are amicably served. Same problems have also been experienced when within a country, a river passes through more than one states. But here problem is solved by the interference of the Central Government or by the Apex Court of the country. Kaveri water dispute beaten Karnataka and Tamil Nadu, the two Indian states, is the best example. We have noted above that a dam serves dual purpose, regulated supply of water and generation of power. When a dam is built the supply of water which was previously uninterrupted gets hampered by the dam. This might cause problems within a state or between some states of a country.

To meet this kind of problems, one solution, which is quite appealing and practicable, is to link the rivers of the state or states so that the supply of water within a state or among the states could be maintained. India has this kind of plan. But the problem with this kind of move is that it would involve a large quantity of money and will have no guarantee of proper flow of water throughout the region. If it is successfully done in India, it will provide a good feedback to other countries.

693. We have noted above that presently in Malaysia the contribution of the hydroelectric power generation is not so significant. But the country is constructing Bakun dam, which will significantly increase the power generation. We have also noted that for the dam project, a comprehensive EIA has been done, and about 10,000 households that were affected have amicably been rehabilitated. In the whole process, the pointers suggested by the Energy Commission were followed by the Bakun Dam Management, which was responsible for construction of the dam and subsequently running the hydroelectric project. Before the project was formally started, the residents of that area and NGOs interested in giving their opinions were given opportunity to express their views. Malaysia also has several prototype hydroelectric projects tapping the river currents and waterfalls, but their contribution is not significant. It is notable that under the Ninth Malaysia Plan, renewable energy sources, including these, will be given special attention, as the Government wants to increase the ration of these energy sources from 2% to 5%.

694. TNB in its write up, published in April 2009, expressed support to the target to have 350 MW of grid-connected renewable energy electricity by 2010. The previous target of having 5% by the year 2005 was not reached because of the difficulty of the interested developers in securing the financing. This problem has been mitigated by the more favourable commercial terms and conditions offered. Renewable energy has been widely accepted by the global energy industry as a necessary means of reducing the emission of GHGs to address the problem of global climatic warming. To date, TNB has signed nine renewable energy power purchase agreements (REPPAs) with Small Renewable Energy Power (SREP) developers in Peninsular Malaysia with a total export capacity of 49.8 MW. Recently, TNB has entered into a Memorandum of Understanding (MoU) with Felda Palm Industries

Sdn Bhd and Japan's J-Power to develop a biomass power plant at Jengka, Pahang. The renewable energy project is planned for completion by the end of 2010. Fuel to generate electrical energy will be sourced from palm oil empty fruit bunches (EFB). Occupying an area of 4.6 hectares, the plant complex will house EFB processing and storage areas, a biomass boiler firing on EFB fuel, a steam turbine complete with the generator unit and other related auxiliaries. To ensure full compliance to DOE requirements, the plant will be equipped with stringent environmental control and monitoring systems. Upon completion, the plant will have a generation capacity of 10 MW and will be connected to the TNB 11 kV grid network that supplies electricity to the local surrounding areas.

695. Presently, Malaysia used to get in 2010 around 11% of the total power generation from hydroelectric sources; it rose up to 13% in 2016. Hydroelectric power generation plants are three: (1) Hydroelectric power plants that require no reservoir. The example is, Sungai Piah, which produces about 50 MW of power. (2) Mini-hydroelectric power plants that cost around MYR 1 million and produce enough power to cater a small village. (3) The medium-class hydroelectric plants that require medium type of dam to play dual role – flood control and power generation. Its example in the country is Temenggor dam of Sungai Perak. (4) Among the big hydrometric plants, presently operative is Kenyir dam, which produces 1,600 MW of electricity, and the other one will be the Bakun dam. Malaysia's most recent hydroelectric project is Pergau, which began operations in 1997. When Bakun Dam is commissioned, the substantial part of the power supply in the East Malaysia will be from it.[152]

Source	*Percentage of Output*
Temenggor Dam	20%
Pergau Dam	25%
Kenyir Dam	45%
Sungai Piah	10%

Source: *New Straits Times*, 24 August 2005.

696. In April 2008, the TNB in its write up stated:

> When we cross the year 2010, hydropower is expected to play a prominent role to achieve a balanced generation mix in Peninsular Malaysia from its current contribution of 11% to 20% by the year 2020. The development of several large hydroelectric projects under the Sarawak Corridor of Renewable Energy (SCORE) spanning over a period of 22 years has the potential to generate 28,000 MW of electricity once fully developed. Amongst the projects, which are already under way to be developed are the Murum dam (990MW), Balleh dam (950MW) and Pelagus dam (770MW) in the upper reaches of the Rejang

152. See *New Straits Times*, 24 Aug. 2005.

river in Sarawak. Plans are also underway to export 5,000MW of power to Peninsular Malaysia via 500kV high-voltage direct current via overhead and undersea cables. TNB has also recognized potential hydropower sources to be developed in Peninsular Malaysia, i.e. the Ulu Terengganu and Ulu Jelai hydropower projects. We do expect that this should bring in diversity to the current energy mix and reduce the dependence on coal for generation of electricity. In February 2017, in Peninsular Malaysia hydropower was 11-13 Percent, in Sarawak with the commissioning of the Bakun Dam, it was 77 percent, and in Sabah it was only 5 percent.[153] (See the figures above).

697. The work on the Bakun Dam in Sarawak, which is the Joint Venture of Malaysia and China, is second highest concrete rock-fill dam of 207 m height. Its reservoir is 70,000 hectares, and upon completion, it will generate 2,400 MW of clean energy. It will become operative soon. Once it is commissioned, the ratio of percentage of the hydroelectric power will tremendously increase.[154] The Bakun Dam was commissioned in 2011. It is operating now in its full estimated capacity of 2,400 MW. It is now operative under the Sarawak Energy Bhd. The dam has increased the energy generation mix of the Sarawak state.[155] In 2016, this source of energy gave 13% of the total generation mix.

698. Malaysia has the potential and capacity to substantially increase the hydroelectric power generation in the country. If the sea current is also exploited, this source of clean energy can be maximized. At the world level also, it is estimated that our planet's hydroelectric capability is greater than world's entire oil supply. It can stay longer and cater the energy needs of the growing population. Basically, dams serve dual purpose, mitigating the flood and power generation. It can also boost the eco-tourism. For example, over 4,000 foreign and local tourists visited Tasik Kenyir in 2004, which generated MYR 1 million. This is in addition to the income to the transport sector and the rise of income of local residents. Resorts around this are still coming up. The income, therefore, is going to multiply.

699. This is true that hydrometric power generation plants are the best clean energy sources. They can also promote eco-tourism. Nevertheless, the loss of the environment in clearing the land, replacement of forest inhabitants, disturbance to the ecological balance and the danger due to possible breach of dams are the economic factors appended to this source of energy to be taken care of properly. This source of energy has to be environment-friendly; then, only it will be a viable source of energy, otherwise not. These can be done by pre- and post-EIAs followed by eco-auditing. It is imperative that dams should properly be maintained, and water level

153. Ministry of Energy, Green Technology and Water, 'Malaysia Energy Policy: Focussing on Sustainable Energy Development and the Way Forward', at: http://bseep.gov.my/App_ClientFile/df08bc24-99fb-47a3-937f-dc25df9d3997/Assets/BSEEP%20NCA2017/PAPER%204%20-%20KETTHA_Malaysia%20Energy%20Policy_04052017.pdf (accessed on 12 Mar. 2018).

154. See <www.bakundam.com/home.html>, 15 May 2010.

155. See Hydroworld.com at: https://www.hydroworld.com/articles/2017/03/state-of-sarawak-purchases-2-400-mw-bakun-hydropower-project-on-island-of-borneo.html (accessed on 12 Feb. 2018).

must also be maintained. This is also imperative that when dams become old and need to be replaced, replacement should be done immediately.

§7. Ethanol

700. Ethanol is one of the sustainable and a less polluting energy source, which is generally being generated and used in transport and agricultural sectors in some countries, especially in Latin American countries. Brazil is one of them. It manufactures this fuel by fermenting and distilling its sugarcane crops and using it in transport sector. Brazil is the biggest manufacturer of this other energy source. Presently, seven out of ten new cars sold in the country are using ethanol known as 'flex-fuel'. Engines of cars have been so designed that they can be run with petrol, or ethanol or a mixture of both. A computer sensor inside the engine decides what will be the best mix of whatever is in the tank for optimum performance. Finding ethanol is not a problem in the country. Almost all filling stations have one pump for this. The mixture of petrol and ethanol is more popular and it is generally used by motorists. It is known as 'gasohol', which has 25% of ethanol and 75% of petrol. It is notable that ethanol creates a cleaner burn than petrol. It does not have sulphur, lead and harmful hydrocarbons. It also releases less quantity of CO_2. Thus, it is environment-friendly. It is engine-friendly too, because engine does not require frequent cleaning. The only down side is that ethanol engines require 25% more fuel than petrol if run with pure ethanol. But if mixture of petrol and ethanol is used the fuel consumption relatively reduces. This contra factor is not an issue in Brazil because ethanol is 60% to 65% cheaper than petrol. This is notable that this alternative source of energy came into use after 1970 price hike of oil. Since then, the ethanol industry of the country has saved billions of dollars for the country. Recent technological developments have overcome many of the disadvantages traditionally associated with ethanol, such as its corrosive effect on tanks and engines. Fuel engine starters and the computer system in the flex-fuel engines mean that starting cars in the cold is no longer an issue and the sluggish performance of ethanol-run engines is the thing of the past. In view of the fast-growing economy with greater emphasis on the transport and agricultural sectors, Brazil has decided to double its production by the year 2013 and making all efforts to reach the target. Some other countries including Mexico are using corn, sugar beets, wood chips, grass and organic wastes rich in carbohydrates; among them, corn is being used in manufacturing ethanol at commercial scale.[156]

701. It is, thus, rightly said and proven in Brazil and Mexico that ethanol, which is a type of alcohol generally produced by corn and sugarcane, is more energy efficient and it is the high time to venture into manufacturing it at a large scale so that it becomes a potent source of energy and dependency on the traditional sources of energy especially oil and gas is considerably reduced. While some critics have said that the push for ethanol is based on faulty science and mostly benefits the farm lobby. But this does not seem to be true. The countries that have surplus corn or

156. See *New Straits Times*, 3 Feb. 2006.

sugarcane or both can easily venture in manufacturing ethanol and can use it as a potent alternative source of energy. Some scientists support this. Alexander Farrell of the University of California is of the opinion that ethanol can contribute significantly to both energy and environmental goals. However, ethanol made by corn meets only the energy goals. He and his colleagues looked at six studies used to argue for and against the development of ethanol as an energy source. 'One of the main purposes is to explain why the studies found in the scientific literature have such divergent results,' Farrell said. Currently, ethanol is not a significant source of fuel, but is blended into gasoline in some states in the US. Environmentalists hope it could be developed as a cleaner source of energy than oil and gas. The 15.5 billion litres of ethanol blended with gasoline in 2004 amounted to 2% of all gasoline sold by volume and 1.3% of the total energy used. This disproves the charge that ethanol cannot be a potential source of energy. Farrell argued that the engine made to suit ethanol will be an expensive venture. This argument is also not tenable because in Brazil engines are being manufactured at fairly affordable cost. Even if it is true the overall benefit will compensate the high cost of the engine. However, Farrell has rightly argued that the environmental cost comes entirely from making fertilizer, running the tractors over the farm and operating the biorefinery. According to him, better methods now being investigated would use the woody parts of plants using what is known as cellulosic technology, a really good fuel for the United States. At the moment cellulosic technology is just too expensive. If that changes, we might see this technology enter the commercial market within five years. Japanese scientists have successfully manufactured fuel cell using methanol, another kind of alcohol. The company that has done this research plans to commercialize it at large scale used in cars very soon at international level and make it as an alternative energy source. This will be economically viable and environmentally friendly. It is also said that in future a soldier will take with him a couple of fuel cells made up of methanol rather than taking several huge batteries for lighting nights. Some have doubts about this research, but if it proves successful, it might be of great help and will be a good source of energy.[157] No one can deny that. But right now the technology of manufacturing ethanol should further be augmented so that we get more with least consumption of materials to be used in manufacturing the fuel. It is suggested that states should give this research priority in the area of scientific research.

702. Bioethanol has a bright future. Its manufacture and use is going to multiply. The United States, China and India are also taking interest in establishing ethanol refineries. This is because bioethanol can be produced by using wastes like wood chips, corn stalks and switch grass that requires no fertilizer. These waste materials can easily be converted into ethanol by some kinds of microscopic fungi. The US Energy Department has announced that Washington is offering USD 160 million for establishing three cellulosic ethanol refineries. Similar plans are there in Canada also.[158] Presently, total global production is 45,993 million tonnes. The present state of bioethanol production can be seen in the Table below:

157. See *New Straits Times*, 5 Feb. 2006.
158. *New Sunday Times*, 4 Jun. 2006.

Country	*Production*
US	16,141
Brazil	16,001
China	3,801
EU	2,521
Others	7,529
Total	45,993

§8. Renewable and Other Sources of Energy

703. On the basis of above discussions, it is rightly said in view of the Paris Accord that the agenda to reduce CO_2 emissions is actually to maximize the renewable and other sources of energy. This is because energy efficiency and fossil fuel have their own limits. The survival of the world thus depends on the maximum use of renewable energy. Presently, this source of energy does not have significant contribution in the total energy supply of the world. We have already noted a troubling fact that a large section of the world's population is deprived of electricity and proper energy supply for cooking. They squarely depend on biomass burning or use of coal for it. To supply clean and healthy energy to all of them is a big challenge. To meet this challenge, we should increase the power generation, and we will have to diversify the use of the power of the country. But if renewable energy is not properly supplemented to it, the problem will never be solved. Thus, solution for sustainable energy for sustainable development lies in maximizing all kinds of renewable and other sources of energy. They are expensive ventures. However, efforts worldwide are being made by all means to increase their ration in the total power generation, because the future of economic development depends on them. It has been decided in the Bonn Conference that by the year 2020, they must account for 20% to 30% of the total power generation in the European Union countries. Developing and less developed countries should also take similar determinations. Among all these, hydroelectric power generation plants and offshore windmills can provide a long-term solution. China's efforts in these areas are remarkable. As the fossil fuels and uranium are exhaustible resources, the sustainable energy sources are all kinds of renewable energy sources. Country like Germany has already declared the end point of use of fossil fuels as sources of energy. They will totally be taken over by renewable energy sources. Other developed countries are also striving hard to fastly replace them. Developing countries, including Malaysia, with less technological advancements, availability of fossil fuels and deficient economic resources will follow their footsteps relatively late.

Chapter 3. Renewable Energy Sources, Energy Efficiency and Conservation Practices in Malaysia

§1. Renewable Energy

704. As renewable energy sources are clean and do not depend on use of any exhaustible natural resources, they are becoming more popular. Their importance has increased with the acceptance of Paris Accord 2015. The REthinking Energy 2017: Accelerating the Global Energy Transformation report stated that in 2015 there was increase of these sources of energy by 9.3% on 2014 accounting it to about 23.5% (5,660 TWh) of the global power generation capacity. Among them hydropower, wind and solar energy were prominent. There is need to maximize the solar PV and wind because they have lot of potentials. Developing countries, especially India and China, are keen in these because their energy demand is going to rise which can be met only with nuclear power generation and renewable energy sources. Other developing countries are also laying emphasis on these. It has been noticed that investment in renewable energy sector in developing countries is increasing fast.[159] The solar energy in Malaysia has tremendous scope at household level and as well as at large scale. At small scale, houses can be made self-sufficient with the use of photovoltaic cells in households. This is being encouraged by all means by the Malaysian government. However, in spite of these efforts photovoltaic cells have a limited purpose to serve. It is being used only for heating water to be used in washrooms. Only in some countries, it is being used for large-scale production. Efforts, therefore, are being made to maximize the use of this source in its original form or with the use of some advanced technology. Towards this direction, the Proton Energy Systems' HOGN renewable energy hydrogen generator has played a critical role in powering the first fully sustainable house in the world that runs entirely on hydrogen. Malaysia's Eco-House, an ambitious solar hydrogen-powered home cited at the University Kebangsan Malaysia, utilizes a photovoltaic electricity production and storage system in conjunction with Proton's HOGEN renewable energy hydrogen generator and a fuel cell to capture, store and regenerate the electricity necessary to power household appliances. Sunlight gathered by 42 PV panels located on the roof of the house is converted into electricity, which in turn feeds the HOGEN renewable energy hydrogen generator inside the house. The generator uses that electrical energy to electrolyse the water, producing oxygen and hydrogen. The hydrogen then is stored in a 1500-litre storage tank at 13.8 bars. When needed, the stored hydrogen is used to feed a fuel cell that powers the household appliances. This technique has been designed to maximize the intermittent renewable energy.[160] This breakthrough is remarkable. If it is made cost-effective, it can make a large number of households as self-dependent, especially in remote areas. But in the near future, it is not going to be so. The solution therefore lies, in

---

159. 'The Rapid Transformation of Global Renewable Energy', *Energy Malaysia*, Vol. 11, 2017, pp. 38–40.
160. For details, refer to the website of FUEL Cell TODAY.

maximizing the renewable energy sources at a commercial scale and to supply electricity generated by projects engaged with this through appropriate grids. At the World Engineering, Science and Technology Congress, Kuala Lumpur, 17–18 June 2010, a Malaysian scientist emphasized on use of hydrogen as an energy source. He said in times to come, it could be 10% of the total energy generation in the country. It will reduce the present heavy reliance on fossil fuels. He appreciated the Malaysian breakthrough of hydrogen-fuelled motorcycle manufactured by Malaysian scientists, which is being appreciated in the country and abroad. The author is of the opinion that if research continues with this pace, hydrogen fuel will constitute substantial part of the energy sector, along with hybrid cars, which are already popular around the world, including Malaysia. It is notable here that this technology is not new. Western countries, especially the United States, are much ahead in this technology; it had sixty-three hydrogen filling stations in 2007. The figure must be quite high now.[161]

We have noted above that Malaysian GreenTech Financing Scheme (GTFS) under the Ministry of Energy, Green Technology and Water is giving away soft loans to encourage renewable energy sector. The Minister stated that the original scheme provided RM 2.96 billion in funding 272 local green technology entrepreneurs. The scheme will continue until 2022 with a USD 1.12 billion allocation.[162] In 2017, the Minister of Energy, Green Technology and Water launched the Green Technology Master Plan (GTMP), which outlines Malaysia's strategic plans for green technology development to create a low-carbon and efficient economy with targeted revenue of RM 180 billion by 2020.[163]

705. We have noted above that about 80% of the energy is produced from fossil fuels in Malaysia. The transport sector and power generation plants mainly consume oil and gas. We have noted above that the country is using its own oil and gas. Gas is being imported from Indonesia also. On a long-term contract basis, the country is converting oil into LNG to be exported to Japan. Coal reserves are estimated to be between 400 and 500 million metric tonnes. Because of low-quality coal and availability of oil and gas on affordable price, coal was not preferred for power generation. The rising oil and gas price and availability of coal in the country have compelled the country to use its coal reserves for power generation. This is notable that two new coal-fired power generation plants in Sarawak, where coal reserves situate, have already been commissioned.

706. We have noted above that presently about 90% of the total power generation is with the use of fossil fuels; other 10% is from other sources. Use of coal is still there, but use of gas in thermal power generation has tremendously increased. Among them, hydroelectric source is significantly notable. Renewable sources of energy are also being augmented, but the ratio of these sources of energy is not encouraging. Efforts are being made to make it 5% of the total power generation in

161. See Professor Hamdani Saidi, 'Green Energy Security – A New Concept', paper presented at the World Engineering, Science and technology Congress, Kuala Lumpur, 17–18 Jun. 2010.
162. Foot 147.
163. See 'The Green Master Plan', *Energy Malaysia*, Vol. 13, 2017, pp. 45–46.

the near future. If this target is achieved, the country can save huge amount of money by cutting on the import of oil and coal. Biomass, together with solar energy, accounts for 90% of the total renewable energy potential of the country. Malaysia is diversifying renewable energy sources by introducing biodiesel, which can easily be produced in the country from palm oil. In 2001, the country launched Small and Renewable Energy Project (SREP) programme, which aims at fast-tackling small-scale power plant projects utilizing renewable sources, such as wood-based residues, palm oil biomass, mill residues and hydropower. A SREP developer can apply for getting priority status in the Income Tax Act 1967 and can sell electricity to the utility company of the country, Tenag Nasional Berhad (TNB) through the distribution grid system. They can also export electricity. These projects generally get twenty-one-year licence. A National Special Committee on Renewable Energy (SCORE) under the Ministry of Energy has been set up. Application has to be made to it. To date there are around sixty-six approved such projects.

707. The National Programme on Grid Connected Palm oil Biomass Power Generation and Cogeneration was launched in 2002. It aims at developing the energy potential of the country so that the 5% target is soon achieved. These projects have five components: information services and awareness enhancement, policy studies and capacity building, financial assistance, developing demonstration projects and biomass energy technology development. This is notable here that these projects are short of raw materials, and only two of them are connected to the national grid. They are also facing a problem that because of low purchase price of the utility company, they are unable to make enough profit.

708. A project development study on Malaysian Building Integrated Photovoltaic Project (MBIP), 2003, aimed at a study to produce deliverables that would facilitate the eventual implementation of a successful and replicable national BIPV project and promote building integrated PV applications for new and existing buildings with energy efficiency potential. Such kinds of projects, especially Grid-Connected Rooftop Solar PV, are also being augments by the TNB. It has completed one project covering six locations. The objective of such projects is to demonstrate the technical capability and to evaluate the commercial viability of Grid-Connected PV System in Malaysia. Enterprise 4 of Technology Park Malaysia is the largest grid-connected power project in Malaysia. It has a solar-powered grid-connected system with UPS battery bank, and a generator back up that ensures uninterrupted power supply to the facilities of the building. In case of insufficient power generated by solar panels, additional power from the grid is taken. In case the power generated by the solar panels is excess, it can be stored in the battery bank, which can be used in case of power failure. In fact this is a successful model of utilizing solar power in the country. The plan is to maximize this kind of projects so that the load on normal electricity supply is reduced.[164]

164. See Lynette Ann & Marie Pichoo, 'The Largest Photovoltaic Grid Connected Power Project in Asia Pacific', *Symbiosis* (February 2002).

709. Malaysia has to go a long way in trapping the solar energy and use it for developmental activities. Recently, SOLAR system producer SOLAR in Holdings (M) Sdn Bhd plans to build three more plants in Malaysia to produce a wider range of solar-based products for global distribution. The company is in the midst of developing Solar Valley, a MYR 1 billion project comprising twenty-one plants, spread over thirty-two hectares of land in Terengganu. Construction of Solar Valley will be completed by the middle of 2007. All the plants will produce solar panel cells, raw materials and solar-powered computers, phones and chargers. The proposed new plants will be in Malacca. The company has planned to produce solar-powered motorbikes and other solar-powered facilities. These will be achieved in collaboration with Denmark Solar Agency.[165]

It is projected, which is achievable, that by 2020, renewable energy will be: Solar PV 9%; Mini-Hydro 24%; Biogas 12%; Biomass 38%; and Solid Waste 17%. They together will generate 2,080 MW.[166]

710. So as to support renewable sources of energy in the country, the Income Tax Act 1967 provides initial allowance and annual allowance and shortly the money invested on such energy projects are paid back to the taxpayer. Projects engaged in renewable energy sources can get priority status for additional financial benefits. All kinds of renewable projects, including hydropower not exceeding 10 MW and solar power without any such limit, qualify for such fiscal incentives (for a detailed account, see *infra*).

711. This is notable here that in spite of all efforts made to popularize renewable sources of energy, baring few countries, these sources, especially solar PV and wind energy sources, are not satisfactorily growing. Investment in them are increasing but not so encouraging. The Malaysian government, therefore, as noted above has created a floating fund to provide financial assistance in form of soft loans as and when proponents of new projects and the owners of the existing projects need. This kind of fund will provide a boost to this sector of power generation, but this will also not help much. The main thing is that the production cost of electricity from renewable sources should be reduced. The fiscal measures practised and the proposed loan facility will certainly reduce the price. The position will improve only when the purchase rate of the electricity produced by renewable sources is high. The low rates offered by utility companies are seriously affecting the Small and Renewable Energy Programme (SREP). The Energy, Water and Communications Ministers have pointed this out. They pointed out that these projects are facing financial difficulties. They could not take loan from banks as they were hardly making any profit. These projects were too small and together can produce only 330 MW. According to him another big problem is low rates offered to these projects by the utility company. This is particularly so in the Peninsular Malaysia where the rates

---

165. *New Straits Times*, 10 Jul. 2006.
166. Ministry of Energy, Green Technology and Water, 'Malaysia Energy Policy: Focusing on Sustainable Energy Development and the Way Forward', at: http://bseep.gov.my/App_ClientFile/df08bc24-99fb-47a3-937f-dc25df9d3997/Assets/BSEEP%20NCA2017/PAPER%204%20-%20KETTHA_Malaysia%20Energy%20Policy_04052017.pdf (accessed on 20 Apr. 2018).

offered by the TNB, the main utility company of the country, is from 14 to 17 Malaysian cents per kilowatt, when the cost to produce that amount of electricity is 13 cents. This is notable here that the purchase price is fixed between the power generator and the utility company under an agreement for certain duration. The power generator cannot revise the rate accepted by the agreement unless the utility company agrees for it.

712. This is notable here that the TNB has shown its interest to increase purchase through REPPA and distribute renewable energy in the country. Under the agreements, power generation from renewable energy fuels is linked to the national grid. Five such agreements have been signed in the peninsular Malaysia to date, with a total generation capacity of 26.2 MW fuelled by palm oil waste, landfill gas and municipal waste. TNB is also negotiating REPPA with developers of small government-backed renewable energy programmes utilizing mini-hydro, landfill gas and other biomass resources such as wood waste and rice husk. It is notable here that if the purchase rate of such energy is reasonably increased, there are chances that the output of renewable sources of energy will increase and diversify.[167]

713. According to Datuk Dr Mohd Anas, the then Chairman of the Energy Commission of Malaysia, the Energy Commission attempted to address the challenges faced by producers of renewable energy from biomass under the Ninth Malaysia Plan. Presently, in spite of incentives provided to it, its contribution is not more than 2% to 3% of the electricity need of the grid. Efforts will be made to increase this ratio. It is popular only in the palm oil industries. The total power generation from this source is around 1,000 MW, but only a small part of it is commercialized. The Government has started Small Renewable Energy Programme (SREP). Under the programme, those producing 10 MW or more may be connected to the grid through the TNB or Sabah Electricity Board. He wants to review this system of power generation from all aspects. He is of the opinion that sale price of renewable energy to utilities of the country should be increased. He expressed hope to provide solutions to all problems pertaining to renewable sources of energy in the Ninth Malaysia Plan.[168] It is notable here that SREP did not do well. It could not substantially contribute to the clean energy sources.[169] It is hoped that GTFS will work well.

714. Besides the price issue, projects engaged in renewable energy sources are facing with the fuel security problem. They are currently using empty palm oil fruit bunches (FEB). The competing use of FEB for mulching and fertilizer in palm oil plantations and the production of biodiesel leads to reduce the supply to power generation. This has also increased the price of FEB. The problem seems to worsen, unless alternative sources are made cost-effective by all means. For this, along with the financial aids and fiscal incentives provided to projects engaged in generating energy from renewable sources, the purchase price of the energy also has to be

167. *New Straits Times*, 23 Aug. 2005.
168. See *New Straits times*, 14 Jun. 2005.
169. See Benjamin Sovacool and Ira Martina Drupady, 'Examining the Small Renewable Energy Power (SREP) Program in Malaysia', *Energy Policy*, 39(11): 7244–7256.

increased. This is notable here that in Malaysia, investors in renewable energy qualify for incentives as Annual Investment Tax Allowance under the Income Tax Act 1967 (See infra). Where the project engaged in renewable energy sources and has obtained status of a pioneer industry under the Promotion of Investment Act 1986, the project gets special allowance under the Act.[170] This may be noted that among the ASEAN countries Malaysia provides electricity at the cheapest rate.[171] The utility companies, especially TNB, are not making much profit. They are pleading to increase their tariffs. Datuk Leo Mogi, who is the Chairman of the TNB, is of the opinion that every sector in the economy has its fair share of sustainable development process of the country. In the power sector, utility companies play a vital role. For ensuring sustainable power supply for sustainable development, it is necessary that utility companies should have enough resources and pace of development so that they are able to meet the future power demand amicably. Their sustainability depends on the profit margin that they can have. If the profit margin is low, they cannot match with the ever-growing power needs of the country. He says that unfortunately, as in the case of the country's national utility the TNB, its rate of return does not commensurate with the growth of electricity demand that it is expected to serve. If it should be unable to access the capital and debt market to secure the required funding to invest in new assets to supply electricity, TNB may have to resort to cutting down on its genuine expenditure that is warranted. As a result, it would get into a vicious circle of not being able to build new production assets to meet the increasing demand for electricity. We know the argument about increasing efficiency and cutting costs. But one can only squeeze to the extent that the company can easily bear. After that there has to be a fundamental examination of the overall cost structure. A look at some comparative figures on return on capital employed by different utilities versus their corresponding electricity growth rate shows that in 2003–2004, TNB's return on capital employed was 6.3% compared to 12.5% for EGAT in Thailand, 5% for KEPCO in Korea, 8.5% for Singapore Power and 14.9% for China Light and Power. The corresponding growth in electricity demand was 8% per annum for Malaysia, 9.2% for Thailand, 5.7% for South Korea, 2.4% for Singapore and 4.3% for Hong Kong. However, even though the demand growth in South Korea, Singapore and Hong Kong was lower than Malaysia's, the returns to these utilities were higher than TNB's. The position of TNB has not improved. There is also a correlation between the electricity tariff charged by utilities and System Average Interruption Duration Index (SAIDI), which also indicates the level of efficiency of a particular utility. The lower the number, the better the reliability of the system will be. In Peninsular Malaysia, the SAIDI figure was at 106, compared to Thailand at 1496, Hong Kong at 5, and Singapore at 2, and Japan at 6. The corresponding average tariffs charged by the utilities – at 22.3 sen/unit for TNB, 43 sen/per unit for China Light and Power, 24 sen/unit for Thailand, 65 sen/unit for Japan and 34 sen/unit for Singapore – show that high reliability is invariably related to higher tariff. Singapore consumers pay 65% more than the rates we pay to enjoy higher reliability of supply, while Japanese consumers pay even more,

170. See the Chapter on Tax Incentives to Renewable Energy Sources in Malaysia.
171. See at: https://themalaysianreserve.com/2017/07/28/malaysias-electricity-tariffs-among-lowest-asean/ (accessed on 12 Jan. 2018).

almost three times more. It is notable here that in Malaysia the tariff rate has been slightly increased with an incentive to the poor section of the consumers who do not consume electricity more than certain prescribed limit. The current electricity sale rates per unit per cent are: Taipower, Taiwan 36.7; TNB, Malaysia 39.45; PLN, Indonesia 39.69; KEPCO, Korea 40.84; EGAT, Thailand 47.31; CLP, Hong Kong 48.43; Singapore Power, Singapore 63.44; MERALCO, Philippines 69.85; TEPCO, Japan 101.5.[172] So far quality and reliability are concerned, Malaysia's SAIDI figure of 106 is in fact better than that of utilities in developed countries. This is based on the Electric Power Research Institute's (EPRI) research for the year 2004, which recorded SAIDI figures for Canada, the United States, United Kingdom, France, Spain, Australia and New Zealand at 220, 214, 70, 53, 179, 182 and 128 respectively. Based on another conventional measure of power supply quality, System Average Reduction Frequency Index (SARFI), which measures the frequency of voltage sags or voltage dipped over a period of one year, TNB recorded an average figure of 5.3 occur-rences per year in 2004 at 132 kV. This in comparison with figures of 9.4 for Canada, up to 35 for South Africa, 40.5 for Norway and up to 31.4 for the United States, again showed that TNB was at par or even better than many other utilities. These figures are also not greatly altered.[173] Utilities can only provide the quality of service modern consumers expect if they earn a fair return to allow for continuous investment in capacity building and upgrading of existing networks. Malaysian price was among the lowest. Utilities cannot be expected to continue providing First World infrastructure at Third World prices. It is, thus, important for consumers to appreciate the role and challenges faced by utilities such as TNB in the right perspective. The reality is that sooner or later the present tariff structure will have to be changed. The higher cost would be recommended if the utility becomes unable to maintain a reasonable margin between production cost and the tariff collections. Many nations have been experimenting with the competitive model in the hope of letting market forces determine the price of electricity and weed out weak and inefficient players. Despite the early enthusiasm that accompanied such a model in the late 1980s and early 1990s, success had been evasive so far and has created instability in the supply system even for countries where demand growth has established. It happened in the United States in 2001 and 2003. It also happened in Europe in 2003. Even now, there are still some concerns about the level of investment in the transmission network in some countries in Europe. The state of affairs where returns are less than the cost of capital is not a sustainable state of the utility. In Malaysia, TNB has a central role in the power sector. It is, therefore, essential to ensure its financial viability and continued sustainability as a prerequisite of the sustained growth of the country.[174]

715. In view of the rising oil and gas prices in 2008, the Minister Datuk Leo Mogi's (as he then was) arguments for increasing the electricity tariff in the country

172. See 'Comparing Electricity Selling Prices', *Energy Malaysia,* pp. 30–33.
173. See at: https://www.researchgate.net/publication/266594846_LBNL-5268E_An_Examination_of_Temporal_Trends_in_Electricity_Reliability_Based_on_Reports_from_US_Electric_Utilities/figures?lo=1 (accessed on 20 Mar. 2018).
174. See *New Straits Times*, 18 Apr. 2005.

were considered laudable. The increased electricity rates prompted the utility to increase the purchase price of electricity generated by renewable sources. In fact, the renewable sources of energy were at that time also a priority area and this had to be supported by all means. This is true that for the sustainable energy in the country, there has to be sustainable growth in its production, and for a sustainable production, the utility companies should also have enough financial resources to grow. If they do not grow at the required pace, the whole idea of sustainable energy for sustainable development will frustrate. However, rise of electricity charges by TNB will have economic impacts also. Therefore, before accepting any increase, the economic assessment of the increase and the bearing capacities of consumers in the country have also to be made. This is because the rise of electricity tariff will have immediate inflation, and if this cannot be absorbed by the economy, it might yield undesired results. We have noted above that the tariff rate in Malaysia has been revised but those who consume up to certain prescribed limit have to pay less. This incentive-based tariff rise is a welcome feature.

716. It has been stated in the Ninth Malaysia Plan that utilization of renewable energy will further be intensified in the Plan period. Towards this end, efforts will be made to foster a more conducive environment to support implementation of SREP projects. In this regard, the review of the terms and conditions of the REPPA was made favourable to the producers. It was ensured that producers get regular fuel supply. The CDM of the Kyoto protocol was also be utilized to provide support for the implementation of the SREP projects. Renewable energy projects utilizing municipal waste also got support. By 2010, in the West Malaysia, about 300 MW was expected to be produced through various renewable energy projects. Additional 50 MW will be produced in Sabah. We have noted above that these figures have already been surpassed. There are now new projections under the 11th Malaysia Plan.

§2. Energy Efficiency

717. We have noted above that to meet the challenges of electricity demand in the country, along with fostering the renewable energy sources, efforts should be made to increase energy efficiency at all levels, households, companies and other institutions. The loss of electricity due to poor quality of electric appliances and less efficient insulation is common and rampant in all countries, developed and developing. Even in the United States and EU countries this is considered to be a serious problem. By increasing the energy efficiency and reduction in the use of power, there will certainly be reduction on the burden of total electricity demand. Towards this end, development of high quality of electrical appliances that have efficient performance with less consumption of electricity, high quality of insulated wires to carry the electricity, electrically efficient houses that consume less electricity for cooling or heating as the case may be and generating public awareness among the people to save electricity and cut unnecessary use of power are some imperatively demanded endeavours that all states should follow. It does not mean states are not making any efforts in the area of increasing electricity efficiency. Measures are on at scientific, fiscal and social levels. Significant among them is providing fiscal incentives to energy-efficient taxpayers and generating consciousness among the people to adopt energy efficacy measures suggested by the government. Malaysia is also working remarkably in this area. It has clearly been stated in the Eighth Malaysia Plan that productivity and efficiency improvements will remain the focus of the energy sector so as to enhance the competitiveness and resilience of the country in the energy sector.

718. Malaysian Industrial Energy Efficiency Improvement Programme (MIEEIP) is a major energy efficiency programme in the country. It is co-funded by the Government of Malaysia and UNDP-Global Environmental Funding (GEF) and private sectors. The total cost of the project is estimated as USD 20,790,200. Its main goal is to remove barriers to efficient energy use in the industrial sector in Malaysia. The focus of MIEEIP is on eight energy-intensive manufacturing sectors namely (1) wood, (2) food, (3) glass, (4) cement, (5) rubber, (6) pulp and paper, (7) iron and steel and (8) ceramics. Under the MIEEIP project, an Energy Efficiency Project Lending Scheme (EEPLS) has been established. GEF contributed MYR 4 million and same amount of money was allocated by Malaysia towards the MIEEIP fund. The objective of the EEPLS is to provide soft loans to ESCOs and industries to implement energy efficiency measures. ESCOs have to implement the project measures through an Energy Performance Contract. The Master services Agreement for the first demonstration project under this scheme was signed on 7 April 2003 between HeaveBoard Sdn Bhd, a wood-based factory, and Mrnsilin Holdings, an ESCO. It has been able to reduce the company's energy bills significantly by changing the oil-based boiler to a wood waste boiler. The factory could use waste readily available from the factory such as bark and wood sawdust as a fuel source.

719. Energy efficiency efforts in buildings started as early as 1980s in Malaysia. The new office premises of the Ministry in Putrajaya are an example of it. It is a large GOM office building specifically designed following the energy efficiency imperatives. It is known as low-energy office. This office building has recently won the ASEAN award. It is hoped that other offices and other buildings will follow the pattern adopted by the Ministry building. These buildings have to be energy efficient by saving considerable amount of energy by all means, for example high-energy-efficient electrical equipment, good-quality insulation system. These kinds of buildings save a lot on their electricity bills. In due course of time, they prove to be energy-saving and means of regular saving of money that facilitates the recovery of the money invested in due course of time. The National Building Code has been made, which is a part of the National Uniform Building Bye-Laws. If the Code is followed properly, the energy-saving can be maximized up to 100 Kilowatt hour per meter square per annum. It has been estimated that energy-efficient buildings will cost only 10% more than the normal cost, but in the long run they will be quite beneficial to residents as well as the country.

720. In Malaysia, energy efficiency and conservation of energy are becoming a matter of priority. Towards this end, it is being suggested by the government that energy-efficient lighting, cooling and other equipment that consume comparatively less power should be preferred. The Government has come out with a plan to start air conditioners one hour late in the morning and close one hour before in the evening. People are being suggested to use fans and have a house that has good insulating walls and consume less power. The job has been started at various ministries, which has to be followed by other government buildings and private buildings. This is a welcome move. Five days week will also save electricity. The suggested strategies are not compulsory, but in future, they might be made obligatory. It will be better if for conservation of energy and energy efficiency suitable legislations are made. It is rather imperatively demanded.

721. The Ninth Malaysia Plan emphasizes that implementation of energy efficiency programmes will focus on energy-saving features in the industrial and commercial sectors. In this regard, all energy efficiency features will be encouraged to be used. Towards this end, efforts will be undertaken to introduce the Efficient Management of Electrical Energy Regulations, amend the Uniform Building By-laws and labelling of electrical appliances. To further support the implementation of renewable energy and energy efficiency initiatives, existing financial and fiscal incentives, such as Accelerated Capital Allowance, will be improved during the Plan period.

722. So far energy efficiency is concerned, there are two levels of productions and use of energy-efficient equipment like hybrid car technology, invertor technology for fridges and air conditioners, LED lighting technology – we have already noted above about their efficiency one-to-five-star certification – and educating the people to internalize these technologies in order to save energy for the country and money for themselves. These are in line with the emphasis areas of the Eleventh Malaysia Plan. Towards the end, the Home Energy Report (HER) programmes are there in place. It is designed to provide informations from time to time for consumers to learn about energy-saving techniques and devices. The first phase of the programme was completed, which had 250,000 TNB customers. They saved 13,979 MW hours. Phase two was launched in August 2017 for one year involving 450,000 customers.[175] Other important thing in this regard is development of the National Energy Efficient Master Plan (NEEMP) within the Tenth Malaysia Plan (2011–2015). It aimed and successfully achieved saving of 4,000 kilo tonnes of oil (ktoe) by 2015.

§3. Energy Efficiency Auditing

723. So as to recommend necessary changes to be made in existing buildings, government and private, an auditing system has been developed. The auditing team is acting in the country since January 2002 and has proved to be very successful in auditing government buildings. In view of this, it may be suggested that every state should have its own auditing team funded by the state government and non-governmental organizations (NGOs).

---

175. 'Nurturing an Energy Efficient Society', *Energy Malaysia*, vol. 11, 2017, pp. 18–21.

§4. Centre for Education and Training of Renewable Energy and Energy Efficiency (CETREE)

724. Centre for Education and Training of Renewable Energy and Energy Efficiency (CETREE) was created in 2000. It is located at the University Science Malaysia, Penang. Its chief objective is to bring about wariness among people at all levels, and walks of life about renewable energy sources and Energy efficiency. The target groups are students and households. CETREE in collaboration with the Ministry of Education has developed books to be taught to students. It has also developed a two credit hours course on renewable energy and energy efficiency to be offered at undergraduate level. In addition to these, for awareness of general public, mobile exhibitions are also being organized. For this purpose, a van has been developed that has all facilities that normal household can have and all these facilities are dependent only on the solar energy. It is interesting to note that the engine of the van is run by biodiesel. It is true that without proper awareness programme use of renewable sources of energy cannot be popularized. It is easier to convince people to save electricity because it will ultimately save money. The task of adopting renewable energy sources might be a bit difficult because, although it will also save money to those who resort to these sources of energy, it requires initial investment and demands after installation care for their sustained use.

§5. Fiscal Incentives to Energy Efficiency

725. The Budget 2003 introduced fiscal incentives to energy efficiency. Companies providing energy efficiency services can be granted priority status under the Promotion of Investment Act 1986. Once they get this status, they can get 70% of tax exemption up to five years. Alternatively, they qualify for investment allowances, initial and annual under the Income Tax Act 1967. On imported equipment, there will be no duty; and purchases of locally manufactured equipment are exempted from sales tax.

726. The foregoing paragraphs reveal that the Malaysian Government is making potent efforts to encourage the use of renewable energy and alternative energy sources. It is also making efforts for saving energy and conservation of energy by using more efficient and less power consuming electrical appliances. However, it has to go a long way. It has recently announced biofuel strategy, which provides a plan, proposals and incentives for promoting biodiesel, a mixture of diesel with 5% of palm oil. It has a plan to have a National Biofuel Policy and a comprehensive legislation for regulating production, storage, consumption and export of biodiesel along with incentives on manufacturing biodiesel engines and vehicles using. It will certainly be fulfilment of a long-awaited desire as the demand of biodiesel in the world is increasing at the rate of 25% per year, and Malaysia has the potential and capability to fulfil the demand substantially. It is suggested that the country should also have a comprehensive legislation on alternative source of energy and energy efficiency.

727. In view of the soaring oil price, major consumers are looking forward to dramatically increase their use of biofuels, made from sugar cane, or vegetable oils. Home-grown crops offer consuming nations the opportunity to cut hefty oil import bills, reduce GHG emissions and revitalize agricultural incomes. They could also help the country in meeting the challenges of briskly rising consumption of motor fuel, which has pushed the oil industry to the brink of its capacity and helped inflate world prices. But biofuels have a long way to go before they will register on the global markets. In 2004, world produced about 30 billion litres of this fuel from fermenting and distilling mainly sugar or corn. In oil terms, that is more than 500,000 barrels per day, 2% of the global gasoline use. Although biofuel is taking off in a number of areas, in terms of absolute volumes it is still relatively small. According to the Paris-based IEA, the real potential is in the longer term. Under the most optimistic scenario, ethanol could make up 10% of world gasoline by 2025. For that to happen, bioenergy will have to clear a number of hurdles – high cost, diminishing land and water availability and mixes policy initiatives. But the pay off would be tremendous. Assuming 1.5% annual growth in gasoline demand up to 2025, ethanol fuel consumption will rise to 3.4 million barrel per day.

728. Substantial high oil prices renewed worldwide interest in biofuel and other clean energy sources, such as solar and wind energy, as well as liquid fuel produced from gas and coal. While major consumers have given some incentives to spur development, largely to help meet Kyoto Protocol emissions targets, few have established mandatory levels that would help organic-based fuels take a significant market share. The European Union set in 2004 a non-binding target of 5.75% biofuel content by 2010, but it is likely to miss a more modest 2% target in 2005. Japan has allowed use of ethanol up to 3% in 2005. The United States, the world's top oil consumer and number two biofuel producer, is taking bigger strides as it sees domestic crops as way to curb its growing dependence on foreign oil. Brazil, the world's biggest producer of ethanol accounting for nearly half of the global output, already blends its domestic gasoline with 25% ethanol and is looking to US, Japan and India to market it. In the South East Asia, Palm oil has the potential to produce biodiesel.[176] In the world, from 1996 to 2004, world biodiesel production has increased fourfold from 591,000 tonnes annually to 2.5 million tonnes. The US produced 0.5 million tonnes, and EU countries are producing around 1.9 million tonnes. By June 2006, Malaysia will produce 60,000 tonnes per annum. It is expected to register further increase.[177]

729. Tan Sri B.C. Shekhar has highlighted the potential of *Jatropa Curcas*, which is extensively grown, even in adverse weather conditions in South Asian and South East Asian countries and mainly used as lubricant and manufacturing soap, to be a potential source for making biodiesel. According to him, it can easily be grown by villagers in Malaysia and elsewhere. It can also be grown along with palm oil plantations. He suggests to grow it at large scale and to set up two mills crushing, extracting, refining oil and ultimately making biodiesel from the oil by mixing it

176. Reuter, *New Straits times*, 10 Jun. 2005.
177. See *New Straits Times*, 27 Jun. 2005.

with diesel. The percentage of the ratio will almost be the same like making with palm oil. He also recommends for establishment of a central government agency that would purchase seeds from farmers and would be responsible for the processing of the oil as well as providing improved strains of the plants to the farmers engaged in growing it. If the dream of Tan Sri Shekhar comes true, which seems to be a possibility, it will revolutionize making biodiesel even at larger scale. At the same time it will bring livelihood to a large number of poor populations of the region.[178]

It may be noted that production and use of biodiesel and other biofuels are high now. Efforts are being made to maximize their production because they are relatively less carbon generating fuels. They are being encouraged by the governments around the world, including Malaysia. Fiscal incentives provided to them are also there in place, but they are suitably revised from time to time. (For Malaysia, see Chapter 9 infra).

178. See *New Straits Times*, 19 Mar. 2006.

Chapter 4. Renewable Energy Act 2011 (Act 725)

§1. PART I: PRELIMINARY

730. The Renewable Energy Act 2011 is a specific legislation enacted for the establishment and implementation of FiT system for renewable energy installations in Malaysia.

731. The term 'renewable energy' is defined in section 2 to mean electricity generated or produced from renewable sources. Similarly 'renewable energy installation' is defined in section 2 to mean any installation, which generates renewable energy and includes any technical facility of installation which converts mechanical, chemical, thermal or electromagnetic energy directly into electricity. This definition encapsulates the meaning of 'renewable resources' provided under the Act, which means the recurring and non-depleting indigenous resources or technology set out in the first column of the Schedule to the Act. The resources include: biogas, biomass, small hydro, solid waste, solar photovoltaic and other forms of renewable energy resources.

732. Section 2 identified the SEDA which was established under the Sustainable Energy Development Authority Act 2011 as the implementing body for the Renewable Energy Act. Under the Act, the energy generated from renewable sources are subject to FiT which means: a special tariff payable to feed-in approval holders in consideration for renewable energy generated and sold to a distribution licensee.

§2. PART II: FIT SYSTEM

733. Under law, the basic mechanism for the implementation of the Act relies on the FiT system, eligibility to participate, application procedure and condition of approval or refusal sections 2–11.

I. Establishment of the FiT

734. For eligible individual and corporate bodies who intend to invest in renewable energy installation, method of application and condition of feed-in approval is provided under the Act. The FiT system is established under section 3 with specific provision on connection point for renewable energy generated, priority energy purchase and the FiT to be paid to feed-in approval holders.

735. Pursuant to section 3(3), due consideration must be given to the renewable energy policy of the government, amount of money in the renewable energy fund, need for sustainability of renewable resources and fair competition and transparency. The provisions of the Act and its administration of the FiT are under the Authority of Sustainable Energy Development Agency.

II. Eligibility, Application and Grant or Refusal of Feed-In Approval

736. Persons or investors shall be eligible to apply for feed-in approval and participate in the FiT system if the person proposes to generate renewable energy with an installed capacity of not more than thirty megawatts or as approved by the minister (section 4). The Act refers to the minister in this regard as the minister in charge for the responsibility of matters related to the supply of electricity.

737. Application for feed-in approval may be made to the Authority pursuant to section 5 either by electronic medium or by electronic transmission. According to section 6, the Authority is empowered to request the eligible producer for additional documents at any time within specified period failure of which the application will be deemed withdrawn. The Authority has the duty to communicate to the eligible producer, a written decision grant or refusal of feed-in approval as soon as practicable (section 7(2)). Pursuant to section 3 of the Act, the written notice of grant or refusal must state the conditions of the approval or the reason for the refusal. The transferability or assignment of grant of a feed-in approval to any other person is subject to a prior written approval of the Authority (section 7(4)).

III. Condition, Variation and Revocation of Condition of Feed-In Approval

738. After approval of feed-in approval, standard conditions and special conditions may be imposed on the holder as prescribed or as the Authority thinks fit (section 8(1)). According to section 3, a feed-in approval holder who fails to comply with imposed conditions commits an offence, and upon conviction is liable to a fine not exceeding MYR 500,000 or imprisonment for a term not exceeding three years or both.

739. In furtherance of the powers of the Authority under the Act, additional conditions for feed-in approval may also be imposed, varied or revoked by the authority (section 9(1)). The procedure for additional imposition, variation or revocation of conditions of feed-in approval is identified in section 9. Before proceeding with the decision, section 9(1) of the Act mandates the authority to give a written notice on its intention with a draft copy of the imposition, variation or revocation as the case may be. The holder must be given an opportunity to make a written submission or response to the written notice within a specified period not less than thirty days.

740. The Authority shall consider the any written submission of the approval holder after the expiration of the specified period, make its decision to take no further action (section 9(3)). A written notice of such decision or no decision must be given to the feed-in approval holder as soon as practicable including the effective date of the decision.

IV. Feed-In Approval Revocation and Appeal

741. Feed-in approval may be revoked by the authorities for several reasons which are itemized in section 10, paragraphs a–f. The reasons include: feed-in approval holder's non-compliance with provision of the Act, the Electricity Supply Act 1990 and any other relevant legislation; failure to comply with approval conditions; where the approval was illegally or improperly obtained; where the holder has been convicted of an offence under the Act, the Electricity Act or any other subsidiary legislation, where a liquidation order or receiver has been appointed over approval the whole or substantial part of the holder's asset and such appointment is not annulled after sixty days; where a change of circumstance occur to defeat the entitlement of the holder under the Act.

742. Section 10(2) provides the requirement of written notice stating the intention of the Authority to revoke the feed-in approval. In addition, the holder must be given an opportunity to make a written submission within specified period, which shall not be less than thirty days. Upon the expiration of the specified period in the written notice, the Authority shall consider the written submission and decide for or against the revocation of the approval. [Section (3)]. Subsection 4 provides that the Authority must notify the holder of its decision under subsection as soon as practicable.

743. Pursuant to subsection 5, no compensation whatsoever shall be due to the approval holder where a revocation is made in accordance with section 10. In furtherance therewith, the revocation of the feed-in approval takes effect on the date stated on the written notice or thirty days from the date the notice is served on the holder (section 10(6)). Henceforth, the feed-in approval holder will immediately cease to participate in the FiT system and not entitled to FiT payments. [section 10(7)].

744. Pursuant to section 11 of the Act Appeals may be brought against grant or refusal of approval, imposition of additional conditions, variation or revocation made by the Authority under the Act within thirty days of the being notified of the any such decision. Such appeals must be made to the Minister in a prescribed manner while the Minister may confirm, reverse or vary the decision of the Authority. (Section 11(3)) The effect of decision of the Minister is final and binding (section 11(3)).

§3. Part III: Connection, Purchase and Distribution of Renewable Energy

745. Upon securing the feed-in approval from the Authority under section 7(2), approval holder must execute a renewable energy PPA, apply for connection to supply electricity through a distribution licensee and comply with priority of purchase and other technical and operational requirements stated in sections 12–15.

I. Renewable Energy PPA

746. Upon receipt of a written notice of approval under subsection 7(2), a feed-in approval holder shall enter into a renewable energy PPA with a distribution licensee (section 12(1). However, subsection 12(2) provides that a distribution licensee shall be not be obliged to enter the agreement with the approval holder where the approval holder refuses, where the Authority opines that a change of circumstances have defeated the grant of feed-in approval or it is just and reasonable for the distribution licensee not to enter into the agreement.

747. Pursuant to subsection 3, the form of the renewable energy PPA shall be as prescribed by the Authority and any deviation shall be with prior written approval of the Authority. In prescribing the form of the agreement, the Authority shall consider the renewable resources involved and the capacity of the proposed renewable energy installation (section 12(4)). After execution of the renewable energy power purchase agreement, the approval holder is required to submit the certified copy of the executed PPA to the Authority for registration (subsection 12(5)).

According to subsection 12(6), the registration of the purchase agreement is subject to the satisfaction of the Authority that the agreement is consistent with the provisions of the Act and relevant legislations. The registration gives legal effect and enforceability to the agreement (subsection 12(7)). In addition, subsection 12(8) of the Act provides that a register of PPAs shall be maintained by the Authority. The distribution licensee who contravenes the PPA is liable to a fine of not more than MYR 1,000,000 upon conviction (subsection 12(8)).

II. Connection to Supply Line

748. Upon conclusion of the renewable energy power purchase agreement under section 12, an approval holder may apply to the distribution licensee for connection of the energy installation to a supply line and the distribution licensee must connect the energy installation to a supply line connection point as may be prescribed by the Authority, Subsection 13 (1 and 2). The location of the connection point shall be determined by the distribution licensee without prejudice to the technical and operational requirements contained in section 15.

III. Priority of Purchase and Distribution

749. Pursuant to section 14(1), the Act confers priority of purchase and distribution on renewable energy installation over other non-renewable energy sources purchased and distributed within the supply line. However, the Authority may exempt the distribution licensee from this priority of purchase for certain period having regards to public safety and private safety (section 14(2)). The priority of purchase for renewable energy is protected under the Act, and contravention of the priority is an offence which attracts a fine of MYR 1 million upon conviction (section 14(2)).

IV. Technical and Operational Requirements

750. Connection to supply line by the distribution licensee pursuant to section 13 must be in accordance with governing rules technical and operational requirements laid down by the Authority with the concurrence of the commission (section 15). The distribution licensee and feed-in approval holder must comply with these rules in the connection of supply lines. The rules cover duties of both parties to the PPA; time period for compliance with specific requirements; apportionment of cost; and procedure of submitting plans, specifications and other documents. (Section 15, paragraphs a–d).

§4. Part IV: FiT

751. The rate payable to the feed-in approval holder under a renewable energy purchase agreement is administered pursuant to sections 16–22 of the Act. The FiT rate, payment, degression, readjustment and review are subject to the provision of Part IV of the Act. Similarly, the recovery of moneys under the Renewable Energy Fund (REF) is established in section 23, and administrative fee and grid parity criteria are set out in under these sections. Part II concludes with sanctions in the use of other renewable resources as an act of dishonesty.

I. Payment, Duration and Degression of FiT

752. A distribution licensee has the duty to pay a FiT to the feed-in approval holder as entered in the renewable purchase agreement based on applicable rate or as adjusted under the Act (subsection 16(1)). The criteria to be met by any energy installation for the purpose of paying a FiT rate are to be determined under the rules set out by Authority. Similarly, section 17(1) provides for a progressively reduced FiT which takes effect from the rate commencing on 1 January every year. The annual reduction or regression is subject to review and readjustment at least once every year which is aimed towards improving the overall performance of the FiT system under the Act (section 18). However, no further reduction of FiT rate after the commencement dates.

753. In reviewing the tariff, the authority must consider the provision of subsection 3(3); return on investment for the feed-in approval holder; the prevailing cost of maintaining a renewable energy installation for the particular resources; the efficiency of the energy installation based on prevailing technology and any other factor the Authority deem relevant [subsection 18(2)].

Pursuant to subsection 18(4), the Authority is required to submit recommendation for adjustment or degression of tariff rate to the Minister in charge of electricity supply for Approval. The Minister may refuse any recommendation made in the report but where it is approved the minister must revise the degression rate as soon as practicable (subsection 18 (4) &(5)). Such approved degression rate shall not apply retrogressively in respect of feed-in approval holders existing before the revised rate took effect.

II. Recovery of Money from Renewable Energy Fund, Administrative Fees and Grid Parity

754. The entitlement of a distribution licensee is recoverable from the Renewable Energy Fund established under section 23. The sum recoverable is equivalent to the difference between (a) the amount of FiTs paid by the distribution licensee to feed-in approval holders in accordance with section 16 and (b) the cost which the distribution licensee would have otherwise had to incur to generate the same amount of electricity generated by such feed-in approval holders based on prevailing displaced cost.

755. Pursuant to section 20, administrative fee is to be charged on the fund and may be payable to the distribution licensee and the Authority for administering the FiT system under the Act. Similarly, the determination of grid parity level for renewable energy installations shall be determined the duty of the Authority. Upon the energy installation achieving grid parity, the Authority must notify the feed-in approval holder and the distribution licensee (section 21(2)). The effect of this notification of the grid parity is that the entitlement to the owner of the renewable energy installation under the FiT will cease but shall instead be paid by the distribution licensee a tariff that is based on the prevailing displaced cost for the remaining duration. On the other hand, the distribution licensee shall cease to benefit from the recovered money under the Renewable Energy Fund under section 19 but shall continue to receive administrative fee under paragraph 20 (a).

III. Offences of Dishonest Use of Resources to Generate Electricity

756. According to the provision of section 22, it is an offence to generate electricity from renewable resources other than the resources stated in the feed-in approval for the purpose of receiving higher payment. This act of dishonesty attracts a fine of MYR 1,000,000 or imprisonment for a term not exceeding five years or both.

757. The prima facie evidence for this dishonest act is a written statement by an officer of the Authority stating the amount of loss to the Fund resulting in payment and the person liable for the amount of loss. (subsection 22(2)a). The person mentioned in the statement shall be requested to pay the amount of loss, otherwise the amount will be treated as a civil debt due to the Authority which shall be recoverable via civil action. Subsection 22(3) and (4).

§5. Part V: Renewable Energy Fund

758. The Act established the Renewable Energy Fund known as 'the Fund' which stipulates the allocation of electricity tariffs payable into the fund, investments made from the fund, expenditures to be charged and account keeping with respect to the fund. Sections 23–27.

I. The Fund and the Allocation of Electricity Tariff

759. Pursuant to section 23 the fund is to be administered and controlled by the Authority based on the sums provided by the parliament; sums paid by the Authority; sums paid as required under subsections 22(4), 24(1) and 24(5); sums derived from investments including interest; and all other monies lawfully received by the Authority on behalf of the fund.

760. A portion of the tariffs levied on the distribution licensee shall be allocated for payment into the Fund based on an order of the Minister published in the *Gazette*. The tariff shall be in accordance with the rates payable under section 26(1) of the Electricity Supply Act 1990. (subsection 24(1)). Following a recommendation of the Authority, the minister may revoke the order to pay the tariff allocation by an order published in a gazette. Such order must be made subject to the satisfaction of the Minister that there is sufficient fund to meet the objectives of the Act (subsection 24(6)).

761. Pursuant to (subsection 24(2)), failure of the distribution licensee to pay the allocation from electricity tariff into the fund is an offence and on conviction will be liable to a fine not exceeding MYR 1,000,000. Subsection 24(4) and (5) provides that, the prima facie evidence of the offence shall be a statement of an officer of the Authority stating the unpaid amount due and the distribution licensee liable to the Fund. The amount shall become a civil debt recoverable by the Authority through civil action against the distribution licensee.

II. Expenditure Chargeable on the Fund

762. Section 25 of the Act specifies the main purposes for which the Fund will be expended with reference to recovery for distribution licensee and administrative fee under the FiT system provided in sections 19 and 20. In addition, the Fund shall be channelled towards paying for other expenditure for carrying out the purposes of the Act.

763. The Authority is permitted under the Act to expend the Fund on investment but subject to the approval of the Minister in concurrence with the Minister of Finance (subsection 26(1)). According to (subsection 26(2)), The Authority is empowered under the Act to operate and hold money in the fund with a bank account or accounts in Malaysia as it thinks fit. Such decision to hold money in a bank must be after consultation with the Minister and the Minister of Finance.

764. The Act mandates the Authority to keep proper accounts and reports of activities of the fund must be kept and prepared for every financial year by the Authority. The specific records are statement of accounts including a balance sheet, an account of the contributions and expenditure; and statement of activities under the Fund (subsection 27(1)). The statement of account must be certified by the auditors and submitted along with the auditors' report to the Minister who shall cause them to be laid before both Houses of Parliament (subsection 27(1)).

§6. Part VI: Information Gathering Powers

765. The Act empowers the Authority to collect information for performance audit and related purposes. This power can be exercised directly by the Authority or by an appointed auditor. Whoever is in possession of documents, records or any publication may be requested to provide such information. It is punishable offence under the Act to refuse information request made by the Authority. Sections 28–35 of the Act provides for the above information gathering powers and persons applicable.

I. Performance Audit and Provision of Information

766. In order to ensure efficiency, the Authority is empowered pursuant to section 28 to carry out audit operation at any time. An Auditor may be appointed by the Authority to evaluate the compliance level of any distribution licensee and any feed-in approval holder subject to written notice of not less than twenty-four hours.

767. Beyond the distribution licensee and the feed-in approval holders, the Authority may request any other person to provide information or any document or give any evidence relevant to the performance of the Authority's function (section 29). By a written notice, the Authority is empowered to order such person to provide any of the following to an authorized officer within a specified period in such a manner specified by the authority: (a) to give information to authorized officer; (b) produce any document, physical or in electronic media; (c) make copies of any relevant document; (d) for an individual, to appear at a private hearing; (e) for body corporate or public body, to cause a competent officer to appear at a private hearing; (f) for partnership, to cause an individual who is a partner or an employee to appear at a private hearing. According to subsection 29(2), it is the duty of such person called upon to ensure that the information or documents provided are accurate, true and complete.

II. Proof of Compliance and Retention of Documents by the Authority

768. In exercising his powers, the Authority is empowered to call upon any person in writing for the purposes of providing any document and information in relation to compliance with the provision of the Act or its subsidiary legislation in any particular case (section 30).

769. Pursuant to section 31, the Authority is allowed to deal with any document provided by any persons under Part VI in such manner specified in the Act. The document may remain in the possession of the authority for as long as necessary, and a certified true copy may be supplied to the person who provides as soon as practicable (subsection 31(2)). The provider of the document is permitted to inspect, take extract or make copies of the original until the certified copy is supplied by the Authority (subsection 31(4)). When the certified copy is supplied, it is deemed as the original for the purposes evidence in courts and tribunals (subsection 31(3)). The retention of the original document made under subsection 31()1 may be reversed by the Authority where it is satisfied that it is no longer necessary.

III. Access to Records, Record or Information and Publication

770. An Authority may at any time request information by writing a notice and appointing an authorized officer or auditor to access the records; sections 32(1) provides that such person must grant access to records for the purposes of carrying out the functions of the Authority under the Act. Non-compliance with this provision is an offence, which attracts a fine not exceeding MYR 200,000.

771. Section 33 provides that the record of all information or documents received in compliance with subsection 29(1) shall be maintained by the Authority and may be made available to the public. Before the Authority can publish any information, considerations must be given to the commercial interest of the parties (subsection 34(2)). Similarly, The publication will not be published if it is likely to prejudice the fair trial of a person or involve unreasonable disclosure of personal information about an individual including deceased persons (subsection 34(3) paragraphs a and b). Section 35 provides a fine not exceeding MYR 50,000 or imprisonment for a term not exceeding six month or both for non-compliance with the general orders made by the Authority under Part VI.

§7. PART VII: ENFORCEMENT

772. The nature of Enforcement of the general provision of Act, its procedures, personnel, investigative powers, search and seizures with or without warrant have been extensively provided for under Part VII, that is sections 36 to section 55. Access to Computerized data, admissibility of defective warrant and handling of seized things are provided for under the Act notwithstanding the provision of Criminal Procedure Code [Act 593]. In addition, provision with respect to examination and admissibility of evidence obtained during enforcement cost of holding equipment and obstruction of enforcement are detailed in this part including compoundable offences and prosecutorial powers under the Act.

I. Authorized Officer and Investigative Powers

773. In accordance with section 36(1) and (2) of the Act, power of enforcement may be exercised by any public officer, officer of the Authority or the commission upon a written authority by the Minister. Such authorized officer is deemed to be a public servant as envisaged under the Penal Code [Act 574]. For the purposes of enforcement, each officer must carry an authority card signed by the Chief Executive Officer of the Authority [section 37(1)]. Subsection 37(2) provides that the officer must produce the card upon demand by person against whom the enforcement is being executed.

774. Section 38(1) provides for the investigative powers of authorized officers over activities of the feed-in approval, distribution licensee or other persons in relation to an offence under the Act. Any authorized officer may undertake any powers in relation to police investigation excluding arrest without warrant given under the Criminal Procedure Act [section 38(1)].

II. Search, Seizure, Warrants and Computerized Data

775. Pursuant to section 39(1), search of premises may be undertaken with or without assistance or by force subject to a warrant issued by a Magistrate. An officer named in the warrant may enter the premises at night or by day to search for and seize any evidence or thing. Postal article, telegram or any document in custody of postal or telegraph authority requires a warrant issued by the High Court.

776. Subsection 39(2) provides that the warrant issued by the Magistrate court authorizes the officer to search persons or seize any item believed to contain evidence of any offence. The items may include the following: copies of books, accounts or documents including computerized data and any equipment or instrument. Subsection 39(2) provides that items, which could not be seized by reason of its nature, size and amount, may be sealed by the seizing officer. Unlawfully breaking or tampering with the seal is an offence, which attracts a fine not exceeding MYR 50,000 or imprisonment for a term not exceeding six months (Subsection 39(7)).

777. Search of the premises includes search of any persons who is in or on the premises (section 39(3)). Subsection 39(4) permits the authorized officer to take possession, seize or place in safe custody all things, which may be evidence of the offence other than the necessary clothing found upon the person. Search of persons must be conducted with regards to decency by persons of same gender (section 39(5)).

778. Pursuant to section 42, any defect, mistake or omission in the warrant does not affect the admissibility in evidence of documents or equipment seized during the execution. Section 40 provides an exception to search and seizure with warrant under section 39. Search and seizure may be undertaken by an authorized officer where he has reason to believe that delay in obtaining warrant would adversely affect evidence of the commission of an offence. In other words, the evidence is likely to be removed, damaged or tampered with before the issuance of a warrant.

779. According to section 41, an authorized officer conducting a search under section 39 or 40 must be given access to computerized data. Subsection 41(2) defines access to include 'necessary password, encryption code, decryption code, software or hardware and any other means', and the meaning assigned under the Computer Crimes Act 1997 [Act 563].

III. List of Things and Release of Things Seized

780. Where seizure of things is made under this Act, the seizing officer is required under subsection 43(1) to prepare a list of things seized and place they are respectively found. A copy of the list must be signed by the occupier of the premises or his agent at the premises. In case of unoccupied premises a list of things seized must be conspicuously posted on the premises (section 43(2)).

781. Release of things seized may be made at any time by the authorized officer who effected the seizure if he is satisfied that the seized items is not required for the purpose of any proceedings under the Act. The Federal government, the Authority or any person shall not be liable to any proceeding by any person if the seizure and release of things had been effected in good faith (section 44(1)).

782. Section 44(2) further provides that within seven days of the release, a record stating the release and the details circumstance and the reason must be made by the authorized officer. A copy of the record must be sent to the Public Prosecutor and the Inspector General of Police.

IV. Attendance, Summons, Examination of Persons and Admissibility of Statements

783. The Act empowers an authorized officer to require the attendance of any person who appears to be acquainted with the circumstance of the case (section 45(1)). Subsection 45(2) provides where a person refuses to attend, the officer may report to the Magistrate who issues summons to secure the attendance of such person.

784. Any person acquainted with the investigation may be orally examined by the officer while the person is legally bound to answer all questions relating to such case (sections 46(1)). Pursuant to subsection 46(4), an authorized officer must inform the person about answers which may expose the person to criminal charge, penalty or forfeiture and the legal duty to make true statement as provided in subsections subsection 46(2) and (3). Sections 46(5) provide the validation of statement made under this circumstance. The statement must be reduced into writing, read to the maker and given opportunity to make corrections. It must be signed or affixed with thumbprint by the person who made it.

785. Any written or oral statement made by a person charged with an offence under the Act or its subsidiary legislation shall be admissible in evidence during trial. Such statement may also be used in cross-examination and for the purpose of impeaching a witness (section 47(1)). According to section 47(2), such statement shall be inadmissible where it is a result of threat, inducement or promise from a person in authority with reference to the proceeding, or where the person made the statement after arrest and the court is satisfied that the person was cautioned. However, statements made before the person is cautioned shall not be rendered inadmissible in evidence but the caution can be administered as soon as possible (section 47(3)). The caution does not bind a person accused of an offence under the Act to answer any question relating to the case (section 47(4)). In other words he may refuse to answer.

786. Pursuant to section 48 of the Act, upon completion of investigation, the authorized officer is enjoined to immediately handover the all information relating to the offence to a police officer in charge of a police station who may arrest persons who committed an offence under the Act.

V. Holding of Equipment and Damages Recoverable

787. Section 49 provides that the cost of holding seized items and equipment in the custody shall be borne by the person found to have committed an offence. This cost shall be a recoverable debt due to the government. Similarly, no proceeding before any court shall grant entitlement, cost or damages or other relief with respect to any equipment or items seized except such seizure was made without reasonable cause (section 50).

VI. Obstruction of Enforcement, Compounding Offences and Prosecutorial Powers

788. Obstruction of an authorized officer in the execution of any duty imposed under the Act is an offence (section 51). Upon conviction, such person will be liable to a fine not exceeding MYR 2,00,000 of imprisonment for a term not exceeding two years. The obstruction by persons may include: denying an authorized officer access to any premises; assault, hinder or delay the entry of authorized officer and refusal to give any information relating to an offence or suspected offence which he has in his knowledge (section 51 paragraphs a–c). Section 52 of the Act grants additional powers to the authorized officer to require the production of records, accounts, computerized data kept by the feed-in approval and to require the production of any identification document from any person.

789. Subsection 53(1) provides that offences under the Act may be made compoundable through a regulation made by the Minister. In furtherance of the regulation, the Authority may with the consent of the Public Prosecutor compound any offence committed under the Act. A written offer may be made to the person suspected to have committed the offence by paying to the Authority an amount not exceeding fifty per centum of the maximum fine for that offence within a specified period stated in the order (section 53(2)). Such offer may be made at any time after the offence has been committed and before the prosecution has been instituted. Failing to pay the offer within the specified period, the Authority may commence prosecution against the person (section 53(3)). In addition subsection 53(5) provides that all sums of money received under section 53 must be paid to the Federal Consolidated Fund.

VII. Prosecutorial Powers

790. Section 54 provides that the prosecution of any offence under the Act must be made either by or with the consent in writing of the Public Prosecutor. The section further provides for the situation where the offence was committed by an individual or corporate body. Where a body corporate commits an offence under the Act, any person responsible for the management of the body corporate for the time being, that is the director, chief executive officer, chief operating officer, manager secretary, may be charged. Such officers may be charged severally, jointly in the same proceeding with the body corporate; and if found guilty, such persons shall be deemed guilty as well (section 55(1) paragraphs a and b). Furthermore, any person charged may prove that the offence was either committed without his knowledge, consent or connivance, and that he had taken all reasonable precautions and due diligence to prevent the commission of the offence.

791. Subsection 55(2) confers the liability for an offence committed by an agent and employee upon the principal or employer. The punishment or penalty of an employer or principal under the Act shall be the same with the employee or agent where such act was committed in the course of his employment; agent must be acting on behalf of that person; or in the course of the agent in the course of his employment by his agent or on behalf of the agent acting on behalf of that person (section 53(3)).

§8. Part VIII: General

792. Part VIII of the Act provides for general provisions on issues such as FiT performance reporting, compliance with other laws, directions by the Authority, powers to make regulations, powers to make rule and penalties for subsidiary legislation among other matters. (sections 56–63).

I. Report Implementation and Performance of FiT System

793. Section 56(1) mandates the Authority to monitor the implementation and performance of FiT system and submit a report to the Minister at the end of each financial year. In addition, pursuant to subsection 56(4), the Authority is mandated to publish the report in a manner it deems appropriate as soon as practicable. The report shall be based on indicators deemed appropriate by the authority (subsection 56(2)). Subsection 56(3) specifically itemized the matters to be considered in the report which include: operations and administration of the Act; the applicable FiT and degression rates; the Fund; any non-compliance by any person; grant or revocation of feed-in approval; deficiencies in the scope and operation of the Act; and other matters the minister thinks necessary.

II. Compliance with All Other Laws and Directions by the Authority

794. A feed-in approval holder is expected to comply with the provision of the electricity Supply Act 1990 and its subsidiary legislation. In other words, the Act did not exempt approval holders form the Electricity Supply Act 1990 (section 57). Section 58(1) provides that the authority is required to issue directions to any person on the compliance with any condition of the feed-in approval including remedying any breach.

795. The issuance of any direction by the authority must follow the procedure set out in subsections (2), (3), (4), (5), (7), (8) and (9). Such directions issued under the Act must be via a notice written to the person regarding the compliance required with a grant of opportunity to respond in writing within a specified time on the reasons for the conduct. The decision of the Authority shall consider the reason provided by the person in its decision (section 58(3) and (4)). In furtherance of the decision, a written notice containing the direction will be issued as soon as practicable ensuring that the person should take a specified action or desist from further contravention of the condition (section 58(5)).

796. The effective date of any direction issued under part viii shall be the date of registration or a date specified in the direction while the expiration is on a date specified in the written notice or until revoked (section 58(8) and 9). The revocation or variation of any direction must follow the procedures set in subsections (2), (3), (4), (5), (7), (8) and (9). Section 58(6) provides that any person in respect of which a direction is issued must comply, failure to comply is an offence, on conviction, be liable to a fine not exceeding MYR 200,000 or a term of imprisonment not exceeding two years or both (section 58(6)).

797. The Act provides that any direction, variation or revocation made under this section must be maintained in a register (section 58(12)). Pursuant to section 59, any person may inspect or make a copy of, or extract of the register upon payment of a specified fee.

III. Powers of Minister to Make Regulation and Powers of Authority to Make Rules

798. The powers to make regulations and rules under the Act reside in the hands of the Minister and the Authority respectively sections 60 and 61. The specific purposes and prescriptions for regulations made by the minister are mentioned in section 60 para a-e *vis-à-vis*: criteria for particular renewable energy installation; matters relating to the Fund; compoundable offences and the forms, method and procedures to be used; manner of appeal and all other matters that are necessary for giving effect to the Act.

799. Similarly, the authority may make rules with respect to the following items mentioned under section 61, paragraph a-g *vis-à-vis:* application of feed-in approvals, eligibility, manner of application and standard conditions; form and substance of PPAs; technical and operational requirements; criteria for receiving a particular feed-in approval rate; procedures of recovery of moneys from the Fund and the methods of calculation of amount payable to the distribution licensee; fees payable under the Act; and any other matter expressly assigned to the Authority.

800. Any subsidiary legislation, direction, regulation, rules made under this Act may provide for penalties of fines not exceeding MYR 300,000 or imprisonment for a term not exceeding three years or both. Schedules in the Act may be amended by the Minister by order published in the *Gazette.*

§9. Part VIII: Savings and Transition

801. This part provides certain provision which applies to existing renewable energy installations and licensees prior to the coming into force of this Act.

I. Existing Renewable Energy Generators and Existing Licences

802. According to section 64, there are two options available to an eligible producer who has executed an agreement with a distribution licensee prior to the coming into operation of this Act. The first option is to apply to participate in the FiT system, terminate the agreement with the consent to the licensee and enter into a new PPA under this Act.

803. The second option is for the continuation of the existing agreement and not participation in the FiT system. The effect of termination of the agreement and applying to participate in the FiT system is that sections 5, 6, 7, 8, 9, 10 and 11 will apply *mutatis mutandis* to the eligible producer based on the FiT system (section 64(2)). Upon grant of the feed-in approval to the eligible producer, Parts III and IV of the Act shall apply *mutatis mutandis* to the approval holder except the reduction of the effective period from the time the energy installation had generated electricity for commercial sale to the distribution licensee before the grant of approval.

804. Pursuant to section 65, the duration of licence issued under section 9 of the Electricity Act 1990 shall not be reduced or extended by any provision in this Act.

Chapter 5. Sustainable Energy Development Authority Act 2011 (Act 726)

§1. Part I: Preliminary

805. The Renewable Energy Act 2011 is a specific legislation enacted for the establishment of the SEDA Malaysia, its functions, powers and related matters. Section 2 of the Act provides legal interpretation for certain terms used in the legislation. Such terms include but not restricted to: sustainable energy, renewable energy, FiT, Authority among others. The Act creates an interface with the Renewable Energy Act 2011 under section 2, which provides that for the FiT, renewable energy and sustainable energy laws subject to this Act, the Renewable Energy Act 2011 and any legislation or subsidiary legislation under which the Authority is to perform its function. This provision is in tandem with the provision of section 2 Renewable Energy Act 2011, which identified the SEDA known as 'the Authority' for implementing the provisions of Renewable Energy Act.

§2. Part II: The Authority

806. The establishment of the SEDA Malaysia, its legal status, common seal and membership is provided under Part II of the Act (sections 3s–5). Other important provisions include: the powers of the minister, appointment of member, tenure, remuneration, and revocation, vacation of office and disclosure of interest. (Sections 6–12).

I. Establishment of the Authority and Common Seal

807. The SEDA Malaysia or the Authority is established as a body corporate pursuant to section 3(1) of the Act. The Authority has perpetual succession, common seal and may sue or be sued in its corporate name. (Section 3(2) and (3)). In addition, the Authority may enter into contracts, acquire, hold, convey, mortgage or reassign movable or immovable properties (section 3(4)).

808. According to section 4, the common seal of the Authority shall bear any device approved by the Authority and may as altered or made anew from time to time. The common seal shall be proof of valid execution of deeds, documents or any other instrument of the Authority (Subsection 4(4)). The safe keeping and custody of the common seal shall be with the Chairman or any person so authorized while authentication is required by either the Chairman or such person so authorized by the Chairman in writing. Subsection 4(6) provides that the common seal shall be officially and judicially noticed.

II. Membership of the Authority and Tenure of Office

809. The membership of the Authority, appointments and composition are determined under sections 5 of the Act. Such persons to be appointed by the Minister include the Chairman, 2 to 4 representatives of the federal government, 3 to 5 other members and the Chief Executive Officer. The persons appointed by the minister must be qualified by experience, capacity in sustainable energy, finance, and engineering or possess special knowledge suitable for the appointment or academic qualifications. (Section 5(2)). Where the office of the Chairman is vacant, the Chairman is absent or unable to perform the duties of his office, section 6 of the Act empowers the Minister to appoint any member of the Authority temporarily.

810. The provision of the schedules shall apply to members of the Authority as amended by the minister and published in the *Gazette* (section 7). Pursuant to section 8 of the Act, any member of the Authority who holds any office or employment whether or not the office is remunerated shall require the Minister's written approval to hold another office. The tenure of office for members of the Authority is provided pursuant to section 9, which provides that members shall not exceed a term of two years. However, such member may be reappointed for a maximum period of three consecutive terms. Section 9(2) excludes the Chief executive Officer from the application of section 9.

III. Remuneration, Allowances, Revocation and Vacation of Office

811. According to section 10 of the Act, the remuneration and allowance of the Chairman and the allowances for other members of the Authority have to be determined by the Ministers. However, this specific provision is not applicable to the Chief Executive Officer (section 10(3)). With respect to revocation and resignation of appointments section 11 provides that the Minister may revoke the appointment of any member of the Authority other than the Chief Executive Officer while any member of the Authority other than the Chief Executive officer may resign his appointment at any time subject to giving a written notice to the Minister.

812. Vacation of office and similar circumstances of a member of the Authority are provided under section 12 of the Act. Subsection 12(1) provides the circumstances where member dies and has been convicted on a charge of fraud or dishonesty, offence of corruption or under section 45 or any other offence which is punishable by imprisonment exceeding two years. Other circumstances, which lead to vacation of office include: bankruptcy; unsound mind or incapability to discharge his duties. With respect to the Chairman and other members of the Authority, para (e) and (f) respectively provides that the absence for three consecutive meetings of the Authority without leave of the Minister will amount to vacation of office while for other members, absence from three consecutive meetings without the leave of the Chairman applies. Similarly, the acceptance of resignation or a revocation of appointment by the Minister implies vacancy of office for both any member of the Authority and the Chairman (section 12(1) paragraphs g and h).

IV. Committees and Disclosure of Interests

813. The establishment of committees, composition and membership, its mode of operation, records and allowances and among others is provided under section 13 of the Act. Similarly, the Act authorizes the disclosure of direct or indirect interest of any member of the Authority or any committee pursuant to section 14.

814. Where considered expedient or necessary, section 13(1) empowers the Authority to establish a committee to assist in performing its functions. Any of the members of the Authority may be elected as the chairman while other persons may be appointed as member of any committee (subsection 13(2) and (3)). Pursuant to subsection 13(3) and (4), the tenure of any member of a committee shall be specified in the appointment letter and subject to reappointment. Any appointment of committee member may be revoked or the member may resign at any time after a written notice to the chairman of the committee. (subsection 13(5) and (6)). Although Subsection 7 provides that a committee may regulate its own procedure, such procedures must be in accordance with any directions given by the Authority pursuant to subsection 9. The constitution of any committee may be altered by the Authority.

815. Meetings and proceedings of a committee are subject to procedures mentioned in subsections 13(10)–(16). The venue of any committee meetings shall be as determined by the chairman of the committee while minutes of all meetings must be signed, kept in proper form and submitted to the Authority as soon as practicable subsection (10) and (11). Such minute of meeting is admissible in legal proceedings as evidence without further proof only if duly signed. Pursuant to subsection 13, a meeting can be deemed to be duly convened and all members duly qualified to act where the minute is made in accordance with this section.

816. Any person may be invited to a committee meeting for advisory purposes only and such invited person is not entitled to vote at such meeting (subsection 13(14)). Pursuant to subsection 15, the allowance and other expenses may be paid to the invited person as determined by the Authority. An act done or proceedings under this Act shall not be defeated or questioned on the basis of vacancy, defective membership or constitution of a committee; or defect or omission not affecting the merit of the case (subsection 13(14)). Subsection 13(15) provides for the payment of allowances and expenses to any invitee as may be determined by the Authority.

817. Section 14(1) provides that members of the Authority or any of its committee shall disclose any direct or indirect interest in relation to any discussion of the Authority or committee. Such interest which may be of himself, member of his family or associates must be disclosed and recorded in the minutes of meeting of the committee (section 14(2)). Member of his family and associate are as defined under subsection 14(5). The effects of the disclosure are that the member shall not be present in any discussion about the matter and shall be disregarded for the purpose of constituting a quorum of the meeting (section 14(2)(a) and b).

818. According to subsection 14(3), any member who fails to disclose interest pursuant to the Act upon conviction shall be liable to a fine not exceeding MYR 100,000 or imprisonment for a term not exceeding two years or both. In addition, failure to disclose interest by any member shall not invalidate any act or proceeding of the Authority or committee (section 14(4)).

§3. Part III: Functions and Powers of the Authority

819. Part III of the Act provides for the functions of the Authority, its powers, subsidiary legislation, directions by the Minister, report and returns, and powers to participate or establish corporate bodies (sections 15 and 21).

I. Establishment of the Authority and Common Seal

820. Pursuant to section 15 of the Act, the functions of the Authority are as conferred on it under all sustainable energy laws in Malaysia. In addition, specific functions are itemized under para a to l. The functions are as follows:

(a) advise the Minister and government on matters relating to sustainable energy, including recommendations on policies, laws and actions;
(b) promote and implement the national policy objectives for renewable energy;
(c) promote, stimulate, facilitate and develop sustainable energy;
(d) implement, manage, monitor and review the FiT system, including to carry out investigations, collect, record and maintain data, information and statistics concerning the FiT system;
(e) implement sustainable energy laws and to recommend reform;
(f) promote private sector investment in the sustainable energy sector, recommend and fiscal incentives applicable to such investment;
(g) carry out or conduct of researches, assessments, studies and advisory services, collate, analyse and publish information, statistics and factors influencing or relevant to the development of sustainable energy, and to disseminate such;
(h) conduct, promote and support, in such manner as the Authority deems fit, research and innovation activities relating to sustainable energy;
(i) conduct, promote and support, programmes relating to the development of human resources and capacity building the sector;
(j) implement measures to promote public participation and to improve public awareness on matters relating to sustainable energy;
(k) act as a focal point to assist the Minister on matters relating to sustainable energy and climate change matters relating to energy; and
(l) any other function conferred by or under or supplemental, incidental to any sustainable energy law or any functions specified in this section.

II. Powers and Additional Functions of the Authority

821. Sections 16 and 17 of the Act specify the powers and additional functions of the Authority respectively. Generally, the Authority shall have powers expedient and necessary in connection with the performance of its function under the sustainable energy laws (subsection 16(1)). Subsection 16(2) paragraphs a–h specifically itemize powers of the Authority without prejudice to the general powers in subsection (1). The powers are as follows:

(a) carry on all activities which appears to the Authority to be requisite, advantageous or convenient with the performance of its functions;
(b) cooperate or act in association with any Government Entity, any company or corporation, or any body or person, whether local or foreign;
(c) directly or indirectly approach, liaise with, and disseminate relevant information to, any investor or potential investor or any financier or potential financier, whether local or foreign in the sustainable energy sector in Malaysia;
(d) appoint such agents, experts or consultants as it may deem fit for the purpose of performing its functions;
(e) impose fees, costs or any other charges as it deems fit for services rendered by it;
(f) formulate and implement human resource development and funding and cooperation programmes for the proper and effective performance of its functions;
(g) grant loans and scholarships to employees of the Authority for such purposes as may be approved by the Minister; and
(h) do anything incidental to any of its functions and powers.

822. Pursuant to section 17(1), the Act imposes additional functions on the Authority to undertake and exercise powers and expend moneys for such purposes as the Federal Government may assign. In so doing, the Authority shall be deemed to be fulfilling the purposes of the Act. Furthermore, the Authority must apply the Act in expending and undertaking such functions and exercising such powers. Subsection 2 provides the money expended for purposes mentioned under subsection 1 which shall be kept separate from the Fund and the renewable Energy Fund in accordance with the Renewable energy Act 2011.

III. Delegation of Authority's Functions and Subsidiary Powers

823. Section 18(1) provides that the powers and functions of the Authority may be delegated in writing to the Chairman; a member of the Authority; a committee; or an employee of the Authority. However, such powers to borrow money raise loans or to make subsidiary legislation may not be delegated. On the other hand, such delegation does not preclude the Authority from exercising at any time of the delegated functions or powers (subsection 18(5)). Without prejudice to subsection 1, the Authority may delegate a member of the Authority or committee or an employee to sanction expenditure from the Fund or any other moneys under the control of the Authority up to such limit specified by the Authority (subsection 18(2)).

824. According to subsection 18(3), any member so delegated shall be bound by all conditions and restrictions, requirements, procedures and matters imposed and specified by the Authority. In addition, such delegated function or power shall be performed and exercised in the name and on behalf of the Authority (subsection 18(5)).

IV. Direction by Minister, Reports and Accounts, and Participation in Bodies Corporate

825. The role of the Minister in the Authority, reports and accounting processes and participation of the Authority in bodies corporate are provided for under sections 19, 20 and 21 of the Act. Pursuant to section 19(1) and (2), the Authority shall be responsible to the Minister who may give directions on general character consistent with the provisions of the sustainable energy laws while the Authority shall give effect to such directions.

826. In furtherance of the responsibility of the Authority to the Minister, section 20(1) provides that the Authority shall furnish the Minister with returns, reports, accounts and information with respect to its finances and activities as the Minister may require or direct. In addition, after the end of every financial year, the Authority shall cause a report of activities and dealings of the preceding financial year to be transmitted to the Minister and, if so directed by the Minister, to any public authority (section 20(2)).

827. According to section 20(3), the form and content of the reports, returns, accounts and information shall be relating to the proceedings and policy of the Authority as may be specified by the Minister from time to time. Section 21 provides that the Authority with the approval of the Minister and the concurrence of the Minister of Finance may establish and participate in any body corporate to carry out the management on behalf of the Authority any project, scheme or enterprise.

§4. Part IV: Employees of the Authority

828. Part IV of the Act provides for the appointment by the Minister of any person to serve as the Chief Executive Officer of the Authority. It also specifies his responsibilities, duties and remuneration. Similarly, the appointment of other employees is also provided along with their conditions of service, retirement benefits, loans and scholarships among other regulations

I. The Chief Executive Officer, Responsibilities and Duties

829. Section 22 of the Act specifically provides for the appointment and responsibilities of the Chief Executive Officer of the Authority. Subsection 1 authorizes the Minister to appoint the CEO and determine the terms and conditions, remuneration and allowances of such appointment. The person to be appointed must possess capacity, professionalism and experience in matters related to sustainable energy, finance, engineering, business or administration, or possess special knowledge, experience or academic qualification in the opinion of the Minister (section 22(2)). According to subsection 7 the CEO shall be an employee of the Authority.

830. Pursuant to subsection 22(3) to (5), the responsibilities and duties of the CEO include the overall administration and management of the day-to-day affairs of the Authority and general control of the employees and other functions that the Authority may determine. In performing his duties, the CEO must take cognizance of the general authority and direction of the Authority (section 22(6)). Section 23 of the Act provides for circumstance where the Minister may appoint any employee of the Authority to act as the Chief Executive officer. Para (a) to (c) identified the period as when the office of the CEO is vacant; the CEO is absent from duty or from Malaysia; or any other reason where the CEO is unable to perform the duties of his office.

II. Other Employees of the Authority, Condition of Service, Retirement, Loans and Adoption of Regulations

831. Pursuant to section 24 the Authority may appoint such number of employees as the Authority think necessary and upon terms considered appropriate. The conditions of service for such employees shall be as determined by the Minister (section 25). Similarly, section 26 provides for a situation where an employees' retirement benefits, pensions, gratuities and other allowances may be arranged and determined by the Authority.

832. In the same vein, section 27 empowers the Authority to grant loans, advances and scholarships to its employees for purposes and terms which the Authority may determine. In exercising its powers on any matter under Part IV, the Authority may adopt any government rules, regulation, circulars, directives by the Federal government with such modifications as it deems fit.

§5. Part V: Finance

833. Part V of the Act provides for the establishment of the 'Sustainable Energy Development Authority Fund' under the control and administration of the Authority. Sections 29–38 of the Act include matters in relation to expenditure to be charged on the Fund, conservation of the Fund, borrowing powers, contracts limitation, investment, financial procedure, accounts and reports of the Fund.

I. The SEDA Fund

834. Pursuant to section 29(1) of the Act, the SEDA Fund is established to be administered and controlled by the Authority. The composition of the Fund is provided under subsection 29(2) as follows:

(a) such sums as may be provided by the Parliament for the purposes of this Act from time to time;
(b) fees, costs, levies, contributions and other charges imposed by or payable to the Authority;
(c) moneys derived as income from investments by the Authority;
(d) moneys derived from the sale, disposal, lease or hire, or any other dealing with, any property, mortgage, charge or debenture vested in or acquired by the Authority;
(e) all moneys earned from consultancy and advisory services and any other services provided by the Authority;
(f) sums borrowed by the Authority under section 33;
(g) such sums as may be paid to the Authority from time to time for loans made by the Authority;
(h) moneys earned by the operation of any project, scheme or enterprise financed from the Fund;
(i) donations and contributions received from within or outside Malaysia;
(j) other sums or property which may in any manner become payable to or vested in the Authority in respect of any matter incidental to its functions, powers and duties; and
(k) other moneys lawfully received by the Authority.

835. In relation to financial limit specified under paragraph (2)(b), subsection 29(3) provides that any moneys in excess of the financial requirement of the Authority may be paid into the Federal Consolidated Fund.

II. Expenditure to Be Charged on the Fund

836. Section 30 provides for the purposes of expending the Fund. Paragraph a to g of the section provides the purposes as follows:

(a) paying any expenditure lawfully incurred by the Authority but excluding expenditure to be paid from the Renewable Energy Fund pursuant to the Renewable Energy Act 2011;
(b) paying for the remuneration, allowances and other expenses of the members of the Authority, members of the committees and employees of the Authority, including the granting of loans, scholarships and advances, retirement benefits, medical benefits, pensions, gratuities and other allowances;
(c) paying any other expenses, costs or expenditure in relation to the procurement of goods and services, including the engagement of consultants, legal fees and costs and other fees and costs properly incurred or accepted by the Authority in

the performance of its functions or the exercise of its powers under the sustainable energy laws, but excluding expenditure to be paid from the Renewable Energy Fund pursuant to the Renewable Energy Act 2011;

(d) purchasing or hiring plant, equipment, machinery and materials, acquiring land and other assets, and erecting buildings, and carrying out any other works and undertakings in the performance of its functions or the exercise of its powers under the sustainable energy laws;

(e) repaying any moneys borrowed under section 33 and the interest due on the borrowed moneys;

(f) investment under section 34; and

(g) generally paying any expenses for carrying into effect the provisions of this Act.

III. Conservation of the Fund, Bank Accounts, Power to Borrow

837. According section 31 of the Act, it is the responsibility of the Authority to conserve the Fund through the exercise of its powers and functions. Similarly, the revenues of the Authority must be secured sufficiently to meet all sums chargeable to its revenue account. In relation to the Fund, the Authority shall maintain an account or accounts with such banks in Malaysia which shall be managed in such a manner and purpose as the Authority may authorize (section 32).

Pursuant to section 32, the Authority may borrow money to meet its obligations or discharge its duties subject to in such forms and terms as may be approved by the Minister with the concurrence of the Minister of Finance.

IV. Investment, Limitation on Contracts and Financial Procedure

838. Under section 34 of the Act, the Authority may invest moneys of Authority in so far such moneys are not immediately required to be expended. Such investment must be made in the manner as may be approved by the Minister with the concurrence of the Minister of Finance. Section 35 places financial limits on contracts which the Authority may enter. Without the approval of the Minister and the concurrence of the Minister of Finance, the Authority is prohibited from entering into any contract, which the Authority is to pay or receive an amount exceeding MYR 10 million.

However, section 36 provides that the general financial procedure of the Authority shall be subject to this Act and the approval of the Minister.

V. Financial Year, Accounts and Reports

839. Section 37 specifies the financial year of the Authority, which will begin on 1 January and ends on 31 December of each year. Consequently, the Authority shall prepare a reports of its financial activities and accounts at the end of each financial year: a statement of account and a report of its activities section 38(1)(a) and (b). Subsection 38(3) provides that the Statutory Bodies (Account and Annual Reports) Act 1980 [*Act 240*] shall apply to the Authority. Subsection 38(3) provides that the copies of the statement of account shall be certified by the auditors while the auditor's report and a copy of activities shall be sent as soon as possible to the Minister and the minister shall lay same before both Houses of Parliament.

§6. Part VI: General Provisions

840. The general miscellaneous provisions of the Authority are provided under Part VI of the Act. As contained in sections 39–49, matters covered in this part include symbols of the Authority, unauthorized modification of information, prosecution, obligation of secrecy, application of the Public Authorities Protection Act, powers to make regulations among others.

I. Restriction, Symbol and Representation of the Authority

841. Pursuant to section 39(1) of the Act, the Authority shall have the exclusive right to create a symbol or representation to be displayed in connection with its activities and affairs. According to subsection 2, such symbol must be published in the *Gazette*. Any person who uses or creates a symbol in semblance of the Authority with the likelihood to deceive or cause confusion commits an offence which upon conviction is liable to a fine not exceeding MYR 200,000 or imprisonment for a term not exceeding two years or both (section 39(3)).

II. Unauthorized Modification of Information and Prosecution

842. The Act prohibits any unauthorized modification of any information, statistics or other data in the possession or control of the Authority. Any person who does this will be guilty of an offence and upon conviction liable to a fine not exceeding MYR 300,000 (section 40(1)). Similarly, subsection 40(2) also prohibits any act to cause unauthorized modification whether in electronic form or otherwise with the intention of causing injury as defined in the Penal Code [*Act 574*], upon conviction will be liable to a fine not exceeding MYR 500,000 or to imprisonment for a term not exceeding three years or both.

843. Subsection 40(3) specifies that the section applies irrespective of the fact that the unauthorized action is not directed towards any particular information, data or statistic, whether permanent or merely temporary, or method which caused the modification (para a to b).

The prosecution of any offence under this Act shall not be instituted without the written consent to the Public Prosecutor.

III. Public Servant, Protection Against Legal Proceedings and Public Protection Act 1948

844. In the discharge of their duties, all members, employees, agents of the Authority or any of its committees shall be deemed to be public servants within the meaning of the Penal Code (section 42). Section 43 of the Act protects the Authority and certain persons from prosecution, action, suit or proceedings in any court with respect of any act, neglect, omission or default committed in good faith. Such persons include the following:

(a) the Minister;
(b) the Authority;
(c) any member of the Authority, any member of a committee or any employee or agent of the Authority; or
(d) any other person lawfully acting on behalf of the Authority.

845. According to section 44, the Public Authorities Protection Act 1948 shall apply to any action, suit or proceedings against the Authority, a member of a committee and an employee or agent of the Authority in respect of any act, neglect or default in his capacity.

IV. Obligation of Secrecy and Representation in Civil Proceedings

846. Pursuant to section 45(1), it is prohibited to disclose any information relating to the affairs of the Authority, except for any civil or criminal proceeding under any written law or where authorized by the Authority. This obligation to secrecy applies to any member of the Authority or any of its committee during or after a meeting or after his tenure of office (para. a). In addition, any person who has any means of access to information or document relating to the affairs of Authority.

847. Any person who contravenes the secrecy obligation commits an offence and is liable upon conviction to imprisonment not exceeding six months or to a fine not exceeding MYR 50,000 or both.

848. The representation of the Authority in civil proceedings is provided for under section 46 of the Act notwithstanding any other written law. The Act specifies that any person may be authorized on behalf of the Authority for the purpose of instituting a proceeding or make appearances, representations and applications in any civil proceedings by or against the Authority, and any other civil proceedings in which the Authority is entitled to be represented.

V. Power to Make Regulations and Power to Employ

849. The authority has the power to make regulation where expedient or necessary for the purpose of giving full effect to the provisions of the Act (section 47). In addition, in the performance of its functions and discharge of its duties, the Authority may employ, transact any business and pay agents, technical and financial advisers, advocates, consultants and any other persons for the purposes of giving effect to this Act (section 48).

850. Certain acts or things done on behalf of the Authority in preparation for or in anticipation of the enactment of this Act are protected under section 46. The provision further states that any expenditure, obligation and rights incurred in relation thereto shall be deemed authorized under this Act, in so far as the acts are consistent with the general intent and purposes of the Act. The Act has 1 Schedule with reference to Subsection 7(1) specifically on meetings of the Authority, invitation of other persons to attend, resolutions of meetings, minutes, meeting procedure and related matters.

Part V. Interaction Between Energy Law and Environmental Law

Chapter 1. Environmental Law Pertaining to Energy in Malaysia

851. Environmental law pertaining to energy in Malaysia is contained in the Environmental Quality Act 1974 and Regulations made under it. Under sections 22–29A, there is a total prohibition on air pollution, open burning, water pollution, soil pollution, noise pollution and marine pollution. A licence holder has the authority to pollute and that too within the pollution standards prescribed in various regulations. Therefore, premises used for power generation will have to take permission, have to undergo a mandatory EIA and have to be within the limits of standards prescribed under relevant regulations. Vehicles using fossil fuels will also have to follow standards prescribed in the regulations made for them. This is notable here that the technical terms like environment, pollution and pollutants have been defined by the Act, and the definitions are compatible with their universally accepted definitions. Violation of this substantive law is subjected to punishments that are comparatively high.

§1. Air Pollution

852. Section 22 of the Act says that no person shall, unless licensed, emit or discharge any environmentally hazardous substances, pollutants or wastes into the atmosphere in contravention of the acceptable conditions specified in Regulations. The section has the following deeming provisions: (1) Placing any matter in a place where it may be released into the atmosphere. (2) Causing or permitting the discharge of odours, which by virtue of their nature, concentration, volume or extent are obnoxious or offensive. (3) Burning any wastes of the trade, process or industry. (4) Using any fuel burning equipment not equipped with any device or control equipment required to be fitted to such equipment. For air pollution, there is fine not exceeding MYR 100,000 or imprisonment for a period not exceeding five years or both. If the offence continues, there will be additional fine of MYR 1,000 a day for every day that the offence is continued after a notice by the Director General of the DOE.

853. This is notable here that in Malaysia, a trend of building power generation plants that pollute comparatively less air has been started. Towards this end, the

TNB has commissioned its first PD1 power generation plant at Port Dickson, which is burning nearly half as much fuel as the older plants to which it has replaced. With the result of that, the level of emission from the plant is 25 parts per million (ppm). The old plant had 60 ppm. The company has the plan to start its PD2 by 2010, which might have even more sophisticated equipment and thus more environment-friendly.[179] Incinerators are a must for a country like Malaysia, especially in the Klang Valley area and industrialized states like Penang and Johor. We have noted under the Malaysian profile on energy that all new coal-fired power generation plants are using new technologies thus releasing relatively less carbon dioxide. They cause air pollution problems similar to that of coal-fired power generation plants; rather, more because they are responsible for emitting dioxine and furon and their management is difficult because dioxine changes on a very high temperature and comes again when temperature goes down. Its chemical management is quite expensive. For these reasons, incinerators require proper site selection and efficient EIAs and SIAs. It is for this reason that a specific regulation under the Act has been made. This prescribes, along with other relevant things, standards of emissions from incinerators. So is the case of nuclear power generation plants. The enrichment process and fission processes have to be in controlled conditions; otherwise, they might cause serious kind of radiation, which might yield disastrous results. It is notable here that Malaysia does not have any nuclear power generation plant. It has a prototype reactor at the Malaysian Institute of Nuclear Technology (MINT) for facilitating nuclear research. Only recently the Government of Malaysia has started thinking to have one nuclear power generation plant. It means in the near future there will not be this source of power generation.

§2. Noise Pollutions

854. According to section 23 of the Act, no person shall, unless licensed, emit or cause or permit to be emitted any noise greater in volume, intensity or quality in contravention of the acceptable noise levels prescribed under regulations. The provision of fine in this case is also the same.

855. Old power generation plants were relatively noisy. New power generation plants are comparatively less noisy. It is thought that in future there will be even better power generation plants. This will be better if standards prescribed by the World Health Organization (WHO) are followed. This is notable that the levels of noise prescribed under the appropriate Regulation for industries and vehicles are very close to the WHO standards.

§3. Soil Pollution

856. Section 24 of the Environmental Quality Act sets out that no person shall, unless licensed, pollute or cause or permit to be polluted any soil or surface of any

---

179. *New Straits Times*, 23 Aug. 2005.

land in contravention of the acceptable conditions. This section has the following deeming provisions: (1) Placing in or on any soil or in any place where it may gain access to any soil any matter whether liquid, solid or gaseous. (2) Establishing on any land a refuse dump, garbage pit, soil or rock disposal site, waste-injection well or otherwise used land for the disposal of or a repository for solid or liquid wastes so as to be obnoxious or offensive to human beings or interfere with underground water or be detrimental to any beneficial use of the soil or the surface of the land. Penalty in this is also the same like air pollution.

857. This is notable here that thermal power generation plants are generally not responsible for soil pollution, which results in pollution of underground water. Recently, due to dumping of wastes closer to watercourses, water supply system got polluted. The problem was considered to be serious because 114 dumpsites were closer to one or the other watercourses. They were responsible for causing latchet. This type of problem can be solved by selecting such sites carefully and by getting EIAs done by competent experts. It is notable that dumpsites that are closer to river courses have been ordered to be relocated. This is also notable here that from some of the dumpsites methane gas is utilized as a source of energy, but it is not significant at all. Power generation plants are not so responsible for soil pollution.

§4. Water Pollution

858. Section 25 of the Environmental Quality Act deals about pollution of inland waters. It provides that no person shall, unless licensed, emit, discharge or deposit any environmentally hazardous substance, pollutants or wastes into any inland waters in contravention of acceptable conditions. This section has three deeming situations of water pollution: (1) Placing any wastes in or on any waters or in a place where it may gain access to any waters. (2) Placing any wastes in a position where it falls, descends, drains, evaporates, is washed, is blown or percolates into any waters, or knowingly or through his/her negligence, whether directly or indirectly, causes or permits any wastes to be placed in such a position. (3) Causing the temperature of the receiving waters to be raised or lowered by more than the prescribed limits. The quantum of penalty is the same.

859. According to the Act, 'inland waters' means any reservoir, pond, lake, river, stream, canal, drain, spring or well, or any part of the sea above the low-water line along the coast, or any other body of natural or artificial surface or surface water. This is notable here that the definition is too wide to include even a part of the seawater. Textile industries, food and beverages industries, hotel industries, paper industries, metal industries, chemical industries, construction industries and animal farms are mainly responsible for water pollution. Few years ago, in addition to untreated sewage, palm oil industries, hotel industries and rubber-based industries were also responsible, but due to proper compliance of regulations especially made to address the problem of wastes generated by them, they are not so significantly responsible. In big cities, including the Klang Valley, sewage is being properly treated. Thermal power generation plants are not so responsible for water pollution.

§5. Pollution of Malaysian Territorial Waters

860. Section 27 of the Environmental Quality Act states that no person, unless licensed, shall discharge or spill any oil mixture containing oil into Malaysian waters in contravention of the acceptable limits prescribed under the International Treaties of which Malaysia is also a member. Penalty in this case is also the same. But unlike previous sections, this section does not provide any penalty for repeat offences.

861. Based on the treaty norms, section 28 of the Act provides the following defence to prove that the person charged can take: (1) It was done for securing safety of the vessel. (2) It was done for saving human life. (3) All reasonable steps were taken to prevent the spillage or discharge. (4) The result of leakage, which was not due to want of care, and that all reasonable steps were taken to stop or reduce the leakage. (5) The result of effluent produced by operation for the refining of oil, and that all reasonable steps had been taken to eliminate oil from the effluent and that it was not reasonable or practicable to dispose of the effluent otherwise than by discharging or spilling it into the Malaysian waters. Section 29 of the Act is about discharge of wastes into Malaysian waters.

862. This is notable here that ships and oil exploration activities are mainly responsible for oil pollution. Accidents of oil tankers have caused extensive damage to the marine environment, boats and establishments at the coast. The most vulnerable area along the Malaysian coast is the Straits of Malacca. Due to accidents, dumping of oil and desludging the condition of straits has deteriorated. It has badly affected the condition of the marine environment in the Straits. Due to narrow and shallow watercourse, it is one of the most polluted straits of the world. The littoral states, with the help of the International Maritime Organization and Japan, are making all possible efforts – by enhancing surveillance and proper channelling of ships passing through the Straits – to meet the challenges posed by a large number of ships passing through this narrow watercourse, but due to lack of resources, trained personnel and lack of support by the states who really benefit from it, the condition of the Straits is not improving fast. This is causing worry to the littoral states. The worry has doubled now because of the eminent danger of any possible terrorist attack. Supposedly, if terrorists used an oil tanker as a bomb and hit it with any cruiser or a port, the result will be unimaginably disastrous. So as to ward off any such possibility, the three littoral states are doing joint military patrolling of the straits of Malacca. It is suggested that these states should take help from the benefiting states also. Other states can provide tugboats and sophisticated equipment that can enhance the military surveillance of the Straits of Malacca.

863. This is also notable that the three-tier compensation mechanism contained in the Civil Liability Convention (CLC) and the Fund Convention, along with Protocols made thereunder, has been able to provide compensation to a large number of countries and their people, who suffered damage due to vessel-source oil pollution damage. These conventions are enforced through local legislations. For this purpose, Malaysia has Merchant Shipping (Civil Liability and Compensation for Oil

Pollution) Act 1998. Exclusive Economic Zone Act 1990 and the Environmental Quality Act 1974 also have some punitive measures. Together they constitute a workable legal regime that can have sufficient deterrence provided they are properly enforced. In the whole process is the surveillance. The Strait of Malacca is too long and too busy. This has made the surveillance a real problem. The problem can be solved only when shipowners are law abiding and instead of dumping the sludge and other hazardous pollutants, they give them to the reception facilities. It is notable that Malaysia has only one reception facility. It has plan to have reception facility at all of its ports, but that might take some time. The process of having more reception facilities can be faster only when benefiting states come forward and extend all kinds of help building them.

§6. Licensing Mechanism

864. We have noted above that no polluting activities can be carried out except without proper licence granted by the Director General of the DOE, and these licensed activities have to be within the Regulations governing the activities. Sections 10–17, read with the Environmental Quality (Licensing) Regulations 1977, of the Environmental Quality Act 1974 deal with the licensing mechanism. The following licences are required by the Environmental Quality Act 1974: (1) section 18 – Licence to occupy and use prescribed premises. (2) section 22 – Licence to emit or discharge wastes into the atmosphere in contravention of the acceptable conditions specified in applicable Regulations. (3) section 23 – Licence to emit or cause or permit to be emitted any noise greater in volume, intensity or quality in contravention of the appropriate Regulations. (4) section 24 – Licence to pollute or cause or permit to be polluted any soil or surface of any land in contravention of the conditions prescribed in appropriate Regulations. (5) section 25 – Licence to emit, discharge or deposit any wastes into any inland waters in contravention conditions contained in the appropriate Regulations. (6) section 29 – Licence to discharge wastes into the Malaysian waters. Under section 11 of the Act an application for a licence or renewal of licence or transfer of licence can be made in a prescribed form. Licence is generally granted appended with certain conditions. These conditions have to be followed. Licence can be granted for a temporary period also. Director General can revoke any licence or put it under some more conditions to be fulfilled for continuing with the licence. He does it only after thorough investigations required to be made under section 11(4) of the Act. The Director General under this power may require the licence holder: to repair, alter or replace any equipment in or on any premises specified in the licence; to install and operate pollution control equipment in or on any premises specified in the licence; to repair, alter or replace any pollution control equipment installed in or on any premises specified in the licence; to conduct on his/her own expense a monitoring programme designed to provide the Director General with information concerning the characteristics, quantity or effects of the emission, discharge or deposit in respect of which the licence was issued; to carry out any of the requirements imposed on him/her under any provisions of the Act. Likewise, the Director General has the power to refuse the request made by the licence holder for altering or replacing any pollution control equipment installed in or on the premises. On non-fulfilment of any of the conditions, licence can be revoked or suspended for a period as decided by the Director General. This may be noted here from the practical point of view suspension of licence amounts to revocation unless suspension order is not lifted. Revocation or suspension is operative from the date of the issue of the order. Licences are generally renewable. This is notable here that conditions appended to the licence by the Director General are appealable. They do not become operative unless the appeal period is expired.

865. Duration of any licence is prescribed in the licence. In case duration has not been specified on the licence, the licence will be valid only for one year. After that, the licence will have to be renewed; and as stated above, a renewal application is required to be made three to four months before the expiry of the existing licence on the prescribed form along with the prescribed fee. Where the premises, with respect to which licence have been granted, is transferred to another person, that person will have to apply for the approval of the transfer. In that case, the same licence will continue. On the contrary, the new possessor of the premises will have to take new licence.

866. In case of failure to comply with any of the terms and conditions appended with the licence, there will be a penal liability. Thus, any holder of a licence in such situations will be liable to a fine not exceeding MYR 25,000 or to an imprisonment for a period not exceeding two years or to both, and to a further fine of MYR 1,000 for every day that the offence is continued after a notice by the Director General requiring him/her to comply with such term or condition specified therein has been served upon him/her. Likewise, occupation or use of premises, prescribed by the Minister, without licence is an offence under section 18 of the Environmental Quality Act 1974. The Minister also prescribes vehicle or ship to be used for movement, transfer, placement or deposit of wastes. Using them without such licence will be an offence under section 18 of the Act. Section 18 has the following exceptions: (1) A person is already possessing such vehicles or premises and takes licence within the prescribed time. (2) Who, whereby virtue of any order made by the Minister from time to time amending any previous order made under section 18, premises not previously prescribed premises become prescribed premises, is consequent upon the order, the occupier of the prescribed premises, and who within the prescribed period, after the application of the order makes application for a licence in respect of those prescribed premises. (3) Who has made application for the transfer to him/her of the licence in respect of any prescribed premises and made the application within the prescribed period after he becomes the occupier of those prescribed premises. The amount of penalty in section 18 is RM 50,000 with imprisonment not exceeding two years or both, a further fine of MYR 1,000 per day as above.

867. Under section 19 of the Environmental Quality Act, prior written permission is also required before carrying out any work on any vehicle or ship, or premises to become a prescribed conveyance or prescribed premises, as the case may be; or construct on any land any building designed for or used for a purpose that would cause the land or building to become prescribed premises. It is, therefore, required under section 20 of the Act that for every application to carry out any work, a plan has to be submitted to the Director General with the following information: (1) The plans and specifications of the proposed work, building, erection or alteration together with details of the control equipment if any to be installed. (2) A layout plan indicating the site of the proposed work, building, erection or alteration which will take place in relation to surrounding areas. (3) The details of the trade, industry or process proposed to be carried on in such premises. (4) Description of waste constituents and characteristics. (5) Any other information that Director General requires. Director General may grant permission on the application with suitable conditions, if any, warranted for the protection of the environment.

§7. Environmental Impact Assessment (EIA)

868. Section 34A read with Environmental Quality (Prescribed Activities) (Environmental Impact Assessment) Order 1987, which came into force on 1 April 1988, prescribed a mandatory Environmental Impact Assessment (EIA) with respect to the following activities that are related to energy: (1) Petroleum – (a) Oil and gas fields development; (b) Construction of offshore pipelines in excess of 50 km in length; (c) Construction of oil and gas separation, processing, handling and storage facilities; (d) Construction of oil refineries; and (e) Construction of product depots for the storage of petrol, gas or diesel (excluding service stations) which are located within 3 km of any commercial industrial or residential areas and which have a combined storage capacity of 60,000 barrels or more. (2) Power Generation and Transmission – (a) Construction of steam-generated power stations burning fossil fuels and having capacity of more than 10 MW; (b) Dams and hydroelectric power schemes with either or both of the following: (i) dams over 15 m high and ancillary structures covering a total area in excess of 40 hectares; (ii) reservoirs with a surface area in excess of 400 hectares; (c) Construction of combined-cycle power stations; and Construction of nuclear-fuelled power stations.

869. The Environmental Quality (Prescribed Activities) (Environmental Impact Assessment) Order 2015 is the new Order on EIA, which replaced the 1987 Order. It has changed certain prescribed activities. So far petroleum is concerned, they are in the First Schedule: (1) development of oil field; development of gas field; or development of oil and gas field. (2) Construction of 30 km or more in length of offshore pipelines, onshore pipelines or offshore and onshore pipelines. (3) Construction of oil separation, processing, handling storage facilities, or construction of gas separation, processing, handling and storage facilities, or both. (4) Construction of product depot for the storage of petrol, gas or diesel which has the combined storage capacity of 60,000 barrels or more (excluding service station) within 3 km from any commercial, industrial or residential area. With respect to power generation and transmission, the prescribed activities are: (1) Construction of steam-generated power station using fossil fuels (other than coal) and having the capacity of 10 MW or more, with or without transmission line. (2) Construction of combined-cycle power station, with or without transmission line. (3) Construction of transmission line in environmentally sensitive areas. In the second schedule, they are: (1) Construction of oil refineries, construction of gas refineries of construction of both. (2) Construction of coal-fired power station and having the capacity of 10 MW or more with or without transmission line, and Construction of nuclear-fuel power station with or without transmission. (3) Construction of dam or impounding reservoir for the purpose of irrigation, flood mitigation control of siltation, 100 hectares or more. (4) Dam of hydroelectric power scheme with either or both of: (a) dam of 15 m or more in height and ancillary structures covering a total area of 40 hectares or more; (b) reservoir with surface area of 100 hectares or more. (5) Using radioactive materials and generating radioactive wastes.

870. As a matter of general rule, EIAs are prepared by the registered expert(s), according to the guidelines issued by the Director General for making various EIAs, by the proponents of projects, for which to have EIAs approved by the DOE is a mandatory requirement. EIAs are submitted to the DOE and experts at the DOE scrutinize them. Public opinions are taken on them. The DOE then approves with or without conditions, or rejects, or sends back to proponents for revision. The EIA mechanism in Malaysia is in line with the National Environmental Policy of the country, which says:

> a systematic interdisciplinary approach which will ensure the integrated use of the natural and social sciences and the environmental design in planning and in the decision making which may have an impact on the environment.

I. Meaning and Scope

871. The 'Assimilative Capacity Principle', which was the outcome of Principle 6 of the Stockholm Declaration, has been replaced by the 'Precautionary Principle', contained in Principle 11 of the UN General Assembly Resolution on World Charter for Nature 1982, because scientific opinions are never constant; they change with change of information. The Supreme Court of India in *A. P. Pollution Control Board v. Prof. M. V. Naydu*, AIR 1999 SC 812, explains this in the following words: Due to uncertainty in scientific opinions, in the 11th Principle of the UN General Assembly Resolution on World Charter for Nature 1982 emphasis was laid on the 'Precautionary Principle', and this was reiterated in the Rio Conference of 1992. In other words, inadequacies of science are the real basis that has led to the development of the 'Precautionary Principle'. It is based on the theory that it is better to err on the side of caution and prevent environmental harm, which may indeed become irreversible. Generally speaking, the principle of precaution involves the anticipation of environmental harm and taking measures to avoid it or to choose the least environmentally harmful activity, or not at all to introduce something into the environment or do any act the effect of which on the environment cannot be determined with surety. More appropriately, in case if there is no surety about the adverse effect on the environment of introducing something or performing any act, it will be better not to introduce or perform as the case may be. It also emphasizes on repeated research on safety concerns. If scientists become sure, that thing can be introduced or the activity can be performed. It is based on scientific uncertainty. Environmental protection should not only aim at protecting health, property and economic interest but also protect the environment for its own sake. Precautionary duties must not only be triggered by the suspicion of concrete danger but also by (justified) risk potential. The 'Precautionary Principle' became the basis for a wide acceptance of EIA in the world as a preventive measure to protect the life and the environmental itself around the selected proposed or existing projects, because this only can tell about any potential risk. If the experts are not sure, the principle will apply. It has been made mandatory in respect to certain activities, including development in sensitive areas like hill, slopes, islands and water catchments area.[180]

872. Generally speaking, an EIA is a process for identifying the likely consequences for the biological, geological and physical environment, as well as human health and welfare of implementing particular activities, and for conveying this information to those responsible for sanctioning the proposal at a stage when it can materially affect their decision. The Environmental Quality Act 1974 does not define the term. The EIA Handbook defines it as: 'Environmental Impact Assessment is a study to identify, predict, evaluate and communicate information about the impacts on the environment of a proposed project and to detail out the mitigation measures prior to project approval and implementation.' An EIA process requires: identification and prediction of significant deleterious effects, immediate and in the long term, of the proposed project on the environment; choosing the best from the alternatives of doing the proposed job; finding means to mitigate the predicted harmful effects and suggesting means to mitigating them. In short, an EIA is a scientific prediction of probable adverse effects on the environment, direct or indirect, secondary and cumulative, short-term, and permanent and temporary from any project of development to be undertaken or already in existence. This is a widely accepted definition. The author feels that this definition should be given a wide connotation so that it may have wide application. For instance, the word 'probable' should mean 'likely to affect the environment'; and the word 'likely' should mean 'a real chance or possibility'. Likewise, the phrase 'adverse effect on the environment' should mean 'degradation of the environment', which may affect any of the parts of the environment – biosphere, lithosphere, hydrosphere including marine life or atmosphere including outer space. The projects of development, where forest is proposed to be cleared, should include the following: cleaning the forest for development, for example, housing, industrialization, mining, construction of dams for irrigation or for hydroelectric purpose or for both, roads and other infrastructure, logging activities beyond certain limits, housing projects, development of the area for sport and plantation. This should not be taken as exhaustive, and some other projects, if the state thinks fit, may be added.

873. Almost all developed states and most of the developing countries, including Malaysia, had made it a mandatory requirement in respect to certain projects.

180. See Abdul Haseeb Ansari, 'Meaning, Scope and Implementation of Precautionary Principle: A Critical Appraisal', *Indian Journal of International Law* 43, no. 4 (2003): 625–660.

But, the idea received impetus from the Agenda 21. Resultantly, many more countries enacted law for this, and those who already had it in practice widened the scope to bring in some more activities. To prepare an EIA pertaining to the above-mentioned activities is a complex job, which involves experts from many related disciplines, including from law and economics. Therefore, there are all chances of divergent views. To meet this type of situations, states have provided guidelines. EIAs are prepared based on these guidelines, and efforts are made to give an amicable input of all related disciplines.

II. Mechanism and Public Participation

874. Section 34A of the Environmental Quality Act 1974 prescribes the procedure. It requires that the proponent of the project will get an EIA report prepared from an individual or a firm registered for this purpose. The report will be submitted to the DOE for approval, which may be approved with or without conditions, or may be rejected for the given reasons. Where certain conditions are appended with the approval of the report, these must be complied with later according to instructions, if any. In case of rejection, a new report may be submitted after removal of the objections. The proposed project can be started only after approval of the project submitted for approval. In contravention of the procedure, the person who has contravened, if charged, may be subjected to an imprisonment of maximum five years or a fine not exceeding MYR 500,000 or both.

875. For preparing EIAs with respect to various prescribed activities, the Director General has made guidelines and an EIA report review checklist. These guidelines and the checklist must be followed. The object for making these is to facilitate the consultants and to bring about uniformity in EIAs pertaining to same type of projects. The guidelines have provisions for making EIAs available to the public. If any person makes a request for any report, it can be made available to him/her on payment of certain money. This provision is to encourage the public, including NGOs, to make fruitful comments so that with their input reports become more realistic and protect the environment and the inhabitants around the proposed projects in a better way. The guidelines provide for public participation at three stages: the proponent of the project can obtain it; it can be given when the detailed assessment report is kept open for public comments; and affected members of the public of the proposed project can go in appeal against the decision under section 35(e) of the Environmental Quality Act 1974. Public participation is in line with the Principle 10 of the Rio Declaration. Advantages of public participation in environmental matters have best been stated by the Royal Commission in its 10th Report, *Tackling Pollution–Experience and Prospects.* It can be summarized in the following words: It enhances the confidence in environmental decision-making; it will lead to a better choice; industries then can take the imperatives of protection of the environment seriously; the idea that the decision of environmental officials will come under scrutiny will bring about serious decision-making; and it strengthens the democratic system of decision-making.

876. Public participation can highlight certain things that might adversely affect the environment and that was not anticipated by the officials of the DOE. One of the best examples of public comments in respect to any proposed development project is the 1991 MYR 500 million worth development project in Penang Hill area. Some 1,400 Penangites showed their concern by writing letter to the Director General of the DOE, and the Department had to disapprove the project. It is said that this epoch-making event could be possible only with the help of the Consumers Association of Penang. The second best example, where public participation played a significant role, has been the proposed Selangor Dam project. People tried to prove that the project should not be started, because the available alternative means, bringing water through the pipe, would protected the firefly colony, would not displace the people presently living on the dam site and would be cheaper. But in respect to other projects, people's participation has not been so significant. The DOE is of the opinion that people now are not coming forward, though reports are put on display. They do not come forward to the consultants or the project proponents also, when the reports are in the process of making.

877. It can hardly be denied that people's participation is important, especially of those who live around the proposed project or who have to be displaced due to the project, because they are immediate affected ones. If they come forward and speak up independently or with aid and assistance of NGOs or individual activists, and if they are given due consideration in promoting proposed projects, there will be proper input to the SIAs with EIAs. The author is of the opinion that both must be done together or concurrently, because in most of the cases, both are closely related to each other. Even in situations they are not so closely related, they have to be done simultaneously if both are necessary. If SIA is not done, then there might be all chances that by the time the socio-economic problems of the affected people are noticed and solutions to them are thought upon or provided, the loss they have suffered might become irreparable or might involve much more money than estimated. For example, for constructing a dam some 5,000 households have to be replaced. There is a time-bound programme for their resettlement, but since houses for them are not ready, they are put temporarily in a longhouse and they finally move after six or seven years to houses built for them, close to agricultural lands assigned to them and jobs generated for them. In this situation, they will eat up the interim grant, because they might have uncertain life and might come across inconveniences. In addition, if developers wish to do justice with them, they will have to spend several times more than they had allocated for their resettlement. Dr Denison of the Foundation for Community Studies and Development and Colin Nicholas of the Centre for Orang Asli give some examples where due to lack of proper SIAs in the process of resettlement people had to suffer a lot.

878. We have noted above that in order to get a greater public participation, DOE wants that the proponent of the project should take public feedback before the EIA for the project is submitted. To this effect, the expert assigned the job of making the EIA should also consult members of the public. In addition to these, for greater response of the public, the report is kept open for the public for comments for two to three months. Nevertheless, people's response in respect to some projects has not been very encouraging. This is agitating the minds of planners and environmentalists. Some environmentalists have made efforts to find reasons for the apathy of the people and have also offered certain suggestions. The factors within the EIA process, which prevents or discourages public participation, may be one or more than one of the following.

879. Lack of transparency in the whole process is the first and the foremost factor. It is said that the recent trend in the EIA processes reveals that project proponents, state governments and the DOE are not as transparent as they should be. Therefore, it has been proposed that there should be proper information to the public right from the stage when a project, which requires a mandatory EIA, is proposed, and it should continue until the project report is finally approved. When an EIA has been submitted by the project proponent, it should be displayed in the DOE office at more than one place. For instance, if the proposed project is situated in Sarawak, it will be appropriate to display the EIA submitted by the proponent of the project in Sarawak and some other places, including the Kuala Lumpur office of the DOE. It will be in the fitness of the thing, if the Kuala Lumpur office has EIAs of all proposed projects, so that any individual or representative of any NGO, if wants, may look into them and submit comments later in the same office. This will make the process faster and efficient, because most of the NGOs have their office or at least a representative in Kuala Lumpur. Another pertinent point is that the DOE should give sufficient time for public comments. This may be decided on the basis of the volume of the project, involvement of money and number of people affected by the project. It is notable here that two to three months will be enough.

880. It should be made clear to the public that their names will be kept confidential, and they should make comments fearlessly. If this is not done, general public might have inhibition that they may be subjected to any kind of legal action(s). Rather, efforts by all means should be made to encourage the people, especially those who might be affected by the proposed project, to come forward to make fruitful comments. In Malaysia, people, who might be affected by a project like construction of a big dam, are not literate or conscious enough to come forward and assert for their rights. This is also necessary in view of *locus standi* requirement for legal actions.

881. In case of mega projects, pre-emptive approach is not advisable. Projects should be allowed to start only when EIAs concerning to them have been approved, because once a project has been started, it will be difficult to stop it; sometimes it might not be advisable for many reasons, to abandon the project. The best approach will be not to have a presumption that the planned project will go ahead. Cautious approach is better, if we have really to protect the environment and the people.

882. Use of English is important, but it should not be the only choice. EIAs should be prepared at least in two languages, one in English and the other in the local language. In case the affected people belong to more than one communities of Malaysia and the number of the communities is considerably high, then in addition to English more than one of the local languages, as the case may be, should be followed. EIAs should not only readily be available, but the price fixed for them should possibly be low, because the whole idea enshrined in the process of doing EIAs is to protect the environment and the people from the immediate and prospective adverse and deleterious effects, which proposed projects might cause.

883. Public education and awareness is also as important as the other preceding points are. The DOE can best do this by itself. The best way doing it is to hold a public gathering at the site of the proposed project, and to explain the people living around the project about the pros and cons of the project. The DOE should keep some experts to do this job, including some from the community, which is going to be affected. The other way can be to distribute booklets having all the details about implications and benefits of the proposed project. This is in fact a prerequisite for the success of the EIA process.

884. Another area, which relates to the post-approval monitoring, is auditing of the execution of the project. The DOE, in fact, is keen to implement this. The former Director General of the DOE Mr Tan Meng Leng stressed on this requirement on one occasion. The author is of the opinion that if auditing is seriously enforced through properly trained personnel of the Department, it can prove to be a very successful preventive measure. This is in line with sections 34A(7) and 31A of the Environmental Quality Act 1974.

885. With respect to sensitive areas, like high lands, slopes, islands, lakes, water catchment areas, some states have made EIAs as a mandatory requirement for developers of all projects. Pahang, Selangor, Perak, Melaka, Sabah, Pinang and Kelantan have taken the lead. These states have made it a requirement to conduct EIAs for development of high lands, ex-solid waste dumping grounds and ex-mining lands. The Selangor state has taken a step further by requiring a macro-EIA to be undertaken for a mixed development project in a hilly terrain covering an area of 30 hectares. The state of Pahang requires an EIA be done for development projects in hilly areas involving 2.5 hectares of land. In Sarawak construction of buildings exceeding four stories on hill land with slopes of 20 degree or more and establishment of golf course are subjected to the Natural Resources and Environment (Prescribed Activities) Order 1994, which requires approval of EIAs as a condition precedent for starting such projects. The DOE has appreciated the initiatives of the states, but it wants that the state's EIA law should be in line with the central legislation. This is a welcome move, because if the job is to be done by the state machinery, it can be entrusted to the municipal corporation under which the proposed project falls. Since the job is highly technical and demands a lot of expertise, states must work under guidance and supervision of the DOE. For this purpose, the DOE should increase the number of its staff at its state offices and a close cooperation between them and state officials should be enhanced.

886. This should be noted here that the Sarawak State has a separate system of EIA under its own legislation, namely the Natural Resources Ordinance 1949 and the Natural Resources and Environmental (Prescribed Activities) Order 1994. Under this law, to take public feedback is not a mandatory requirement. In other words, a project can be started without inviting public comments on its EIA if the project is fully situated within the state. This was held in *Ketual Pengarah Jabatan Alam Sekiar & Anor v. Kajing Tubek & Ors and Other Appeals*, [1997] 3 MLJ 23. The Court gave the following reason:

> Since the environment in question, by reason of item 2(a) of list II and item 13 of list III A of Schedule 9 of the Federal Constitution, lay wholly within the legislative and constitutional province of the State of Sarawak, that state has exclusive authority to regulate by legislation, the use of it in such manner as it deemed fit. The Environmental Quality Act thus does not apply … Parliament, when it passed the Environmental Quality Act, did not intend-and could not have intended- to regulate so much of the environment as falls within the legislative jurisdiction of Sarawak.

Environmentalists are not happy with the verdict of this case law. The author feels that the Sarawak law on EIA should be in line with the central law.

887. The above paragraphs clearly reveal that the EIA mechanism of Malaysia is workable. It will be in the interest of the environment and the people living around proposed projects, if the suggestions mentioned above for improvement of the mechanism are given due consideration by the DOE. In addition to those suggestions, the author feels that the following points should also be taken as a part of the process:

(1) For avoiding unnecessary delay in the approval of an EIA submitted to the DOE or the state department, as the case may be, there should be a time limit, and within the time limit the whole process at the DOE or the state department should be completed. If an EIA was returned to the proponent of the project with certain objections, and the report has again been submitted after necessary amendments made based on the objections, this time limit should reasonably be extended. Two months' time will be appropriate for the DOE or the State DOE. The time limits will protect proposed projects from an unnecessary delay, which may adversely affect the projects.

(2) The post-approval monitoring is also a very important tool for total compliance of the EIA. This is possible by an auditing to be done by competent personnel of the DOE. Therefore, for this purpose, the DOE should employ sufficient number of experts to carry out this job. Alternatively, auditing can be done by any independent body employed for this purpose by the DOE. But the first one should be preferred, when the DOE has a wing for research and development comprising enough experts and the job of auditing is entrusted to that wing. For increasing the credibility of the DOE, all audit reports should also be published.

(3) It is normal for the results of scientific research to be published. Unfortunately, much of the works, which are done for EIAs, remain in reports; they never become part of scientific literatures. These reports are often prepared at a considerable expense, and yet they quickly disappear into oblivion, far from

any accessible database. Indeed, many contracts, including those of government agencies, contain a secrecy clause that prevents a consultant from communicating his/her results with his/her professional colleagues. But this does not apply to the EIAs. Rather, they have to be open and transparent to encourage for enough public participation. The author suggests that there should be a database, prepared based on EIA reports approved by the DOE. If this is done, it will be a valuable source of guidance for future EIAs. With the result of that, the quality of EIAs will improve and they can be finalized in a comparatively less time.

(4) Input of EIAs in every development planning has been accepted as a *sine qua non* in many countries. In Malaysia also, this has been started. The author is of the opinion that the scope of this should be maximized, so that all development planning becomes safe.

888. The idea of area-wise comprehensive EIA should be given priority. It will be a helpful instrument in protecting sensitive areas. Otherwise, there will be all chances that EIAs in these areas can be avoided. With the result of that, a sensitive area can be brought subject to development or other activities, which will later prove to be detrimental. For example, no country can afford to face highland disasters, as it brings atrocities to a large number of people and wastes a lot of money.

889. The existing Malaysian law pertaining to EIA is one of the best in the world. In some respects, it is even better than the law of some developed countries. It can be a good guide for developing countries, especially tropical countries, in developing law on EIA. However, for toning up of the law the suggestions made above should be given due consideration. In addition to this, it is also important that Malaysia should try its best to enforce the law properly.

It may be noted here that in Malaysia, the Director General may issue a prohibition order stopping the operation of any project if there is no approved EIA, or if there is violation of any of the conditions appended to the approved EIA, or the work is not being carried out in a proper manner. The work may be stopped absolutely or conditionally, or for a short period, or until certain remedial measures are not incorporated. In contravention of the order, there will be liability of fine of MYR 500,000 or an imprisonment not exceeding five years or both, and additional penalty for continuation of the contravention as MYR 1,000 per day.

890. EIA in India is not done like Malaysia. There, it is a part of the process of taking Environment Clearance Certificate (ECC) before operating any project/activity that might adversely affect the environment. In addition to this, the Environment Ministry makes an impact study in respect to certain major projects under the 1994 notification (as amended in 1997), issued under section 3 of the Environmental (Protection) Act 1986, before sanction is given. In respect to some other projects, EIAs are approved by the respective states. On any representation made by affected persons or when guidelines made by the Central Government have been ignored, the Central Government can review EIAs approved by State Governments. At both the levels, in respect to the scheduled projects, public participation is a mandatory requirement. As per the regulation, this has to be completed within three months. This may be noted that in many cases, EIAs are not done seriously, and in many other cases EIAs are not done at all. For not doing so, excuses of paucity of manpower and multiplicity of projects are given. It is surprising that in a country like India, where judiciary is making tremendous efforts to protect the environment, legislature has not yet enacted a law for making an EIA as a mandatory requirement in respect to certain projects, including all projects in sensitive areas, which have widely been accepted around the world to be vulnerable to the environment. The Indian Supreme Court on reports of experts constituted by it, that certain projects are adversely affecting the environment, has never hesitated in making orders to stop those projects. For example, in Doon Valley Litigation the Court, in view of the air pollution, river pollution, destruction of hydrological system and loss of vegetation, ordered to halt the mining operations in the valley, except required in the interest of the defence of the country or for safeguarding the foreign exchange position in the country. Likewise, in *TN Godavaraman Thirumuspad v. Union of India,* AIR 1997 SC 1228, the Supreme Court, in view of the State Forest Report 1997, which revealed that between 1995 and 1997 some 17,777 km^2 of forests in the country were logged, imposed a ban in respect of felling of trees in forests irrespective of the nature of the forest, that is, whether the forest is a public forest or private, reserved, protected or otherwise, except according to working plans of states. In respect to seven northeastern states the exception was allowed for the defence of the country and government purposes, if certified so. Section 2 of the Forest (Conservation) Act 1980, which does not have retrospective effect, provides that no state or other authority will make any order, except with a prior approval of the Central Government, directing: (i) Dereservation of any reserved forest; (ii) Use of any forestland for non-forest purposes; (iii) Assignment of forestland by lease or otherwise to anyone other than government; and (iv) Clear natural forest for reforestation. The Supreme Court has given strict interpretation to this section; and the Court has been liberal in cases of disapproval orders given by the Central Government, provided they were based on the prime object to protect the environment. Various High Courts have also followed the Supreme Court. Thus, in *Veerabhadrappa T. v. Ministry of Mines and Steel, New Delhi,* AIR 1998 Kant. 412, the Karnataka High Court upheld the disapproval of the application for renewal of the mining lease on the ground that mining operations will result in accelerated soil erosion in the leased areas.

891. It has been mentioned above that India does not have a developed legal framework for EIAs like Malaysia. Nevertheless, it has an effective restrictive mechanism for protecting its environment from being degraded from developmental activities. This may be noted that section 3 of the Environment (Protection) Act 1986 has authorized the Central Government to take measures to protect the environment in respect to certain matters, including 'restriction of areas in which any industries, operations or processes or class of industries, operations or processes shall not be carried out or shall be carried out subject to certain safeguards'. Rules 2, 3(d) and 5 of the Environment (Protection) Rules 1986, made under the Act, also contain restrictive provisions. Under these provisions, while prohibiting or restricting the location of industries and carrying on the processes and operations in an area a set of procedure, made by the Central Government, has to be followed. The Central Government is authorized to issue a notification inviting objections. All objections pertaining to the project will be considered before taking decision. In exercise of the power conferred by these provisions, the Ministry of Environment and Forests issued a notification dated 27 January 1994, which was amended on 10 April 1997. The procedure prescribed by the notification may be summarized under the following points: (1) Any person who desires to undertake any prescribed new project or the expansion or modernization of any existing industry or project will submit an application along with the project report and an EIA. (2) The report and the EIA submitted by the proponent are evaluated and assessed by the Impact Assessment Agency, which may consult a committee of experts constituted by the Agency itself or by any delegated authority. (3) It is obligatory for the Impact Assessment Agency to interact with the local people, to take their opinions and to give them due consideration before giving decision.

892. Thus, under the Indian law, public participation in the process of granting permission to an industry or any other project has been given importance. Any persons or NGOs, including local residents, who might be directly affected, have right to give their opinions. The provisions pertaining to taking public opinion concerning any industry or project has been thoroughly considered by the Gujarat High Court in *Centre for Social Justice v. Union of India,* AIR 2001 Gujarat 71. The following points have received greater emphasis: (1) The venue of the public hearing should be in the close proximity of the proposed project or the affected people and in any case their venue of hearing shall ordinarily not be away from the headquarters of the taluka (local area) in which the proposed project is coming up or of the taluka which includes most of the area of the settlements of the affected people. (2) The Pollution Control Board shall cause the notice of public hearing to be published in two newspapers widely circulated in that area and one of them should be in the vernacular language of the concerned (affected) people. The Board shall also send a copy of the public notice to the village committees, if any, of the village or town likely to be affected by the project with a request to bring it to the notice of the people likely to be affected by the project. (3) The date of first public hearing should be only after thirty days of the notification. It should also be made sure in the meantime that the copies of the executive summary of the project furnished to the Board are made available at all local places mentioned in the notification at least thirty days prior to the date of public hearing. (4) As far as the EIA report submitted to the Board along with the application for environmental clearance certificate is concerned, the summary of such EIA report in the local language shall also be made available to the concerned persons on demand. It will be open to the Board to charge reasonable money for supplying copies of such summary or copies of the report, but in any case the request shall be acceded to within one week from the date of the demand. (5) The Board on demand and on payment of reasonable charges shall furnish the minutes of the public hearing. When any demand for such minutes is made and the charges are paid, the minutes shall be supplied as expeditiously as possible and in any case within one fortnight from the date on which the minutes are sent to the Environmental Impact Agency or to the Central Government in the Ministry of Environment and Forest. (6) There is no hard and fast rule for the number of public hearing. Looking at the size of the project and its impact on the environment, the committee will take its own decision. While doing this, the committee will consider the following Central Government's observation expressed in a letter dated 17 July 1998 addressed to the Board: 'In respect of certain projects such as laying of pipelines, highways and projects located in inaccessible regions, clarification has been sought weather the public hearing should be conducted at one place or number of places, etc. The matter has been examined. It has been decided that venue and number of public hearing to be conducted for a particular proposal may be left to the discretion of the State Pollution Control Board. The State Pollution Control Board / Pollution Control Committees, as the case may be, may take a decision on the venue and number of public hearings for projects which require environmental clearance certificates as per provisions of the EIA Notification keeping in view the nature of the project, its environmental ramification and feasibility of grouping of people at the nearest convenient locations.' (7) As far as the environmental clearance certificate is concerned, as soon as such clearance is granted, the State Government or the Central Government, as the case may be, shall cause publication of the epitome of such clearance certificate in the newspapers in which the notice for public hearing was published by the Board for the particular project in question.

893. It can be noted that in India, for ensuring the public participation in the process of granting environmental clearance certificate, the State Government or the Central Government, as the case may be, has to ensure that the proposed project will not adversely affect the environment. In the whole process, for bringing about objectivity in the decision, public participation has rightly been given due importance. However, the author feels that there should be a proper regime for approval of EIAs and Environmental Clearance Certificates. This law should be made by the Central Government and should uniformly be applied in the country. If this is done, the law pertaining to EIA will be certain and uniform in the country. This law must specify certain projects in respect to which EIAs should be a mandatory requirement. Clearing of forests for any purpose 50 hectares or more and every developmental activities on hill slopes must be subject to an EIA followed by Environmental Clearance Certificate. If India does so, it will be nothing but to show its allegiance to the 'Precautionary Principle' of the World Charter for Nature, the Agenda 21, the 'Forest Principles' negotiated at the Rio Conference, and the Principle 17 of the Rio Declaration. In addition to this, law should also be made pertaining to auditing and ecolabelling. The Malaysian practice can be a good guide for India.

894. In addition to approving EIAs, SIAs and granting environmental clearance certificates, as the case may be, as a matter of policy pertaining to developments on hills, which involve clearing of large areas of forests and threatens widespread disaster and environmental damage, the author supports the following suggestions: (1) Development at hills should be an exception. (2) If development is very necessary, alternatives should be explored and the one that is less detrimental to the environment should be adopted. For example infrastructure development, like roads or railway tracks, making tunnels should be preferred over laying them on the surface. (3) Cost and benefit assessment should be done. (4) Water catchment areas should not be disturbed. (5) An assessment of the biodiversity should be made. If development causes a serious irreparable loss to the biodiversity, the proposed development should be abandoned. (6) The development projects should be monitored by an appropriate government agency and if the loss to the environment seems to be unsustainable, the development activity should immediately be stopped. (7) For every project, big or small, public opinion should be taken. If the opinion of experts and NGOs working for conservation of the environment is against the development project, it should be abandoned. (8) Environmentally sensitive areas should be identified and extra care should be taken for all developmental activities in these areas.

895. In India, there is a welcome feature that mega projects like dams, especially when proposed to be built on hills and barrages, are subjected to intensive testing at the Poona Institute. There, a miniature project with exact surroundings is made and testing continues for months. Projects are approved with appropriate preventive suggestions after that. The best example for such testing is the recent bridge of Japan. Testing for it continued for about ten years. The author is of the opinion that all mega projects on hills, which demands clearing of a huge forest area and involves widespread risk on accident, must be subjected to an intensive risk testing. This type of testing should be followed in Malaysia also, because they have been proved in India and elsewhere very successful.

896. The EIA-making process pertaining to energy in Malaysia has to be done according to the law made for this purpose, the law contained in the EQ Act regulations made thereunder and Guidelines issued by the DOE. Once a power generation project has been started it may have to undergo through an environmental audit if asked by the Director General under section 33A of the Environmental Quality Act 1974. If auditing reveals that the conditions appended to the approved EIA are not being complied with or the project is adversely affecting the environmental processes, necessary actions can be taken by the DOE.

897. It may be noted here that the importance of EIAs and input of public hearing in them have been recognized by the Indian Supreme Court in a number of cases. The court is of the opinion that EIAs should be genuinely done by the States' EIA approval body.[181] The Court wants an EIA Regulator in the country working under the Central Government having its branches in every state so that genuineness of EIAs could be ensured.[182]

181. See at: https://www.casemine.com/search/in?q=environmental+impact+assessment+requirements (accessed on 20 Mar. 2018).

182. *Times of India*, 'Supreme Court wants regulator for environmental clearance of projects', 7 Jan. 2014.

§8. Environmental Regulations Pertaining to Energy

I. Environmental Quality (Clean Air) Regulations 1978 and Environmental Quality (Clean Air) Regulations 2015

898. It may be noted at the outset that the 1978 Regulations have been replaced by the 2015 Regulations. For a complete picture of past and present, we will discuss both sets of Regulations.

A. *The 1978 Regulations*

899. This piece of subordinate legislation was applicable to power generation plants. Regulation 4 states that without prior permission of the Director General of the DOE, any plant or machinery that may discharge or emit smoke as dark or as darker than the shade no. 1 of the Ringelmann Chart cannot be installed within (a) the premises situated within an area designated as a residential zone having clearly demarcated boundaries as defined and which appear in the gazetted local plan prepared by the appropriate local planning authorities under part III of the Town and Country Planning Act 1976. In the absence of such plan it will mean that such premises are situated within a housing estate. This may be noted here that according to the Regulations air impurities include smoke, soot, dust ash (including fly ash) solid particles of any kind, inclusive of gases, fumes which are generated as a result of combustion of fuels and the like, or a result of use of electricity as a heat source. Regulation 14 states that the occupier of any industrial premises shall not cause, suffer, allow or permit smoke emissions of any colour from any new facility except fuel burning equipment utilizing solid fuel and including but not limited to any chimney which appears: (1) to be darker than that designated as shade No. 1 on the Ringelmann Chart; or (2) when observed or recorded with prescribed equipment to be darker than that; or to be of such capacity as to cause obscuration to a degree equivalent darker than that. This has to be noted here that for fuel burning equipment utilizing solid fuels, shade No. 2 of the Ringelmann Chart is applicable. According to Regulation 15, permissible dark smoke limit for existing such facilities is shade No. 2 on the Ringelmann Chart.

900. For achieving that these standards be followed, the occupier of any premises in or on which any smoke emitting facility, including industrial plant or fuel burning equipment is situated, shall if so directed by the Director General provide a means to his/her satisfaction whereby any person in charge of such facility may at all times readily ascertain without leaving the control room whether or not smoke is discharging from any chimney or such premises. Such means may include one or more of the following: (1) A smoke density indicator and alarm, installed so as to indicate adequately in the control room the density of smoke being discharged. (2) A window or other opening through which an unobstructed view of the top of the chimney may be obtained from the control room. (3) One or series of mirrors so placed as to reflect the top of the opening or chimney, which reflection shall be visible from the control room. (4) A closed circuit television installation with the receiver located in the control room. (5) Any other device that may be approved by the director general. The occupier of the premises, if so required, will install, operate, maintain and calibrate as may be determined by the Director General and to keep records of volume and density of smoke generated for inspection by the Director General.

901. Standards of compliance are contained in Regulations 24 to 30, which have the following essential standards to be followed: (1) According to Regulation 25, in any trade, industry, process, fuel burning equipment or industrial plant (other than plant or equipment used for the heating of metals) in the operation of which dust or other particles are emitted, the concentration at any point of any smoke, shoot, dust, ash (including fly ash) or other solid particles of any kind shall be such that the total mass of such solid particles before admixture with air, smoke or other gases does not exceed Standard A: 0.6, Standard B: 0.5, Standard C: 0.4 gram in each normal cubic meter of effluent gases. Likewise, Regulation 27 says that in any trade, industry or process, certain indicated gases should not be emitted more than the prescribed limits. With respect to emission of noxious or offensive substances is concerned, Regulation 32 says that they have to be within the prescribed limits. This is notable here in connection of power generation that smoke, grit, dust, carbon monoxide, hydrocarbons and fumes from petroleum works have been classified as noxious and offensive substances.

902. It is notable that for being within the prescribed limits power generation plants will have to install air pollution control equipment. If they do not do that, they will be considered to have violated the statutory provisions contained in the Environmental Quality Act 1974 and will be indicted for that. However, under section 45 of the Act with respect to offences which in the opinion of the inspecting officer a fine of not more than MYR 2,000 can be issued, a compound summon up to MYR 2,000 can be issued by the officer. Compounding of offences are done according to the Environmental Quality (Compounding of Offences) Regulations 1978. In addition to these, in case of any damage caused by the offender, the Director General can recover the costs and expenses incurred in connection of such violation.

903. As a matter of emergency requirement, where the Director General is satisfied that the failure in operation of any equipment, etc., or any control equipment used on any premises may cause accumulation of air impurities attaining such level as to threaten the public health, safety or welfare, or the quality of the environment, he may by writing require the occupier of such premises to provide within such period and to his/her satisfaction: (1) A comprehensive standby plan detailing the equipment, etc. (2) To install such necessary public warning or alert system. (3) To keep in adequate stock such equipment as may be required in such an emergent situation.

904. Where, in the opinion of the Director general the emissions of air impurities from one or a group of trade or industrial premises are of such volume, types, constituents and effects that the prescribed conditions or standard set forth in these

Regulations will not adequately protect public health, safety and welfare, the Director General may, under section 31 of the Environmental Quality Act, by notice in writing require the occupier of those premises to do the following within the stipulated time: (1) Install and operate control equipment or additional control equipment. (2) Repair, alter or replace any equipment or control equipment on those premises. (3) Erect or increase the height of the chimney. (4) Emit, discharge or deposit the air impurities. (5) Carry out his/her trade, industry or process or operate any equipment or industrial plant.

B. 2015 Regulations

905. The Environmental Quality (Clean Air) Regulation 2014 has replaced the Environmental Quality (Clean Air) Regulation 1978. It has made provisions about: measures to reduce emission, air pollution control system maintenance of records, change in occupancy limit values and technical standards, prohibition of emission dilution, periodic monitoring, emission declaration, accidental emission, standard method of sampling and analysis of emissions, prohibition order in certain cases and prohibition of giving false and misleading information. The salient features are: (1) Any change in operation or structure cannot be carried out without prior permission. (2) Efforts will be made to reduce emissions with the best available techniques. (3) Premises will have appropriate pollution control equipment. (4) Records will be maintained. (5) Change of occupancy will be notified. (6) The prescribed standards about emissions will be followed. (7) There will be no dilution of emissions. (8) Efforts will be made to adopt the best practices of emission of hazardous substances. (9) There will be periodic monitoring and continuous emission monitoring. (10) Accident must immediately be informed. (11) Prohibitory orders must be followed.

906. Giving false or misleading informations will be subject to a fine not exceeding MYR 100,000 or imprisonment not exceeding two years or both. Likewise, anyone who contravenes the regulations will be liable for a fine not exceeding MYR 100,000 or a jail not exceeding two years or both.

II. Environmental Quality (Control of Emissions from Diesel Engines) Regulations 1996

A. Control on Diesel Engines

907. The following points from Regulations 3 to 8 are notable: (1) Installed or replaced diesel engines must comply with the standards prescribed in the First Schedule. (2) From 1 January 1997, all motor vehicles must comply with the standards prescribed in the Schedule. (3) Notwithstanding this, the Director General may accept: (i) an engine type which is covered by a type test certificate in accordance with the Japanese Six Model Exhaust Emission Test (ii) or an engine type complying with such emission standards and test procedures approved by the Director General. (4) If desired by the Director General, there have to be periodical tests also.

B. Smoke Emission Control

908. This is governed under Regulations 9 to 19. The salient points are as follows: (1) The applicable standard to all kinds of vehicles is Ringelmann No. 2 of the Ringelmann Smoke Chart for a continuous period of more than ten seconds of emission form the exhaust pipe. (2) The maximum density of smoke should not be more than 50 HSU or other equivalent smoke units. (3) prohibition order may be issued as specified in the Seventh Schedule prohibiting the further operation of any motor vehicle that: (i) has undergone a smoke test as prescribed in the Regulations and the test result exceeds 70 HSU or other equivalent or (ii) has contravened the acceptable conditions within the period of three months preceding the smoke test. (4) More stringent standards may be issued if so required. (5) Vehicles under the prohibitory order cannot be operated until the prohibition period has expired or the defects have been fixed to the satisfaction of the Director General. (6) The exhaust pipe has to be straight and free of any attachment for the last 150 mm when the exhaust gas is finally discharged into the atmosphere. (7) The engine has to be stopped if the vehicle has to be stationary for more than three minutes. (8) Smoke tests can be carried out only at approved locations and the cost will be borne by the owner of the vehicle. (9) There should be a logbook having the details of the test and it will have to be made available for inspection.

909. First Schedule prescribes standards for diesel engine tested at steady speed. The parameters test about Co, HC and NO_x. These parameters are different with respect to heavy vehicles. Second Schedule contains different parameters pertaining to CO, HC NO_x and mass particulate matters for new models of motor vehicles. Schedule Three shows the Ringelmann Smoke Chart.

III. Environmental Quality (Control of Emission from Petrol Engines) Regulations 1996

A. Control of Petrol Engines

910. Regulations 3 to 8 deal about this. The important points to be noted are: (1) For all vehicles, standards have been prescribed in the First Schedule, including vehicles having an engine capacity of 700 cubic centimetre and below and 1,020 kg and below. (2) On or after 1 January 1997, new model cars will comply with the standard prescribed in Second Schedule. (3) After 1 January 2000, new models of motor vehicles, except vehicles used for racing designated racing circuits and approved racing events, will comply with the emission standards contained in the Third schedule.

911. Third Schedule is more stringent; according to it, if Director General so desires, he may recommend for even more stringent standards and test procedures as prescribed in previous points. (6) The assembler or manufacturer may be required to conduct necessary tests and to repeat such tests with interval of the prescribed period and to take certificate of the tests and keep them.

B. *Control of Gas Emissions*

912. The following are the notable points: (1) Every petrol engine shall comply with the emission standards prescribed in Schedule Four. For existing models, when the Regulations were brought into operation, CO had to be 4.5% and HC had to be 800 ppm. For all new models, it has to be 3.5% and 600 ppm respectively. These standards are meant for Regulation 10, which has general application. (2) Test will be conducted and certificates will be taken according to Schedule Six. (3) An appropriate officer can issue a prohibitory order with respect to any vehicle. This order is for three months. Within this period the order can be expunged if the engine is fixed and made efficient to comply the given emission standards. (4) The exhaust pipe has to be straight and free from any attachment for the last 150 mm. (5) Tests have to be conducted only by the approved facilities and test results have to be maintained in the logbook made for this purpose, which will be made available for inspection.

913. This has to be noted here that First schedule prescribes general standards about CO, No_x and HC emissions for Regulation 4(1) and (2) and Regulation 7. Emission standards for new models on or after 1 January 1997 are prescribed in the Second Schedule. Third Schedule prescribes standards to be applied for new vehicles on or after 1 January 2000.

C. *Contravention Licence*

914. Contravention licence can be issued by the Director General, when application is made to that effect, with respect to: (1) Motor vehicles to be used solely for testing. (2) Motor vehicles intended for assembly or already assembled before the coming into force of these regulations. (3) Motor vehicles to be used for military, combat or tactical purposes. (4) Motor vehicles that are in transit through Malaysia.

IV. Environmental Quality (Control of Emission from Motorcycles) Regulations 2003

915. The standards for all kinds of motorcycles locally manufactured and imported have been prescribed in the First schedule. So as to ensure the compliance, there is a mechanism of testing and certification. Violation of the requirement has been subjected to a stringent penalty, a fine of MYR 100,000 or an imprisonment of five years or both. The Director General may prescribe more stringent standards and test procedures. The standards are similar to that of EEC Council Directive 97/24/EC of 17 June 1997. With respect to two-stroke engines, standards are: CO 8 gm/km, HC 4 gm/km and NO_x gm/km.

Part VI. Interaction Between Energy Law and Tax Law

Chapter 1. Environmental Tax and Fiscal Incentives to Conservation of Energy and Renewable Energy Sources

916. In 1980s and 1990s, the idea of imposing pollution taxes, especially carbon tax on supply of fossil fuels and supply of electricity generated by thermal power generation plants, was seriously considered by many developed countries. This was inspired by the idea of shared responsibility, 'polluter pays' principle, and shifting the tax burden from taxing labour and investments to polluting acts and consumption of products that are produced not in environment-friendly manner, totally or partially. Almost all developed countries now have some kind of pollution taxes. Initially, the idea of imposing pollution taxes did not appeal developing countries, including Malaysia, because it was thought that they would impede economic development of those countries. This notion is becoming weak now. Some industrialized developing countries seem to go on board to impose carbon tax. Ever since the idea of imposing pollution taxes has been entertained, the base of imposition and modality of such taxes and utilization of financial resources generated from them have been the area for intellectual exercises.

917. The idea of imposing pollution taxes received strength when it was potently and persuasively argued that exaction of these taxes enhances environmental justice as their impositions are in conformity with the 'polluter pays' principle, and they enhance the equity in taxation in the sense that who pollutes more will pay more, and who consumes more of goods manufactured by non-environment-friendly ways will pay the cost of pollution burden accordingly.

918. At the same time when imposition of pollution taxes was stressed for these reasons, it was argued that we should tax 'bads'(polluting activities and goods manufactured in non-environment-friendly ways) rather than taxing 'goods' (labour and investments) or 'sins' (alcohol and tobacco). For these reasons, in 1997, when many developed nations were already imposing some kind of pollution taxes, more than 2,500 economists, including eight noble laureates, signed a petition suggesting to policymakers that carbon taxes or auctions of various emissions be used to curb emissions thought to be reasonable for global climate change. This is notable here that when this call was made, some developed countries were already imposing some kind of carbon tax, prominent among them were taxing supply of fossil fuels and increasing the tariff on electricity supply by a considerable percentage, where electricity was generated by thermal power generation plants using coal, oil or gas, because inflation of cost of electricity generated at thermal power generation plants is nothing but internalizing the external costs on power generation. This call strengthened the political will of many states, developed and developing, and then these states started widening the taxing net by imposing newer kinds of pollution taxes, like landfill tax, aviation tax, tax on pesticides and taxes on plastic bags. Some developing countries that have achieved certain limit of industrialization, their people are imminently suffering from the scourge of pollution and have to painfully bear the cost of pollution, are also exploring the possibility of imposing pollution taxes suited to their developing economies.

919. On the contrary, a sizable minority of economists is of the opinion that pollution taxes will unnecessarily increase the tax burden that will slow the economic growth. If a pollution tax is imposed on the supply of goods and services and the tax is not properly designed, consumers will suffer. The apprehensions of developing countries are not far from reality. Economies in these countries have to grow and the cost of pollution taxes cannot be internalized by weak economies. In spite of these apprehensions, some developing economies like Malaysia, India, Philippines and China are planning to have some kind of pollution taxes in the near future. Malaysian sales tax on petroleum is comparatively lower: petrol, 0.5862 Malaysian cents per litre; diesel, 0.1964 Malaysian cents per litre; and gas, 0.010 Malaysian cents per litre. The low rates have to be seen in light of gradual withdrawal of the subsidy on these. Nevertheless, there is a scope to levy some kind of carbon tax on their sales, but the country has not yet decided in its favour probably because the country is gradually withdrawing subsidy given on oil and gas and an economic study for imposing a carbon tax in this situation, which is necessary to be made, has not yet been made.

920. The idea of imposing pollution taxes seems to be simple and laudable but it suffers from numerous socio-economic and legal questions that have not yet been answered to the satisfaction of many. In spite of such doubts, developed countries opted for environmental taxes and imposed taxes on activities that caused deleterious effects on the environment. Prominent among them is carbon tax, a tax on supply on/and burning of fossil fuels. Other taxes ranged from taxing emission of NO_x, SO_x, landfill tax, surcharge on aviation, taxing supply of electricity and tax on use of inorganic fertilizers. These taxes got popularity in developed countries because they have double benefits: one, as a burden of the polluting activities; and, secondly, by mobilizing financial resources that could be utilized for cleaning up activities and reducing the burden of the traditional taxes. However, developing countries except China and few others still have economic doubts about these taxes. They think if these taxes cannot be internalized by their fragile economies, they will leave adverse effects on them.

§1. CARBON TAX

921. As a matter of first phase of tax reform, carbon tax is a popular pollution tax. It is being imposed in various West European countries, including EU countries, to fulfil their commitments to the Kyoto Protocol. This is widely accepted that carbon taxes – tax on sale or purchase of mainly fossil fuels, or tax on the end product of their consumption, like energy – will help in meeting the challenges of global warming. This is because the immediate impact of this kind of tax will affect consumption of fossil fuel or electricity. This is called the 'price effect' of the tax. Article 17 of the Kyoto Protocol of 1997 made under the UNFCCC also paves the way for imposing such taxes. Eminent environmental economists like William Cline, a Senior Fellow at the Institute for International Economics, and the Centre for Global development, Washington, Harvard University Professor Robert Mendelsohn, and Stanford University Professor Alan Manne have also supported this for this obvious reason. This has to be noted here that coal contains the largest amount of carbon. So, it has to be taxed at the highest rate. Oil is next to it and gas comes next to oil. As a matter of strategy for alleviating CO_2 emissions in those countries that have to adopt cut on CO_2 emissions under the Kyoto Protocol, tax can suitably be imposed in any of the following forms: a tax on supply of fossil fuels according to the content of carbon in them; a tax on the supply of electricity generated by thermal power generation plants; or tax on emission permits (emission trading). Each one of them has its merits and demerits. In addition to these, there can be low road tax rate on economy cars, and comparatively high tax rates on big cars, heavy vehicles and dieselized cars so that they bear the cost of polluting the environment according to their capacity to pollute it. These considerations are also viable in case of imposition of carbon tax. British Columbia is the best example of this. One thing has to be noted here that since heavy transport vehicles are part of the economic system of big industries, due consideration to this aspect will have to be given while designing a viable tax structure. Likewise, as has been pointed out in some of the European countries, it has been observed that pollution tax will put additional burden on middle-class and lower-middle-class people. They would not be able to use cars or other vehicles so frequently; their economic activities with the result of that might ultimately suffer. The example that is frequently given is of farmers. It, therefore, pointed out that the tax structure must consider this factor. Thus, *Guardian* highlights this issue in the following words:

> The study of professor Paul Ekins and Dr. Simon Dresner of the Policy Studies Institute, UK, shows consumption of energy, water and waste disposal services in poorer homes is disproportionately high in relation to their income. The same is true of petrol and diesel for those who own cars. Consequently, flat-rate environmental taxes or charges would be regressive – claiming a greater share of income from poor people than from better off households. Most unintended social consequences could be removed by giving green taxes a structure that increase the tariff or charge those most able to pay – or by making compensation available for low-income households through state benefits. However, it is warned that use of environmental resources varied widely within income groups. This means that even if most low-income households were to

> be protected by charging or compensation schemes, a minority would still end up as net losers. On energy use, and a potential impact of a carbon tax on household energy consumption, it was noted that many low-income households already experienced 'fuel poverty', defined as needed to spend more than ten per cent of their income on keeping warm. After analyzing 13 different models for tax and compensation schemes the researchers could conclude that it would be possible to designed systems based on interests of average poor households.

In view of this, it has to be noted here that the EU on 27 October 2003 adopted new laws on energy taxation, but with many consumer friendly exemptions. A proposal to broaden the scope of existing energy taxation laws to include all energy products was adopted. The directive, thus, intended to boost competitiveness and reduce GHG emissions. But numerous exemptions included in the final proposal means consumer petrol and diesel prices will not be affected in any Member State until 2010 at the earliest. And the law will not affect the public transport system or international air and sea transport. Modality will be simple: enforcing quota system on consumption of petrol diesel for poor consumers; and subsidizing the transport industries.

The new directive will see all other uses of coal, gas and electricity subjected to minimum tax rates across Europe. Member States will be able to offer companies tax breaks if they work to reduce their energy emissions. The new law has come into effect from January 2004 and suitable legislations are being made to meet the requirements on the EU Directive. Countries that impose tax on energy are always conscious about the international competitiveness of the products of energy-intensive industries. To keep such industries competitive at the international scale, lower rate of carbon tax, for example, is imposed on them. Other industries are taxed at normal rate. A study on OECD countries has revealed that this strategy has proved to be successful. The above discussions are based on the basis of experiences of developed countries. They may be useful in industrialized developing countries with strong economic indicators if they wish to impose carbon tax on supply of fossil fuels, or a comprehensive tax on supply of energy produced in thermal power generation plants, or a pollution tax on the products of energy-intensive industries or products that consume fossil fuels. This has to be noted that before entertaining the idea of imposing such a tax, the development strategy of the country, total energy consumption, and total emissions of CO_2 will have to be taken into consideration. Blind emulation of developed countries by developing or less developed countries might yield undesired results. Malaysia, for example imposes sales tax comparatively at very low rate. In spite of the fact that the country is gradually withdrawing the subsidy given on oil and gas, there is a scope to impose a carbon tax at a moderate rate on their sale, or at any other level, provided an economic study permits for imposing it. In many developing countries, including Malaysia, down town areas are crowded with vehicles and the air is highly polluted. In addition to other strategies to ease the problem, a toll on vehicles at the entry points can be considered. It is the modest type of pollution tax that will squarely help in solving the air pollution problems in these areas.

I. Carbon Tax Versus Emissions Trading

922. Carbon tax and emissions trading, as it was, were considered the two policy instruments in the area of pollution taxation. Although an international emissions trading system did not necessarily preclude imposition of carbon tax, both are considered suitable means to reduce CO_2 emissions. Both of them were considered to have advantages and disadvantages, and both could be practised. We have noted above that carbon tax is price related; it increases the price of services and goods, which decreases the demand of such goods and services. Emissions trading (trading permits), on the other hand, is quantity based, which fixes the total amount of carbon emitted and allows price level to fluctuate according to market forces. Thus, under this system, the quantity of emissions is fixed (often called as 'cap') and the right to emit becomes a tradable commodity. The 'cap' (say 10,000 tonnes of carbon) is divided into transferable units (say 10,000 permits of 1 tonne of carbon each). Permits are often referred to as 'greenhouse gas units', 'quotas' or 'allowances'. To be in compliance, actors participating in the system must hold a number of permits greater or equal to their actual emission level. Once permits are allocated (by auction, sale or free allocation) to the actors participating in the system, they are tradable. This enables emission reductions to take place wherever costs are lower. Kevin Baumert, while supporting the case of emissions trading, says that a well-functioning emission trading system allows emission reductions to take place wherever abatement cost is lower, regardless of international borders. Since cost associated with climate change, for example, coastal flooding, loss of crop or damage by drought, etc. have no correlations with the origin of carbon dioxide emissions, the rationale for this policy approach is clear. If emission reductions are cheaper to make in one country than in another country, emissions should be reduced first in the former country where cost will be lower.

923. Emission trading had the advantage of fixing of certain environmental outcome – the aggregate emission levels were fixed, and institutions had to pay the market rate for the right to pollute. This also attempted to make emissions trading more conducive to international environmental agreement – Kyoto Protocol – because specific emission reduction levels can be agreed upon more easily than tax rates or policy instruments, which may vary in appropriateness and applicability between states.

924. 'Emission trading' was thus considered to be more appealing to private industries, because by decreasing emissions, firms could actually profit by selling their excess GHG allowances. Thus, creating such a market for pollution could potentially drive emission reductions below targets. In general, transferring resources between private entities was more appealing than transfers to government. 'Emission trading' was better equipped than taxes to deal with all GHGs mentioned in the Kyoto Protocol under one comprehensive strategy. Each gas has its own greenhouse effect. Thus, business installations emitting more than one GHG had more flexibility in making reductions. Permits adjust automatically for inflation and external price shocks, while taxes do not. For example, the US has already experienced an extended period of stable GHG emission levels because of high oil prices. Taxes, therefore, have to be designed to adjust for such external shocks. No doubt, 'emissions trading' is an alternative to carbon tax and that can also be practiced, but when we compare it with a carbon tax, we find that a carbon tax has more advantages than the 'emission trading'. Some of the advantages are: (1) A carbon tax would relate a commercial organization and also an individual, because it relates to consumption of fuels that have carbon content in them, or it will relate to the products manufactured in energy-intensive industries. (2) In case of a carbon tax there are no intermediaries. It also does not involve commercial intricacies. It is, thus, simple to operate. (3) Through pollution taxes incentives can be granted to those who strive for emission reduction and achieve success. It can also provide incentives to the poor populations, small- and medium-scale industries, priority industries and units that consume less energy, like small cars, portable electricity generators, small pumping sets used for irrigation purposes. (4) Pollution taxes are not susceptible to strategic 370 behaviour of industries and NGOs, which may harm the contractual environment of the market. NGOs or even private individuals that object to the concept of purchasing the 'right to pollute' may purchase large number of permits to drive up cost of CO_2 emissions abatement. Likewise, industries may hoard permits, driving up the prices of competitors. These will not set healthy practices. (5) Pollution taxes are simple than the other choice. (6) Pollution taxes provide a choice to shift the burden of tax from 'good' to 'bad' as has been mentioned above.

925. In spite of these advantages of imposing a carbon tax, the United States supports the 'emission trading'. This was because the US believes that carbon tax will impede their economy and their products will be less competitive in the international market. Trading allowed the US companies to purchase emissions allowances from those countries that had not to accept any cut on the CO_2 emissions now. The United States pleaded that this would benefit both a developing country from where the 'tradable permits' would be purchased and the US companies that would purchase them. On the contrary, the EU also had to accept a cut on the threshold accepted in the Kyoto Protocol, but it supports, for the above reasons, a suitably designed carbon tax. With the result of that, EU Member States opted for carbon tax rather than supporting 'emissions trading'. This has been unfortunate that in spite of the EU opposition to the idea of 'emissions trading', it was made a part of the Kyoto Protocol. Developing countries rightly have the cautious approach, because they know that the system of 'emission trading' could be financial resources to them, but that could not help in fighting the menace of global warming. In the long run, therefore, could suffer more than the financial benefits they could get. They thus want permit allocations based on population rather than historic national emissions levels. This was not acceptable to the United States and Japan. The author is of the opinion that from the environmental and economic point of view, to impose a carbon tax is a better choice. It will certainly reduce emissions levels of CO_2, which is mainly responsible for the phenomenon of global warming. It will also keep the economic balance. The worst economic effect of 'emission trading' might be that the industries of developing countries will never have competitiveness of their products in the era of globalization because industries in developed countries will buy the 'emissions permit' and will continue to maintain their competitive edge in the global market.

926. Even though developing countries are in favour of imposing carbon tax first if they positively consider for imposing pollution taxes, the actual difficulty with them is that they are in the process of withdrawing subsidy that they give on petrol, diesel and gas. This is being opposed by a section of the people on the argument that it would increase the prices of these commodities, and in turn there will be higher rate of inflation, which unnecessarily increase the burden on the poor population. If in addition to this a carbon tax is also imposed, it will further escalate the prices of fuel and that will result in further rise of prices of essential commodities. Perhaps for this reason, developing countries like India, Malaysia and Thailand talk about imposing carbon tax, but have so far abstained from resorting to this source of revenue mobilization. They can, thus, think of imposing some kind of environmental levy on consumption of electricity. If they do so, they can easily protect the interest of the poor population inhabiting in rural areas by either levying it on per household basis, per pumping set basis or at comparatively lower rate. In this case they will have to be watchful about commercial use of the electricity. In case electricity is used for commercial activities other than agricultural activities, the lower rate that is applicable to agricultural activities should not be applicable. In commercial activities, however, incentives through tax rates or rebate can be provided to SMIs and priority industries. Free supply of electricity to the rural mass is not advisable, because if electricity is free, the chances of wastage of electricity and its misuse will be unimaginable.

It is notable here that some countries, including Malaysia, are imposing FiT between 1% to 2% on higher electricity consumers to finance power generation by renewable sources. As noted above, Malaysia imposed at the rate of 1% on those who consume electricity worth RM 100 or more. The proposal is to raise it to 2%. This is in effect a kind of carbon tax to be paid by energy consumers and to be utilized for encouraging those engaged with power generation by renewable sources. This seems to be a better option in developing countries, as it has an element of equity in it.

II. Input Versus Output Tax

927. We have noted above that a carbon tax has to be internalized by industries that emit GHGs so that they bear the burden of it on the society and the society is given proper incentives from the proceeds of the tax. We have also noted that in case of power generation units, a carbon tax can be imposed on the sale or purchase of fossil fuels (tax on input), or on the end product, electricity (output tax). These two tax schemes contain their good and bad aspects. The input tax means taxing each power producer according to its own GHG emissions. The output tax puts burden on the supply of electricity or goods manufactured by use of electricity generated from fossil fuels. An output tax, thus, taxes electricity bought by consumers according to the average GHG emission, regardless of electricity's origin. In theory, according to Boris Cournede and Stephen Gallon the first option of taxation is expected to be the best since it discriminates between the producers according to the damage they cause to the environment; whereas, option two does not give any incentive to make the producers reduce their GHG emissions as all producers face the same tax when selling electricity to consumers. Nonetheless, the option two, which will reduce the electricity demand, is much easier to implement and does not create distortion in the competitive electricity market. According to them, each option has to be assessed on the charge of electricity prices, load curve, power generation plants, taxation revenues for the state and GHG emissions. They found, in the French context – after testing both on these parameters that in the short term – that both options will lead to a rise in electricity price and fall in electricity demand and in GHG emissions. Nonetheless, in the long term (once the power generation system gets fit to the reduced demand), the second option will lead to rise 7% of GHG emission. On the contrary, the first option will help reducing GHG emissions by 40%. Ultimately, the option 2 will become counterproductive. This is concluded from the fact that in the long term, due to option two the French producers will turn more heavily to fossil fuel-fired power generation plants that are more suitable to meet the reduced demands. We have noted above that that second option is easy to administer and can easily be put together with various suitable incentives. The author is of the opinion that from the point of view of environment also the second option can be preferable because emissions of GHG can be controlled by suitable regulations and incentives provided in the income tax law.

§2. Pollution Funds

928. Internationally and nationally for compensating environmental victims, especially damage caused by oil spills, funds have been created, especially for compensating environmental victims. There has been a practice to compensate victims of pollution, where it is difficult to identify the polluter responsible for the pollution damage, to undertake clean-up operations and enhance the environmental processes, and to provide alternative source of drinking water where the source of water is contaminated, from a fund created from the pollution taxes levied on those who are jointly and severally liable for degradation of the environment in general and damage sustained by the people in specific. Initial examples of creation of such funds are: Japanese Air Pollution Health Fund and Netherlands's Air Pollution Fund. The Japanese fund was created, out of the levy on the industries that emitted Sulphur Dioxide gas, to deal with the problem of health hazards caused by emissions of this gas. The Netherlands's fund was to deal with the general health hazards resulted by pollution. This was created on the revenue derived from general taxpayers. In this case the claimant had to exhaust other remedies available in the legal system. An advantage of the Japanese fund was that it was based on 'polluter pays' principle and it provided incentives to the industries to reduce their liability by emitting less.

929. The Japanese experience provides an example of a viable Environmental Enhancement Fund (EEF). After the original compensation fund was closed to new claimants in 1988, a new Compensation and Prevention Association (CPA) was set up, financed by a fund consisting of an initial endowment from the Japanese Government, which was invested and supplemented by a compulsory levy on industries responsible for air pollution. The Association implemented various health and environmental educational projects directly and disbursed grants to local governments to carry out environmental clean-up and conservation projects, including tree plantations.

930. The feasibility of such funds was thoroughly discussed by the European Commission in 1993 with a predominant question whether they should exist alongside individual civil liability so as to 'maintain a preventive effect'. The Commission after considering the compensation scheme contained in the International Convention on Civil Liability for Oil Pollution Damage 1992 (CLC) and the International Convention on the Establishment of an International Fund for Compensation for Oil Pollution Damage 1992 (the Fund Convention), supported for creation of such funds. This may be noted here that both of these conventions are effective together in case of marine oil pollution damage. A claim is first established under the CLC and compensation is claimed within the given limits of compensations. If the compensation awarded under the CLC falls short, a petition for additional compensation is filed before the Director General of the IOPC fund, created under the Fund Convention on the basis of the definite contributions given by the countries on their oil importations. This two-tier system of compensation is working very successfully.

931. Since then, European countries are keen to establish viable environmental funds. Significant among them is the French Model. Since 1993 through the Law No. 92-1444 of France, the country has provided for a Noise Fund based on the taxation of airline operators. As a result, those living along the Paris airports are compensated for exposure to excessive noise levels. The tax is proportionate to the number of lights, the noise level of the aircraft and the category of airports. The Swedish Environmental Damage Act 1986 requires those who obtain regulatory approval under the Environmental Protection Act to subscribe to compulsory insurance provided by fire insurance companies through a system of prescribed levies. The product of the insurance is applied to those situations where liability compensation under the Act of 1986 is considered inadequate, usually because the party responsible cannot be identified or because a responsible company is insolvent, or because a claim is time barred. This scheme is also followed by Finland under Environmental Damage Insurance Act 1998.

932. Section 36A of the Malaysian Environmental Quality Act 1974 provides for imposition of a cess on the waste generation. Along with other money, money mobilized by the cess will become part of the Environmental Fund. Section 36D provides that the Minister may require any person, engaged in exploration, extraction, refining, production, bulk movement, distribution or storage of oil and environmentally hazardous substances, or engaged in bulk movement or storage of wastes, to contribute to the fund. The fund can be utilized under section 36E for: coordinating research in relation to any aspect of pollution or the prevention thereof; prevention or combating the spillage, discharge or dumping of oil or discharge or deposit of environmentally hazardous substances or wastes; and encouraging conservation measures against any damage to the environment. In the Act, there are provisions for imposing some kind of environmental levy. It can be anticipated that the scope of the fund can be widened by imposing carbon tax and making the financial resources, mobilized through it, part of the fund.

933. As a matter of conclusion it can be said that developing countries, including Malaysia, should conduct an intensive economic study for imposing some kind of carbon tax. If its imposition does not leave a significant adverse economic effect, it can be imposed because it has its own positive effects on the environment and the money mobilized by this source can be utilized in fighting environmental damage and possibly in reducing the other tax burden on person and property. This kind of stuff is necessary because in these countries presently on the agenda is to gradually withdraw the subsidy given on petrol and diesel. Can a carbon tax be imposed on along with withdrawal of subsidy is a big economic question, which can be answered only when a thorough economic study on it has been conducted. This is notable here that Western countries do not have oil totally free from subsidy. This fact will have to be kept in mind.

§3. Renewable Energy Sources and Fiscal and Other Incentives to Them

934. Environmental taxes are supported for protection of the environment and mobilizing financial resources. They are known as double dividends. One best use of that money may be for funding conservation processes of the environment. These taxes are also supported because they aim to substitute taxing ‘bad’ from ‘good’, that is, taxing polluting activities and exempting labour and investment. For this reason, in the energy sector, sale, purchase and use of fossil fuels are subjected to a tax with a predominant idea to reduce their consumption. Towards this end, subsidy on them is also being withdrawn gradually. In view of the fact that oil and gas are exhaustible natural resources, emphasis was laid on augmenting renewable energy sources. But renewable sources of energy are not becoming popular because they are not cost-effective. So as to mitigate their costs, various fiscal and other incentives are being resorted to. Malaysia is also granting tax incentives to these energy sources.

935. Renewable energy sources, atomic energy source and hydroelectric energy source, are cleanest and reliable energy sources. They are being considered to be reliable and in the long run they will be the only viable renewable energy source. This perception is getting strength. It is, therefore, suggested that about these thorough environmental and safety investigations should be done. Among these, hydroelectric can be less dangerous provided before starting the project thorough environmental impact assessment is done and it is followed by regular competent auditing mechanism. In the area of renewable energy sources solar energy, wind energy, geothermal energy, underwater turbines, biomass energy and biofuels can be fruitful. Many countries are already successfully resorting to them. Their importance has increased with the forging of the Paris Agreement to put a cap on continuous increase of the average global temperature with the excessive emissions of carbon dioxide and other greenhouse gases. Some of them have great potential in Malaysia too. But the greatest problem with them is that they are presently not cost-effective. States, notably India and China, are making efforts by declaring these areas, especially Solar PV, as priority areas and are providing fiscal incentives and financial assistance so that they could substantially contribute to the total power generation of the country. Western countries have set a target that by the end of this decade the ratio of renewable sources of energy will be more than 30% of the total power generation. Among them, Germany notably has declared to totally phase out fossil fuels. Developing countries, including Malaysia, have also set a target through their development plans in order to keep their promises made to the UN to internalize the targets of the Paris Agreement, and are making all positive efforts to achieve the targets. It can be suggested here that in this process developed countries should help developing countries. It is necessary because reliability of developing countries on burning wood and fossil fuel with less advanced technology will escalate the global warming problem.

§4. Tax Incentives on Energy in Malaysia

936.

- In many countries, the most popular incentive provided to certain activities or institutions is depreciation allowance. In some countries, this allowance is granted on the basis of commercial expediency. In some other countries it is allowable at the rates prescribed in the taxing statutes. In these countries, higher rate of depreciation allowance is granted with respect to certain plant and machinery, including pollution control equipment, to which incentives have to be provided. Depreciation allowance in these countries is enhanced when the business activity is carried out in extra shifts also. India is the best example of this practice. Enhanced depreciation allowance is the most popular way of providing incentive to machinery and plant, used for conservation and protection of the environment, including machinery and plant used for conservation of energy and producing and using renewable and other environmentally friendly energy generation sources. Such incentives are also provided for producing energy-efficient equipments. India allows 100% depreciation allowance on purchase of pollution control equipment by a company if used in running the business or machinery and plants used in generating, and supplying renewable and other energy sources. It is given on the straight-line basis and can be set off against the income and carried forward and set off against incomes of subsequent years. India provided 80% depreciation allowance on power generation by wind, and ten years of tax-free benefits on investments in this sector. In 2017, this 80% has been brought down to 40%. This is not considered to be a good policy by the Indian Wind Power Association.[183] The position of solar PV is maintained. The Government is considering similar incentives to be provided to rooftop solar power. In order to

183. *The Hindu,* 11 Nov. 2017.

achieve its 175 GW by small hydro, biomass, rooftop solar, wind and solar PV by 2022, the Electricity Act 2003 provides up to 100% FDI. There are following incentives also:

- Some imported products are exempt from payment of excise duty. For instance, certain components of wind energy electricity generators and solar photovoltaic (PV) ribbons are liable for full exemptions.
- Select components for the manufacture of solar modules, solar water heaters and associated systems are granted complete or partial Basic Customs Duty (BCD) waivers.
- Solar and wind power projects are excluded from inter-state transmission charges or taxes on transmission losses for twenty-five years from the date of commissioning.
- The Goods and Services Tax (GST) on solar and wind energy components is limited to 5%.

The solar PV and wind energy sources are also supported by the following financial incentives:

- Wheeling charges (charges for transmission of electricity over the grid on a per mega watt hour basis) are comparable with those offered to fossil fuel-based power. Considering the irregular nature of wind and sunshine, this is a vital incentive offered to companies.
- Viability Gap Funding (VGF) assistance, up to a maximum of USD 153,846.2/MW, through reverse auction for ultra-large solar power projects of 5,000 MW capacity, which will be implemented by the Solar Energy Corporation of India (SECI).
- A subsidy of 30% of project costs, after which off-grid solar projects can also avail soft loans.
- 40% accelerated depreciation in a written down value (WDV) basis.
- Rooftop solar installation as accommodated in housing loans provided by banks or National Housing Boards.

In Malaysia, depreciation is calculated by the company, but it is not a deductible expense under the Income Tax Act 1967. Instead of this, Malaysia grants capital allowances, given on investments pertaining to certain activities and plant and machinery, computed in the prescribed manner. The term 'plant and machinery' has not been defined in the Income Tax Act. This has to be understood, therefore, in the light of decided cases in Malaysia and elsewhere. Courts have given it a widest possible connotation so that the scope of the incentive is widened. In Malaysia, its scope had further been widened by paragraph 2 of Schedule 3 of the Income Tax Act. This paragraph was not applicable to renewable energy sources. It was suggested that renewable energy sources should also be brought within the ambit of paragraph 2 of Schedule 3 of the Act. This will encourage investment in this area. Capital allowances in the country initially were in form of initial allowance on initial investment and annual allowance with respect to certain machinery and plants under paragraphs 15 and 19 of Schedule 3 of the Income Tax Act. It provided initial allowance of 40% to plants and machinery used for managing schedule wastes, generating electricity from renewable sources. Initial allowance at this rate was allowable with respect to investments in acquiring plants and machinery providing natural gas at petrol stations and acquiring and running monogas buses. In addition to this, annual allowance of 20% with respect to environmental protection equipment, and plant, machinery and equipment required in providing natural gas at petrol stations was also deductible. Annual allowance at the same rate is granted to companies operating monogas buses.

937. This is notable here that although renewable sources had not been mentioned here, the allowance was supposed to be available under the first category with respect to plant and machinery used in generating and transmitting renewable energy because use of renewable source of energy is a sine qua non for protection of the environment. This is also notable that the total of allowances became 60% in the first year and in subsequent years it was at the rate of 20% on straight-line basis.

938. The system of capital allowances worked well. However, the system of depreciation allowance given with respect to plant and machinery pertaining to protection and conservation of environment in India is working efficiently and has not been subjected to criticism. In view of this, it will be appropriate to say that both the systems are economically viable and suited to all economies. It can, however, be suggested that the annual allowance provided to environmental protection equipment, plant, machinery and equipment required in providing natural gas at petrol stations, and monogas buses should have been given annual allowance at the rate of 40%. It can also be suggested that the scope of this allowance should be widened to include other aspects of conservation and protection of the environment.

939. In addition to the two allowances mentioned above, conservation of energy and renewable energy qualified for accelerated capital allowance and expenses incurred on scientific researches pertaining to these qualify for double deduction. These have provided the real boost to conservation of energy and renewable energy sources. Nevertheless, renewable energy sources are not people's choice. The Government thought to provide financial assistance to projects venturing in this area of energy generation by creating a floating fund. It is already there in place.

940. The present position **of** tax incentives provided to clean energy sector are:

(1) From October 2009 until 2004, green building projects were entitled to get 100% tax exemption on additional capital expenditure. This could be used to set off against 100% statutory income. Buildings and residential properties owners were also eligible for stamp duty exemption based on the additional cost to obtain Green Building certification.
(2) In 2014 budget a general incentive scheme – known as Green Technology Incentives – was introduced to support green technology meeting the criteria specified in the National Green Technology Policy, which also covered green buildings. The incentive is in the form of Investment Tax Allowance and tax exemptions.

(3) For investment tax allowance eligible companies are companies that undertake investments in promoted projects that encourage sustainability and green environment either for own use or business purposes. This is 100% of qualifying capital expenditure incurred within a period of five years to be utilized against 100% of statutory income for each year of assessment. It is available until 2020.

(4) The companies must be engaged with projects pertaining to renewable energy (excluding solar FiT projects), energy efficiency, green building, green data centres, and integrated waste management (notably recycling, treatment and recovery).

(5) The conditions for the companies are: It must be registered under the Companies Act 1965. It must have achieved the following green results: minimizes the degradation of the environment or reduces greenhouse emissions; promoted health and improved environment; and conserves the use of energy and/or other forms of natural resources or promotes the use of renewable energy or recycles waste material resources.

(6) From the energy point of view they may be: companies providing energy conservation services, and companies which incur capital expenditure for conserving energy for own consumption.

(7) Companies rendering green technology services are entitled to income tax exemption of 100% of statutory income from the year of assessment until the year of assessment 2020. Green technology services related to renewable energy, energy efficiency, electric vehicles, green buildings, green data centres, green certification and verification, and green townships can qualify for this tax incentive.

(8) Investment tax allowance of 100% of qualifying capital expenditure on green technology assets from the year of assessment 2013 until the year of assessment 2020. The allowance can be offset against 70% of statutory income of the year of assessment. Unutilized allowance can be carried forward and set off until fully absorbed.

(9) Pioneer status companies are entitled to get tax exemption for ten years. Otherwise, companies providing green services that support investment in green technology are entitled for tax exemption of 100% of statutory income from the year of assessment 2013 until year of assessment 2020. Green services are: Renewable related to renewable energy; energy-efficient services; green building-related services; Green data services; certification or verification bodies; green township advisory or consultancy or design services; and electric vehicles (installation, maintenance, and repair of EV charging equipment, infrastructure and EV charging station. Operation of EV charging station, and maintenance, repair and overhaul of EV. The criteria for these are: company must be registered under the Companies Act 1965 and had started operation before 25 October 2013; it should have at least one personal expert in the green technology of the area; it must be green policy-friendly to the environment; 100% of company's income must be derived from green technology services.

(10) All applications have to be processed through Malaysian Investment Development Authority (MIDA). Decisions are taken based on the evaluation made by the Energy Commissions.[184]

It is hoped that the incentives provided above will help gradually shifting of power generation from fossil fuels to renewable energy sources, as these incentives will certainly encourage investment in green technology pertaining to these sources of energy, energy conservation and energy efficiency. This will also encourage companies to buy green technology assets verified by the Malaysian Green Technology Corporation (MGTC) that are listed under the MyHijau Directory.

The Energy Commission was established as a statutory body under the Energy Commission Act 2001 on 1 May 2001; it became fully operative from 1 January 2002. It aims to balance the needs of consumers and providers of energy to ensure safe and reliable supply of electricity at reasonable prices, protect public interest and foster economic development and competitive markets in an environmentally sustainable manner. Towards this end, it is regulating the energy sector specifically the electricity and the piped gas supply industries in Peninsular Malaysia and Sabah.

§5. CONCLUSIONS

941. Malaysia is an industrialized developing country. It is growing at a relatively faster rate. Due to rapid industrial development, an increasing number of cars and commercial vehicles and rapid urbanization, its energy needs are growing faster than many other developing countries. Presently, the country is mainly relying on thermal power generation plants. Among them, gas-fired thermal power generation plants are significant. The country's oil and gas reserves are being extracted, and efforts are being made to discover new reserves. It exports its good-quality oil and imports crude oil mainly from the Middle East for its refineries. The country is using its gas reserves moderately and was importing gas from Indonesia to support the total gas consumption. Malaysia is also third largest exporter of gas. However, LNG export in 2015 was valued at RM 47 billion, lower than RM 64 billion in 2014, due to lower price. The first biogas plant began production in 2016. Since the country has huge generation of palm oil mill effluents, this sector has potential to grow fast.

184. See, Japheth Lim, 'New Tax Incentive for Green Building Malaysia (2013-2020)', at: http://blog.japhethlim.com/index.php/2016/11/04/new-tax-incentive-for-green-buildings-updated/ (accessed on 20 Mar. 2018); Energy Commission, 'Energy Efficiency Incentive Through Investment Tax Allowance and Pioneer Status', at: file:///Users/ahaseeb/Downloads/EE%20Incentive%20By%20Norazrin.pdf (accessed on 19 Mar. 2018); Zabidah Daud, 'Tax Incentives for Green Technology Industry', 18 Apr. 2017, at: file:///Users/ahaseeb/Downloads/MIDA_Tax%20Incentives%20for%20Green%20Technology%20Industry.pdf (accessed on 12 Feb. 2018); 'Mastering Energy Efficiency Initiatives Into High Gear', *Energy Malaysia*, vol. 10, 2016, pp. 8–12.

We have pointed out above that ASEAN countries are seriously working on establishing a network of gas supply among Member States. Malaysia is actively participating in this project. Malaysia is trying hard to maximize its oil and gas production. It has got considerable success. It is said that a time will come when Malaysia will become net oil exporter in the region.

942. The country does not have any nuclear power generation plant. There is a plan to have a nuclear power generation beyond 2030. Right now, the country has one prototype nuclear reactor at the MINT for research purposes. However, in view of the ever-increasing power demand – about 5% per year – in the country and escalating oil and gas prices and their exhaustible nature, the federal government has indicated that it is considering to build one or if need be more than one after 2030. It is notable here that Malaysia is a member of the IAEA. Therefore, its future nuclear power generation programme will have to be transparent and within the non-proliferation rules.

943. We have noted above that atomic power generation is being considered by some industrialized and fast-growing economies, especially India and China. They will have few more additions to their existing nuclear power plants. Malaysia does not have such plans for the near future as until 2020 the country will not face energy crisis. It has one small reactor for research purposes only. India and China feel that without this, their future demand of energy cannot be met. The idea to increase dependency on nuclear power generation has gained strength due to high power demand and the soaring prices of oil and gas. It is notable that policymakers and scientific advisors in these countries are of the opinion that future development depends on atomic power generation plants. This tendency has its impact on other countries, including Malaysia, also because the IAEA supports the peaceful use of atomic reactors. In view of this, it can be said that a country such as Malaysia, where energy demands are growing fast, should keep the option of atomic power generation plant(s) open. It is pertinent to suggest here that a country should venture to this source of energy only when it is sure about the safety aspects of such power generation reactors, safe movement and treatment of wastes generated from reactors, and the capability to treat the nuclear wastes generated. The most challenging task is ensuring that atomic materials will not pass into the hands of terrorists.

944. As noted above, presently, electricity is mainly generated by thermal power generation plants using coal and gas. This is the position in countries that have coal reserves. India and China are fast-growing economies, but their power demands are mainly fulfilled by thermal power generation plants, mainly coal-fired power generation plants. In Malaysia also, the position, more or less, is the same. Only recently, in Sarawak, which is a state in East Malaysia, two coal-fired thermal power generation plants have been commissioned. There are plans to have few more such plants in the West Malaysia also. But the best thing is that these plants nearly follow international standards. Sarawak has coal-fired power plants because the state has coal reserves, the power needs of the state are growing and the prices of oil and gas are becoming unbearably high. It is notable here that the country is venturing into this area of power generation due to some compelling factors. Malaysia believes in having the cleanest possible thermal power generation plants. This is proven by the fact that Malaysia is revamping its old thermal power generation plants. In the State of Malacca, two old plants have already been renovated. Renovation is placing a monetary burden on the country, but the work has been undertaken to achieve cleaner and more efficient power generation plants. It is planned to modify other old coal-fired thermal power generation plants. It can rightly be understood that in many coming years Malaysia's main power generation will be based on gas thermal power generation units. Coal-fired power generation plants will partially supplement them. The country is taking benefits of Clean Development Mechanism under the Kyoto Protocol.

945. In addition to thermal power generation plants, Malaysia also has embarked on hydroelectric power generation, on both a large and prototype scale. Initially, the ratio of this source of energy was not that high, but with commissioning of the Bakun Dam of Sarawak, the ratio has substantially increased. In Sarawak, thus, the hydropower is the main source of power generation.

946. Malaysia is ambitious to manufacture, export and use locally its biodiesel (it is called as EnvoDiesel), manufactured by blending 7% palm oil with natural diesel (B7). This has proven to be a successful venture. It is expected that the country will soon start producing B10. Currently, biodiesel manufactured in the country is being exported to the European Union, and the importing countries are using it to run trains. However, because of the recent EU Regulation, its export to EU countries is badly suffering. It is in this perspective that the Malaysia and Indonesia are trying hard to block its enforcement against them. There is a great demand for biodiesel elsewhere because it is cheaper and causes comparatively less pollution as it contains less carbon and hydrocarbons. Malaysia is venturing into this area because the country is one of the biggest palm oil manufacturers. Towards this end, palm oil manufacturers and other relevant parties are fast converging. It was decided that by the end of 2006, there will be six large units producing biodiesel. This further grew in 2007. In 2006, the federal government invited applications for establishing a biodiesel industry in the country. It received an overwhelming response. In 2000, one person applied to produce biodiesel and his application was approved. In 2002, two people applied and both applications were approved. In 2004, three applications were made and all of them were approved. Until 2004, the total production was estimated at 27,000 tonnes per year. In 2006, when the government invited applications, ninety-eight applications were made, of which fifty-seven were approved. Taking these new producers into account, the estimated total production of biodiesel would go beyond 5,200,000 tonnes per annum. This will help to protect the environment and will be a means of generating profit for a country like Malaysia. It is estimated that the consumption of B7 in 2018 will be 400 million litres. It is estimated that the export of B10 biodiesel may further rise. However, in view of maintaining a meaningful and practicable balance between the use of palm oil in manufacturing biodiesel and its other uses, especially as cooking oil, only some applications were approved; some others are kept in abeyance. They might be considered when the production of palm oil in the country increases further. The author is of the opinion that research in the country and elsewhere should be augmented with regard to increasing the ratio of palm oil in biodiesel and that other kinds of biodiesel should also get due consideration because they are relatively less polluting. Ethanol is one of its examples.

947. In the area of bioethenol and hydrogen-based power generation, research in the country is at full swing. Scientists are attempting to produce ethanol by using industrial wastes, especially palm oil mill effluents (POME). However, its potential seems to be weak. This source of energy is being successfully used in countries that are producing surplus corn and sugar, such as Brazil, Mexico and the United States. Hydrogen fuel is at the experimental stage in the country. It is popular in the United States and few other countries. There are several filling stations in the United States now. It seems that in future, this source of energy will be proven to be one of the most successful scientific breakthroughs, but the price of such vehicles is worrying the scientists: it is currently very high, but might fall in the future. So is the case of hybrid vehicles. However, if we look at them from the point of view of cost and benefit analysis, it will prove to be a profitable venture. In this area, Malaysian scientists have the capability to augment research. Hydrogen Fuel Technology Sdn. Bhd. recently spent MYR 20 million on research, and conducted this research in collaboration with Malaysian, European and American scientists. It claims to have developed a useful technology to run cars, which will save 50% fuel and will not require a new engine (although it would need a water tank in the boot). A high compression-processing canister divides water into hydrogen and oxygen particles, which are then injected into the petrol fuel line. The mixture of petrol, hydrogen and oxygen will flow into the carburettor and the engine, enabling the car to run. Initially, the technology will be used to run cars, but it may be further expanded for use in running heavy vehicles.[185] There is a chance that this technology will prove to be very useful in the country and elsewhere. This technology should be further excelled and diversified so that it has the possibility of becoming a potent means of saving oil. It is notable here that some scientists in Malaysia have already had success by way of developing a motorcycle to be run on hydrogen fuel technology. It was displayed at several scientific expos between 2006 and 2009. It bagged several gold medals as has been considered a great achievement by those who are working on developing this technology.

948. Malaysia is seriously searching for other renewable energy sources. Although the percentage of these sources is too low and mainly limited to generation by using biomass, solar PV and prototype hydroelectric projects, it is the target that, in years to come, the ratio of renewable energy sources will become 10% of the country's total power generation. It may be noted here that the country has promised under the UNFCCC to generate 35% reduction in carbon emission on its own, and 45% with the help of developed countries. In order to achieve the target, the country is striving hard. It is submitted that this target can be achieved only when, together with cash and fiscal incentives, the rate of purchase of electricity by the utility companies, especially TNB, from generators is also encouraging. There

185. *New Straits Times*, 11 Feb. 2006.

is a need to attach power generated from these sources to the national grids. The dimensions of the alternative energy sources should also be diversified. This has to be taken care of by the federal government. Positive endeavour towards supporting renewable energy can be seen in form of various incentives in the Ninth Malaysia Plan and the Tenth Malaysia Plan. The Eleventh Malaysia Plan has reincentivized the renewable sources of energy and other green energy-related activities. Presently, as stated above, alternative sources of energy are mainly limited to thermal power generation by burning biowastes and prototype hydroelectric plants set up at some rivers that have relatively fast water currents; only recently the Bakun Dam has given a boost to them. This must be diversified. Being a tropical country, Malaysia has the potential to exploit solar energy. Efforts towards this end are being made, but the endeavours are not so encouraging. It is, therefore, suggested that efforts should be made to maximize the exploitation of this energy source. Malaysia also has tremendous potential to exploit wind energy by building offshore windmills. Although this is an expensive venture, the benefits will outweigh the costs and the country can afford it. It is notable here that China is venturing into this source of energy: it is currently building two such plants in the country and plans to build more in the near future. Why then, can Malaysia not build such plants?

949. Presently, the supply of renewable energy through the grid is too low. The position will increase with the increase of power generation through various renewable energy sources. TNB and other utility companies will have to have a greater degree of responsibility in this area. It is hoped that with the passing of the Renewable Energy Act and new pricing mechanism, this energy sector will get support.

950. Together with maximization of alternative energy sources, it is necessary to maximize efforts on energy efficiency and conservation of energy. In fact, these go hand-in-hand because they are directly related to the demand and supply of energy. Less consumption and more efficient consumption reduces the burden on energy generation and leads to the productive use of energy. It is notable here that conservation of energy and energy efficiency are among the top priorities of the country. This has been reiterated in the Ninth Malaysia Plan to Eleventh Malaysia Plan. It is notable here that the Malaysian government is now supporting 'green technology' in a big way. There is huge allocation of money for this purpose. It is also notable that towards this end, the government has started to enforce strategies pertaining to both of these priorities through government buildings. The Ministry's building is a model of self-sufficiency with regard to electricity. It proved to be very successful. It is notable that this building also won the ASEAN award. It is planned to extend these strategies to other buildings in the near future. It is suggested that these strategies should compulsorily be enforced through appropriate legislation. There should be some incentive-based schemes for those buildings that have 90% or more compliance levels. To begin with, some of those buildings should be made self-sufficient with respect to generation and consumption of electricity. This can be achieved by installing sufficient photovoltaic cells on the roof and walls of the building. Buildings can be suitably designed for this purpose and should be known as 'smart buildings' and qualify for monetary support and tax incentives.

951. It is significantly notable that in Malaysia, efforts are being made to increase awareness among the general public regarding energy efficiency and conservation. For this purpose, the media, especially newspapers and televisions, are being used. People are learning now to use more efficient electrical equipment and use electricity only when necessary and to use it moderately. The media are conveying messages that this will save energy, which can be used in industries, and people will be able to reduce their electricity bills. Mr Gurmeet Singh, a notable environmentalist of the country and recipient of the Langkawi Award, can be quoted as a model example. He travels by public transport and has specially designed walls in his house so that he does not need to run air conditioners. Not everyone can be as committed as he is, but people can try hard to emulate him. It will be a great help to the country.

952. As far as the concept of 'green cars' is concerned, there are various options. Among them, the use of gas instead of oil and diesel has proved to be very successful. The best example is in New Delhi. There, based on Supreme Court's order, all commercial vehicles in the town have to use liquefied gas in place of oil. This has resulted in a relatively clean Delhi in terms of air pollution. The other success story lies with the use of ethanol and biodiesel. These are also less polluting sources of energy. We have noted above that Malaysia has decided to maximize the use of biodiesel by commercial vehicles. We know that in EU countries, especially France and Germany, biodiesel and other biofuels are popular. Position in the United States is also worth mentioning. It will be beneficial if the use of ethanol and biodiesel is maximized, because it is cleaner and a less expensive source of energy. Malaysia, being one of the biggest palm oil-producing countries, will certainly reap financial benefits as it will have to import fewer diesels. Hydrogen technology has proven to be successful. This is the cleanest source of energy, but the problem of producing hydrogen and the high cost of the vehicles are two significant disadvantages, which are real impediment in popularizing this technology.

953. Another preferred option is hybrid vehicles. Cars have been manufactured to be run with both petrol and electricity. These cars are first run by using petrol and when the in-built battery is charged, the engine switches to that source of energy. It has proved to be a very successful technology, as it saves petrol and pollutes the environment at less than half the rate of normal cars. This kind of car may cost relatively more, but the cost is not exorbitantly high. The high cost can be reimbursed in due course of time. The author is of the opinion that a country such as Malaysia should by all means augment the production and use of hybrid cars.

954. Various laws pertaining to the generation, storage and supply of electricity and gas are generally based on international standards. It is suggested that these laws should be amended if need be to bring them in line with the international laws, especially laws followed in EU member countries. It is true that laws have to be commensurate with the local conditions and technological advancement. It is submitted that in the area of energy, Malaysia should emulate EU countries because the country does not differ significantly in this regard.

955. We have noted above that the Income tax Act provides a fair number of incentives for the use of renewable energy sources and conservation strategies. The law pertaining to income tax on energy also supports investment in the energy sector. Towards this end, the law has established a low rate of income tax and provides a considerable number of incentives in the form of deductions and double deductions. The author is of the opinion that these incentives should be enhanced so that the energy sector is further boosted, which is imperatively demanded.

Selected Bibliography

Arnold, Wayne. 'At the Mercy of Oil'. *New York Times*, 10 June 2004. (Reprinted in *New Straits Times*, 11 June 2004).

Ansari, Abdul Haseeb. 'Socio-Economic and Legal Perspective of Withdrawal of Subsidy on Diesel and Petrol and Possibility of Imposition of an Energy Tax: A Study with Special Reference to Malaysia'. *The Law Review* (2009): 45.

Asia Pacific Energy research Centre. Electricity Sector Degradation in the APEC Region, 2000, Tokyo. 'Malaysia – Energy Overview', at: <www.ieej.or.jp/aperc/01Malaysia.pdf>.

Basin, Yusuf. 'Pushing the Case for Biodiesel, Palm Oil'. *New Straits Times*, 27 May 2010.

Bradbrook, A. 'Energy and Sustainable development'. *Asia Pacific Journal of Environmental Law* 4, no. 4 (1999): 309–317.

Bradsher, Keith. 'Why Asia Is Thinking Anew on Oil Subsidy'. *New York Times*, 8 September 2005. (Reprinted in *New Straits Times*, 9 September 2005).

Brundtland Commission Report. 'Our Common Future'. Chapter 7, at: <en.wikipedia.org/wiki/World_Commission_onEnvironment_and_Development>.

Economic Planning Unit, Prime Minister's Department. 'Eight Malaysia Plan', at: <www.epu.jpm.my/RM8/c11cont.pdf>.

Energy Information Administration. 'Malaysia', <www.eia.doe.gov/emeu/cabs/malaysia.html>, 2002.

Energy Information Administration. 'Malaysia', <www.eia.doe.gov/emeu/cabs/malaysia.html>, 2002.

'Extract from the Survey of Energy Resources 2001', <www.worldenergy.org/wecgeis/edc/countries/Malaysia.asp>.

Field, B. & M. Field. *Environmental Economics: An Introduction*. McGraw Hill, 2002, Chapter 5.

Fecher, Harald Winkler et al. 'Energy and the World Summit on Sustainable Development: What Next?'. *Energy Policy* (Winter 2003): 34–51.

Gavigan, R. 'Siberia's Environment: A Challenge to Traditional Thinking'. *Georgetown International Environmental Law Review* 8 (1996): 333.

Goldemberg, J. 'Development and Energy'. In *Energy Law and Sustainable Development*, edited by Adrian J. Bradbrook, et al. IUCN, 2003, 1–9.

Grassi, I.G. 'Potential Bioenergy Impacts of Bioenergy Activity on Employment'. *Proceedings of the 9th European Bioenergy Conference* 1 (June 1996): 419–423.

Guraja Jayarao. 'Financing Energy for Sustainable Development', paper presented at the First IUCN Conference, 4–6 November 2003.

Gururaja, Jayarao. 'Energy for Sustainable development: Framework and Methodology'. *Natural Resources Forum* 27 (2003): 58.

Selected Bibliography

Hodas, David R. 'Energy, Climate Change and Sustainable Development'. In *Energy Law and Sustainable Development*, edited by Bradbrook, Adrisn J., et al. IUCN, 2003, 11–29.

Husniarti, T. 'Malaysian Energy Policy: An Overview', paper presented at the Malaysia–Japan Workshop on Energy Supply and Demand Forecasting, March 1998, Kuala Lumpur.

International Energy Agency and Organization of Economic Cooperation and Development. 'Energy Balance of Non-OECD Countries', Paris, France: OECD/IEA 2000. 1990–2000.

Institute of Energy Economics, Japan, 'Malaysia-energy Overview', at: <www.ieej.or.jp/aperc/o/Malaysia.pdf>.

IPCC – Relevant Reports.

Jaafar, Mohd Zamzam. 'Malaysia's Energy Plan: The Way Forward', Malaysian Energy Centre, at: <www.ptm.org.my>.

Jaafar, Mohd Zamzam. 'Greener Energy Solutions for a Sustainable Future: Issues and Challenges for Malaysia'. *Energy Policy* 31 (2003): 1061–1072, at: <www.sciencedirect.com>.

Jaafar Mohd Zamzam. 'Malaysia's Energy Plan: The Way Forward', paper presented at 4th APEC Coal Trade and Investment Liberalization and Facilitation Workshop, 6–8 March 2002, Kuala Lumpur, at: <www.apec-egcfe.fossil.energy.gov/TILF_2002_KL_jaafar.pdf>.

Jeffert, Micheal I. 'Capacity Building for Sustainable Energy Regimes and Effective Compliance and Enforcement: Foundations in University education', paper presented at the First IUCN Colloquium, 4–6 November 2003, Shanghai.

McDonald, S. *Petroleum Conservation in the United States: An Economic Analysis*. John Hopkins University Press, 1971.

Mak, Kui-Nang & Fredrick Soltau. 'A United Nations Perspective on Law and Energy for Sustainable Development', paper presented at the First IUCN Colloquium, 4–6 November 2003, Shanghai.

Mariyappan, Komathi. 'Status of Renewable Energy and Energy Efficiency in Malaysia', at: <www.isep.or.jp/spens/countryreports/malaysia.htm>.

'Malaysia: Energy Profile and Future Estimations', at: <www.bu.edu/cees/classes/binna/304/energyprofiles/malaysia.html>.

Mienik, O. & J. Goldemberg. 'Covering to a Common Pattern of Energy Use in Developing and Industrialized Countries'. *Energy Policy* 28 (2000): 503–508.

Ministry of Energy, Communications and Multimedia, Malaysia. 'Notable Energy Developments', paper presented at EWG 18, November 1999, Willington.

Mukherjee, Krittivas. 'India Finds Prosperity, Still Depends on Coal'. *New Straits Times*, 8 December 2009.

Nagarajan, M. 'Biofuel Development in Malaysia', paper presented at the International Symposium and Agriculture and Biofuel Policy', 25 February 2008, Bangkok.

New Straits Times.

Omer, A.M. 'Energy, Environment and Sustainable Development'. *Renewable and Sustainable Energy Review* 12, no. 9 (2008): 2265.

Ottinger, Richard L. 'Biofuels: Potentials and Solutions'. *Environmental Law Review* (2009): 56.

Ottinger Richard L. 'Notes from Copenhagen Blog' at: <http://web.pace.edu/page.cfm?_id=35345>.

Ottinger, R.L. *Environmental Cost of Energy*. Oceana Publication, 1989.

Reddy, A.K.N. 'Energy Technologies and Policies for Rural Development'. In *Energy for Sustainable Development*, edited by T.B. Johansson & J. Goldemberg. IIIEE and UNDP, 2002.

RWEPD Field Document 50, 1997, 'Regional Study of Wood Energy Today and Tomorrow in Asia', at: <www.rwepd.org>.

Ministry of Energy, Communication and Multimedia, Malaysia. 'Proceedings of World Renewable Energy Congress (WREC)', December 1999, Kuala Lumpur. Also see, Proceedings of 8th and 9th World energy Congress 2004 and 2005 respectively at: <www.elsevier.com>.

Robinson, Nicholas A. 'Foreword'. In *Energy Law and Sustainable Development*, edited by Adrin J. Bradbrook & Richard L. Ottinger. IUCN, 2003.

Robinson, Nicholas A. 'Befogged Vision: International Environmental Governance, a Decade after Rio'. *Law and Policy Review* (May 2002).

RWEPD Field Document 47, 1997. 'Review of Wood Energy Data in RWEPD Member Countries', at: <www.rwepd.org>.

RWEPD Field Document 47, 1997. 'Biomass Energy in Asean Member Countries', at: <www.rwepd.org>.

'The Trends in Malaysia's energy Consumption up to the Year 2020', at: <www.ptm.org.my/ptmnews/issues5-ED20.html>.

UNDP, World Energy Assessment: Energy and the Challenges of Sustainability, 2000.

UNDP, UN DESA & WEC. *World Energy Assessment: Energy and the Challenge of Sustainability: An Overview*. UNDP, 2001.

Umera, Yushimitu. 'Utilization of Biomass as Energy Source in Malaysia', paper presented at the World Engineering Science and Technology Congress, Kuala Lumpur, 17–18 June 2010.

Vespa, M. 'Climate Change 2001: Kyoto at Bonn and Marrakesh'. *Ecology Law Quarterly* 29 (2003): 395.

Weaver, Jacqueline Lang. 'Sustainable Development in the Petroleum Sector'. In *Energy Law and Sustainable Development*, edited by Adrian J. Bradbrook, et al. IUCN, 2003.

Writh, D. 'The Sixth Session (Part 2) and Seventh Session of the Conference of Parties to the Framework Convention on Climate Change'. *American Journal of International Law* (July 2002): 45.

Energy Commission Malaysia: *Malaysia Energy Statistics, Handbook 2016.*

Ministry of Energy Malaysia, *Malaysia Energy Policy: Focussing on Sustainable Energy Development and The Way Forward, June 2016.*

Energy Commission Malaysia: *Energy Malaysia Vol. 11, 12. 13 of 2017.*

EIA: US Energy Information Administration: Country Analysis Brief: Malaysia, 26 April 2017.

World Energy Council: World Energy Resource, Oil, and Gas, 2016.

World Energy Outlook, 2017.

Selected Bibliography

List of Acts and Statutes

Atomic Energy Licensing Act 1984
Efficient Management of Electricity Regulations 2008
Electricity Supply Act 1990 (Act 447)
Electricity Supply (Amendment) Act 2015 (Act A1501)
Electricity Supply (Successor Company) Act 1990
Electricity Regulations 1994
Electricity (Amendment) Regulations 2013
Electricity (Amendment) (No. 2) Regulations 2014
Electricity Supply (Compounding of Offences) Regulations 2001
Energy Commission Act 2001
Energy Commission (Amendment) Act 2010
Environmental Quality Act 1974 (Act 127)
Environmental Quality (Prescribed Activities) Environmental Impact Assessment) Order 1987
Environmental Quality (Clean Air) Regulations 1978
Environmental Quality (Control of Emission from Diesel Engines) Regulations 1996
Environmental Quality (Control of Emission from Petrol Engines) Regulations 1996
Environmental Quality (Control of Emission from Motorcycles) Regulations 2003
Gas Supply Act 1993 (Act 501)
Gas Supply (Amendment) Act 2016 (Act A1515)
Gas Supply Regulations 1997
Gas Supply (Amendment) Regulations 2014
Gas Supply (Amendment) Regulations 2017
Petroleum Development Act 1974 (Act 144)
Petroleum Regulations 1974
Petroleum Mining Act 1966 (Act 95)
Petroleum Mining Rules 1968
Petroleum Safety Measures Act 1984 (Act 302)
Petroleum (Safety Measures) (Transportation of Petroleum by Pipelines) Regulations 1985
Petroleum (Safety Measures) (Transportation of Petroleum by Water) Regulations 1985
Petroleum Income Tax Act 1967 (Act 543)
Petroleum (Income Tax) (Qualifying Plant Allowance) (Cost of Provision Computer Software) Rules 2003
Petroleum (Income Tax) (Qualifying Plant Allowances) (Computers and Information Technology Equipment) Rules 2003

List of Acts and Statutes

Petroleum (Income Tax) (Qualifying Plant Allowances) (Secondary Gas Recovery) Rules 2003
Petroleum (Income Tax) (Qualifying Plant Allowances) (Environmental Protection Equipment and Facilities) Rules 2004
Petroleum (Income Tax) Deduction for Audit Expenditure) Rules 2006
Petroleum (Income Tax) (Deduction for Expenditure Incurred for the Provision of an Expenditure Incurred for the Provision of an Approved Internship Programme) Rules 2012
Petroleum (Income Tax) (Accelerated Capital Allowances) (Marginal Field) Rules 2013
Petroleum (Income Tax) (Marginal Field) Regulations 2013
Petroleum (Income Tax) (Deduction for Participation in and Approved Career Fair) Rules 2013
Renewable Energy Act 2011 (Act 725)
Sustainable Energy Development Authority Act 2011 (Act 726)
Deduction of Research Expenditure Rules 1989
Deductions for the employment of Disabled Persons Rules 1989
Deductions of Insurance Premiums for Importers Rules 1989
Deductions of Abandonment Expenditure Rules 1997

List of Cases

Abdul Ghani hamid v. Abdul Nasir Abdul Jabbar & Aor, [1995] 4 CLJ 317.
Allen v. Jumbo Holdings Ltd, [1980] 1 WLR 1252.
Ashtiani v. Kashi, [1968] 3 WLR647.
Center for Social Justice v. Union of India, AIR 2001 Gujrat 71.
Claybricks & Tiles sdn Bhd v. Nenaga Nasional Bhd, [2007] 1MLJ 217.
D. P. Vijandaran v. Majlis Beguam, [1995] 3 MLJ 576.
Everhome Furniture Manufacturing (M) Sdn Bhd v.Tenaga Nasional Bhd, [2009] MLJ 715.
Jaswant Singh v. Central electricity Board, [1967] 1 MLJ 272.
Kamalanathan Ponnumbalan v. Tenaga Nasional Berhad, Civil Suit No: MT(3)22-585-1998. Decided on 7 March 2006
Karupasamy a/l Silliah and Others v. Tenaga Nasional Bhd, [2006] 3 MLJ 347.
Lembaga Letrik Negara tanah Melayu v. Syarikat Klang Electric, [1974] 1 MLJ 209.
Nikmat Maju Development Sdn Bhd v. Tenaga Nasional Berhad, Civil Appeal No: W-02(NCVC)(W)-949-04/2013 (CA)
Ong See Teong & Anore v. Tenaga Nasional Bhd, [2008] 5 MLJ 717.
Pepper v. Hart, [1993] AC 593.
Sabah Electricity Sdn. Bhd. v. Kkip Power Sdn Bhd. Civil Appeal No. S-02(w)-1123-06/2016 (CA)
TN Godavaraman Thirumuspad v. Union of India, AIR 1997 SC 1228.
Tenaga Nasional Bhd v. Calsonic Compressor (M) Sdn Bhd, [2009] 8 MLJ 793.
Tenaga Nasional Bhd v. Dolomite Industrial Park Sdn bhd, [2000] 1 CLJ 695.
Tenaga Nasional Bhd v. Teck See Plastic Sdn Bhd, [2007] 5 MLJ 430.
Tenaga Nasional Bhd. v. Teobros Development Sdn Bhd, [2008] 6 MLJ 391.
Tenaga Nasional Bhd v. Trans Resources Corp Sdn Bhd, [2009] 5 MLJ 673.
Tekali Prospecting Sdn Bhd. v. Tenag Nasional Bhd and 1 or, [2002] 1 MLJ 113.
Tenaga Nasional Bhd v. Tekali Prospecting Sdn Bhd, [2002] 2 MLJ 707.
Tenaga Nasional Bhd. v. Ong See Teong & Another, [2010] 2 CLJ 1
Tenaga Nasional Berhad v. Pearl Island Development Sdn Bhd, Civil Appeal No. P-02 (NCVC) (W)-897-04/2013. Decided on 13 January 2015.
Third Chandris Corporation v. Unimarine, [1979] 1 QB 645.
Virabhadrappa T v. Ministry of Mines and Steel New Delhi, AIR 1998 Kar. 412.
Yusoff v. Central electricity Board, [1964 1 MLJ 374.
Z Ltd v. A, [1982] 1 All ER 556.

Index

The numbers here refer to paragraph numbers.

Index

Made in the USA
Monee, IL
09 March 2026

45790296R00256